SEEKING SUCCESS IN E-BUSINESS

IFIP – The International Federation for Information Processing

IFIP was founded in 1960 under the auspices of UNESCO, following the First World Computer Congress held in Paris the previous year. An umbrella organization for societies working in information processing, IFIP's aim is two-fold: to support information processing within its member countries and to encourage technology transfer to developing nations. As its mission statement clearly states,

> *IFIP's mission is to be the leading, truly international, apolitical organization which encourages and assists in the development, exploitation and application of information technology for the benefit of all people.*

IFIP is a non-profitmaking organization, run almost solely by 2500 volunteers. It operates through a number of technical committees, which organize events and publications. IFIP's events range from an international congress to local seminars, but the most important are:

- The IFIP World Computer Congress, held every second year;
- Open conferences;
- Working conferences.

The flagship event is the IFIP World Computer Congress, at which both invited and contributed papers are presented. Contributed papers are rigorously refereed and the rejection rate is high.

As with the Congress, participation in the open conferences is open to all and papers may be invited or submitted. Again, submitted papers are stringently refereed.

The working conferences are structured differently. They are usually run by a working group and attendance is small and by invitation only. Their purpose is to create an atmosphere conducive to innovation and development. Refereeing is less rigorous and papers are subjected to extensive group discussion.

Publications arising from IFIP events vary. The papers presented at the IFIP World Computer Congress and at open conferences are published as conference proceedings, while the results of the working conferences are often published as collections of selected and edited papers.

Any national society whose primary activity is in information may apply to become a full member of IFIP, although full membership is restricted to one society per country. Full members are entitled to vote at the annual General Assembly, National societies preferring a less committed involvement may apply for associate or corresponding membership. Associate members enjoy the same benefits as full members, but without voting rights. Corresponding members are not represented in IFIP bodies. Affiliated membership is open to non-national societies, and individual and honorary membership schemes are also offered.

SEEKING SUCCESS IN E-BUSINESS

A Multidisciplinary Approach

IFIP TC8 / WG8.4 Second Working Conference on E-Business: Multidisciplinary Research and Practice June 9–11, 2002, Copenhagen, Denmark

Edited by

KIM VIBORG ANDERSEN
Copenhagen Business School, Denmark

STEVE ELLIOT
University of Sydney, Australia

PAULA SWATMAN
University of Koblenz-Landau, Germany and Deakin University, Australia

EILEEN TRAUTH
Pennsylvania State University, USA

NIELS BJØRN-ANDERSEN
Copenhagen Business School, Denmark

KLUWER ACADEMIC PUBLISHERS
BOSTON / DORDRECHT / LONDON

Distributors for North, Central and South America:
Kluwer Academic Publishers
101 Philip Drive
Assinippi Park
Norwell, Massachusetts 02061 USA
Telephone (781) 871-6600
Fax (781) 681-9045
E-Mail <kluwer@wkap.com>

Distributors for all other countries:
Kluwer Academic Publishers Group
Post Office Box 322
3300 AH Dordrecht, THE NETHERLANDS
Telephone 31 78 6576 000
Fax 31 78 6576 254
E-Mail <services@wkap.nl>

Electronic Services <http://www.wkap.nl>

Library of Congress Cataloging-in-Publication Data

A C.I.P. Catalogue record for this book is available from the Library of Congress.

Seeking Success in E-Business: A Multidisciplinary Approach
Edited by Kim Viborg Andersen, Steve Elliot, Paula Swatman, Eileen Trauth and Niels Bjørn-Andersen
ISBN 1-4020-7450-6

Printed on acid-free paper.
Printed in United Kingdom by Biddles / IBT Global

Contents

Foreword

In the foreword to this volume of conference proceedings for IFIP Working Group 8.4, it is appropriate to review the wider organization to which the Working Group belongs. The International Federation of Information Processing (IFIP) is a non-governmental, non-profit umbrella organization for national societies working in the field of information processing that was established in 1960 under the auspices of UNESCO. IFIP's mission is to be the leading, truly international, apolitical organization which encourages and assists in the development, exploitation and application of Information Technology for the benefit of all people.

At the heart of IFIP lie its Technical Committees that, between them, count on the active participation of some two thousand people world-wide. These Groups work in a variety of ways to share experience and to develop their specialised knowledge. Technical Committees include: TC1. Foundations of Computer Science; TC 2: Software: Theory and Practice; TC 3: Education; TC 6: Communication Systems; TC 7: System Modelling and Optimization; TC 9: Relationship between Computers and Society; TC 11: Security and Protection in Information Processing Systems; TC 12: Artificial Intelligence and TC 13: Human-Computer Interaction. The IFIP website www.ifip.org) has further details.

Technical Committee 8 (TC8) is concerned with Information Systems in organisations. Within TC8 there are different Working Groups focusing on particular aspects of Information Systems.

Working Group 8.4 (see also www.econ.usyd.edu.au/ifip84) focuses on promoting collaboration across disciplines in E-business Information Systems research and practice. Our intention is to extend the IFIP community's focus on E-business to recognize, acknowledge and facilitate research and practice as it crosses the boundaries of IS, organizational, consumer, community, industry and national domains.

Successful implementations of E-business frequently require additional interaction between elements that extend beyond technology and organizational issues to include environmental (eg infrastructure, national culture, national and international payment mechanisms) and consumer factors.

These issues were explored in detail at the very successful 2002 conference hosted by Copenhagen Business School. In response to the theme: 'Seeking success in E-business: A multi-disciplinary approach' the Conference attracted 65 delegates from 12 countries to its refereed research presentations and to its expert panels.

Congratulations are offered to all involved with the conference organization, particularly Kim Viborg Andersen, Niels Bjørn-Andersen and Vicki Antosz.

Steve Elliot

Chair, IFIP WG8.4

SEEKING SUCCESS IN E-BUSINESS

IF E-BUSINESS IS DIFFERENT, THEN SO IS RESEARCH IN E-BUSINESS

ROGER CLARKE
Xamax Consultancy Pty Ltd, Australian National University

Abstract: Information systems research is challenging enough, but information systems research in the e-business domain presents even greater difficulties, because its characteristics are in direct conflict with the implicit assumptions underlying most academic research. Approaches are suggested whereby relevant research into e-business can be undertaken. The delivery of real-world value while achieving sufficient rigour to satisfy the guardians of academic standards will, however, remain problematical.

1. INTRODUCTION

Electronic commerce burst onto the scene in the early 1990s (see, for example, Clarke 1993). Of the many disciplines whose techniques can be brought to bear on electronic commerce, Information Systems is an important one (Clarke 1990, 1992). Practitioners of the Information Systems discipline, in searching for appropriate ways to undertake research in the domain, have been confronted by many challenges. This paper's purpose is to identify and discuss those challenges, and propose appropriate ways of conducting research.

The paper commences by reviewing the nature of scientific research, and the assumptions that are implicit in it. It contrasts this against the rather different assumptions inherent in two primary alternative approaches, interpretivism and engineering research. The characteristics of e-business are delineated, and a description is provided of the expectations that real-world audiences have of research in the e-business domain.

Preliminary results of an assessment of published e-business research are presented, and substantial weaknesses in the body of work undertaken to date are identified. Suggestions are made as to how I.S. practitioners can go about addressing the challenges, and improving the quality of research into e-business.

2. IMPLICIT ASSUMPTIONS IN SCIENTIFIC RESEARCH

The nature of scientific research is the subject of a large literature. For a discussion and a substantial collection of references, see Clarke (2000a). This section confines itself to a few key observations that enable development of the argument pursued in the rest of the paper.

Following Popper (1959, 1968), a theory is scientific if and only if it generates inferences that are refutable by reference to the real world. Following in particular Kuhn (1962), key **features of the process of scientific research** are as follows:

- it investigates 'research questions' within a 'domain';
- it is driven by theories that:
  - are founded on axioms, which are unchanging;
  - comprise trees of deductive inference; and
  - enable the generation of 'hypotheses' that are explicit, unambiguous and refutable;
- research design has the following objectives:
  - to empirically test the hypotheses. This involves undertaking observation and measurement of the real world, in such a manner that the hypotheses, if false, will be shown to be so;
  - to exercise control over confounding variables; and
  - to be sufficiently well-documented to be replicable;
- its outcomes:
  - in most cases, refine, extend or articulate the theory;
  - in some cases, are not entirely consistent with the theory;
  - result in the gradual accumulation of 'anomalies'; and
  - enable, from time to time, a more general theory to be formulated, which accommodates the anomalies, and results in a 'paradigm shift'.

The following terms are used in this paper with the following meanings:

- **'research technique'** refers to a specific means, approach or tool-and-its-use, whereby data is gathered and analysed, and inferences are drawn;
- **'research method'** refers to the manner in which a particular project is undertaken. It comprises one or more research techniques; and
- **'research methodology'** refers to the study of research methods. It is a singular that does not admit of a plural.

Inherent in scientific research are some **meta-physical assumptions** that are less frequently expressed, but that are nonetheless critical, in particular:

- there is a 'real world';
- the phenomena in that real world are stable;
- data can be gathered by observing the real world;
- such data are factual, truthful and unambiguous;
- the domain of study is unaffected by the research;
- the domain of study is unaffected by the researcher; and
- the language in which theory is expressed is unambiguous, and contains no value judgements.

From these assumptions, combined with my observation of the application of the scientific method within the information systems discipline, I suggest that the following attitudes are inherent:

- rigour is paramount, in order that theories can be built;
- where relevance conflicts with rigour, relevance has to be a secondary consideration;
- to be cohesive, a body of theory needs to exist within a single clearly-defined discipline. It may draw on reference disciplines for axioms, but should not be inherently multi-disciplinary;
- instability of the phenomena within a research domain is highly inconvenient;
- perturbability of the phenomena by research and the presence of researchers is also highly inconvenient;
- the rapid accumulation of anomalies is also highly inconvenient, and is a sign of an insufficiently mature body of theory.

3. ALTERNATIVES TO CONVENTIONAL SCIENTISM

There are substantial advantages in the scientific approach. At least when applied to social phenomena, however, its inherent assumptions create difficulties. As the information systems discipline has matured, it has increasingly questioned those assumptions, and the techniques associated with scientistic research (e.g. Klein & Lyytinen 1985).

An alternative approach that was dominant in western thought for more than a millenium is to focus on the ideal world of thought, and regard the physical world as an imperfect and temporary inconvenience. Given the argument developed below concerning the needs of the audiences for e-business research, however, it would clearly not be satisfactory to resort to **contemplation** alone, and abandon the empirical orientation and the preference for theories to relate to the imperfect physical world.

Interpretivism has provided an alternative basis for research, and during the last two decades has become well-accepted in the information systems discipline. It embodies alternative assumptions, which run counter to those of the scientific approach. In particular, these include the following:

- the observer's perspective is a factor:
  - in the selection and formulation of theory;
  - in the formulation of hypotheses;
  - in choices made in the research design process;
  - in the selectiveness of observation; and
  - in the process of observation;
- scientific objectivity is infeasible:
  - in general; and
  - especially where the domain includes entities that exercise what appears to be free will.

A further alternative, usefully described as **'engineering' research**, focuses away from the social setting, and towards artefacts. These may be designed and constructed, or protoyped and trialled, in order to enable effective interventions to be undertaken in a particular domain; or existing artefacts may be experimented with, in order to identify the limits of their applicability, effectiveness or usefulness.

4. CHARACTERISTICS OF E-BUSINESS

In order to assess the applicability of the various research approaches, it is necessary to identify key features of the e-business domain. This in turn requires working definitions for the main terms.

Since 1993, I have used a series of broad definitions to define the scope of the domain (Clarke 1997a). By 'electronic commerce' and 'e-commerce', I mean the conduct of trading with the assistance of telecommunications and telecommunications-based tools. Correspondingly, 'electronic business' or 'e-business' is the conduct of business generally, with the assistance of telecommunications and telecommunications-based tools. e-business therefore encompasses a wide range of activities such as e-commerce (Clarke 1993), e-publishing (Clarke 1997b) and electronic services delivery (Clarke 1999). Its scope extends across the business activities of all categories of organisations and individuals, whether undertaken for profit, or as a service to some community.

In recent years, there has been a trend within the U.S.A. to adopt a much narrower interpretation of the term 'e-business'. This restricts it to business enterprises alone, and focuses on their internal processes. See, for example, Alter et al. (2001). Such narrowness seems to have been inspired by the belated adoption of a trade-marked semi-graphical representation of 'e-business' by a major information technology provider. It would be a serious disservice to the discipline if such a narrow and industry-driven interpretation were to become mainstream.

The terms e-commerce and e-business have been applied retrospectively to the use of electronic data interchange (EDI) and value-added networks (VANs) and various forms of on-line services, which commenced as early as the late 1960s, and became mainstream during the 1980s. The currency of the terms dates, however, from early-mid 1990s, reflecting the explosion of public use of the Internet, and of key services enabled by the Internet, particularly email and the World Wide Web.

The domain has become considerably segmented during its first decade, in particular through the discovery that significantly different factors are at work in the various relationships among businesses, governments, consumers and citizens, giving rise to a 3x3 (or possibly 4x4) matrix. Of these 9-12 contexts, only B2B and B2C have been subjected to intensive study, although C2C is now attracting greater attention.

Some key features of e-business distinguish it from most other domains that have been of interest to I.S. researchers. It is **new and exciting**, and with that comes a lack of circumspection, a very high level of 'marketing hype', and downright exaggeration. This has been a key factor in the casino mentality of the late 1990s, in which dot.com fervor turned investors into gamblers, and encouraged an unworldly belief in the economics of business having been re-written overnight.

The newness of the domain has meant that no one was well prepared to participate in it, much less conduct research into it. Awareness and then reflection necessarily precede understanding, general principles take time to be extracted, courses have to be devised, and most of the pioneers are by definition too busy doing it to explain it or train people in it. As a result, a great deal of the early development and application of new technologies has a high 'turkey-factor', and the opportunity for latecomers to apply '20-20 hindsight' is enormous.

Associated with this is the complete **lack of stability in the phenomena** within the domain. Technologies keep being re-defined. Perceptions of the purposes and potentials of the technologies change rapidly. Participant behaviour is dependent on perceptions at the time a technology or its application is first experienced, but is subject to learning, which in some cases is very brisk. The perceptions of the needs that are being addressed migrates. Technologies diverge, then converge, and products re-combine. Underlying all of this is a high degree of terminological confusion, with technologists and thoughtful observers struggling to apply existing words and phrases, and invent new ones, all the time having their contributions undermined by marketers whose understanding of the technologies is vastly exceeded by their enthusiasm, their imprecision, and their avarice.

A further crucial aspect of e-business is its reach and borderlessness. Beyond the hype, this means to researchers that there are some **significant additional confounding variables**. One of these is the difficulty of defining populations, population segments, and sampling frames. Another is the inability to rely any longer on geographical extent as a proxy for cultural commonality. Suddenly, key cultural factors have to be identified and controlled for, because, if due attention is not paid to the cultural setting(s), the results will be patent nonsense. This is an enormous challenge, given the utter inadequacy of theories of cultural definition and behaviour, and the lack of clarity even about the dimensions of what 'culture' means in the contexts of business services and electronic participation.

5. THE PRACTICE OF E-BUSINESS RESEARCH

Despite the many challenges identified above, journal editors encourage submission of papers on e-business topics (e.g. Zwass 1996), and stimulate special issues. Many I.S. academics have grasped the nettle, and conducted research into many different aspects of e-business. An important question that arises is: what are the audiences that are expected to read the results of this research?

A great deal of research in the I.S. discipline, as in many others, is conducted primarily for the purpose of publication in research journals and presentation at research conferences, and hence as a means of progression within the academic profession. The audience is therefore **other I.S. researchers, in particular the gatekeepers**, i.e. editors, program chairs, referees, and assessors of research grant applications (a group that is conventionally, but rather misleadingly, referred to as 'one's peers').

There are many further categories of people, however, who are interested in the outcomes of research into e-business. Among those desperate for insights are the developers of new technologies; the professionals, managers and individual workers who apply them; and process specialists who devise approaches whereby the technologies can be effectively applied within organisational contexts. Investors are equally eager for information that will enable them to select among the plethora of bright ideas that are in need of capital. A final category of real-world audience is policy analysts, particularly within government and applied social research organisations, but also in associations of corporations, consumers, citizens and workers, and in large corporations.

Those **real-world audiences** have interests very different from the research community. Their focus is on 'proof-of-concept' prototyping, the development of products and services, demonstration applications, understanding about users' reactions to them, and appreciation of how their features can be communicated to prospects. Particularly once they have developed a significant capital and/or psychic investment, they have a strong preference for the 'right' answers, or at least not the 'wrong' ones. They are uninterested in researchers whose choice of topic, hypotheses, method, analysis and timetable, are dictated primarily by the demands of journal editors.

This leads to a need to analyse several aspects of research that are often left to one side by academics. One of those aspects is **the motivation for the research activity**. The following alternatives need to be distinguished:

- **'pure research'**. This is typified by the wish to conquer something "because it's there". More prosaically, research of this kind is undertaken with the primary intention of contributing to abstract, theoretical understanding. It is the approach that is most acceptable for academic journals and research conferences;
- **'applied research'**. This can be depicted as "I have a hammer, so go and find me a nail". This still falls within the realm of academic research, because it can be reasonably strongly theory-driven. It is more attractive to businessmen and practitioners than pure research, but still falls short of their needs. For example, the cluster of techniques referred to as operations research has long been subject to the deprecatory description of being 'a tool-kit looking for a problem to solve';
- **'instrumentalist research'**. The catchcry of this approach is "I have a problem, so go and find me a solution". This provides a good fit to the interests of real-world audiences. On the other hand, research driven by this motivation is very difficult to report on in formal research outlets. It is not sufficiently theory-driven, and is very likely, in its search for answers, to cross boundaries into multiple disciplines.

Another distinction that needs to be drawn might be referred to as **the focus of the research**. The following alternatives exist:

- the technology or process, which is oriented towards the question 'what is this thing?';
- applications of the technology or process, which involves the question 'what do I do with it?';
- adoption and impediments to adoption, which asks 'how do I make sure it gets used?';
- impact, which is interested in 'what will its first-order effects be?'; and
- implications, which is concerned with 'what will its second-order effects be?'.

Activities can also be differentiated according to **the nature of the research outcomes**. The alternative forms they may be in are as follows:

- descriptive outcomes, providing a depiction of a behaviour or a domain;
- explanatory outcomes, providing either:
  - statistical correlations among factors that appear to be associated with particular behaviours; or
  - systemic explanation of how behaviours arise, possibly extending to an ascription of the causes of occurrences in the domain;
- predictive outcomes, which offers answers to such questions as 'what behaviour will arise, and how?', 'what occurrences will arise within the domain?', and 'what effect will a particular intervention have?'; and
- normative outcomes, which state which interventions are likely to achieve a desired outcome, subject to various environmental circumstances.

The rigorous research that is attractive to journal editors is most commonly explanatory (especially where it involves statistical correlation) or perhaps predictive in nature. Normative outcomes must by their nature involve discussion of, and perhaps even adoption of, value-judgements. They are highly desirable for real-world audiences, but anathema to journal editors.

Keen (1980) and others have drawn attention to **the eternal tension between relevance and rigour**. Associated with rigour are independence from sponsors' interests, through pure research motivation, explanatory outcomes, and quantitative data, with a preference for the ratio scales that enable the tools of statistical analysis to be brought to bear. Associated with relevance, on the other hand, are instrumentalist motivation, predictive and normative outcomes, and whatever data is collectable.

Researchers in the e-business domain are confronted by enormous challenges. Those who value publishability in major academic journals well above the impact of their work on practitioners are well-advised to conduct their research in other, less dynamic domains.

6. WHAT E-BUSINESS RESEARCH IS PUBLISHED?

Despite the serious challenges, some e-business is being published, and not only in refereed proceedings such as those of the premier annual event in Bled (now in its 14th year), but also in journals.

A colleague and myself have been cataloguing e-business research publications in the primary information systems journals. Assessment is not yet complete of the small number of specialist EC journals, primarily the 18 issues of the International Journal of Electronic Commerce since mid-1996, Electronic Markets (in particular the 10 issues since February 1999) and the 6 volumes of Journal of Electronic Commerce Research since February 2000.

Cataloguing of 5 major research journals (MISQ, ISR, Information & Management, Decision Science and JMIS), and of the primary 'emergent issues' journal (Commun. ACM) has been completed. The period assessed is that since the explosion of e-commerce in about 1993, until late 2000. The following conclusions can be drawn:

- 37 e-business articles were published in the 5 selected research journals and 38 in the leading 'issues' journal;
- in the issues journal, 25 of the 38 were theoretical-only. Of the 13 that included empirical work, the research technique used comprised 1 survey, 8 case studies, and 4 field studies;
- in the 5 research journals, 10 of the 37 were theoretical-only. In the 27 papers reporting on empirical research, 11 involved surveys, 3 interviews, 14 case studies, and only 1 a field study.

EDI was the topic in 16 of the 37 research articles, but not a single one of the 38 in the issues journal. EDI is a technology of long standing, relatively stable, well-understood, and used by many organisations. It therefore qualifies as a suitable topic for research and publication in learned journals. It is utterly atypical of e-business, however, because it is batch-oriented and not interactive, and highly structured rather than open-ended. The results are unlikely to be of high value to practitioners in coping with the problems they face. Reflecting this change in priorities, the leading specialist international conference, held in Bled, Slovenia each year, was an EDI conference 1988-93, in transition 1994-95, but has been an e-commerce conference since 1996.

In short, the evidence from this limited study suggests that rigour continues to heavily dominate relevance in the selection of research topics for publication in refereed journals.

7. WHY E-BUSINESS RESEARCH IS MOSTLY OF LOW QUALITY

The author has reviewed a great deal of research in the e-business domain, generally as a member of the community, and as a referee and conference program chair and member. This section explains why he considers that most e-business research is not of high quality, with little of it satisfying journal editors, little of it satisfying non-academic audiences, and almost none of it satisfying both.

The first observation that has to be made is that good research in any social domain that is multi-segmented, young and changing rapidly, is extremely difficult to devise and to implement. Established theories are in short supply; terminology is distorted; such source data as is available is tainted; models of participant behaviour are lacking; the researcher is frequently also a participant and even a protagonist; the populations being studied are poor survey-subjects; the staleness factor makes publication urgent; and the strong demand that exists for populist reports stimulates premature release.

In addition, **the management of research** presents challenges that are particularly acute in the context of e-business. These include:

- insufficient relevance to attract industry funding, or (at the other extreme) excessive influence by the sponsor over topics, techniques and outcomes;
- inadequate resourcing to achieve the aims by supporting all of:
  - researcher time;
  - supervisor time;
  - travel costs;
  - infrastructure costs;
  - support staffing; and
  - host-institution levies;
- inadequate timeframe, arising from such sources as:
  - slow cycles of grant request, grant approval, candidate search, and candidate preparation; and

- the need for time-variant phenomena to be subjected to longitudinal study, over a period longer than a candidature or research assistantship.

Some of the low quality in e-business research, however, is not excusable on the grounds discussed above. One recurrent poor **research practice** is the unquestioning application of convenience reference theories such as Hofstede's cultural factors theory, Rogers' innovation diffusion theory, and transaction cost theory. These have some applicability to e-business, but they suffer serious weaknesses, yet are commonly applied without any assessment of their relevance.

There are also problems with the selection and implementation of reesearch techniques. Semi-structured interviews frequently masquerade as case studies, without the combination of depth and breadth that triangulation demands, and that is needed for any validity to be claimed. Meanwhile, consultancy work poses as [action] research.

Many problems are routinely evident in reports on **surveys**. These include:

- surveys are used as the sole technique even when:
  - in-depth information is needed as well; and
  - in-depth information is needed instead;
- effort is invested merely in questionnaire design, with the many other aspects of survey design short-changed. Particular problems include the following:
- survey objectives are ill-defined;
  - the population, the sampling frame and the sample are not clearly defined;
  - population stratification / segmentation is overlooked or over-simplified, in deference to the need to have enough responses to be statistically meaningful. In particular:
    - the mythical 'SME' is not classified into micro, small and medium-sized enterprises, nor divided into independent, loosely-controlled subsidiary and closely-controlled subsidiary categories;
    - no distinction is made among large single-function companies, cohesive multi-divisional business enterprises, conglomerates of operationally independent subsidiaries, multinational corporations, and virtual business enterprises;

  - government agencies are not differentiated according to the various functions that they perform (in particular, service delivery, regulation and policy-formation); and
  - non-profit/not-for-profit organisations are not differentiated by function;
- convenience samples are used with no apology and even no recognition, including proxies (such as the researcher's Masters class) instead of principals, and whoever responds to an emailed request;
- no account is taken of the principal-agent problem, i.e. the assumption is made that an employee speaks reliably on behalf of their employer;
- no account is taken of the simple fact that what people say and what people do are not the same thing;

– data analysis pays attention to the syntax (statistical correctness) but overlooks the semantics. In particular:
  - enormous respondent diversity is inadequately controlled;
  - questionnaires use highly ambiguous terminology that is differentially interpreted by respondents, without control being exercised;
  - long lists of 'Likert or not' data masquerade as information, without control being exercised over respondent comprehension, boredom, and the ease of providing semi-random answers;
  - the low response-rates and response-counts that are inevitable from over-surveyed and uninterested populations are routinely ignored; and
  - the sources and impact of non-response bias are inadequately considered.

Some research practices go beyond the question of quality to that of morality. As a contribution to a panel session at ICIS'2000, Clarke (2000b) identified a raft of **ethical issues** that arise in relation to the submission of papers arising from research, including matters relating to sponsorship, authorship, 'school of' manoeuvres, the depiction of the research method used, plagiarism, references and citations, depiction of the research's significance, consideration of the research's implications, economic factors, 'political correctness', and choice of submission venue(s).

8. TENABLE RESEARCH TECHNIQUES FOR E-BUSINESS

This paper has portrayed a grim picture. It has identified many difficulties presented by e-business, and drawn attention to a litany of problems that arise even in conventional I.S. research, and which are yet more challenging to master in a new and dynamic context. This section sets out to re-build some confidence in the conduct of research in e-business, but on new terms. It is intended to complement more general guides regarding the selection of research techniques, such as Galliers (1992).

The first observation is that there is progress. As evidenced in the section above on e-business research publications in journals, there is an e-business research literature, however limited; and hence the domain is no longer entirely 'virgin territory' or 'a green-fields site'.

In a relatively young discipline, focussing on a very new domain, non-empirical techniques have a considerable amount to offer. One is reviews of existing literatures, within the discipline, in cognate disciplines, and in less familiar reference disciplines. Conceptual research (often referred to as 'arm-chair reasoning', like this paper) can provide impetus to research, and assist empirical work to avoid weaknesses.

Other non-empirical techniques that can offer assistance in particular circumstances include the following:

- scenario-building;
- futurism, especially Delphi rounds;
- game- or role-playing; and
- simulation.

Among the scientific techniques, laboratory experimentation, and where feasible field experimentation and quasi-experimental designs offer prospects.

Interpretivist techniques that are directly relevant to various problems that instrumentalist e-business research can address include:

- descriptive/interpretive work;
- grounded theory;
- focus groups;
- action research; and
- ethnographic research.

A number of relevant techniques lie at the boundary of the scientific and interpretivist research approaches, and are used within both traditions. These include:

- secondary research, drawing on existing sources, including meta-analysis;

- questionnaire-based surveys, provided that their limitations are taken into account and acknowledged, and their weaknesses are addressed through the use of complementary techniques;
- interview-based surveys;
- case studies, but provided that proper attention is paid to the deep and multi-sourced nature of the technique; and
- field studies.

Finally, engineering techniques offer a great deal to some kinds of investigations, including:

- construction of an artefact, including:
  - conception (based on a body of theory);
  - design / creation / prototyping / testing; and
  - application;
- destruction of an artefact, including:
  - testing (but on real people, not proxies); and
  - application.

The following suggestions are made about particularly suitable research techniques:

- **Field Study through Observation**. e-business is characterised by a lack of theory and models. There is a need for foundation work to be performed, relatively free from the constraints of theory. Several techniques in the interpretivist tradition lend themselves to this purpose;
- **Case Studies**. Where a body of theory is available, it can be brought to bear through the combination of documentary research, interviews, small, targeted surveys and observation, in order to achieve triangulation. Care must still be taken to reflect the body of knowledge that exists on the scope for, and limitations of, the case study method;
- **Laboratory Experimentation**. Because many artefacts are very new, and the impact and implications of the intervention, and of particular features of it, are uncertain, there is scope for the development of prototypes, and the laboratory use of prototypes and alpha- and beta-versions of new products, initially perhaps by proxies, but primarily by members of the target population;
- **Field Experimentation**. Particularly in such areas as user interface and the comprehensibility and usefulness of new functionality, opportunities exist for field trials to be undertaken in large

organisations, with metrication designed in, and with experimental and control groups in different locations;

- **Surveys**. Although their limitations are substantial, circumstances exist in which responses to questions can be reliably and usefully gained from tightly-defined and -segmented populations.

Finally, the observation is offered that, of all of the aspects of e-business research, consideration of **implications** is the least often addressed. Because of the enormous import of information technology, Clarke (1988) issued a plea for implications to be researched in conjunction with at least applications of technology, and preferably right at the source, in the engineering, experimentation and trial usage phases. The intervening 13 years have seen the power of I.T. explode, the convergence of computing and communications completed, the convergence with content make great advances, location and tracking of devices and people become mainstream, and early steps taken towards the integration of robotics within I.T.

The need for social impact assessment is now seriously overdue, if errors yet worse than those of nuclear scientists and engineers of the first half of the twentieth century are to be avoided. Areas in especial need of attention include:

- workplace behaviour, stress, and skills formation;
- employment / income-distribution mechanisms;
- urban, regional, rural and remote accessibility and use;
- consumer and citizen behaviour;
- consumer and citizen rights;
- privacy (as distinct from mere security and data protection); and
- marketing, including permission-based, consensual, micro-, 1-to-1 and other forms of non-mass communications.

9. CONCLUSIONS

E-business research involves focusing a still-young discipline on a very young domain. The challenges of rapid change in technologies and behaviour, combined with inadequacies in research activities, are compounded by the confrontation between the academic demand for rigour and the real-world need for relevance.

It is easy to draw negative conclusions, such as that research will continue to be under-funded and inadequately performed, and that academics at the outset of their careers would be well-advised to choose less exciting domains in which to undergo their research training.

Some positive conclusions are possible, however. e-business must be perceived as a research domain, and the mistake avoided of regarding it as a new discipline. It needs the insights and methods of established disciplines brought to bear on it. In many circumstances, it is essential that multiple disciplines be carefully integrated within a single research project. This is because existing theories are inadequate to provide a basis for describing, let alone understanding, and far less predicting, the behaviour of individuals, organisations and mechanisms such as e-communities, marketspaces and e-enhanced societies.

The research methods devised to address particular research questions need to achieve both depth and breadth of understanding. In general, this requires either a compound technique such as case studies, or multiple complementary techniques, such as semi-structured interviews and surveys. Holistic approaches, and the integration of the insights of multiple disciplines, present special challenges, because they inevitably derive from distinct bodies of theory developed in order to describe rather different phenomena.

For real-world audiences to be attracted and informed, and for support to be gained from them, e-business research must be motivated by instrumentalism. Hence relevance needs to be regarded as the primary objective, and rigour as the constraint, rather than the other way around. This will create challenges for academics who need to achieve a modicum of publication in the highest-ranking and inevitably academically very demanding journals. It is therefore a responsibility of senior academics, who are less seriously impacted upon by the 'publish or perish' imperative, to devise, acquire funding for, and manage, e-business research programs.

Finally, the focus of research must not be limited to technology, applications of technology, and adoption of applications, but must also extend to their impact and their personal, legal, social and economic implications. Descriptive and explanatory outcomes must be complemented by predictive value, and must extend to normative outcomes, in order to inform the vital policy debates that surround e-business.

REFERENCES

A substantial list of references is provided at Clarke (2000a).

Alter S., Ein-Dor P., Markus M.L., Scott J. & Vessey I. (2001) 'Does The Trend Toward E-Business Call For Changes In The Fundamental Concepts Of Information Systems? A Debate' Commun. AIS 5, 10 (April 2001), at cais.isworld.org/articles/5-10/cais.isworld.org/articles/5-10/

Galliers, R.D. (1992) 'Choosing Information Systems Research Approaches', in Galliers R.D. (ed., 1992) 'Information Systems Research: Issues, Methods and Practical Guidelines', Blackwell, 1992. pp. 144-162

Keen P. (1980) 'MIS Research: Reference Disciplines and a Cumulative Tradition' McLean E. (Ed.), Proc. 1st Int'l Conf. Info. Sys. 1980, 9-18

Klein H.K. & Lyytinen K. (1985) 'The Poverty of Scientism in Information Systems' in Mumford E., Hirschheim R., Fitzgerald G. & Wood-Harper T. (Eds.) (1985) 'Research Methods in Information Systems' North-Holland, 1985, pp. 131-161

Kuhn T. (1962) 'The Structure of Scientific Revolutions' Uni. of Chicago Press, 1st Edition 1962, 2nd Edition 1970

Popper K.R. (1959) 'The Logic of Scientific Discovery', Basic Books, 1959

Popper K.R. (1968) 'Conjecture and Refutations' Harper & Row, 1968

Zwass V. (1996) 'Electronic Commerce: Structures and Issues' Int'l J. Electronic Commerce 1,1 (Fall 1996) 3-23, at www.mhhe.com/business/mis/zwass/ecpaper.html

THE INTERNET AND AN OPPORTUNITY TO RE-INVENT THE BANKING SYSTEM

MICHAEL S.H. HENG[1] and STEVE C.A. PETERS[2]
[1]*School of Accounting and Information Systems, University of South Australia*
[2]*Faculty of Economics, Vrije Universiteit, Amsterdam*

Abstract: This is an opinion paper. It argues that conditions are ripe for the re-invention of a core component of the banking system by having an autonomous institution to house the deposit accounts of individuals and companies. This institution would own and operate the payment and settlement systems. There would be no government guarantee for deposits with commercial banks, thereby removing one important factor of moral hazard. Governments would not need to worry about the collapse of the payment and settlement systems. The proposed set-up would constitute an important building block in a new international financial architecture. Banks could continue to thrive but they would need to innovate and earn their revenue by providing value-added services to their customers.

1. INTRODUCTION

In the last three to four decades, a profound and irreversible revolution has occurred in the world's financial markets and institutions. The hallmarks of this change are innovation, globalisation, and deregulation (Fabozzi et al 1994). Direct results of such changes are more intense competition in the business world and widespread use of information technology. Between them, they have reduced the traditional role played by banks as intermediary and indispensable players in payment and settlement systems.

Generally, banking activities fall into five categories: (1) payment systems, (2) custody of deposits, (3) provider of loans, (4) trading in stocks and asset management, (5) advice, namely in merger and acquisition. We argue that the sea change presents us with an opportunity to re-organize the first two activities of banking systems in economically developed countries before doing so elsewhere in the world. The central idea is to establish an independent institution to house the deposit accounts of individuals and companies. All payment transactions including the clearing between banks would happen there. This institution, which we shall call the Deposit Giro (DG), would function as the payment system within a country. It is autonomous and its independence is enshrined in the constitution. It is not profit-orientated, and will be managed by experienced bankers reputed for their competence, prudence and integrity. With this structure, governments no longer need to worry about the collapse of the payment system should one major bank go bankrupt. Moreover, there is no real threat to banks that live up to the standards of good banking practice. This new set-up will be an improvement on the status quo and because it is just one step beyond an emerging trend, it stands a chance of being implemented.

The new structure does not provide deposit guarantee for commercial banks, thereby removing a key factor of moral hazard. One manifestation of moral hazard was the reckless lending practices of banks in rich countries to East Asian companies and this was a crucial factor in the Asian economic crisis (Friedman 1999). By encouraging banks to be more prudent in their lending habits, the new set-up would contribute to a sounder financial system in emerging economies and a sounder international financial architecture. We suggest that the IMF encourage the set-up of such a Deposit Giro.

Anything new is likely to encounter resistance, and in this case we expect it from the banking industry. The American banking industry has one of the most powerful lobbies in Washington (Friedman 1999). Instead of fighting the tide by political lobbying, banks should welcome innovation and support the re-invention of the banking system. The new construction should not trouble banks that are prudent with their own capital and their customers' money. They would continue to flourish by providing value-added services to their customers. Four such services include: (1) acting as financial manager for small and medium-sized companies, (2) insuring businesses against foreign exchange losses at an affordable premium, (3) functioning as a knowledge system for their clients, and (4) providing services to support electronic commerce.

The rest of the paper is organised as follows. Section 2 reviews the major trends in the world of financial, which gives rise to shocking crises treated in Section 3, and also gives rise to an emerging opportunity to re-invent the banking system, treated in Section 4. The outline of the proposed new set-up is discussed in Section 5, which also leaves room for customers with choices (Section 6). The new environment is challenging to banks which are prepared to provide value-added services to their customers, and some possibilities are described in Section 7. The conclusion is in Section 8.

2. MAJOR TRENDS

A reading of business newspapers reveals that commercial banks are being exposed to some major structural changes. To ordinary bank customers, the trends are visible. Banks are trying to be bigger as a defensive measure; they are adopting multi-channel approaches, closing small branches and introducing account managers into their system. These changes are certainly not the result of some international conspiracy but that of wider forces at work, namely deregulation, globalisation, advances in information technology and the accompanying growth in importance of financial markets.

The last few decades witnessed a continuing trend towards the erosion of banks' intermediary role. The first disinter mediation involved savings, and the growth of mutual funds, specialized pension funds and life-insurance policies at the expense of bank deposits. In the second, the capital markets assumed some of the banks' traditional role as providers of loans. In the third, technology helped to streamline back-office operations. The threat associated with the Internet is the fourth, where the distribution of banking products is being disintermediated (Long 2000).

The Internet as a technological platform is to financial transaction what money as a common medium of exchange is to the economy. Just consider the convenience and flexibility provided by money in economic activity. The beauty of Internet banking lies in its low cost, convenience and availability. It enables banks and financial companies to offer services with the following qualities: 24-hour, seven-days-a-week availability, convenience, fast delivery, customer focus and personal service. The commercial use of the 128-bit encryption opens the way for secure on-line financial transaction. A pure Internet bank does not need brick and mortar branches, which means a lower entry barrier for newcomers and lower operating costs. Newcomers see the Internet as an opportunity to offer attractively priced products, higher interest rates for savings deposits, and lower service charges. They hope to beat the more established banks with a solid, easy-to-use, reliable and secure Internet banking services. The dreadful scenario for incumbent banks could have been such: embracing the Internet would mean destruction of banks in their current form; to do otherwise means opting out of banking.

Fortunately, what has come to pass is more benign. The pure Internet banks' single channel solution does not seem to work. The current trend is more towards multi- channel distribution than single channel banks. Yet the challenge remains. Banks have large legacy systems and a rigid culture. It takes them several years to accommodate a new channel like the Internet and to profit from the opportunities offered.

The business of acting as money intermediary is yielding lower profit. Under such conditions, some banks may not survive at all. The fierce competition could be a welcome challenge to provide better and cheaper services to customers. The problem is that banks tend to engage in risky, speculative activities in order to earn more profits and this can sow the seeds of financial crises.

3. MORAL HAZARD, BANKING CRISES AND DEFINING MOMENT

Banks take risks in the knowledge that should they be lucky, the profits are theirs to reap. Should they blunder, there is a safety net provided by the government. And there has been no shortage of blunders. "The past 20 years have seen more than 90 serious banking crises, each of which resulted in bank losses that, in proportion to GDP, exceeded the costs of banking collapse during the Great Depression (Beddoes 1999:6)." As Blinder (1999: 53) correctly observes, "The current system breeds too many crises that are too severe."

This problem of moral hazard partly encouraged by the safety net is getting more serious now for two reasons. The first is the upshot of globalisation, which has reduced governments' ability to raise taxes (Castells 2000). This means less money with which government can weave the safety net. Moreover, taxpayers are revolting against the costs of bailing out failed banks. Secondly, inter-bank loans are growing. In America it rose from $74 billion in 1980 to $170 billion in 1995. Turnover in foreign exchange market, in which banks are the main players, has reached to $1.2 trillion a day, almost double the figure in 1989. Banks are doing more business with each other. If one of the big systems breaks down, the banks would be the first to be hit hard, followed quickly by the rest of the economy (Giles 1996).

The crises from Mexico (1994) to East Asia (1997), Russia (1998) and Brazil (1999) are shocking in their frequency, virulence, contagion and scale. The crises highlight how interconnected and vulnerable the world's financial systems have become (Blustein 2001). This series of events constitutes a defining moment in the history of international finance, with the Mexico crisis described by the former managing director of the IMF as the first crisis of the 21st century (Summers 1995). They have led to the most serious re-thinking of the structure of the international financial system since the breakdown of the Bretton Woods system in 1971 (Fischer 1999). They are crises caused by interaction between weaknesses in domestic sector of those countries and free flow of international capital, magnified by financial innovations and speeded up by advanced information technology. A crisis erupts "when investors lose confidence in the country's banking system, stock market, or public debt management and when their scramble for the exits, facilitated by the existence of an open capital account, brings the financial system and the currency crashing down (Eichengreen 1999:5-6)." The sad story is that financial crises hurt hundreds of millions of innocent bystanders who play no part in the speculative excesses but suffer when the bubbles burst (Blinder 1999).

A simple answer to the problem of moral hazard is to tighten regulation dramatically, while retaining comprehensive deposit insurance. However, there are several problems with this approach. For a start, it may not work, because banks are old hands at finding loopholes in the law. Worse, an attempt to tighten the screws might simply drive business to more lightly regulated offshore havens. It would certainly impose an even heftier burden on banks, which would pass it on to their customers (Giles 1996:31)

In examining moral hazard, we should distinguish the hazards associated with different types of international lending. "The problem is far more serious for inter-bank lines of credit than for equity investment. The responsibility for dealing with the moral hazard problem for inter-bank lines of credit lies as much with the government of the lender as with the borrower government, for it is the former that supervises and tends to protect its banks. Lender supervisory authorities will have to recognize the responsibilities of their institutions to participate in bail-ins and work out procedures (Fischer 1999:14)." Herein lies the significance of improving the banking system in the rich countries as a contribution to the new international financial architecture.

4. AN EMERGING OPPORTUNITY

The dilemma of moral hazard encouraged by the safety net has prompted some people to propose the idea of a two-tier system of banks – the narrow banks whose accounts are guaranteed by the government and subject to very strict supervision. The other type of banks, which are not covered by the safety net, are not subject to strict supervision and are free to operate like any other ordinary business (Bryan 1991). The proposal generated heated debate (Seidman et al 1991), and enjoyed attention for a while. However, whatever the merits of the two-tier system, the idea is less exciting now that a new opportunity is emerging.

Currently, banks are being squeezed from the deposit and payment system side as well as the lending side (Claessens et al 2000). On the deposit and payment system side, many deposit substitutes are emerging and many non-banks such as mutual funds are offering transaction accounts. With Internet banking, consumers no longer have to pay high prices to transfer money from one country to another. On the lending side, technology and deregulation allow non-deposit-taking financial institutions and capital markets to serve many more segments of borrowers including small and medium size borrowers. Transaction costs are lower, information more widely available and better credit scoring and secularisation techniques are designed. Banks are losing their proprietary information about borrowers who do business with more than one bank and financial firm.

Historically, banks have played a dominant role in the provision of loans to finance trade and industrial development. By promoting development rather than passively following the course, they have helped to advance the development of incipient industrialization. In his study of history of American banks Bodenhorn (2000) found that they formed long distance relationships that promoted geographic capital mobility, thereby assuring the direction of short-term capital towards socially desirable ends. There existed an inherent tension between banks' duty to depositors and their responsibility to foster economic growth. Such responsibility is diminishing by virtue of new development in the capital market. Today, the technology and the economic environment have greatly reduced the need for banks' involvement in the provision of credits for such purposes. Many corporations have made good use of financial instruments such as stocks and bonds to raise capital. Blue chip companies enjoy higher credit ratings than commercial banks. As for new and promising companies, they can lean on the support of venture capital.

We concur with Claessens et al (2000) in arguing that current developments in technology and deregulation are eroding the special nature of banks. An opportunity presents itself for governments to re-evaluate the overall need of a public safety net.

The new environment provides a new opportunity for governments and the financial world to re-invent the banking system. Consider an independent institution created to house the bank deposits of individuals and companies. All payment transactions would happen there. In other words, the institution would function as the payment system and depository within a country. With this construction, governments no longer need to worry about the collapse of the payment system should one major bank go bankrupt as a result of its speculative activity. The system will continue to function regardless of the ups and downs of the financial market.

5. RE-INVENTING THE BANKING SYSTEM

The Deposit Giro we are discussing is already existing in a nascent form in West European countries, in the form of the clearing house used by commercial banks and financial firms to process their payments. It is currently owned and operated by commercial banks. The transaction services are yielding very marginal revenues for their operators thus reducing the government's difficulty in taking over the clearing bank. In fact, banks might welcome the Deposit Giro because it rids them of expensive payment systems. The Deposit Giro will also act as the custodian for individuals and companies to deposit their money. As a result of developments on the money market over the last few decades, this custodian function is yielding little profits for banks. There could be two sources of opposition. The first comes from banks which will still like to operate with the safety net and use the customers' money to indulge in high-risk business activities. The second objection comes from those customers who like to earn more interests with a high-risk profile. These two points will be discussed in the next two sections.

With due preparations and by designing the payment infrastructure on a non-competitive basis, banks can be persuaded to co-operate and benefit from this non-partisan, technical institution.

An independent body is established to manage this Deposit Giro. This body will own, control and operate the payment system serving the banking and financial community. The Deposit Giro enjoys autonomous status and its independence is enshrined in the constitution. Its board of management must consist of experienced bankers known for their competence, prudence and integrity. It is free from political interference and its guidelines are based on professionalism, not political expediency.

On the whole, the Deposit Giro is thoroughly clear in its mission, and transparent in operation. It is easy to manage provided it is embedded in a tight set of regulations and legislation. It is purely a clearing institute in the technical sense, avoiding all the trappings of commercial banks.

The Deposit Giro is not profit-orientated. While serving as a custodian of deposits, it pays out modest interests to savings account, and lends money in the form of buying government bonds and other gilt-based investments where no risk is involved. This modus operandi serves two purposes. It rewards its customers and earns an income to pay for all its expenses. At the same time, it provides liquidity to the capital market.

Another possibility is for the Deposit Giro to earn its income from transaction and not from interest margins. It is a place to keep your money safe without interest and to be able to pay your bills. Your salary is put into that account, without any special costs related. Electronic transactions at that scale cost almost nothing, so let the companies which pay their employees using Deposit Giro bear that cost. It can, in fact, operate as the post office does i.e. the sender pays. This was how the old post bank of the Netherlands worked. Its task was only in money transfer. It gave no interest and could not act as a financial intermediary.

In the new construction, commercial banks and other loan providers can be given permission by a customer to look at that customer's financial profile, based on income and expenditure information stored at the Deposit Giro. These banks can analyse the data before making decisions on whether or not to give loans to those individuals and companies. The privacy of the customers is not compromised as only high level information revealing the required pattern of income and expenditure (and not the detailed information) is made available to third party. Because the DG is non-profit orientated there is no incentive to sell information to other parties. Hence, there is less danger of infringing on the privacy of account holders.

To whom should the DG be accountable? To the society. Some of the features of the Deposit Giro are already there in the form of the central bank, which operates under very strict rules, and is non-profit orientated. Just as the central bank, it should generate enough revenue to pay for itself and to offer sufficient incentive to attract good people with integrity and skill. It is worth considering making the Deposit Giro a joint stock company with no majority shareholder. Such a stock or certificate pays, say, only one percent dividend and retains profits for upgrading the payment systems. The public should be encouraged to have an interest in this socially and monetarily useful institution. Its stocks can be classified as a socially responsible investment (or ethical investment as it is referred to in some countries) whose dividend is tax-exempted. By having a thinly spread out ownership (e.g. trade unions, church organizations, central banks, financial watchdogs and regulators, and university endowment funds) there is a wider involvement and control by the general public.

Within the euro zone, the European Central Bank should take the initiative to establish the Deposit Giro to serve member states.

The recent series of financial crises has highlighted the urgency and importance of strengthening banking systems and reforming international financial systems. It is instructive to remember that in the 1920s-1930s the fragility of the international financial system helped turn a slump into the Great Depression (James 2001). That the global economy is not as bad as the 1930s has ambivalent implications. On the one hand, a healthy economy masks bad lending. On the other, the current relatively benign business environment is favourable for planning and implementing a new structure. It makes sense to carry out much needed surgery when the body is strong enough to cope with the physical trauma rather than postpone it to a point of crisis. Although the idea of an operation may be more readily accepted when there is "no choice", the body, at that point, may not be able to take it. Shock therapy is a last resort for those without foresight and lacking in discipline.

We suggest implementing the scheme first in the Western countries, where the trends are most advanced. Over time, with the benefit of experience, the scheme would become more robust. It is then appropriate to let the scheme diffuse to other countries. There is no need to rush to apply the idea world-wide in a short period.

6. THERE SHOULD BE ROOM FOR CHOICES AND RISK TAKING

There may be people who like to keep their money with commercial banks and financial firms to earn higher interests. The choice should be open to them, but they must be told that they run the risk of losing their money. Having deposits with these banks and firms would be basically similar to buying bonds or owning company stocks. To give themselves the guarantee of their savings, depositors can buy insurance, very much like stocks owners buying put options. The insurance providers would have to continuously monitor the risk exposure of these banks and firms, and if need be, impose some form of discipline on them. Their reliability is also indicated by the ratings provided on a regular basis by rating agencies.

Banks would no longer be special. Gone would be the days where, upon a major bank going bankrupt, other banks would be pressured by the authorities to cough up princely sum to help in bailing out the failed bank. Moreover, commercial banks can insure themselves against whatever risks in which they are engaged. Largely the market would now handle the control function traditionally exercised by the government.

Although government would no longer act as guarantor of deposits, it will still have to supervise and regulate the banks. It does so directly in the form of legislature and indirectly by establishing independent supervisory boards, just as it is doing now with the stock exchanges, insurance companies and pension funds. The reason is quite clear. The government must exercise its duty to protect the interests of the people by preventing fraud and embezzlement, partly because individual depositors are not good at monitoring their banks. This forms part of the institutional infrastructure needed for a free market to function properly. It will not hamper the banks in performing their usual function of financing promising and innovative, but risky, business ventures (Bodie and Merton 1998).

The DG set up is not a panacea. Financial crises and bank failures will still happen, fuelled by human shortcomings such as greed, panic, hubris, corruption, incompetence and mismanagement. Because of these deep-seated flaws in the human condition and weaknesses of the system, volatility and contagion cannot be banished. Financial crises and panic have been taking place for centuries (Kindleberger 1978; MacKay 1841), and they will be with us for a long time to come (Garten 1999). In many countries, the central bank is given the responsibility to maintain the stability of the financial system. It is in this context of preventing panic-induced declines in money stock and mitigating financial crises, that the central bank takes on the role of "lender of last resort" (Humphrey 1975; Fischer 1999). While acting to stabilize the system, the central bank should follow the famous advice of Bagehot (1873): that in a crisis the lender of last resort should lend freely, at a penalty rate, on good collateral. Companies that would be bankrupt in normal times should be left to disappear.

In other words, the new structure would not exorcise the demons of reckless speculation which is a part of business life. To deal with the problem, we need (1) official regulation, (2) monitoring and self-regulation by the private sector, (3) imposition of costs on those who make mistakes including, when appropriate, the enforcement of bankruptcies (Fischer 1999).

7. BANKS TO FLOURISH ON A FIRM BASIS

This section examines four areas where banks can do well by providing value-added services to their customers, based on which they earn their revenue. Banks may know a lot about their customers, but do they use the information to help them improve management of their financial affairs?

7.1 As Financial Manager of Small and Medium-Sized Companies

Medium-sized businesses form the backbone of the vast majority of the rich economies and the emerging economies. In terms of products, technology, marketing and customer service, they usually have the needed critical mass. But in financial management many do not have the size to support the competence they need (Drucker 1999). Typically they operate with a woefully low productivity of capital and have either too little or too much cash. Banks can add value to their customer service by providing money management services for their clients' businesses. Related to this is the conversion of their needs into investment products for the retail investor.

7.2 To Insure a Business against Foreign Exchange Losses

Another service for business clients is in developing financial instruments to protect a business against catastrophic foreign exchange losses. They convert currency risks into another ordinary cost of doing business. In the words of Drucker (1999), the need is desperate, mostly among the world's huge numbers of medium-sized businesses that suddenly find themselves exposed to a chaotic global economy. Only aggregation, which subjects the risks to probability, could protect these businesses against such risks.

7.3 As a Knowledge System for Their Clients

Risk management and information management are the two major tasks of financial institutions (Saunders 1994). Competent information management cannot be divorced from business knowledge, as evidenced from the use of data mining technology to supplement database technology. Credit risk analysis requires in-depth knowledge of the business, as illustrated by the work of venture capital. Besides risk assessment, the venture capitalists serve as a source of early capital and as a locus of high-tech investment expertise and services to start-up companies. In the USA the role of venture capital firms in high-tech companies in the Silicon Valley is well known (Cohen and Fields 1999).

Knowledge-intensive services provided by banks in the more "traditional" activities are the vetting and tracking of growth companies, assisting clients in finding partnership abroad, identifying export opportunities, financing projects that promote sustainable economic development, etc. New types of knowledge services are emerging. For example, a vehicle lease company in the Netherlands combines the use of its knowledge about cars and information technology to create values for the stakeholders (Heng and Peters 2001). An important point to emphasise here is that bank needs to position itself as player in the knowledge intensive economy and to *consciously* see itself as a knowledge network to serve its customers.

7.4 To Provide Services To Serve Electronic Commerce

Commerce in our age inevitably involves monetary transaction. It would thus come as no surprise that e-commerce could affect banking in a very fundamental way, and could be affected by the approaches banks take to respond to the new demands. For example, e-commerce will further undermine the power of bank branches (Lawrence et al 1998). It has created a demand for low cost facility for micro payments (Choi et al 1997). Some areas for banks to develop products and services are: protection for e-commerce participants against fraud arising from misrepresentation of identities, assistance to small business entries into e-commerce, provision of electronic billing services and provision of technology for business-to-business e-commerce (Wenninger 2000). In short, the new form of commerce may provide banks a new playing field.

8. CONCLUSION

The global capital markets have got so huge, so unruly, and so panic-prone that the IMF can be easily overwhelmed when crises arise, and this is especially true if the IMF's response is confined to large loan packages and demands for economic reforms in the country involved (Blustein 2001). The recent series of financial crises shows the urgency of strengthening the international financial system. Our paper is essentially a proposal to build an institution to cope with systemic volatility of global financial markets. We have not seen it being proposed this way, either in academic journals or in serious newspapers like *The Economist*. The whole endeavour will not be easy. It would not be easy for the usual reason that opposition would come from those banks which have a vested interests in being protected by the safety net. It will not be easy because we would be embarking on a project to build social-economic institution under a new historical condition. But the benefits in the form of more prudent use of taxpayers' money and, more crucially, a sounder and more stable international financial system are too enormous for the governments of the rich countries not to strive for it. Writing in the closing chapter of his recent book on the changes associated with the Internet, Castells (2001) says, "Systematic volatility of global financial markets and vast disparities in the utilization of human resources require new forms of regulation, adapted to the new technology and to the new market economy. It will not be easy. Particularly it will not be easy to enact effective, dynamic regulation of global financial markets .... Yet, since no one has really tried, we really do not know. It would be wise to find sensitive ways of channelling global finance before a major crisis forces to do it under more strenuous conditions (ibid: 279)."

In an interesting way, some of the factors responsible for these crises are creating the conditions needed for re-inventing the banking system. We suggest the formation of an institution to house the deposits of individuals and companies and to operate the payment and settlement systems. It is non-profit orientated and its independence is enshrined in the constitution. Government would no longer need to provide deposit guarantee, thereby removing one key factor of moral hazard. Governments are right in perceiving their responsibility as creating a benign environment for business firms to operate. Re-inventing the banking system in the new technological and economic conditions fits this scheme well. In so doing, they contribute to a sounder international financial architecture.

The new banking system would kiss goodbye to the strange capitalistic practice of privatising the profits and socializing the losses. It would put an end to the burden on innocent taxpayers brought about by the moral hazards. Though there is no need for deposit guarantee, there is still need for lender of last resort to cope with sudden actual, or potential, breakdown of the system in a financial crisis.

ACKNOWLEDGEMENT

We are grateful to Dr Sven Fischer, Mr Chen-Ie Lie, Mr Jaap Peters and Mr Cees Quirijns as well as the three anonymous reviewers of the IFIP WG8.4 conference for their thoughtful comments on an earlier version of this paper. The usual disclaimer applies.

REFERENCES

Bagehot, W 1873, Lombart Street: a description of the money market, London: William Clowes & Son

Beddoes, M. 1999: Global Finance survey, The Economist, 30 Jan 1999 p. 1-18

Blinder, A S 1999: Eight steps to a new financial order, Foreign Affairs, vol.78, no.5, p.50-63

Blustein, P. 2001 Chastening: Inside the Crisis that Rocked the Global Financial System and Humbled the IMF, Public Affairs

Bodenhorn, H. 2000: A History of Banking in Antebellum America : Financial Markets and Economic Development in an Era of Nation-Building, Cambridge: Cambridge University Press

Bodie, Z and Merton, R C 1998: Finance, London: Prentice-Hall

Bryan, Lowell L. 1991: A Blueprint for financial Reconstruction, Harvard Business Review, May-June

Castells, M 2000: The rise of the network society, revised edition, Oxford: Blackwell

Castells, M 2001: The Internet galaxy, Oxford: Oxford University Press

Choi, S Y et al 1997: The economics of electronic commerce, Indianapolis: Macmillan

Claessens, S, Glaessner, T and Klingebiel, D. 2000: Electronic finance: reshaping the financial landscape around the world, Presented at the joint conference of the World Bank, the IMF and *International Finance,* 11 July 2000 Washington DC, available at www.worldbank.org/research/interest/conf/upcoming/papersjuly11/papjuly11.htm

Cohen S S and Fields G 1999: Social capital and capital gains in Silicon Valley, California Management Review Winter, p. 108-130

Drucker, Peter 1999: Innovate or die, The Economist, 25 Sept.

Eichengreen, B 1999: Toward a new international financial architecture: a practical post-Asia agenda, Washington, DC: Institute of International Economics

Fabozzi, F J, Modigliani, F and Ferri, M G 1994: Foundations of financial markets and institutions, New York: Prentice-Hall

Fischer, S 1999: On the need for an international lender of last resort, Talk delivered to the joint luncheon of the American Economic Association and The American Finance Association, New York, 3 Jan 1999 www.imf.org/external/np/speeches/1999/010399.htm

Friedman, T 1999: The lexus and the olive tree, London: HarperCollins

Garten, J E 1999: Lessons for the next financial crisis, Foreign Affairs, March/April

Giles 1996: Survey on International Banking, The Economist April 27, p. 1-44

Heng, M S. H. and S C.A. Peters 2001: Domain knowledge as corporate resource of financial firms Proc. of 3rd International Conference on Enterprise Information Systems, Setubal, Portugal

Humphrey, T 1975: The Classical Concept of the Lender of Last Resort, Federal Reserve Bank of Richmond Economic Review, 61 (February), pp. 2-9.

James, H 2001: The end of globalisation: lessons from the Great Depression, Boston: Harvard Business Press

Kindleberger, C 1978): Manias, Panics, and Crashes: A History of Financial Crisis, New York: Basic Books.

Lawrence, E et al 1998: Internet commerce, New York: Wiley

Long, S. 2000: Survey of on-line finance, The Economist, 20 May 2000

MacKay, C 1841: Extraordinary Popular Delusions and the Madness of Crowds. (Reprint, 1932). New York: Farrar, Straus and Giroux

Saunders, A 1994: Financial Institutions management: a modern perspective, Burr Ridge, Ill: Irwin

Seidman, L W et al 1991: What is the future of banking? (debating Lowell L Bryan's article) Harvard Business Review July-August

Summers, L 1995: Ten lessons to learn, The Economist, 23 Dec 1995

Wenninger, J 2000: The emerging role of banks in e-commerce, Current Issues in Economics and Finance, vol.6, no.3, p.1-6

FAILING WITH SUCCESS

A study of e-commerce adoption and knowledge transfer to small and medium-sized enterprises in Sweden

FRANK ULBRICH
Stockholm School of Economics, Department of Information Management, Sweden

Abstract: An e-commerce dissemination project for small and medium-sized enterprises is analyzed to determinate its successfulness. After a theoretical discussion of different success measurements, different phases of the dissemination project are examined from different perspectives by representing the three different groups of participants - project management, consultancies, and small and medium-sized enterprises (SMEs). Understanding the process of carrying out a dissemination project will help to identify determining factors for the successfulness of such projects which in fact depends on the different perspectives presented in this paper.

1. INTRODUCTION

The European Union (EU) supports many information and communication technology (ICT) dissemination projects, even if the rate of success is questionable.

Over the past years, European politicians expressed their wish to strengthen Europe's economic wealth, resulting among others things in the EU's e-Europe initiative. Turner (2001) describes how Europe might achieve a leading position in the global market. He emphasizes that companies of all sizes need to improve their competitive advantages. Callon (1996) believes that this can be achieved by widely using modern and innovative ICT. One example for innovative ICT is e-commerce. The EU expects e-commerce to become a technology that will give European companies competitive advantages in the global market. This assumption is confirmed by the fact that many e-commerce projects were initiated and/or funded by the EU or its

memberstates in recent years.
But are the high expectations really justified? And what price do companies have to pay to obtain a competitive advantage through e-commerce?

Shapiro and Varian (1998) point out the risk of becoming dependent of technology even if it probably will help to achieve competitive advantages. Porter (2001) states that the majority of basic economic principles will most likely not change when adopting e-commerce and that technology per se will not generate any benefits or competitive advantages. McKenna (1997) shows that modern technology will significantly influence the way of doing business by helping companies to meet their customers' demands. Following the customers' requests to provide more individual services, Davis and Davidson (1991) state that companies need to capture and utilize information about their customers at each stage of contact, and not only a few. This will, according to Hagel and Armstrong (1997), revamp competitive and managerial situations. Consequently, ICT becomes more and more a significant part of doing business.

However, it has to be asked whether companies are prepared to handle the new situation. Especially small and medium-sized enterprises (SMEs) do not often have enough knowledge about how to use a new technology efficiently. Here, ICT dissemination projects come into the picture. Different projects are run to accelerate the implementation of e-commerce among European SMEs, aimed to help European companies to quickly become more competitive.

Considering the great amount of ICT projects carried out, it is of particular interest to investigate whether such projects actually succeed.

1.1 Objective of the paper

The objective of this paper is to deal with a particular ICT dissemination project, which was conducted in Sweden, to determine its rate of success. After discussing success criteria, different perspectives from the project management, consultancies, and SMEs will be used to find factors and interrelations between them to determine the successfulness of the dissemination project.

The findings are considered to be of primary interest for those dealing with project management in similar projects and/or those deciding to fund such projects.

2. A SHORT PROJECT DESCRIPTION

An e-commerce dissemination project run by the Blekinge Institute of Technology during the year 2000 was the starting point for this study. The project was called "Companies in cooperation meeting tomorrow's challenges" (in Swedish: "Företag i samverkan möter framtidens utmaningar"). Its objective was to raise the participating SMEs' ability of being competitive by supporting them in the process of implementing electronic commerce (cf. Länsstyrelse Blekinge 1999).

At the point the project was granted it could be observed that smaller companies would be forced more and more by larger companies to implement some form of e-commerce. Therefore, the participating companies should be helped to survive in an increasingly competitive market. The project focused on subcontractors to larger Swedish companies, and the basic idea to start with the larger companies' demands.

Initially, the dissemination project was designed to consist of three different phases:

1. The first phase included competence improvement, where companies should have been made more aware of benefits with e-commerce. As a measurable result, 150 companies should participate in such activities and even more should be reached by mailing information about such activities.
2. The second phase was planned to consist of cooperation and collaboration between the participating SMEs. During this phase, at least 25 companies should have created local networks, partly in order to discuss problems and ideas with each other, partly to see whether there could be some cooperation between them.
3. Finally the third phase should include analysis of the 25 project participants' businesses in order to present individual action plans on how to implement e-commerce. The third phase was meant to be accomplished by external consultancies.

3. METHODOLOGICAL APPROACH

Some researchers believe that there is no such thing as a best research method. Often, a combination or modification of research methods is used for certain purposes. Schein for example argues, "there is no one best way, and that what we must strive for is a deeper understanding of each of the many ways to further our knowledge of human systems" (Schein 1986, p. 9).

Therefore, it is actually irrelevant to question whether to use quantitative or qualitative research methods or techniques in isolation. "Important is, instead, the congruence between the scope of the research and the method we have chosen in order to realize this scope." (Berg 2000, p. 9). In order to gain a better understanding in the research object it is therefore important to perceive reality as it is. Lundeberg (1993) believes that shifting between different perspectives will help the researcher to better perceive reality as it really is. Therefore, three different perspectives are used when describing and analyzing the empirical data: a) a project management perspective, b) a consultancy perspective, and c) a SME perspective. Data collection was conducted by participating observation and interviews with participants.

4. BACKGROUND

4.1 Small Enterprises

The average company that participated in the analyzing phase of the dissemination project had between 25-50 employees and was family-owned. Three areas were focused on in the literature review. These areas were connected to: 1) SMEs economic growth; 2) expectations for the future; and 3) enhancement of working conditions in SMEs. These areas were chosen partly because of their connection to the objective to achieve better positions in competing markets, partly because of the SMEs motivation to participate in the project.

Emling (2000) shows that family-owned companies in Sweden are usually not especially interested in economic growth, but rather like to know how costs would develop in the future. Many of the companies seemed to be pleased with their current situation and did not strive to become a larger company. Schumacher (1975) already described this behavior when arguing for keeping a business small instead of focusing on expansion.

Concerns about the future were also expressed, primarily on how technology could be used to improve a company's competitiveness. Many previous studies showed that companies could achieve competitive advantages through the use of modern innovative ICT (cf. e.g. Hardes et al 1993; Callon 1996).

Finally, improving working conditions and life-style of the owners was an addressed field. Enhancing the owner's quality of life was found to be important in SMEs (cf. Westhead et al 1996; Ulbrich 2000). Here the main concerns of owners were about getting more spare-time and /or higher revenues, which they could benefit from.

4.2 Success and failure criteria

Success and failure are concepts that are used in different ways by different authors. Mirvis and Berg (1977) e.g. describe success and failure from an organization development context and state that, besides demands from organizations, our understanding of success and failure even is characterized by cultural influences. They mean that parents e.g. hope for a better life for their children. Mirvis and Berg (1977, p. 8) state that, "to foster and sustain these values our culture associates success with hard work and competence. At the same time it equals failure with indolence and inability."

Our perception of success and failure is influenced by what we learn from parents, teachers, institutions and so on. Therefore, success and failure are often measured in terms that people consider being good or bad at a certain time in a certain cultural environment. Trying to measure if something has been successful or not, has kept researchers busy for decades. They are often looking for objective measurements such as productivity. Marrow (1972) did so when e.g. describing whether changes in the automotive industry had been successful or not. He could find that productivity, and by those means, success, was influenced by technology. If new technology had been applied in a way that increased productivity, a successful implementation had taken place.

Other explanations for success can be found in an encyclopedia. In Brockhaus (1979) e.g. one explanation is connected to economics and measured as profit and loss within an organization, meanwhile another one is based on psychology. The second states that success is the experience of confirmation when successfully realizing a self-set target, which is specified by one's own level of claim and performance motivation. This explanation is totally subjective and can therefore only be measured by the person who set his/her own goals.

Consequently, success and failure can be measured in different ways. Therefore, one has to decide how and what to measure. Kahn (1975; 1988) e.g. measures success and failure in export industries. He initially decided to use an objective and a subjective criterion when measuring failure and success. Kahn (1975) decided to use pre-tax profit and sales as a criterion for objective measurement. This is in accordance with others, such as Marrow (1972), where success or failure can be expressed in numbers and economic terms. As a subjective measurement Kahn (1975) uses an internal assessment to measure the degree of success and failure of a given venture. He investigates the degree to which expectations are met by comparing actual outcomes with expected outcomes regarding a number of criteria such as costs, export volume, profitability etc. This way of measuring success and failure is in line with the psychological explanation of the encyclopedia (Brockhaus 1979) and puts individuals and their perceptions to the forefront. Several years later, Kahn (1988) decides to change some of the subjective measurements to what he calls semi-objective. The degree to which expectations are met compared to the actual outcome, is moved from subjective to semi-objective and only individual statements are left as subjective. Furthermore, Kahn (1988) could observe that success and failure were not measured in equal terms in Sweden and Japan and confirmed Mirvis and Berg's (1977) statement on cultural differences in our understanding of what success and failure is.

When discussing and measuring success and failure in this paper, a trisection, as suggested by Kahn (1988) with minor modifications for the purpose of investigating ICT dissemination projects, is used: 1) objective, pre-tax profit and sales; 2) semi-objective, as a degree to which outcomes fulfilled project requirements; and 3) subjective, as an internal assessment to which individuals' expectations were met compared to the actual outcome.

5. PROJECT ACCOMPLISHMENT

The dissemination project was performed in three successive phases. But in contrast to the three phases the project was initially divided into (cf. A Short Project Description), project management decided to change the order of these sequences. Phase two (cooperation and collaboration between the participating SMEs) and three (analyzing businesses of 25 project participants) were performed in parallel and before the first phase (competence improvement). Project management decided to do it in this way, as it felt the need to inform the local SMEs about definite findings from the region, rather than theories on electronic commerce or best practice from companies the local SMEs could not identify themselves with.

5.1 Phase I: Initializing

The dissemination project started with an initializing phase where project management's tasks were to rewrite the original project plan and to receive approval. Activities and states of Phase I are pictured in Figure 1.

After creating the new version of the project plan, the next activity was to inform SMEs and external consultancies about the project. It was necessary to find at least 25 SMEs that wanted to participate in the project. One of the project managers had been working at the Chamber of Commerce and Industry of Southern Sweden previously and had been in contact with several local SMEs, which would give him access to more than 200 SMEs.

Project management decided to contact those companies where they assumed or knew that the SMEs could be interested in participating in an electronic commerce project. In this way participating SMEs were hand-selected without spreading information about the project's existence to a broader audience.

In parallel, project management decided to contact a number of consultancies that could fit the project's requirements. The project budget included financial means for only some external consultancy hours. Therefore, consultancies that were willing to donate some of their services, seeing the participation in the dissemination project as a strategic investment into their future electronic commerce ventures, were attracted to the dissemination project. In return a so-called Round Table was set up for consultancies to share ideas and discuss all kind of issues encountered during the project. Furthermore, the consultancies were promised early access to the results from the other consultancies before the participating university would publish any findings about the project.

Three consulting firms were contracted and meetings between one consultancy and 8-12 SMEs were conducted. During the meetings the invited SMEs were informed about the purpose of the project as well as the consultancy's way of carrying out individual analyses of the SMEs.

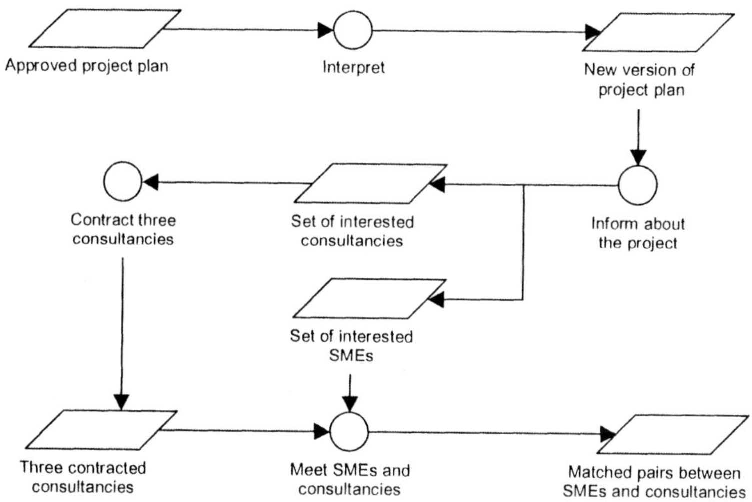

Figure 1. Initializing phase

After the initial meetings some of the SMEs dropped out and others were considered inappropriate for the project due to lack of interest or preconditions such as the size of the business. Project management and the consultancies decided together which SMEs would participate in the second phase.

5.2 Phase II: Accomplishment

In the second phase (cf. Figure 2) the "real work" was carried out. The participating SMEs had a number of individual meetings with their assigned consultancy. Project management's role in this phase was to help the consultancies to establish contact with the SMEs and to keep alive a discussion between the consultancies, which was done by organizing three Round Tables where results and problems with the project were discussed.

In parallel with activities in Phase II, project management prepared the third phase.

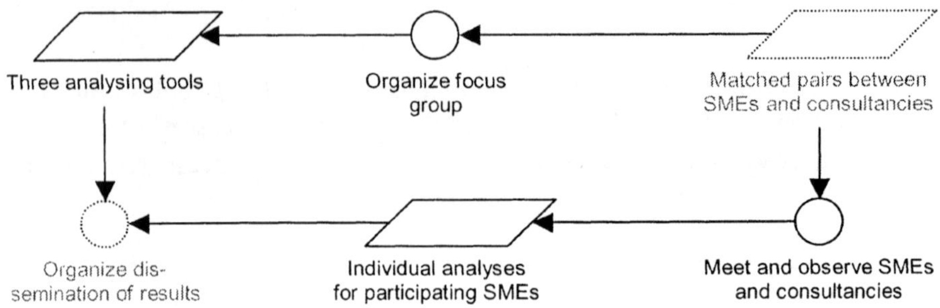

Figure 2. Accomplishment phase

5.3 Phase III: Dissemination

The last phase concentrated on dissemination and evaluation of the project (cf. Figure 3). According to the approved project plan, information about electronic commerce needed to be spread to at least 150 SMEs in the region. Project management invited local SMEs to an e-commerce conference where the purpose was to inform about e-commerce in general and possible solutions for SMEs in particular. The consultancies were also invited to talk about their experiences of the project using one or two companies as case studies.

After the conference, findings from the projects and some further project documentation were collated in a final project report. This report was circulated to all participants and invited companies at the conference.

In addition to the synthesis, two researchers from the Blekinge Institute of Technology evaluated the project. Their evaluation showed that the project was performed according to the requirements stated in the revised project plan.

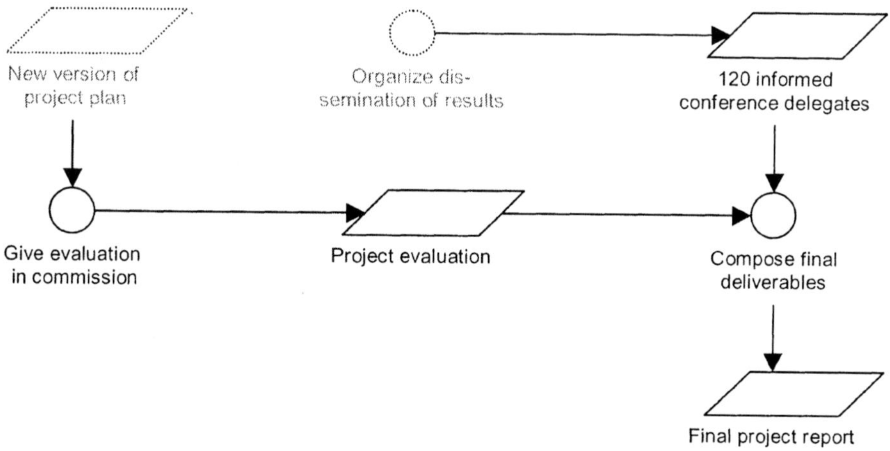

Figure 3. Dissemination phase

5.4 Was it a success?

The final project evaluation concluded that the project had been performed according to the requirements. The external evaluators could only evaluate the visible surface of the project using a semi-objective perspective. An insider might have had more insight as to the project's progression and all the problems that had been handled at certain times. Therefore, an observer who had the possibility to monitor all different stages in the process would have had more opportunity to look beyond the black box and beyond the surface, to question whether the project was a success.

6. UNDER THE SURFACE

In the first phase it seemed that project management put a lot of effort into selecting the 25 SMEs that would be asked to participate in the project. The project manager, coming from the Chamber of Commerce and Industry of Southern Sweden, performed this task, as he already knew many of the regional SMEs. He contacted 32 SMEs in the selection process that he thought might be interested in participating.

One reason behind the fast selection process was because the time frame for the project was quite limited. It was already spring when the first companies were contacted and individual analyses should be finished by the end of autumn. It is very difficult to set up meetings during the long Swedish vacation period (mid-June to mid-August). Therefore, the project manager wanted to finish the selection process as quickly as possible.

At the first general meeting between 11 SMEs and one of the consultancies it come to light that the selection process had not been very effective. After a presentation about how the consultancy wanted to carry out the project, the SMEs were asked how they thought electronic commerce could make a contribution to improve their businesses. From the answers some of the participants' expectations about the project and their knowledge about e-commerce could be derived. While one person e.g. could state exactly what his company needed-which was an implementation of an EDI solution in order to be able to stay in business as subcontractor in the Swedish car industry-another did not even know why he was joining the meeting-which he expressed by the statement that his boss had sent him to the meeting just to hear what it was about. These statements also show the wide array of understanding about e-commerce. Companies which already knew about e-commerce and how it might be adopted in their businesses, were much more engaged in the initial meetings and appeared more motivated to participate in the project than those without pre-knowledge. Pre-knowledge on electronic commerce would be one factor that would probably influence the outcome of such a project.

Even the relation between project management and the SMEs influenced the motivation factor. Earlier contacts and probably also personal relations between persons in the SMEs and the project manager, who earlier worked at the Chamber of Commerce and Industry for Southern Sweden, may have influenced the relationship between the project manager and the SMEs. This could be observed, since it appeared that some SMEs did not join the project because of its content. In many cases companies accepted the invitation to participate in the project because the CEO and project manager knew each other and sometimes it may have been commanded by feelings such as guilt ("I have to help them with this unpromising situation."), rendering a service ("Well, in return for my service they will have to help me next time.") or avarice ("If we participate now, it will look good to get something for free in the future."). Thus, Motivation to be part of the project was influenced both by feelings and personal contacts that were based more on content.

The relationship between the abovementioned factors could be summarized as a group of driving forces for the SMEs (cf. Figure 4).

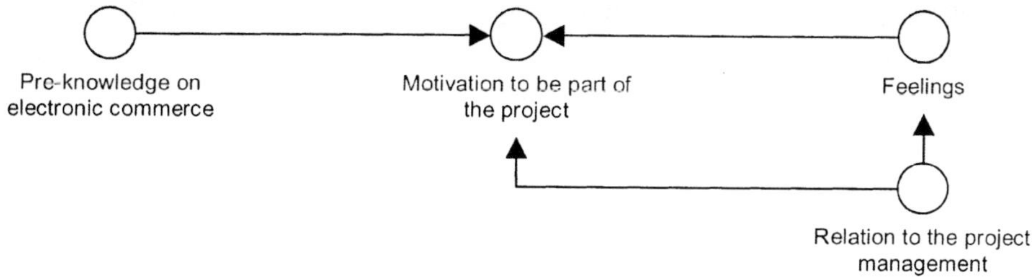

Figure 4. Driving forces for SMEs

Motivation and pre-knowledge are factors that affected the project's progress. Overall it could be stated that those companies who had pre-knowledge and were more motivated also played a more active role in the second phase of the project. In these companies, meetings with the consultancies went without mentionable incident, whereas the other companies sometimes felt compelled to cancel an appointment or did not show up with the personnel that were required. For instance, one of the SMEs called a project manager and asked him to move a meeting with the consultancy to the day after because they wanted rather to meet with a client. It was obvious for the project manager that the new meeting with the client would not be critical for the company's survival in the future, but they preferred it anyway. In another example an SME did not call all responsible managers to a meeting with the consultancy even if they earlier agreed to do so. The CEO simply did not see the need of having all managers gathered at the same time and he considered himself as the one who knew the company best of all.

This shows that tactical issues came before strategic. As the project was more of strategic nature, the degree of active participation in the SMEs was directly influenced by motivation and pre-knowledge.

Active participation also influenced two goals of the projects. One was directly influenced, the degree to which extent suggestions would be usable for SMEs, i.e. the degree of how likely SMEs will adopt the suggestions of the consultancies after the project was completed. An unexpressed goal for project management was that 80% of the participating SMEs should declare that the project was useful for them in the future. But the consultancies doubted from an early stage whether this could have been achieved. The inability to adopt new ways of thinking how to conduct business by using electronic commerce seemed to affect this goal. The other goal was to establish at least three new networks among the participating SMEs, as stated in the project plan. To establish new networks, of course, depended on the SMEs' wish to be included. If SMEs could see good reason to join the network they probably would have done so, but to create an Interest to join a network was influenced by the SMEs motivation as well as active participation.

During the second phase the interrelation between different factors affecting the outcomes of the project from the SME perspective increased the driving forces and active participation as shown in Figure 5.

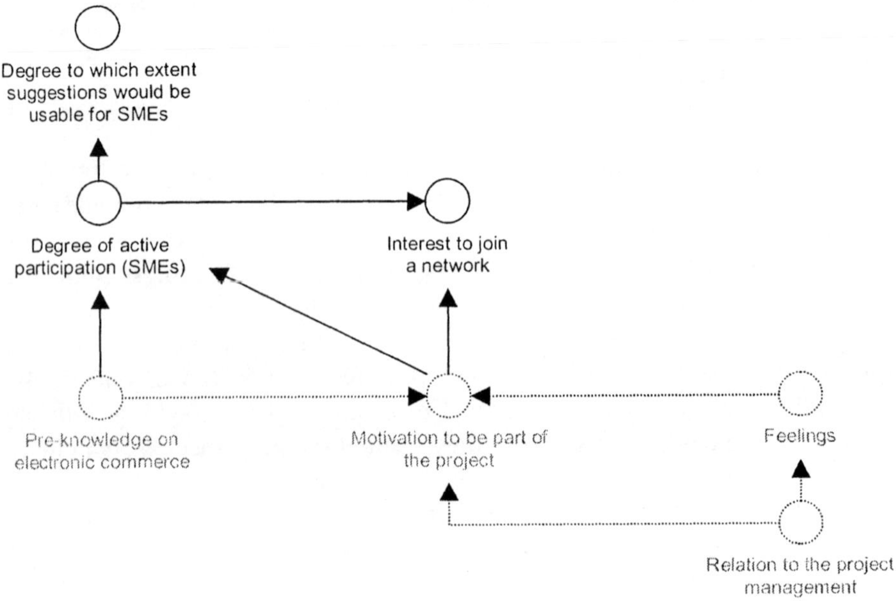

Figure 5. Driving forces and active participation in SMEs

6.1 Shifting perspective

To achieve a high degree of usability is not only dependent on the SMEs. So far we have only discussed factors that described levels and states to the SMEs and how these will affect the outcomes of the project. We already started to see connections to the project management as well, but for now let us leave the SME perspective and look closer at what happened within the three consultancies.

The degree of usability is e.g. to a high degree dependant on the efforts of the consultancies. It was shown to be a problem that the three consultancies were all large well-established consultancies. One of them operated on a global level, one of them on the European market and one of them on the Swedish market only.

The average customer for these consultancies usually were large, often multi-national, companies with long-term commitments in fields such as outsourcing, system development and user training. Assignments like the one in this project, to analyze an SME within a fraction of hours they usually could use for similar task within larger companies, demanded a new way of thinking. So it seemed crucial that the consultancies would succeed in developing new ways to produce usable consultancy reports. New methods and tools for analysis were needed in order to carry out analysis under the circumstances the project demanded.

As already stated in the short project description, getting access to each other's analysis tools should partly compensate the consultancies. So it was not only the development of analyzing tools but also the consultancies' willingness to cooperate, those were factors behind the desired degree of usability (cf. Figure 6).

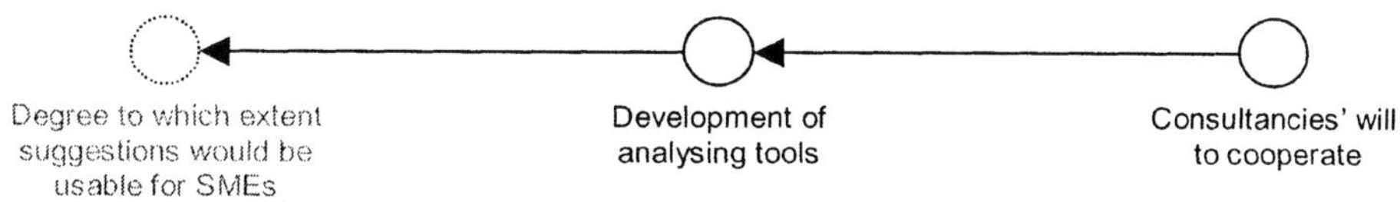

Figure 6. Creating preconditions for analysis

The development of the analysis tools was incumbent on the consultancies, but in order to share experiences from an early stage and to learn from each other, the consultancies agreed to participate in Round Table meetings.

The Round Table meetings turned out to be the place where the consultancies were more willing to listen than to share their new ideas. Information that was shared with the other consultancies was mostly information that was later documented in the consultancies' reports, but did not offer much to the development of new analysis tools. One of the consultants summarized the Round Table meeting by stating after the last one, that nothing was actually achieved that was not already known. His observation turned out to be correct. The desire to cooperate in order to achieve competitive advantage against other consultancies, who had not participated in the project, was overshadowed by the fact that the companies still saw themselves as competitors. Some ideas about how to do such an analysis might have come up at the consultancies, but they were neither discussed at the Round Table, nor reflected in the analysis tool description that each consultancy provided in the end of the project. One consultant reported afterwards that there was no profit in SME e-commerce, and this might explain why one of the three consultancies did not show much interest at the Round Table meetings and did not apply much effort on developing new analysis tools.

6.2 Shifting perspective

For the project management it was a preferred goal to achieve some common analysis tools. The project management expected that such a tool should even be valid for SMEs without the help of a consultancy in order to increase SMEs pre-knowledge before taking further steps to implement electronic commerce and before even talking to a consultant. Therefore, increased pre-knowledge could result in a positive circle with higher degrees of motivation and active participation. But the consultancies did not wish to develop such tools that should be given away for free. Thus, the Development of free tools for SMEs was strong depending on the Consultancies' will to provide free tools (cf. Figure 7).

Figure 7. Supporting SMEs in knowledge build-up

Unfortunately, this never happened during the project. The consultancies either did not develop such tools, or did not inform the others that they did so. The only tools they used were different kind of questionnaires where SMEs were asked to prepare themselves before a meeting but these questionnaires were not transparent for the SMEs and therefore did not serve the knowledge build-up in SMEs.

7. CONCLUSIONS

Regardless of how the project ended, the participating organizations learnt about themselves and how they could apply e-commerce in the future. Whether it is really concrete, such as a forthcoming implementation project or just the insight that the organization is not ready to use e-commerce at the moment, organizations might benefit from participating in the project from an organizational development standpoint. Even if one might call the project a failure the insights can be useful for the single participating organization. Therefore, the project can be seen as a success.

Others might say that the project where only the formal goals were achieved, but the participants decided not to pursue their own implementation, was a complete disaster. In this case, projects that are indicated not to be followed up or carried on by the participants should neither be supported nor started at all.

From a third point of view, it could be argued that the project was a success despite some failures. This means that the project management could not be hold responsible for what the participants would do after the project and that it is only of interest that the formal project requirements were fulfilled.

Concluding it can be stated that the particular project described in this paper could be classified as a success, a complete disaster or a success despite failure, depending on how one would like to look at the results. A combination of the three different views could be called as "Failing with Success".

REFERENCES

Berg, P. O. (2000), *Is There a Clinical Research Method?* Stockholm School of Entrepreneurship, draft.

Brockhaus (1979), *Der grosse Brockhaus*, Bielefeld: Bertelsmann Verlag.

Callon, J. D. (1996). *Competitive advantage through information technology*, New York, McGraw-Hill.

Davis, S. and Davidson, B. (1991), *2020 vision*. New York, Simon & Schuster.

Emling, E. (2000), *Svenskt familjeföretagande*, Stockholm: The Economic Research Institute.

Hagel, J. and Armstrong, A. G. (1997), *Net gain: expanding markets through virtual communities*, Boston, Mass.: Harvard Business School Press.

Hardes, H. D., Krol, G. J., Rahmeyer, F. and Schmid, A. (1993), *Volkswirtschaftslehre*, Tübingen: UTB für Wissenschaft.

Kahn, M. S. (1975), *A study of success and failure in the Swedish export industry: an empirical study of fourteen firms in three manufacturing industries*, Stockholm: Stockholms Universitet - Forskningsrapport.

Kahn, S. (1988), *Success and failure of Japanese companies' export ventures in high-tech industries: a comparative study of Japanese and European manufacturing companies' export marketing and investment strategies in ASEAN, the NIEs and the People's Republic of China*, Stockholm: Almqvist & Wiksell International.

Länsstyrelse Blekinge (1999), 'EG:s strukturfonder beslut 1999-10-25', Dnr. BL 2.41-41-99, Karlskrona.

Lundeberg, M. (1993), *Handling change processes: a systems approach*, Lund, Bromley: Studentlitteratur, Chartwell-Bratt.

Marrow, A. J. (1972), *The failure of success*, New York.

McKenna, R. (1997), *Real time: prepearing for the age of the never satisfied customer*, Boston, Mass.: Harvard Business School Press.

Mirvis, P. H. and Berg, D. N. (1977), *Failures in organization development and change: cases and essays for learning,* New York.

Porter, M. E. (2001), 'Strategy and the Internet', *Harvard Business Review*, March 2001, pp. 63-78.

Schein, E. H. (1986), *The Clinical Perspective in Fieldwork,* Qualitative Research Methods Series 5, Beverly Hills: Sage Publications.

Schumacher, E.F. (1975), *Small Is Beautiful,* New York: Harper & Row, Publishers, Inc.

Shaprio, C. and Varian, R. (1998), *Information Rules,* Boston, Massachusetts: Harvard Business School Press.

Turner, C. (2001), 'Accelerating the development of the European information economy: the European Commisson's eEurope initiative.' *European Business Review* **13**(1), 60-66.

Ulbrich, F. (2000), A Decision-Support Framework for Electronic Commerce in Small and Medium-sized Enterprises, *in* 'Conference Proceedings: Innovation Through Electronic Commerce IeC 2000', Manchester, UK, Nov 14-16, pp. 211-221.

Westhead, P., Cowling, M. and Storey, D. J. (1996), *The Management and Performance of unquoted Family Companies in the United Kingdom,* Centre for Small and Medium Sized Enterprises, Warwick Business School, The University of Warwick.

MODELS OF TRUST IN BUSINESS-TO-CONSUMER ELECTRONIC COMMERCE

A Review of Multi-Disciplinary Approaches

VIVIENNE FARRELL, RENS SCHEEPERS and PHILIP JOYCE

School of Information Technology, Australia

Abstract: The issue of trust in Internet-based business-to-consumer electronic commerce has been explored from a number of different perspectives. The current body of research is diverse and fragmented. This paper critically reviews recently published models pertaining to trust in business to consumer e-commerce. For analytical purposes we categorize the literature in three main streams: technological, design and sociological/psychological. Based on our analysis and our own empirical observations we raise four main areas of concern that warrant further research attention: an oversimplification of the trust concept, a uni-directional view of trust, discipline centred approaches to modelling trust and a lack of empirical grounding and testing. In the light of these concerns we recommend avenues for further research

1. INTRODUCTION

We continue to witness the growth in the global business community of the Internet as a platform for electronic commerce. Much attention is dedicated to the Web, its potential and the risks that it holds for marketing and selling products and services online. In the context of business-to-consumer (B2C) electronic commerce, the consumer not only compares product and pricing alternatives, but also the risks of conducting the transaction online. The notion of trust is especially relevant in the online context where the intended purchase may be from a supplier that is operating in a different country, time zone, currency and legal system. In the B2C context products are typically paid for in advance and only received after the transaction. Consequently the issue of trust in Internet-based B2C electronic commerce is receiving much research attention.

Research into trust in e-commerce has been approached from different perspectives and as a result the current body of research is diverse and fragmented. We draw on this rich interdisciplinary base to rationalise the current thinking pertaining to trust in B2C contexts.

We believe that the research within this area has reached a level of maturity where it now requires a more integrative approach to foster a richer understanding for both practitioners and researchers alike. Indeed, we outline some of the dangers of a continued fragmented approach, especially the conceptual deficiencies that prevent a more cohesive understanding of B2C trust. Within this paper we analyse a number of current models of B2C trust and critically reflect on the current streams of research. We highlight main areas of concern in the light of our review and also in the light of our own empirical observations.

This paper is structured as follows. Firstly we revisit the notion of trust in the B2C context and we isolate recent streams of research in this area. We then categorise sixteen models of B2C trust within the main streams of research. This categorization enables us to reflect critically on a number of conceptual concerns and omissions due to the fragmented approach of much of the current research. We discuss our concerns and highlight specifics that we argue need to be addressed in further research efforts in this field.

2. METHODOLOGY

A preliminary literature review of B2C trust research was carried out by drawing on recent studies from prominent peer reviewed journals and conference proceedings. The review not only centred on publications addressing B2C trust models, but also closely related topics. In preparation for the review, we liased with a number of research colleagues in the field in order to identify prominent outlets for trust publications in e-commerce. This preliminary review yielded in excess of 50 relevant studies of B2C e-commerce trust models. Although we do not claim this to be an exhaustive review our approach was to be inclusive rather than exclusive. In examining the results of the preliminary review we noted that there was considerable overlap between the different studies. Many of the models were extrapolations or interpolations of previously published concepts and models. Our primary focus was on identifying novel and original studies as opposed to adaptations and extensions of existing models. These studies were subsequently analysed by the authors both independently and collectively. This analysis was complemented by the reviewers independently in light of their current empirical fieldwork. This approach compares to similar reviews of this nature (e.g. Tornatzky & Klein, 1982). A greater emphasis was placed on research studies that displayed a high level of rigour in terms of methodology in its establishment of concepts and models.

We found we could classify the literature review into three main focal areas: technological, design and sociological/psychological perspectives. This again emphasised the interdisciplinary approach we adopted within this study indicating the main thrusts and models of B2C e-commerce trust. It also allowed us to question some of the contemporary thought emanating from the current literature. We expand on these classifications in the following sections.

2.1 Trust in a B2C Context

There is no consensus in the current literature as to a commonly accepted definition for the notion of trust in the B2C context. This observation is echoed by McKnight et al. (2001) where they state "there is no agreed upon definition of trust due to different definitions coming out of varying disciplines". Ambrose (1998) proposes that trust is related to task risks, that is trust varies depending on the task the user is undertaking. Cheung et al. (2001) argue that there is confusion by some between the understanding of trust as an outcome and antecedents. This problem manifests itself in testing for effectors of the trust in design and the marketing of the B2C web site when the antecedent decision to purchase has already been made in the individual's antecedents of trust. Cheung (2001) also recognise two effectors of Internet trust, trustworthiness of Internet vendors and their external environment, and the division of types of trust proposed by personality theorists, sociologists and economists, and social psychologists.

In an attempt to collate the varying factors affecting trust, Papadopoulou (2001) discusses different trust categories of system shopping process, vendor, individuals and firm trust in e-commerce, separating out consumer and vendor related trust.

No matter what the context, discipline or the trust beliefs of the consumer, most researchers agree that trust in an e-commerce, B2C relationship is related to risk, or more precisely, inversely related to risk. It is from this perspective that we will consider trust in a B2C, Internet based, e-commerce relationship.

There is little correlation between the studies and the independence of the variables posed as being responsible at some level for the mistrust in e-commerce technologies. The area of e-commerce itself is multi-disciplinary and requires the integration of technology, visual design, business acumen, human computer interaction, sociological and psychological considerations. To this end the research approaches seem to have followed the discipline from which the author's orientation belongs.

It is from this position that we bring together the research and evaluations that have been undertaken to date. We will now analyse and discuss the perspectives of B2C trust, the pertinent models that exist in recent literature and the major issues raised.

2.2 Perspectives of B2C Trust

A number of perspectives on B2C trust were apparent from the literature. These emanate from the variety of disciplines that have an interest in electronic commerce and B2C electronic commerce in particular. From our preliminary review we have isolated three main perspectives across the various disciplines for categorizing the research studies pertaining to B2C trust. These are technological, design and sociological/psychological perspectives. We will provide a brief overview of each of these research streams by focusing on some central areas of emphasis.

2.3 B2C Trust from a Technology perspective

This stream of research deals with trust issues such as encryption, verification and authentication of vendors and consumers. Studies cover the application of technologies such as third party validation certificates, fulfilment methods, order tracking and handling of consumer data. There are a number of avenues within this stream that focus on the techniques to make the technologies adopted "more visible" to the consumer in order to foster trust.

Many studies have attempted to test the consumer's perception of technology usage and its level of importance in creating an environment of trust in B2C e-commerce.

2.4 B2C Trust from a Design perspective

This stream of research broadly deals with the influence of design issues such as aesthetics, metaphor and usability on trust in B2C contexts. Many design issues such as ease of use, tailoring, amateurism, perceived business size and reputation, and enjoyment have been raised over time especially within the area of Human Computer Interaction (HCI).

Design issues however, extend beyond HCI and cover research efforts aimed at simulating real world experiences and processes online in order to foster a familiar and trustworthy environment for the consumer. This includes the use of well-known metaphors such "shopping carts" and design of the website to simulate a physical "bricks and mortar" store layout.

Research efforts in this stream deal with design guidelines that seek to engender consumer trust of websites. Design issues such as the incorporation of company logos, privacy statements, style and their impact on trust, and perceived reputation all fit into this vein of research.

2.5 B2C Trust from a Sociological/Psychological Perspective

This stream of research encompasses studies that examine issues that are external to the e-commerce artefact but intrinsic to the individual's socio-psychographic makeup. Such studies relate to the individual's propensity to trust. The latter is based on preconceived beliefs, attitudes and intentions towards e-commerce in general, technology in general and ultimately how these should be considered in terms of web site design, marketing, advertising etc.

It is claimed by some studies that fears and concerns can be allayed by carefully crafted B2C implementations and the use of effectors of trust such as testimonials, transitional reputation, trusting beliefs, propensity to trust, perceived usefulness and usage of brand name.

This stream of research seeks to establish correlations between these effectors and the behaviour of study subjects, site usage statistics and ultimately purchasing behaviour.

3. REVIEW OF PERTINENT B2C TRUST MODELS FROM LITERATURE

We now classify and summarise the various themes addressed by the B2C models in the studies in our review within each of the perspectives as outlined above. The classification reported here enables the analysis following later in this section. Where elements of some studies could reside in more than one category we have classified them as such. In addition, for each model that we included in our final review, we have assessed the nature of the trust relationship being model (e.g. from the vendor's or consumer's viewpoint) and we also assessed whether the model was empirically tested (and if so, how this was achieved). A summary of the findings appears in Table 1.

3.1 Technological perspectives

In the relatively new B2C e-commerce environment the ground rules for security have yet to be set and understood by both the consumer and the vendor. The use of credit cards, the most popular mode of transacting in B2C e-commerce is seen as a potential means to fraudulent behaviour. A lack of understanding as to how secure an encrypted transaction, or how to know if the latest encryption techniques are being used leads to a perception of substantial risk (Salam et al., 1998). Personal information being passed to an entity into a world of technology that is not necessarily understood by the consumer can cause concern to the consumer (D Harrison McKnight et al., 2000).

The availability of technologies, such as encryption, reduces the ability to tamper with data during transmission. There are regulations, laws and privacy policies to protect the consumer and the vendor and assist the consumer in assessing the level of risk that is to be taken. Although a B2C site may include all of the technology available to secure the site, it is not certain that the consumer understands the relevant technology symbols used or if the symbols make a difference to the consumer's intention to purchase (Farrell et al., 2001).

A variety of technology mechanisms that may engender trust has been researched. Grazioli (2000) presents the *Model of Internet Consumer Behaviour* that represents trust mechanisms such as testimonials, company size, reputation and assurance mechanisms such as seals warranties, news clips and physical location. Grazioli (2000) considers the *assurance mechanisms*, their relationship to trust and the *trust mechanisms* and their relationship to trust, leading to the shopper's attitude towards purchase. These technological issues are empirically tested on the Internet students, who were given the challenge of perceiving fraud within the site. This research found that deception by the vendor had only a moderate effect on the subjects' opinion of risk and trust.

Tan & Theon (2000-2001) relate *control trust* to *party trust* and propose an equation that models the behaviour of trust in e-commerce. Control trust relates to the control mechanisms that are in place for the transaction to take place, i.e. the technology that is available. "If you understand a control mechanism then you can evaluate your trust in it" (Tan & Thoen, 2000-2001). Party trust refers to the trust in the party with whom you are doing business; this can be applied from either the vendor's or consumer's position. This trust is developed through knowledge of the other party and an understanding of the knowledge that the other party possesses. The *Generic Trust Model* takes the perspective of the vendor in regards to the control mechanisms required to obtain trust for the vendor and from the consumer. The model depicts risk, risk attitude and potential gain as internal to the person's attitude towards trust in an e-commerce environment. Externally the model suggests trust in the other party and trust in the control mechanisms affect the level of trust. Tan & Theon consider that once we understand who we are dealing with and the mechanisms for transaction we can evaluate our trust in the transaction.

The importance to industry of fostering a trustworthy relationship can be seen by the extent to which the business community have engaged in research to identify effectors of trust. In an industrial study six formal characteristics of web sites are identified that claim to communicate trustworthiness from the consumer's perspective (Cheskin Studio Archetype/Sapient, 1999). The empirical testing is done from the consumer's perspective. The characteristics are brand navigation fulfilment, presentation, up-to-date technology and logos of security-guaranteeing firms (Cheskin Studio Archetype/Sapient, 1999). The study also presents a level of trust that is required as a base before a transaction can take place ranging from mistrust to an intrinsic level of trust.

3.2 Design perspectives

From the included research literature, methods pertaining to web site design were identified that are considered to improve the confidence of the consumer. The Theory of Reasoned Action (Fishbein & I, 1975) leads to the consequence that the buyer's belief about a site affects the buyers' attitude toward the site (Grazioli & Jarvenpaa, 2000). Careful design of an Internet site is maintained to portray a look and feel that will engender substantial size and professionalism of the company while emanating traditional aspects relating to consumer confidence and trust. The literature suggests that in doing so the web site designers are able to reduce the perceived risk potentially experienced by the consumer. It is recognised by the researchers that it is not essential for a vendor to outlay a substantial financial commitment in order to trade on the Internet, hence the possibility of a "fly by night" business exists (Einwiller et al., 2000). Therefore it is considered that trading with an unknown business demands a higher level of trust on the behalf of the consumer than a face-to-face purchase (Choi, 1998). For Internet start-up companies it is therefore suggested that they should present themselves as being professional and able to fulfil any transactions that are established.

From the literature relating to design perspectives, it is proposed that careful design can be incorporated to create a site that presents the look and feel of a pervasive, professional organization that follows traditional trustworthy practices. It is also argued that amateurism and difficulty to navigate through a site or transaction may question the professionalism of a business, leading to a diminished trust. Another aspect of design said to create a trusting environment is one that recognizes the consumer by tailoring to their individual requirements, giving importance to the consumer as an individual. These issues have been recognized and included in models that lead to e-commerce B2C trust and consequently perceived reduction of risk.

The *Internet Consumer Trust Model* of Jarvenpaa et al (1999) depicts consumer trust as a result in the consumer's view of the perceived size of the store and reputation. The resultant trust in the store is then reflective of the attitude and risk perception of the consumer. Perceived reputation and size of the business as effectors of trust are considered to offer a significant contribution. Jarvenpaa et al. (1999) consider the positive effects that perceived reputation and size have towards trust in a store that leads to eventual purchasing intention.

The TAM model (Technology Acceptance Model) (Fishbein & I, 1975; Davis, 1989) has been adapted and extended to identify its relevance to B2C e-commerce. The *Proposed Conceptual Model,* an extension of the TAM, includes perceptions of privacy and security (Pavlou, 2001) that attributes TAM with social aspects. A survey of students found that the factors of privacy and security perceptions affect trust and therefore perceived risk. The survey of 52 students is said to substantiate the initial premise of the TAM model, indicating a correlation between perceived usefulness and perceived ease of use on intention to transact.

Design is also discussed within the literature from a Human Computer Interaction perspective. Such issues as the look and feel of a web site to project an image of establishment and security are foremost in the discussion. Fogg et al. (2001) set out to discover what gives a web site the perception of credibility. Fogg's study is a large-scale on-line survey that considers the consumers' perspective of the factors that are said to portray a strong sense of credibility. Seven web site design factors and their effects on credibility were tested; "real world feel", ease of use, expertise, trustworthiness, tailoring, commercial implications and amateurism. It was found that amateurism was the greatest deterrent of web trust while a real world feel gained the greatest acceptance. From the study, Fogg et al (2001) have proposed guidelines in order to assist web site design to engender trust in a B2C e-commerce environment.

McKnight et al. (2000) use terminology from the HCI discipline in relationship to e-commerce design, such as the effects of icons from "trusted" third parties. The paper discusses the movement of the consumer from the exploratory stage to the commitment stage and how the consumer's commitment is effected by the inclusion of third party recognition on the site. The authors indicate that the model is to be empirically tested by using students and an online survey.

Egger's (2000) *Model of Trust for E-Commerce* (MoTEC) considers the usability, overview and appeal from the design perspective of an e-commerce site. Egger (2000) proposes that traditional HCI analysis and design methods are relevant in addressing design issues in B2C e-commerce incorporating 'User Centred Design' methodologies. Egger's model includes interface properties of appeal, overview, usability and informational content of products and services, company, security, privacy and communication. Egger (2000) does not consider these to be the only effectors of trust but recognises that reputation, attitude to technology and propensity to trust need to be considered.

In a second study McKnight et al. (D. H. McKnight & Chervany, 2001) identify linkages between trusting beliefs to trust related Internet behaviour in the *Interdisciplinary Trust Constructs Model*. Trusting beliefs are said to be a product of web vendor interventions including design issues such as privacy policies and third party seals and customer interaction. McKnight discusses vendor interventions (certification, etc.) as having strong direct links to *trust* but recognizes that *trusting beliefs* and *trusting intentions* have a large effect on trust in e-commerce.

3.3 Sociological/Psychological perspectives

Within the selected literature individuals are recognized as bringing to the e-commerce B2C environment preconceived ideas regarding technology, electronic commerce, purchasing behaviour and a propensity to trust (Jarvenpaa et al., 1999; D. H. McKnight & Chervany, 2001). Individuals are also purported to be influenced by external factors such as experiences of others, media exposure, advertising and use of brand name (Einwiller et al., 2000). The factors considered to have an influence on consumer trust have been acknowledged as possibly having either a positive or negative impact depending on the knowledge and experience of the individual. Much research attention is dedicated to determining how much impact, if any, each of these factors have on e-commerce. Methods and models relating to the neutralising of any negative effectors of trust relating to individual beliefs and environmental issues have been proposed and tested. In an attempt to alleviate concerns felt by the individuals, vendor's sites are tested with contrary factors that appear external to the vendor such as testimonials of satisfied customers and transitional reputation that often relies on the 'good name' of a known product. It is anticipated by the researchers that by reducing the negative preconceived views of e-commerce and improving the environmental issues, purchasing behaviour can be modified to include e-commerce as a trustworthy environment in which to conduct business.

The theme of propensity to trust is modelled by Ambrose (1998), *A Trust Based Buying Behaviour Model*, and includes seller and buyer characteristics as part of the model. This was developed from Mayer et al (1995) and proposes that the vendor can improve the trustworthiness from the consumer's view of the site by managing its appearance of ability, benevolence and integrity. It is also proposed within this model that the consumer must have a need, capacity and willingness to purchase as trust is not the only criterion for purchasing behaviour. This model has not been empirically tested.

Effectors on trust such as propensity to trust, word of mouth and institutional characteristics are depicted in the *Research Model* by K. Kim & Prabhakar (2000). Kim's research considers the factors influencing trust, in particular initial trust, categorising the factors into economics based, institution based and personality based. Propensity to trust, word of mouth referrals and institutional characteristics are said to influence initial trust and when considered with the perceived risk and trust in the institution will lead to trusting behaviour by the consumer. The model has been pre-tested by students in an online survey and is to be tested further in regards to the banking industry utilizing an online survey.

Cheung & Lee (2001) have developed a 30 item list of sociological and psychological effectors that affect trust in e-commerce as a measurement instrument reliability and validity of an e-commerce transaction. The list of 30 items covers consumers view of security, privacy, integrity of vendor, competence of vendor, propensity to trust, cultural background positive experience with the Internet, third party recognition, legal aspects, trust and perceived risk. It does not cover HCI design aspects. This instrument was initially empirically tested by a student survey and subsequently tested indicating cultural differences in trust of e-commerce (Borchers, 2001).

Kini & Choobineh (2001) conducted empirical testing on the issues relating to propensity to trust and developed an instrument named the *trust scale* leading to a *Research Model for Studying Trust in WWW Commerce*. This model, which was tested on students by means of a questionnaire, includes tendency to trust, risk involved, and information provision as influencing factors for trust in banking e-commerce. The findings from the consumer's perspective show that tendency to trust was not a significant influence on trust in the banking environment, which is contrary to many other studies, in particular those who have revised the TAM model. Their research also found that trust is related to the task that is being undertaken and suggests that therefore not all tasks may be suitable for Internet commerce.

Considerations other than personality based trust characteristics are identified by Kim, E. (2001) who adds to personality based trust with environment based trust and process-based trust. The Model of Sustainable Trust discusses four possible factors that affect trust that are ability, willingness, familiarity and affection. Kim, E. (2001) suggests that personal tendency may be too contingent to be managed, whereas environment and processes are factors that are under the control of the vendor and legal system. Kim, E. (2001) suggests factors that may affect sustainable trust rather than initial trust as ability, willingness, familiarity and affection. This model has not been empirically tested.

More intently focused on the environment as a factor affecting trust in e-commerce, Salam (1998) suggest in the proposed model, *A Priori Theoretical Model,* that institutional trust and economic incentive are the main reasons for trust and purchasing in an e-commerce environment. The paper claims that these two social factors lead to consumer perceived risk and are in fact inversely proportional to consumer perceived risk. This model was tested using an online survey of web users. Einwiller et al. (2000) propose that recognition of a trusted symbol or transference of trust can give trust to a vendor's site. This research discusses the concept of corporate branding as a method of engaging trust in e-commerce distinguishing branding processes by targets, content and methods. Einwiller et al. (2000) have collated a table of methods said to improve the level of trust by including in the contact with the consumer either personal or imparted experience by phone or chat rooms, increasing familiarity through brand naming, creating affiliations with membership, being transparent in all matters of security and privacy. These methods include assuring that the web site meets the demands of the consumer, press coverage, financial coverage such as turning customers into shareholders and corporate advertising and design. These influencing factors have not yet been empirically confirmed.

Extending from these individual sociological, psychological Papadopoulou et al. (2001) collate research in e-commerce trust and theoretical models for the formation of trust in customer-business relationships. The authors present a model of *Trust Formation Through Promise Fulfillment Within E-Serviscape that* considers the building and retention of trust from the consumer perspective throughout the e-commerce process. The underlying aspects of trust creation considered include trusting intention, behaviour and beliefs. The model is based on the argument that trust is built through repeated interactions that include fulfilment of promises, and is yet to be empirically tested.

Table 1 provides an overview of the pertinent research that we have reviewed as outlined above. We refer to the perspectives adopted by the researchers in developing their models and the research testing procedures and collated the data accordingly. Table 1 also displays the direction from which the trust is considered, i.e. trust by the consumer of the vendor or trust by the vendor of the consumer.

Reference	Perspective			Empirically tested
	Technological	**Design**	**Sociological/ Psychological**	
Ambrose & Johnson, 1998			Consumer	No
Cheung & Lee, 2001	Consumer		Consumer	Yes (students)
Kini & Choobineh, 2001			Consumer	Yes (students)
Egger, 2000		Vendor	Vendor	No
Einwiller et al., 2000			Consumer	No
Fogg et al., 2001		Consumer		Yes (online)
Grazioli & Jarvenpaa, 2000	Consumer	Consumer		Yes (online students)
Jarvenpaa et al., 1999		Consumer		Yes (students)
K. Kim & Prabhakar, 2000			Consumer	Yes (students pretest only)
E. Kim, 2001			Consumer	No
D Harrison McKnight et al., 2000		Consumer		No
D. H. McKnight & Chervany, 2001		Consumer	Consumer	No
Papadopoulou et al., 2001			Consumer	No
Pavlou, 2001	Consumer		Consumer	Yes (students)
Salam et al., 1998			Consumer	Yes (not directly)
Tan & Thoen, 2000-2001	Vendor	Vendor		No

Table 1: Comparisons of trust models from current literature indicating major perspectives, consumer/vendor trust direction and empirical testing status

4. DISCUSSION

It could be argued that the diverse and fragmented nature of the studies we reviewed is typical of an emerging field of research. Indeed, pluralistic research approaches are generally considered to be conducive towards establishing a broader understanding of emergent phenomena (Nissen et al., 1991). However, there is also now a need for more integrative research efforts that are cognisant of the current body of knowledge. In addressing this need it is necessary to revisit existing assumptions, points of departure and to critically reflect on the progress to date. In these respects we raise four main concerns that warrant further research attention. We base the discussion on the analysis of the research studies as outlined above and some findings from our own empirical field studies.

4.1 An oversimplification of the trust concept

A key criticism of much of the current literature concerns the conflation of the trust concept. Many of the current studies view trust (and especially consumer trust) as a singular notion: the consumer trusts the vendor. Such a simplistic view is not only inconsistent with our own empirical findings, but may also become a conceptual liability in addressing specific consumer concerns. We argue for an "unbundling" of the trust concept. For example, a distinction could be made between trust in the integrity and trust in the ability of a vendor. A consumer may trust a vendor to be honest and to make every effort possible to deliver on the products as requested (integrity), however the consumer may not trust the same vendor's ability to ensure the safety of their transaction over the Internet (a point supported by Tan & Thoen, 2000-2001). An unbundling of the trust concept can isolate different facets of trust with much richer insights in terms of addressing specific consumer trust concerns. In addition we advocate the need to acknowledge the richness and multiplicity of the trust concept.

4.2 Uni-directional view of trust

As mentioned earlier, in a B2C context consumers are typically required to pay for the transaction up front in the expectation that the goods or services will be received as promised. In addition, consumers often need to furnish additional (and possibly sensitive) personal details (e.g. home addresses) that could be misused. It comes as no surprise that in the trust models reviewed these facets are well accounted for.

From Table 1 we can however see that very few of the studies acknowledge other stakeholders' perspectives on trust. In our own empirical fieldwork, it is clear that the vendor also expects a level of integrity in fulfilling an order that has been placed (Scheepers, 2001). The recently reported high levels of credit card fraud, in particular the Asia Pacific Region, contributes to this vendor expectation. The perpetrators of fraudulent transactions use stolen credit card numbers and try to obtain goods from trusting vendors (O'Brien, 2001). Since the stolen credit card details are valid, basic credit card authorisation processes fail to register the fraudulent use.

In addition financial institutions (e.g. credit card companies) and governments for example, also have a vested interest in B2C transactions being conducted in an environment of high integrity. Hence we argue that multiple stakeholder perspectives on the trust relationship should be reflected in B2C trust models.

4.3 Discipline centred approaches to modelling trust

The review suggests theoretical and empirical frameworks on which to base an integrative approach to understanding the complexities of human behaviour, design, technology and the business world. As can be seen from Table 1, the presented models reviewed depict trust in an e-commerce environment as coming from mainly singular and at best dual perspectives that the authors have adopted in their study. While each suggested model has equally justified its reasons for concerning itself with its chosen discipline/s, in taking these isolated views they have diminished the relevance of the factors that are found to be intrinsic to e-commerce trust by other modellers. In moving towards an understanding in e-commerce we need to understand the consumer, the vendor, the technology and the surrounding influences that involve all parties and how they all interact with each other. In particular, consideration needs to be given to the overlap of each of the three disciplines that can give a clearer picture of the trust effectors and their relationships. Clear guidelines are needed for the business community that will create an environment where both the consumer and vendor feel secure in all stages of transactions in B2C Internet e-commerce. We therefore argue for more collaborative research efforts across disciplines to address the fragmented body of knowledge.

4.4 Lack of empirical grounding and testing

Other issues of concern with most of the current documented models on B2C trust are the lack of empirical grounding and the lack of rigorous testing. As can be seen from the models in Table 1, few of the models have been subjected to empirical testing. In those cases where the models have indeed been tested, the test subjects are often students. We argue that this does not constitute a sufficiently rigorous test base. Hence we suggest there is a need for research approaches aimed at testing current models. We also suggest future research in this area should clearly indicate how proposed models should be tested.

5. CONCLUSION

In this review we have drawn on recent studies from prominent peer reviewed journals and conference proceedings on B2C trust models in an Internet e-commerce environment. From this literature we classified the various models into three main focal areas: technological, design and sociological /psychological perspectives with minimal overlap of perspectives. We found that each of the researchers had considered the question of trust from the direction of either the vendor or the consumer, limiting the outlook and consequently the requirements of trust creation on an Internet e-commerce site. It was also evident from the literature that although there were many differing definitions of trust there appeared to be an oversimplification of trust concepts. To realise a model for trust requires the unbundling of the trust in the vendor and trust in the vendor's ability to fulfil a transaction. Within the literature reviewed it appeared that the grounding for the models and the empirical testing was not rigorous in all cases with the use of students and online surveys. This method of testing did not address the full extent of the transaction, e.g. the financial obligation that is intrinsically part of Internet commerce.

The reviewed models have suggested theoretical and empirical frameworks on which to base an integrative approach to understanding the complexities of human behaviour, design, technology and the business world. It can now been seen that the question of trust within the e-commerce discipline is diverse, possibly beyond that of the individual researcher, raising the need for more collaborative research efforts across disciplines to address the fragmented research. We also advocate that multiple stakeholder perspectives on the trust relationship should be considered and reflected in B2C trust models. Furthermore the concept of trust needs to be unbundled from its simplistic roots in order to isolate different facets of trust, allowing a greater understanding of the trust concerns and recognizing the multiplicity of the trust concept. Finally we suggest there is a need for rigorous research approaches aimed at testing current models and that future research in this area should clearly indicate how proposed models are to be tested.

ACKNOWLEDGEMENT

We thank Lorraine Johnston for her useful comments on this research.

REFERENCES

Ambrose, P. J., & Johnson, G. J. (1998). A Trust Based Model of Buying Behavior in Electronic Retailing, *Proceedings of Americas Conference on Information Systems (AIS '98)*, Baltimore, Maryland, 263-265.

Borchers, A. (2001). Trust in Internet Shopping: A Test of a Measurement Instrument, *Proceedings of Americas Conference on Information Systems*, 799.

Cheskin Studio Archetype/Sapient. (1999). *E-commerce Trust Study*.

Cheung, C., & Lee, M. K. O. (2001). Trust in Internet Shopping: A Proposed Model and Measurement Instrument, *Proceedings of Americas Conference on Information Systems*, 681 - 686.

Choi, S. Y. S., D.O; Whiston, A.B. (1998). Intermediation, Contracts and Micropayments in Electronic Commerce. *Electronic Markets, 8* (1), pp 20-22.

Davis, F. D. (1989). Perceived Usefulness, Perceived Ease of Use, and User Acceptance of Information Technology. *MIS Quarterly, 13* (3), 319-340.

Egger, F. (2000). Towards a Model of Trust for E-Commerce System Design, *Proceedings of CHI 2000*, Zurich.

Einwiller, S., Ulrike, G., & Markus, W. (2000, 05/2000). Engendering Trust in Internet Businesses using Elements of Corporate Branding. In Chung, H. M. (Ed.), *Proceedings of 2000 Americas Conference on Information Systems (AMCIS 2000)*, pp. 733-739,.

Farrell, V., Farrell, G., & Leung, Y. (2001). E-Commerce: The Net Generation - A study in youth perceptions of security and trust, *Proceedings of In Proceedings of the IFIP TC8 Working Conference*, Salzburg.

Fishbein, M., & I, A. (1975). Belief, Attitude, Intention and Behaviour: An Introduction to Theory and Research. In Addison -Wesley Reading, M. (Ed.).

Fogg, B. J., J., M., Othman, L., Osipovich, A., Varma, C., Fang, N., Paul, J., Rangnekar, A., Shon, J., Swani, P., & Treinen, M. (2001, 31-3-2001). What makes web sites credible? a report on a large quantitative study., *Proceedings of CHI 2001*, Pages: 61 - 68.

Grazioli, S., & Jarvenpaa, S. (2000). Perils of Internet Fraud: An Empirical Investigation of Deception and Trust with Experienced Internet Consumers. *IEEE Transactions on Systems, Man and Cybernetics, 30*, 395-410.

Jarvenpaa, S., Tractinsky, N., & Saarinen, L. (1999). Consumer Trust in an Internet Store: A Cross-Cultural Validation. *JCMC, 5* (2).

Kim, E. (2001). A model of sustainable trust in B2C e-markets, *Proceedings of American Conference on Information Sytems*, USA, 804-809.

Kim, K., & Prabhakar. (2000). Initial trust, Perceived Risk and the Adoption of Internet Banking, *Proceedings of International Conference on Information Systems 2000*, 537-543.

Kini, A. D., & Choobineh, J. (2001). An Empirical evaluation of the factors affecting trust in web banking systems. *Americas Conference on Information Systems 2000*, 185-191.

Mayer, R. C., & Schoorman, F. D. (1995). An Integrative Model of Organizational Trust. *Academy of Management Journal, 20* (3), 709 - 934.

McKnight, D. H., & Chervany, N. L. (2001, 2001). Conceptualizing Trust: A Typology and E-Commerce Customer Relationships Model, *Proceedings of 34th Hawaii International Conference on System Sciences -2001*, Hawaii.

McKnight, D. H., Choudhury, V., & Kacmar, C. (2000, December 10-13). Trust in E-Commerce Vendors: A Two Stage Model, *Proceedings of Twenty-First Annual International Conference on Information Systems*, Brisbane, Australia, 532-536.

Nissen, H.-E., Klein, H. K., & Hirschheim, R. A. (Eds.). (1991). *Information systems research: contemporary approaches and emergent traditions*. Amsterdam: Elsevier Science Publishers B.V. (North-Holland).

O'Brien, T. (2001). *Guard against credit card fraud*. Available: http://www.webstrategy. com.au/ ver20/tip_view.asp?ID=6226 November 2001].

Papadopoulou, P., P, K., & D, M. (2001). Investigating Trust in E-Commerce: A Literature Review and a Model for It s Formation in Customer Relationships, *Proceedings of Americas Conference on Information Systems 2001*, 791-798.

Pavlou, P. A. (2001). Integrating trust in electronic commerce with the technology acceptance model: Model Development and Validation, *Proceedings of Americas Conference on Information Systems 2001*, p. 816.

Salam, A. F., Rao, H. R., & Pegels, C. C. (1998). An Investigation Of Consumer Perceived Risk on Electronic Commerce Transactions: The Role of Institutional Trust and Economic Incentive in a Social Exchange Framework, *Proceedings of America's Conference on Information Systems (AIS '98)*, , Baltimore, Maryland, p. 335.

Scheepers, R. (2001). Supporting the Online Consumer Decision Process: Electronic Commerce in a Small Australian Retailer, *Proceedings of the Twelfth Australasian Conference on Information Systems(ACIS 2001), Coffs Harbour, NSW, Australia.*

Tan, Y.-H., & Thoen, W. (2000-2001). Toward a generic model of trust for electronic commerce. *International Journal of Electronic Commerce, 5* (2), 61-74.

Tornatzky, L. G., & Klein, K. J. (1982). Innovation characteristics and innovation adoption-implementation: a meta-analysis of findings. *IEEE Transactions on Engineering Management, EM-29* (1), 28-45.

CONCEPTUAL FRAMES OF REFERENCE AND THEIR INFLUENCE ON E-COMMERCE SYSTEM DEVELOPMENT

GLEN L. VAN DER VYVER and MICHAEL S. LANE
Department of Information Systems, University of Southern Queensland, Australia

Abstract: The complexity and uncertainty that is inherent in the e-commerce environment poses a number of challenges to the development of e-commerce applications. Key stakeholders consistently use heuristics to make sense of the challenges they face. The most pervasive of these heuristics is framing, whereby people rely on a conceptual set to organise their perceptions. This process has some benefits but it can also lead to a narrow approach, ignorance concerning important elements of the decision environment and an absolute reliance on a specialist area of knowledge. This has significant implications for coherence of effort and vision, elements crucial to the success of e-commerce projects. This paper uses a case study, qualitative approach in order to establish whether there is evidence for the operation of the framing heuristic, particularly within the context of risk perception, within a variety of e-commerce system development environments.

1. INTRODUCTION

E-commerce is without doubt one of the key indicators of the arrival of a new global economy, even a new global society, with new imperatives and new ways of thinking. Those who foresaw the coming revolution just a couple of decades ago did not speak of e-commerce directly but of a business environment characterised by rapid change and paradigm shift (Drucker, 1988; Marchand and Horton, 1986; Peters, 1987). In the new economy, the well-learned and dependable skills, methods and procedures that worked well in the past are becoming obsolete and we only have a vague conceptualisation of what will replace them. (Earl, 1997; Gue Henno, 1995)

This paper focuses on the use of the framing heuristic by key stakeholders in the complex and uncertain environment of e-commerce. The paper reports on the potential influence of the framing heuristic when stakeholders attempt to make sense of complex and uncertain e-commerce system development environments and explores the social construction of e-commerce reality. Such an approach will help facilitate and inform strategic management issues in the e-commerce environment.

The paper is structured as follows. First, we discuss the inherent complexity and uncertainty that exists in the e-commerce environment and its impact on the way in which key stakeholders strive to make sense of that environment. Then, we discuss the use of heuristics, particularly the framing heuristic, in situations where there is significant uncertainty and ambiguity. Next, we present and discuss a risk model for e-commerce. Then the research issue is outlined and the research method is described and justified. Next, the potential impact of the framing heuristic within the context of e-commerce system development is investigated in a number of case organisations, and the findings are discussed. Finally, there are some concluding remarks regarding the potential significance and relevance of the framing heuristic in the development of e-commerce systems.

2. DEALING WITH THE COMPLEXITY AND UNCERTAINTY IMPOSED BY E-COMMERCE

The cataclysms of the past twelve months in the e-commerce arena, coming as they did on the crest of a wave of unbridled confidence, lend all the more credence to the fundamental premise that the modern economy is more unpredictable and uncertain than ever. There is now a substantial body of evidence which indicates that rational responses become all the more difficult as the levels of uncertainty and ambiguity in social systems become more prevalent (Simon, 1976; Douglas and Wildavsky, 1982; Handy, 1989). The markets of two years ago largely reflect this, based as they were on a frenzy of investment in unknown companies with no track record operating in an uncertain and undefined business environment. Many investors could not envisage the prospect of large-scale corporate failures because they were trapped in a perception environment where they had never seen failure. Most of these people did not rationally plan their investment decisions by attempting to forecast the likelihood of future events. Rather, they were seduced by the irrational belief that the past and present somehow tell us what will happen tomorrow, that today is part of some mysterious pattern which may fluctuate slightly tomorrow but whose course to inevitable success is assured.

Not all individuals or corporate cultures are equally imbued with the capacity to manage complex and uncertain environments. (Smart and Vertinsky, 1984; Webber, 1997) Some, indeed, are doomed to failure from the outset as they are inherently incapable of managing uncertainty. Webber (1997) speaks of the 'vision thing', and argues that many professionals today are so overwhelmed by the complexities of the task at hand that they struggle to make informed decisions. They are unable to focus on issues unrelated to their area of expertise. This has profound implications for the development of e-commerce systems where a narrow approach is untenable. e-commerce systems development requires a multidisciplinary, team-based effort. Perhaps more than anything else, it requires vision and a critical mind. It requires people who are prepared to question whether the tried and trusted methods of the past are applicable to the new business context.

3. USE OF HEURISTICS TO COPE WITH COMPLEXITY AND UNCERTAINTY

People do not even attempt to deal with all the complexities in any but the most simple of situations. (Simon 1976). They seek to construct a simplified model of the world based upon their values, knowledge and experiences. Central to this process is the use of heuristics, or subconscious mental rules of thumb which allow us to make sense of novel, ambiguous or uncertain problems. These heuristics are essential because they make the incomprehensible comprehensible. That is not to say that that they lead to rationality. It might be better to say that heuristics make us think that we comprehend something. The decisions we make, the conclusions we reach and the explanations we offer are often based on our judgements of the likelihood of uncertain events (Kahnenman & Tversky 1974). People do not as a matter of course follow the principles of rationality or probability theory when making judgements. Indeed, 'irrational' heuristics often have a pervasive but unconscious influence on the cognitive processes involved in the determination of a course of action.

The operation of cognitive decision structures in uncertain environments was examined and it was concluded that humans need to simplify and structure perceptual materials in order to make sense of their environment (Walsh 1988). This is emphasized succinctly by Walsh (1988):

> 'Managers routinely confront ill-structured, complex problems that challenge their cognitive capacities. They must meet such challenged with limited

information-processing capabilities . . . managers construct belief structures that are simplified representations of their worlds. These belief structures are considered indispensable to any decision maker, for without them individuals would be overwhelmed by an information world of staggering complexity'

4. FRAMING TERMS OF REFERENCE

A wide variety of heuristics and biases have been identified and much work has been done on their influence on human cognitive and perceptual processes. Enduring problems with this research have included isolating the effect of individual heuristics, measuring the potential for interaction effects and determining the cumulative influence of a variety of heuristics acting in concert. Russo and Shoemaker (1990, 1992) address some of these problems when they argue that there exists an overall or higher-level heuristic which they call framing. They argue that people structure decision environments in terms of a conceptual set, using cognitive structures to make sense of the world. These structures are clearly heuristic in nature but Russo and Shoemaker argue that overall conceptual style dominates individual heuristics. Their work builds upon the seminal work of Douglas and Wildavsky (1982) on risk perception.

Risk perception is subjective, based upon conceptual frameworks (Douglas & Wildavsky, 1982).. The fundamental point of departure is that it is impossible for any individual, corporation or society to ever know the totality of risks that it faces. At a macro level, risk selection is a social process. Thus, people from different cultures might have risk sets that are totally different, where risk set refers to the totality of risks that culture admits into its collective consciousness. At the micro level, risk selection is an individual process, dependant upon the conceptual style of the individual decision maker.

Framing is both very useful and very dangerous (Russo & Shoemaker 1992). In an increasingly complex world, it is simply impossible to function without conceptual frames of reference. While this process does allow us to function it is also insidious, sometimes leading to wildly inaccurate decisions and even a world concept that is far removed from reality. Often the partial view of the problem which the frame of reference encompasses precludes the identification of the correct course of action, literally forcing an incorrect decision or course of action. Alternatively, outdated rules of thumb may be used or a particular rule of thumb may be applied to an inappropriate situation.

5. ROLE OF HEURISTICS AND FRAMING OF TERMS OF REFERENCE ON DECISION MAKING OF KEY STAKEHOLDERS IN E-COMMERCE SYSTEM DEVELOPMENT

Information Technology professionals are by no means above decision errors (Wiseman 1988). Many companies are constrained by their own culture and unable to make rational decisions about Information Technology. Acting as some companies do within a defunct paradigm, their IT solutions are doomed to failure. Thus, identifying good information systems and potential risks depends upon the conceptual perspective of the people involved, the perspective of the corporate culture, even the mores and values of the society in which the action is situated. E-commerce is an activity whose whole being is permeated with uncertainty and ambiguity. It has a short history and continues to evolve rapidly. Relatively few rules or guidelines exist, which is not surprising as the encompassing paradigm is itself fluid. Although an increasing volume of research is devoted to e-commerce systems development, e-commerce risk management and the like, we are not sure that this work has made much impact at the coalface.

We are concerned here with the way process, problem areas, potential risks and even the meaning of e-commerce are conceptualised by various participants in the construction of e-commerce technologies. Cognitive theory would suggest that there could be significant differences in perception between companies and industries but, more important for our purposes, even between people participating in the same project. We do not speak here of conflicting viewpoints or corporate politics but of different conceptual frameworks. Thus, two people working on the same project may not even assign the same meaning to the term e-commerce. They may very well fall back in terms of what they know, whether that is a well-worn and wholly inappropriate paradigm or a narrow reliance on an expert field of knowledge. Surely, this would be a recipe for failure.

6. E-COMMERCE RISK MODEL

APRA Insight (2001) identified that electronic commerce poses a number of potential risks such as operational risk, reputational risk, outsourcing risk, strategic risk, legal risks, increased liquidity risk and narrowing of margins (see figure 1 Dimensions of risk in E-Commerce). A discussion of these different types of e-commerce risk follows.

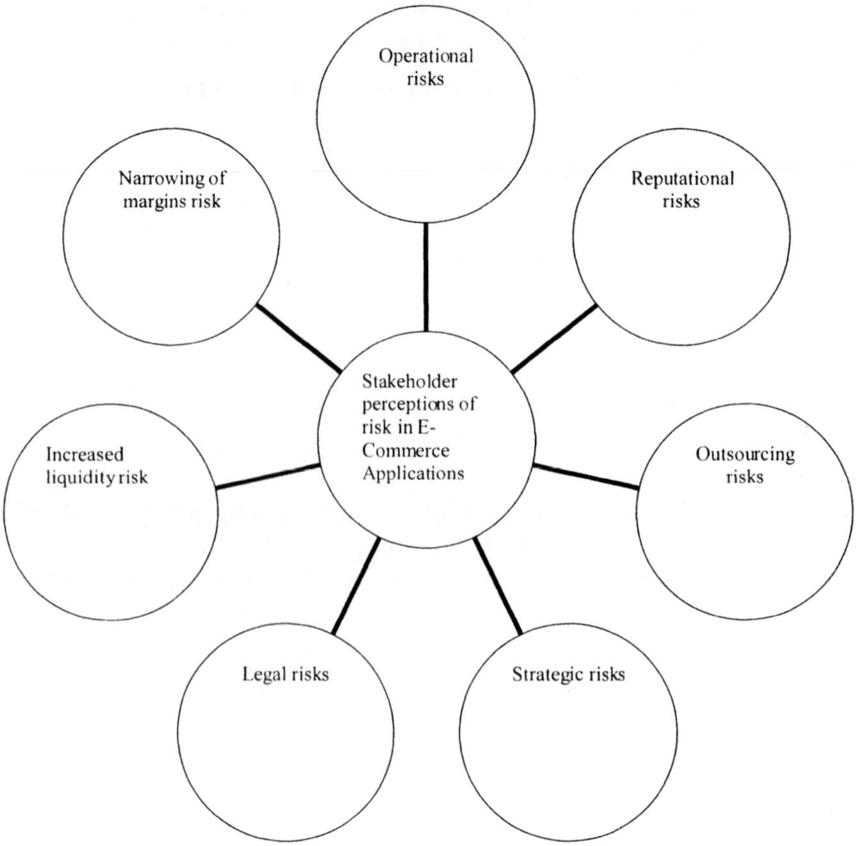

Figure1. Different dimensions of risk in E-Commerce System development

Source: APRA Insight 2001

Electronic commerce is highly dependent on system reliability and integrity and, as a result, highly vulnerable to operational risk. In particular, security raises significant concerns. By its very nature, the Web is very public and anything published is technically accessible to anyone. Reputation risk implies that there is also an expectation from the public that a web site is available 24X7. While there are considerable benefits from outsourcing, increased reliance on third parties for provision of services, products and infrastructure also increases risk. Strategic risk arises from the pace of innovation in electronic commerce and the considerable costs involved keeping abreast of new technologies. The rights and obligations of various parties to an electronic transaction can be unclear and open to legal challenge, with existing laws and regulations not keeping pace with electronic commerce developments. Increased liquidity risk may arise from the ability to rapidly transfer funds between accounts and institutions resulting in a virtual bank run on funds. The openness of the Internet creates a dilemma in that customers can easily compare products and services offered by institutions resulting in a narrowing of profits. Many of these risks are applicable to any organization conducting electronic commerce using a web site.

This dimensions of risk model was used to assess the perceptual differences in key stakeholders in relation to risk in e-commerce systems. We argue in this paper that perceptual differences in key stakeholders frames of reference has significant implications for the development of e-commerce systems This model was developed within a particular context, the financial services industry. It is interesting to note that most of the potential risks seem to apply equally to e-commerce in general. The model focuses on a relatively few risks at a high level. Clearly, there are many other potential risks but it does seem possible to make some sense of all the factors as a collectivity. Yet, it is clear that each risk factor could spawn many subcategories. When this happens, we believe that people will begin focusing on a few areas, or even one, because there is a limit to the number of risks we are able to think about at any given time.

7. RESEARCH ISSUE AND METHOD

This study was designed to investigate the use of the framing heuristic in the decision making processes of key stakeholders in the e-commerce system development process. E-commerce systems are becoming increasingly complex and sophisticated with many systems supporting extensive information, communication, distribution and transaction capabilities (Angehrn & Meyer 1997). As a result the key stakeholders in e-commerce system development are faced with making decisions in a complex and uncertain environment.

Individually, key stakeholders will use differing sets of heuristics and framing of terms of reference in their decision making in relation to e-commerce system development. This may result in misalignment of the business strategy and objectives of an e-commerce system and the increased risk profile and likely failure of these systems. The management of potential differences in the terms of references of key stakeholders in e-commerce systems will reduce the risk and potential failure associated with such types of systems.

A qualitative approach was deemed appropriate as this line of research is in the exploratory stage (Galliers 1994, Yin 1994). A case study method was used as it allows the researchers to investigate in-depth the phenomena of interest, the research issue` in a real life context (Gable 1994). There is also a lack of empirical research on the potential differential effects of heuristics and framing in the e-commerce system development process. In the first phase of this research, data collection involved analysis of the perceived risk of e-commerce in four case organisations that have been involved in developing e-commerce systems. These case organisations were purposely chosen because two of the cases are banking institutions that followed a traditional informed path to e-commerce system development. The other two case organisations were chosen because they are new Internet start up companies with no background or tradition in information systems development. A number of key stakeholders were interviewed from each case organisation. The heuristics and frames of reference that they used in their decision making in relation to the various levels of risk inherent in the e-commerce system development process were compared. We will explore the following:

1. Do people perceive e-commerce systems development as uncertain and / or risky. Are there clear intra-organisational and / or inter-organisational differences.
2. Do people from different areas of the corporation perceive e-commerce in different ways.
3. Do people from corporations operating in different sectors of the economy perceive e-commerce in different ways.
4. What appears to be the most significant characteristics of the frame/s of reference people use to conceptualise the method, procedures and problems associated with e-commerce system development. In particular, we are interested to determine whether people are attempting to understand e-commerce in terms of frameworks that are no longer valid.

8. OVERVIEW OF CASE ORGANISATIONS

Two of the case organisations that were chosen for this study are large financial institutions that have relatively sophisticated Internet banking presences. These case organisations have Internet banking sites which are an aggregate of organisation content and banking applications. The ongoing development of these Internet banking sites involves a diversity of key stakeholders both internal and external to the case organisations. The migration of traditional banking and relevant banking content to e-commerce environment poses many challenges in the ongoing development of e-commerce systems. The other two case organisations chosen for this study were involved selling products online. These case organisations are new Internet start-up companies with extensive previous history in the traditional way of business but no previous history in information systems development. Their web sites were designed to be largely functional sites that facilitated the purchase of products online.

Case A is a medium sized financial institution that is based in Toowoomba. The organization has been in existence for over 100 years and currently employs over 1000 people in its financial institution banking operations. It has had a web presence since 1997, and Internet banking capability since 1998. The general IT manager, marketing manager, IT operations manager, managing director of a Queensland based software company that builds and hosts Internet banking solutions for financial institutions and the Queensland state manager of a regulatory authority that monitors financial institution operations including Internet banking were interviewed.

Case B is large financial institution which has branches nationwide. The organization has been in existence since 1909 and currently employs over 7,700 people nationally. It has had a web presence since 1996 and has had Internet banking capability since 1998. The content manager, two business analysts, the Internet banking project manager, and Internet architecture manager were interviewed.

Case C is an online pharmacy and has been an operational entity for little over 18 months. Case C's web site is primarily concerned with the sale of pharmaceutical products online. Retail pharmacy is a highly regulated industry, hence there were considerable constraints on the operation of online pharmacy. The Manager Director, Customer Relationship Management Employee and the External Web Developer were interviewed.

Case D is a pure Internet organization. The company is based in Armidale and operates a florist relay network. It was one of the first Internet based Florist Relay Networks to be established in the world. The organization has had a operational web site which supports secure transactions over the Internet since 1994. The organization employs about 10 people full time with three employees involved full time with developing and maintaining the web site. A fourth employee is involved in web site maintenance and enhancement on a casual basis on two to three days a week. The other employees are involved supporting in the call centre, order processing and fulfillment. The organization has annual turnover of 10 million dollars per annum. The chief executive, marketing manager and the external web developer were interviewed.

9. FINDINGS AND DISCUSSION

The risk perceptions of key stakeholders in the four case organisations were analysed on the basis of the dimensions of risk in e-commerce model presented in figure 1. The following tables 1, 2, 3 and 4 present the summarised findings in each relation to each case organisation and research objectives of this study. Each case organisation will now be discussed in relation to the findings. A number of direct quotations are included to highlight the different frames of references that key stakeholders use to construct their perception of risk in the development of e-commerce systems.

Case A	Operational Risk	Reputational risk	Outsourcing risk	Strategic risk	Legal risk	Increasing liquidity Risk	Narrowing of margins risk
Marketing manager	Acknowledged to some extent	Very important	Not acknowledged	Acknowledged to some extent	Very important	No acknowledged	Not acknowledged
CIO	Very important	Very important	Acknowledged to some extent	Very important	Very important	Not acknowledged	Not acknowledged
IT operations manager	Very important	Very important	Not acknowledged	Acknowledged to some extent	Important	Not acknowledged	Not acknowledged
External system developer (CEO)	Very important	Important	Not acknowledged	Acknowledged to some extent	Important	Not acknowledged	Not acknowledged
Regulatory authority state manager	Very important	Very important	Important	Important	Very important	Important	Important

Table 1. Summary of Case A - Key stakeholder perceptions of risk in relation to E-Commerce

In Case A, *operational risk* was considered important by most of the key stakeholders as the e-commerce development team was small and consisted of both management and technical people. This meant that all of the key stakeholders interviewed were very informed about all of the key issues in relation to Internet banking. The following comment by IT operations manager emphasises that Case A were a small team and communicated well in regard to e-commerce system development.

> " Yes a reasonably small group of people generally speaking. We're of common mind and therefore the politics of different peoples views don't necessarily have a ...impact on where we're going" (A3:T314:316).

Reputational risk was considered important by all of the key stakeholders in Case A. They were acutely aware of the consequences of a security breach of their Internet banking systems on the reputation of Case A and on the confidence of their mutual membership. The following comment by the CIO emphasises the importance of reputational risk and the potential impact of a security breach on Case A's incredibility.

> "Absolutely, you have a security breach as I said, you pack it up and put it in a box because nobody will us it. It's paramount. I'm just" (A2:T182:183).

Outsourcing was not acknowledged by Case A key stakeholders as being a serious risk. This was not surprising as outsourcing was a significant part of their Internet strategy and rather was seen as a way to compete with the big players in the Australian banking industry. The following comment by the CIO emphasises outsourcing was a critical component of Case A's approach to Internet banking.

> "Now going forward we can't do everything in house. This takes up twenty percent of A1's time, it takes up thirty percent, third of my time, its growing, I don't have web designer, I don't have a in house resource.

One of the key stakeholders interviewed was the developer and provider of their Internet banking system. This stakeholder emphasised that they had to reach strict requirements of the banking regulatory authorities such as Australian Prudential Regulatory Authority (APRA). The state manager of APRA reiterated that part of its role was monitor and regulate Internet banking solutions providers. In fact, Case A's strategy to counter the strategic risks imposed by the e-commerce environment was to rely heavily on outsourcing to provide Internet banking solutions. The *legal risks* were apparent to all of the key stakeholders and it is an issue that has to be dealt within the banking industry. Therefore it is merely a case of ensuring that necessity legal requirements of banking are dealt with in the e-commerce environment and that adequate checks and balances are put in place to ensure that this happens. Not surprisingly, increased liquidity risk of Internet banking was considered an important issue by the state manager from the banking regulatory authority in general terms. But this may not be an issue for Case A given that it is a mutual society and its membership is regionally focused. *Narrowing of margins* was acknowledged to some extent by the key stakeholders but since the primary Internet banking strategy was not cost containment and migration of membership to Internet banking, it was not a major concern.. The following comment emphasises that narrowing of margins was not a concern and that Case A's main focus was on providing value and service to its mutual members.

> "My perspective, is customer service, customer choice if we can make banking easier or user friendly that's costly then we're providing value to the. membership. Everything we do is about providing value to our membership" (A2:T734:737).

Case B	Opera-tional risk	Reputa-tional risk	Outsour-cing risk	Strategic risk	Legal risk	Increa-sed liquidity risk	Narrow-ing of margins risk
Content Manager	Acknow-ledged to some extent	Important	Not acknow-ledged	Important	Important	Not acknow-ledged	Not acknow-ledged
Business Analyst for EC projects	Very important	Very important	Not acknow-ledged	Very important	Very important	Not acknow-ledged	Import-ant
Business Analyst for EC Projects	Acknow-ledged to some extent	Important	Acknow-ledged to some extent	Acknow-ledged to some extent	Important	Not acknow-ledged	Import-ant
Web site project manager	Acknow-ledged to some extent	Acknow-ledged to some extent	Not acknow-ledged	Acknow-ledged to some extent	Acknow-ledged to some extent	Not acknow-ledged	Not acknow-ledged
Web infra-structure manager	Very important	Acknow-ledged to some extent	Not acknow-ledged	Important	Acknow-ledged to some extent	Not acknow-ledged	Not acknow-ledged

Table 2. Summary of Case B:
- Key stakeholder perceptions of risk in relation to E-Commerce

For Case B, two stakeholders that emphasised *operational risk* was very important had significant hands on experience in developing and maintaining e-commerce systems since the beginning of the commercialisation of the Internet. Web infrastructure manager have been involved Internet banking since its inception in Australia in 1996 while the

Business analyst have been involved in setting up a number of Internet start up companies prior to working for Case B. *Reputational risk* was considered important by a number of the key stakeholders in Case B and this was no doubt influenced by the communication of Case B's e-commerce strategy ‚Best Bank' to all of its employees. The following comment by the content manager emphasize Case B stakeholders perceptions of reputational risk were influenced by Case B's Internet banking strategy *Best bank strategy implied a strong element of reputational risk.* As part of the Best Bank strategy, Case B needed to be seen to be seen as being a leader in Internet banking in Australian market place.

> "Because most of the projects that we are doing at the moment come under the umbrella of BEST bank, all the projects do so we have our own methodologies but there is also a best bank method" (B1:T1030:1032).

The following comment by the e-commerce business analyst indicates professional experience also influences perceptions of reputational risk.

> "I think its huge, I think that the reputations that people get with web sites both good and bad is huge and it will become more so more and more companies will be judged by the standard of their web presence" (B2:T163:166).

Not many of the key stakeholders interviewed were acutely aware of the potential risk associated with *outsourcing e*-commerce system development in e-commerce. It should also be said that Case B had countered this risk to some extent as most of its e-commerce system development was in house and it have acquired a number of firms that were involved in specialised E-commerce system development such secure payment gateway.. External developers were also required to follow e-commerce system development standards set in place by Case B. The following comment by e-commerce business analyst B3 emphasises how Case B handled the risks associated with outsourcing.

> "Yeah when external companies do web development obviously we have to communicate in the internal business unit to make sure what is delivered by the external companies up to our internal standards" (B3:T202:206).

The perception of outsourcing risk was guided by in house development procedures that required external developers to meet Case B's IS development standards. It is also maybe true that the very procedures that deal with outsourced development may also reinforce a sense of over confidence in relation to the potential risks of outsourcing E-Commerce system development.

Strategic risk associated with the e-commerce environment was also acknowledged by a number of the key stakeholders due to their extensive experience in developing e-commerce systems from concept through to product. The following comment by the web infrastructure manager indicates a level of confidence from a long involvement in e-commerce.

"Firstly I have got a technical background and I have been involved with e-commerce Internet in particular for the past ten years. From the beginning then when the Web took off in Australia" (B5:T7:9).

Not surprisingly *legal risks* presented by the e-commerce environment were well understood by all of the key stakeholders as legal risks transcend across traditional and electronic banking. The potential of increased liquidity in Internet banking was not considered an important issue by any of the key stakeholders in Case B but regulatory bodies are concerned about the potential for Internet banking to facilitate a run on a banking institute's cash reserves. Obviously, checks should be in place in Internet banking systems that alert organisations if such a situation is arising. *Narrowing of margins* was acknowledged as being important. A number of the key stakeholders had realised the benefits of Internet banking may be offset by the significant costs of developing and maintaining Internet banking and the need to retain traditional banking infrastructure. The following comment by E-Commerce business analyst emphasises that cost savings of Internet banking may be misleading.

"We replaced three staff down in lending services so that's great yet you hired one web developer, yes that's three to one No No those three people cost $90,000 your web developer costs $120,000 you are actually $30,000 behind now no one is doing that maths so I think it is a bit of misnomer that the fact that it reduces costs when we talk about reduced costs what we do we talk about replacing people that what the banks seem to be concerned about, I think that there " (B2:T177:183).

Case C	Operational risk	Reputational risk	Outsourcing risk	Strategic risk	Legal risk	Liquidity risk	Narrowing of margins risk
Managing Director	Very important	Very important	Important	Very important	Very important	Not applicable	Very important
Customer relationship manager	Important	Acknowledged to some extent	Not acknowledged	Very important	Important	Not applicable	Not acknowledged
External web developer	Important	Important	Not acknowledged	Not acknowledged	Important	Not applicable	Not acknowledged

Table 3. Summary of Case C:
- Key stakeholder perceptions of risk in relation to E-Commerce

For case C, *operational risk* was a key issue for the managing director and external web developer. The managing director was aware that a successful E-Commerce site needed to be reliable, efficient and easy to use. The external web developer was also aware of the importance of a web site that was operationally functional and facilitated the online purchase of pharmaceutical goods. The following comment by the external web developer indicates the importance of having a viable operational E-Commerce site.

> " There's a lot of factors - there's money and then there's I guess, your marketing, the effectiveness of your marketing, how well you target your users, and on the technical side how well it works, how quickly the users get the information they want. You know, how intuitive is the interface. I mean you want to make it intuitive for an e-Commerce site. They're coming in - they're either going to be just having a general browse and then they might find something that they want to buy or they're coming in to purchase something specifically. So you've got to cater for them and you've got to get them through seamlessly. You can't confuse them - there can't ever be a stage where they're going 'where do I go next'. It's " (C2:T549:558).

Case C operated in a highly regulated industry, retail pharmacy. The managing director was highly aware that the online *reputation* of Case C was of paramount importance to its survival and acceptance in the industry.. There were a number of government and industry regulatory bodies that could easily shut down Case C's E-Commerce site at a moments notice if it was seen to be acting illegally or unethically online. The following comment by manager director indicates an awareness of the reputational risks associated with an online pharmacy.

> "The other thing you should be looking at is – no other Internet website with pharmacy in Australia at the moment does this. We're the only one who does it. So I've actually had the Pharmacy Guild out here watching me and the particular reason I did that was I wanted to show them what we do here, because we're all being cast at the moment in the same pot" (C1:T115:120).

Reputational risk was less of an issue to the external web developer who was more concerned with delivering technical solutions to meet the managing director's requirements. The customer relationship manager was aware of the importance dealing promptly and courteously with customer orders and inquiries, and that customers needed to be ensured that shopping online was safe and secure. The managing director was aware of the consequences of the outsourcing of the Case C's E-Commerce site and appropriate legal documents have been drawn up to protect the intellectual property and business assets of Case C.

"C3.... Development Company is what they're called – the programmers. And document that was drawn up by the legals – ensured that the possession of intellectual property....and who owned everything and we own the domain name, we own the information, we own the rights to anything that was created by us and to actually build the site. So that was a very important document – about 30 pages. " (B1:T1422:1477).

Outsourcing was not acknowledged as an issue by the external web developer and the customer relationship manager. The external web developer was providing the outsourced development and maintenance of Case C's E-Commerce site while the customer relationship manager was not actively involved in the development process. On the other hand, the managing director was aware that outsourcing posed legal risks concerning ownership of the intellectual property. The *strategic risks* of E-Commerce system development were considered to be very important by the managing director and the external web developer. There needed to be a balance between providing the necessary sophistication in an E-Commerce site and the resource limitations of a small organisation like Case C. Again, this was not an immediate concern of the customer relationship manager in relation her perception of risk in E-Commerce. *Legal risks* were considered important by all of the key stakeholders as retail pharmacy is a highly regulated industry and there are significant legal requirements that need to met when selling pharmaceutical goods. The following comment by the managing director emphasises the importance of addressing legal risks that arise from selling retail pharmaceutical goods online.

"And you're right; liability is a big issue. You know in our game if you give out the wrong, like if you're selling beer and you give out the wrong type of beer who cares! But here if you give out the wrong drug – the implications. So you're correct – the liability on our side is massive and cost me a lot of money to address those, through lawyers but we feel confident with what we've covered" (C1:T95:101).

Increased liquidity was not applicable to this case. *Narrowing of margins* was acknowledged by the managing director and was actually one of the reasons that had prompted the managing director to consider the viability of an online pharmacy. Traditional retail pharmacy was actually facing a narrowing of margins due to increased competition from the supermarket chains and looming threat of deregulation of the industry.

In Case D, the *operational risks* associated with an E-Commerce site were acknowledged by the managing director and by the marketing/customer relationship manager and the external web developer to a lesser extent. The following comments by the managing director that he considered a viable operational site needed to attract users through search engines.

Case D	Operational risk	Repu-tational risk	Out-sourcing risk	Strategic risk	Legal risk	Liqui-dity risk	Narrow-ing of margins risk
Managing Director	Very important	Very important	Important	Very important	Very important	Not appli-cable	Important
Marketing/ Customer relation-ship manager	Acknow-ledged to some extent	Important	Not acknow-ledged	Acknow-ledged to some extent	Important	Not appli-cable	Not acknow-ledged
External web developer	Very important	Important	Not acknow-ledged	Acknow-ledged to some extent	Not acknow-ledged	Not appli-cable	Not acknow-ledged

Table 4. Summary of Case D:
- Key stakeholder perceptions of risk in relation to E-Commerce

> "That also means that your website needs to designed to be friendly to the search engines not the Yahoos not the directories but the Alta Vistas who actually visit you site and crawl over it. Now you are probably familiar with Hallway and Doorway technology You'll find that less than half about a third of our website is actually visible to you two thirds of it is not see by the consumer it is only seen by the search engines. That is not pages that is two thirds of the pages that we have are what we call doorway pages they are designed to get into a search engine by a certain criteria so if you type in Flowers Toowoomba we would be trying very hard" (D1:T220:227).

The managing director also considered that the site should be functional and facilitate purchasing online.

> "It is quite important that it is functional and processes you quickly in my opinion. So what we want to do is people have arrived at a website they want to consume because that is why they are going there. We see our job as getting to the consuming page as fast as possible. So we would say the speed, high speed plenty of. speed is I think more critical than anything. Product range is not too much because too much product range confuses them and the other thing that you need to establish very quickly on your web site is creditability - why should I deal with this " (D1:T342:350).

The external web developer was employed on a part time basis. The managing director was heavily involved in any new development of the E-Commerce while the marketing/customer relationship manager and external web developer were largely involved maintenance work. *Reputational risk* was considered important by all of the key stakeholders as Case D was dependent on the commercial viability of its E-Commerce site. This was particularly evident in Case D's approach to customer relationship management. The philosophy was that the customer is always right and that any florist in the relay network that behaved unethically towards the retail customers was given one warning only. *Outsourcing* was only considered an issue by the manager director in that he was reliant on the external web developer to maintain the E-Commerce site on a part time basis. *Strategic risks* associated with an E-Commerce site were only considered by the managing director as he had total control over the development of the E-Commerce site and the other key stakeholders involvement was directed development and maintenance. The following comment by the managing director indicates that he was driving the E-commerce system development and adoption of new web technologies.

> "Yes they serve us. I don't really think of them as stakeholders we use self employed individuals rather than corporations, I don't think I wouldn't call them stakeholders. We would certainly listen to their advise but they wouldn't give us" (D1:T152:155).

This may be both a strength and a weakness given that his perceptions of strategic risk will be governed by his particular frames of reference. As with all businesses, *legal risks* need to be addressed but the flower industry is not a highly regulated industry, and only normal legal issues associated with doing business needed to be addressed. *Increased liquidity* was not an applicable in Case D's industry and narrowing of margins was only of concern to the manager director. As was noted in Case C, the *narrowing of margins* had actually occurred in the traditional business model of Case D. The move to an E-Commerce presence was an attempt to remain viable in the long term in an industry that had been impacted on and rationalised by the advent of the Internet. The following comment by the managing director emphasises that he considered that the move toward an E-commerce presence was critical to the long term survival in the industry.

> "Well we went on the Web in 1994 business started in 92 with the Web as we know it or the Web itself actually ..... We visited America in 94 and heard about the internet there and the forecast was that in our industry, our American counterpart said they expected 30% of their business to be lost to the Web inside 5 years and they were pretty accurate actually so we were both excited and depressed by that and put all our florists on the web and as far as I know I think we were the first florist relay service in the world to have a website and have all our florists on the website" (C1:T10:20).

10. CONCLUSIONS

This paper seeks to explore the relationship between E-Commerce and a psychological construct. It does not seek to make definitive statements; rather, it explores potentialities. There appear to be some between-organisation differences in terms of the perceived risk of E-commerce. While it could be argued that this is simply a reflection of the different industries in which these organisations operate and the different imperatives peculiar to those industries, it could equally be argued that this is a strong indicator of the framing heuristic in action. While it may very well be true that a corporation needs to pay heed to the requirements of its particular markets, there is some evidence to suggest that this focus can lead the corporation to ignore more general risks that apply across the broader spectrum of E-Commerce activities.

We were initially surprised at the extent to which all four cases were aligned with the financial institution risk perception model suggested by APRA. We were interested to see that the non-banking companies recognised some of the risks which are apparently more significant in a banking environment. Overall, the APRA model does seem to apply to a variety of contexts On closer analysis, this is perhaps more of a weakness than a strength. The factors are simply too general. Once people began speaking about individual concerns, the general factors began to narrow into highly-focused, specific concerns. Thus, one individual was indeed concerned with operational issues but his concern was highly focused on the technical capabilities of search engines. This concern emerged nowhere else.

The two smaller companies also come across as innovative and sensitive to the business environment whereas the financial institutions rely on the strength of their procedures. They believe that the traditional SDLC approach to engineering systems is adaptable to development for the Internet. Indeed, in their opinion it is the best way to address concerns regarding security. This issue is beyond the scope of this paper but it must be mentioned that there is some debate about the best way in which to conduct development for the Internet Some would favour RAD and prototyping approaches in environments which someone like Peters (1987) would describe as unpredictable and chaotic, requiring rapid and continuous adaptation from the corporation.

The intra-organisational differences are somewhat more striking. There is evidence to indicate that different organisational levels and functions view E-Commerce in divergent ways. There is also evidence that the `us and them` attitude is as strong as ever, and herein lies the most interesting finding of the study. In two of the organisations, management complained that their IT departments were not delivering. I.T departments are referred to as `whingers` who offer excuses and not solutions. These managers speak about the need for speed, customer focus, ongoing redevelopment and customisation. To these people, the key risks relate to lack of speed and not meeting the market. Developers, on the other hand, seem to focus on traditional techniques and procedures as the best tools to manage risk. They complain that management expects too much and does not understand what they do. One developer focuses on the way in which detailed change management helps in efforts to control risk.

It seems to us that these differences in perception is one of the reasons many E-Commerce projects have run into trouble. On the one hand, management does not understand the level of complexity of the technology or its rapid pace of change. On the other hand, I.T. developers do not understand that margins are under pressure and time is of the essence. While it is true that traditional systems development has not been free of the same differences of opinion that we see now, it could be argued that software engineering approaches made the whole development process more predictable and we cannot now blame I.T. people for wanting to use these techniques. The problem is: are these techniques applicable to today's requirements?

We suggest that our case study supports the following general arguments:

1. People continue to view E-Commerce systems development as uncertain and / or risky. Indeed, even when they are speaking about E-Commerce in general terms the topic of risk emerges in a variety of guises.
2. People from different areas and levels of the corporations studied did indeed view the process and goals of E-Commerce system development in different ways. Of course, some of these differences can be explained in terms of the fact that the people involved occupied different occupational roles. The framing heuristic has a wide influence, however, and encompasses perceived occupational role and distinctive corporate influences.
3. Although there was a relative degree of convergence in terms of inter-organisational risk perceptions, this only applied when the risks themselves were framed in the most general of terms. Dominant concerns tended to be much more specific and varied widely.
4. In at least two organisations, people who filled boundary-spanning roles were highly focused on innovation, rapid adaptation and the external environment whereas those involved in development were focused on control, security and measured change.

It may be that chaotic development exists within apparently structured organisations and procedures due to the different perceptual frames of references that underpin the thinking of key stakeholders. Of course, it is possible that a wide variety of opinions and perceptions make for good E-Commerce systems development due to some undefined symbiotic element. It is our experience, however, that when a wide variety of perceptions exist, one set comes to dominate. If that set is bound by a paradigm out of touch with commercial reality, the consequences are likely to be unfavourable.

We also believe the cases suggest that the uncertain and complex world of E-Commerce systems development does indeed make people withdraw into their own limited specialist worlds where they feel secure in their perceived expertise and view people from other parts of the organisation with suspicion.

It would appear that a challenge, in the face of the increasing complexity and uncertainty of E-Commerce systems, is to align the perceptions of key stakeholders towards risk, process and corporate exigencies in order to have a coherent and focused E-Commerce system development approach. More work is required in this area of research and current information systems development approaches do not acknowledge potential impact and significance of differing frames of reference in the development of information systems. In particular, development of E-Commerce systems exasperate the problem given that key stakeholders are dealing with uncertainty and complexity using frames of reference which may or may not be appropriate.

REFERENCES

APRA Insight 2001, Prudential Issues in Electronic Commerce, Ist Quarter 2001

Angehrn, A and Meyer, A (1997) Developing mature Internet strategies, Information Systems Management, Vol. 14 No. 3, pp. 37-43.

Galliers, R. (1994) Choosing Information Systems Research Approaches, in:

G. R. Henley (Ed) *Information Systems Research: Issues, Methods and Practical Guidelines*, Alfred Walker, pp. 144-162 .

Douglas, M. And Wildavsky, A. (1982) How can we know the risks we face? *Risk Analysis 2*

Drucker, P.F. (1988) The Coming of the New Organisation. *Harvard Business Review,* Jan-Feb

Earl, M. (1997) *Management in the Information Era.* cited in: Bickerstaffe, G. (ed.) Mastering Management: Pitman:London

Gable, G (1994) Integrating case study and survey methods: An example in information systems, European Journal of Information Systems, vol. 3, No 2, pp. 112-126.

Gue Henno (1995) *The end of the Nation State.* Minneapolis: Unviversity of Minnesota Press

Handy, C. *The Age of Unreason.* Business Books:London

Kahneman, D. And Tversky, A. (1974) Judgement of under uncertainty: Heuristics and Biases, *Science, No 185,* September

Marchand, D. And Horton, W. *Infotrends.* John Wiley and Sons: London

Peters, T. (1987) *Thriving on Chaos.* Pan: London

Reichardt, C. (1992) The Fallibility of our Judgements. *Evaluation Practice* volume 3

Russo, E. And Shoemaker, P.J. (1991) *Confident Decision Making*. Piatkus: London

Russo, E. And Shoemaker, P.J. (1990) The Overconfidence Quiz. *Harvard Business Review*, September

Russo, E. And Shoemaker, P.J. (1992) Managing Overconfidence. *Sloan Management Review*, Winter

Simon, H.A. (1976) *Administrative Behaviour*. MacMillan: New York

Smart, C. and Vertinsky, I. (1984) Strategy and the Environment: A Study of Corporate Responses to Crises. *Strategic Management Journal*, July-September

Walsh, J.P. (1988) Selectivity and Selective Perception. *Academy of Management Journal*, Volume 31 number 4

Webber, R. (1997) *Modern Imperatives*. cited in: Bickerstaffe, G. (ed.) Mastering Management: Pitman:London

Wiseman, C. (1988) *Strategic Information Systems*. Irwin: Illinois

Yin, R. K. (1994) *Case Study Research - Design and Methods* (Thousand Oaks, California, Sage).

AN EVALUATION OF INTELLIGENT AGENT BASED INNOVATION IN THE WHOLESALE FINANCIAL SERVICES INDUSTRY

MARY-ANNE WILLIAMS and STEVE ELLIOT
University of Technology, Sydney and University of Sydney, Australia

Abstract: It is now widely accepted that success in providing wholesale financial services will depend on the industry's ability to develop flexible ebusiness models and strategies, as well as its ability to develop innovative systems for knowledge management and customer relationship management that can communicate effectively with legacy systems. In this paper we describe the problems and challenges facing Australian corporations in the Wholesale Financial Services sector and describe a research model which seeks to assess the impact of emerging Intelligent Agent enabled e-business initiatives, particularly in the area of system architecture and mass customisation. The purpose is to assist these firms achieve a level of international competitiveness in this area through (a) the investigation and longitudinal monitoring of the current status of and further developments in intelligent agent technologies, and (b) the investigation of emergent applications and successful approaches for the adoption and implementation of these key technologies in the provision of improved value-added customer services. We argue that a multi-disciplinary integration of e-business strategy, finance, intelligent agent architectures and knowledge technologies offer a previously unexplored solution to the documented challenges confronting Australia's Wholesale Financial Services industry. Agent architectures transcend traditional information system designs for applications that require complex, highly customized transactions in an open exception rich environment where responsiveness is imperative. We show that agent architectures naturally support e-business innovation by providing a framework for genuine dynamic information system development, which in turn leads to the kind of system agility that is crucial in the current highly competitive global financial environment. Agents can evolve over time iteratively and independently, without impacting other agents. A key difference between agent architectures and more traditional architectures is that instead of building relationships between software components at design time, agent architectures allow relationships to be formed on the fly at run-time. This results in highly responsive systems that are sensitive to the dynamic financial services context and that may be opportunistic in any competitive complex business environment. The ability to be opportunistic is particularly important in the current highly competitive global wholesale financial services industry.

1. INTRODUCTION

In the current increasingly efficient business environment, customers and businesses enjoy instant access to information and a wide array of product choice, a situation leading to intensive comparison shopping [7, 25]. Electronic business facilitates conditions for *perfect competition* and forces a knowledge shift from sellers to buyers [15, 25]. This massive power shift occurs as buyers gain advantage through rapid access to high quality information [7,13]. Sustaining competitive advantage in this highly competitive complex business environment era of e-commerce is challenging.

In this paper we describe the problems and challenges facing Australian corporations in the Wholesale Financial Services sector and describe a multi-disciplinary research model that seeks to assess the impact of emerging Intelligent Agent enabled e-business initiatives, particularly in the area of system architecture and mass customisation. The purpose is to assist these firms achieve a level of international competitiveness in this area through (a) the investigation and longitudinal monitoring of the current status of and further developments in intelligent agent technologies, and (b) the investigation of emergent applications and successful approaches for the adoption and implementation of these key technologies in the provision of improved value-added customer services.

We focus on the wholesale financial services throughout, and suggest a multi-disciplinary approach [5, 6] to evaluate and monitor intelligent agent architectures and knowledge technologies within the financial services context that may offer significant benefits when applied to the recognised problems facing the industry.

Intelligent agents are software entities that are capable of independent action in open, unpredictable environments, and as such they have become a promising information management technology. Indeed, one could argue that they are emerging as a new way of thinking, and as a consequence they are dramatically changing the way we design and build information systems in a wide variety of fields.

Agent architectures transcend traditional information system designs for applications that require complex, highly customized transactions in an open exception rich environment where responsiveness is imperative. Agent architectures support innovation by providing a framework for genuine dynamic information system development, which leads to the kind of system agility that is crucial in the current highly competitive global financial environment.

Agents are autonomous, and as such can evolve over time iteratively and independently, without impacting other agents. A key difference between agent architectures and more traditional ones is that instead of building relationships between software components at design time, agent architectures allow relationships to be established on the fly at run-time. This results in highly responsive systems that are context-sensitive and that can be opportunistic in a competitive complex business environment. The ability to be opportunistic is particularly pertinent and important in the current highly competitive global wholesale financial services industry.

Another important advantage intelligent agents offer business is the ability to forge and nurture relationships with their customers [27]. Intelligent agents offer mechanisms to fulfill and anticipate customer needs [2,3]. Intelligent agents can be used to increase the scale and efficiency of existing CRM strategies by employing mass customization techniques.

The challenge lies in the identification of relevant information to provide to the customer that will enable them to make good decisions and that will assist them to reach their goals.

A wide range of radically new business models is emerging that challenges existing business methods and IT architectures. New business models need new IT architectures and infrastructure to support them. Traditional solutions are too inflexible. Indeed it is this inflexibility that has lead to the phenomena of new businesses taking the lead in ebusiness and leaving the bricks and mortar businesses behind or putting them out of business. Businesses must interact with other businesses information systems i.e. customers, partners etc. A key capability of Amazon.com is its capacity to interact with DHL's to give customers specific information about book purchase deliveries. Agent solutions have an intrinsic capacity for establishing and managing the formation and evolution of business relationships. Early adopters of technological innovation typically immerse themselves in a learning environment where they can "play" and experiment with technology where they can develop novel approaches to problems quickly and effectively. This means that their systems must be flexible and extensible.

2. PROBLEMS IN INDUSTRY

A successful, robust, and vibrant wholesale financial services industry is crucial for Australia's future. The range of services provided by the industry includes bonds, cash management, deposit, equity, foreign currency exchange, investment, loan, settlement and other facilities for enterprises and government organisations in support of their commercial operations. It is has become widely accepted that long term success in providing wholesale financial services will be dependent on the industry's ability to develop flexible ebusiness models and strategies, as well as its ability to develop innovative systems for knowledge management and customer relationship management that can communicate effectively with legacy systems [7, 28].

Unfortunately, this necessity to develop new strategies and systems represents a significant challenge for the Australian Wholesale Financial Services industry. The industry is not known for its early adoption of e-business innovation. The major benefit of e-business lies in its potential to transform traditional business practice. Substantial business risk is associated with structural transformation of organizations and industries and financial services firms are traditionally risk averse. Based on interviews with 23 senior executives with responsibility for ebusiness in 18 corporations in 2000 - 2001, a recent industry report suggests that a significant transformation needs to take place in order for the industry to be able to seize the opportunities presented by ebusiness. Furthermore, if it fails to do so then its future and Australia's hopes are in serious jeopardy [7].

The reasons for the current concerns stem from a number of systemic problems in the industry including the following [as identified in 7]:

1. The poor state of integration between a bank's internal systems. The range of services offered by firms (as listed above) is typically provided by separate, incompatible systems. Apart from challenges in establishing a degree of integration across systems that would enable the recognition and treatment of customers in a consistent manner, there are also serious issues surrounding the necessity to maintain and to extend existing legacy systems.
2. Difficulties in achieving Straight Through Processing (STP). STP is the concept that transactions should be able to be processed completely through both customer and service provider systems without the necessity for manual intervention. STP is significant as 'it represents huge potential cost savings and increased margins without exposure to competitive threat or market risk'. The greatest barrier to STP in any organization is its legacy systems. The nature of the products, and the

relationships with suppliers and customers are also important. 'The potential gains from STP will drive industry-wide cooperation in developing common standards and systems for trading capture and settlement.' [7].

3. Information on customers is held in silos and is not integrated. This lack of integration is often an organizational issue, not just a technological one. Traditional information system architectures tend to closely mirror organizational structure and constraints. The close coupling presents significant obstacles for change.
4. There are difficulties linking the businesses information systems with client information systems. "All banks will face the common necessities of linking their processing systems more closely with those of their clients" [7].
5. The wholesale banking industry is not uniform. For example, low-value, high-volume commoditisable markets such as foreign exchange, the focus is on improvements in process efficiency. For high-value, low volume markets such as funds management, the focus is on adding value to the products.
6. Some product types, such as those in the funds management sector, are not easily commoditisable and require human intervention.
7. High cost of conventional customized information systems.
8. Large volume of data in many applications.
9. Regulatory nature of the financial sector.

In the following sections we argue that agent technologies can be used to alleviate many of the problems above. For example, agent technology offers the ability to support alliances and to build collaborative advantage - an important capability for business in the future. It also supports new forms of collaboration, which will result in providing seamless experiences for customers.

3. AGENT TECHNOLOGIES

Intelligent Software Agents are innovative technologies that have the potential to become one of the most important information management tools of this century. Intelligent agents are autonomous computational entities capable of making decisions independently and without the intervention of other entities, e.g. humans [31]. They can be proactive, purposeful and exhibit goal-directed behaviour, as well as reactive and responsive to changes in the environment. They can interact and modify their environments, and most importantly they can interact with other agents. A key feature of an agent is autonomy [17]. Being autonomous distinguishes them from objects in the object-oriented paradigm [12]. Autonomy allows system development to be enhanced with the embedding of desired actions into modular units, which can operate individually and independently. As a consequence they lead to more flexible designs, and since the processing is distributed, better performance can be obtained in practice.

Agents are most suited to applications that involve communication between heterogeneous information systems. Electronic business transactions in a global economy typically involve interactions between numerous heterogeneous systems. Intelligent agents have the ability to reason and draw inferences and as a consequence they can perform sequences of complex operations based on their internal beliefs, goals and the information/messages they receive [20]. They can use explicit representation of their internal beliefs, the services they offer, and their overall goals, which can then be communicated and shared with other agents.

Traditional software systems are often unable to model rational behavior and experience a great deal of limitation in a real time environment where information is typically incomplete and susceptible to change [29, 30]. Agents, on the other hand, thrive on the need for applications to exhibit rational, human like decision making in their respective problem domains [11]. These properties give agents the edge in the information and process rich environment of e-commerce, which creates the need for agent based programming as the solution for current and future business needs [10]. Although still in the phase of development, agent-oriented programming has already shown much promise in a variety of real-time applications such as air traffic management, air simulation, and distributed business systems.

The kinds of agent architectures we have in mind for the Wholesale Financial Services Industry is illustrated in Figure 1 below. In essence each client will have an agent, or family of agents, that acts as the go-between. The *customer agent* possesses information about the customer including information gleaned from the customer's corporate databases. The *customer agent* interacts with the *business agent* by sharing information pertinent to the transaction being negotiated. The *business agent* obtains information from the corporate databases and also from other sources that might involve automatically generated user profiles.

4. APPLYING AGENT TECHNOLOGIES TO WHOLESALE FINANCIAL SERVICES

Agent architectures support innovation by providing the framework for genuine dynamic development, which leads to the kind of system agility that is crucial in the current highly competitive global financial environment. Traditional architectures force businesses to accept a trade-off between scalability and agility. Enterprise-wide systems are typically rigid, and they provide the classic example of how agility is sacrificed for scalability. Inevitably traditional system development solutions result in relatively inflexible systems that reduce an organisation's responsiveness to change in both the short and the long term. Agent architectures, on the other hand, can be developed and enhanced iteratively because each agent is completely autonomous. Therefore, one of the main benefits of agent architectures is their scope for incremental deployment, progressive refinement and experimental elaboration – components and processes can be added, removed or changed independently.

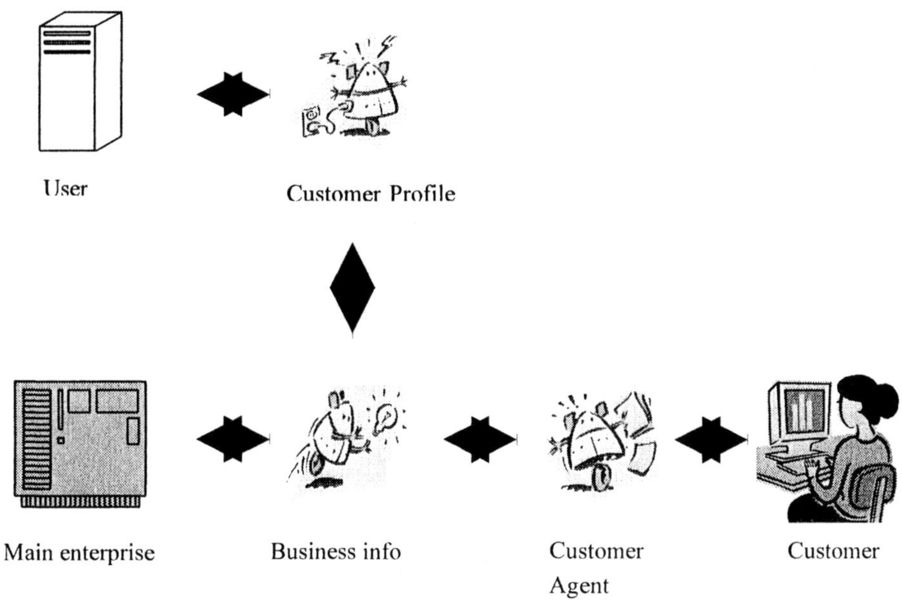

Figure 1. Agent Architecture for the Wholesale Financial Services Industry

Instead of building relationships between software components at design time, agent architectures allow relationships to be context-sensitive and to be formed at run-time. This results in highly responsive systems that can be opportunistic in a competitive business environment. The ability to be opportunistic is particularly important in the current highly competitive global wholesale financial services industry.

4.1 Agent based Business Process Management

Business process management in industry typically involves seamless end-to-end processing across multi-step business activities and multiple heterogeneous systems and people, in possibly one or more organizations. A major goal of business process management is to harness and enhance the value chain.

Many wholesale financial services enterprises have developed first generation process management systems, usually custom built combinations of workflow, document management, or systems automation with bubblegum-code "gluing" it all together.

Although Enterprise Application Integration and Enterprise Resource Planning systems attempt to provide a systematic end-to-end solution, there is no single system that has been capable of providing a complete solution. As a result the industry is left with overly complex monolithic and cumbersome legacy systems that are relatively inflexible when it comes to change.

As the industry tries to automate and enhance their customer-oriented operations and leverage Internet connectivity with suppliers, customers and partners, system complexity has increased dramatically and change has become even more difficult. In the current economic environment, industry is challenged to deliver bottom-line improvements through a combination of significant cost savings and increased responsiveness to customers. The industry is in desperate need of a pathway to sustained competitiveness and profitability. The answer to these problems lies in the adoption of innovations that will lead to significant improvements in the industry's agility in an increasingly competitive global economy.

Agent technology offers a way to integrate large complex heterogeneous systems. They provide a mechanism for integrating legacy systems with newly developed information systems. Agents are well suited for middleware applications that translate information and implement information systems interfaces that meet a wide variety of requirements.

In many applications, system developers have legacy code that performs some unique function, which is needed in their new applications. An agent can be used to invoke and execute this legacy code. The capability to enable execution of native software and legacy code is crucial for the financial services industry.

Agent architectures present tremendous possibilities for solving many industry problems. They can not only communicate with legacy systems, but even more importantly they alleviate many of the traditional design problems system developers face. In particular, the developers do not have to anticipate and explicitly design for all conceivable situations and potential scenarios. Developers using traditional means identify all possible execution paths during the design phase of the system development life cycle, which are later hard coded as links between the sub-processes. For large-scale applications, the number of interprocess links tends to grow exponentially. In practice this means that there are too many situations to code for and as a consequence, systems become sensitive to exceptions, i.e. they fail when something unexpected occurs. The problem of having to anticipate every conceivable situation at design time leads to the fundamental development dilemma: scalability or business agility.

Agent architectures differ with traditional solutions in fundamental ways. For example, how the various agents (and subprocess) come together and interact is determined at run time. The developer has only to specify properties and behaviours of the agent, does not need to dictate how it will respond in every possible situation.

Conventional software architectures do not handle the following financial services problems effectively:

1. The high volume of events or service requests: large online transaction and decision support systems such as foreign exchange and OTC services invoke many complex processes; many of those transactions requiring significant human intervention to be completed.
2. The high volume of configurations for example funds management: need a high level of process customization to handle all the possible scenarios; the number of permutations to code becomes rapidly too large.
3. The high volume of exceptions: those systems encounter many unplanned situations or exceptions, significantly reducing efficiency; self-service applications over the Internet, such as loan processing cannot be successfully automated due to numerous exceptions.

Integrating wholesale financial services will be a time-consuming and expensive exercise. Automating large-scale business processes has essentially been limited to back-end operations such as financial reporting systems. Such systems are typically custom-coded and therefore very rigid. However, they generated adequate returns on investment because of the stable and predictable nature of the processes and configurations. As companies began to automate their customer-oriented operations, they searched for flexibility to personalize handling of each customer and adapt to changing business policies and processes. Opening the environment of the enterprise resulted in increased complexity, rapid change and more unpredictable situations. New computing approaches such as workflow systems, e-process servers or rules engines have been use as the basis for Enterprise Application Integration solutions and other platforms and applications. However, customization resulted in significant custom coding and consulting support, close to back-end systems. With the extension of these applications to Internet-based connectivity, corporations are faced with unprecedented unpredictability that made it impossible to achieve high-performance, large-scale, yet agile business process management. A fundamentally new computing infrastructure is necessary to deliver in a single solution performance and agility and, at the same time, dramatically reduce the cost of developing and maintaining business automation systems.

Agent technologies have significant potential to address the industry's technology-based systemic problems and to improve its efficiency and competitiveness. Many systemic problems arise from incompatible legacy systems. Agent technologies present a possible cost-effective solution to systems integration. The promises of tight coupling between bank and client systems and adding value through customization of products and services in a high volume market may also be realised by the potential of agents to:

1. Support technology-based customized services to mass markets.
2. Enable integrated service provision to specific customers.
3. Eliminate margins based on customers' limited capability for price discovery.
4. Increase the rate of providers' responsiveness to market changes.
5. Reduce the time and cost of product and service provision.
6. Assist customers to migrate to online channels
7. Link disparate systems, eg financial service provider' and client's systems.
8. Enable collaborative advantage between providers.

4.2 Mass Customization

One advantage intelligent agents offer the industry is the ability to forge and nurture relationships with their customers. Intelligent agents offer mechanisms to fulfill and anticipate customer needs [2,3]. Intelligent agents can be used to increase the scale and efficiency of existing CRM strategies by employing mass customization techniques.

Data mining can be used to help build context sensitive customer profiles and models of customer behavior as they interact with a business system, see how customer profile building fits into our proposed architecture in Figure 1. Customization is nontrivial. First, different visitors carry different intentions and are attracted to the different elements and offerings of a business' website. Second, different visitors perceive the same site differently and may use it differently against the designer's expectations. Third, the same visitor may log in to the same site with new intentions.

The challenge lies in the identification of relevant information to provide to the customer that will enable them to make good decisions and assist them reach their goals. Many advanced solutions have come about in response to this challenge. All too often though these approaches are based on human interaction-input (user profile) such as Firefly [27]. These static inputs feed the system to produce the same non-dynamic personalized presentation, as the profile ages. Agent technology paired with web mining techniques will yield more favorable results because more meaningful exchanges of information can be achieved.

A number of approaches have been developed which focus on automatic personalization based on user-web site interaction. For instance Schechter et al [22] came up with the technique using user path profiles to predict further web usage, which can be used for network and proxy caching. Other researchers, Perkowitz and Etzioni [18] suggested the idea of optimizing on the Web site based co-occurrence page patterns. Clustering of user sessions to predict future user behavior were used by Shahabi et al [24] and Nasraoui et al [16]. Mobasher, Cooley and Srivastava [14] provided several techniques in which the user preferences are automatically learned from the web usage data to keep a constant rejuvenated user profile. Similarly, Spiliopoulou et al [26], Cooley et al [4], and Buchner and Mulvenna [3] have applied data mining techniques to extract usage pattern from web server logs [14, 16, 18]. Perkowitz and Etzioni [18] again, proposed a cluster based mining algorithm together with data mining algorithm to analyze log servers in attempt to synthesize the index page.

5. PROPOSED RESEARCH MODEL

This research seeks to assist Australian corporations in the Wholesale Financial Services sector to assess the impact of emerging Intelligent Agent enabled e-business initiatives, with particular attention to system architecture and mass customisation. The purpose is to assist these firms achieve a level of international competitiveness through a multi-disciplinary research project for the:

- investigation and longitudinal monitoring of the current status of and further developments in intelligent agent technologies,
- investigation of emergent applications and successful approaches for the adoption and implementation of these key technologies in the provision of improved value-added customer services.
- determination of appropriate applications of these technologies to address identified problems confronting the Wholesale Financial Services industry, particularly in mass customisation.

The research also seeks to support a national priority to establish Australia as a regional financial services centre by ensuring that Australian financial services organisations have ready access to the latest developments in and applications of intelligent agent technologies in their provision of value-added customer services. In response to significant industry challenges identified in interviews with senior executives in 18 corporations in 2000-2001 [7], our research aims to:

a) identify the current 'best of breed' levels of capability in intelligent agent technology and to determine the current capacity of these technologies to support value-added customer services in the financial services sector;
b) identify emergent, relevant developments in intelligent agent technologies and their applications through a program of longitudinal monitoring of international activities;
c) identify factors that drive and inhibit the potential for intelligent agent technologies to create and sustain value in value-added customer services;
d) describe key elements of success in the understanding, planning, development and effective application of intelligent agent technologies;
e) provide the basis for assessing progress, in understanding and use, of each successive wave of innovation in applications of intelligent agent technologies to value-added customer services; and
f) incorporate a set of industry and national benchmarks for critical dimensions of intelligent agent effectiveness.

The research focus lies in the multi-disciplinary conjunction of information systems, knowledge representation, intelligent agent technologies, adoption of innovations, Australia's Wholesale Financial Services sector and business-to-business e-commerce. Research questions include:

a) What is the current level of applications of intelligent systems relevant to value-added customer services and mass customisation in the Wholesale Financial Services sector?
b) How can the impact of intelligent agent technologies be reasonably and reliably measured by organisations, industries and nations?

c) What are the likely impacts of developments in intelligent agent capabilities on organisations, industries and nations over the next 5 years?
d) What factors drive or inhibit the strategic level adoption and diffusion of intelligent agent technologies for mass customisation?
e) What factors, processes and practices influence the effective development and implementation of intelligent agent based value-added customer services?

The objectives are to proceed with parallel investigations into the technologies and their international applications in the Wholesale Financial Services industries. There will be regular reporting to Australian firms and other interested bodies of developments through industry-oriented publications, seminars, demonstrations and briefings. Suitable evaluation criteria will need to be developed for each research area.

A characteristic of this project is its multi-disciplinary approach with a single applied focus – determination of the potential of intelligent agent technologies to deliver internationally competitive, value-added, customised services. It will be implemented through integrated, parallel investigations into the technologies and their international applications relevant to the Wholesale Financial Services industries. The technologies investigation will be achieved through monitoring of and participation in internationally significant projects in intelligent agent technologies. The applications investigation will be achieved through a series of longitudinal case studies of organizations implementing relevant intelligent agent initiatives. In addition, through the establishment and collection of appropriate metrics, using interviews and surveys, the study will assess the on-going impact of intelligent agent initiatives on the financial services sector, the broader Australian economy and internationally.

6. DISCUSSION

Challenges confronting the Australian Wholesale Financial Services sector have been identified in a White Paper, launched by the Federal Minister for Financial Services in March 2001 [7]. Success in meeting these challenges will depend on the sector's ability to develop and to effectively implement flexible ebusiness models and strategies. A critical implementation challenge will be to develop innovative systems for knowledge management and customer relationship management that can communicate effectively with legacy systems.

Agent technologies offer a potential solution to specific industry problems. We have proposed a research model that seeks to assess the impact of emerging Intelligent Agent enabled e-business initiatives, particularly in the area of system architecture and mass customisation.

Intelligent agent architectures and knowledge technologies offer the potential for significant benefits in the wholesale financial services industry.

Agent architectures transcend traditional information system designs for applications that require complex, highly customized transactions in an open exception rich environment where responsiveness is imperative. Furthermore, they naturally support innovation by providing a framework for genuine dynamic information system development, which in turn leads to the kind of system agility that is crucial in the current highly competitive global financial environment. This results in highly responsive systems that are context-sensitive and that can be opportunistic in a competitive complex business environment.

REFERENCES

Bratman M. E.. 1987. Intentions, Plans, and Practical Reason. Harvard University Press, Cambridge, M.A..

Bratman, M. E, Isreal, D., and Pollack, M. E.. 1988. Plans and resource-bounded practical reasoning. Computational Intelligence, 4:439-355.

Buchner, A. and Mulvenna, M. D., 1999. Discovering Internet marketing intelligence through online analytical Web usage mining. *SIGMOD Record*, (4) 27.

Cooley, R., Mobasher, B., and Srivastava, J., 1999. Data preparation for mining World Wide Web browsing patterns. *Journal of Knowledge and Information Systems*, (1) 1.

Elliot S. (ed) 2002. *Electronic Commerce: B2C strategies and models*. JohnWiley Series on Information Systems, Chichester UK, February. ISBN: 0471487058.

Elliot S., Andersen K.V., Swatman P. and Reich S. (eds) *E-Business: Multidisciplinary research and practice*. Proceedings of TC8 Conference, Salzburg, June 2001. BICE Press, Ourimbah. November 2001.

Elliot, S. and Briers, M, 2001. *E-Business Challenges for Australia's Wholesale Financial Markets: An Industry White Paper*. SIRCA Australia.

Ernst and Young. 1999. Special Report Technology in Financial Services. E-commerce. Customer Relationship Management. [Online] http://www.ey.com/

Fensel, D., 2001. *Ontologies: A Silver Bullet for Knowledge Management and Electronic Commerce,* Springer Verlag, Berlin.

Finin, T., Yannis Labrou, and James Mayfield. 1997. KQML as an agent communication language, in Jeff Bradshaw (Ed.), ``Software Agents", MIT Press, Cambridge.

Georgeff M. P. and F. F. Ingrand. 1989. Decision-making in an embedded reasoning system. In *Proceedings of the International Joint Conference on Artificial Intelligence*, Detroit, MI.

Jokelainen, A.S 1998. Autonomous Agent in Artificial Intelligence Research. Object oriented software and intelligent agents in future automation systems - Seminar Autumn 1998 [Online] http://www.automation.hut.fi/edu/as84360/autumn98/jokelainen/jokelainen.htm

Kierzkowksi, A., Mcquade, S., Waitman, R., Zeisser, M. 1996. Marketing to the digital consumer The McKinsey Quarterly, 1996 Number 2, pp. 180-183.

Mobasher, B., Cooley, R., and Srivastava, J., 1999. Automatic Personalization Through Web sage Mining, Technical Report TR99-010, Department of Computer Science, Depaul University.

Morrisette S,. April 1998 The Retail Power Shift Forrester Report [Online. http://www.forrester.com/ER/Research/Report/Excerpt/0,1358,3861,FF.html]

Nasraoui, O., Frigui, H., Joshi, A., Krishnapuram, R., 1999. Mining Web access logs using relational competitive fuzzy clustering. To appear in *the Proceedings of the Eight International Fuzzy Systems Association World Congress*, August.

Nwana, H.S., 1996. Software Agents: An Overview. In: The Knowledge Engineering Review, October/November, Volume 11, Number 3, pages 205-244.

Perkowitz, M. and Etzioni, O., 1998. Adaptive Web sites: automatically synthesizing Web pages. In *Proceedings of Fifteenth National Conference on Artificial Intelligence*, Madison, WI.

Perkowitz, M. and Etzioni, O., 2000. Towards Adaptive Web sites: Conceptual Framework and Case Study Artificial Intelligence Journal, v 188, n1/2.

Rao, A.S. 1996. Decision Procedures for Propositional Linear-Time Belief-Desire-Intention Logics, in Wooldridge, M. Müller, J.P. Tambe, M. (Eds.), Intelligent Agents II: Agent Theories, Architectures, and Languages, Springer-Verlag, Berlin and Heidelberg, Germany, pp.33-48

Robert Frances Group. 1999. A Knowledge Shift Becomes a Power Shift -- Anticipate it or Vanish [Online]. www.rfgonline.com/unprotectedarchive/research/060399nt.html.

Schechter, S., Krishnan, M., and Smith, M. D., 1998. Using path profiles to predict HTTP requests. In *Proceedings of 7th International World Wide Web Conference*, Brisbane, Australia.

Shardanand, U., Maes, P., 1995. Social information filtering: algorithms for automating "word of mouth." In *Proceedings of the ACM CHI Conference*.

Shahabi, C., Zarkesh, A. M., Adibi, J., and Shah, V., 1997. Knowledge discovery from users Web-page navigation. In *Proceedings of Workshop on Research Issues in Data Engineering*, Birmingham, England. 25.

Shern, S and Crawford, F. 1999. The 2nd Annual Ernst &Young. Internet Shopping Study. The Digital Channel Continuous to Gather Steam. [Online]. http://www.ey.com.au

Spiliopoulou, M. and Faulstich, L. C., 1999. WUM: A Web Utilization Miner. *In Proceedings of EDBT Workshop WebDB98*, Valencia, Spain, LNCS 1590, Springer Verlag.

Terpsidis, I. S., Moukas, A., Pergioudakis, B., Doukidis, G., and Maes, P., 1997. The potential of Electronic Commerce in Re-engineering-retailer relationships through Intelligent agents. *Proceedings of the European Conference on Multimedia and E-Commerce*, Florence, Italy 1997

Webley, M., Coates, A., King, S., 1999. Knowing your customer. A research report into customer information. KPMG Consulting. [Online. http://www.kpmg.com.uk (1999, Aug. 17)

Williams, M.A., 1997. *Anytime Belief Revision*, in the Proceedings of the International Joint Conference on Artificial Intelligence, Morgan Kaufmann, 74-80.

Williams, M. A., 1998. Applications of Belief Revision, in Transactions and Change in Logic Databases, LNAI 1472, Springer Verlag, 285 - 314.

Wooldridge, M and Jennings, R., J. 1995. Agent Theories, Architectures, and Languages: a Survey, "in Wooldridge and Jennings Eds., Intelligent Agents, Berlin: Springer-Verlag, 1-22.

ENHANCING MOBILE COMMERCE: INSTANT MUSIC PURCHASING OVER THE AIR

J. FELIX HAMPE[1] and GERHARD SCHWABE[2]
[1]*University of Koblenz, Institute of IS Research, Germany*
[2]*University of Zürich, Institute of Computer Science, Switzerland*

Abstract: The advances of electronic commerce had an tremendous impact on the media industry already. In this paper we take a closer look on the audio industry and summarize major considerations found in the relating media theoretical literature. This leads to the main topic under study: the much more significant impact mobile commerce might have. We discuss present and future technology options, which could offer new distribution mechanisms as well as significant changes in the underlying value chains. By presenting an existing prototype development for ordering music via air we afterwards even extend the discussion to the consideration of seeing mobiles of third generation networks as a download and distribution devices. From the discussion of optional features of the prototype we return to the general discussion of a relevant subset of open research questions.

1. INTRODUCTION

The distribution and delivery of information, and especially that of music as a product has always been subject to significant changes due to technology shifts. Whereas broadcasting through licensed radio or TV stations seems well understood in terms of established models for fee collection, the invention of records, music cassettes or compact disc - digital audio (CD-DA) simply allowed charging via the physical media. But clearly, with MP3 coding of audio data (IIS, 2001) and approaches like Napster (Napster, 2001) or Gnutella (Gnutella, 2001) etc. those considerations of distribution, delivery and pricing have gained an overwhelming relevance.

Internet based peer-to-peer services as used by Napster had been around for a long time (primarily in universities), but never before have we seen an approach for a very specific commercial domain with such a strong impact on its industry.

With a constantly growing user base of those systems for music distribution, there are significant technology implications when one thinks they all still require PC-equipment at the customer side, at least for the download of files. Surely it is possible to think of another distribution channel with nearly ubiquitous access, which can be connected to any PC?

So what are the implications if we look at music download services offered to an even larger user-base of the continuously growing mobile networks? As is well known, mobile e-markets show at least five major aspects of relevance (for an extended discussion we refer to (TIMElabs, 2000, pp 20):

- it is one of the fastest growing markets
- it offers ubiquitous, instant and fast access
- it will support mobile payment, thus allowing for instant settlement of transactions
- it promises around the clock service and thus continuous customer relations
- with IMT-2000 (UMTS) location based services could be implemented

With the emergence of the 2.5 or 3G mobile networks, an additional distribution channel for music (and later video, too) will be available, allowing for title selection and download, as well as accounting and billing over the air. This could be seen as a value added service, generating additional air time and specific revenue for mobile operators seeking to refinance their investments for spectrum licenses, both in terms of infrastructure and maintenance.

The question arises as to who will take over the role of (new) intermediary to set up this distribution channel. As will be argued in this paper, a variety of distribution channels will continue to co-exist, but the wider alternatives will allow radio stations to extend their business by offering instant shopping of music distributed via air, production and distribution of consumer customised audio products of any type and e-shop services offering all standard media products.
By introducing some major building blocks of a much more general prototype, the paper provides a proof of concept with respect to the technical feasibility of this solution. CYS : Catch Your Song is a prototype based on

Web and WAP technology which fulfils most of the requirements stated above.

This paper is based on a theory guided literature analysis and the development of a prototype as a prove of concept. Schwabe&Krcmar (Schwabe/Krcmar 2000) argue based on Szyperski (Szyperski, 1971), Nunamaker (Nunamaker/Chen 1990) and the understanding of the German IS community (Heinzl et al. 2001) that designing sociotechnical innovations is an important task of Information Systems Research.

2. RADIO STATIONS AND THE MUSIC CONTENT PROVIDERS

In the following discussion we concentrate on the literature relating to the German music market, but our conclusions are equally valid for other European and overseas media markets.

2.1 The current situation of the radio stations

In Germany, competition in the radio business began about 15 years ago with the appearance of private commercial radio stations (Filk, 1996). Up to then, there were only public radio stations. Competition has forced public radio station marketing to the point where critics no longer see any significant difference from private radio. Furthermore the listener market has changed: with the increasing abundance of other media, radio has become a byproduct consumed during other activities (i.e. a 'stand-by-medium'), e.g. while driving a car. This has made it increasingly difficult to bind listeners to a certain program; and radio stations therefore prefer to try to bind listeners to their station. Typical components of modern radio marketing strategies are (see (Seidel/Libertus, 1993; Heinrich, 1994; Heinrich 1999; Mühl-Bennighaus/Zerdick, 2000; Schumann/Hess, 2000)):

- The creation of a station identity that is transferred through jingles, and the structure of programs etc. The listener should feel "at home" with his radio station. Similarity of program structure makes orientation easier and reduces the listeners' tendency to switch to another radio-station.
- The building of a listeners community (see e.g. the community of SWR3 (SWR3, 2001)). This community receives extra benefits (e.g. reduced entrance fees to music events) and extra information (mostly over Websites), has the opportunity to communicate with the radio moderators

and is involved in running the radio program. As most German radio stations are local or regional, listener communities have a 'natural' geographic basis. For the radio station, a strong listener community is a source of considerable commercial and political power (the latter is particularly important for public radio).

– the creation and marketing of events with visibility beyond radio. The transmission of live concerts has been a traditional task of radio stations. Modern radio stations go much further: They create their own music festivals (broadcasting only small fractions of them) and co-market tours of famous artists. They thus both create their own content and make their communities more attractive (for further information on community building ref (Kim, 2000)). During the 1990s new media and product alliances between radio stations and the music industry led to merchandising opportunities for both partners.

The latter two efforts have led to an increase in collaboration between the radio stations and their content providers. Both have become close content partners, each one owning a different distribution channel. The characteristics of the distribution channels are actually so different that radio and CDs are seen as two different products by the general public (for an extended treatment see (Zerdick et al., 1999; Goldhammer/Zerdick, 1999; Szyperski, 1999). An increasing number of radio stations have discovered the Internet as an additional broadcasting medium. While currently the traditional program is mainly broadcast, radio stations are already taking command of the market for future value added services. This potential will significantly increase once digital audio broadcast (DAB) is introduced more widely into the market (Digitalradio, 2001).

2.2 The current situation of the content providers

There is tremendous pressure on the music industry for change (Middelhoff, 2000; Marathe, 2001). Music is a non-physical product and can thus be delivered entirely over the Internet. Recent inventions in audio compression, increasing network bandwidth (see the discussions further below) and the lack of law enforcement have led to an explosion of – largely illegal – distribution of music content over the Internet (for a discussion see (Dernbach et al., 1998; Neverla, 1998; Ludes/Werner, 1997; Goldhammer/Zerdick, 1999)). Music listeners have not only learnt to like over-the-net distributed music because it is free, but also because it provides easier and more flexible access to a larger volume of music titles than can be found in conventional record shops. Music content providers[1] have to find ways for online music marketing and reestablishing legal distribution. One approach is to make the internet "safer", i.e. to establish mechanisms on the net that allow content providers to collect royalties for their music. Technically, this requires a music-format that allows control over the copying of music titles, as well as avoiding illegal playback. The Secure Digital Music Initiative (SDMI 2001) has been formed with this objective, but has failed to produce tangible results. As the MP3 format is already very widely used, establishing a new standard that incorporates no further significant advantages for the consumer is at the very least an up-hill-battle, and more likely a hopeless task. Institutionally, "safe" music distribution over the Internet implies the build-up of legal electronic commerce sites for music distribution. As an example we refer to the “Music on Demand” platform of Deutsche Telekom (AOD, 2001). A prerequisite is a suitable business model for marketing music over the Internet. The recent takeover of Napster by Bertelsmann shows that music content providers are beginning to become more proactive in distributing their content over the Internet. Still, legal music distribution over the Internet may always stay problematic.

With respect to our topic of using mobile networks as distribution channels we note the following arguments which should attract content providers:

Mobile systems based on cell phones may become a much more attractive distribution channel:

1. The control of copyright in mobile networks could be realized more easily, because user authentication is performed by the subscriber identity module.
2. The customer base of mobile phones is already larger than that of Internet users and market penetration will increase in the foreseeable future (Durlacher, 1996).
3. Customers are already used to paying for mobile phone services (which is not the case for Internet services).

[1] For the purpose of this paper, the general term 'content provider' means all elements in the value chain of the music industry from the invention of the music piece by the artist to the production and multiplication of the music media, excluding the distribution and marketing. For a discussion of the value chain ref. later sections of this paper.

Despite these obvious advantages it will not be technically and economically feasible and reasonable to distribute all music exclusively over mobile phone networks for some time to come. But diversification of distribution channels as in similar branches will be observable. Thus, any mobile service for music marketing will also rely on other media channels for the transfer of content. Here radio stations may be the ideal partners for content providers. The remainder of this paper will introduce a concept for such a partnership.

2.3 Division of labor and value chain

The fundamental requirement to form such partnerships is the adjustment of current value chains or the creation of new ones. For the justification of this statement it makes sense to analyse the current value chains. Roughly, the value chain up to now shows the following traditional players (see figure 1) according to the detailed discussion in (Zerdick et al., 1999) and especially (Kulle, 1998).

Artists create their work (e.g. a pop song) and originally hold the rights. The work is then (traditionally) published and/or performed in collaboration with (concert) organisers and publishers. The third step is the recording of the piece and the production of the master tape. The organisational and technical environment for this step is supplied by producers and studios. This is also the last step in which the artist is directly involved. Media factories afterwards multiply the audio media (e.g. a CD-DA) and publish it. The product is then sold by shops and clubs (i.e. primary exploitation). If the music titles are publicly preformed or radio stations broadcast them, license fees result in a second stream of revenue (i.e. secondary exploitation). The consumer then buys the pieces, listens to them and copies the content privately (within and beyond the legal limits).

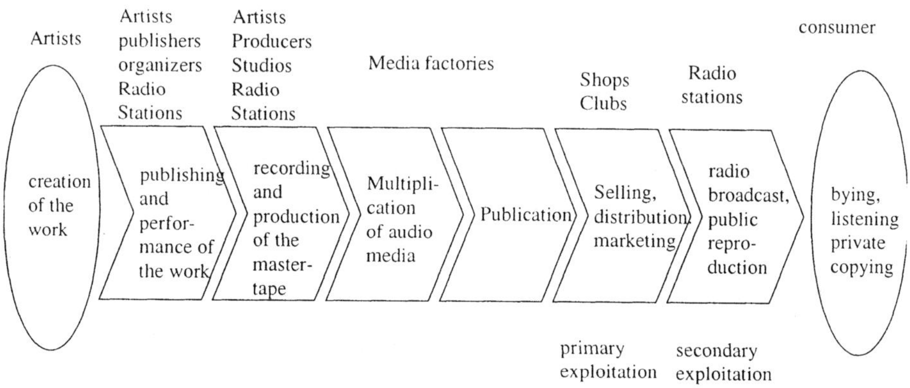

Figure 1. Value Chain of the Music Industry (based on (Kulle, 1998))

This value chain is heavily threatened by internet based electronic commerce: The whole value generation process may get cut off, if the consumers copy and distribute most of their music titles privately without paying royalties. The digital recording has provided a format that allows copying (almost) without loss of quality. The resulting private copying and selling of CD-DA has been the biggest source of loss for the music industry. An even much more significant threat is, however, seen in the illegal distribution of music over the Internet. Here, the music industry faces an illegal distribution channel for music titles that is far better organised than schoolyard CD-DA markets. In many senses an Internet-based value chain is also superior to the traditional value chain in terms of flexibility, availability, time to market and cost: traditional multiplication of audio media, publication and selling, distribution and marketing can be replaced by Internet-based value generation processes. For a sound and detailed discussion of the structural changes to the value chain through online-music-distribution we refer to (Kulle, 1998).

These highly visible changes have moved other changes to the value chain into the background. One such important change of the last decade is the increasing involvement of radio stations into value generation prior to the secondary exploitation stage. Radio has traditionally been involved in the phase of performance of work, particularly in terms of classical music. These performances have also been recorded by (public) radio stations. Furthermore, radio stations are increasingly involved in the selling and distribution of music titles in three ways:

1. Radio stations broadcast commercial advertisements on new music media.
2. Content Providers and radio stations co-market events (concerts etc.) and implicitly the underlying music
3. Radio stations select and broadcast new music titles and thus have a decisive influence on the attention a music title or an artist gains.

Broadcasting of music content is less harmful to the economic value than broadcasting of video content by TV-stations, because music is a repetitive good: if one likes a song, one is inclined to listen to it over and over again. Even though a listener can copy the content from radio broadcast, the music industry has learnt to live with it because radio delivery had several important restrictions:

1. Quality: Radio delivery is typically of lower quality than digital originals; the widespread delivery of radio programs over cables has increased quality significantly. With the diffusion of digital audio broadcasting, quality will cease to be a problem.
2. Content selection: Radio is a push service without history and without future: The moderator selects a title and plays it; typically the listener does not know in advance when a certain title will be played and does not have an opportunity to access a played song afterwards (A minor exception to this is play lists published to communities in advance as an extra service to members only (SWR3, 2001).
3. Reimbursement: The content providers are reimbursed for their content by the radio companies through public intermediaries. However, reimbursement is low in Germany and a source of constant conflict between radio stations and content providers (Kulle, 1998, p. 276).
4. Legal Limitations: Radio programs typically play only selections of albums, but very rarely the total album.

The music industry and the radio stations have co-existed in a relative stability that was based on balanced market power as well as a symbiotic relationship to one another. The sources and critical aspects of this "equilibrium" are:

1. mutual interdependence: the vast majority of all music titles broadcast is owned by the music publishing houses, but no music title has a chance for commercial success if it is not broadcast by the radio stations.
2. control over the artists: Artist are typically controlled by the music industry (through contracts). This control is a major source of power for the music industry.
3. control over the listeners: Radio stations have instant access to the vast majority of all listeners and the ability to influence public opinion.
4. protection of the radio stations by law: The market for radio broadcasting is regulated by law. In Germany, these regulations entitle radio stations to broadcast content for a non-negotiable and low fee.

The most fundamental source for a stable and mutually accepted co-existence is, however, that both players target different listeners needs and thus effectively different markets. This stability may very well end soon as both players move into one another's markets. The music industry can and very likely will build up its own music-communities. It can offer for each community or even for each individual radio-like programs for a monthly flat rate. The radio stations can use their wide user basis and direct access for selling content. This latter opportunity will be focused on in the remainder of the paper. We will introduce concepts and a prototype for mobile commerce based on radio programs.

3. THE POTENTIAL OF MOBILE SYSTEMS

Mobile systems have technically diversified over the last few years by the introduction of new standards, e.g. BlueTooth, 802.11 (wireless LAN) as well as UMTS. They all show some similar features, like cellular structure, but in detail they differ significantly. The same holds for the primary type of usage, reach, bandwidth or cost. The field for study is so wide, that it certainly can't be treated in detail within this paper. We summarise therefore a few aspects relevant for the discussion of the prototype solution.

3.1 Technical potential

The first issue is bandwidth. As is known from streaming audio, acceptable but low quality music playback can be achieved with common modem transfer rates (verifiable by using the Windows Media Player option 'Radio Tuner'). The basic idea here is buffering before playback, slightly higher connection speed than the audio transfer rate and sufficient processing power. But in downloading MP3 files which provide higher audio quality, more bandwidth has to be available. Compared to regular CD-DA less storage is needed for the recording of music. MP3 allows for compression ratios of approximately 1/11 if nearly CD-quality is required (bitrate of 128kbs). But the resulting file size is still huge. An example may clarify this: the title from Mariah Carey's album labeled '#1's' called 'When you Believe' has a playtime of 4'35'' or 275 sec. Per second we would have to transfer 176400 byte (44,1kHz sampling frequency and 16 bit per sample, stereo). With MPEG 1.0 layer 3 coding and a bit rate of 160kbs (for even superior quality) the resulting file size is 5.3 MB, whereas the original file size is 46.4MB. For an extended technical treatment of MP3 coding and its successor AAC we refer to (MPEG, 2001) and (AMM, 2001).

The bandwidth offered today in GSM standard based mobile networks is 9.6kbs and will effectively increase to about 43kbs with GPRS only, but with EDGE or UMTS we will realistically approach 384kbs (Durlacher, 2001, p. 13]. Whereas the former compares with the low quality music transmission via modem connections, the latter is sufficient for higher quality MP3 transmission. While listening to it the transferred data could be stored in the mobile device for further use.

The playback of MP3 files is no problem, as can be seen from the variety of mobile phones with onboard MP3 players available today. As an example we refer to the SIEMENS SL45 allowing for an optional memory extension of 128MB (Siemens, 2001). Thus we could have about 25 songs as above.

As has been evident over the last few years, memory capacity and size of handsets is no longer a critical issue. The technology found in other devices like digital cameras is offering micro disks with 1GB and certainly we will see even higher capacities soon (IBM, 2001).

3.2 Business Potential

Mobile commerce per se has some interesting features which are worth considering briefly:

- identification of users via SIM authorisation leads to regarding a mobile as a very personal piece of equipment and fosters the concept of non repudiation
- with respect to the stored directory information or other PDA type data the device incorporates personalised information to a large extent, thus lowering barriers to store personalised data on directly related web frontends
- in most contracts for mobile phone utilisation the payment for any service is coupled with direct debit facilities, thus converting the mobile to support instant payment to third parties
- by use of the CallerID one could realise a personalised versioning of any data stream prior to downloading, thus allowing for copy right protection or at least watermarking
- as location-based services become available, it will be interesting to see closely related business opportunities emerging, e.g. receiving audio data containing tourist information if the mobile is located close to a monument and the specific channel has been subscribed etc.

With those considerations in mind, areas of opportunity for mobile commerce have been seen in many areas, primarily in ticketing and ordering, mobile banking and payment as well as edutainment, see (TIMElabs, 2000) and (Durlacher, 2001). With respect to audio data we will concentrate here on instant ordering for later access via any other media channel or spontaneous download and listening.

Whether a pay-per-listen or pay-per-download approach will be followed depends on many factors. One is certainly the pricing scheme for content and for transfer time, while another might be the ease of use or access.

As was shown by the early disappointment of the Short Message Service, followed by its late but ongoing tremendous business success, the acceptance of new services is difficult to predict and seems not be related to established patterns found in other media. SMS not only offers an anachronistic user interface for sending very limited strings of max. 160 characters, but is also an extremely expensive communication environment compared to common prices on the internet.

For sending one SMS the average transfer charge is between € 0,08 (network internal) and 0,20 for external messages within the German mobile networks. Those fixed prices ignore the effective length of the message. Assuming that one could really send the full 160 chars for € 0,20, the extrapolation for transferring 1 MByte indicates an amount of more than € 1.310,- which would be a staggering price in the IP-world. We do not consider that this extrapolation is really meaningful, but it clearly indicates that users of mobile networks are used to, and willing to, pay significantly higher prices for basic services compared to the internet. Furthermore, mobile users are used to paying for transfer and for content, as many of those SMS-based instant messaging services, e.g. stock market or specific news channels, as well as unified messaging services indicate.

4. AN INSTANT SHOPPING APPROACH FOR MOBILE DEVICES: CATCH YOUR SONG

4.1 Business Idea

Regular CD shopping, as found for example with amazon.com, can be set up by use of nearly any web-shop platform. Extending this service to allow order placement via mobile handsets is substantially more challenging, as the user interface design for the selection process of titles is non trivial. The idea of CYS does not tackle those general problems. But the approach allows the user to order any song whilst it is being played on the radio, without knowing any details such as title or artist etc.

There might be many situations where people listen to radio. Without any further empirical analysis (which could certainly be undertaken with currently available commercial media data), we can imagine that listening to the radio while driving in the car might be a typical occasion. As soon as a new song is released, most radio stations will introduce it to their audience, thus fulfilling their marketing contracts or simply by facing the competition of staying up-to-date compared with other stations. That is the very moment instantaneous buying might offer a competitive advantage. As the customer has subscribed to a community of one or more radio stations, s/he dials a specific number or URL via his/her mobile and connects to a dialogue which shows those titles played within the last minutes (e.g. the actually played title and the one before that). With one further selection and an accept click the ordering, the delivery and payment process will be executed. A variety of delivery forms are possible, i.e. direct download via air interface into the mobile which owns the feature of an MP3 player, or storage on a web host for later download are possible options. The authentication of the user has been performed prior to the connection setup via calling line identification. The billing process could be - as today in many call-by-call solutions - handed over to the mobile carrier, which receives a call detail record from the service provider for any single transaction. The associated accounting data are kept by the service provider (i.e. the radio station) and could be used for further cross- and up-selling activities as well as marketing campaigns. Certainly, this will work only in a legal world with explicit user allowance for dealing with those data.

At any time the customers may access their personalised web-store and rearrange, delete or enlarge their title selection. They may order any form of delivery on any medium in any format at any time, or even may generate different title arrangements and send them as gifts or loyalty bonuses to friends or business partners. The radio station, obviously working with subcontractors at least for the logistics, will take over the role of traditional intermediaries via this e-business approach. Beyond the production phase of a master tape, record or digital audio stream, the complete later phases of the value chain could be influenced by the service provider.

So far we have concentrated our considerations exclusively on the radio stations, but it goes without saying that either Music-TV stations of today or any interactive TV-station of tomorrow could offer this service, too. The reason we have concentrated on music is, in fact, the bandwidth availability today and in the near future – but in principle the idea could be extended to, or beyond, any movie material.

An important consideration is the issue of dis-intermediation of traditional music shops on the one hand, and the re-intermediation by those service providers on the other hand. We argue that radio stations are well prepared and positioned to adopt this role. Revenue generation could be achieved by access and / or content fees, by sophisticated forms of advertising, by cross or up selling via all accessible media channels, or even by selling data collected from profiling (obeying the law of customer protection). For an extended treatment see, for example, (TIMElabs, 2000, pp. 155]. In the following section we describe the functionality of the mobile ordering component within CYS in more detail.

4.2 Functionality of the prototype

CYS (Catch-Your-Song) has two components:

1. A web-based component for the individual music archive and for the participation in a music community. This system can be used on any conventional computer connected to the Internet with a standard browser.
2. A mobile access component for "catching songs" that are currently on the air in selected radio stations. This mobile access system is currently

based on a WAP-enabled mobile phone, but could also be integrated into a car-radio etc.

The system should be used in the following manner: interested radio listeners firstly register their radio stations and personal interests, using the web-based components, and subscribe as members of a music community. Whenever they hear a song on the radio, with a few clicks they can "catch" the song. We refer in the following description to the sequence of screen shots in figure 2.

Assuming they have selected SWR3 (first picture), they will see the current song in the cellphone interface and catch it with one selection (second picture and third picture). They can then either finish the transaction or continue processing the song (fourth picture): Either they order the single, order the album, download the song onto their cellphone or send an electronic greeting mail with the song attached. Finally, they decide on their preferred payment method. Once the users return to their desktop with Internet access, they will find a list of the radio stations and their programs, as well as an updated list containing their personal library of all songs caught. At this point they are once again offered all ordering options.

We now discuss the technical feasibility of this concept from the point of view of the service provider and discuss alternative options of the service concept.

Currently we have realized a CYS prototype, which simulates radio stations with a random selection of music titles from a database. We have not completely implemented the payment system, but simply generate a record entry in a payment database for each transaction as needed for accounting and billing processes. The remaining features of CYS including the interaction between WAP and the Internet has been implemented and tested. A major challenge has been the design of the interface allowing for minimal interaction on the mobile phones as well as sufficient ease of use for the web-system.

Figure 2. WAP-Interface CYS2[2]

A real service provider would certainly face some more technical challenges:

[2] Screendumps are reproduced in low quality to reduce file size. A published version will have high-resolution screendumps.

- The system should be scalable, allowing for heavy peak loads
- In a legal environment each delivery should be watermarked using the CallerID or any other suitable item for unique identification of this specific customer
- Transaction logging has to be performed for later claims etc.
- Considerations of insufficient connectivity (especially for transfer via air) have to be undertaken and formulated into contract clauses
- General security policies with respect to the web-shop operation have to be applied

Most interesting is the security issue once the mobile platform has been left, as it leads to the well known problems in general web-commerce requiring high level trust centre functionality.

Economically, the timing of the payment is crucial. On the one hand, payment issues should be hidden as much as possible. Settling payment can distract listeners from their current activity (e.g. driving a car). From this point of view, it would be preferable that the users initiate those transactions in non-mobile situations from their desktop. This approach, however, might have the following disadvantages:

- instant, emotional decisions are the dream of marketing. If the listener is just hearing the song and finally deciding on buying it, s/he is in a happy mood (because of having just listened to a song s/he obviously likes) and must decide on a relatively small amount of money (for one song). Once listeners have returned home, they might get second thoughts, particularly if they realise the summed cost for a larger number of songs.
- postponed buying is hardly possible, if there is large-scale illegal music distribution over the internet; listeners could collect the title information with catch-your-song and then get the songs from the Internet instead of buying them!

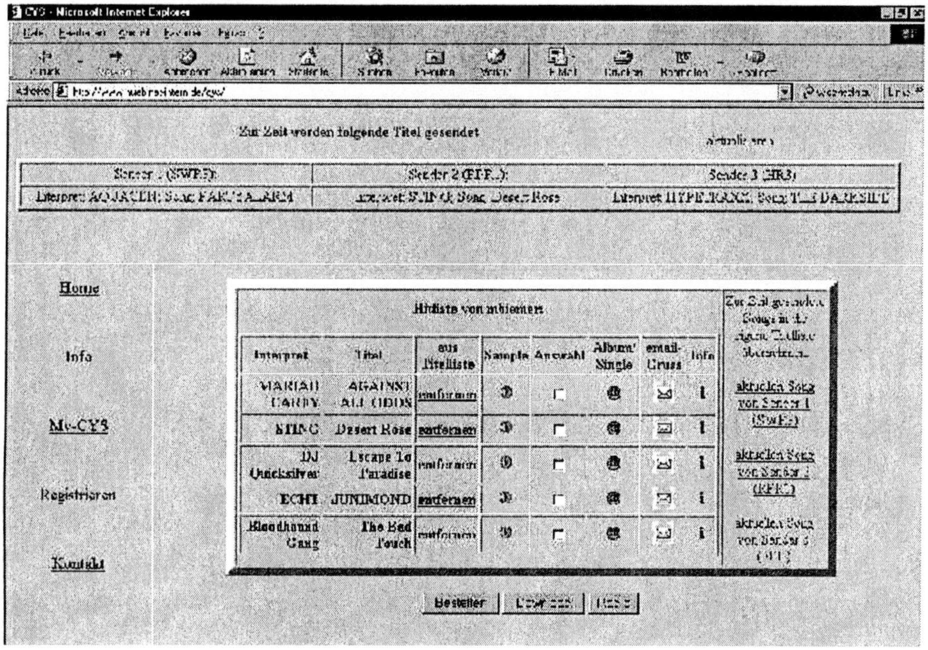

Figure 3. Internet Interface

Thus, ideally, catching a song and purchasing it is combined into one transaction performed by a very few clicks. In fact, the average length of the transfer process might induce some non trivial problems with respect to complete delivery, non repudiation of delivery etc.

CYS song is only the beginning of radio service diversification, the path to future features is sketched in figure 4.

A CYS-user cannot just listen to radio songs, but can also order the song using his/her WAP-mobile and access the selections over the Internet. We have shown that this can be implemented. The newest generation of mobiles will be full-featured MP3 players with infrared or BlueTooth connectivity to notebooks, desktop or hybrid multimedia devices. Thus, as soon as bandwidth becomes less expensive, songs can be downloaded to those mobiles or PDAs and listeners can carry their individual current best-of-selection in their pocket. With the option of transferring those downloads, the problem remains how to avoid illegal peer-to-peer distribution. But certainly the system design should allow that any data should be freely transferable by the owner and is not restricted for limited use with only one single device.

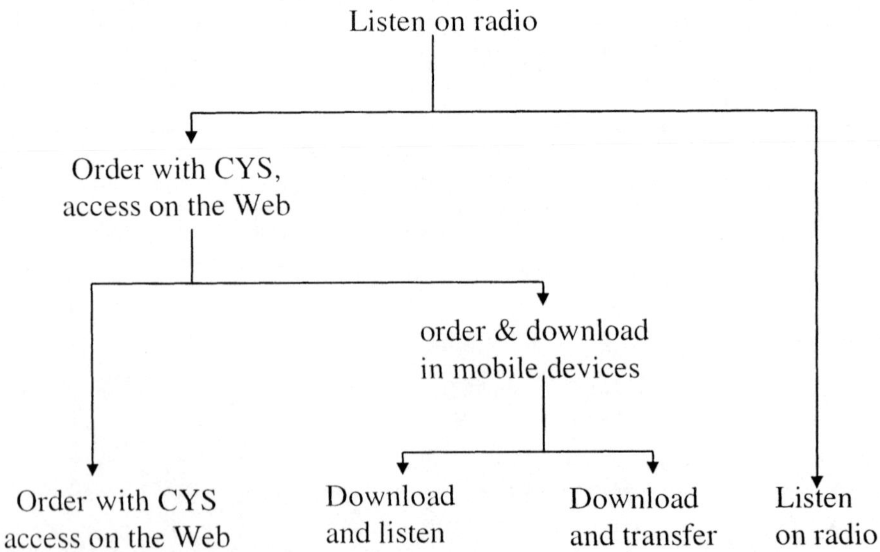

Figure 4. Service diversification

4.3 Implications

New business ideas like CYS open a new era of co-opetition between radio stations and the major media companies. Both have a lot to gain from cooperation but inevitably there will be an increasing overlap in their activities. The most fundamental issue will be: "who owns the customer"? One argument is that customer ownership comes with payment. This argument would imply that the music industry will very likely run CYS and any other advanced services, since they are in a much better position to build up a new payment system. The radio would just become one interface for digital music commerce among others. Another argument is that customer ownership comes with community ownership. This argument implies that the radio stations will run CYS, since they are in a much better position to create and support communities. While we will see automatic, radio-like selection and broadcast of music content as a service in the near future, a real listener's community life also consists of enthusiastic radio moderators and a carefully selected mixture of music pieces, information and interaction. Both the majors and the radio stations have a lot to gain from "owning the customer". The following sections will discuss these potential issues.

4.4 Challenges and opportunities for the radio station

Data mining on aggregated buying patterns allows the radio stations to gain knowledge about their listeners which, in turn, could be immediately fed into their program design. For example, the buying behavior might be an excellent basis for pop music charts. Here we identify a complete feedback loop: Songs are in the charts, because many listeners ordered them and many further listeners can order the song, because it is frequently played on the radio. If there are some cheap buying options (not only: pay once- play forever, but also: pay per listen, pay per period .etc.), there is a good chance that many will buy a song in order to contribute to the music charts and thus become customers for CYS. Information from CYS can also give feedback on the quality of program components and the program structure (e.g. the sequence of songs or: who prefers what kind of music when?).

Thus we consider that a distribution channel like CYS can have a significant impact on the value chain as indicated in figure 5. We foresee a movement of radio stations into the selling, distribution and marketing element of the value chain, integrating primary and secondary exploitation. It remains an open question, whether they will also move into the publication and multiplication of audio media. Electronic distribution makes large sections of commercial multiplication of audio media obsolete; we rather see prosumers (Tapscott, 1996) not only consuming the audio media, but also configuring their own audio selection[3].

If selling songs becomes a source of revenue for radio stations they might lose their innocence and credibility in the eyes of the listener; how much influence can or should cross-selling have on the design of the radio program? At one extreme, public radio stations will lose their special status if they become too commercialised. At the other extreme, private radio stations may become even more commercialised than they are today and other subjects of the music value chain may become interested in buying radio stations and using them as their distribution channel.

[3] It is a discussion beyond the scope of this paper, whether radio stations might also step up their efforts to publish, produce and sell their own content. As 'good' content is extremely expensive, we cannot yet imagine radio-stations participating in or even controlling the whole value chain.

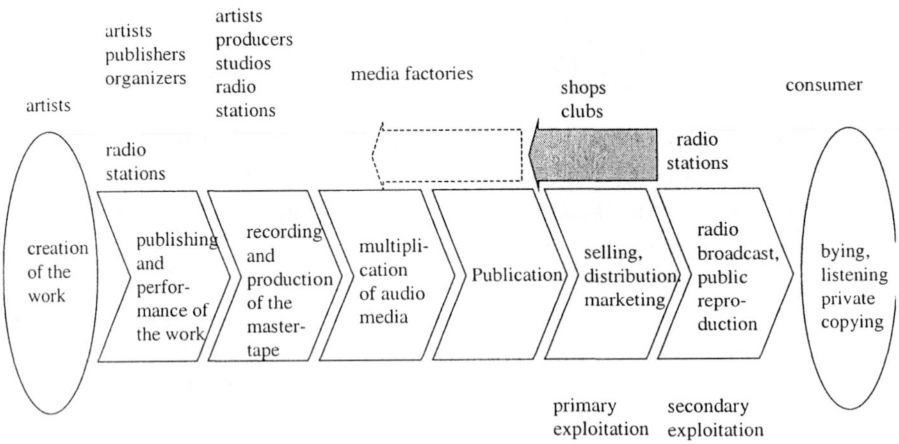

Figure 5. Radio stations' new role in the music industry value chain

4.5 Challenges and opportunities for the content providers

CYS can be more than an additional distribution channel for content providers – it can be the beginning of one-to-one marketing for music titles. As an additional channel it is only as valuable as its potential to generate additional revenue. Here it is an open question if CYS-buying would replace conventional purchasing or be on top of it. We would argue that instant buying has the potential to generate additional revenue because it originates from an emotional buying situation, but we do not yet have the empirical data to substantiate this assertion.

If the content provider persuade the radio stations to share the ownership of customer, or even leaves customer-ownership to the content providers, they can use the customer data for one-to-one marketing. This marketing then includes CYS, but can also be used for other channels, e.g. personalised follow-up-marketing ("If you like these two songs from this album, why don't you buy this album?"). Aggregated customer data can be used to configure and price new albums or other music selections. Allowing random configuration of titles might, however, lead to legal problems as current contracts frequently require the artist's consent to using his/her titles in other contexts.

5. FURTHER RESEARCH QUESTIONS

Although the legal problems might not been solved in the near future, most challenging would be to set up a test bed with a radio station and a mobile carrier. This could generate, over a limited period and for a closed user group, some empirical evidence concerning the acceptance and price sensitivity of this type of service. By starting with short audio clips instead of full length titles, the experimental study could be started even before the roll out of UMTS.

Later we see many more challenging research questions. A whole complex worthy of study are the interdependencies and stability of customer ownership scenarios.

From a more operational point of view it would be interesting to analyse the problems:

- If we assume we can receive superior media response data when counting visits to personalised web-pages and correlate them with buying transactions: how do we measure these data?
- What are the challenges of setting up sufficiently scalable and secure systems for mass traffic?
- Will the value chain be cut off by peer-to-peer approaches due to lower cost, as any new song can be digitally transferred without any loss of quality and with minimal delay by Gnutella-like systems? (Does this mean that even CYS will be too late?)

The general discussion on mobile commerce value chains mostly focuses on the later phases of the value chain. Figure 6 depicts such an understanding, and a similar example can be found in (Durlacher, 2001).

As can be observed, it summarises the value chain of the music industry in the "content provider" element. We have endeavoured to show that one element of the traditional value chain – the radio stations – have the potential to change the rules of the game. This leads to the question of whether those general models are really helpful in explaining the sophisticated mechanisms inherited from traditional domain-specific business-to-business interaction. Is it true that neither intermediaries nor carrier operators are found in pole position? Couldn't be the example presented here serve as a counter-example, if we consider re-intermediation by the radio and TV-stations?

We clearly see many more questions and problems, but our research so far has convinced us that mobile commerce will shift the opportunities and understanding of e-business into new dimensions.

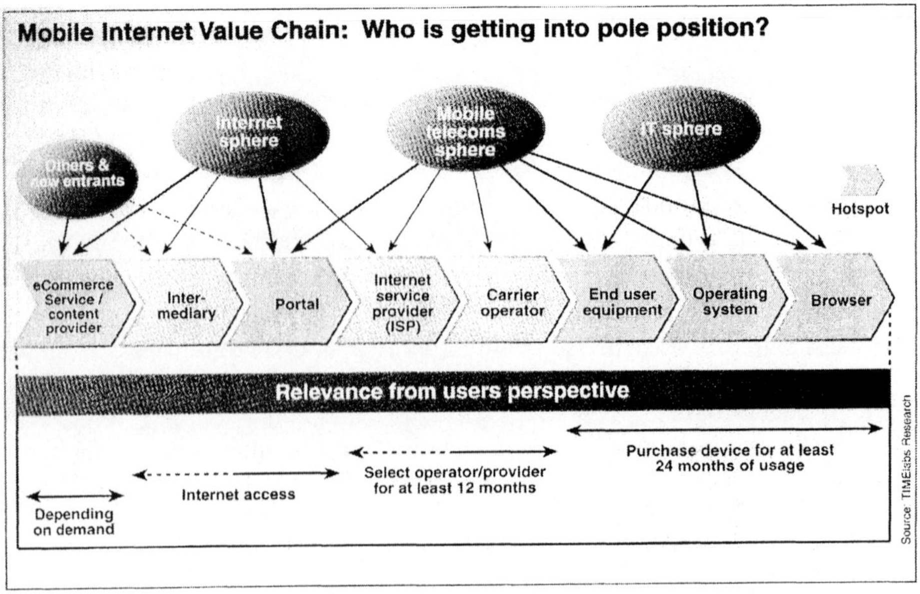

Figure 6. Generic mobile commerce value chain, taken from (TIMElabs 2000, p.36)

6. ACKNOWLEDGEMENT

We would also like to thank our Students Michael Biemer, Sascha Moschfeghi and Mustafa Oeren for the valuable input, particularily for implementing the CYS prototype.

REFERENCES

AMM (2001) www.iis.fhg.de/amm/ [Version: 6.2.2001]

AOD (2001), www.audio-on-demand.de/ [Version: 6.2.2001]

Dernbach (1998), Dernbach, B. et al. (ed.) (1998): Publizistik im vernetzten Zeitalter: Berufe - Formen - Strukturen, Westdeutscher Verlag Opladen, Wiesbaden.

Digitalradio (2001), www.digitalradio-info.de/ [Version: 6.2.2001]

Durlacher (2001), Durlacher Research. Mobile Commerce Report. www.durlacher.com/ research/res-reports.asp [Version: 6.2.2001]

Filk (1996), Filk, C. (1996): (Teil-)Dereguliertes Fernsehen: Eine kurze Rekapitulation. In: Friedrich-Ebert-Stiftung (ed.) (1996): Jahrbuch der Akademie der politischen Bildung 1996: Medien, Politik, politische Bildung, Friedrich-Ebert-Stiftung Bonn, S. 96-102.

Goldhammer/Zerdick (1999), Goldhammer, K.; Zerdick, A. (1999): Rundfunk Online: Entwicklung und Perspektiven des Internets für Hörfunk- und Fernsehanbieter, Vistas Verlag Berlin.

Gnutella (2001), gnutella.wego.com/ [Version: 6.2.2001]

Heinrich (1994), Heinrich, J. (1994): Medienökonomie, Band 1: Mediensystem, Zeitung, Zeitschrift, Anzeigenblatt, Westdeutscher Verlag Opladen 1994 (Reprint 2000).

Heinrich (1999), Heinrich, J. (1999): Medienökonomie, Band 2: Hörfunk und Fernsehen, Westdeutscher Verlag Opladen, Wiesbaden.

Heinzl et al. (2001), Heinzl, A.; König, W.; Hack, J.: Erkenntnisziele der Wirtschaftsinformatik in den nächsten drei und nächsten zehn Jahren. In: Wirtschaftsinformatik Vol 43, No. 3, p. 223.

IBM (2001) www.storage.ibm.com/hardsoft/diskdrdl/micro/datasheet.htm[Version: 6.2.2001]

IIS, (2001), www.iis.fhg.de/amm/techinf/layer3/index.html[Version: 6.2.2001] GmbH, Eschborn.

Kim (2000), Kim, A.: Community Building on the Web, Peachpit Press, Berkley.

Kulle (1998), Kulle, J.: Ökonomie der Musikindustrie, Peter Lang, Frankfurt et al.

Ludes/Werner (1997), Ludes, P.; Werner, A. (ed.) (1997): Multimedia-Kommunikation: Theorien, Trends und Praxis, Westdeutscher Verlag Opladen,Wiesbaden.

Marathe (2001), Marathe, J. (2001): Impacts of Digital Distribution on the Music Industry. Durlacher Research Report, http://www.durlacher.com/downloads/music.pdf [Version: 15.05.2002]

Middelhoff (2001), Middelhoff, T.: Auf in den digitalen Alltag der Musik!. Eröffnungsrede auf der Popkomm, 18. 8.2000, Köln. www.bertelsmann.de [Version: 6.2.2001]

MPEG (2001), www.mpeg.org/MPEG/aac.html [Version: 6.2.2001]

Mühl-Benninghaus/Zerdick (2000), Mühl-Benninghaus, W.; Zerdick, A. (ed.) (2000): Ökonomie der AV-Medien, Band 1: Fernsehen, Vistas Verlag Berlin.

Napster (2001), www.napster.com/ [Version: 6.2.2001]

Neverla (1998), Neverla, I. (ed.) (1998): Das Netz-Medium: Kommunikationswissenschaftliche Aspekte eines Medium in Entwicklung, Westdeutscher Verlag Opladen, Wiesbaden.

Nunamaker/Chen (1990), Nunamaker, Jr. J.F.; Chen, M.: Systems Development in Information Systems Research. In: Journal of Management Information Systems, Vol. 7. No. 3, 1990/91 p. 631-640.

Schumann (2000), Schumann, M.; Hess, T.: Grundfragen der Medienwirtschaft, Springer Berlin, Heidelberg.

Schwabe/Krcmar (2000), Schwabe, G.; Krcmar, H.: Piloting a Sociotechnical Innovation. In: Proceedings of the 8th European Conference on Information Systems ECIS 2000, Wirtschaftsuniversität Wien, Wien, S. 132-139.

SDMI (2001), www.sdmi.org [Version: 6.2.2001]SWR3 (2001), www.swr3.de/ [Version: 6.2.2001]

Seidel/Libertus (1993), Seidel N.; Libertus, M. (1993): Rundfunkökonomie: Organisation, Finanzierung und Management von Rundfunkunternehmen, Gabler Wiesbaden.

Siemens (2001) www.ic.siemens.com/mySiemens?product=SL45 [Version: 6.2.2001]

Szyperski (1971), Szyperski, N.: Zur wissensprogrammatischen und forschungsstrategischen Orientierung der Betriebswirtschaft. In: zfbf Vol 23 1971, S. 261-282.

Szyperski (1999), Szyperski, N. (ed.) (1999): Medienwirtschaft: Kompetenz - Akzeptanz - Geschäftsfelder, Josef Eul Verlag Lohmar, Köln.

Tapscott (1996) Tapscott, D. (1996): The Digital Economy. Promise and Peril in the Age of Networked Intelligence. New York.

TIMElabs (2000), TIMElabs Research Center. Winning in Mobile eMarkets. Diebold Deutschland

Zerdick et al. (1999), Zerdick, A. et al.: Die Internet-Ökonomie – Strategien für die digitale Wirtschaft, Springer Berlin, Heidelberg.

E-BUSINESS AND DOT.COM DRIVEN TRANSFORMATION– A COMPARISON OF AUSTRALIAN AND INDIAN EXPERIENCES IN THE TELECOM SECTOR

CHANDANA R. UNNITHAN[1] and PAULA M. C. SWATMAN[2]

[1]*Deakin University, School of Information Systems, Faculty of Business and Law, Melbourne, Australia*

[2] *Deakin University, School of Information Systems, Faculty of Business and Law, Melbourne, Australia AND University of Koblenz, Institute of Management, Faculty of Informatics, Koblenz, Germany*

Abstract: The global telecommunications sector has been transforming rapidly as a result of deregulation; privatisation; competition from smaller telcos due to their ability to list on NASDAQ index; convergence of media and communication sectors; and driven by rapid uptake of Internet-related activities. Like many businesses, telcos expected to increase market capitalisation through dot.com floats, perceived broadly as a measure of profitability. Despite the recent spate of dot.com crashes, telcos have been actively promoting dot.coms, and even developing electronic markets. Our exploratory study investigates this phenomenon, studying the eBusiness-driven transformation, taking into account the move towards new technologies such as broadband delivery. The paper describes our qualitative, document-based investigation of the Australian and Indian telecom sectors, together with a preliminary quantitative analysis of the impact of dot.coms on market capitalisation within the sector. We have applied the theory of Transaction Cost Economics to the quantitative analysis to explain the reduction of costs through dot.com floats. Further, by applying theories of telecoms liberalisation, such as neo-liberal and alternative accounts (Bagchi, 2000); theories of adoption such as innovation-diffusion (Roger, 1995) and catch-up, forge-ahead, fall-behind theory (Abramovitz, 1986) to the synthesised findings, we have derived cross-economy perspectives in the eBusiness driven growth of the telecoms sector. The paper provides practical assistance to telcos and policy makers in the economies reviewed and have the potential to contribute to academic research in eBusiness and telecommunications more generally.

1. INTRODUCTION

Corporate involvement in Internet-based activities and content provision on the Web is increasing, and appears to be becoming compulsory in infrastructure sectors such as telecommunications (Berryman *et al*, 1998). Pitroda (1993) suggests that telecommunications is a powerful force for economic development, necessary to co-ordinate development activities, conduct business and operate markets. Cyranek and Bhatnagar (1992) observe that telecommunications is essential for providing access to market information and transactions globally.

In this paper, we study the drivers for change in the evolution of the telecommunications sector. We then look at the opportunities and challenges offered by new technologies, which support and promote eBusiness – both generally and in two disparate economies, Australia and India. These findings are further synthesised from a broad review of the telecoms industry and from a quantitative analysis, making use of market capitalisation as a measure of profitability for telcos. Finally, we have applied three popular economic theories to the findings to gain further insights into our findings.

2. METHODOLOGY

This paper is part of an ongoing research project into eCommerce diffusion within the banking and telecoms sectors, which seeks to identify the effectiveness of dot.coms as an indicator of eBusiness diffusion and success on a sector-by-sector basis. The study takes a positivist approach, where social realities are viewed as a complex of causal relations between events – themselves depicted as an emerging patchwork of relations between variables (Blaikie, 1993).

A brief historical trend analysis of the telecoms industry in Australia and India, using document analysis, has revealed major drivers and barriers for the rapid transition of this sector and for the uptake of new technologies such as broadband. Neuman (1997) suggests that document analysis is the systematic analysis of a particular topic, using news media, annual reports, employment records, unpublished and published articles, white papers, industry and consultancy reports, etc. In a field as diverse and as rapidly-growing as the telecoms industry, such an approach enables researchers to gather a wide variety of data and to grasp the essence of a market quickly and effectively.

The document analysis was augmented by a quantitative analysis, using the least squares method, which tested dot.com viability for telcos. Dot.coms are regarded by telcos as a channel for increasing market capitalisation –

broadly perceived as a measure of profitability. To test this general view, a preliminary analysis was conducted on three major telcos over a two-year period, in the two economies. We then applied transaction cost theory (Williamson and Winter, 1993; Pant and Hsu, 1996) to the results to provide a more in-depth explanation than was possible from the statistics alone.

Subsequently, the dominant (or neo-liberal) and alternative theories of telecom liberalisation (Bagchi, 2000); as well as two well-known theories relating to the uptake of technological innovation – innovation-diffusion theory (Roger, 1995) which classifies the adoption patterns in a society from innovators to laggards, and the catch-up, forge-ahead, fall-behind hypothesis (Abramovitz, 1989) which explores why certain economies *catch-up* while others *forge ahead* or *fall behind*, were applied to the synthesised results to gain a social perspective on the phenomena identified.

The combination of these quantitative and qualitative methods (see, for example, Gable 1994; Mingers and Brocklesby 1997; or Pinsonneault and Krämer 1993 for a more thorough discussion of the benefits of combining qualitative and quantitative research methods) enabled us to gain a better understanding of the impact of new technologies/eBusiness to telcos in these disparate economies.

3. DRIVING FORCES IN TELECOMMUNICATIONS

To compete in the global market, exploiting the opportunities presented by innovation, businesses are increasingly putting pressure on governments worldwide to revise their policies, regulation and the structure of the telecoms sector (Jain, 2001). Quiggin (1998) notes that until the 1980s the telecoms industry was a publicly owned enterprise in most economies. The 1980s ushered in two critical changes – deregulation and the privatisation of telcos; and the build up of competition in the sector.

Bagchi (2000) identifies two competing theories about policy changes and liberalisation in the telecom sector – *the dominant (or neo-liberal) account, and the alternative account* (see also McDowell, 1997). The dominant account suggests that liberalisation is a set of policies which reduce social and political control over market forces, and over the building of production, exchange and property relations more closely, approximating those found in ideal competitive markets (Bagchi, 2000). Telecoms liberalisation, in other words, would allow increased use of market mechanisms to guide social, economic and political life, loosening State control. The application of this theory is underpinned by the fact that telecommunications are becoming integrated into economic structure and the global environment far more broadly, through participation in international treaties such as the Global Agreement on Tariffs and Trade (GATT) and the International Telecommunications Union (ITU); and through the convergence of technologies (McDowell, 1997).

By contrast, the *alternative theory* argues that the historical process of liberalisation in the telecoms sector was linked to a number of distinct national and international issues and processes. This theory portrays the liberalisation of the telecoms sector as a case of the First World winning over the interests of Third World states (McDowell, 1997; Bagchi, 2000). Westland and Clarke (1999) suggest that with the development of new technologies, customers are demanding innovative communication products, which keep pace with rapid transitions in technology. Many authors (Uehara 1990; Glynn 1992; Kima and Yoon 1992; Ladlaw 1994) comment that the impact of restructuring in many countries has been to encourage telcos to become more responsive to business and consumer needs, evolving continuously to remain competitive. Developed countries, in particular, have recognised the need for a responsive, business-focussed, technologically innovative telecoms sector for the growth of the economy (Jain, 2001).

4. EBUSINESS OPPORTUNITIES & CHALLENGES

Mandel and Hof (2001) suggest that the promise of the Internet is dependent on both the widespread introduction of broadband telecommunications delivery to the home, and on the development of high-speed wireless telecommunications[4]. These technologies will not only enable effective business and personal communications from any location, but will enable always-on access and effective work practices from home as well as from networked office environments.

For cellular operators, wireless Internet access represents considerable revenue potential, as shown by the success of Japan's digital telecom industry (Yamada, 2000). In May 2000, Yamada (2000) reported in Industry Standard that 20,000 subscribers join the net every day. However, with the delay in introducing UMTS and other third generation standards and products (NTIA, 2000) most telcos, particularly those which have paid high

[4] In August 2000 there were 570 million mobile users. It is estimated that by 2002/3 there will be one billion subscribers and 1.6 billion by 2010. Penetration rates (users in % of the population) in Europe are expected to reach 80% in 2005 (Barnett/Hodges/ Wilshire). Thus, there will be almost universal coverage within Europe. Even on a global scale penetration rates are forecast to be over 30% in 2005 (UMTS-Forum 2000).

prices for third generation licences, are feeling the financial pressure of supporting existing services and this is slowing the rollout of broadband. There is an increasing likelihood that a number of small telecom providers may fall by the wayside, as may subscriber growth in second and third-tier markets (Pelline, 1996; Deloitte, 2001). It is already clear that charges for high-speed Internet access products such as ADSL (Asynchronous Digital Subscriber Line) are increasing in a number of countries (Harrison *et al*, 1998) resulting in a decrease in consumer numbers, and the overall profitability of telcos (Michael *et al.*, 2001).

Pastore (2001) points to significant consumer interest in obtaining multiple communications services (local, long distance, cable TV, cellular, paging, Internet and high speed access) from a single provider (convenience, single billing, integration, etc). Nonetheless, in many economies smaller telcos have managed to create effective competition in niche markets, often providing services such as cheap international or Internet access by purchasing and rebundling from the larger providers, (for example, Primus Telecom in Australia, Satyam Infoway in India) and have managed to float on the stock exchange, spurring the growth of the entire sector.

4.1 The Australian Telecoms Experience

Australia's National Office of the Information Economy suggests that eCommerce is having a remarkable impact on the communications industry. Telecommunications carriers have an obvious role to play in providing the communication lines and bandwidth to make network access and ultimately eCommerce possible (NOIE, 2000c).

Holmes (2000) notes that in 1989 the independent telecommunications regulator AUSTEL was created to develop increased service competition, private networks and value added network services (VANS). The former PTT monopoly, at that time comprising Telecom Australia and the Overseas Telecommunications Corporation (OTC), was corporatised and partially privatised taking the name Telstra (Quiggin 1998; Holmes 2000). New entrants to the Australian marketplace resulted in a fixed-network duopoly between Telstra and Optus (a Cable & Wireless dominated conglomerate); as well as a mobile oligopoly between Telstra, Optus and the then British-owned Vodafone. In 1997 the country was opened further to competition with open network competition permitted. Competition and technical regulation were provided through the ACCC (Australian Competition and Consumer Commission) and the ACA (Australian Consumer Authority), which offered consumer and competitive safeguards.

According to Holmes (2000) the costs and benefits of deregulation included the clearing of transaction costs, maximising self-regulation or co-regulation, cost recovery through regulatory charges and relatively non-intrusive regulation. Massive demand growth from 15% annually for voice to 150% for Internet subscription, new investment of US$5 billion, improved efficiency of operators, improved customer focus and service levels, continuous price reductions with costs falling and far more limited margins for service providers, were some other cost benefits (Holmes, 2000). Evans and Bonugli (2001) estimated the Australian telecommunications market to be worth A$27 billion in 1998. Orange, the flagship brand of Hutchinson Telecoms, listed on the Australian stock exchange in August 1999, and received licenses for a unique wire-free service which combined local loop with mobile telephony, covering certain metropolitan areas (Orange, 2001).

Australia has significant advantages from the point of view of telcos, including access to state-of-the-art telecommunications infrastructure, and a highly educated, very technophilic population. In addition to Telstra, which manufactures hardware and provides a solid and significant telecommunications infrastructure, most of the major telecom manufacturers including Ericsson, Nokia, Siemens, etc. have established a presence within Australia. Fels (2001) suggests that the rollout of new telecommunications and infrastructure in Australia has been one of the most important drivers of new competitive forces in the market. The new technologies of broadband and wireless communications are being used to provide comprehensive service packages to household consumers, including pay-television, telecommunications, data and Internet services, and a range of business-to-business applications.

Fels (2001) also suggests that broadband infrastructure is of particular importance to the future of digital services. The potential to utilise the existing copper telephony network, which already passes every Australian house, to provide high speed Internet access opens the possibility of achieving high levels of broadband penetration via services such as ADSL. Telstyle (2001b) estimates the number of DSL connections in Australia will grow to 200,000 by mid 2002 from 59,000 in 2001. Optus was a leader in alternative access with DSL, offering new levels of flexibility. Fels notes, however, that the rate and ultimate extent of such services will depend on the price charged for such services and on demand. Australia has already seen the impact of overly high pricing for new telecommunications services, when ISDN was priced so high that only a very few businesses took it up – with the result that this technology, which is almost a standard for European households, is effectively not used in Australia (Moon, 1999).

The current hot issues for Australian telcos include broadband IP and Internet connections; local loop bundling; competitive provisioning of universal services in uneconomic areas, convergence and the impact on broadcasting, telecom, and information service markets; and the three year audit of telecoms regulation under the 1997 legislation (Holmes, 2000). Clear legislative objectives of continuing user benefit through competition at all levels of the market, and consolidation of the competition is required in the telecoms sector (Legard, 2001).

Eastham (2001a, 2001b) suggests that online marketplaces represent a significant eBusiness opportunity for telcos in Australia, both to provide higher value services over simple voice and data connections, and to draw them closer to customers. He argues that the main benefits of joining an eMarketplace are reduction in transaction costs for buyers and suppliers; the opportunity for suppliers to find new buyers; and for buyers to find cheaper suppliers. The major telcos in Australia, Telstra and Optus, have already entered the eMarketplace arena (Eastham, 2001a). However, two of the major Telstra-enabled eMarketplaces closed down i.e. mySAP.com (a joint venture with German enterprise software developer SAP[5]) and TBX (an e-marketplace for SMEs) following the dot.com meltdown, taking the company out of the online marketplace race against its main rival, Optus (Eastham, 2001a). Optus has continued to provide eMarketplaces with its Marketsite, a business-to-business trading service. Initially, the company was targeting large corporations but, with the launch of Marketsite, has moved into the SME sector, because 300 buyers and suppliers happened to be SMEs (Eastham, 2001b). Boston Consulting Group research reports suggest that there are 250 eMarketplaces operating in Australia, and that by 2002 there will be 53 (Eastham, 2001b).

Colquhoun (2001a) suggests that the real future for telcos lies in understanding customer requirements and in a willingness to customise service levels, supported by agreements and penalties for non-delivery. The author points to Macquarie Corporate Communications, an Australian telco with a dedicated focus on the corporate market. It is moving away from the traditional voice market with the help of DSL to provide a wider suite of services and is offering tiered levels of service, from entry level to business and first class. Colquhoun (2001a) argues that this kind of initiative will take telcos up the value chain into the area of IT and managed services. The Australian Telecommunications Industry reports suggest that the major telcos are still 80% reliant on the voice market, which is declining rapidly (i.e. from revenues of 13% in 2000 to 3% in 2001) (Colquhoun, 2001a). Therefore, more telcos are considering the provision of business services, enabled by eBusiness.

[5] Note that mySAP.com continues to operate outside Australia

Eastham (2001b) suggests that telcos in Australia need to consider whether they should move away from their core competencies. However, there seems to be little choice for telcos other than following market trends, consolidating and re-engineering themselves for competition. As Budde Communication suggests, those that survive will integrate IT offerings with broadband, to form true business partnerships with consumers (Colquhoun, 2001a).

4.2 The Indian Telecoms Experience

Many developing countries have noted the constraint of a state monopoly in telecoms as standing in the way of spurring internal growth and competing in an increasingly global economy (Jain, 2001). Even though it is a century since telecommunications emerged, developing nations such as India still do not share the benefits of a universally distributed telecom service (Maxwell, 2000). Granting monopolies in the sector to create a barrier to market entry is most common in emerging economies. Jain (2001) notes that the process of introducing new telecoms reforms and structures is complex in a country like India. Maxwell (2000) adds that with the advent of Internet telephony, there is a serious threat to the national telecoms providers. Emerging economies are trapped between the need to attract private capital to upgrade their telecoms network and the conflicting desire to develop their strategic goals – both of which require significant funds.

The Indian telecoms sector was wholly under government ownership until 1984, and was characterised by under-investment, outdated equipment and growth below the potential of the market (Jain, 2001; India Infoline, 2001; Sinha, 1997, Dhar, 2001). The Post and Telegraph was separated from the sector in 1985 to form the Department of Telecoms or DOT (Jain, 2001; India Infoline, 2001; Sinha, 1997). Subsequently, DOT set up two public sector corporations, Mahanagar Telephone Nigam Limited (MTNL) and Videsh Sanchar Nigam Limited (VSNL).

While MTNL took over the operation, maintenance and development of telecom services in the metropolitan areas of Mumbai and New Delhi, VSNL was set up to plan, operate, develop and accelerate international telecom services in India (Jain, 2001; India Infoline, 2001; Sinha, 1997). MTNL enjoyed a monopoly position in the two metropolitan cities, until recently; but VSNL was given a monopoly over all international access to India through its gateways (India Infoline, 2001). The Indian government created these corporate organisations in order to allow greater decision-making autonomy and flexibility. However, realising that major decision making including policy formulation and that regulation of the sector remained with DOT, the government created a new organisation named the

Telecom Commission, with representatives from many government departments including electronics and finance (Jain, 2001; Dhar, 2001). In 1997, a separate regulatory body, the Telecom Regulatory Authority of India (TRAI) was formed by an act of Parliament, with the main function of finalising toll rates and settling disputes between the main players (India Infoline, 2001; Bagchi 2001). However, TRAI was not given regulatory authority over DOT, and the telecoms sector itself still remained under the control of DOT.

Following the National Telecom Policy of 1994, the government announced private participation in basic and cellular services. The country was divided into 20 'circles' and one private operator was allowed to compete with the DOT in each of these circles. However, DOT was to give the licenses to operators with a fee. This was the major flaw – DOT was able to drive out much of the competition with heavy license fees and tariffs (Bagchi, 2001). This led to the announcement of the National Telecom Policy of 1999, taking into account the convergence and existing anomalies in the sector (Bagchi, 2001).

Jhunjunwala and Ramamurthy (2001) argue that telecoms sector revenues are basically boosted by Internet connections. The introduction of private ISPs has contributed greatly to this momentum. Following the National Telecom Policy of 1999, 70 ISPs have become operational in India. The government also allowed several ISPs to set up international gateways to the Internet, bypassing the VSNL monopolised gateway (Bagchi, 2001) In addition to opening up international telephony, the government also decided to end VSNL's monopoly, two years before the WTO-set deadline of 2004.

Jhunjhunwala (2001) argues that the availability of telecoms equipment and technology is crucial for the development of the sector in a developing country. To build research and develop technology suited to Indian climatic conditions, the Centre for Development of Telematics, an autonomous organisation, was set up in the early 1980s (Jain, 2001). CDOT was able to champion the idea of technology for the masses, with rural automatic exchanges designed specifically for Indian climatic conditions. Many regional areas including villages, small towns and B class cities were connected and public telephone booths became part of Indian society. An indigenously developed technology, adaptable for Indian conditions, was successful and, by end of the year 2000, 10 million of the 20 million lines installed in India were using CDOT exchanges (Jain, 2001).

However, as Jain (2001) points out, DOT had a detrimental impact on the success of CDOT exchanges by not accepting this technology until some time during the early 1990s, pushing indigenous manufacturers into financial difficulties. At the same time, multinationals used this policy to their advantage, by raising the price of imported exchanges. The success of CDOT did, however, help the government in negotiating cheaper prices for other imported exchanges in the following years (Jhunjunwala, 2001).

Several technological changes made it imperative for the government to view IT, telecoms and broadcasting legislation in a coherent and convergent manner, which led to the drafting of the Information, Communications and Entertainment Bill (Jain, 2001). In 2000, the Communication Bill 2000 had the objective of facilitating the development of a national infrastructure for an informed society. This Act of Parliament will establish a licensing framework for carriage and content of information in the converging areas of television, broadcasting, data communications, multimedia and other technologies. The Bill aims at creating a super regulator for the broadcasting and telecoms industries (Bagchi, 2001).

India only has an approximate tele-density of only 2 fixed lines per 100 persons (India Infoline, 2001), as compared to Australia's tele-density of 1 fixed line per 1.5 persons (Worldroom, 2002). However, telephone penetration is not dependant on phone ownership. As in many developed countries, private space in houses is not abundant, and phones tend to be shared. In many interior areas, public call offices or telephone booths tend to be used (Jain, 2001). The socio-economic changes within the country spurred by the Internet have seen the emergence of cyber cafes and computer institutes all over the country. Interestingly, this development has been accentuated by the growing need for technology education within the country, essentially facilitated by the growing software industry. Although telephones may not have reached every home, cyber cafes are in great demand.

The Indian telecoms sector is considered one of the fastest growing in the world, growing at an average of more than 20% over the last 4 years. It is expected to witness rapid growth in cellular, radio-paging, value-added services, Internet and global communication by satellite (GMPCS) services. The government is currently undertaking several regulatory and policy initiatives, making India an ideal environment for foreign direct investment (investindia, 2001). In July 2001, CIOL (2001c) reported that the telecoms sector in India is attracting foreign direct investment, despite the bureaucratic hurdles. The new regulatory policy does not seem to have constrained this flow of funds. While 44% of these investments were for cellular mobile services, 27% was aimed at telecoms companies which manufacture telephone equipment. With the entry of national long distance providers, domestic investments in the sector have also remained steady.

In November 2001, a Reuters report in CIOL (2001b) claimed that the Indian mobile telephone market had over five million subscribers and, according to ABN Amro, this is expected to reach 34.1 million by March

2006. Over the single year of 2000, the market grew by more than 90%. It is estimated that the number will cross 25 million in 2005 and rise to 77 million by 2010. ABN Amro expects the market to expand at 57% CAGR[6] for the next 5 years. In contrast, India's fixed line business, which had 32.4 million lines at the end of March 2001, is expected to grow at only 15% CAGR, to touch 66.5 million lines by March 2006. ABN Amro further predicts growth in the pre-paid segment, increasing the number of subscribers. However, it is still Mumbai and New Delhi, which are leading the increase in subscriber numbers (CIOL, 2001b).

The broadband market in India is expected to soar (CIOL, 2001a). As India has the highest cable penetration percentage of 46.8% among low telephone penetration countries (Nagaraj, 2001), the market for broadband is very active (CIOL, 2001a). However, according to IDC although cable is widespread across the country, the existing broadband infrastructure is not suitable for two-way communication and the price of upgrading this technology is very high. Despite these problems, there is a drive for cable modems, particularly by work-at-home households and Internet users. Future expansion of the data-over-cable market is expected to be driven by increased Internet use and development of compelling image/video rich applications and IP telephony services (CIOL, 2001a).

The DSL market is expected to grow, but is still plagued by distance limitations, regulation issues, installation and provisioning challenges, competition from other broadband technologies, cable modems on the residential area, fixed wireless and other high-speed technologies from the business market (CIOL, 2001a). Fixed Wireless Access (FWA)[7] is becoming attractive, as it allows competitive providers to bypass the local loop generally controlled by incumbent carriers. FWA is also well suited for rural and regional installations. Satellite is still an unexplored broadband access technology, which has immense potential for a country as large as India. IDC has estimated direct access subscribers will reach 2.1 million in 2005 with a CAGR of 114% (CIOL, 2001a).

Major telcos such as MTNL and VSNL have recognised the fact that eCommerce is a key to their future success, with private competition arriving at an increasing rate. MTNL, for example, has put in place several IT systems such as CSMS (Customer Support Management System), FRS (Fault Repair System), DQ (Directory Enquiry), FMS (Financial

[6] Compounded Annual Growth Rate.

[7] Fixed wireless access is the use of wireless technology to replace copper to connect subscribers to the telephone network (Trinkwon, 1996).

Management System), IVRS (Interactive Voice Response System) and accounting and billing systems. Projects for Dataware housing, call centres, e-commerce billing mediation, new IT policy consultancy projects are also in the pipeline (MTNL, 2001) VSNL plans to open more international gateways, satellite and cable communications. Currently, it offers many services online to individuals and business consumers. In February 2001, Tata – India's biggest and most trusted conglomerate won 25% stake in this telco (Menon, 2002). This strategic move and the subsequent global networks, which these moves imply, are bound to take VSNL further into eBusiness success. However, eCommerce revenues are still nascent and unpredictable for the sector.

5. DOT.COM VIABILITY - AN ANALYSIS

The document analysis provided in the preceding sections of this paper, while providing a foundation for research into the sector, lacks generalisability. To understand whether dot.com floats had any effect on the growth of market capitalisation for telcos in Australia and India, we conducted a statistical analysis using the least squares method. Three significant telcos from each economy were selected for this analysis, on the basis of their comparability, size and visibility in the economy.

The model estimated is:

$$\mathbf{SIZE}_{it} = \beta_{oi} + \mathbf{DA}\ \beta_{1i} + \beta_{2i}\ \mathbf{Trend} + \beta_{3i}\ \mathbf{DA\ Trend} + \varepsilon_{it}\ \mathbf{(4.1)}$$

where $\mathbf{Size}_{it}$ is the market capitalisation of the telecoms organisation **i** in period **t** ; **Trend** is a linear time period (which increments each period); **DA** is a dummy variable which takes the value of **0** before the organisation floated a dot.com and **1** after the company floated a dot.com; β_{0i} , β_{1i} , β_{2i}, β_{3i} are unknown company-specific parameters to be estimated; and ε_{it} is assumed to be N $(0,\sigma^2{}_i)$.

The results of analysing the telecoms sector sample are reported in Table 1.1. The selected organisations within each economy are given in the first column. The table reports least squares parameter estimates, **P** values in parenthesis and the last column provides adjusted $\mathbf{R^2}$ β_{1i} reports the immediate change in market capitalisation following dot.com float, β_{2i} reports the trend growth in market capitalisation before the dot.com float and β_{3i} reports the trend growth after the dot.com float.

Company/Economy	β_{2i}	B_{1i}	β_{3i}	R2(Adjusted R^2)
ONETEL/Australia	18.501 (0.877)	-4597.954 (0.078)	166.625 (0.177)	0.875
TELSTRA/Australia	2753.446 (0.424)	33228.24 (0.645)	-733.295 (0.831)	0.726
OPTUS/Australia	1374.988 (0.000)	89801.90 (0.000)	-3653.930 (0.000)	0.439
Satyam/India	304.699 (0.747)	-242478.0 (0.000)	8478.399 (0.000)	0.741
VSNL/India	-1076.258 (0.133)	-165801.1 (0.000)	5855.64 (0.000)	0.520
MTNL/India	131.491 (0.000)	-228922.5 (0.000)	8074.456 (0.000)	0.753

Table 1. Results of telecoms sector organisations' analysis

The p value of β_{2i} (the rate of market capitalisation growth before floating the dot.com) was indicated as statistically significant for only one organisation out of the three investigated, per economy. For Australia, the range of β_{2i} was between 18.501 and 2753.446. However, only Optus with the β_{2i} value of 1374.988 had a significant p value of 0.000. Similarly, for India, the β_{2i} values ranged between 131.491 and -1076.258, and only MTNL indicated a significant β_{2i} of 131.491 with a p value of 0.000.

From these disparate results, it appears that floating a dot.com entity was rather insignificant or negative for Australian telcos, but was indicated small but positive growth levels for Indian telcos. It seems possible that telcos in Australia are driven by the 'long term' benefits which have not yet shown up, while Indian telcos are capitalising on the 'new economy aura' of telecommunications created by the media. It is intriguing that, despite these disparate results, and the apparently low impact on market capitalisation, telcos in both economies still seem keen on floating dot.coms and developing this channel. We explore this insight, applying the transaction cost theory to these results, in the next section.

5.1 Transaction Cost Theory – Application to Telcos

Transaction Cost Theory (Pant and Hsu, 1996) suggested that 4 types of transaction costs could be reduced through web-based business: bounded rationality, opportunism, market uncertainty, and asset specificity.

Bounded rationality refers to the fact that human beings have limited information storage, retrieval and processing capacity, adding to transaction costs. Web based businesses can use the global facilities of information storage, retrieval through powerful search engines, and accessibility across the organisation and virtual linkages to other organisations, extending the value chain, without incurring additional costs. While the Indian telcos seem to be enthusiastic about eliminating the expensive systems by imbibing the Internet based new technologies and systems, Australian telcos have taken the further step of migrating to the Web, which initially is not cost-effective. However, the telcos seem to be enthusiastic about a network effect[8] within a technophilic population, which will in the longer term reduce their transaction costs.

Opportunism refers to the way in which information is distorted when reaching the consumer. It is becoming essential to become 'net certified' or transparent to enable evaluation and feedback by consumers on the Web. Driven by the growth of 'informed customers' in India and the demands of the younger generation, telcos in both economies are using the dot.com channel as a profitable, yet low transaction-cost venture.

Market uncertainty is a transaction cost involved in market research. With globalisation and increasing reach of products and services in the telecom sector, tools such as online surveys are not only reducing costs, but are also empowering the consumer through 'design your own' options. The uneven, high population volume in India and the long distances in Australia - both attract high transaction costs in the area of market research. The telcos can reduce their costs in this area, in the longer-term, by making use of web-based technology.

Asset specificity is a transaction cost associated with the Web, which is changing the business scenario from competition to collaboration. The move is towards standardisation, through systems such as Web Based EDI and, which reduces overall transaction costs for all collaborators within a supply chain. In both economies, telcos are moving towards collaborative networks through online ventures to reduce transaction costs.

Although floating a dot.com entity may or may not have benefited the telcos significantly, the integration of online services through dot.com floats

[8] Network effect refers to the phenomenon in which the value of any product or service increases with the number of users adapting it.

is bound to help them remain profitable in today's volatile, and competitive marketplace. Clearly, there is an opportunity for progressive telcos to benefit from using online ventures to promote and offer their services.

6. CROSS-ECONOMY PERSPECTIVES

In this section, we have synthesised the document based investigation and the quantitative analysis by applying various theories, deriving a cross-economy perspective to the telecoms sector.

The application of the *neo-liberal* account to the Australian and Indian contexts would suggest that both countries, to a certain extent, had to increasingly become a part of the global integration of telecoms through participation in GATT and international institutions such as the International Telecommunications Union. In addition, with the increasing convergence of technology, policy liberalisation has become imperative. From the *alternative theory* perspective, the opening up of the telecoms sector and the introduction of foreign capital investments have been part of India's response to general World Bank structural adjustments and First World interests have played a significant role in precipitating a large mass market in India (Mody, 1995).

The experiences of these two countries suggest that government policy; deregulation and demand are critical for growth in the telecoms sector. Having gone through the process of de-regulation in the 1990s, and with technology convergence adding a further dimension to the alternatives available, the hold of government over the telecoms sector is loosening. Interestingly, this formerly bureaucratic sector seems to have benefited to a large extent from IT/eBusiness diffusion, which is reflected in the convergence bills proclaimed in both countries studied. In Australia, Telstra (still majority-owned by the State) has more or less controlled competition through license fees and restricted entry to competition in critical areas. Similarly, in India, DOT has more or less controlled the sector, restricting entry through high license fees and union-supported influence on government policy. It has been market forces, rather than government fiat, which has introduced effective competition to these two megalithic organisations.

The well-researched *innovation-diffusion* theory of Rogers (1995), extended lately by many authors (Sonnenwald et al 2001, Agarwal et al, 1998; Sellitto 2001) classifies adoption patterns within social groups into innovators, early adopters, early majority, late majority and laggards. *Innovators* are classified as highly venturesome, mobile, daring and risk taking, usually found in societies, which are able to absorb unprofitable innovations and apply highly complex technical knowledge with a higher degree of uncertainty. *Early adopters* are upwardly mobile, successful opinion leaders who form role models in any society. *Early majority* are deliberate before adopting an innovation although they are keen to be active in the uptake of new technology, while the *late majority* are cautious and respond only to necessity. *Laggards* are usually isolated, suspicious of innovation, and have limited resources.

Applying these variables to the Australian telecoms scenario, the society is more or less spread between *innovators, early adopters* and the *early majority*. This technophilic mindset, spurred also by the demands of the upwardly mobile younger generation, has enabled telcos to further experiment with eBusiness ventures. There is more or less early/rapid adoption of telecoms innovations in Australia. The country is also able to absorb unprofitable ventures and is a test-bed for many innovative telecoms services (for example, Orange One). By contrast, the Indian telecoms scenario indicates more a picture of *late majority to laggards,* if the statistics are any indication. The society has had limited resources to absorb unprofitable innovations and the majority of the population has historically responded only with caution and economic necessity. Interestingly, the growing upper-middle class, characterised by the computer professionals, is increasingly driving the diffusion of technological innovation. Many of these professionals are non-residents willing to invest in innovative telco ventures, as they are seen as progressive icons for the economy. The increasing popularity of mobile phones in metropolitan cities, broadband and DSL seems to indicate this move.

This analysis may be further augmented and explained through the *catch-up, forge ahead, fall behind theory*, developed by Abramovitz (1986), which argues that some economies try to catch-up with others, others fall behind, and yet others forge ahead as a result of the attitude of the population in general. Telcos in developed economies such as Australia are finding it harder to migrate their population to ever-renewed technology variations. Although technophilic and rapid adopters of new technology, the population is sceptical of the 'media hype' surrounding telcos, which are typically classified as 'new economy' ventures. The decline in dot.com stocks, especially telcos, has further added to this scepticism. To forge ahead and keep up with their counterparts, telcos in Australia need not only to innovate consistently, but also to be visibly cost-effective for the consumer.

Developing economies such as India, by comparison, are plagued by weak infrastructure, especially in terms of telecommunications. However, unlike Australia, telcos are viewed as 'new economy' icons by the rapidly growing upper-middle-class professionals, driven by the *catch-up* attitude.

These role models are pressuring the government to develop new initiatives, for a faster, more innovative, yet more cost-effective spread of telecoms services country-wide, harnessing the power of eBusiness. In a bid to *catch-up* with developed economies, the government has, in turn, become responsive to this demand. However, the legacy of bureaucratic government ownership still casts a shadow on the sector, slowing its progress.

7. CONCLUSIONS

Clearly, despite the threats of new entrants and technologies, there is enormous opportunity for dynamic telcos to capitalise on the opportunities offered by eBusiness. This paper has highlighted the importance of technology infrastructure, together with population size and distribution, as well as the general attitude towards innovation and adoption in the growth of telcos.

Australia, a high-technology country with a well-developed infrastructure, has been able to take advantage of many of the current telecommunications advances, but is hampered by a saturated market, a small population (which makes it difficult to support a large number of telcos), and a very expensive, geographically wide-spread rural sector. India, by contrast, has a huge population, which is much more evenly spread geographically (despite the dominance of two very large cities), but is hampered by the slow spread of technological infrastructure and a strongly bureaucratic development style.

In these very disparate economies, the growth of the telecommunications sectors has proceeded in a surprisingly similar manner – although the two countries have reacted differently to the dot.com floats by telcos. Our statistical analysis indicates the Australian share purchasers have not responded positively to this development – possibly seeing the telecoms sector as a less attractive vehicle for quick share profits. Indian purchasers, by contrast, have shown more enthusiasm for telcos floating dot.coms, with a resultant increase in market capitalisation, although this increase is still marginal. The application of innovation-diffusion and catch-up theory appears to suggest that India may be able to by-pass its weak infrastructure developments, harnessing the power of eBusiness and with the support of the growing 'catch-up' attitude of the public. Ironically, Australia may actually be suffering from its wealth of existing infrastructure and scepticism concerning telcos by the public as it attempts to take up the wireless/broadband challenge of the 21st century.

Clearly, these results can only be considered preliminary in nature. We plan to extend our analyses to other countries to test the tentative explanations suggested here. One particularly interesting comparison will be with the Accession countries of the former Eastern bloc, such as Poland, Hungary, the Czech Republic, etc. – many of which have also decided to by-pass the creation of wide-spread fixed telephone networks. Their decision to move directly into wireless telephone networks will provide a fascinating comparison with India's experience.

REFERENCES

Abramovitz, Moses (1989) Catching-up, forging ahead and falling behind, *Thinking about growth and other essays on economic growth and welfare*, Cambridge University Press, USA

Agarwal R, Ahuja M, Carter PE, Gans M (1998) Early and late adopters of IT Innovations: Extensions to Innovation Diffusion theory, Florida State University Working Paper.

Anderson, Chris (2000) The future of telecommunications, Address to SA Great-South Australian Business Forum, 13th July 2000. Available [online] http://www.cwo.com.au/content/1,1463,87,00.html. Accessed on 6th December 2001.

Bagchi (2000) Telecommunications Reform and the State in India: The contradiction of Private Control and Government corporartion, Center for Advanced Study of India, CASI Occasional Paper #13, December Available [online] http://www.sas.upenn.edu/casi/reports/Bagchipaper120000.pdf. Accessed on June 10th, 2001.

Berryman K, Harrington L., Layton-Rodin D, Rerolle V(1998) Electronic commerce: Three emerging strategies, *McKinsey Quarterly*, no.1 pages 152-159

Blaikie (1993) Approaches to Social Enquiry, Blackwell Publishing, UK

CIOL (2001a) Broadband market to touch Rs.66 crore by 2005:IDC, CIOL Bureau, October 23, 2001. Available [online] http://www.ciol.com/content/news/repts/101102312.asp?nl=ctd-Oct231 Accessed on 24th October 2001.

CIOL (2001b) Cellular market will be 34 m by 2006, Reuters, November 26th. Available [online] http://www.ciol.com/content/news/repts/101112606.asp?nl=ctd-112601 Accessed On 27th November 2001.

CIOL (2001c) Telecoms Sector attracts FDI despite bureaucratic hurdles, Cyber News Service, July 27th. Available [online] http://www.ciol.com/content/news/repts/101072716.asp?nl=ctd-July27. Accessed on 30th July 2001.

Colquhoun, Lachlan (2001a) Telecommunications: Telcos won't take the plunge, BOL Australia, Available [online] http://www.bolweb.com/magarticle.asp?doc_id=13509

Cyranek G and Bhatnagar SC (1992) *Technology Transfer for Development: The Prospects and Limits of Information Technology*, Tata McGraw-Hill, New Delhi

DCITA (2001) The Department of Communications, Information Technology and the Arts, Home Page. Available [online] http://www.dcita.gov.au Accessed on 21st February 2002.

Deloitte (2001) Telecommunications in Australia: Wireless, but with strings attached. Available [online] http://www.deloitte.com/internet/items/friendly.asp?id=341&frames=no. Accessed on 25th October 2001.

Dhar, Surindher (2001) Indian Telecommunication Liberalisation and Development, A report, Essar Comvision Limited, India.

Eastham, Jaime (2001a) Telecommunications: Telcos seel e-market solutions, BOL Australia. Available [online] http://www.bolweb.com/magarticle.asp?doc_id=13506. Accessed on 26th September 2001.

Eastham, Jaime (2001b) Telecommunications: Telcos seel e-market solutions, BOL Australia. Available [online] http://www.bolweb.com/magarticle.asp?REL_DOC_ID=25726. Accessed on 26th September 2001.

Eastham, Jaime (2001c) Telecommunications: Telcos seel e-market solutions, BOL Australia. Available [online] http://www.bolweb.com/magarticle.asp?REL_DOC_ID=257267 Accessed on 26th September 2001.

Evans and Bonugli (2001) The future of business in electronic age, Telstyle Pty Ltd, AAPT Connexus Magazine, 4Q98, Available [online] www.telstyle.com.au/other/aapt_business_a.htm. Accessed on 18th October 2001.

Fels, Allan (2001) Regulation and the future of the telecoms industry, Australian Telecoms Cisco Lecture Series,26th March 2001, Sydney, Available [online] http://www.accc.gov.au/speeches/2001/Australian_Telecoms_Cisco_Lecture_Series.htm. Accessed on 6th December 2001.

Gable, G., "Integrating Case Study and Survey Research Methods: An Example in Information Systems," European Journal of Information Systems, (3:2), 1994, pp. 112-126.

Glynn (1992) The Telecoms Review, India Infrastructure Report.

Harrison, J, Fifi E, Pereira F, Worthington R (1998) ADSL Prospects and Possibilities, Centrefor Telecomsmunication Management, Report prepared for ADSL Forum, Available [online] http://www.adsl.com/store/mrp_exec_summary.html, Accessed on 21st February 2002

Holmes, Jim (2000) Telecommunications deregulation: Lessons from the Australian Experience, *Ovum*. Available [online] http://www.ovum.com Accessed on 5th December 2001.

India Infoline (2001) Telecoms, Indian Telecoms Industries Sector Report Available [online] http://www.indiainfoline.com/sect/tesp/ch01.html Accessed on 7th December 2001.

Jain, Rekha (2001) The Telecoms Sector, *India Infrastructure Report 2001*, IIM Ahmedabad, Available [online] http://www.iimahd.ernet.in/ctps/iir8.pdf Accessed on 7th, December 2001.

Jhunjunwala Aand Ramamurthy B(2001) Enabling Telecoms and Internet Connectivity in Small Towns and Rural India, India Infrastructure Report 2001.

Kima and Yoon (1992) cited in Jain (2001) The Telecoms Sector, A Review of Indian Telecoms Sector, Indian Infrastructure Report.

Ladlaw (1994) cited in Jain (2001) The Telecoms Sector, A Review of Indian Telecoms Sector, Indian Infrastructure Report

Legard, David (2001) OneTel's Failure hits Australian Telecoms Competition, IDG, May 31st. Available [online] http://www.idg.net/ec?external=1&content_source_id=200&remote_addr=&doc_id=5506 Accessed on 5th December 2001.

Lucent (1999a) OneTel signs AUD$430 M contract with Lucent Technologies to build GSM1800 network in Melbourne, Adelaide and Perth, Lucent Technologies, September 30th. Available [online] http://www.lucent.com/press/0999/990930.cob.html Accessed on 5th December 2001.

Mandel MJ and Hof RD (2001) The rethinking of the Internet, Dataquest DQ-BW E-Biz Section, Available [online] http://dqindia.ciol.commakemainsection.asp/01060101.asp. Accessed on 4th July 2001.

Maxwell, Christine (2000) Global trends that will impact universal access to information resources, Submitted to UNESCO, July 15th.

McDowell, Stephen D (1997) Globalisation, Liberalisation and Policy Change: A political economy of India's Communications Sector, St Martin's Press Inc, New York.

Menon (2002) India's privatisation: standing on the crossroads, CIOL, February 4th. Available [online] http://www.ciol.com/content/news/repts/102020414.asp?nl=ctd-020402 Accessed on 5th February, 2002.

Michael DC, Sutherland G, Lang NS (2001) Digital Dragons – How Asia Pacific's Large Companies can generate value from consumer eBusiness, *The Boston Consulting Group*, July Available [online] http://www.bcg.com Accessed on September 17th 2001.

Mingers, J. & Brocklesby, J. (1997). Multimethodology: Towards a Framework for Mixing Methodologies. OMEGA, International Journal of Management Science, 489-509.

Mody, Bella (1995) State Consolidation through liberalisation of telecoms, Journal of Communication, 45(4).

Moon, Olaf (1999) Bandwith requirements for the Australian Training and Education Sector, Chapter 7, eDna Online publication, Available [online] http://www.edna.edu.au/showpage.html?file=%2Fpublications%2Fbandwidth%2F6restraints.html

MTNL (2001) Company Research Report – MTNL, Available [online] http://profiles.wisi.com/profiles/scripts/corpinfo2.asp?cusip=C35662570 Accessed on 9th July 2001.

Nagaraj, Sudha (2001) India to post 49.5% growth in Internet users, *The Economic Times*, June 27th. Available [online] http://www.economictimes.com/today/27tech01.htm. Accessed on 4th July 2001.

Neuman William L(1997) *Social research methods : qualitative and quantitative approaches*, Allyn and Bacon, Boston

NOIE (2000c) *eCommerce beyond 2000*, Commonwealth of Australia Available [online] http://www.noie.gov.au/beyond2000 Accessed on June 2, 2000.

NTIA (2000) The Council of Economic Advisors - The Economic Impact of Third-Generation Wireless Technology, Available [online] http://www.ntia.doc.gov/ntiahome/threeg/ceareportoct2000.pdf, Accessed on 21st February 2002

Optus (2001) Speeches: The future of telecommunications, Chris Anderson, CEO, Available [online] http://www.cwo.com.au/content/1,1463,87,00.html Accessed on 5th December 2001.

Orange (2001) Company Profile Available [online] http://www.orange.net.au/aboutus/company.htm Accessed on 5th December 2001.

Pastore (2001) Consumers Prefer Local Telco for Bundling, Available [online] http://cyberatlas.internet.com/big_picture/hardware/article/0,,5921_899271,00.html Accessed September 27th, 2001

Pelline, Jeff (1996) Say goodbye to small ISPs, CNET News.com, Available [online] http://news.com.com/2100-1023-222758.html?legacy=cnet Accessed on 21st February 2002

Pinsonneault, A. & Kraemer, K.L. (1993). Survey Research Methodology in Management Information Systems: An Assessment. Journal of Management Information Systems, 75.

Pitroda, Saumen (1993) Development, Democracy, and the Village Telephone, *Harvard Business Review*, November-December, page 66-79

Quiggin (1998) The Premature burial of natural monopoly: Telecomsmunication reform in Australia, Agenda 5(4), 427D440.

Rogers E (1995) *Diffusion of Innovations*, The Free Press, NY.

Sellitto, C (2001) Developing an Ecommerce Best Practice Model for Victorian Wineries: An Agenda for Research, RMIT Working Paper.

Sinha, Sidharth (1997) The Risks of Financing Telecoms Projects, Indian Institute of Management, Ahmedabad, Vikalpa: The Journal of Decision Makers, Volume 22, no.3, July-September, pp 1- 15. Available [online] http://www.iimahd.ernet.in/vikalpa/past/v022n03.htm#ab5 Accessed on January 4th, 2001.

Sonnenwald DH, Maglaughlin KL, Whitton MC (2001) Using Innovation theory to guide Collaborative Technology Innovation: Work in Progress, IEEE 10th International Workshop on enabling technologies: Infrastructure for Collaborative Enterprises, USA.

Telstyle (2001a) Sidebar: The local telephony market. Available [online] http://www.telestyle.com.au/feature/local_call_sidebar_a.htm. Accessed on 18th October 2001.

Telstyle (2001b) DSL market growing rapidly in Australia, Newbytes Asia, October 10th. Available [online] http://www.nua.com/surveys/index.cgi?f=VS&art_id=905357281&rel=true. Accessed on 18th October 2001.

Trinkwon, David (1996) Technology of Fixed Wireless Access, Seminar presentation, Columbia University, Available [online] http://www.citi.columbia.edu/wireless/!citi_fw.htm, Accessed on 21st February 2002.

Uehara (1990) cited in Jain (2001) Review of Indian Telecoms Sector, The Telecoms Sector Report.

UMTS Forum (2000) Enabling UMTS/Third Generation Services and Applications, Report No. 11, October 2000 Available [online] http://www.umts-forum.org/reports.html, Accessed on 21st February 2002

Westland JC and Clarke T H K (1999) *Global electronic commerce – theory and case studies*, The MIT Press, Massachusetts.

Williamson O. E. & Winter S.G. (eds.), (1993), *The Nature of the Firm: Origins, Evolution and Development*, Oxford University Press, N.Y.

Worldroom (2002) Teledensity, Australia Available [online] http://www.worldroom.com/pages/wrnsyd/fastfacts/syd_fastfacts.phtml Accessed on 21st February 2002.

Yamada, M M (2000) Web Cell Phones a Ringing Success in Japan, The Industry Standard, Available [online] http://www.thestandard.com/article/display/0,1151,15377,00.html, Accessed on 21st February 2002

A STRATEGIC COMPREHENSIVE FRAMEWORK FOR EVALUATING IS INVESTMENTS

- a proposed checklist for evaluating E-Business investments

ARJEN WASSENAAR
Department of Business Information Systems, Faculty of Technology and Management, University of Twente

Abstract: Because of the strategic importance of IS investments, it is essential to incorporate in strategic IS management effective managerial evaluation practices. Therefore this paper aims to develop a checklist for comprehensive evaluation of e-business (EB) investments as a part of strategic IS management. An IS (investment) plan is considered as a contract between involved internal stakeholders like department managers and external stakeholders like customers and suppliers. In the evaluation of investments we have to consider the variety in their impacts on objectives and interests of stakeholders. Therefore this checklist is based on six different foci on IS investments. Firstly, from an internal perspective, we distinguish the IS cost savings focus, the management information quality focus and the strategic aligment focus. Secondly, from an external perspective, we distinguish the IT infrastructural platform focus, organisational transformation focus and business scope redefinition focus. The checklist is elaborated for an EB investment evaluation.

1. INTRODUCTION

Our research objective is formulated and the structure of the paper is presented.

1.1 Background

In this paper e-business (innovation) is considered as:

"A general (innovation) concept covering the application of IT for transforming any form of business transactions between stakeholders such as customers, suppliers and other partners by adoption, implementation and institutionalisation of information systems (IS)".

Companies are becoming aware of the many potential benefits provided by e-business such as lower data communication costs (using the inexpensive internet infrastructure), cost reductions through deployment of electronically supported transactions, strong relationships with customers and suppliers and expansion of the market reach that goes beyond any border. Because of the intangible nature of some of the benefits it is difficult to evaluate the e-business investments and to manage these projects ensuring that real profits are realised (Giaglis et al., 1999, Kettinger et al., 1995). The impression is that in practice e-business projects are often managed too technically and little attention is paid to the business case. The practical need for evaluating and measuring e-business performance is confirmed by a field study in bricks-and-mortal, click-and-mortal and dot.com firms. (Adams et al., 2001).

1.2 Aim and structure of the paper

To summarise, because of the strategic importance of EB investments and the high risks, it is essential to have effective managerial practices for IS investment evaluation (Van der Zee, 1999). In IS WORLD, IS researchers have identified strategic management, assessment and evaluation of e-business as the two most important research questions in the near future. Till now, IS research is studying too often strategic planning and evaluation of IS investments as two separate topics. However, there is a strong relation between these two topics. Therefore, we will consider evaluation as an integrated part of strategic IS management. In previous work we developed an eclectic strategic management concept (Wassenaar and Gregor, 2001). This concept recognises explicitly that many stakeholders are involved in IS planning. Thus a number of questions have motivated this paper. How should we evaluate e-business investments (innovations) as integrated part of strategic IS management? What can we learn from past IS evaluation research? How can we integrate existing IS evaluation and strategic IS management knowledge for improved e-business investment evaluation? Our ultimate research (on-progress) objective is:

To develop a comprehensive framework and a checklist for IS investment evaluation as an integrated part of strategic IS management.

Section 1 introduces the subject, aim and structure of the paper. Section 2 presents a generic strategic evaluation model and a historical review of the existing evaluation literature. Section 3 introduces a framework for evaluating IS investments elaborated in an EB investment evaluation checklist. Finally, section 4 gives some conclusions and final remarks.

2. THEORETICAL BACKGROUND

We explore the concept of evaluation resulting in a general strategic evaluation model and present an historical overview of the IS investment evaluation literature.

2.1 A generic strategic evaluation model

Our generic model (figure 1) is based on the EMIOS framework (Wassenaar and Gregor, 2001) encompassing a constellation of stakeholders with partly overlapping, and partly conflicting interests, interacting in:

- an intervening mode by implementing (development, conversion, testing and acceptance) and institutionalising (use, maintenance and continuous improvement) of an agreed (portfolio of) IS investment in the realisation system and
- a reflecting mode by planning (contracting) common objectives and allocation of resources (IS investments plans) of stakeholders and evaluating courses of actions (IS
- investments) in the planning and evaluation system.

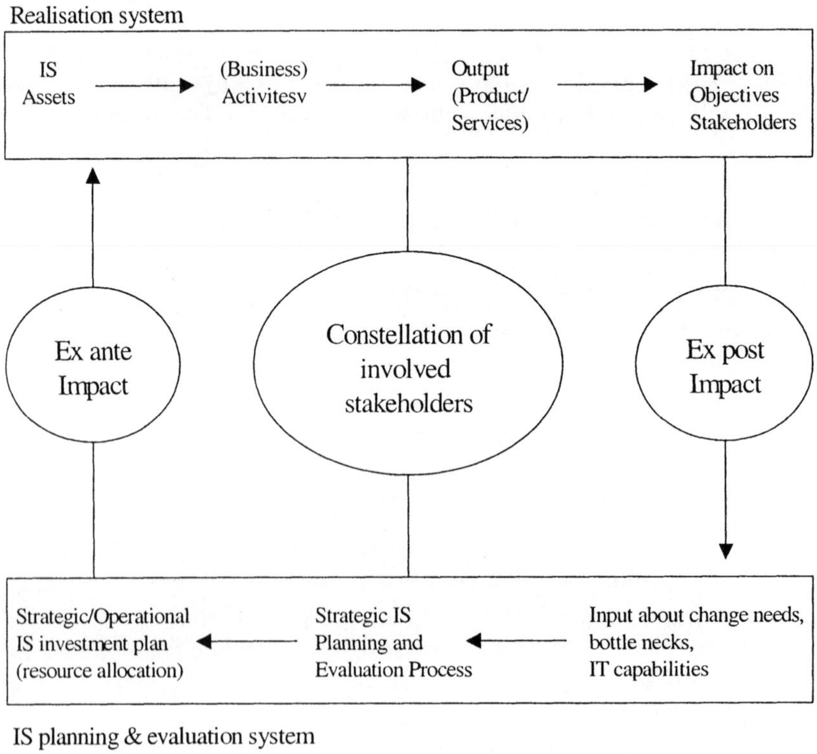

Figure 1. Generic Strategic Evaluation Model

Strategic IS management behaviour is exposed (formed) in the realisation system and reasoned (formulated) in the planning and evaluation system. IS evaluation is considered as an integrated part of the reasoning. IS investments are affecting enterprise IS assets, and enabling improved business activities resulting in improved or new products and services impacting interests and especially costs and benefits of the involved stakeholders like managers, customers, suppliers, employees and shareholders. The IS investment plan is considered as a contract between involved stakeholders. Based on Farbey et al. (1999) IS evaluation is defined as a process that takes place at different points in time or continuously for searching and making explicit, qualitatively or quantatively, ex ante or ex post, impacts of IS investments and their risks for all involved stakeholders (in the realisation system).

Ex ante evaluation is mostly defined as an appraisal of investments in future information systems aiming a selection/ranking of one of the several (portfolio) alternatives and establishing expectation measures or performance metrics for the future. Ex post evaluation is defined as assessment of investments in current information systems at different stages in their life cycle: during implementation (on portfolio, programme, project/subproject level) and institutionalisation (on level of application, IT function, enterprise, stakeholder, industry and economy as a whole).

2.2 Historical overview IS evaluation literature

Our review is based on Van Reeken (1995) identifying different stages in IS investments and their different impacts in organisations. We prefer to speak about different evaluation foci divided after an internal, IS oriented, versus an external oriented perspective.

2.2.1 Internal, IS oriented, perspective

This perspective is starting from (1) the existing information and accounting information systems function (IS cost savings focus) (2) the existing decision making and business processes (management information quality focus) and (3) the existing business strategy (strategic alignment focus). Because the existing internal IS situation of the firm is the starting point for evaluation we will label this perspective as the "inside-out" approach.

1. The (first) automation stage during the fifties and sixties, or what we will call the IS cost savings focus, refers to computers which were used to automate administrative work in isolated operational business functions done by hand like registration and calculation. Consequently, these investments should be evaluated on their improvements in efficiency (especially of the IS function) and their technical IT risks. The financial criteria based methods for evaluating direct financial tangible cost savings embraces financial oriented techniques like (1) the pay back period, (2) average return on investment (ROI), (3) net present value and (4) internal rate of return.

2. The (second) informatisation stage during the seventies, or what we call the management information quality focus, computers were used not only to automate existing work but also to support decision-making processes by management information systems. Galbraith (1974) is relating management information capacity, decision-making quality and their impact on business process performance. Investments in (management) information processing capacity can improve decision-making quality and (indirectly)

business processes and their performance. Therefore these types of IS investments should be evaluated on their tangible and intangible impact on business processes and their performance. The (specification) risks of these IS investments depends on the possibility to specify unambiguous the decision making process and especially the decision algorithm character (routine or heuristic), decision frequency and the degree of formalisation of language. Parker, Benson and Trainor (1988) presented new techniques for evaluating indirect tangible benefits like value linking and value acceleration based on Porter's value chain concept. So, they explore the value of IS investment in terms of their implication on (operational) decision making quality and impact on business process performance. Bedell (1995) faces in his multi-criteria based method the problem of intangible benefits by suggesting a ranking and scoring system for evaluation and prioritisation relating the contribution and importance of IS investments. Strassman (1990) evaluates management and information activities and their added value to the company.

3. In the third strategic information systems stage during the eighties, partly parallel with the informatisation stage, emerged the strategic alignment focus (Earl, 1989) oriented on the appraisal of strategic information systems (SIS) to support the existing business strategy. Strategic IS planning methods were introduced in order to align (top down) IT with business (unit) strategy. So, strategic alignment implies that IS investments have to be evaluated and justified on their increased competitive advantages and competitive risks. Many authors (see for an overview Earl, 1989) classified SIS (based on the concept of Porter , 1980) after their influence on the five competitive forces and impact on (sustainable) competitive advantage. However many of the competitive risks are exogenous, uncontrollable and are of a temporal nature because these systems are imitated by their competitors (Jurison, 1996)

2.2.2 The external oriented perspective

This perspective is rooted in the need for radical improvement of enterprise responsiveness in a fast changing dynamic environment. Therefore we distinguish based on Ansoff and Brandenburg (1971) and Volbeda (1998) (1) the IT infrastructural platform focus aiming operational or technical responsiveness, (2) the organisational transformation focus aiming organisational responsiveness and (3) the business scope redefinition focus aiming strategic responsiveness. Because this perspective starts from the external turbulent environment of the firm, we will label it as the "outside-in" approach.

4. At the end of the eighties/beginning of the nineties, with phenomena like outsourcing and insourcing of parts of the IS function emerged the stage of anticipating on the future by IT infrastructure or what we will call the IT infrastructural platform focus. Enterprises recognised that they had an insufficient insight in the future. Therefore they could use an IT infrastructure in order to anticipate and create more flexibility just like buying an option. According to Saaksjarvi (2000) corporate IT infrastructure consists of IT components like common hardware, software, communication technology, databases and standards providing the base for shared services between a large range of business applications. It differs from business applications because it serves a shared and common enabling foundation for the future applications and services of all business units. However these IS investments in infrastructure are very difficult to justify, it is more a formulated general policy than a calculation of costs and benefits. Saaksjarvi (2000) suggest to evaluate these type of IS investments on their compatibility with new technologies and applications of external vendors, connectivity with emerging (future) suppliers, customers, strategic partnerships and other collaborative networks. Other evaluation criteria suggested in literature (Duncan, 1995; Van Grembergen et al. 2002) are on time deployability for shortening the development and implementation cycle of new applications, accumulation capability of technical skills which makes the imitation of the infrastructural services difficult, and portability which is defined as the degree to which resources are sharable and reusable across the enterprise.

5. In the business process reengineering (BPR) stage during the nineties, partly parallel with the IT infrastructure stage, emerged what we will call the organisational transformation focus. IT was considered as an enabler for total business performance and quality by organisational transformation. The first category of a business process reengineering projects like ERP systems are oriented on horizontal value chain restructuring by eliminating time lags and costs of intermediate stocks in the (primary) activities. Another category is oriented on the vertical management (command and control) chain restructuring by downsizing, eliminating managerial levels, and empowerment. Their ultimate goal was improving organisational responsiveness on the fast changing customer needs. IS is not any more an isolated factor but becomes one of the organisational design variables, just like task division, organisational department structure and overall planning and coordination structure (Lucas, 1995). Evaluation of these IS investments regards the impact of the whole transformed organisational form on organisational responsiveness and their change/implementation risks. Therefore, these investments have to be evaluated by general business

performance measurement methods like Balanced Scorecard (BSC) launched by Kaplan and Norton (1992,1996) the total quality management oriented EFQM model (Hardjono, 1993) and learning models (Argyris and Schon, 1978; Senge, 1990).

6. In the middle of the nineties, with phenomena like WWW, Internet and E Commerce emerged the stage of reinventing business or what we call the business scope redefinition focus (Venkatraman, 1994). Firstly, IS investment are initiating new product/market combinations, extending the business scope by offering new products to existing markets or offering new or existing products to new markets by using electronic channels (Hoogeweegen et al.1998). Secondly, IS investments aim to create a new business network of cooperating companies restructuring the existing industry. The ultimate goal is improving strategic responsiveness in a fast changing turbulent environment. These investments have to be considered in the context of the often information intensive products in IT based industries like the publishing, banking and insurance sector and has to be evaluated on their strategic responsiveness and their strategic risks.

3. A COMPREHENSIVE IS INVESTMENT EVALUATION FRAMEWORK AND AN E-BUSINESS INVESTMENT EVALUATION CHECKLIST.

We are developing a comprehensive evaluation framework, which is elaborated in a e-business investment evaluation checklist.

3.1 A comprehensive IS evaluation framework

This framework is combining the generic strategic evaluation model, distinguishing three objects in the realisation system and the distinguished internal and external oriented foci identified in the historical overview. Riggens et al. (2001) suggest a similar framework for EC applications, but is limited to internal issues such as efficiency benefits (our cost saving focus), effectiveness benefits (our management information quality) and strategic benefits (our strategic alignment focus). Especially in the turbulent era of e-business, a more external oriented perspective has to be added. Therefore we propose in figure 2 a comprehensive IS evaluation framework especially for e-business investments based on the combination of the internal oriented foci (inside-out approach) and external oriented foci (outside-in approach).

Object Approach-Foci properties	**IS assets (Configuration)**	**Business/ decision activity structure**	**Output product/ service portfolio**
Inside - out			
Focus	Cost saving	Management Information Equality	Strategic alignment
Type of investment	Automation IS function	Informalization processes value chain	Strategic Information Systems (SIS)
Aimed impact	Cost savings Existing IS function	Benefits improved process equality	Competitive position (advantages)
Uncertainty	Technical risks	Process modeling risks	Competitive risks
Outside - in			
Focus	IT infrastructural platform	Organisational transformation	Business scope redefinition
Type of investment	Infrastructural reengineering	Business process reengineering	Business network reengineering
Aimed impact	Technical responsiveness	Organizational responsiveness	Strategic responsiveness
Uncertainty	Technical risks	Change/ implementation risks	Entrepreneurial interorganisational risks

Figure 2. A Comprehensive IS Evaluation Framework

3.2 An e-business evaluation checklist

Our framework will be elaborated in a EB investment evaluation checklist, consisting of a set of evaluation issues especially for EB investments.

3.2.1 Inside-out approach.

In this "inside-out" approach, the starting point is the existing IS situation of the firm.

IS cost savings focus:

The central question is: What are the impacts of EB investments based on a cost savings perspective derived from improvement of total costs of ownership and the generated cash flows (revenues and expenditures) of the IS function?

The checklist for evaluation of EB investments from a cost savings point of view explores the impact on the IS expenditures during the defined life time for the following categories:

1. Hardware (processing, storage, data communication, in/output devices, fall back facilities) and their operating expenditures (including basic facilities, maintenance, insurances and supplies) based on an estimated service level;
2. software expenditures based on the initial cost, expected future releases and yearly software maintenance and optimalisation expenditures based on estimated (increasing) number of users and features;
3. additional expenditures for training, support and IT management.

The cost savings are the result of the comparison of the costs in the old and new situation assuming the same service/performance levels for availibility (average system availibility, average downtime, maximum downtime) security and safety. Some general investments in overall supporting hard-, soft- and knowledge-ware are joint costs which has to be distributed to IS systems for different stakeholders.

Management information quality focus

The central question is: What are the impacts of EB investments based on the management information quality perspective derived from improvements of business process performance and their underlying decision making quality?

The checklist for evaluation of EB investments from a management information quality point of view explores for each business process in the value chain the impact on the direct and indirect tangible and intangible benefits of the involved stakeholders. Examples of tangible benefits are lower inventory cost and production costs (resource utilisation, less reruns) by improving operational planning, coordination and logistic decisions and lower cost of (working) capital by faster invoicing and lower stocks. The indirect benefits can be traced by value linking (improvement of the billing process makes it easier for sales to identify credit risks of customers) and value accelerating techniques (speed up the billing process can result in a one time accelerated benefit of interest expense savings).

Strategic alignment focus

The central question is:What are the impacts of EB investments based on a strategic alignment perspective derived from improvements of sustainable competitive advantage of the existing business strategy by strategic information systems?

The checklist for evaluation of EB investments from a strategic alignment point of view explores the impact on the sustainable competitive advantages (rooted in the existing business strategy) by assessing the following issues (Rangone et al. , 1999):

- level of bargaining power towards suppliers and customers;
- position competitors in relation to the possibility for new business models based on on-line trading;
- level of internal rivalry, competitors strengths and weaknesses and the underlying competitive advantage by looking at determinants like market growth rate, level of concentration, competitive diversity, fixed costs/added value ratio, product differentiation and brand identity and at direct and indirect competitors and their marketing mix embracing place (site), product/service, price, promotion and delivery and virtual community;
- level of existing barriers and threat of new entrants by examining determinants like economy of scale (critical mass of customers and/or suppliers), loyalty building, brand identity, cost of switching, cost advantages, capital requirements, access to distribution channels and strategic alliances;
- threat of substitution traditional channels by electronic channels (inter channel competition)

This part of the checklist can be used especially for a more detailled evaluation of the "strategic importance" of EB investments, which is often a general justification statement without any further argumentation.

3.2.2 Outside-in approach

This "outside-in approach" is rooted in the need for enterprise responsiveness in a dynamic environment and has its starting point in innovation of the firm.

<u>IT infrastructural platform focus</u>

The central question is: What are the impacts of EB investments from a IT infrastructural platform perspective derived from improvements of firm's technical responsiveness in a dynamic technical IT environment by an IT infrastructure?

The checklist for evaluation of EB investments from an IT infrastructural point of view has to explore the impact on technical responsiveness and flexibility by assessing the following topics:

- portability (compatibility) or the degree to which IT resources are sharable and reusable across the enterprise by standardising their web services and used tools;

- connectivity or the degree to which IT resources enable interaction across the enterprise and their (future) partners like customers, suppliers and strategic partners;
- deployability or the implementation time for integrating new emerging technology and standard applications and tools in the existing technical infrastructure;
- scalability or the degree to which the infrastructure is capable to process a strong growth in transactions;
- accumulation capability or the capability of integrating technical skills across the enterprise which gives added value to infrastructural services and makes it difficult for imitation by competitors.

Organisational transformation focus

The central question is: What are the impacts of EB investments from an organisational transformation perspective based on improvements in organisational responsiveness in a dynamic environment by organisational transformation?

The checklist for evaluation of EB investments from an organisational transformation point of view has to explore the impact on the overall organisational quality and responsiveness by assessing the following topics

- customer satisfaction in general and especially (1) cycle time defining the company's ability to satisfy customer requirements including new product development cycles, order to delivery cycles and service cycles (2) quality, including both product and service quality and (3) service levels, including levels of customer satisfaction as determined by opinion surveys:
- business process quality and especially the value drivers in four basic processes product design, product development, manufacturing/building and marketing (BSC framework) or in the enabling processes (EFQM framework): leadership, resource management, people management, policy and strategy and the (primary) processes. For each of these identified processes should be explored how they affect customer satisfaction, measured in three ways: cycle time, quality and productivity;
- organisational learning and sustaining innovation, change and improvement by looking after (1) the capability for market innovation (introducing continuously new products and services), (2) continuous improvement by measuring the rate of improvement in performance over an extended period and (3) intelectual capital (human resources) by measuring the importance of knowledge workers and their contribution or added value to company's revenues;
- shareholders value by analysing the profitability and value of the firm based on the shareholder value principle but also explicitly the value gaps

in the belief that, if management does not recognise and deal with them, then other actors in the marketplace will.

Business scope redefinition focus

The central question is: What are the impacts of EB investments from a business scope redefinition perspective based on improvements in strategic responsiveness in a dynamic environment by a reengineering external relations (business networks)?

The checklist for evaluation of EB investments from a business scope redefinition point of view explores the impact on strategic responsiveness by assessing the same topics of above mentioned strategic alligment focus but then regarding the new defined business (network) strategy.

4. CONCLUSION AND FINAL REMARKS

4.1 Conclusions

This research is based on the assumption that strategic IS management can be more effective by integrating managerial evaluation practices in strategic IS planning. Many impacts of EB investments are uncertain and difficult to quantify. However in a first preliminary review of this checklist in a few cases, it seems useful that the impacts have to be described and debated from different viewpoints. A special problem in EB investments are the distribution of the costs and benefits over the involved stakeholders. Often is the case that costs are displaced from one stakeholder to another stakeholder. Further the distinction between the organisational transformation and business redefinition focus was not clear for practioners. One of the suggestions was that business scope redefinition has to be broadened to network redefinition embracing EB investments in collaboration of organisations in virtual networks aiming cooperative and not competitive advantages. The checklist requires a time consuming extensive collection of data from many different sources. Therefore one of the suggestions was to integrate strategic (IS) planning and especially the generation of strategic options with the evaluation in order to reduce the data collecting efforts. Finally, the involvement of many internal and external stakeholders in EB investments introduced a negotiation element in the evaluation of EB investments with respect to the distribution of the "negative and positive" impacts.

4.2 Final remarks

The proposed checklist will be more explored and improved in practice. Especially attention will be paid to the relation with strategic IS planning, completeness and understandability of the checklist by managers. There will be reviewed more literature especially regarding the business redefinition focus and especially in the field of business networks and their value.

REFERENCES

Adams, C., Kapashi, N., Neely, A. and Marr, B. (2001). Measuring eBusiness performance, Cranfield University School of management/ Accenture,http://www.accenture.com.

Ansoff, H. I. and Brandenburg, R.G. (1971). A Language for organization design: parts 1 and 2, *Management science*, 17/12; B705-31.

Argyris, C., Schon, D. (1978). *Organisational learning. A theory of action perspective*, Reading , MA; Addison Wesley Publishing Co

Bedell, E.F.(1985). *The computer solution: strategies for the information age*. Dow-Jones-Irwin, Homewood, Illinois 60430, USA.

Duncan, N.B.(1995) Capturing Flexibility of Information Technology Infrastructure: A study of resource characteristics and their measure, *Journal of Management Information Systems*, vol. 12 no. 2 (fall), 1995.

Earl, M.J. (1989). *Management strategies for Information technology*, Prentice Hall International UK.

Farbey, B., Land, F. and Targett, D. (1999). IS Evaluation: A process for bringing together Benefits, Costs and Risks, *Rethinking Management Information Systems*. W. Currie and B. Galliers(ed) Oxford University Press , New York.

Galbraith , J.R. (1973) . *Design complex organizations*, Reading, Mass.: Addison-Wesley.

George, B. (2000) A Framework for IT evaluation research, *Proceeedings AMCIS Conference*.

Giaglis , G.M. , Paul, R.J., Doukidis, G.I. (1999). *Dynamic modelling to assess the business value of E-Commerce*, International Journal of Electronic Commerce, vol. 3 , no 3, pp. 31-51.

Grembergen Van , W. , Amelinckx, I. (2002). Measuring and Managing E-Business Projects through the Balanced Scorecard, *Proceedings of the 35th Hawaii International Conference on Systems Science* , Hawaii.

Hardjono, T.W., and Hes, F.W. (1993). *De Nederlandse kwaliteitsprijs en Onderscheiding*, Deventer , Kluwer.

Hoogeweegen, M.R., Streng, R.J. and Wagenaar, R.W. (1996). A comprehensive approach for assessing the value of Edi, *Proceedings of the 3th European Conference on Information Systems* , Lisbon-Portugal , July 2-4

Jurison, J.(1996). The temporal Nature of IS Benefits: A longitudional Study. *Information and Management* , vol. 30, pp. 75-80

Kaplan, R.S. and Norton, D.P. (1992). The balanced Scorecard-measures that drive performance, *Harvard Business Review*, january-february 1992 , pp 71-79

Kaplan, R.S. and Norton, D.P. (1996). *Translating Strategy into Action: The balanced Scorecard*, Harvard Business School Press

Kettinger, W.J., Grover, V. (1995. Do strategic systems really pay off?. *Information Systems Management* , vol 12 , no 1, , pp. 533-542.

Lucas, H.C.(1995*), The T-form organization*, Jersey-Bas Publishers, San Francisco.

Parker, M.M. , Benson , R.J., Traitor , H.E (1988). *Information Economics : Linking business performance and Information technology* , Prentice Hall Inc. New Jersey

Porter, M.E.(1980). *Competitive Strategy: Techniques for Analysing Industries and Competitors,* The Free Press, New York.

Rangone , A. and C. Capriotti (1999). A strategic frameworkto analyse a business to consumer e-commerce project, *Proceedings of the 2nd International Conference IeC'99* , Manchester

Reeken van, A.J. (1995). Justifying Investments in Information Technology and Systems: Dependence on the investment vision, *Proceedings third SISnet Conference* , Berne, Swiss

Riggens. F.J. and Mitra, S. (2001)- A Framework for developing E-Business Metrics through Functionality interaction, internal paper.

Saaksjarvi, M. (2000). The role of Corporate IT infrastructure and their impact on IS effectiveness, *Proceedings of the 8 th ECIS conference* , Vienna

Senge , P.M. (1990). *The fifth discipline: the art and practice of the learning organisation*, New York , Doubleday.

Strassman , P. A. (1990). *The business value of computers*, New Canaan

Venkatraman, N.(1994). IT-enabled business transformation: from automation to business scope redefinition, *Sloan Management Review*, Winter .

Volbeda, H.W. (1998). *Building the flexible Firm: How to remain competitive* , Oxford University press.

Wassenaar, D.A and Gregor, S.D. (2001). E-Business Strategy formulating and forming: new wine in old bottles? *Proceedings 9th European Conference on Information Systems*, Bled, Slovenia.

Zee Van der, J.T.M. and De Jong , B. (1999), Alignment is not enough: Integrating Business and Information Technology Management with the Balanced Scorecard, *Journal of Management Information Systems*, Fall, vol 16, no 2 pp. 137-156

SUPPORTING CLEAR: A STRATEGY FOR SMALL AND MEDIUM SIZE ENTERPRISE ADOPTION OF E-BUSINESS PRACTICES IN ATLANTIC CANADA

DAWN JUTLA and TERRANCE WEATHERBEE
Faculty of Commerce, Saint Mary's University, Halifax, Nova Scotia, Canada

Abstract: The successful adoption of e-business practices for small and medium sized enterprises involves creating a business environment for an innovation-based economy. The necessary environment does not yet exist in investment-based economies, such as Canada, that depend on natural resource wealth. In Canada, excellence in providing a business environment for the knowledge-based economy is being created in silos amidst a mix of formal and informal efforts at various levels of government. This paper describes university support for CLEAR, an acronym for Coordinated Learning for E-Business Adoption, Research, and Resources, which is a strategy designed to accelerate e-business adoption in SMEs (Small and Medium-sized Enterprises) in Atlantic Canada. Addressing problems such as isolated silos of excellence, poor communications, and non-existent knowledge sharing, mentoring, delivery, and measuring mechanisms for e-business, CLEAR is anchored on a network of strong research collaboration with universities, private and public sector associations, private sector firms, private and public sector institutions and agencies for innovation and value creation. What is novel about CLEAR is that the management of the CLEAR network activities is to be hosted in university business schools versus government agencies, thereby leveraging the research capacities and business expertise in the region. The expected value lies in the aggregation and alignment, of resources, capacities, and capabilities in e-business with the needs of the SME firms.

1. INTRODUCTION

According to Michael Porter (2001), more sophisticated strategies by companies require more skilled people, better information, more advanced infrastructure and stronger competitive pressures. More sophisticated strategies for developing an innovation-based economy from governments require much of the same. The business environment for the knowledge economy is created and sustained when at least six types of infrastructure are strategically and tactically addressed: (1) knowledge and innovation, (2) communications and information infrastructure and access (3) regulatory, trust, and financial infrastructure, (4) human infrastructure, (5) e-government, (6) content (Jutla et al, 2002a, b). Most countries support initiatives to address the fulfillment of the infrastructure pieces (e.g. IEI (2000), IntIsland (2000))

CLEAR is a complementary strategy, initiated in Weatherbee (2000), to accelerate adoption of e-business practices in SMEs in Atlantic Canada thereby helping some businesses to use, and others to create innovation for competitive advantage. CLEAR's strategy builds, through consensus, an innovation network of SMEs, SME associations, local boards of trade, government agencies, provincial governments and municipalities, universities, and regional community colleges. CLEAR adds an integrative layer that enables the multi-disciplines within business to play active roles in creating and sustaining an innovation economy.

Recognizing that the CLEAR strategy is not being formed in a vacuum, required elements include alignment, collaboration, and non-duplication of the partners' existing services and programs that are already deployed, or that are in development. Initiatives to support federal and municipal-level strategies for SME adoption of e-business practices are common in many countries. Universally, we see non-alignment of federal and municipal strategies as they are independently created in parallel. For example, from consultation through interviews, a number of local governments in Canada appear oblivious of federal strategies to promote SME adoption of e-business practices. Clearly only minimal efforts are being made to align e-government strategies in Canada. Superficial evidence is readily apparent by simply surfing the various local municipal web sites and viewing the unpredictability in naming city or municipal sites, inconsistency in formatting content, and non-uniformity of navigation paths (Jutla et al, 2002c). Nonetheless, despite seemingly ad-hoc efforts, Canada was recently acclaimed as a leader in e-government (Accenture 2001). Early successes are more quickly visible in Canada, the second largest country in the world, because of its relatively high level of connectivity but relatively small population of less than 30 million people. Compared with Canada, countries like the United States with 10 times the population, and hence scale, require much more formality to show early successes for strategies. However, excellence will only become widespread in Canada if more formal infrastructure and mechanisms are set in place.

This paper outlines support for a strategy advocating formal mechanisms and structure for the acceleration of e-business adoption in SMEs in Atlantic Canada. In turn, the CLEAR strategy is intended to support the federal-level SME adoption initiative. The paper is organized as follows. Section 2 describes federal initiatives to create an innovation-based economy and also the Canadian Roundtable SME e-Business Adoption Initiative. Section 3 explains the Atlantic Canada business environment. Section 4 lists CLEAR's services, and presents the support for the CLEAR strategy. Finally, a summary and concluding remarks are provided in section 5.

2. E-BUSINESS READINESS AND SME E-BUSINESS ADOPTION INITIATIVES IN CANADA

We will examine Canadian advances with reference to the model for creating an e-business readiness climate presented in Jutla et al (2000b). The model proposes that the key infrastructure for country-level e-business readiness lies in: (1) knowledge and innovation processes, (2) communications and information infrastructure and access (3) regulatory, trust, and financial infrastructure, (4) human infrastructure, (5) e-government infrastructure, and (6) content infrastructure.

Knowledge and ability to innovate has strong impact on SMEs (Craig, 2000). Lefebvre and Lefebvre (2000) illustrate how R&D and knowledge intensity in SMEs are positively related to their export effectiveness suggesting a strong link to job creation potential. In 2000, the OECD highlighted the challenges that SMEs face in industry-science relationships and suggested that governments must help to enhance the ability of national firms, especially SMEs, to partner with public research institutions as well as to access global research networks and markets (Barre and Guinet, 2000). Canada has made several billion Canadian dollars available for the creation of knowledge and innovation through various federal-level research and development funding agencies over the past few years. The Canadian Foundation for Innovation grants, that top universities and researchers in Canada compete for, are provided from a federal billion-dollar fund. Other funding bodies for support of innovation include CANARIE, Canada's

Advanced Internet Development Organization that in 1998 initiated the first project in the world to create a purely optical-based national network (CANARIE, 2002). Presently, Canada has the world's longest purely optical network at 6000 km long. According to CANARIE, "CA*net 3 is being used as a model for the next generation of networks in other countries, (CA3, 2002)." In late 1999, Canada was leading the rest of the world in communications infrastructure by almost a year. However, by early 2001, most other countries had leapfrogged to install similar infrastructure with transmission speeds at 2.5 Gbps. Canada is reported to have delivered 10 Gbps speeds in 2001. Most networks in the Gbps range are only currently available to universities and research institutions where resident scientists can develop applications of great impact to society. However we are starting to see SMEs being encouraged to collaborate on broadband applications research with universities. For example, CANARIE provides funding for SMEs who want to do research in broadband content applications as well as virtual cluster development. Since the CA*net3 network is not yet available to SMEs, except through research partnerships, Canada's lead in technical infrastructure is not enough to affect the SME economy today, but certainly impacts on their future as dependent innovations are diffused to the business world.

Outreach programs to the SME community are ongoing in the government's communications effort to get the message about e-business practices out. In 2000 and 2001, agencies of Industry Canada conducted dozens of workshops and seminars on e-commerce for the SMEs across Canada. While uptake is good on email and informational marketing web site applications, there is a marked lack of uptake on more sophisticated e-business applications such as customer relationship management and content management. Also we see inconsistency on how e-business is defined by local SME associations leading to inconclusive measures of e-business adoption.

Canada has made many advances in establishing information infrastructure, increasing access, and upgrading skills. In terms of access to lower speed communications infrastructure, by March 1999, Canada had connected each school and public library, under the SchoolNet (2002) and LibraryNet initiatives. Through the community access program (CAP, 2002), Canada intends to connect 10,000 communities. The VOLNet (2002) initiative connects a further 10,000 voluntary organizations.

On the regulatory front, Canada's Personal Information Protection and Electronic Documents Act (Bill C-6, 2002) recognizes the equivalence of electronic signatures and documents to their physical counterparts. It also legislates the privacy aspect of security for businesses and their customers. Canada has proposed a Seal of Seals for regulating trust providers. Industry

Canada provides a support site (www.strategic.ic.gc.ca) that provides details on e-business elements including security. Since 1998 the banking sector and third parties have responded to barrier issues such as expense of credit card processing fees and now offer inexpensive online credit card processing services to merchants. Canadian insurance companies are now designing insurance policies to cover "data and phone bandwidth interruption", and "data integrity insurance", and extended clauses on "good name" insurance to cover web site defamations and negative publicity from security attacks. However these are not ready for Canadian businesses as yet, and probably will not be offered to SMEs for almost another year.

On a national level, SMEs are asking for leadership, consistency, and signs of stability from the local, provincial and federal governments who have a tendency to take different approaches to setting standards (e.g. security standards), and building systems. From SME associations and the National Liberal Caucus Economic Development Committee are recommendations for beneficial tax treatments on e-business related SME expenditures, similar to those given for Y2K in 1999.

Workforce skills are well recognized as being an essential element to e-readiness (Jutla et al 2002a, McConnell 2001, International Development Center 2001, European Union 2001). Canada also uses the International Computer Driving License curriculum for professionals and teachers to upgrade IT skills. In a train-the-trainer program, the Student Connection Program (SCP) hires and trains university and college students to act as Business Advisors on Internet and e-business to SMEs.

Government Online (2002) or "GoL" is Canada's naming of e-government, another key factor in an e-readiness strategy. All provinces are mandated to place a large percentage of services online to all citizens by 2004. Behind the scenes, the Canadian government has enabled a network of government departments and agencies that service SMEs to co-ordinate and exchange research projects, experiences, and programs as an initiative under its "e-Business Growth Strategy." To complement the public sector activities, a Canadian e-Business Opportunities Roundtable (eTeam, 2002) comprising of mainly private sector representatives was formed in mid-1999 to "accelerate Canada's leadership in the digital economy." Six subteams led by Roundtable members form the e-Team Canada umbrella.

Digital collections for organized content focused on culture, science, geography, and so on can be found at collections.ic.gc.ca/. Most of the collections are created within a Youth Employment program where students aged 15-30 create the web sites using content from Canadian museums, and other archives. Canada's efforts at organizing content for SMEs are best found in the strategis (http://strategis.ic.gc.ca) web site – a site that provides databases of information for trade, supply, export, legal research, business financing, patents, matches on private sector and university-based expertise to name just a few.

The subteam for the SME e-Business Adoption Initiative, created under the Canadian e-Business Opportunities RoundTable e-Business Acceleration team to encourage Canadian SMEs into becoming sophisticated users of e-business technologies, has added content to the strategis.ic.gc.ca/ebizenable site. The latter site addresses breaking barriers to e-business adoption. The March 2001 report (Ivis 2001), from the SME Adoption subteam, streamed the top-level barriers inhibiting SME e-Business adoption into 4 categories: information and education, costs and benefits, e-business resources, and security. The report recommends an assessment of the resources and materials available from and to the public and private sectors, as well as the creation of an SME eBusiness Toolkit. According to the Ivis (2001), "SMEs not using the Internet cite ROI and cost as primary inhibitors, those using the Internet cite the lack of e-business strategy as the barrier, and those implementing transactional capability say that security is the barrier." Lack of leadership and managerial skills are also commonly identified business success barriers in SMEs in Canada.

One recommendation from the subteam for the SME e-Business Adoption Initiative is for the creation of a toolkit of resources for helping the SMEs to overcome these barriers. In October 2001, the "toolkit" was provided in the strategis collection (EbizEbable, 2002). While the content on strategis is generic to all SMEs, a great deal of localization and syndication is still needed to enable the effectiveness of the toolkit throughout disparate regions in Canada.

Results of the combined efforts of government, and private sector show that approximately 630,000 of Canada's one million businesses are now online. Small and medium enterprises employ 6 out of 10 working Canadians. The majority of Canadian businesses are very small. 97% of the one million Canadian businesses have less than 50 employees. 78% has less than 5 people. Thus the growth of the SME sector is extremely important to the Canadian economy.

The numerous multi-level and fragmented initiatives and support sites described in this section provides the foundation and backdrop for development of a strategy to support rapid e-business adoption in SMEs in Atlantic Canada. Next we will provide a short description of the business environment in Atlantic Canada.

3. ATLANTIC CANADA: PROBLEMS AND OPPORTUNITIES

Atlantic Canada comprises 4 out of 10 of Canada's provinces: Nova Scotia, New Brunswick, Prince Edward Island, and Newfoundland. This region represents only 6% of the national economy - even with over 8% of the population. As the Atlantic Provinces' private sector remains under-developed, in comparison with other parts of Canada, e-business awareness levels are lower than the national average. The Atlantic Provinces have lower levels of human capital that are working in greater numbers in smaller businesses than other regions (ACOA, 1997). Additionally, while fully 49% of the Atlantic workforce is employed in areas where the capabilities of e-business and knowledge economics (StatsCan 1996) are directly applicable, there is little of the expected development in e-business technologies. The SMEs in Atlantic Canada have, generally speaking, been slower to adopt new technologies than the remainder of Canada. The latest Canadian (CFIB, 2000) Internet survey of SMEs states that "while Nova Scotia has a high Internet penetration rate (73 percent), the prevalence of e-businesses (26%) is below the national average.

While businesses in other regions of the country are investing in the benefits of e-business, most Atlantic Canadian SMEs are not. There are several reasons for this relative regional disparity within Canada. They include (Weatherbee, 2000):

a) The 'high-knowledge' industrial sectors are currently the fastest growing sectors in Atlantic Canada representing an opportunity for learning and information exchange horizontally across sectors;
b) One of the highest per capita density of degree granting institutions in the continent, situated particularly within Nova Scotia, representing an untapped wealth of human capital and expertise that is not being utilized;
c) Regional cost advantages within the 'knowledge management' sector, as well as quality of life benefits which could be leveraged to gain a competitive advantage for the development of this sector within the region; and
d) A strategic presence at the midpoint between North American and European markets which presents an opportunity for e-business value-added activity for both knowledge and supply chain activities.

The region also has a number of potential opportunities that may be exploited in the arena of e-business. These include:

a) The continued forecasted growth and importance of information/knowledge based industries. This trend is forecasted to continue for the next two decades (APEC, 2000) and investment in this area will produce higher returns on investment than current resource based industries while growth will outpace traditional manufacturing sectors;

b) Competitive potential for non-geographically reliant value-added activities as geography becomes less of a limitation within knowledge-based businesses or through utilizing e-business tools;
c) An information and communications infrastructure on par with the remainder of the country which can provide ready access to business within the region and provides a competitive foundation that may not be available to competing organizations within the balance of the continent or internationally;
d) A large potential for university and private sector joint ventures leveraging the density of learning and educational institutions within the region; and
e) The ability to take advantage of the growing clusters such as the Halifax Regional Municipality 'Industrial Cluster' (ACOA, 1997), the Fredericton-Moncton corridor or the Saint Johns cluster; which have sufficient critical mass to support knowledge exchange, a learning environment and horizontal synergy within and across sectors.

4. CLEAR AND ITS SUPPORT STRUCTURE

CLEAR is a Pan Atlantic strategy to accelerate e-business adoption in the over 12000 SMEs in Atlantic Canada. The CLEAR concept and its underlying partnership-based model are initially detailed in (Weatherbee, 2000). CLEAR proposes the setting up of an innovative knowledge-sharing mechanism and formal partnership network among various levels in the education, government, and private sectors in the region. It intends to play a coordinating role in creating a value web that will increase knowledge and innovation output, raise business and IT-based skill sets, promote e-government practices in all municipalities, and facilitate strong linkages between innovation research in universities and SMEs.

Initial services from the CLEAR implementation will include:

1. Coordination and hence alignment of regional research to create and transfer innovation to SMEs;
2. Aggregation of resources, capabilities, and capacities of public sector research infrastructure, human capital from local and international researchers, government agency employees, SME association employees, and private sector employees;
3. Creation of new channels for communication among stakeholders for value creation;

4. Creation of new social capital for SMEs. Social capital is a construct essential to the success of innovation networks (Cooke, 1999);
5. Peer-reviewed research grant funding mechanism for research projects targeted at breaking down the barriers to e-business adoption in SMEs as well as projects targeted at creating business process innovations in partnership with SMEs;
6. Development and validation of new methods and models for e-business adoption in SMEs;
7. Development of new business processes, methods, technologies to support SME needs;
8. Development of new databases to support reduction of barriers to e-business adoption and follow-through;
9. Self- and external measurement of service success;
10. Knowledge sharing and knowledge protection mechanisms such as sophisticated intellectual property proposals;
11. Knowledge transfer of non-codifiable knowledge;
12. Alignment of regional standards to national standards;
13. Facilitate the creation of Pan-Atlantic standards for trust and regulatory infrastructure;
14. Connect SMEs with funding mechanisms; and
15. Strengthen the ability of SMEs to absorb new technologies

In a nutshell, CLEAR's mechanisms will be designed to aggregate and align capabilities, capacities, and resources in Atlantic Canada for maximum value creation. The CLEAR network of partnerships, referred to the CLEAR network for brevity in the rest of this paper, is built on consensus through leadership and sharing of a common vision. In practice, the leadership and original concept for CLEAR emerged from a business school in Atlantic Canada. The leaders shared their vision with other business schools in each of the 4 Atlantic provinces, provincial and federal government agencies, community colleges, law and computer science institutes, SME associations, local boards of trade, government and university-managed business development centres, community colleges, private sector, and SMEs. One major private sector partner is Aliant Inc., the regional telecommunications company, and one of only 4 major businesses in Atlantic Canada. One example of a SME association that has joined is the Canadian Federation of Independent Businesses. International partnerships are currently being sought.

Numerous research articles in Etzkowitz and Leydesdorf (1997), document the importance of the third role of universities, that of industrial participation, for transfer of knowledge and innovation to SMEs. Strengthening linkages between university and industry will increase innovation transfer. Interlocking and other necessary factors for creation of innovation include shared vision, leadership, management skills, availability of funding, and a high degree of partnerships to name a few. Furthermore, many researchers (e.g. Cohen and Levinthal, 1989, Fountain 1998, Cossentino 1996) show the importance of social capital to SME ability to innovate and eventual success. Social capital is created in a rich partnership model such as that on which CLEAR is built. Social capital involves tangible assets of goodwill, fellowship, sympathy, and social intercourse (Hanifan 1920), and social relationships to promote or aid in the development of valued skills and characteristics (Loury 1977).

Opening communication channels across partnership boundaries often causes acquisition of new skills by participating professionals. It also costs in terms of participating employees' time to manage and service the channels. According to Cooke (1999) "communicating across firm and cultural boundaries (as within a rich partnership network) is a profoundly social, interactive process where great care, attentiveness, and patience must be developed." It is area where government and universities with a history of facilitation, partnership and slow, careful decision-making have experience.

The proposed structure of CLEAR is outlined in the organization chart shown in Figure 1. CLEAR consists of five organizational components that are discussed below.

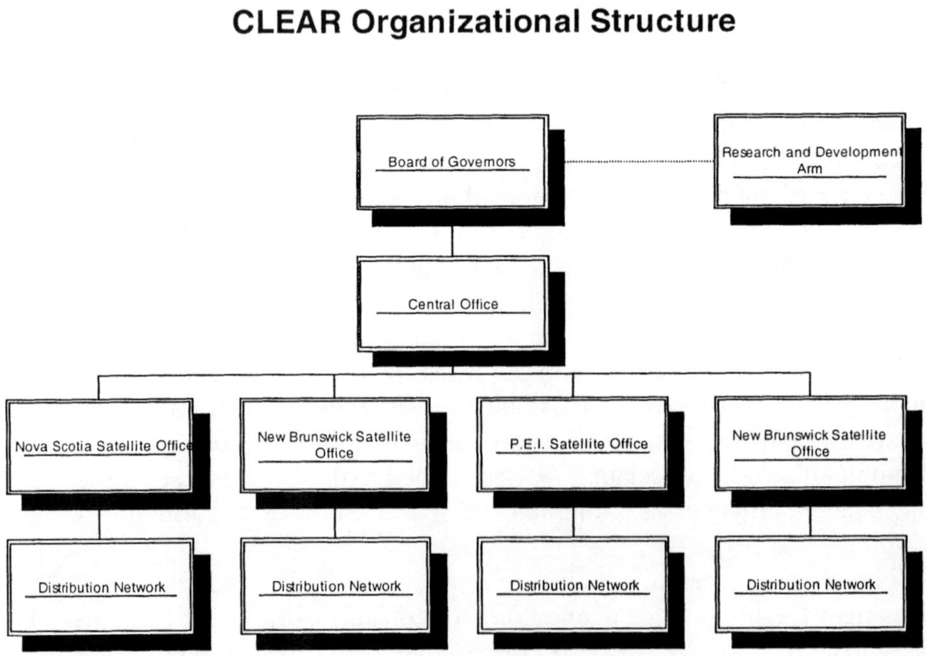

Figure 1. CLEAR organizational structure

4.1 Board of Governors

A board of governors will provide oversight for CLEAR. The board will include representation from institutional partners, business representatives and government partners from the federal and provincial levels. The role of the board is to provide strategic direction, resource allocation, and accountability.

4.2 Central/Head Office

CLEAR will include a central implementation office, which will be responsible to the board of governors for the operations of CLEAR. The role of the central office will be to create and execute the overall strategy for CLEAR, aggregate and align cross-provincial efforts, coordinate research & development initiatives, and coordinate the development of online and offline content. CLEAR's central office is responsible to the board of governors for the operations of CLEAR. The office consists of a full-time director of operations, a full-time director of communications, a stipended strategy director and a stipended research director from the lead agency's business school. The role of the central office will be to implement the overall strategy for CLEAR, coordinate research & development initiatives, and coordinate the development of online and offline content, and the development and growth of partner participation and delivery mechanisms.

4.3 Research and Development Arm

The research and development arm contains the set of Atlantic Canada researchers working on projects that are targeted to breaking the e-business barriers for SMEs. The value of the R&D component is in its knowledge and innovation creation, and innovation building capability and capacity. A research director at the head office's R&D arm will coordinate research efforts for all the provinces. Appointed lead researchers for each province will report to the research director. 4.4 Provincial Satellite Nodes.

CLEAR will establish a physical presence, or satellite office, in each of the four provinces. It is anticipated that these will be hosted by the business schools of institutional partners This is a strategic association since content and enabling tools developed by researchers are critical to the success of

CLEAR, and it creates a strong linkage between innovation from public research and SMEs. Additionally, the largest problem facing SMEs in developed countries is the absence of sufficiently organized content. Even the most connected countries still need to facilitate the organization of content around verticals and clusters for SME participation and aggregation. Online collections are important for lifelong learning, and the weaning from dependencies on more expensive off-line services.

The role of the satellite offices will be: (1) to provide a coordination role in SME e-business initiatives within the satellite's province to create content and enabling tools for the SMEs (2) to bring potential partners together and to promote SME clustering (3) to serve as a direct channel for gathering input and feedback from SMEs and other provincial bodies back to CLEAR and its researchers, and to transfer knowledge/innovation back to the SMEs (4) to input into the content of the field consulting services via a distribution network to SMEs within their province (5) to deliver training and content to the provincial distribution network

The Sobey's Business School at Saint Mary's University, the Electronic Commerce Centre at the University of New Brunswick at Saint John, the PJ Gartner School at Memorial University, and business school at UPEI are the recommended hosts in their respective provinces. Each satellite office will include a satellite director, and 2 operations staff, (one dedicated to communications and the other operations), with the exception of the PEI office (requires small geographic coverage), which will have one operations staff. Each satellite office will also have a lead researcher who will supervise in the development of applied research and content of specific relevance to the local environment for the host province.

4.4 Link and Distribution Network

The link and distribution network is the mechanism for CLEAR's delivery of localized e-business services directly to the SMEs, and for delivery of SME needs to the university and public sector researchers. The precise structure of the distribution network across the region will depend upon the structure of partners/networks as developed by the satellite offices. It is anticipated that provinces will select different delivery structures, depending on existing infrastructure. The University Business Development Centre network has already been identified as the distribution partner in Nova Scotia, and the New Brunswick Community College system as the partner in New Brunswick. Holland College in UPEI and the community college system in New Foundland are proposed for PEI and Newfoundland respectively. The value of these delivery partners are that (1) they have the trust of the SMEs in that they are already familiar with the SMEs' bankers, lawyers, and accountants, (2) they have excellent geographic coverage of the whole Atlantic region, and (3) they already act as consultants for business services to many SMEs. For these reasons they are perfect partners to provide the mentorship and handholding required for effective acceleration of movement of e-business practices into SMEs. In Nova Scotia, particularly there is an advantage for receiving SME needs into university research, since the university business development centres are acting as the link and delivery channel. Many of the Nova Scotian business development centres have provided very low cost services (sometimes free services when there is a lot of student involvement) to small businesses in the region. It has built a lot of goodwill for the universities in the SME firms. Services include writing business plans and developing strategies.

5. POTENTIAL BARRIERS AND RISKS FOR CLEAR

There are number of barriers and risks facing CLEAR. Obtaining funding for CLEAR will be a major barrier, especially in the aftermath of the meltdown of the dot com stocks. Governments, like SMEs, are also unsure of calculating return on investment, even though the concept may make sense. Because of CLEAR's scale, funding will come from many sources and infused at different stages. Mismatch of initially identified funding requirements and projected timelines with actual requirements and completion times can emerge. Management of the numerous applications for funding and providing reports to funding bodies with diverse accountability standards could be onerous. Once funding is obtained, the risk of limited commitment on the parts of faculty members at the various business schools can prevent success. There is a risk that incentive schemes for faculty members working in CLEAR may conflict with the usual reward structures for a university faculty employees. The mismatch between university careful and studied cultures and the SMEs needs for quick and sometimes dirty solutions can possibly lead to friction and dissatisfaction for the partnerships. Careful management of expectations among partners will be necessary.

The cause of most economic development schemes that fail in Atlantic Canada has been identified as a lack of a good business plan. Such a plan needs to cover aspects of identification of critical success factors and priorization of tasks. Should insufficient funding be a problem, critical positions should less likely be cut with a reasonable business plan.

6. RELATED WORK

The CLEAR strategy requires (1) the building of a strongly-linked collaborative network, or "network of networks" for coordination and alignment, (2) instituting knowledge management processes between universities and SMEs, and (3) complementary infrastructure (technological, human, regulatory, trust, financial, content, and e-government leadership). On surveying strategies with similar goals in various countries, we find that some have two separate strategies to address the above points; while some combine all three in one innovation strategy. For example, Germany has INSTI (www.insti.de), a 5-year collaborative project designed to facilitate effective technology transfer between research institutions and industry. According to INSTI's website, " 32 mainly private enterprise partners from the invention and patent sector have joined the INSTI Project: patent attorneys, regional patent information centres, information brokers, regional inventor support centres, business consultants, technology agencies and transfer agencies of higher education institutions and research institutes."

Countries start from different places when creating strategies for strengthening links between university research and SMEs. For example, Europe has millions of SMEs; in contrast Canada hosts a total of one million businesses, with under 50 000 in Atlantic Canada. Thus one reason that European strategies will differ will be due to disparities in scale. The EU programme titled "innovation and participation of SMEs", launched in 1999, aims to "stimulate, disseminate, and exploit the results of research, in particular for the benefits of SMEs (CORDIS, 1998)". It is under the umbrella of the Fifth Framework programme (coordinating body) and complements other specific 5th Framework programmes and, coordinates schemes such as CRAFT, with its own distinctive initiatives. CRAFT is a program wherein SMEs can outsource co-operative research to university institutions. The overall aim is "to improve the economic and social impact of research, by ensuring better dissemination and exploitation of its results, and encouraging the transfer and dissemination of technologies. " (CORDIS, 1998).

The European "Go Digital" initiative is aimed squarely at SMEs for adoption of e-business. The European Commission claims that e-commerce in the European Union is hampered by lack of consumer trust. 66% of small companies have Internet access, but only 6% of small businesses transact business online in real-time. The most important influences on SMEs' future uptake of e-business awareness and opportunities may come from the roles of associations and governments.

In the Netherlands, partnerships among private and public sector firms, institutions, and associations is brought together in the Electronic Commerce

Platform (www.ecp.nl) to accelerate innovation creation and use. The Dutch Syntens is a business innovation network for small businesses that promotes the adoption of technologies in SMEs.

In late 1998, in Singapore, a national level Electronic Commerce Co-ordination Committee (EC3) was formed to manage e-readiness efforts. The Local Enterprise Electronic Commerce Programme has to-date assisted more than 500 local enterprises in their e-readiness efforts, mostly on a cost-sharing basis.

7. SUMMARY AND CONCLUSIONS

Proposed in this paper are university business school involvement, and an accompanying formal infrastructure to support the CLEAR strategy, that facilitates widespread diffusion of e-business practices, processes, and opportunities in SMEs in Atlantic Canada. Working with government agencies, other disciplines, and various SME stakeholders, business schools in universities can advise, collaborate, and provide services to build the environment for aggressive e-business adoption in SMEs, and hence grow the digital economy.

Copying another's successful innovation network is not an instant recipe to success (Novakovic and Sturn 2000). Localization factors, such as the structure and characteristics of national R&D systems including incentives, are critical success factors. To this end, we illustrate a novel strategy for business schools in universities, in the Atlantic Canada setting, to work together to impact on the SME adoption rate of e-business in their regions. CLEAR builds on other existing and growing infrastructure, in terms of, communications and information, human, content, e-government, regulatory and trust, knowledge and innovation infrastructure, and existing distribution networks. Countries with similar problems and opportunities as those found in Atlantic Canada may benefit from examination of the CLEAR strategy, and perhaps contribute new ideas to the CLEAR work.

Even though, e-business research is being heavily quoted from the IS (information systems) and marketing fields (IFIP84, 2002), in many countries, such as Canada, business research is comparatively under-funded in the national R&D systems (Renaud, 2001). CLEAR defines infrastructure, pro-active roles and ownership of tasks, and opportunities for researchers from business sub-disciplines such as management (including human resources, SME), economics, accounting, marketing, management science, finance, and information systems to contribute to the digital economy. In addition to the potential positive impact that the business researchers can have on SMEs, cheaper and quicker means of identifying needs and collecting data (e.g. through partnership with SME associations) becomes apparent.

REFERENCES

Accenture (2001). Rhetoric vs. Reality – Closing the Gap. (AC111 30/03/01 6:27 pm). Second Annual Survey of e-government. Available at www.accenture.com /xd/xd.asp?it=enWeb&xd=Industries%5CGovernment%5Cgove_study.xml. Viewed February 2002.

ACOA (1997). Prospects for Growing Knowledge Based Industrial Clusters in Atlantic Canada. Atlantic Canada Opportunities Agency Report. Ottawa: Nordicity Group Ltd, Syntel Consulting Inc (Halifax), & Horizons Consulting Ltd. (St John's), 31 July 1997.

APEC (2000). Our University Students: The Key to Atlantic Canada's Future. APEC and AAU Report. January 2000.

Barre, R. and Guinet, J. (2000). Benchmarking industry science relationships. A publication of the Federal Ministry of Education and Research, and the OECD. Available at www1.oecd.org/dsti/sti/s_t/inte/prod/tip2001barre.pdf. Viewed February 2002.

CA3 (2002). Advanced Networks. Available at www.connect.gc.ca/en/ar/1002-e.htm. Viewed January 2002.

CANARIE (2002). Canada's Advanced Internet Development website. Available at www.canarie.ca. Viewed January 2001.

CAP (2002). Community Access Program: Connecting Canadians. Available at cap.ic.gc.ca/english/5000.shtml. Viewed January 2002.

CFIB (2000). E-Business Update: Internet Use among Small and Medium Sized Firms. Canadian Federation of Independent Businesses Survey. August 2000.

Cohen, W. and Levinthal, D. (1999). Innovation and Learning: The Two Faces of R&D. The Economic Journal. 99, 569-596.

Cooke, P. (1999). Small firms, social capital, and the enhancement of business performance through innovation programs. Small Business Economics. 13(3), 219-234.

CORDIS (1998). Introducing the "Innovation and participation of SMEs programme – the key to making the most of the Fifth Framework Programme. European CORDIS database. As of 9 June 1998.

Cossentino, F., Pyke, F. and Sengenberger, W. (1996). Local and Regional Response to Global Pressure: The Case Study of Italy and Its Industrial Districts. International Institute for Labour Studies.

Craig, J. and Jutla, D.(2001), eBusiness readiness: a customer focused framework. Boston: Addison Wesley.

EbizEnable. (2002). SME e-business Information Toolkit. Available at strategis.gc.ca/SSG/ee00240e.html and strategis.gc.ca/sc_indps/ebiz/engdoc /homepage.php. Viewed January 2002.

ECPlatform. (2002). Electronic Commerce in Nederland. Available at www.ecp.nl. Viewed January 2002.

ETeam. (2002). Electronic Commerce in Canada. Available at "e-com.ic.gc.ca /eteam/mission.html. Viewed January 2002.

Etzkowitz, H., and Leydesdorf, L., (eds.) (1997). Universities and the Global Knowledge Economy, A Triple Helix of University-Industry-government Relations, eds. London: Printer.

EUScoreboard. (2001). The European Innovation Scoreboard: October 2001. Available at www.cordis.lu/innovation-smes/scoreboard/. Viewed December 2001.

Fountain, J. (1998), Social Capital: A Key Enabler of Innovation. Investing in Innovation. L. Branscomb and J. Keller (eds.), Cambridge: MIT Press, 85-111.

GoL (2002). www.gol-ged.gc.ca/index_e.asp. Viewed January 2002.

Hanifan, L. (1920). The Community Center. Boston: Silver, Burdette and Co.

Hosmer, L.T. (1995). Trust: The connecting link between organizational theory and philosophical ethics. Academy of Management Review, 20(1), 379-403.

Hull, D. (2000). Connecting Canadians: an agenda for the knowledge economy and society. Information Highway Applications Branch of Industry Canada, Distinguished Lecture Series. Halifax: Dalhousie University.

IEI (2000). Information Economy Initiative. Available at www.gov.ns.ca/govt/accountability/tssaccrpt01.pdf. Viewed February 2002.

International Development Center (2001). Harvard University: International Development Center e-readiness guide, Available at www.readinessguide.org. Viewed January 2002.

IntIsland (2000). IT2000: Realizing an Intelligent Island. Available at www.s-one.gov.sg/overview/it2k01.html. Viewed January 2002.

ICDL (2002). International Computer Driving License. Available at www.icdl.org.za. Viewed January 2002.

IFIP84 (2002). Call for papers - Seeking success in e-business: a multi-disciplinary approach. Available at www.ifip2002.cbs.dk/. Viewed February 2002.

Jutla, D., Bodorik, P. and Dhaliwal, J. (2002a). Government Support for e-Readiness of Small and Medium Sized Enterprises. Hawaii International Conference on Systems Science. IEEE: e-Governance track.

Jutla, D., Bodorik, P., and Dhaliwhal, J. (2002b). Supporting e-Business Readiness of SMEs: Approaches and Metrics. Internet Research Journal. In Press 2002.

Jutla D., Bodorik, P., Weatherbee T., and Hudson B. (2002c), e-Government in Execution: Building Organizational Infrastructure. European Conference on Information Systems, ECIS, Gdansk, June 6-8, 2002.

Lefebvre, E. and Lefebvre L.A. (2000). SMEs, Exports, and Job Creation: A Firm Level Analysis. CIRANO and Polytechnique de Montreal. Available at strategis.ic.gc.ca/SSI/ra/op26_e.pdf. Viewed February 2002.

McConnell International LLC and WITSA (2001). Ready? Net. Go! Partnerships Leading the Global Economy. Available at http://www.witsa.org/papers/e-readiness2.pdf Viewed February 2002.

Novakovic, M. and Sturn, D. (2000). Start-up on Campus – European models for the stimulation of academic spin-offs. Available at www.tig.or.at/bilder/45.doc. Viewed February 2002.

Porter, M. (2001). The Global Competitiveness Report 2001-2002. World Economic Forum. Oxford, 2002.

Renaud, M. (2001). Presentation on SSHRC New Economy Initiative, Saint Mary's University, Halifax, 20 April 2001.

SchoolNet. (2000). SchoolNet's On-line Connectivity Survey: Final Report. Available at www.schoolnet.ca/home/e/Research_Papers/Research/SchoolNet_Research/Final_Survey_Report_2000(English).htm. Viewed May 2001.

StatsCan. (1996). Statistics Canada Labour Force Report, 1996 Census, available at www.statcan.ca/english/Pgdb/People/Labour/labour45a.htm, Viewed January 2002.

VolNet. (2002). Connecting voluntary organizations to the Internet. Available at www.volnet.org/. Viewed January 2002.

Weatherbee, T.G. (2000). A Proposal for A Centre of Learning: for e-Business Awareness and Resources – (CLEAR). Report FMS#01-01. Saint Mary's University.

MULTIDISCIPLINARY E-FORENSICS METHODOLOGY DEVELOPMENT TO ASSIST IN THE INVESTIGATION OF E-CRIME

AMY TENNYENHUIS and RODGER JAMIESON
SEAR – Security E-Business Assurance Research Group, School of Information Systems Technology and Management, University of New South Wales, Australia

Abstract: E-Crime in e-business is rising at an ever increasing rate with nations positioning themselves through alliances to fight this threat - evidenced by thirty countries recently signing a new cyber crime treaty. In order to combat this threat, law enforcement and other government and private organisations are turning to computer forensics, which is a new field that deals with investigating computer-related crimes. This paper describes the identification of research issues for methodology development via a Delphi study and the development of a standard methodology for computer forensics to assist in the investigation of e-Crime by use of semi-structured questionnaires and interviews.

1. INTRODUCTION

E-Crime in e-business is rising at an ever increasing rate (CSI, 2001) with nations positioning themselves through alliances to fight this threat evidenced by thirty countries signing a new cybercrime treaty (IDG News Service 23 Nov 2001). E-Crime has increased the exposure to e-business and has strengthed the resolve of organisations to increase security and control of their e-commerce applications (Cerpa & Jamieson, 2001). In order to combat this threat, law enforcement and other government and private organisations are turning to computer forensics, which is a new field that deals with investigating computer-related crimes. Computer forensics, also referred to as electronic discovery, electronic evidence discovery, computer forensic analysis, digital discovery, computer examination and computer analysis, is the process of methodically examining computer systems, computer networks, computer media and peripherals for evidence (Rehman, 2000).

The Commissioners of Police of Australasia have recognised that unless law enforcement acts quickly, society could be seriously affected by unchecked electronic crime (Virtual Horizons - ACPR, 2000). It is therefore important to have a standard methodology developed to ensure proper procedures are followed so that these e-crimes can be detected, evidence adequately collected and presented in a court of law so that the perpetrators of e-crime can be brought to justice.

In Australia there is currently no standard methodology in place for computer forensic investigation and analysis. This is due to the many variables that affect the way a computer forensic investigation takes place, for example, the operating system, software applications, hardware platforms, legal system, and international boundaries (Rude, 2000). As such, many methodologies have been developed that take into consideration each of these factors, and the addition problem that digital evidence is hard to present as evidence in court or show the jury due its digital form. Despite their differences, it is important to understand the need for a standard computer forensic methodology and the factors influencing its development. A methodology is required as it establishes a protocol by which electronic evidence (physical and logical) is gathered and handled, to reduce the potential for this evidence to be corrupted or tainted.

This paper will discuss the research issues associated with and the structure and development of computer forensic methodologies. First the objectives of the research are set out followed by the theoretical foundation to the research. Secondly, the research methods are outlined together with the research results and progress to date.

2. RESEARCH OBJECTIVES

The aim of this research is to investigate and develop a framework for the development of a standard for computer forensic methodologies. The research aim may be broken down into related research objectives:

Identifying issues related to computer forensics methodologies from a multidisciplinary perspective;

- Investigating and developing a framework for a computer forensic methodology standard; and
- Investigating and documenting the skills and competencies required by a CFA to conduct a computer forensic examination (this last objective is outside the scope of this paper).

The result of this study should provide a list of competency variables from which a standard can be devised. Additionally, for methodologies, a list of the main steps in the process, the main functions, rules and guidelines and the main quality control specifications will be devised.

This research will have a number of outcomes:

- A validated normative computer forensic model developed from the literature;
- A high-level computer forensic methodology framework, consisting of major phases, steps, guiding principles and documentary requirements. Sound computer forensic methodologies can then be developed using this framework;
- A list of skills, knowledge, qualifications and experience that a computer forensic analyst must posses. This will form the basis for a competency standard;
- A taxonomy of emerging issues that have been rated and ranked by experts in the field; and
- Contacts and ongoing research between the University and the Australian Computer Crime Managers Group, in the form of a sub-group called the Computer Forensic Research Group. This joint research has been ratified by Australian Police Commissioners.

3. THEORETICAL FOUNDATION

3.1 Background

There has been a call for the development of best practices and standards in the computer forensic field. The Virtual Horizons paper (Virtual Horizons - ACPR, 2000) developed by the Australian Centre for Police Research has outlined world wide strategies for combating computer crime. One of the main associations dealing with international computer crime, the Association of Chief Police Officers Computer Crime Working Group have stated in a memorandum that 'forensic standards for retrieving and authenticating electronic data for use in criminal investigations and prosecutions must be developed and employed' (ACPO). Additionally, the International Hi-Tech Crime Forensics Conference and Workshops (IHCFC) held in London 1999, recommended that principles for evidence handling should be developed, an accreditation device should be provided, and the term 'forensically competent' should be defined (ACPO). Interpol has developed a Computer Crime manual which includes flowcharts to aid complicated investigations.

The G8 summit held in 1997 included as part of a Statement of Principles concerning computer crime that law enforcement personnel must be trained and equipped to address high-tech crimes and forensic standards for retrieving and authenticating electronic data to be used in criminal investigations and prosecutions must be developed and employed (Virtual Horizons - ACPR, 2000). The UK National Criminal Intelligence Service has recognised the importance of partnerships and international cooperation in terms of standardisation of investigative and forensic techniques (Virtual Horizons - ACPR, 2000).

In Australia, a study done by Wieszyk (1998a) found that only three out of eight police departments has guidelines for search and seizure. The Wieszyk report recommended that 'guidelines for the collection, analysis and presentation of computer evidence be developed to an Australian law enforcement standard and investigators be made aware of these guidelines'. The result of this has prompted may institutions in Australia to undertake studies to develop procedures and training for investigations. The Victoria Police Computer Crime Investigation Squad (CCIS) has included in its list of current e-crime objectives to 'develop computer crime investigation and computer evidence handling procedures and practices throughout the force, provide a force-wide field response capability for computer search and seizure operations; and to develop and manage internet investigations procedures and practices' (Virtual Horizons - ACPR, 2000).

The National Office for the Information Economy (NOIE) and the Action Group into the Law Enforcement Implications of Electronic Commerce (AGEC) have been researching into creating standards for computer forensics. Similarly the Australasian Computer Crime Program (ACCP) established the Computer Investigation techniques (CIT) program whose objectives were to 'establish links with national and international agencies/individuals in the area; identify, acquire and develop investigative tools; disseminate tools and information; and develop and provide a training regime for police investigators' (Virtual Horizons - ACPR, 2000).

As it can be seen there have been a number of national and international strategies for combating electronic crime.

3.2 Need for Methodologies

Many influences and success factors (Tennyenhuis and Jamieson, 2001) highlight the need for any methodology to be independent of the low-level details such as specific tools and methods to be used. As such, a computer forensic methodology can be broken down into logical layers. Computer forensics encompasses four functional areas: identification, preservation, analysis and presentation of digital evidence. At a high level these areas and corresponding principles form the basis for any computer forensics methodology. Due to the complexity of the computer forensic investigative process any methodology should include high-level steps, principles of examination, and standard operating procedures (SOP's). SOP's are guidelines how to go about analysing digital evidence at the process level. For example, part of the standard operating procedure could include details on how to backup a piece of media without specifying the software or the media.

By viewing the process as a three-levelled model the methodology is more flexible, as each layer is independent of the layer below. This means that the top two layers are independent of the many factors that make the computer forensics field dynamic such as changing technology and diverse software and evidence. The highest level should include the basic phases involved in the methodology as discussed above. The second level should comprise of a set of principles, which are structural guidelines that apply to forensic examinations (FBI, 2000a, FBI 2000b)

For example, the high level 'analysis' phase can be approached three different ways: Applications approach, modified operating system approach and black box approach (McKemmish, 1998).These methods are highly dependant on the tools and the operating environment. Details of these approaches should be documented at the lowest level of the methodology. Due to privacy reasons, law enforcement often do not want to divulge the tools and techniques they use at the lower layer. Using this model, it is possible for the law enforcement to follow the public methodology and then devise their own lower layer as long as it conforms to the principles set out in the second layer. This model allows us to understand the concept of the different layers of complexity and detail in a methodology. The flexibility is increased by the independence between the layers of the methodology as shown in this model. The first two levels will always be applicable as they are independent of tools and media.

After this initial understanding of what influences the structure and development of many of today's computer forensic methodologies, existing methodologies will be examined to determine their strengths and weaknesses.

3.3 Existing Methodologies

Throughout the world there is no standard methodology but rather a whole set of different methodologies devised by different specialists and organisations. The issue has been raised as to whether it is valid to produce a world standard for computer forensic methodologies (CRFG, 2001). In reality, a high level framework for developing computer forensic methodologies would be beneficial world wide. The majority of these methodologies differ only in terms and minor details. The major steps in each methodology are similar. Therefore, it would not be of much use to go through each methodology in turn and highlight the major phases, principles and techniques. Instead this paper will provide a view of existing methodologies by highlighting common steps and suggested rules and guidelines (in the next section) that are common to the documented methodologies of today.

There are six phases in the standard computer forensic methodology: preparation, identification, preservation, analysis, presentation and documentation, which are discussed below:

Preparation - The preparation stage involves preparing the personnel, materials and tools required for the investigation. During this stage the paperwork is prepared for the investigation and details are distributed to the personnel working on the case. The specialists are made aware (if they do not already know) of the various different forms of evidence that may be at the crime scene when they arrive. A preliminary plan is drawn which details what each specialist will be doing once they arrive at the scene, and the order in which each type of evidence is to be collected.

Identification - On arrival the team must approach and secure the crime scene. This involves protecting the crime scene from unauthorised personnel, determining whether to disconnect computers from remote access such as telephone lines, and determining whether to unplug machines from network access.

After the scene is secured, all computers, devices and all other aspects of the crime scene are documented. All evidence is identified, photographed, documented and tagged. This involves determining what evidence is present, where it is stored, in what format and determining what tools and procedures are required to facilitate the recovery of the evidence. (AIC, 1999). Documentation is especially important at this stage as it provides support for any accusations of negligence or charges that the investigator knowingly tried to hide evidence.

Preservation - Once the location and state of all evidence has been documented it should be backed up, protected and preserved so that no damage can be done.

All procedures performed on the evidence should be documented in the evidence log, which should detail the original state of the evidence, the procedure performed, the time it was performed and the investigator who performed the procedure. This evidence log is especially important as it will help to show that continuity of evidence was maintained. Continuity of evidence is a means of accounting for every move and change to the evidence including who touched it, when, why and for how long. Not maintaining continuity of evidence can quickly render evidence inadmissible in court as "Failure to substantiate the evidence's chain of custody may lead to serious questions regarding the authenticity and integrity of the evidence and the examinations rendered upon it" (Saferstein, 1998, 48).

Analysis - Once the evidence has been identified and secured, the search, recovery and analysis of the digital evidence is performed. This involves the extraction, processing and interpretation of the digital data. A plan should be devised describing the approach to be taken in analysing the evidence. This is particularly important as different types of digital evidence and media have different levels of volatility. Once all evidence has been found it should then be copied and analysed. This may involve searching for and retrieving deleted files, running word searches on file systems and documenting all evidence found and all procedures performed.

Presentation - Once the evidence has been processed and all the necessary preparation has been carried out the evidence should be prepared for court. This involves making sure all documentation such as evidence logs are readable and in an appropriate format for court. Investigators should prepare reports on what they did during the investigation and should be prepared to provide expert testimony. Evidence should be presented in a manner which is easy to read and which does not over complicate the evidence by disguising it in a mass of technical jargon. It is important to note that the complete and accurate evidence will be of little value in court if it is not presented in a way that can be understood by all members of the court, especially the jury.

Documentation - This phase of the methodology is perhaps not a phase as such but a continuing process. Throughout the investigation documentation should be constantly updated. The documentation may include various types of logs such as an evidence log, transport log, evidence lab analysis log and many other documents which together provide an accurate and detailed description of events that occurred from first arrival on the crime scene to the courts.

These six phases are common to the traditional computer forensic methodologies of today. They outline the major steps taken in an investigation. As mentioned earlier, there is little in the way of documented methodologies for computer forensics.

3.4 Comparison of Methodologies

There are several documented computer forensic methodologies, principles and guidelines that are available today. The IOCE and ACPO have developed draft standards guidelines and principles for computer forensics. The US Department of justice has released guidelines for the search and seizure of computers. However, this document is very detailed and specific to the US law. Timothy E. Wright, Peter Stephenson, Mathew Braid, and Thomas Rude have all documented their own computer forensic methodology. Additionally, the model developed by Rodney McKemmish will serve as a good guide on the development of a framework (refer Figure 1). These principles, guidelines and methodologies will be synthesised to create a normative methodology model, which will be discussed following a brief description of the critical success factors, influencing factors, existing principles, guidelines and methodologies.

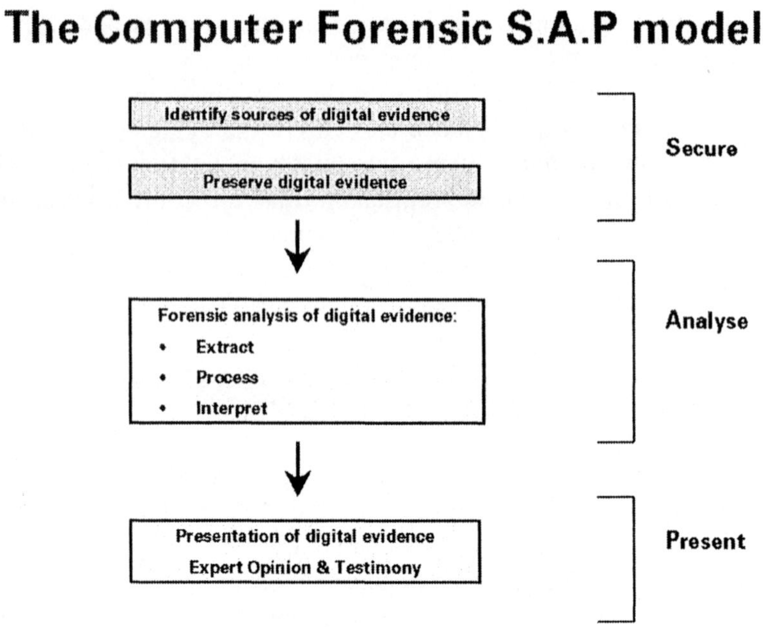

Figure 1. CFSAP Model (McKemmish, 2001)

From the literature review of existing methodologies it is possible to develop a methodology matrix, which illustrates the corresponding phases of the existing methodologies with the phases of a normative methodology. This normative methodology was developed by a synthesis of the existing methodologies. This methodology is a hypothetical model of the possible phases in a methodology. This matrix set out in Table 1 gives support to the normative methodology showing the comparison of each phase with the existing methodologies.

Phase of the normative model	Description	Stephenson 2000	Wright 2000	McKemmish , 2001	Braid, 2001	Rude, 2000
Preparation	The preparation stage involves preparing the personnel, materials and tools required for the investigation	Launch	Formulate plan	Secure		Preparation
Identification	The identification phase involves securing the scene and identifying the evidence	Launch	Approach and secure Crime Scene, Document crime scene layout	Secure: Identification	Identification	Snapshot
Preservation	The preservation phase involves backing up, protecting and preserving the evidence to prevent tampering and damage	Launch		Secure: Preservation	Preservation	Transport, Preparation for Examination
Analysis	This involves the extraction, processing and interpretation of the digital data.	Incident Analysis	Search for evidence, Retrieve Evidence, Process evidence	Analyse: Extraction, processing and interpretation	Analysis	Examination
Presentation	This stage involves preparing the case and evidence for court	Evidence analysis and Report preparation	Process Evidence	Presentation	Presentation	

Table 1. Comparison of Computer Forensic Methodology Phases

4. RESEARCH METHODOLOGY

The research methodology consists of the following phases: literature review; conduct of a research forum on e-crime and computer forensics;

Delphi study arising from the forum to determine the major issues surrounding computer forensics methodologies; semi-structured questionnaires and interviews with personnel from key law enforcement and private investigation agencies at both federal and state levels; construction of a normative computer forensics methodology; comparison of the normative methodology with those used by expert practitioners; refinement of a standard computer forensic methodology; review of the methodology by expert practitioners.

4.1 Data Collection and Methods

The collection of data in this research will be based around the formation of a normative methodology model. This normative model will help to collect the various actions, principles and steps that a computer forensic investigator performs into a framework. This is consistent with the retroductive strategy where, according to Blaike (2000, 71), 'the literature review may provide some assistance in the construction of hypothetical explanatory model", when conducting retroductive research.

The methods used to collect data must be able to capture the accounts of the computer forensic specialists in a precise and conducive way. According to Blaike (2000, 234) "the qualitative interview, particularly the in-depth variety, can get close to the social actors' meanings and interpretations". Similarly, written questionnaires and research forums are data collection methods that can be used when undertaking exploratory research.

This research is primarily exploratory in nature and therefore this study positions itself as the basis for further research in the area. The results of this study will need to be validated and further explored in future research as the framework is the first step in an iterative process. The issues rose in the research forum and the implications and limitations of this research will form the basis for future research in the area.

This study will use the existing literature in two main ways. First, the literature will be used to develop a normative methodology model, which will be used to formulate and direct the collection of the data. Secondly, prior research in the area of competency standards will help focus the collection of data for competencies. Through the use of a semi-structured written questionnaire, interview, and a research forum, a framework for a computer forensic methodology will be developed. This framework will need to be refined and explored further.

The exploration, description, development and explanation of practices and behaviours relating to computer forensic analysis relies on the generation of theory from in-depth accounts of social actors in the field. Therefore the research methodology adopted by this study will be that of

Grounded Theory. Grounded Theory is a qualitative research methodology that seeks to develop theory that is grounded in data systematically gathered and organised (Myers, 2001). Denzin and Lincoln (1994, 273) define Grounded Theory as a "general methodology for developing theory that is grounded in data systematically gathered and analysed". Prior research in computer forensic search and seizure in Australia has also chosen Grounded Theory as its theoretical framework (Wieszyk, 1998b). This methodology was chosen as it allows theory to emerge rather than verifying or negating hypotheses, whilst also allowing conceptualisation and operationalisation to occur at the same time as data collection and analysis (Wieszyk, 1998b).

4.2 Interviews and Research Forum

There were two rounds of interviews. The purpose of the first round was to undertake exploratory research to determine the main issues and views on methodology and competency standard development and determine whether the subject had a methodology or competency standard in place. The second or main round of interviews will be used to explore specifically the computer forensic techniques and skills used by the various investigators in terms of their own phases and in terms of the normative model developed from the literature. Details on actual steps undertaken in the forensic analysis are explored during the interviews. In line with the methodology of Grounded Theory, transcripts of the interviews were written up and a qualitative data analysis tool called NVIVO was used to code and categorise the answers to the interviews. This tool was then be used to collate, compare and contrast different answers to the questions. NVIVO was used to categorise the answers into groups for each of the phases of the normative model, allowing for easy analysis of the answers to the interview questions.

The purpose of the research forum was to bring together various experts in the computer forensic field in Australia to brainstorm the current and emerging issues in the area of computer forensic methodology and competency standard development. During the brainstorming session, the issues raised were documented. At the end of the discussion, the experts were asked to give a level of importance and a rank to each issue using a Delphi technique (Sarantakos, 1998). Following on from the forum will be three more rounds of Delphi ranking and importance scaling where respondents will rank and give each issue a level of importance whilst also having the chance to raise additional issues.

4.3 Research Subjects

Contacts with subjects for the interviews were made during attendance at an industry e-Crime conference. The study population for this research consists of three main groups:

- Law enforcement agencies and Government Regulators
- Private sector organisations
- Independent associations

The first group consists of representatives from the Australian Federal Police (AFP) and various other law enforcement agencies (including the Royal Canadian Mounted Police - RCMP) and government regulators such as the Australian Securities and Investment Commission (ASIC).

A research group called the Computer Forensic Research Group (CFRG) consisting of representatives from ASIC, AFP, W.A Police, and NSW Police, and UNSW was formed for the purpose of developing a framework for the development of a methodology standard, and exploring competency standards. The law enforcement members of the group were also members of the Australian Computer Crime Managers Group (ACCMG), whose charter covers e-crime and computer forensic. The proposal for this study was presented at the ACCMG leading to the formation of the CFRG, and the launch of this research after approval from the ACCMG.

The second group consists of representatives from the large consulting companies and other private sector companies dealing with computer forensics. The third group consists of representatives from working groups and organisations that are addressing issues relating to computer forensics.

5. PROGRESS TO DATE

5.1 Research Forum Results

From the research forum, a number of issues were determined for the area of computer forensic methodology and competency standards development. These are listed below:

1. Need a definition for computer forensics. There are a number of different areas in computer forensics:
   - Digital Evidence Recovery
   - Cyber/Intrusion Forensics
   - Forensic Data Analysis
   - Research and Development – Keeping tools and processes up to a

standard, and development
across other specialised areas such as electrical engineering (communications)
2. Develop computer forensics as a multi-disciplinary occupation
3. Exploration and development of relationship between forensics, and security in terms of skills
4. Identify skills for computer forensic investigators through putting in place the correct methodologies which will drive the development of competencies.
5. Connections and communication between communities: forensic, legal, security, risk management, law enforcement etc
6. Knowledge and information sharing between public and private sector with regards to competencies and standards
7. Discussion of privacy grades and context
8. Investigate ethical issues and acceptable levels
9. Define what elements or parts of the computer forensic field require or would benefit from the development of standards
10. Technical nature of standards
11. Explore the difference between civil and criminal investigations with respect to standards
12. Why do you need methodologies and standards?
13. Compile a stock take of interests and stakeholders
14. Set up of a Working group/professional body
15. Development of a testing mechanism for the methodology
16. Who to appoint as an accreditation body.
17. Setting up accreditation for various roles involved in investigating computer crimes

Each of the forum attendees filled out a Delphi rating system, rating each issue with a level of importance and also ranking all issues with an importance ranking. From the initial forum round of the Delphi study, the following top five issues relating to computer forensics methodology emerged:

- Need for a definition of computer forensics
- Define what elements or parts of the computer forensic field require or would benefit from the development of standards
- Who to appoint as an accreditation body and the setting up accreditation for various roles involved in investigating computer crimes
- Knowledge and information sharing between public and private sector with regards to competencies and standards

- Identify skills for computer forensic investigators through putting in place the correct methodologies which will drive the development of competencies.

Having derived these seventeen issues from the research forum, they have been sent to representatives from the Australian computer crime managers group who are currently completing the first round of the Delphi study. Following completion of this first round, the averaged results will be the fed back to participants together with their own ratings and rankings, and the participants will be requested to complete the second round of the Delphi study.

5.2 Methodology Development

The five phases of the normative methodology set out in Table 1 form the basis for a normative methodology model. This four-layer model, as shown in Figure 2, is used to illustrate the main components of any computer forensic methodology. The first layer defines the five high-level phases that are to be performed in any computer forensic investigation. Each phase in this layer is dependent on the previous and all phases must visited in turn. This layer is applicable to all cases and should be developed to be independent of factors that may change such as jurisdictions, tools and techniques.

The next three layers support the top layer but have been broken down logically into three layers. The documentation layer supports the top layer by providing a source of reference and repository for all the information gathered throughout the five steps. In essence, the first and second layer can be thought of as one layer where documentation is an ongoing and a cumulative process. The third layer, contains principles which support the above two layers by dictating the how to perform each of the phases. The fourth layer, standard operating procedures details the lo level process description of tools and techniques that are used throughout the process. The layer is technology specific and thus differs between cases, technologies and countries and changes with the dynamic nature of the IT industry. This layer includes definitions of tools, their applicability and expected results. In addition to this, this layer includes several standard operating procedures which detail techniques that are used at the lowest level e.g. how to perform a bit-level backup of a hard disk.

Preparation Identification Preservation Analysis Presentation
Documentation
Guidelines
SOP/Tools/Techniques

Figure 2. The Normative Methodology Mode

The modular structure of the model allows each layer to be interchangeable and independent of the other layers. This promotes flexibility of each component and allows for reuse and customisation of each component for different cases or for use in different jurisdictions or countries. For example, two cases will differ primarily by the different tools and techniques that will be used, and somewhat on the rules and guidelines that are relevant. However, the overlying process that is taken to investigate the crime, as described in the top layer of the model, will be identical for both cases. Similarly, as technology changes, the tools and techniques will change in accordance with the changing technologies. The top layer will remain unchanged despite the subsequent changes to the bottom layer. Differences across jurisdictions and countries should be evident primarily in the middle layer, as different laws will effect the rules and guidelines for handling evidence.In theory, using this model will produce an internationally applicable methodology, which is flexible to the differing rules, standards and regulations and to the changing technology. This model has many strengths:

- It is applicable to many cases.
- The top layer is supported by rules and guidelines
- The structure can cope with changing technology and dynamic environments
- Change will generally only effect the bottom layer (as technology is the most dynamic)
- As the computer forensic field is mainly in the law enforcement industry, dealing with crime, the model is easily adapted to accommodate the sensitive nature of some of the tools and techniques that law enforcement agencies may use. The first three layers can be made public as they

contain little material that is sensitive in nature, and the bottom layer can be proprietary. Thus, the bottom layer is interchangeable. Additionally, because the second layer dictates rules for evidence handling, evidence can be easily exchanged without releasing the method for retrieving the evidence.

- The bottom layer is made up of toolkits and Standard operating procedures (SOP's)

Currently a standard computer forensics methodology has been developed from the literature and derived out of results from the semi-structured questionnaires and interviews. This standard methodology consists of seven phases and forty two steps within those seven phases. A summary of these phases is set out in Table 2.

Phase of the Derived Model	Description
Preparation	The preparation stage involves preparing the personnel, materials and tools and equipment required for the computer forensic examination.
Identification	The identification phase involves securing the scene and identifying the evidence from the data set.
Baseline	The baseline phase involves testing of original evidence to provide a baseline or control result for future verifications to ensure consistency and accuracy.
Preservation	The preservation phase involves backing up, protecting and preserving the evidence to prevent tampering and damage
Verification	The verifications phase involves testing of outputs/results to ensure consistency and accuracy. Failure at this stage may dictate a return to the identification and preservation phases.
Analysis	This involves the extraction, processing and interpretation of the digital data.
Presentation	This stage involves preparing the case and evidence for court

Table 2. Derived Standard Computer Forensic Methodology Phases

To complement the standard computer forensics methodology, a list of twenty seven principles were derived from the semi structured questionnaires and interviews, together with a skills matrix and documentation required for each phase within the standard computer forensics methodology. Three examples of principles would be: storage equipment should be sterilised if possible; comply with search warrant/Anton pillar principles/ or gain users consent at all times: maintaining continuity of evidence -- account for any change to the data set/evidence. The following three examples illustrate the skills required to carry out computer forensics examination: knowledge of possible sources of evidence; computer software knowledge and experience of specific operating system and network operating systems related knowledge; knowledge of and experience with computer forensics tools - their operation and limitations. Examples of required documentation would include: search warrants; mud maps - an initial sketch of surroundings equipment and items; and forensics software log files.

Currently the standard computer forensics methodology, principles, the skills matrix and documentation derived from the research are being reviewed by representatives from the Australian Computer Crime Managers Group. Following this review, the results will be released into the public domain and be published.

6. CONCLUSIONS

This paper reviewed existing methodologies and the discussed the development of a standard computer forensic methodology. The issues raised open possible areas of future research in the computer forensics field for developing best practice or a standard methodology for international computer forensic investigators and investigating agencies. The shortfalls of traditional models, which also needs further investigation, suggest that there may be a better approach that could be taken to combat e-crime. There are also questions regarding the viability of accrediting computer forensic methodologies, techniques and investigators. This area is particularly important, as the results of such research will have influence on the way CFA's conduct investigations, as well as the training required for investigators. The availability of a standard computer forensic methodology and an accreditation device should improve the quality of computer forensic investigations in addition to advancing the computer forensic field to a recognised profession.

The idea of a proactive computer forensic methodology combined with the rules, guidelines and existing experience in the computer forensic field, may lead to an open standard international methodology, which is applicable to most cases and to computer evidence. This new methodology may be able to combat the shortfalls of traditional methodologies.

For certain, any future or standard methodology developed must include evidence handling procedures and principles, and must be independent of the tools and digital media. This will ensure that the methodology will be widely applicable to cases well into the future, despite the ever-changing technology.

ACKNOWLEDGEMENTS

The authors wish to acknowledge the contributions made by the members of the Australian Computer Crime Managers Group, ASIC, AUSTRAC, PWC, Deloitte Touche Tohmatsu, KPMG, for their time and patience in completion of the questionnaires and interviews, and their reviews of the resulting frameworks. Also to the members of the e-Crime and e-Forensics Research Forum held in September 2001 by the Security, E-business, and Assurance Research Group (SEAR- sear.web.unsw.edu.au) for their contributions of research issues leading to the development and conduct of this research. The authors also wish to acknowledge the contribution by Ken Stevens for his help in reviewing the research.

REFERENCES

ACPR (2000), The Virtual Horizon: Meeting the Law Enforcement Challenges - Developing an Australasian law enforcement strategy for dealing with electronic crime, Report Series No: 134.1, Police Commissioners' Conference Electronic Crime Working Party, Australasian Centre for Policing Research, Adelaide.

ACPO, (2000), Memorandum by the Association of Chief Police Officers Computer Crime Working Group URL=www.parliament.the-stationery-office.co.uk/pa/ld199900 /ldselect/ldeucom/95/0031502.htm

AIC (1999), What is Forensic Computing, Australian Institute of Criminology – Trends and Issues No. 118, June, URL=www.aic.gov.au/publications/tandi/tandi118.html

Blaike, N. (2000), Designing Social Research, Polity.

CFRG (2001), Meeting minutes for the CFRG meeting, Australian Computer Crime Managers Group – Computer Forensics Research Group, 15 October 2001

CSI/FBI (2001), 2001 CSI/FBI Computer Crime and Security Survey, Computer Security Issues and Trends, 7 (1), Spring, 1-18.

Cerpa, N. & R. Jamieson (2001), A Security Trust and Assurance Research Framework for Electronic Commerce, Proceedings of the IFIP TC8 Working Conference on Electronic Commerce, Salzburg, Austria, 22-23 June.

Denzin, N.K. & Y. S. Lincoln, (1994), Handbook of Qualitative Research, Sage Publications.

FBI (2000a), Three-Level Hierarchical Model for Developing Guidelines for Computer Forensic Evidence, Forensic Science Communications, October 2000, 2 (4), URL = http://www.fbi.gov/hq/lab/fsc/backissu/oct2000/cmptrf1.htm

FBI (2000b), Recovering and Examining Computer Forensic Evidence, Forensic Science Communications, October, 2 (4), URL = www.fbi.gov/hq/lab/fsc/backissu/ oct2000/computer..htm

IDG News Service (2001), Update: Thirty countries sign cybercrime treaty, IDG News Service, 23 Nov 2001.

Lek, M., Anandarajah, B., Cerpa, N. & R. Jamieson (2001), Data Mining Prototype for Detecting e-Commerce Fraud, Proceedings of the ECIS'2001, Bled Slovenia, 27-29 June.

McKemmish, R. (1998), Report from the 1998 Donald Mackay Churchill Fellowship to Study Overseas Development in Forensic Computing, The Winston Churchill Memorial Trust of Australia, Brisbane.

McKeown, M. & R. Jamieson, (2001). Computer Forensics – Intrusion Detection, SEAR Working Paper, UNSW, Sydney, November, No 2001_3.

Myers M. D. (2001), Qualitative Research in Information Systems, URL = www2.auckland.ac.nz/msis/isworld, October.

Rehman Technology Services. (2000), Computer Forensics, Electronic Discovery, Electronic Evidence Discovery, Digital Discovery, Computer Analysis, Computer Examination, Computer Expert, URL = electronic-discovery.com (2000, October 26)

Rao, V., Cerpa, N. & R. Jamieson, (2001), A Comparison of Online Electronic Commerce Assurance Service Providers in Australia, Proceedings of the Fourteen Bled Electronic Commerce Conference, Slovenia, 24-26 June, 2001.

Rude, T. (2000), Evidence Seizure Methodology for Computer Forensics, September 2000, URL = www.crazytrain.com/seizure.html

Saferstein, R. (1998), Criminalistics: An Introduction to Forensic Science, 6th ed., Prentice Hall, Upper Saddle River, New Jersey.

Sarantakos, S, (1998). Social Research, MacMillan.

SC Magazine (2000), Computer Forensics April 2001, SC Magazine URL = www.scmagazine.com/scmagazine/2000_04/cover/cover.html

Stephenson, P. (1999), Investigating Computer-Related Crime, CRC Press.

Tennyenhuis A & Jamieson R (2001), Computer Forensics Methodologies, SEAR Working Paper, UNSW, Sydney, September, No 2001_2.

Wieszyk, M. (1998a), Computer Evidence Search & Seizure: Results of National Surveys & Interviews – A report for the national police research unit, ACPR, Adelaide.

Wieszyk, M. (1998b), Computer Evidence search & Seizure, Research Masters thesis.

Wong, K., Ng, B., Cerpa, N., & R. Jamieson (2000), An Online Audit Review System for Electronic Commerce, Proceedings of the Thirteen Bled Electronic Commerce Conference, Slovenia, 19-21.

Wright, T. (2000), The Field Guide for Investigating Computer Crime: Overview of a Methodology for the Application of Computer Forensics Part 2, URL = www.securityfocus.com/focus/ih/articles/crimeguide2.html.

THE POTENTIALITIES OF FOCUS GROUPS IN E-BUSINESS RESEARCH: THEORY VALIDATION

Sharman Lichtenstein[1] and Paula M.C. Swatman[2]
[1]*School of Information Systems, Faculty of Business and Law, Deakin University, Australia*
[2] *Institute for Management, Faculty of Informatics, University of Koblenz-Landau, Germany*

Abstract: Focus groups enable the rapid and timely collation, integration and assembly of the views of a variety of different types of stakeholders into plausible theory. This paper examines the usefulness of the focus group as an e-business research method, using an exemplar of focus group deployment for the purpose of theory validation as its illustration. Our results suggest that a focus group can be effective as a strategy in e-business research, providing a useful alternative or complementary method to more traditional empirical methods. We provide a set of guidelines for effective focus groups in e-business research, which may prove useful to researchers contemplating employing the focus group method in a research design.

1. INTRODUCTION

With e-business being a comparatively recent phenomenon, there is still a scarcity of robust research literature to draw on for theory development, necessitating a significant amount of empirical research in order to ground new theory. E-business researchers face important challenges identifying appropriate methods for their needs (Clarke, 2000a). Frequently, issues relating to the multi-disciplinary, interorganisational nature of e-business must be explored (Clarke, 2001). Comprehensive coverage and in-depth analysis of the extensive issues involved often require debating between stakeholders to enable issues in contention to surface. Understanding is sought of "the behaviour of individuals, organisations and mechanisms such as e-communities, marketspaces and e-enhanced societies" (Clarke, 2001). Approaches which facilitate the development of integrated, holistic solutions, and facilitate solutions of relevance for both practitioners and e-business researchers are also key requirements in e-business research.

This wish list of empirical research methods for the e-business domain suggests that there is scope for examining the benefits of alternative approaches to the more traditional approaches – often examplied by case studies and surveys. We believe that the focus group method has significant potential to address the challenges listed above, providing a complementary tool for empirical researchers in this rapidly-growing field of academic endeavour. Focus groups are a relatively recent addition to the repertoire of empirical information systems (IS) research methods, although they have a much longer history in the field of marketing research (see, for example, Hasan and Tibbits, 1999; Law and Lee-Partridge, 2001; Lichtenstein, 2001) so that there has, to date, been little empirical research into their use as a research method for either IS or e-business research. Recently, focus groups were nominated by Clarke (2001) as being amongst the viable methods for e-business research – although it is interesting that he did not single them out in his final recommendations. We believe, however, that focus groups offer some very real advantages for e-business research, in that they enable the rapid and timely collation, integration and assembly of the views of a variety of different types of stakeholders from multiple disciplines and different institutions into relevant, plausible theory, in a relatively short period of time.

The objective of this paper is to investigate the usefulness of the focus group research method for e-business research. We employ the example of a focus group in e-business theory validation, to illustrate the potential effectiveness of focus groups in e-business research.

The paper commences by providing an overview of the focus group research method. The following section articulates some important challenges for e-business research, highlighting the role focus groups can play in addressing these challenges. Next, we describe an example of the use of a focus group for theory validation in an e-business research project, illustrating the advantages of the focus group for our research project. We then present a set of guidelines for effective focus groups in theory validation in e-business research, and conclude by outlining the implications of our research results for e-business researchers and for businesses.

2. THE FOCUS GROUP RESEARCH METHOD

A focus group is a qualitative research method, positioned somewhere between participant observation and in-depth interviews (Morgan, 1997), and often referred to as a group interview. Focus group sessions consist of semi-structured panel discussions between a small group of people representing a specific target audience – for example, key stakeholders – which provide relaxed *fora* for discourse and for the exchange, exploration and testing of ideas, feedback, brainstorming and discovery; while generating valuable qualitative research information representing critical client interests (Edmunds, 2000; Greenbaum, 1998; Morgan, 1997; Morgan and Krueger, 1998; Morrison, 1998; Templeton, 1996). Discussions are led by a moderator, who is able to tap genuine feelings and issues about the research topic, while remaining aloof from the issues under discussion. A focus group can be used as the principal data source, a supplementary data source following a primary method such as a survey, and in multi-method studies where independent data sources are used (Morgan, 1997).

Most commonly employed as a marketing research technique, focus groups typically yield ideas insights and directions for new products, packaging, advertising, and consumer habits, and for screening new concepts. Organisations also use focus groups to investigate their customers' beliefs, attitudes and perceptions about current business policies, programmes and services. Recent developments include the use of synchronous or asynchronous online focus groups (Edmunds, 2000; Murray; 1997; Rezabek, 2000).

Criticisms of the focus group approach have included: their limited generalisability due to the small number of people participating, together with the possibility that these participants may not be a representative sample; their inadequacy for forming conclusive opinions and yes/no decision-making; the significant effect of the moderator, who must maintain control of the forum so that forceful personalities do not sway the group, and in order that the timid and polite get a chance to speak up; the tendency for participants to "play into the hands of the researcher" by agreeing with ideas that they may not believe in reality; and the insufficiency of this research method when employed as the sole source of data (Gibbs, 1997; Nucifora, 1997). Despite these criticisms, however (and which research method does not have weaknesses?), we believe that the genuine benefits which focus groups can offer to e-business research significantly outweigh their weaknesses.

3. ADVANTAGES OF FOCUS GROUPS IN E-BUSINESS RESEARCH

There are some important challenges facing e-business researchers when approaching the selection of empirical methods. We elaborate on these challenges below, and discuss the potential advantages of focus groups for meeting them.

3.1 Multi-disciplinary and interorganisational nature of e-business

The need for multi-disciplinary research approaches to e-business problems is now considered pressing (Kumar and Crook, 1999; Vogel, 2001). Reference disciplines for e-business issues include sociology, anthropology, politics, economics, management, law, computer science, engineering, architecture, health sciences and history (Vogel, 2001), each offering a quite different perspective on any given e-business issue. In addition, stakeholders often include business-oriented and systems-oriented groups, which typically offer discordant views (Gordijn *et al.*, 2001). When traditional empirical methods such as case studies, action research, or surveys are employed, the researcher must frequently interpret and reconcile uncertain and/or conflicting sets of data harvested from a variety of stakeholders and disciplines via interviews and/or questionnaires. Later attempts to resolve contradictions in isolation from the human sources of data can mean that the researcher establishes results which compromise the various viewpoints subjectively, rather than integrating them to produce a broader, holistic solution. For example, the researcher – lacking the opportunity to recycle the developing theory amongst stakeholders to incorporate all viewpoints – may prefer one type of stakeholder's viewpoint over others, or formulate a subjective compromise between several differing stakeholder viewpoints.

Interorganisational issues are regarded as critical to e-business success (Geisler, 2001). Holland and Lockett (1997) and Kampas (2000) argued that interorganisational relations may contribute to an understanding of how e-commerce organisations evolve and succeed, while Johnston and Gregor (2000) advocated the examination of electronic networks of organisations at an industry level. Using traditional empirical methods such as case studies and surveys, there may not be sufficient opportunity to capture and explore the many interorganisational issues involved in e-business research projects, because the opportunity for debate between personnel in the different organisations is lacking in such methods and because comparisons across organisational boundaries are difficult both to establish and to validate (the danger of finding oneself comparing apples and oranges is ever-present in interorganisational empirical research). And yet it is imperative to undertake such interorganisational studies to gain deeper understanding of e-business phenomena of various sorts.

A focus group can be a valuable research method whenever the opinion of a target population is difficult to obtain due to either a multidimensional topic, or to polarised or fluid opinions (Clarke, 2000b): this is a common scenario in the multi-disciplinary and interorganisational e-business domain. Through a focus group, representative stakeholders for the reference disciplines and different types of organisations may be brought together in a controlled environment, in order to: offer potentially discordant opinions and perspectives; discuss previously identified issues; identify and resolve conflicts; uncover new issues; and establish conciliatory yet feasible, integrated, holistic solutions.

3.2 Extensive issues in e-business research topics

There are a large number and variety of issues involved in many e-business topic areas. These have proven difficult to explore and identify comprehensively within the constraints of data collection via either questionnaires or single person interviews – during which issues resulting from potential conflict between different stakeholder viewpoints are unlikely to be uncovered, debated or explored; and during which brainstorming is not facilitated.

Within a focus group session, those issues for which there is ready agreement among participants can be passed over quickly, with most of the time and attention being directed to issues in contention, or to the uncovering of new issues (note that the brainstorming activities characteristic of focus groups are conducive to the discovery and illumination of new information and issues). The potential for researching often-overlooked issues relating to a given e-business research topic thus exists within focus groups and can be used to great advantage in an e-business research project.

3.3 Holistic approaches to e-business research

Technical issues were the focus of IS research until recent years, in accord with the now-outdated technical-economic rationality which assumed an organisational goal of economic efficiency and effectiveness via technology deployment (Kumar *et al.*, 1998; Kling, 1980). The focus has recently shifted in both IS and e-business research toward more holistic approaches which integrate the human, social, organisational and technical issues (Baskerville *et al.*, 2000; Bennetts *et al.*, 2000; Cavaye, 1998; Lichtenstein, 1997; 2001; Lichtenstein and Swatman, 2001; McMichael, 1999; Russo *et a.l*, 2001; Vogel, 2001). It can be difficult for case studies (whether positivist, or utilising more interpretivist approaches such as ethnographic surveys or grounded theory approaches) and surveys alone to yield an integrated holistic solution to an e-business research problem, because the method of collection is a single viewpoint, without opportunity for debate between stakeholders. There are complementary techniques such as Delphi surveys (see, for example Delbecq *et al.*, 1975), or a combination of quantitative with qualitative methods (see Gable, 1994, for a discussion of this issue) which can make a real contribution to linking individual viewpoints to arrive at a solution. While we in no way criticise any of these approaches, focus groups offer an alternative approach with some unique holistic benefits.

Indeed, focus groups – being a moderated interview of multiple perspectives – facilitate debate, which can lead to conflict resolution, theme exploration, pattern identification, and collaborative, holistic solution development. The potential for over-focusing on a single dimension (for example, technology) is minimised in a focus group by the accessibility of differing perspectives from participants with backgrounds in different disciplines and organisations, all of whom can argue their perspectives until they are incorporated in the solution. Human, social, organisational and technical issues relevant to the research problem are all likely to be raised during a session, and a solution can be devised which accommodates and integrates the various dimensions, forming an entity greater than the sum of the individual perspectives.

3.4 Relevance of e-business research

E-business is a highly dynamic area, so that the need to conduct research speedily may be pressing, in order that the research outcomes still have relevance for practitioners and researchers alike (Clarke, 2000a; Gray, 2001; Kock *et al.*, 2001). In a recent ISWORLD debate questioning the relevance of IS research, Amaravadi proposed: "a Kuhnian vision of rationalization of [information systems – of which e-business is a domain] research …that can clarify the channels, make progress visible, make summaries available, streamline the research process and improve relevance" (Weber and Cockcroft, 2001). Relevance versus rigour in IS research has previously been deliberated (Benbasat and Zmud, 1999; Davenport and Markus, 1999), but there is an argument which suggests it is even more an issue for e-business, with its rapid growth, wide-ranging issues and interorganisational focus. Indeed, some experts believe that expediting research and assuring its relevance, while potentially sacrificing a degree of rigour, may well be critical for e-business research (Clarke, 2001).

A focus group can improve e-business research relevance by including representatives from different stakeholder types and reference disciplines, in the group. Furthermore, sessions may be organised quickly, take a short time to conduct – typically, several hours – and can thus yield research outcomes relatively speedily.

4. THE FOCUS GROUP IN E-BUSINESS RESEARCH

We feel focus groups have considerable potential to assist in the validation of e-business research. In any area that is relatively new, business-oriented and multi-disciplinary, theory validation is a constant issue. We used the focus group approach to validate the findings of a major e-business security research project (reported in Lichtenstein, 2001; Lichtenstein and Swatman, 2001). In the project, we investigated the management of Internet security issues for organisations conducting e-business, by an organisational e-business security policy. In particular, we were interested in determining an holistic solution, incorporating the human, societal, technical, organisational and other influential factors. In 1996 at the time the project commenced, there were few guidelines in this topic area. Literature sources from a variety of disciplines were employed to construct an initial framework for organisational e-business security policy (the final version of the highest level model of the framework is depicted in Figure 1). The framework comprised various models and issues at different levels of detail, representing three sets of guidelines—a set of *factors* to be considered when developing the policy, a method for the *development* of the policy, and a model for the *content* of the policy. Details of this framework are found in Lichtenstein (2001), and are not included here due to space limitations.

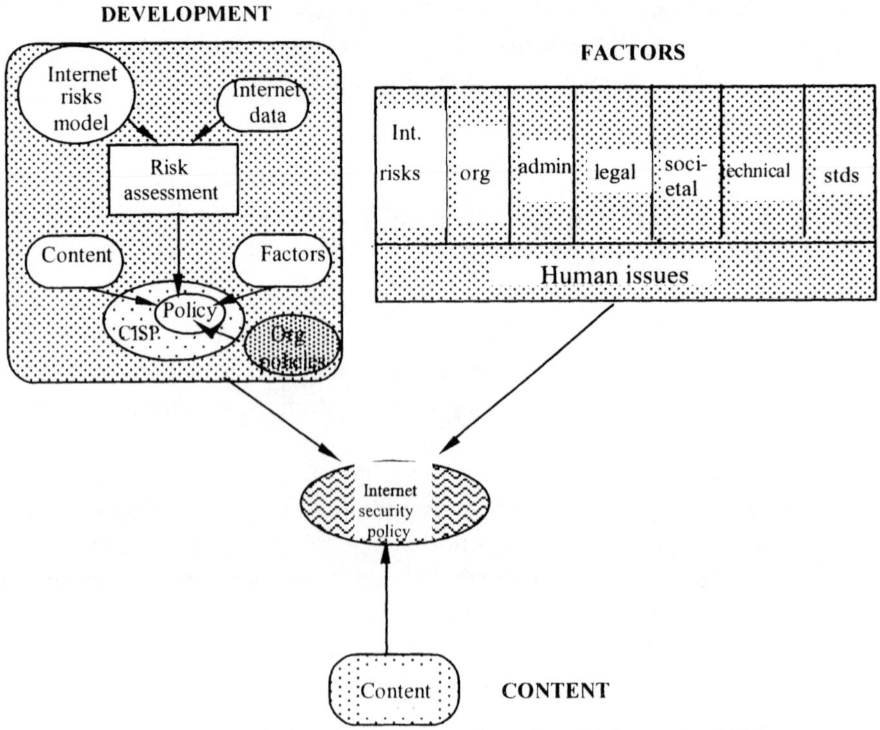

Figure 1. Framework for e-business security policy (Lichtenstein, 2001)

We explored the research topic further via multiple case studies of six large organisations (five Australian and one US), selected for their significant Internet usage at the time of study. We conducted semi-structured interviews with network administrators and IT security managers, who appeared to have the greatest in-depth knowledge of what was actually happening in their organisastions in the complex Internet security area. We analysed the data collected in each case, using the initial version of the framework as a guide for pattern-matching purposes, then performed a cross-case analysis across the six cases, to determine commonalities, trends, and differences, and to draw conclusions from these for the research project.

4.1 Selection of focus group method for theory validation

We then faced the problem of choosing another research method to validate the framework, in order to obtain triangulation for our research results. We examined our research progress at that point and, particularly, identified areas of insufficiency in data collected and solutions devised so far. While conducting the case studies, it had become apparent that there were limitations to the data we were able to collect via single interviews, documents, etc:

- The type of personnel we had selected for interviewing were network administrators and IT security managers, whom we had presumed to be most knowledgeable about the security of their e-business systems. Yet many issues arose about which they clearly lacked the expertise to provide in-depth comments – including social, human resources, legal, engineering, administration and organisational culture issues.
- In several instances, two people from the same organisation were interviewed in the one interview session – for example the network administrator and the IT security manager. In each such interview, conflict and tension were apparent between the two parties, raising some interesting issues that we were not able to explore or resolve, due the constraints of the interview technique. We also suspected that in those interviews there were issues left unraised, due to the reluctance of interviewees concerned to highlight certain problems with co-workers present.
- We suspected that at times interviewees had contributed politically correct responses, while on other occasions they did not appear to be sufficiently stimulated to suggest potential solutions to problems revealed in the interviews (for example, almost all the parties interviewed deemed the control of excessive personal use of the Internet by employees, impossible).
- On occasion, we suspected interviewees were being too agreeable in their responses, inside an interview environment, which was not conducive to challenging the framework components offered for discussion.
- Solutions suggested by interviewees to existing problems were typically one-dimensional in nature (eg an Internet risk management technology) rather than holistic.

When analysing the multiple case data via a cross-case analysis, the inadequacies of our collected data became even more evident. Our framework had identified a plethora of relevant issues, many of which were unclear from the case interviews and other organisational data sources such as policy documents. Could auditors, for example, have provided useful information about the conduct of security audits and about security standards, which would have added to the models? Could human resource experts have added more understanding about employee rights and recommended we include those issues in our models? Would employees think our framework was missing some important problems they faced in

Internet usage? Would a consultant find the methodology suitable for customer approval? The multi-disciplinary nature of e-business was proving to be a thorn in the research agenda. Importantly, we also wondered whether all these different perspectives would clash, and if so, how would contentious issues be resolved to the satisfaction of all? We wondered whether a group of people representing the different perspectives might be able to argue through the issues in the research problem and framework, under the supervision of an impartial moderator fluent in the topic.

It seemed that a focus group could be ideally suited for this purpose. We began investigating the focus group research method for its potential advantages. We anticipated that any solutions arising out of a meeting of diverse experts from different disciplines would be likely to be holistic. We also recognised the potential benefit in selecting participants from different organisations – to stimulate debate over interorganisational issues involved in the research topic. After some deliberation, we chose the focus group method for the validation stage of the research project.

4.2 Establishment and conduct of focus group session

We established and conducted a focus group comprised of a moderator – an academic with a solid background in the research domain – and five experts with different job roles representing different perspectives and disciplines (we have taken some liberty here with the term 'discipline', for the purposes of highlighting the different reference points from which participants were approaching the research problem). Each participant was employed at a different organisation. The roles and reference disciplines of the five participants were: network administrator (within a specifically computer science -oriented domain), telecommunications consultant (engineering, sales and management), auditor (accounting), computer user (human resources), and programmer/analyst (information systems). Note that the views of medium level IT managers had already been heavily polled via interviews with IT security managers in the case studies, so we did not include any of this stakeholder type in the focus group.

A document containing background information on the project as well as the framework itself, was despatched to all participants ahead of the session date. The meeting took place as a three hour session, in June, 1998, in a special observation laboratory designed for such activities, located at Monash University in Melbourne, Australia. The room possessed video cameras and audio recording facilities. The session was video-recorded for subsequent study. One of the researchers was able to view the session from the room next door through a one-way window, as well as listen to the proceedings through speakers. She was also able to communicate with the moderator via a microphone which transmitted to an earpiece worn by the moderator. She employed this communication facility from time to time to request the moderator to follow up issues of particular importance, as well as to ask the moderator to seek clarification where deemed necessary.

The moderator began the session by requesting introductions, and explaining the focus group objectives, which were:

- to determine whether an e-business security policy was considered an important policy for Internet-connected companies;
- to determine whether the proposed framework and its component models could be useful to companies;
- to improve the framework;
- to elicit recommendations regarding the presentation of the framework as a commercial methodology; and
- to determine the overall usefulness of the research project.

Next, he asked each participant to explain his/her company's interest in the research project, and queried participant positions regarding the research topic. He then led the group through a review of the document containing the topics, issues, framework and component models, encouraging a free flow of ideas and brainstorming, and steering the discussion when necessary to determine support or lack thereof for the framework and its models, or to elicit suggestions for changes.

In the interests of limiting the size of this paper, only selected aspects of the session are presented, illustrative of the advantages presented by focus groups for e-business theory validation.

4.3 Status of e-business security policies in organisations

Participants agreed the research topic was important to their companies, few of which possessed e-business security policies, or found them effective when they did have them (recall the session was held in mid-1998). All participants mentioned the difficulty in monitoring and enforcing existing or future policy. They supported one another in a discussion of the depth and importance of this problem. What was painted by the group was a fairly bleak overall picture of diffusion and effectiveness of e-business security policies in the workplace, a picture which had not emerged from the case studies. On reflection, it appeared that the interviewees in the case studies may have whitewashed their company's problems in this area. This part of the session discussion, about the status of e-business security policies, highlights the advantages of a focus group for identifying the level of relevance and importance of a research topic to stakeholder groups.

4.4 Factors in e-business security policy

The focus group discussed at length the special position of the *human issues* factor in the factors model (Figure 2). The network administrator (representing the computer science discipline) was initially convinced that human issues did not need to be treated differently to the various other factors in the model. He did not see why all other issues had to be considered in light of the human issues involved. One participant was adamant that human issues should remain in its current, special position in the model, pointing out that if human issues were treated as just another factor to be considered in policy setting, then not as many human issues would be identified as if the various other factors were seen *through* the filter of human issues. Another participant stressed that his company would not accept the model unless human issues were highlighted as shown in the current model. The remaining three participants were gradually won over in discussion by the arguments raised by the two who clearly saw human issues as critical to all other issues. This discussion highlights the advantage of a focus group for dealing with contentious issues caused by the *multi-disciplinary* and *interorganisational* nature of e-business. It also illustrated the capacity of this method to act as an agent of change in the research domain, and added richness to the detail of the framework.

4.5 Internet risks, organisational factors, and human issues in e-business security policy

Participants suggested *a number of changes* to the proposed models for Internet risks, organisational factors and human issues. For example, one participant identified a new organisational factor, *organisational culture* – a factor which we believe came to light because participants, when acting as a group, appeared to be more in tune with people and soft issues in general, than had been the individual interviewees during the earlier case study (single person) interviews. The moderator may also have played a key role in raising the group's awareness of the people issues involved in the research topic. This part of the session highlighted the advantages of a focus group for exploring extensive issues relating to a complex e-business research topic. It also highlighted the advantages of the focus group for tapping and debating the different perspectives of the representatives of different reference disciplines, from different organisations.

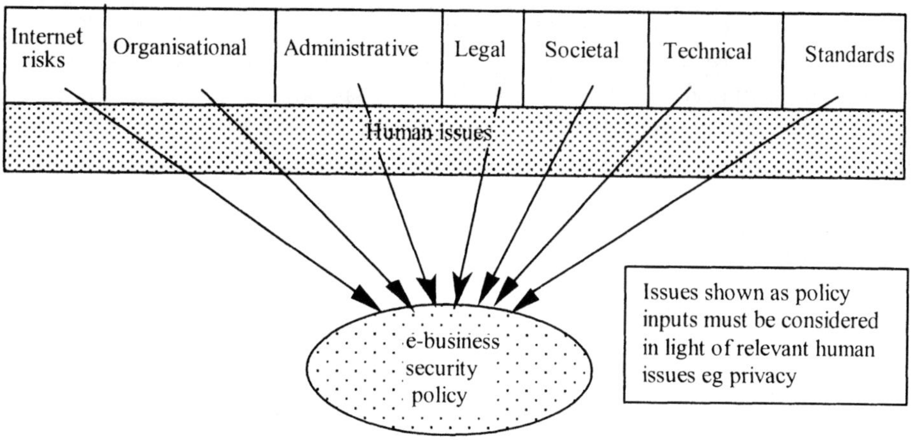

Figure 2. Factors in e-business security policy

4.6 Freedom of Internet use in e-business security policy

Participants engaged in a heated debate about whether there should be restrictions on the freedom to use the Internet for personal reasons in the workplace. Each participant had a different view, depending on their personal perspective, organization represented, and reference discipline. The resulting solution – *limited personal use as necessary* – was an holistic one, highlighting the usefulness of the focus group method for producing holistic solutions.

Altogether, many models and issues were discussed in the session. We have discussed only a small portion of these above, sufficient to illustrate the benefits of the focus group method for e-business research.

4.7 Methodology for e-business security policy

The moderator concluded the meeting by asking participants whether they thought the framework was a good starting point for an organisation to develop an e-business security policy, and whether the framework would have a useful outcome in practice. One participant responded that the framework would be useful as a commercial methodology when polished and expanded as suggested during the session. A second participant commented that the required content was present in the framework and that it met the research objectives, but that its presentation could be improved by a document design expert to make the framework more useable as a methodology for an organisation. A third participant, the auditor, advised that he wished to use the framework, with permission, as a guide for an impending Internet audit. A fourth participant commented, "It (the framework) was great," but added that it needed to be revised by a legal team and a publicising team, prior to finalisation. The fifth participant believed the framework was very comprehensive, and mentioned that if a particular company wanted to use it, they would surely find the means to handle various practicalities that had been mentioned during the session. This conclusion to the focus group highlights the usefulness of the method for suggesting research relevance for practitioners, and for providing an holistic solution that meets the needs of different types of stakeholders.

Clearly, the focus group fulfilled our theory validation needs, as well as providing the specific benefits suggested earlier in Section 3.

5. MAKING FOCUS GROUPS WORK FOR E-BUSINESS RESEARCH

As a result of this study, we have developed the following guidelines for effective use of focus groups in theory validation in e-business research.

5.1 Composition of focus group: multi-disciplinary and multi-organisational

The composition of the focus group should be multi-disciplinary and multi-organisational. While it is clearly infeasible to include within a single focus group session representatives from all types of e-business disciplines and organisations, a considered and balanced selection process will minimise this limitation. In such a selection process, the researcher should attempt to identify a wide spectrum of e-business disciplines and organisational types relevant to the topic area. The researcher should be *au fait* with key issues in e-business. Clearly, the availability of expertise will also be an important factor in the selection process. The researcher must search for a homogenous mix of disciplines and organisations by postulating, evaluating and comparing different combinations, aiming for the most comfortable and productive interactions between participants. The intent is to forge an insightful focus group, whose participants share common goals, but possess the diverse skills and perspectives of the different disciplines and organisational types.

5.2 Direct discussion to conflicting multi-disciplinary, interorganisational issues

The focus group should direct its attention to the conflicting multi-disciplinary, interorganisational issues of e-business. The moderator should draw participants' attention to points of possible discord, which tend to lie in the areas where different disciplines and organisations involved in e-business would have differing perspectives to put forward, debate and resolve. The moderator should encourage the participants to discuss and resolve the issues, without his/her interference if possible. This is more likely to yield a genuine, rather than a contrived, solution.

5.3 Documentation of existing theory must be available and structured

The models which comprise the theory to be validated should be available to participants as documents, both before and during the session. Models should be structured and presented in such a way that participants can easily move back and forth between them as necessary during the session, with minimal disturbance to the flow and momentum of the session. Terminology which may be confusing to participants from different reference disciplines should be clearly defined.

5.4 Encourage discussion of different perspectives

The moderator must carefully lead the participants through the theory, explaining any models and giving ample opportunity for the provision of varied perspectives from participants representing different disciplines and organisations in e-business – particularly on issues that the researcher has highlighted beforehand as likely to be contentious. It is useful if the researcher is able communicate with the moderator during the session, to ask the moderator to seek clarification or more information where needed (although this should be a relatively transparent and seamless process in order not to disturb session momentum; this communication can be performed remotely, using an earpiece and microphone).

5.5 Moderator should promote brainstorming, to elicit new issues

The moderator should make judicious use of brainstorming at key points, to identify more of the many issues often involved in an e-business topic area.

5.6 Moderator should attempt to maintain session momentum until discussion has resulted in integrated, holistic solutions

The moderator needs to be very aware of the need to integrate the differing perspectives of the different types of participants gathered to represent different reference disciplines in e-business. The moderator is aiming for compromise, consensus, and an integrated, holistic solution.

5.7 Moderator must be highly knowledgeable in e-business and the specific research domain

The moderator needs to be well-versed in e-business, as well as the specific theory being validated. S/he also needs to be aware of those issues regarded as likely to cause contention due to differing perspectives from the different disciplines involved in e-business – in order to direct attention to those topics.

5.8 Moderator must search for research relevance

The moderator must continually be aware of the need for the research to have relevance to previously-defined target audiences, such as practitioners and researchers. For example, if the theory is being developed in order to be utilised by businesses, then the moderator should seek such confirmation, at key points during the session.

6. CONCLUSIONS

We have presented in this paper some important challenges facing e-business researchers today, and have argued the potentialities of focus groups for addressing these challenges. Our case study of focus group use in a significant e-business research project provides support for our view of the usefulness of focus groups in e-business research, in particular for theory validation, which is often a problematic stage for researchers seeking an appropriate method. We have presented a set of guidelines for the effective use of focus groups in e-business theory validation. These may prove useful to e-business researchers who are considering using the focus group method for that purpose or indeed, for other stages of a research project. However we consider further research needs to be carried out, perhaps using our guidelines as a starting point, to develop a set of guidelines for effective focus groups in other research stages such as theory building.

One theme which emerged particularly strongly during our study was that there are indeed many perspectives to be considered in any significant e-business topic area, and that there will sometimes be conflict between these perspectives which can be difficult to identify when the stakeholders do not meet face to face. Even then, a skilled moderator is needed to draw the different perspectives from the participants, and to assist them in brainstorming and integrating the issues into an holistic solution. Given the widely varying backgrounds and disciplines of the stakeholders, there are likely to be contentious issues, and the moderator needs to be skilled at handling conflict in a productive way. Vogel and Klassen (2000), building on a significant body of work by Vogel in the area of group support technologies, suggest ways in which asynchronous learning linkages can be used in an e-business environment. Such an approach might well provide an additional method of utilising the focus group concept in a truly global and networked manner – combining some of the advantages currently provided by Delphi surveys (such as global reach and the ability to ignore time zones), with those already provided by focus groups (note also the work of Murray (1997) and Rezabek (2000) in online focus groups for qualitative research).

A second important theme which emerged from our study is the effectiveness of focus groups for devising holistic solutions. Participants when meeting face to face seem less bent on focusing on any single dimension, and are particularly attuned to the all important human issues often neglected in e-business research.

A third theme which emerged is the usefulness of the focus group for identifying priorities and relevance in the research area. In our example, the group highlighted the importance of the need for organisational e-business security policies, and the importance of human issues in organisational e-business security management.

A fourth theme identified is the tendency of a focus group, operating in a social setting, to search for and identify missing social elements of the framework – in our example, organisational culture. These days, it is recognised that the social aspects of e-business solutions are critical to their eventual success, and hence a research method which illuminates those aspects could be most useful.

Clearly, in an era where business demand for new and effective solutions for e-business needs is high and the issue of theory relevance is paramount, speedy research methods such as the focus group should be seriously considered by e-business researchers. We remind the reader here of the comment by Clarke (2001) regarding a critical need to sacrifice a degree of rigour in e-business research, in order to obtain desired relevance. Our research has shown that when a focus group is employed, the potential for relevance is high, as the variety of disciplines and organisations represented provide the opportunity to cover many facets of the topic and produce integrated, holistic solutions, in a timely fashion. If the session is carefully planned and conducted, using guidelines such as those we have provided here, there is every chance of rigor being preserved, also. We can thus provide business with solutions that are effective in practice – e-business solutions, in fact.

REFERENCES

Baskerville, R., Stage, J. and DeGross, J. (Eds.) (2000), *Organization and Social Perspectives on Information Technology*, Kluwer Academic Publishers, Boston, US.

Benbasat, I. and Zmud, R.W. (1999), 'Empirical Research in Information Systems: The Practice of Relevance', *MIS Quarterly*, 23(1), March.

Bennetts, P.D.C., Wood-Harper, A.T. and Mills, S. (2000), 'An Holistic Approach to the Management of Information Systems Development - A View Using a Soft Systems Approach and Multiple Viewpoints", *Journal of Systemic Practice and Action Research*, 13(2).

Cavaye, A. (1998), 'Using a multi-disciplinary research team to carry out research in IS', *Journal of Systems and Information Technology*, 2(1).

Clarke, R. (2000a), 'Appropriate Research Methods for Electronic Commerce', Xamax Consultancy Pty Ltd, http://www.anu.edu.au/people/Roger.Clarke/EC/ResMeth.html

Clarke, R. (2000b), 'Focus Groups', Xamax Consultancy Pty Ltd,
http://www.xamax.com.au/Res/FocusGrps.html

Clarke, R. (2001), If e-Business is Different Then Research in e-Business is too, *in* 'Proceedings of IFIP TC8 Working Conference on E-Commerce/E-Business', Salzburg, 22-23 June, http://www.anu.edu.au/people/Roger.Clarke/EC/EBR0106.html (accessed 16 January 2002).

Davenport, T. H., and Markus, M.L. (1999), 'Rigor vs. Relevance Revisited: Response to Benbasat and Zmud', *MIS Quarterly*, 23(1) (March): 19-23.

Delbecq, A. L., Ven, A. H. and Gustafson, D.H. (1975), *Group Techniques for Program Planning: A Guide to Nominal Group and Delphi Processes*, Scott-Foresman.

Edmunds, H. (2000), *Focus Group Research Handbook*, McGraw-Hill.

Gable, G. (1994), 'Integrating Case Study and Survey Research Methods: An Example in Information Systems', *European Journal of Information Systems*, 3(2), 112-126.

Gibbs, A. (1997) 'Focus Groups', *Social Research Update*, 19, University of Surrey, UK, http://www.soc.surrey.ac.uk/sru/SRU19.html

Geisler, E. (2001), Organizing for e-business: the implementation of management principles in Electronic Commerce, *in* 'Proceedings of PICMET01 – Portland International Conference on Management of Engineering and Technology: Technology Management in the Knowledge Era: Life in the e-World', Dept of Engineering and Technology Management, Portland State University, Portland, OR, US.

Gordijn, J., de Bruin, H. and Akkermans, H. (2001), Scenario Methods for Viewpoint Integration in e-Business Requirements Engineering, *in* Sprague, R.H. (Editor), 'Proceedings of the Thirty-fourth Annual Hawaii International Conference on Systems Sciences', Los Alamitos: IEEE Computer Society Press 2001.

Gray, P. (2001), Editor, *Communications of the AIS*, 6, Association of Information Systems, US.

Greenbaum, T. L. (1998), *The Handbook for Focus Group Research* (2nd ed.), Sage Publications, Thousand Oaks, CA, US.

Hasan, H. and Tibbits, H. (1999), Multiple Perspectives on Electronic Business: A Case Study of a Financial Planning Service, *in* 'Proceedings of ACIS99', Wellington, New Zealand.

Holland, C., and Lockett, G. (1997), 'Mixed Mode Network Structures: The Strategic Use of Electronic Commerce by Organizations', *Organization Science*, 8(5), 475-488.

Johnston, R., and Gregor, S. (2000), 'A Theory of Industry-Level Activity for Understanding the Adoption of Interorganizational Systems', *European Journal of Information Systems* 9(4), 243-251.

Kampas, P. (2000), 'Road Map to the E-Revolution', *Information Systems Management* 17(2), 8-22.

Kling, R. (1980), 'Social analysis of computing: theoretical perspectives in recent empirical research', *ACM Computing Surveys,* 12(1), 61-110.

Kock, N., Gray, P., Hoving, R., Klein, H., Myers, M. and Rockart, J. (2001), IS Research Relevance Revisited: Subtle Accomplishment, Unfulfilled Promise, or Serial Hypocrisy? *in* 'Proceedings of Twenty-second International Conference on Information Systems', New Orleans, US.

Kumar, K., Dissel, H.G.V., and Bielli, P. (1998), 'The merchant of Prato revisited: toward a third rationality of information systems', *MIS Quarterly,* 22(2), 199-226.

Kumar, R. L., and Crook, C. W. (1999), 'A Multi-Disciplinary Framework of the Management of Interorganizational Systems', *Database for Advances in Information Systems,* 30(1), 22-38.

Law, D.Y.F. and Lee-Partridge, J.E. (2001), Sense-making of empirical knowledge management through frames of reference, *in* 'Proceedings of the Twenty-second International Conference on Information Systems', New Orleans, US.

Lichtenstein, S. (1997), Developing Internet security policy for organizations, *in* 'Proceedings of the Thirtieth Annual Hawaii International Conference on Systems Sciences', Nunamaker, J.F. and Sprague, R.H. (Eds.), Hawaii, IEEE Computer Society Press, Los Alamitos, California.

Lichtenstein, S. (2001), 'Internet security policy for organisations', Thesis (PhD) (public version), Monash University, Melbourne, Australia.

Lichtenstein, S. and Swatman, P.M.C. (2001), Effective management and policy in e-business security, *in* O'Keefe, B., Loebbecke, C., Gricar, J., Pucihar, A. And Lenart, G. (Editors), 'Proceedings of the Fourteenth Bled Electronic Commerce Conference', Bled, Slovenia.

McMichael, H. (1999), An Activity-Based Perspective for Information Systems Research, *in* 'Proceedings 10th Australasian Conference on Information Systems', Wellington, New Zealand.

Morgan, D. L. (1997), *Focus groups as Qualitative Research,* 2nd ed. Volume 16 The Sage publications series on qualitative research methods. Thousand Oaks, CA: Sage.

Morgan, D. L. and Krueger, R.A. (1998), *The Focus Group Guidebook: Focus Group Kit Volume 1,* Thousand Oaks, Calif.: Sage.

Morrison, D. E. (1998), *The Search for a Method: Focus Groups and the Development of Mass Communication Research,* Luton, Bedfordshire, U.K.: University of Luton Press.

Murray, P. J. (1997), 'Using virtual focus groups in qualitative research', *Qualitative Health Research,* 7(4), 542-54.

Nucifora, A. (1997), 'Focus groups offer candid feedback', *American City Business Journals*, April 14.

Rezabek, R. (2000), 'Online focus groups: Electronic discussions for research', *Forum: Qualitative Social Research,* 1(1), http://qualitative-research.net/fqs (accessed 8 Jan 2002).

Russo, N.L., Fitzgerald, B. and DeGross, J.I. (eds.) (2001), Realigning Research and Practice in Information Systems Development: The social and organizational perspective, *in* 'Proceedings of the International Federation for Information Processing (IFIP) Working Group 8.2 Conference', Boise, Idaho, US, Chapman & Hall, London

Templeton, J.F. (1996), *The Focus Group: a Strategic Guide to Organizing, Conducting and Analyzing the Focus Group Interview*, McGraw Hill.

Vogel, D. and Klassen J. (2000), Networked Learning as Electronic Commerce: Cultural Change in a Faculty, *in* 'Proceedings of the Thirteenth Bled Electronic Commerce Conference', Bled, Slovenia, June 19-21, 600—615.

Vogel, D. (2001), 'Call for Papers, Working Conference: Developing a dynamic, integrative, multi-disciplinary research agenda in E-Commerce/E-Business (IFIP TC8) ', Salzburg, Austria, http://www.salzburgresearch.at/suntrec/IFIPTC8Conference/ (accessed 20 Feb 2002).

Weber, R. and Cockroft, S. (2001), Discussion of IS Relevance 8-Feb-01 to 21-Feb-01, *in* 'ISWORLD Information Systems World Network', http://www.commerce.uq.edu.au/isworld/research/msg.22-02-2001.html (accessed 22 Dec 2001).

USE OF THE WEB FOR DESTINATION MARKETING BY REGIONAL TOURISM ORGANISATIONS IN THE ASIA-PACIFIC REGION

LOIS BURGESS[1], JOAN COOPER[2], CAROLE ALCOCK[2], KEIRAN McNAMEE[2] and BILL DOOLIN[3]

[1]*Faculty of Business, Auckland University of Technology, New Zealand*

[2]*Faculty of Informatics, University of Wollongong, Australia*

[3]*Department of Management Systems, University of Waikato, New Zealand*

Abstract: The information-intensive nature of the tourism and travel industry suggests an important role for Web technology in the promotion and marketing of destinations. This paper evaluates the level of Web site development in Asia-Pacific Regional Tourism Organisations. The study uses the extended Model of Internet Commerce Adoption (eMICA) (Burgess and Cooper 2000), and highlights the utility of using interactivity to evaluate the relative maturity of commercial Web sites.

1. INTRODUCTION

Conventional wisdom contends that business Web site development typically begins simply and evolves over time with the addition of features as the site takes on more functionality and complexity. Past empirical research of commercial web sites support this notion, contending that firms imitate what others do on the Web, partially in a desire to keep pace with competitors or to gain an advantage over competitors in ones own industry by replicating what firms have done in other industries (Sumner and Klepper 1998), or build expertise in electronic commerce through progressive experience with Internet technologies (Poon and Swatman 1999, Van Slyke

2000). Academic enquiry into this evolutionary process followed by firms is gaining momentum in particular industry sectors. One industry sector that is poised to reap the benefits that e-commerce has to offer is the Tourism Industry.

With reports of travel purchases and reservations being one of the fastest growing segments of the Internet community (Bernstein and Awe, 1999), there is little surprise that the number of tourism operators on the Web has changed considerably over the past few years. Although regions have taken advantage of government assistance to move their business online, they are still lagging behind other industries in the uptake of web technologies (Department of Industry, Science and Resources, 2000).

This paper reports the results of a study of Web site development in the Asia Pacific tourism industry. Tourism and travel are unusual products, in that they do not exist when they are purchased. Tourism and travel exist only as information at the point of sale, and cannot be sampled before the purchase decision is made (WTO Business Council 1999). The information-based nature of these products means that the Internet, which offers global reach and multimedia capability, is an increasingly important means of promoting and distributing tourism and travel services (cf. Walle 1996). The Internet is a potentially significant means of promotion and destination marketing for the Asia Pacific tourism industry.

2. TOURISM IN THE ISLANDS OF ASIA AND THE PACIFIC

Over the centuries, the Asia Pacific has been a vehicle for the exchange of cultures, ideas, crafts, beliefs, peoples and technologies between the East and the West. 1991 saw an awakening of interest in the region with respect to cultural exchange, trade and tourism (WTO, 2001). The number of tourists travelling to the region has grown exponentially. In an industry as competitive as tourism, and with beach tourism forming a considerable sector within the industry, islands have been extremely active in capitalising on the economic benefits from the development of tourism.

The Asia and Pacific region will be the focus of the worldwide tourism industry in the future. Over the last decade, tourist arrivals rose faster than any other region in the world, almost twice the rate of industrialised countries (WTO, 2001). Between 1980 and 1995, tourist arrivals in the region rose at an annual rate of 15% (WTO, 1996). The WTO (2001) projects that by the year 2010, the region will surpass the Americas to become the world's number two tourist region, with 229 million arrivals. The region is now regarded as a major generator and receiver of tourism. This has been attributed to a number of factors including: strong economic growth, increase in disposable income and leisure time, easing of travel restrictions, successful tourist promotion, and a recognition by host governments that tourism is a powerful growth engine and generator of foreign exchange earnings (Singh, 1997).

Tourism is one of the most important sectors in the economies of Asia Pacific countries. In 2000, East Asia and the Pacific recorded record growth to reach 111.7 million arrivals (growth rate of 14.5% over 1999). (WTO, 2000). WTO statistics reveal that the East Asia and Pacific regions will continue to grow. Overall, the region has witnessed a general economic recovery, which has fuelled domestic and international tourism activities (WTO, 2001). Marketing campaigns have been more aggressive and directed towards selected markets. Many of the countries in the region have benefited from assistance provided by the WTO. For example, Malaysia's Rural Tourism Master Plan, aimed at providing guidance for controlled development of rural tourism and consultancy assistance in the areas of policy direction, infrastructure development, marketing and training (WTO, 2001).

The tourism industry provides a wide variety of products and services, including adventure tourism, culture and heritage, transport, accommodation, retail and hospitality. Regional destination marketing organisations called Regional Tourism Organisations (RTOs) form part of the industry structure, and it is these organisations that are the focus of the current study. RTOs form an important layer between central government and the local tourism industry, potentially providing a coordinated and comprehensive marketing effort, and acting as a portal for visitor access to tourism operators and service providers.

The purpose of this study is to evaluate the extent of Web site development in RTOs in the Asia Pacific region. This evaluation is achieved using an Internet commerce adoption metric developed by Burgess and Cooper (2000) in a study of the Australian regional tourism industry, the extended Model of Internet Commerce Adoption (eMICA). The Web sites of 34 Asia Pacific Tropical Island RTOs were evaluated using the eMICA model. Secondary objectives of the study were (1) evaluating the validity of the extended MICA as proposed in the Australian study in different national contexts, and (2) providing a comparative study across countries so as to add to the assessment of the "Net-readiness" of the tourism industry globally.

3. THE EXTENDED MODEL OF INTERNET COMMERCE ADOPTION

The Model of Internet Commerce Adoption (MICA) was originally developed for a study in the Australian metal fabrication industry (Burgess and Cooper 1998). The model proposes that in developing commercial web sites, organisations typically start simply by establishing a presence on the Web and build on functionality over time, as their expertise in the use of Internet technologies increases. In addition, as Web sites build on complexity, so will the number of modules incorporated into the site increase. MICA consists of three stages, incorporating three levels of business process – Web-based promotion, provision of information and services, and transaction processing. The three levels of business processes are similar to those proposed by Ho (1997) and Liu et al. (1997). The stages of development provide a roadmap that indicates where a business or industry sector is in its development of Internet commerce applications.

As sites move through the stages of development from inception (promotion) through consolidation (provision) to maturity (processing), layers of complexity and functionality are added to the site. This addition of layers is synonymous with the business moving from a static Internet presence through increasing levels of interactivity to a dynamic site incorporating value chain integration and innovative applications to add value through information management and rich functionality (Timmers 1998).

Since the original study, MICA has been applied to the government sector (Boon 1999) and tourism industry (Burgess and Cooper 2000) in Australia, resulting in its enhancement as an extended Model of Internet Commerce Adoption (eMICA). The central tenet of the extended model is that while businesses develop Internet commerce applications in stages as proposed by the original version of MICA, complexity and functionality vary greatly between applications, and even between businesses in an industry sector. In line with this, the extended model proposes that a number of additional layers of complexity, ranging from very simple to highly sophisticated, exist within the identified main stages of MICA.

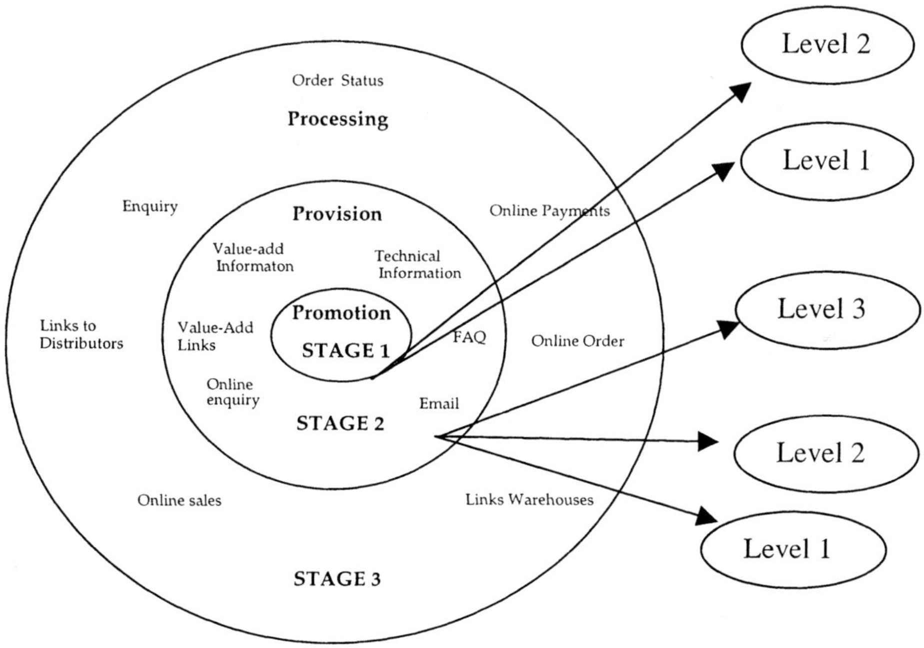

Figure 1. eMICA

The extended model (eMICA) adds several layers of sophistication of functionality and innovation within the three main stages, in order to accommodate the wide range of Internet commerce development evidenced in industries such as tourism. The full eMICA model (Figure 1) is summarised in Table 1 below.

EMICA	Examples of functionality
Stage 1 - Promotion	
Level 1 – basic information	company name, physical address and contact details, area of business
Level 2 – rich information	annual report, email contact, information on company activities
Stage 2 - Provision	
Level 1 – low level interactivity	basic product catalogue, hyperlinks to further information, online enquiry form
Level 2 – medium interactivity	higher-level product catalogues, customer support (e.g. FAQs, sitemaps), industry-specific value-added features
Level 3 – high interactivity	chat room, discussion forum, multimedia, newsletters or updates by email
Stage 3 - Processing	secure online transactions, order status and tracking, interaction with corporate servers

Table 1: The extended Model of Internet Commerce Adoption (eMICA); adapted from Burgess and Cooper (2000)

4. REGIONAL TOURISM

Tourism is a fragmented industry (Gretzel et al. 2000), and tourism promotion is a complex web of International, national, regional and local institutions frequently influenced by politics and personalities (Ryan 2001). RTOs have a role to play in providing comprehensive coverage of products and services in their region, irrespective of whether individual service operators have an independent online presence (Sharma et al. 2000).

RTOs play a major role in destination marketing, pooling the marketing resources of both public and private sectors to achieve a coordinated effect. RTOs play a major role in domestic and international marketing, destination management, regional tourism planning and development, and facilitating provision of services to tourism operators. Gretzel et al. (2000) note that destination marketing organisations often have to struggle with limited financial and human resources, and a lack of technical expertise.

5. METHODOLOGY

The web sites of 34 RTOs in the Asia Pacific region which were obtained from:

- Open Directory Regional Asia Travel and Tourism Website (http://dmoz.org/regional/asia/travel_and_tourism/travel_guides)
- Google Directory Regional Asia Travel (http://directory.ggogle.com/top/regional/asia/travel_and_tourism/travel_guides)

were assessed using eMICA. Each site was examined in detail and the various functions performed by the site were noted in a spreadsheet file. The functions and features across all the sites were then grouped according to their level of interactivity and sophistication. Each RTO site was matched against this ordered list, the results are summarised in Table 2.

6. RESULTS OF THE STUDY

Each RTO site was then assigned an appropriate stage and level in eMICA based on the level of development of the site. The results of the Asia Pacific Tropical Islands' study are shown below in Table 2, together with the equivalent figures from the previous studies of Australian and New Zealand RTOs (Doolin et al 2001).

Stage of eMICA		**Tropical Islands**	**New Zealand**	**Australia**
Stage 1	Level 1	-	-	4.1%
	Level 2	-	3.8%	4.1%
Stage 2	Level 1	21%	30.8%	36.6%
	Level 2	47%	46.2%	40.0%
	Level 3	32%	15.4%	15.2%
Stage 3		0%	3.8%	0.7%
Total		100%	100%	100%

Table 2: Comparison of the Asia Pacific Results

The majority (97%) of the Asia Pacific Tropical Island RTO sites were developed to Stage 2 of eMICA, and incorporated the standard functional attributes of the first stage of development, such as email contact details, the use of photographic images, and a description of regional tourism features. However, the level of functionality and sophistication varied greatly across the three levels comprising this second stage of development, as discussed below. None of the sites evaluated were developed to Stage 3. However one site provided a link to an accommodation provider with the capability of offering secure online credit card payment for accommodation.

The major differentiation in the Asia Pacific Tropical Island RTO sites lay within Stage 2 of the eMICA model. Those sites located within the first Level of Stage 2 had some form of navigation structure such as buttons with links to different parts of the site. They had numerous internal and external links to further information, and incorporated value-added features characteristic of the tourism industry such as key facts (on location, climate, weather and services), maps, itineraries, news and media releases, and a photo gallery. Often, there would also be a more interactive feature such as a currency converter or a Web-based contact form. These sites also contained information on accommodation, attractions, activities and events in the region, usually in the form of a list organised by category and with contact details and/or links to the third-party operator (where available). Some of these lists appeared to be database-driven using technology such as "active server pages" (ASP).

At Level 2 of Stage 2, the value-added tourism features became increasingly interactive, and included electronic postcards, interactive maps, downloadable materials, special offers, guest books, and the use of Web cams. Sites at this Level incorporated some form of online customer support, such as FAQs, a site map or an internal site search engine. User interaction also included the use of Web-based enquiry or order forms. Information on accommodation, attractions, activities, dining, shopping, and events was provided via searchable databases, with searches available by type and/or location within the region. As sites progressed to Level 3, the key feature was the facility to accept online bookings for accommodation, tours and travel. Nine of the sites had advanced value-added features that included multi-language support, multimedia, newsletter updates by email, streaming video, and a QuickTime virtual tour.

Comparing the results of the Asia Pacific Tropical Island RTO Web site evaluations with the Australian and New Zealand studies (Burgess and Cooper 2000, Doolin et al, 2001) indicates that a majority of sites in all three studies are at Stage 2 of development. However at Stage 2 Level 1, there was a variance in that although Australia and New Zealand had a similar result (approximately 30%) there was a smaller percentage (21%) of the tropical island sites at this level. Similarly at Stage 2 level 3 almost double (47%) of Tropical Island websites were at this level of development.

In all cases, most of the organisations in this industry sector are at a relatively advanced stage of adoption of Internet commerce. The majority have incorporated various levels of functionality consistent with the three Levels identified at Stage 2 of eMICA. This is consistent with the focus of this industry sector on tourism promotion and the provision of information and services that enable potential tourists to the regions to make informed travel decisions and choices.

7. DISCUSSION

The information-intensive nature of the tourism industry fits particularly well with interactive media like the Web, and indications are that tourism Web sites are constantly being made more interactive (Goodrich 2000a, Gretzel et al. 2000, Hanna and Millar 1997, Marcussen 1997, WTO Business Council 1999). Moving from simply broadcasting information to letting consumers interact with the Web site content allows the tourism organisation to engage consumers' interest and participation, increasing the likelihood that they will return to the site, to capture information about their preferences, and to use that information to provide personalised communication and services. The content of tourism destination Web sites is particularly important because it directly influences the perceived image of the destination and creates a virtual experience for the consumer. This experience is greatly enhanced when Web sites offer interactivity (Cano and Prentice 1998, Gretzel et al. 2000, Legoherel et al. 2000).

Interactive Web site presentation runs a spectrum from information provision, through brochure ordering and inquiry services, to booking and payment online (Marcussen 1997). A summary of the key features of 25 "best practice" destination marketing organisations, evaluated by the World Tourism Organization, is presented by Goodrich (2000b). These features included navigational assistance and branding on the home page, multiple means of communication (including the use of colour, photographs, maps, symbols, and multimedia), interactivity, rich information on a wide range of topics, the use of managed and updated databases, and multilingual support. Standing and Vasudavan (1999) used a similar list of functions in their evaluation of Australian travel agents' Web sites. Their features included provision of product, service and destination information, transaction capability, customer interaction and feedback, and links to value-added information sources. Although Standing and Vasudavan were evaluating travel agencies, it is interesting to note that relatively few sites provided higher levels of interactivity such as online booking, payment and customer service.

The Web sites of the Tropical Island RTOs display a greater range of functionality than the earlier studies, and can be distinguished on the basis of the level of interactivity they offer to the consumer of tourism information and services. In fact, the eMICA model uses interactivity as the primary means of establishing the various stages of Internet commerce adoption. This study confirms the usefulness of Web site interactivity for this purpose. The results of the study suggest that in the tourism industry, major milestones in Internet commerce development are:

- moving beyond a basic Web page with an email contact, to providing links to value-added tourism information and the use of Web-based forms for customer interaction;
- offering opportunities for the consumer to interact with the Web site through (a) value-added features such as sending electronic postcards or recording their experiences and reading others' experiences in Web-based guest books, and (b) the provision of online customer support via internal site search engines and searchable databases;
- the beginnings of Internet commerce transactions with the acceptance of online bookings for accommodation, travel, and other tourism services;
- full adoption of Internet commerce, where consumers are able to complete transactions online through secure Internet channels.

None of the Tropical Island RTO sites displayed interactivity at this last transactional level. Perhaps, as Burgess and Cooper (2000) note, this is not an unusual finding, given that the organisations in this industry sector are in the business of promoting regions and their unique features and offerings primarily through the provision of value-added information and services. As noted earlier the WTO (WTO, 2001) involvement in this region through provision of support and incentive programs to the Tourism Industry Sector may account for the higher level of development (47% at Stage 2 Level 3) of the Tropical Island RTO websites.

Further adoption of Internet commerce is likely to depend on the future role taken by public and private sector involvement in future development programs.

8. CONCLUSION

This paper has evaluated the Web sites of the 34 Asia Pacific Tropical Island Regional Tourism Organisations. The RTOs generally displayed a high level of interactivity, consistent with their role in providing comprehensive destination marketing for geographic regions in which many local tourism operators lack an Internet presence. However, almost all the RTOs stopped short of offering consumers the capability to complete their tourism and travel transactions online. Progression beyond this point is likely to depend on the overall maturing of Internet commerce use by domestic and international consumers.

The outcome of the research provides further confirmation of the staged approach to development of commercial Web sites proposed by the extended Model of Internet Commerce (eMICA). Further, the comparative results of all three studies suggest that regional tourism organisations in the Asia Pacific Region are at a similar, relatively sophisticated stage of development on the Internet commerce roadmap.

REFERENCES

Berstein, J. and Awe, S.C., (1999) 'Wired travellers: travel and tourism Web sites', Reference Services Review, Vol. 27, No. 4, pp. 364.

Boon, O. (1999) Evaluating the Adoption of the Internet: A Model Towards World's Best Practice. Unpublished Honours thesis, Deakin University.

Burgess and Cooper (1998) The Status of Internet Commerce in the Manufacturing Industry in Australia: A survey of Metal Fabrication Industries. Proceedings of the Second CollECTeR Conference on Electronic Commerce, pp. 65-73. Sydney.

Burgess, L. and Cooper, J. (2000) Extending the Viability of MICA (Model of Internet Commerce Adoption) as a Metric for Explaining the Process of Business Adoption of Internet Commerce. International Conference on Telecommunications and Electronic Commerce. Dallas (November).

Cano, V. and Prentice, R. (1998) Opportunities for Endearment to Place Through Electronic 'Visiting': WWW Homepages and the Tourism Promotion of Scotland. Tourism Management **19** (1), pp. 67-73.

Department of Industry, Science and Resources, (2000) Regional Online Tourism Program 2000-2001 Guidelines [URL: www.isr.gov.au/sport_tourism/publications /grants/ 2000-01_Tourism/RTPGlines.pdf]

Doolin, B., Burgess, L., Cooper, J., Alcock, C (2001) "Internet Commerce Adoption by New Zealand and Australian Regional Tourism Organisations: A Comparative Study Using eMICA" ICECR-4 Dallas, Texas, November.

Doolin, B, Burgess, L and Cooper, J "Use of the Web for Destination Marketing in Regional Tourism" Proceedings 2nd We-B Conference, Perth, Australia, November, 2001.

Goodrich, J.N. (2000a) Internet Distribution of European Travel and Tourism Services. [Book review]. Journal of Travel Research **39** (August), pp. 115-116.

Goodrich, J.N. (2000b) Marketing Tourism Destinations On-Line: Strategies for the Information Age. [Book review]. Journal of Travel Research **39** (November), pp. 240-241.

Gretzel, U., Yuan, Y.-L. and Fesenmaier, D.R. (2000) Preparing for the New Economy: Advertising Strategies and Change in Destination Marketing Organizations. Journal of Travel Research **39** (November), pp. 146-156.

Hanna, J.R.P. and Millar, R.J. (1997) Promoting Tourism on the Internet. Tourism Management **18**(7), pp. 469-470.

Ho, J. (1997) Evaluating the World Wide Web: A Global Study of Commercial Sites. Journal of Computer Mediated Communication **3**(1). Available: http://www.ascusc.org /jcmc/vol3/issue1/ho.html.

Legoherel, P., Fischer-Lokou, J. and Gueguen, N. (2000) Selling Tourism on the Web: Analysis of the Balance of Power Between Seller and Consumer During Information Exchange and Negotiation. Journal of Travel & Tourism Marketing **9**(3), pp. 49-64.

Liu, C., Arnett, K.P., Capella, L. and Beatty, B. (1997) Web Sites of Fortune 500 Companies: Facing Customers through Home Pages. Information and Management **31**(1), pp.335-345.

Marcussen, C.H. (1997) Marketing European Tourism Products via Internet/WWW. Journal of Travel & Tourism Marketing **6**(3/4), pp. 23-34.

Poon, S. and Swatman, P.M.C. (1999) An Exploratory Study of Small Business Internet Commerce Issues. Information & Management **35**(1), pp. 9-18.

Ryan, C. (2001) The Politics of Promoting Cities and Regions: A Case Study of New Zealand's Tourism Organisations. Unpublished paper, Department of Tourism Management, University of Waikato.

Sharma, P., Carson, D. and DeLacy, T. (2000) National Online Tourism Initiatives for Australia. Journal of Travel Research **39** (November), pp. 157-162.

Standing, C. and Vasudavan, T. (1999) Effective Internet Commerce Business Models in the Travel Agency Sector. Proceedings of the Fourth Pacific Asia Conference on Information Systems, pp. 88-99. Hong Kong (June).

Sumner, M. and Klepper, R. (1998) Business Strategy and the Use of Web Sites. International Conference on Telecommunications and Electronic Commerce (November).

Timmers, P. (1998) Business Models for Electronic Markets. Electronic Markets **8**(2), pp. 3-8. University of Texas (2000) 'Measuring the Internet Economy' Austin Center for research in Electronic Commerce.

Van Slyke, C. (2000) The Role of Technology Clusters in Small Business Electronic Commerce Adoption. Proceedings of the Fifth CollECTeR Conference on Electronic Commerce, 8 pp. Brisbane (December).

Walle, A.H. (1996) Tourism and the Internet: Opportunities for Direct Marketing. Journal of travel Research **35**(Summer), pp. 72-77.

World Tourism Organization (1996) WTO Tourism Statistics database [Online] Available: http://www.world-tourism.org/statserv.htm

World Tourism Organization Business Council. (1999) Chapter 1: Introduction. In Marketing Tourism Destinations Online: Strategies for the Information Age. Madrid: World Tourism Organization. Available: http://www.world-tourism.org/isroot/wto/pdf/1133-1.pdf

World Tourism Organization (2000) "WTO in Asia and the Pacific 2000" Available: http://www.world-tourism.org

INTERNET MARKETING COMMUNICATIONS: INTERACTIVITY AND INTEGRATION

BRETT LAWTON[1] and SHIRLEY GREGOR[2]
[1] *Marketing Department, School of Business and Economics, University of Auckland, New Zealand*
[2]*School of Business and Information Management, Australian National University, Australia*

Abstract: This paper reports exploratory research into the role of the Internet in marketing communications and the conceptualisation of integration and interactivity in this context. Three mini case studies of large companies in the fast moving consumer good industry illustrate the application of frameworks developed for the understanding of integration and interactivity. The case studies show uncertainty about the value of the Internet as a communications channel and the use of interactive tools. The more advanced companies exhibit greater integration of communication tools, across marketing functions and across media. The interactive tools/goals framework developed shows how the more advanced companies also use interactive tools that address a wider range of human motivational goals. This framework suggests how opportunities for value-adding through interactive tools can be identified, giving a basis for further work.

1. INTRODUCTION

The Internet has emerged as a significant new business tool with considerable implications for marketing communications (Cross 1994). The potential benefits of Internet marketing communication are many. Communications can be one-to-one or many-to-many, synchronous or asynchronous, and local or global. Variable costs tend to zero. There are exciting opportunities for creativity and innovation.

A number of challenges, however, accompany these opportunities. First, knowledge of how to use the Internet in marketing communications is limited. Managers are still grappling with how to use this new medium effectively, despite widespread adoption by both marketers and consumers (Berthon et al. 1996; Bush 1998). Second, use of the Internet has not been well integrated with existing marketing practice (Schultz 1999; Sheehan 2001). Evidence suggests the use of the Internet in marketing communications has been stand alone and haphazard in nature. Third, although interactivity is seen as crucial to effective use of the Internet (Ghose and Dou 1998; Perman 2001), it has not been well used (Bucy et al. 1999; Geiger and Martin 1999; Ha and James 1998; Perry 2000).

These challenges have led us to three questions:

1. What is the **role** of the Internet in marketing communications? How are organizations using the Internet in their promotional mix in practice and how they should be using it?
2. How should Internet communications be **integrated** into an organization's promotional mix to achieve maximum impact?
3. How are organizations using Internet **interactivity** in their promotional mix efforts?

We propose that understanding of the two concepts, i*ntegration* and i*nteractivity,* are crucial to effectively using the Internet in the promotional mix. We explore each of these concepts in detail.

First, we draw on work in Integrated Marketing Communications (IMC) to provide a theoretical framework to aid in understanding how the Internet can be integrated into the promotional mix. IMC suggests that if Internet communications are integrated with other marketing communications, then synergies will enhance the effectiveness and efficiency of marketing efforts.

Second, we consider the concept of interactivity as a defining aspect of the Internet and as crucial to the effective use of the Internet in the promotional mix. In understanding interactivity, we consider perspectives from psychology, marketing, human communication, and human-computer interaction. A framework for classifying interactive tools in terms of user's motivational needs is developed as a means of showing how interactivity can add value to users' experiences and to marketing communications.

Our study is exploratory. We found it necessary to consider the issues addressed here as a prelude to more wide-scale work The work is significant as prior literature that addresses the challenges of the use of the Internet in marketing communications in a holistic and systematic way is sparse (Berthon et al. 1996; Watson et al. 2000). Key issues of integration and interactivity have been explored to a limited extent (Gallaher, Foster and Parson 2001, Sheehan and Doherty 2001).

The paper proceeds with a review of relevant literature and the development of conceptual frameworks for the understanding of integration and interactivity. Our analytic frameworks were used in the analysis of marketing communications in mini case studies of three organizations. The results of the study are then discussed, with implications for marketing theory and practice.

2. CONCEPTUAL BACKGROUND

The marketing literature contains a number of studies that explore the implications of the Internet for marketing (Balasubramanian and Bronnenberg 1997; Barwise et al. 2001; Peterson et al., 1997, Hoffman and Novak 1996; Quelch and Klein 1996). Several studies consider the marketing communications impacts of the Internet (Berthon, Pitt and Watson 1996; Bush et al. 1998; Bush and Bush 2000; Cross 1994; Deighton 1997, Van Doren, Fechner and Green-Adelsberger 2000). Others have begun to apply established marketing theories to the online environment (for example, Bruner and Kumar 2000; Chen and Wells 1999).

This paper considers the impact of the Internet on the *promotional mix* of an organization's marketing efforts. The promotional mix is that aspect of marketing that relates to a firm's communications with its customers in the hope of influencing the recipient's feelings, beliefs or behaviour. It includes five promotional functions: advertising, direct marketing, sales promotion, personal selling, and public relations (Kotler et al. 1998, Belch and Belch 2001).

To date, advertising has been the major focus of the Internet marketing communication literature. This focus ignores many other forms of Internet marketing communication, such as online communities (Bickart and Schindler 2001; McWilliam 2000), permission-based email (Krishnamurthy 2001), online branding (Davis et al. 2000), chat and discussion groups. No prior studies have been identified that consider these disparate areas of Internet marketing communications in a holistic and systematic way. When Internet marketing communications is approached from this holistic perspective, two issues emerge of central importance – integration and interactivity.

2.1 Integrated Marketing Communication (IMC)

A considerable body of IMC literature exists. IMC is a concept of best practice that seeks to integrate all communication activities of an organization in order to achieve enhanced efficiency and effectiveness of communications efforts. IMC has received widespread support by marketers, academics and advertising agencies (Cornelissen and Lock 2000; Gould 2000).

IMC has been defined as:

> A concept of marketing communications planning that recognizes the added value of a comprehensive plan that evaluates the strategic roles of a variety of communications disciplines (for example, general advertising, direct response, sales promotion, and public relations).... and combines these disciplines to provide clarity, consistency and maximum communications impact (Schultz, 1993).

IMC encompasses the dimensions of *strategic* and *tactical* integration (Sheehan and Doherty 2001). Strategic integration occurs when the objectives of marketing communications are integrated. This means that all communications are moving in the same direction. For example, an advertisement aiming to increase awareness could be complemented by public relations aimed at this same goal. Tactical integration occurs when the elements of tools, such as pictures and colours, are integrated. Strategic integration cannot occur without tactical integration.

Low (2000) measured integration using the concept of consistency. He suggests IMC can be conceptualised as a continuum on which the degree of consistency is measured using three components: (i) the extent to which communications are planned by the same manager (ii) the strategic consistency of communications efforts, and (iii) the commonality of the communications message.

We propose that, to maximise the impact of the Internet in marketing communications, it should be included in the IMC framework. To do this there must be a clear understanding of how the Internet is conceptualised in marketing. Is it a new communications channel or media, or is it a new marketing function?

There is acceptance of the Internet as a new communications channel, similar to television or radio (Hanson 1998; Hochhauser 2000; Wells et al. 2000). Key characteristics of the media have been identified. These characteristics include consumer control, consumer choice, and interactivity (Hoffman and Novak 1996). In addition, there can be any-to-any communication, the content can be perpetually fresh, consumers can select information, communities can form unbounded by space or time, privacy and identity can be refined, and hyper-impulsivity is enabled (Deighton and Barwise 2000). It is thought that best practice use of Internet marketing will involve leveraging the unique characteristics of this new media, such as interactivity.

At times, however, the Internet is referred to as a new "communications function", similar to sales promotion, or advertising (Belch and Belch, 2001; Ritson, 1998). It appears preferable to avoid this usage, and adopt the view which recognizes the Internet as an alternative channel of communication for existing recognized communication functions. This view allows the development of the framework shown below.

2.2 An Internet-Integrated Marketing Communications Framework

To conceptualise the inclusion of the Internet into integrated marketing communications theory, we propose the framework shown in Table 1. The five promotional functions are in the vertical columns. Definitions for each function are given in the Appendix. Promotional channels, including traditional media and Internet media, form the rows of the table. Channels are the means of distributing the promotional functions. For example advertising (a function) is often screened on television (a channel). Different promotional tools are listed in each cell in the table. These tools represent the diversity of applications, execution and creativity possible in marketing communications.

Channels	**Functions**				
	Advertising	**Sales Promotion**	**Public Relations**	**Personal Selling**	**Direct Marketing**
Traditional (Broadcast, Print, Supple-mentary)	Many tools (magazine, newspaper, television advertisements)	Samples Coupons Sweepstakes Rebates Refunds Price-offs Bonus packs Frequency programs Event marketing Premiums	Publicity Sponsorship Crisis management Corporate advertising Marketing Public relations Cause-related marketing Government / community relations	One-to-one selling	Direct response ads Database marketing Direct-mail Mail order catalogues Tele-marketing Database CD-Roms Kiosks Digital TV
Internet (Web, Email)	Organizational website Banners Sponsorship Pop-ups Push technology Links from other websites	Organizational website with many of the above (eg samples, coupons, sweepstakes) Games Puzzles Chat groups Online communities	Organizational website with many of the above. Information dissemination tailored to different audiences (eg press packs, email)	One-to-one selling enhanced with electronic information provision (online shopping)	Direct email Database marketing Infomercials Branding sites Brand communities Permission-based email

Table 1 . An Integrated Framework for Internet Marketing Communications

The tools shown in the framework were identified in a review of marketing activities and literature. The lists in each cell are representative rather than exhaustive. In addition, one tool can serve more than one function or purpose.

This framework allows an analysis of the tools used by an organization from the **organization's viewpoint**. An organization can see which tools it is using for the communications functions in its marketing promotional mix, and which media are, or could be used, to achieve these functions. In addition, this framework allows the level of integration across the promotional mix, both strategic and tactical to be addressed. Ideally, similar strategies would be used across functions (horizontal integration) and across channels (vertical integration).

3. INTERACTIVITY

A number of the Internet-based tools in the framework above involve interactivity, which is seen as the key to using the Internet in marketing communications (Ha and James 1998; Hoffman and Novak 1996; Perman 2001; Rogers and Allbritton 1995).

The use of interactivity in marketing communications, however, has not been as successful as hoped (Bucy et al. 1999; Ha and James 1998, Geiger and Martin 1999). One reason could be the lack of common understanding about what interactivity means and what potential it offers.

In the general marketing literature, interactivity has been defined as "a person-to-person or person-to-technology exchange designed to effect a change in the knowledge or behaviour of at least one person" (Haeckel 1998, p.64). Haeckel identifies the dimensions of interactivity as: impact of interaction, number of entities involved, frequency of exchange, degree of contingency, degree of sensory involvement, degree of cognitive involvement, degree of synchronicity, content of exchange, types of entities involved, and type of media involved.

The communications literature uses the analogy of conversation and interpersonal communication to give a feedback view of interactivity. Key to the notion of conversation is the idea of responsiveness. For example, Rafeali (1988, p.111) defines interactivity as:

> An expression of the extent that in a given series of communication exchanges, any third (or later) transmission (or message) is related to the degree to which previous exchanges referred to even earlier transmissions.

The communications in the exchange can be unmediated, as in face-to-face interpersonal communication, or mediated through use of media such as the Internet.

Interactivity can be seen, not as a characteristic of the media as some have suggested (Steuer 1992, Hoffman and Novak 1996), but rather a potential that the medium offers. The Internet is a medium that has one of the greatest potentials for interactivity. Rafeali (1988) considers that interactivity exists on a *continuum,* meaning that there can be high and low levels of interactivity. High levels of interactivity occur when communication relates to previous responses, for example a response from A to B is based on B's response (Bretz 1983). Low levels of interactivity occur when responses relate to previous exchanges only to a small extent.

The human-computer interaction and other information technology literatures offer further perspectives on the dimensions of interactivity. The dimensions of interactivity identified by Heeter (1989, pp 217-218) include (i) the *effort* users must exert to access information – that is, "the ration of user activity to system activity", (ii) the complexity of c*hoice* available – that is, "the extent to which users are provided with a choice of available information" and (iii) *responsiveness,* or "the degree to which a medium can react responsively to a user". Communication via the Internet is mediated by sophisticated interface design and programming techniques. Knowledge of these is central to effective communication through this medium. Therefore, Internet and interface design principles play an important role in our understanding of interactivity.

Steuer (1992, p. 86) has identified three variables that effect interactivity in mediated communications. "*Speed* of interaction, or response time, is one important characteristic of an interactive media system". Real time interaction is considered the most sophisticated execution of this variable -- for example, the faster the response the more like human interaction. Email is an exception to this rule due to its asynchronous nature. *Mapping* "refers to the way human actions are connected to actions within a mediated environment". The closer the computer response resembles the natural human response the greater the level of sophistication. *Range* is "the number of attributes of the mediated environment that can be manipulated and the amount of variation possible within each attribute". These attributes include spatial organisation, colour, and brightness.

Thus, we propose that an understanding of interactivity in Internet communications lies at the intersection of the communications and human-computer interaction literatures. It involves an appreciation of the different viewpoints expressed above – from both the interpersonal and technological literatures

Further, we propose that a key to understanding how interactivity is used in marketing communications is consideration of how added value is offered to the user – that is, how interactivity allows fulfilment of basic human goals. *Perceived usefulness* has been found to be a strong determinant of the adoption and use of information technologies in general (Davis, 1989). This finding has been observed mostly in industry contexts where users were motivated by the need to accomplish a task related to their employment. With the use of the Internet for marketing communications, we have a more general context where users have many goals, including those relating to social needs and entertainment. For this reason, we suggest that interactive experiences in marketing communication should be evaluated against the different human goals they can help satisfy.

A convenient taxonomy of human goals for this purpose is that offered by Ford (1992). This is a general taxonomy, with no hierarchical ordering of goals, where "each category simply describes a particular kind of consequence that people may desire to achieve" (Ford 1992 p.86). Ford groups human goals as follows:

- affective goals (entertainment, tranquillity, happiness, bodily sensations, physical well-being.),
- cognitive goals (exploration, understanding, intellectual creativity, positive self-evaluations),
- subjective organization goals (unity, transcendence)
- self-assertive social relationship goals (individuality, self-determination, superiority, resource acquisition,
- integrative social relationship goals (belongingness, social responsibility, equity, resource provision), and
- task goals (mastery, task creativity, management, material gain, safety).

The first three goal categories represent within-person goals, and the last three categories represent goals with respect to the relationships between people and their environments. Some goals may, on average, be more compelling than others (eg happiness, physical well-being, belongingness). At this point, we do not consider the relative importance of the goals or categories, though this area could warrant further research in Internet marketing, particularly in respect to which goals motivate particular demographic groups.

The application of both the Internet-integrated marketing communications and the interactivity/tools frameworks is illustrated in the following sections in the analysis of case studies.

4. METHOD

Our exploratory research involved three mini case studies of large companies in the fast moving consumer goods (FMCG) industry. This industry was selected because it tends to use the Internet for marketing communications (rather than, for example, service or distribution). The three organisations chosen were selected because they appeared to be at different stages in their use of Internet communications. Each organisation operates in Australia, marketing multiple consumer product brands.

The *OzProd* company is the least advanced in the use of Internet marketing communications. *EuroNat* is using the Internet for Internet marketing communications activities, but does not attach a great deal of importance to these efforts. *OctoPlus* has been using the Internet for more than five years, is committed to Internet communications and is quite sophisticated in their use. Pseudonyms are used and only limited details given for each organisation for privacy reasons.

Data was gathered in interviews with marketing or marketing communications managers from each of these organisations. In addition, data was gathered from secondary sources including company websites and annual reports.

Interviews were conducted by telephone and lasted about 30 minutes. A standard set of open-ended questions guided the interviews[9]. The questions focused on three areas – the role of the Internet, integration and interactivity. Interview transcripts were prepared following each interview.

In addition, an analysis of each organization's web sites was performed, using the interactive tools/goals framework outlined above.

5. RESULTS

The results of the mini case studies are presented in terms of our three research questions.

5.1 Role and Use of the Internet in Marketing Communications

Table 2 gives an overview of how each case study organization is using the Internet.

[9] The interview guide is available from the authors on request.

Respondents confirmed the view of the Internet as a communications channel, or *another prong in the fork* in reaching the consumer.

The Internet was seen as a *support media* and secondary to traditional media such as television. For OzProd and EuroNat, Internet communications were a relatively low priority. OctoPlus placed more importance on the Internet, considering that it *builds value above the mainstream media.*

OzProd
OzProd is a large Australian-based food company at the first stages of using the Internet in its marketing communications. The company recognizes that *the Internet has been the last on our list.* Some brands have websites, but many are out of date and have not been upgraded from initial versions. A corporate web page is used for the community and investors, with annual reports and consumer feedback sections. Links to brand sites were difficult to find on the corporate website. The company is considering putting a freeze on Internet communications apart from one or two sites until they can be relaunched. *Long-term we see the Internet as having a large role, especially for one-to-one relationships. It can communicate a depth of information and enable a direct dialogue with consumers.*
EuroNat
EuroNat is a very large international food company and an umbrella brand for many consumer product brands. The Internet is used in a range of ways, including corporate and brand websites, product launches, competitions/promotion, market research and Internet advertising. Websites are targeted to specific audiences, such as children. Brand websites are closely linked to brand positioning. The corporate website serves multiple stakeholders and contains clear links to brand websites. Online and offline communications are well integrated, for example product packaging and some sales promotions carry website addresses. Many interactive tools are used. *The Internet is a communication tool to be evaluated against objectives. It allows direct and dynamic communication with customers. It is another media – its use depends on the situation, objectives and target market.*
OctoPlus
OctoPlus is a very large international, branded, consumer goods company. It has been using Internet marketing communications in Australia for over five years. Unlike EuroNat, OctoPlus is not an umbrella brand and is hence invisible to the consumer. Websites are the main form of communication and are used where they add value for the consumer and the organisation. The focus is on using Internet communications to achieve specific objectives. These include building brand equity, relationships, promotions, customer contact, support programs, and advertising. *Advertising on the Web is a way of extending our reach to a different group of people in a cost-effective way. It is especially good for hard-to-get-at consumers like kids who use technology a lot. We use the Internet to build brand equity and build relationships – not for selling. We have a website set up to support* [a safety campaign]. *It is purely about completing a link in a community service.*

Table 2. Internet use in marketing communications.

The Internet was not seen as a new, distinct, promotional function. However, several existing promotional functions were fulfilled through the

Internet. These were advertising, sales promotion, and public relations. Direct marketing on the Internet was not used. Interest existed in using the Internet for direct marketing in the future. For example, OctoPlus uses sales promotions to collect customer information. This information is used to build a database with the intention of using it for direct marketing in the future. There was no personal selling online, which is not surprising for FMCG industries.

Relationship marketing and branding were seen as particularly important. For example, OzProd noted the Internet's potential for one-to-one communications, and EuroNat highlighted the Internet's facility to communication a depth of information - both important in building relationships. All respondents had brand websites and advanced companies, such as OctoPlus, used the Internet to create positive brand experiences. A key issue for respondents was the value proposition of this new media in their communication efforts. Respondents were grappling with how the Internet could add value to both the consumer and its business. For example EuroNat wanted to know: *How does the Internet affect customer attitudes or intentions to purchase?*

5.2 Integration of the Internet in the Promotional Mix

Our second research question focused on how the Internet should be included in the promotional mix for maximum impact. Respondents were unanimous that the best way to include the Internet in the promotional mix was to integrate it. However, implementation did not match these views in all cases.

Integration in this study was assessed using the concept of consistency. Three measures of integration were used (Low, 2000):

- *Planning/Management*: In all case online and offline communication efforts were planned by the same manager.
- *Strategic consistency*: Marketing communications were strategically integrated at OctoPlus and EuroNat. However the marketing communications of OzProd were not strategically consistent.
- *Commonality of messages*: OctoPlus and EuroNat had consistent communications messages, while OzProd did not.

An additional dimension was highlighted in the study, termed *brand positioning*. This is consistent with the marketing literature (e.g. Shultz, 2001). Respondents commented that Internet communications should be consistent with the positioning of the brand. For example, OctoPlus said the Internet *should live, breath and enhance that brand's proposition*. EuroNat and OctoPlus integrated their Internet communications with brand positioning. OzProd's Internet communications did not reflect brand positioning.

Table 3 summarizes the results concerning the integration of the Internet in the promotional mix in the organizations studied. Overall, OzProd did not integrate, keeping the Internet distinct from other promotional activities. EuroNat integrated the Internet with other promotional activities, but was unsure about how it should be included and was still experimenting in this area. The Internet was seamlessly included in OctoPlus's promotional mix and used wherever it could add value.

	Same manager	**Same message**	**Strategic consistency**	**Brand positioning**
OzProd	x	-	-	-
EuroNat	x	x	x	x
OctoPLus	x	x	x	x

Table 3. Integration of the Internet in the promotional mix in the case study organizations

The constructs of strategic and tactical integration were clarified by respondents. These marketing managers believed that strategic integration involved integrating brand positioning and communications strategy. Integrating communication message and creativity was considered tactical integration. Tactical integration was found in all organisations, except OzProd.

Respondents were not questioned directly in terms of the IMC Framework shown in Table 1. It was clear from their comments, however, that they distinguished among the different functions in the promotional mix and were aware of how different Internet tools could be used to address these functions individually:

> If we're target marketing we use the Internet for banner advertising and building awareness. *[EuroNat]*

> The best role at the moment for the Internet in marketing communications is in sales promotion. *[OctoPlus]*

Respondents believed that use of the Internet should be integrated across the tools in Table 1. Verbatim comments show the flavour of responses.

> The Internet should be integrated. *[OzProd]*

> Every piece of communication to consumers communicates a similar message. For example, for *[a product]* the TV and Web site relate to *[concept]*. Communications should be integrated. There should be horizontal and vertical consistency. Strategic integration is the same brand positioning across media and tools. *[EuroNat]*

> We integrate where it's relevant. It's beyond the stage where every product needs a Web site. ... At the end of the day the user expects a similar brand experience. All communications are signed off by the marketing manager. *[OctoPlus]*

Overall, responses showed that companies direct energy at integration across communication tools, or cells within the framework in Table 1, though not all have achieved this. The concept of "branding" occurred frequently and was seen to be of considerable importance.

5.3 Interactivity

The third research question concerned the use of Interactivity. Responses showed varying conceptualisations of interactivity.

> We don't use interactivity.... *[but also commented]* With *[one of our products]* consumers can get recipes, communicate with home economists and get nutritional information. *[OzProd]*

> Interactivity means consumers communicating with your site. Not just receiving messages but doing something... It is a small priority with us at the moment, because we haven't identified reasons for interactivity – in terms of cost. Why is interactivity better for a company that sells products below $10 than billboards or other media? However, we are not ignoring it because of its potential in market research and relationships. Kids and teens especially **expect** a good web site. It comes down to business case decisions. Still, interactivity is an empowering tool for consumers. Consumers can turn it off, whereas with TV we yell at them. We are still experimenting and learning. Getting used to consumers and learning how not to be flicked... Why use interactivity for a product like *[a food bar]?* Are banner ads relevant? *[EuroNat]*

> We see interactivity as a fully integrated part of the mix to enable us to interact with customers. It gives us the ability to reinforce brand propositions. ... There are very few examples of effective use, though banks are a great example.. depends on the industry. Creativity means it is still totally open. *[OctoPlus]*

To analyse the uses of interactivity, we used a framework based on Ford's goal taxonomy as reviewed earlier. Table 4 shows both the analysis framework and the analysis of the three case studies. The first two columns in Table 4 show how different interactive web tools can be grouped against the different motivating goals, and form a framework for analysing an organization's Internet tools. The two social relationship goals have been merged. This framework allows the analysis of interactive Internet tools from the **user's viewpoint.** Some interactive tools (email and search) are so general that they can be used in achievement of almost any goal, so are grouped separately. Other tools could also be used to achieve a number of goals, and we have included them in the categories where they appear to be of primary use. Ford considers that behaviour is often (perhaps usually) guided by multiple goals simultaneously, so it recognized that this classification mechanism is somewhat arbitrary. We could find no tools that clearly addressed the "subjective organization goals" of unity and transcendence. Ford considers that the "exquisitely powerful and satisfying state of 'flow', as described by Csikszentmihalyi (1990) in his theory of optimal experience" exemplifies a kind of transcendent state to which one might aspire. These flow states could occur with a number of interactive experiences, such as searching for information for pleasure or work tasks under certain conditions.

		Organizational usage		
Goal Category	Interactive tools	OzProd	EuroNat	OctoPLus
Affective goals (entertainment, tranquillity, happiness, bodily sensations, physical well-being.)	Promotions		X	X
	Virtual-tour		X	X
	Downloads		X	
	Games			
	Film			
Cognitive goals (exploration, understanding, intellectual creativity, positive self-evaluations)	Puzzles			X
	Games			
	In-depth information provision			
Subjective organization goals (unity, transcendence)	Many tools under specific conditions	?	?	?
Self-assertive and integrative social relationship goals (individuality, self-determination, superiority, resource acquisition, belongingness, social responsibility, equity, resource provision)	Communities		X	X
	Chat			X
	Members' sections			X
Task goals (mastery, task creativity, management, material gain, safety)	Input-response		X	X
	E-forms		X	X
	Downloads		X	X
	Calculators		X	X
	Members' sections			X
	Store locator			
	Promotions			
	Customisation and personalisation			
	Websites that change behaviour			
(All goals)	Search	X	X	X
	Email	X	X	X

Table 4. Application of interactive tools/goals framework to marketing communications

Note that Ford's taxonomy of human goals offers a more extensive categorization of possible human-goal states in the Internet environment than offered previously. Hoffman and Novak (1996), for example, differentiated primarily between "experiential" and "goal-directed" behavior in their landmark work on marketing on the Web. Their interest was primarily in the state of "flow" (Csikszentmihalyi, 1977, 1990).

The last three columns in Table 4 shows the analysis of the case studies using the framework. The websites of the three case study companies were analysed in terms of the interactive tools each company was using. This analysis was performed by the first author. Interactive tools were used mainly to fulfill task, affective and social relationship goals. Interactive applications were available most in task-based situations -- for example, finding prices. Entertainment and social relationship goals were the next most frequent applications available. OzProd used few interactive tools. EuroNat and OctoPlus each made numerous interactive tools available. Note that no attempt was made to classify company's usage of tools in terms of "Subjective organizational goals", as achievement of these goals (eg through "flow") is likely to be very highly subject- and context-dependent.

6. CONCLUSION

We have reported exploratory research on the role of the Internet in marketing communications and the conceptualisation of integration and interactivity in this context.

Three mini case studies of large companies in the fast moving consumer good industry has allowed some grounding of our ideas on how to approach our research questions.

In answer to our first research question, the **role** of the Internet in marketing communications was seen to be to provide an additional communication channel for functions in the marketing mix. The three companies studied were using the Internet mainly for advertising, sales and public relations. For this industry, personal selling is not a priority. There was interest in direct marketing in the future. Relationship marketing and branding were seen as particularly important. A key issue for respondents was the value proposition of this new media in their communications efforts.

In answer to the second question, **integration** was believed to be important in all three companies. Respondents believed that all communication messages should be integrated, including those on the Internet. Integration through brand positioning was identified as a dimension of integration, in addition to the three consistency dimensions identified a priori from the literature. The least advanced company had integration only in the sense that the same manager planned all marketing communications. The two more advanced companies were also integrated in terms of strategic consistency and commonality of messages. The integrated-Internet Marketing communications Framework developed for this study (Table 1) gave a conceptual background to our questioning of integration. This framework identifies tools used in marketing communications in terms of the marketing functions achieved. Thus, in some respects it gives a **push** viewpoint.

Our third research question asked how organizations are using **interactivity**. Interactivity has a number of conceptualisations, depending on the discipline in which it is studied. It appears to be important to maintain a cross-disciplinary view, so that the different dimensions of interactivity are appreciated. Our three case study organizations had different views on interactivity and were unclear as to its value and how it should be used most effectively. An analysis in terms of our interactive tools/goals framework showed the most advanced company was using tools to address the largest spread of human motivational goals, while the next most advanced company was not far behind. The least advanced company had interactive tools that addressed the fewest of users' possible motivational goals. This tools/goals framework categorizes Internet communication tools in terms of user's goals. Thus, in some respects it gives a **pull** viewpoint.

Though our work is exploratory it raises some interesting issues for future work. Organizations were seen to be uncertain about how the Internet, and interactive tools in particular, can add value. We suggest that the tools/goal framework can assist in identifying possible opportunities for use of interactive tools, particularly if the goals of particular demographic groups can be isolated. Our analysis showed that even the advanced companies were not using many tools in some goal categories – for example, for cognitive goals such as exploration and understanding. Demographic groups who are likely to have these goals may be reached more readily by tools in this category. The achievement of subjective organization goals, such as "flow", presents a further challenge, but may bring greater rewards.

In addition, it is interesting to compare the Internet tools in the "push", marketing-oriented framework (lower half of Table 1) against the "pull", consumer-goal oriented framework (left two columns of Table 4). Some tools, such as banner ads, do not appear in the latter framework and it is difficult to see which, if any, consumer goals they fulfil. One interviewee commented: *Are banner ads relevant?* It appears that in the Internet environment, non-passive, "consumer-pull", interactive marketing tools have the greatest potential to add value because of the additional range of human goals they can address.

REFERENCES

Barwise, P. Elberse, A. Hammond, K. (2001) Marketing and the Internet. *London Business School.*

Belch, G.E. Belch, M.A (2001) Advertising and Promotion – An integrated marketing communications perspective. 5th ed. McGraw-Jill Irwin: San Francisco

Berthon, P. Pitt, L.F. Watson, R.T. (1996). The world wide web as an advertising medium: towards an understanding of conversion efficiency. *Journal of Advertising Research.* Vol.36 No.1 pp.43-54

Bretz, R. (1983) Media for Interactive Communication. Sage: Beverly Hills

Bezjian-Avery, A. Calder, B. Iacobucci, D. (1998) New Media Interactive Advertising vs. Traditional Advertising. Journal of Advertising Research. Vol.38 No.4; pp. 23-33

Blattberg, R.C. Deighton, J. (1991) Interactive marketing: exploiting the age of addressability. *Sloan Management Review.* Fall pp.5-14

Bickart, B. Schindler, R.M. (2001) Internet Forums as influential sources of consumer information. *Journal of interactive marketing.* Vol.15 No.3

Bruner, G. C. Kumar, A. (2000) Web commercials and Advertising Hierarcy of Effects. *Journal of Advertising Research.* Vol.40 No.1/2. pp.35-43

Bucy, E.P. Lang, A. Potter, R.F. Grabe, M..E. (1999) Formal features of cyberspace: relationships between web page complexity and site traffic. *Journal of the America society for information science.* Vol. 50 No. 13. pp.1246-1256

Bush, A.J. Bush, V. Harris, S. (1998) Advertiser perceptions of the Internet as a marketing communications tool. *Journal of Advertising research.* Vol.38 No.2 pp.17-27

Bush, A.J. Bush, V.D (2000) Potential Challenges the Internet Brings to the agency-advertiser relationship. *Journal of Advertising Research.* Vol.40 No.4; pp.7-16

Chen, Q. Wells, W.D. (1999) Attitude toward the site. *Journal of Advertising Research.* Vol.39 No.5 pp.27-38

Cornelissen, J.P. Lock, A.R. (2000) Theoretical Concept or Management Fashion? Examining the significance of IMC. *Journal of Advertising Research.* Vol.40 No. 5 pp.7-15

Covielo, N. Milley, R. Marcolin, B. (2001) Understanding IT enable interactivity in contemporary marketing. *Journal of Interactive Marketing.* Vol.15 No.4 pp.18-33.

Coyle, J. R. Thorson, E. (2001) The effects of progressive levels of Interactivity and vividness in web marketing sites. *Journal of Advertising.* Vol.30 No.3 pp.65-77

Cross, R. (1994) Internet: The missing Marketing Medium Found. *Direct Marketing.* Vol.57 No.6 pp.20-24

Csikszentmihalyi, M. (1977). *Beyond boredom and anxiety.* San Francisco: Jossey-Bass.

Csikszentmihalyi, M. (1990). *Flow: The psychology of optimal experience.* New York: Harper Row.

Davis, F. D. (1989). Perceived usefulness, perceived ease of use, and user acceptance of information technology. *MIS Quarterly,* Sept., 319-340.

Davis, R. Buchanan-Oliver, M. Brodie, R.J. (2000) Retail Service Branding in Electronic Commerce environments. *Journal of Services Research.* Vol.3 No.2; pp.178-187

Deighton, J. Barwise, P. (2000) Digital Marketing Communication. *Future Media Research Programme – London Business School.*

Deighton, J. (1997) Commentary on "Exploring the implications of the Internet for consumer marketing. *Journal of the Academy of Marketing Science.* Vol.25, No.4, pp.329-346

Duncan, T. R. Everett S. E. (1993) Client perceptions of Integrated Marketing Communications. *Journal of Advertising Research.* Vol.33 No.3; pp.30-40

Ford, M. (1992). Motivating Humans Goals, Emotions & Personal Agency Beliefs. Sage Publications: London

Geiger, S. Martin, S. (1999) The Internet as a relationship marketing tool – some evidence from Irish companies. Irish Marketing Review. Vol.12 No.2 pp.24-36

Ghose, S. Dou, W. (1998) Interactive Functions and their impacts on the appeal of Internet presence sites. *Journal of Advertising Research*. Vol.38 No.2; pp.29-44

Gould, S.J (2000) The state of IMC research and applications. *Journal of Advertising Research*. Vol. 40 No.5 pp.22-24

Haeckel, S. H. (1998). About the nature and future of interactive marketing. *Journal of Interactive Marketing, 12*(1), pp. 63-71.

Hanson, W. (1998) The original WWW: Web lessons from the early days of radio. *Journal of Interactive Marketing*. Vol.12 No.3 pp.46-56

Heeter, C. (1989) Implications of new interactive technologies for conceptualizing communication. In J.L. Salvaggio & J. Bryant (Eds.) *Media use in the information age* (pp.217-236). Hillsdale, NJ: Lawrence Erlbaum.

Hochhauser, R.M. (2000) The interactive evolution of a direct marketing leader. *Direct Marketing*. Vol.63 No.1 pp.45-49.

Hoffman, D.L. Novak, T.P. (1996) Marketing in Hypermedia Computer-Mediated Environments: Conceptual Foundations. *Journal of Marketing*. Vol.60 No.3 pp.50-68.

Kotler, P. Armstrong, G. Brown, L. Adam, S. (1999) Marketing 4th edition. Prentice Hall: Australia.

Krishnamurthy, S. (2001) A comprehensive Analysis of Permission Marketing. *Journal of Computer Mediated Communication*. Vol.6 No.2

Low, G.S. (2000) Correlates of Integrated Marketing Communications. *Journal of Advertising Research*. Vol.40 No.3 pp.27-35

Mcgaughey, R.E. Mason, K.H. (1998) The Internet as a marketing tool. *Journal of Marketing Theory and Practice*. Vol.6 No.3 1998. pp.1-11.

McWilliam, G. (2000) Building Stronger Brands through Online Communities. *Sloan Management Review*. Vol.41 No.3 pp.43-55

Perman, S. (2001) Enterprise Marketing, Building Brands. *Asia week*. Oct 26 2001.

Perry, M. Bodkin C. (2000) Content analysis of Fortune 100 company websites. *Corporate Communications*. Vol.5 No.2 pp.87-96

Peterson, R.A. Balasubramanian, S. Bronenberg, B. J. (1997) Exploring the implications of the Internet for consumer marketing. *Journal of the Academy of Marketing Science*. Vol.25 No.4, pp.329-346

Quelch, J.A. Klein, L.R. (1996) The Internet and International Marketing. *Sloan Management Review*. Vol.37 No.3 pp.60-76

Rafaeli, S. (1988) Interactivity: From New Media to Comunication. In: Advances in Communication Science, Merging Mass and Interpersonal Processes. Hawkins, R.P., Wieman J.M, and Pingree S. eds. Sage: Newbury Park, CA. 110,34

Rogers, E.M. Allbritton, M.M (1995) Interactive Communication Technologies in Business Organisations. *The Journal of Business Communication*. Vol.32. No.2. pp.177-195

Sheehan, K.B. Boherty, C. (2001) Re-weaving the web: Integrating Print and Online Communications. *Journal of Interactive Marketing*. Vol.15 No.2 pp.47-59

Schlosser, A.E. Shavitt, S. Kanfer, A. (1999) Survey of Internet Users Attitudes towards Internet Advertising. *Journal of Interactive Marketing*. Vol.13 No.3 pp.34-54

Schultz, D.E. (1993) Integrated Marketing Communications: Maybe definition is in the point of view. *Marketing News*. Vol.27 No.2 pp.17-18

Schultz, D.E. (1999) New media, old problem: Keeping marcom integrated. *Marketing News*. Vol.33 No.7 pp.11-12

Schultz, D.E. (2001) The core of integration is the brand. *Marketing Management.* Vol.10 No.1 pp.6-8

Steuer, J. (1992) Defining virtual reality: dimensions determining telepresence. *Journal of Communication.* Vol 42 No 2. pp.73-93

Takacs, S.J. Freiden, J.B. (1998) Changes on the Electronic Frontier: Growth and opportunity of the World Wide Web. *Journal of Marketing Theory and Practice.* Vol.6 No.3 pp.24-38

Ritson, M. (1998) Three possibilities in integrating the Internet. *Marketing News.* Vol. 32 No.10. pp.10-11.

Van Doren, D.C. Fechner, D.L. and Green-Adelsberger, K. (2000) Promotional Strategies on the World Wide Web. *Journal of Marketing Communications.* Vol.6 pp.21-35

Wells, W. Burnett, J. Moriarty, S. (2000) Advertising principles and practice 5th ed. Prentice Hall: New Jersey

Watson, R.T. Zinkhan, G.M. Pitt, L.F. (2000) Integrated Internet Marketing. *Communications of the AMC.* Vol.43 No.6 pp.97-102

APPENDIX

- Definition of Promotional Functions:
(source: Belch and Belch 2001)

Advertising is any paid form of non-personal communication about an organization, product, service, or idea by an identified sponsor.

Direct marketing is where organizations communicate directly with target customers to generate a response and/or a transaction.

Sales promotion is marketing activities that provide extra value or incentives to the sales force, distributors, or the ultimate consumer and can stimulate immediate sales.
Personal selling is a form of person-to-person communication in which a seller attempts to assist and/or persuade prospective buyers to purchase the company's product or service or to act on an idea.

Public relations is the management function which evaluates public attitudes, identifies the policies and procedures of an individual or organization with the public interest, and executes a program of action to earn public under-standing and acceptance. *Publicity* refers to non-personal communications regarding an organization, product, service, or idea not directly paid for or run under identified sponsorship.

E-BUSINESS AND THE FORMATION OF STRATEGIES

SVEN JUNGHAGEN[1] and HENRIK C. J. LINDEROTH[2]

[1] *Department of Management, Politics & Philosophy, Copenhagen Business School*

[2] *Department of Management, Politics & Philosophy, Copenhagen Business School and Centre for Digital Business, Umeå School of Business and Economics*

Abstract: During the last years e-business has become a topic that has gained much attention among scholars and practitioners, and in contemporary business different IT-applications play important roles for transactions in business to business (B2B) relations. But in business to consumer (B2C) relations the results of e-business efforts are mixed. Hence, the issue is what kind of strategic considerations a company has to do when they would engage in e-business efforts on B2C relations? The aim of the paper is to discuss a few possible points of departure for a further inquiry into the relation between a company's strategies and e-business efforts, that could be important to pay attention to in further research on e-business and strategies, or when a company would conduct an e-business effort. The discussion takes its point of departure in different theoretical conceptions on strategy, with the intention to account for a model on strategy formation that can be valid in relation to e-business in B2C relations. The theoretical concepts are then discussed with regards to some s observations mainly build on secondary data. Built on the secondary data and the theoretical conception on strategy formation, the following topics are identified to be highlighted in the process of relating e-business efforts to a overall strategies: (1) A clear conception of the target market, (2) A consistency between the defined market and the product system to be sold, (3) An understanding of the relation between market, product and the delivery/communication system, (4) Act on the values and beliefs of the organisation.

1. INTRODUCTION

During the last years e-business has become a topic that has gained much attention among scholars and practitioners, and in contemporary business different IT-applications play important roles for transactions in business to business (B2B) relations. But in business to consumer (B2C) relations the results of e-business efforts are mixed. From a strategic point of view, management dealing with B2C relations seems to consider how the company would be related to e-business. Should the company enter the e-business scene, or should it stay outside? If a decision is made to enter the e-business scene, the management issue will than be formulation and implementation of e-business efforts.

Recommendations for formulation and implementation of e-business efforts are varying from a process of rigorous planning (see e.g. Hackbart & Kettinger 2000), to an organic process (Brache & Webb 2000). Consequently, it does not seems to be a best way of formulating e-business efforts in B2C relations, but can some common topics be identified for a formulation of e-business efforts? In order to elaborate upon this issue a few perspectives on generic business strategies will be discussed in this paper. Concepts discussed in the theoretical framework will be combined with some empirical observations mainly build secondary data, with the aim of identify and discuss topics that could be important to pay attention to in further research on e-business and strategies, or when a company would conduct an e-business effort. Thus, the aim of the paper is to discuss a few possible points of departure for a further inquiry into the relation between a company's strategies and e-business efforts.

In order to reach this aim, some basic virtues of a company is discussed, which is followed by a discussion on different theoretical conceptions on strategy, with the intention to account for a conceptual framework on strategy formation that can be valid in relation to e-business. This discussion is followed by some observations of e-business attempts, built mainly on secondary data from descriptions of e-business efforts, and a few informal interviews. The following analyses will account for a discussion on these observations in relation to the theoretical framework with the purpose to indicate some possible directions in the quest for integration of e-business efforts into a company's overall strategies.

2. BASIC VIRTUES OF THE FIRM

To put it bluntly, it could be claimed that e-business strategies are completely uninteresting, but e-business as strategy is very interesting. It might seem to be a matter of rhetoric, but solely discussing e-business strategies could in fact be to get into implementation issues, without questioning the basic premises of the chosen path. The discourse on the new e-conomy has been characterised by a strong technological imperative. A predominant part of the literature on e-business and e-commerce has taken its starting point in concepts like e.g. richness and reach in terms of technological possibilities (e.g. Evans & Wurster, 2000) and more or less neglected other traditional business virtues. We do however believe that even though a new e-conomy might be expired today, some basic marketing virtues and strategic virtues are to be remembered and honoured.

One of the most fundamental virtues is that of value creation. Even though it might seem as a very simplified view of a firm, it can stated that if a firm cannot provide a value that someone outside the firm is willing to pay for, the firm will inevitably die. Even if first mover advantage is expired or if a firm have an extensive amount of unique hits on your website, it will not survive without someone willing to pay for what you do. This statement is one important starting point for our perspective on strategy. Another important issue is the relation between overall business strategies and e-business efforts. E-business can be seen as a very broad concept including all activities in a firm, if these activities are in some way incorporated in a digital information system. The focus in this paper will be on activities related to the external relations of a firm, and mainly activities supporting transactions with consumers by means of the Internet. It might be a blunt description, but it can be claimed in a marketing and strategy perspective that the Internet can be seen as a media for communication and for transactions. In some cases, if the product is virtual, it can also be seen as a distribution channel. Put in other words, the Internet can be seen as a communications resource, a content resource and a channel resource (Coupey, 2001). As claimed above, a high amount of hits on a website do not necessarily lead to success automatically, but will enable the site owner to sell this exposure to advertisers. We will not in this paper go into these mechanisms, where Internet can be seen as a pure communications media through an attractive content. Instead, the discussion will focus on strategy formation options in relation to the conception of Internet as a strategic channel resource for products and services, and to illuminate interdependencies of e-business efforts and overall strategies of a firm.

3. A THEORETICAL CONCEPTION OF STRATEGY FORMATION

3.1 A Discourse on Strategy

Strategy might be one of these words we use a lot, without a single unified conception of the "true meaning" of the word. The word strategy is directly derived from the Greek word *strategia*, basically meaning the art of warfare in a supreme command position. Early conceptions of business strategy and corporate strategy are very much related to this basic meaning of the word. Strategy is something that you practice in a command position in a firm, to plan a competitive action against opponents in a market or an industry. The holder of this command position is in Greek called *strategos*. Even though we do not agree fully with the analogy of warfare, there are some dimensions in this generic derivation that deserve attention. First of all, even though there are not enemies, strategy can be seen as something dealing with the external relations of a firm. This might be in competition with others, in co-operation, and even in co-opetition (e.g. Hamel, Doz & Prahalad, 1989). Secondly, even though strategy might not be a phenomenon specifically addressed to a supreme command, it should be regarded as some kind of guided action, by means of a vision, a mission or intent (e.g. Campbell & Yeung, 1991).

The discourse on strategy is clearly diversified, with a number of paradigms and perspectives. Mintzberg et al. (1998) suggest ten schools of thought on strategy, a classification involving thoughts of scholars as well as practitioners. We are not going into all these schools of thoughts in this paper, but the two major categories are worth mentioning, the prescriptive and the descriptive schools of thought. Examples of the prescriptive schools are the planning school and the positioning school, where the fundamental logic of strategy formation is a distinction between decision-making and the implementation of these decisions. Mintzberg also refers to this category as deliberate strategies.

As a reaction to the fact that these normative statements seldom seemed to come true, the descriptive schools of thought on strategy emerged. Instead of giving normative propositions, the descriptive schools rather propose how things actually are done. Examples here are the cognitive school, the environmental school and the learning school. In these schools of thought, strategies are not deliberate, but emergent. Even though it might seem that these different conceptions of strategy are conflicting in terms of explaining the strategy phenomenon, it could argued that the conflict is not on a factual level, but an ideological level. The most important difference is in ontological assumptions. The prescriptive schools are based on an objective ontology, where it is possible to analyse a context and make a decision that will provide a satisfactory outcome. Most of the descriptive schools are more subjective in their ontological assumption, and strategy is formed as for example a consequence of social constructions (e.g. Searle, 1995) as in the cognitive school, or through individual psychological characteristics (e.g. Davidsson 1989; 1996; Thong & Yap, 1995) as in the entrepreneurial school or through collective learning, and so forth.

The main problem in the debate between these schools is that the validation of the explanatory power in the perspective is based on the ontological assumptions underlying the same perspective. In a way, validation tends to be a self-fulfilling prophecy. We do not intend to take an active part in that debate in this paper, but try to provide a theoretical conception of interdependency between e-business and overall strategies that can function as a prescriptive statement based on a view that strategies emerge, rather than are planned.

3.2 The Concept of Business Ideas

A conceptual framework that can function as an overall model of strategy formation is that of business ideas (Normann, 1975). A business idea could be seen as a statement defining the raison d'être for a firm, answering three basic questions: To whom, what, and How? The answers to these three questions include a close description of the specific market, the product system delivered to this market, and finally the system of resources, competencies and structures utilised in order to make it all happen.

The most important part is not just a clear conception of these three levels, but a high level of consistency between the levels. You might have a clear conception of a given market, and the perfect product for this market, but if you do not have a consistent system for delivery, you will not succeed.

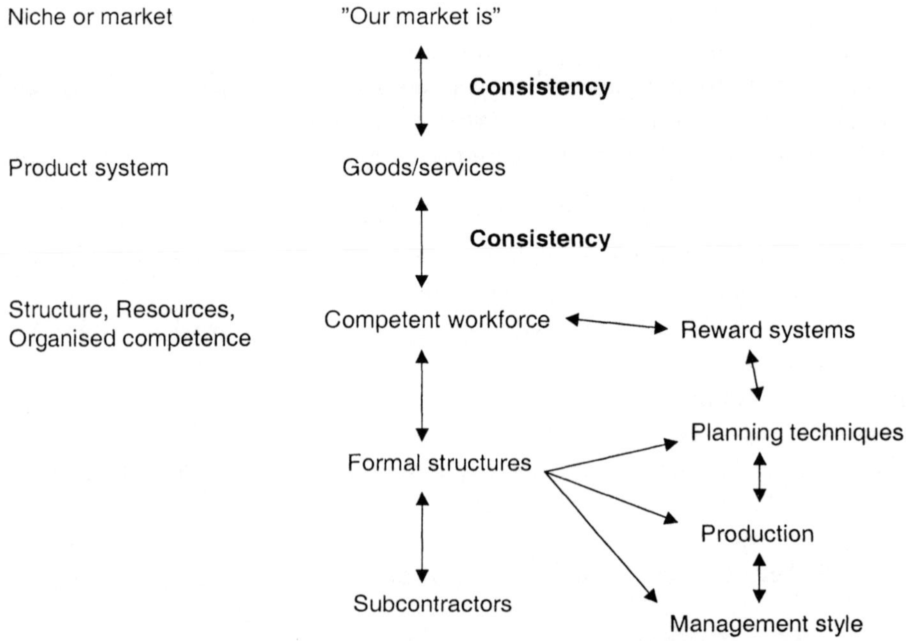

Figure 1. Main characteristics of a business idea (Normann, 1975)

As was stated above, someone outside the firm must perceive the offer as valuable in order for the firm to survive on a long-term basis. A critical reflection might evolve at this stage, since discussions on infrastructure and other structural resources are normally sorted under a discourse on operations management and not strategic management, but that is very much dependent upon a chosen perspective. We believe in inseparability between these elements, the duality of strategy and structure (e.g. Chandler, 1962) basically meaning that we cannot tell whether strategy forms structure or if structure forms strategy. As a consequence, the argument in the introductory section is strengthened, where it was stated that e-business efforts should take overall business strategies into account and support them. By extending this line of reasoning even further, if we believe in inseparability between strategy and supporting structures, e-business efforts should not just support overall strategies, but be an integrative part of strategy formation.

3.3 Strategy formation

If we then direct our focus to formation on a conceptual level, rather than formulation and implementation, it might seem problematic to accept emergent strategies, and in the same time state that e-business efforts should be an integrative part. We do however believe in that strategies emerge within a more or less explicitly defined sense of strategic direction of the firm. As claimed above, this sense of direction could for example be defined through the business idea. The question is then if this implies that a change of strategic direction simply means that the business idea should be reformulated? In order for that to be true, we have to believe in the possibility to plan an action to be implemented later. Since we do not accept that belief, we have to answer negatively and will instead bring forward a model showing the relation between intentions for future change and present conditions. The model shown in figure 2 is built on a conception that there is a relation between the change situation, the organisational structure and the system of values and beliefs in the firm. Any intended change has to take the existing structure and values into account. The values and beliefs of significant actors regarding the identity of the firm may for example be as important for the potential for change as market conditions are.

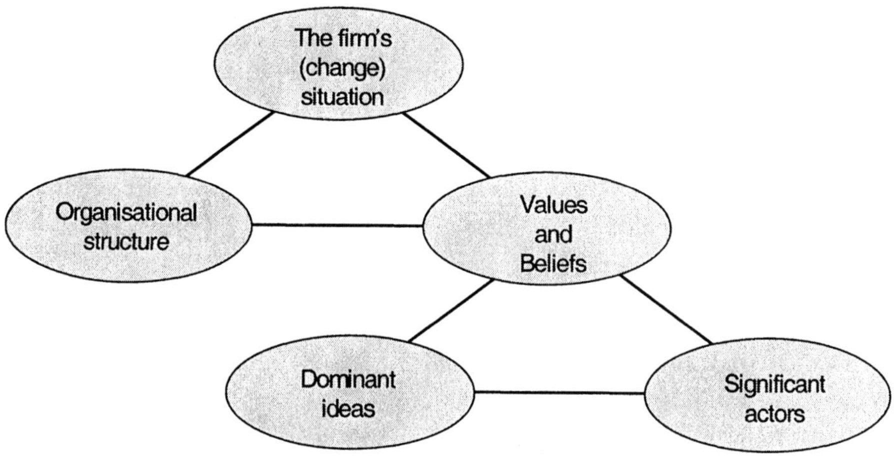

Figure 2. A model of a firm's strategic context (Adapted from Normann, 1975)

The reasoning in relation to Figure 2 can be seen as somewhat analogue to the structurational model of technology, brought forward by Orlikowski & Robey (1991), with the difference that we do not consider information technology as a stand-alone phenomenon, but an integrated dimension of the organisational structure.

To conclude, we cannot provide a complete model, stating appropriate actions for success when forming a strategy for e-business, but must accept the effects of contingencies. In the following section, a number of observations will be accounted for in order to give some examples of contingencies and e-business scenarios.

4. OBSERVATIONS FROM THE E-BUSINESS SCENE

Around the turn of the last millennium the notion of "dotcom death" came into everyone's mind, but not all companies entering the e-business scene was stroked by the "dotcom death". Some companies are still wealthy and expanding their business. But can some tendencies be seen that is sorting out the survivors, from those resting in the virtual graveyards? In order to found a ground for the further search on research directions about formulation of e-business efforts, a few cases those have been more or less successful in surviving on the e-business scene will be shortly described.

4.1 Clas Ohlson

A couple of years ago, word of mouth said that a bicycle repairman founded the biggest e-business company in Sweden back in 1918. Clas Ohlson, located in the small village of Insjön in middle Sweden, started its mail order operations by selling technical handbooks in the beginning of the 1920-s. In 2000 the annual turnover was approximately 140 M€ and the catalogue contains 15 000 products ranging from welding sets and small compressors to shaving foam and paint for the hobby artist. What is common for all products is that they are sold to private consumers and institutions.

In 1996 Clas Ohlson launched their first web site and in 1999 they launched their new website where all products were available for sale. The launch of the website could be seen as logical step in the company's expansion, aiming at building a hybrid channels structure (Boberg & Boborg 2001). In 1989 the company opened its first store outside Insjön, when they went into one of the most central gallerias in Stockholm. Since then another 21 stores has open in central location in major Swedish and Norwegian cities. Last year, 2001, the sales via Internet were about 35% of the total mail order sales, which in turn was around 13% of the total turn over. According to the company the sales via the web has attracted new customer groups like generally younger people and more women. But they don't think that their website will replace the catalogue, because you can bring it to all places in your home, as one company representative stated. The company see three different factors these positively have influenced the sales via the website. First, their base of 500 000 customers; second they have a knowledge about logistics, meaning that at least 98% of the sold products should be delivered to the right place on the right time; third, the need for customer care, 20 people are working at the main location in Insjön to manage customer complaints.

4.2 Net-on-Net

Not only a prevailing customer base and infrastructure seems to be a way to remain on the e-business scene. Net-on-Net is a Swedish web based company selling home electronics and their turnover has grown from approximately 620 000 € in 1999, to approximately 18 M€ in 2001, but they are still struggling to reach a profit. In 2000 the loss was 4 M€, but for the period January-November 2001 the losses had decreased to 2 M€, and according to the monthly report for November the company had 5,2 M€ in cash in hand and bank deposit. According to the company's CEO, companies like Net-on-Net, or pure dotcoms have during the last years, in order of turn over via the net, passed the traditional mail order companies, even if these are bigger in terms of total turn over. A further observation from the interview is that many of the dotcoms that survived, have been in businesses where the business models are similar to traditional mail order. A further interesting detail about Net-on-Net is its location in Borås, the home city of the major Swedish mail order companies since at least 50 years.

4.3 Webvan and Disco

Not only traditional mail order companies, or companies who start up on the Internet with concepts similar to mail order firms, have entered the e-business scene. Groceries have been a product where several attempts have been made. Two companies with a, at the first glance, similar concepts are Webvan and Disco. Webvan was an Internet grocer with a vision of creating 26 massive automated warehouses and a national fleet of vans that would deliver groceries in major US cities (Helft 2001). In order to gain success Webvan had built up a sophisticated logistic system to handle and deliver the right merchandise to the right place in the right time (Platoni 2001):

> "The huge warehouse is a sci-fi workplace where the employees wear bar-code scanners on their fingertips and miniature wrist computers that tell them what to do, where the software driving the machinery is so prescient that it makes sure the potato chips get packed on top of the six-pack of Coke, instead of

underneath. It is also the nerve center of Webvan's Bay Area hub-and-spoke routing system, designed to time deliveries so precisely that your order gets to your house with the ice cream still frozen and the tomatoes unblemished."

Webvan invested heavily in their infrastructure and their website was also regarded as "best of class", but they ran out of money and had to close down in mid 2001 (Schubert & Dettling 2002).

A company with a, at the first glance, similar concept as Webvan is Disco in Buenos Aires, Argentina, a 237-store unit of Dutch food conglomerate Royal Ahold. But there are more differences than similarities between Disco and Webvan (Helft 2001):

> Disco has built the business without the massive customized warehouses and automated distribution systems that cost Webvan hundreds of millions of dollars. Instead, it based the operation on a service that Disco has offered for decades: home delivery. Last year, about 25 percent of Disco's $2.5 billion in sales were delivered. "We have been intimately familiar with the workings and the economics of the home delivery business for a long time," says Pablo García Gili, CEO of Disco's online division Disco Virtual. Another big difference: Disco execs were quick to recognize the discomfort Argentines have with punching their credit card numbers into a computer. Unlike Americans who use Webvan, Disco customers can pay for deliveries with cash or credit cards when the groceries arrive.

However, the virtual branch of Disco share one similarity with Webvan, it has yet to turn to a profit.

4.4 E-commerce in Scandinavia

A further clue to which kind of companies who can survive on the net might found if it is investigated what is sold on the net. A study of how much of the total sales volumes for different product groups that was sold via the Internet in Scandinavia in 2000 is shown in Table 5:

Computer software	18,2%
Computer accessories	12,8%
PC's	10,6%
Music CD's	8,7%
Books	4,5%
Video movies	3,9%
Travels	2,4%
Toys	1,6%
Garment	0,5%
Groceries	0,2%

Table 5. Percentage of sales volume via Internet of total sales volume in Scandinavia 2000 (Jansson 2000)

The observations until now show that tangible goods sold before via mail order, is now also selling well via the net. But selling tangible goods is not a guarantee for survival, which Webvan is an example of. Another example of a company trying to sell tangible goods was Boo.Com, who through its existence burnt about 180 M€ of venture capital (The Irish times 2000). In May 1999 the online sportswear company was launched. The idea was to sell high-end garment via the Internet and retail sites was opened up in 18 countries. But due to technical problems it lasted until November 1999 before the sites were up and running. During its short life Boo.com struggled with financial problems and 17:th of May 2000 the company went bankrupt. The web site of Boo.com was technically rather advanced, but the problem was that it required a high bandwidth that made it too slow for many potential customers. (Glick 2000)

4.5 Intangibles: Lovesearch

However, not only companies selling tangible goods has survived, the net dating site "Lovesearch", which had the American site Match.com as a prototype, has also survived the dotcom death. Lovesearch opened up in the end of 1999 and was founded by the former member of the pop group Army of Lovers, Dominika Peczynski and the fashion designer Camilla Thulin. The members of the site are paying a member fee of 10 € per month. The service is built upon the members' input of information and characteristics about themselves, and characteristics the member wants of the potential partner. Then the computer is doing the job by matching together members with similar preferences and they can send messages or chat with each other. However, Lovesearch was not only built around the matchmaking site. The venture capitalist behind the site is Scandinavian Broadcasting Group who owns the Swedish channel 5, and the intention behind their engagement was to link the site to the companies TV- and radio stations (Edling 2001). One expression for this was the fact that one of the site founders, Dominika Peczynski, was host in Channel 5 for a program called Dating.

The description of the cases has showed that not only mail order companies have managed to survive the dotcom death. Even pure dotcoms selling tangible and intangible goods have survived, while other dotcoms who tried to sell tangible goods are resting in peace. In the next section, observations from the e-business arena will be discussed with regards to the theoretical framework in order to indicate what dimensions are important to relate to when considering e-business efforts.

5. EVOLUTION AS A BEST PRACTICE IN E-STRATEGY?

In order to create a deeper understanding of the integration of a firm's overall strategy and its e-business efforts, the point of departure will be taken in the conception of a company's business idea and an elaboration of the three questions: what, to whom and how? The relation between who and what can be seen to reflect the classical relation between supply and demand, and how determines whether there will be a transaction or not. But the notion of how in the business idea should not only be understood as how the offer is delivered to the customer, if it is via mail order, store or another kind of delivery channel. The notion of how can also have a bearing on what the customer is buying. As stated above, a customer does not pay for a product, but for a perceived value. This expectation of value can of course in many cases be fulfilled, but in many other cases customers perceive value in some dimension that goes beyond the core product. This might be one explanation to why companies like Boo.com failed. Customers not only want to buy high-end fashion garments, they also want the pleasure involved in a shopping experience. This explanation is more or less exclusively directed towards the actual product offer, the "what part". A discussion on the "how part" leads us to an understanding of consumer behaviour. There are not many examples of successful mail order firms selling high-end fashion; it might be so that the target markets for these products do not consider mail order as a shopping alternative. If you cannot sell these products via traditional mail order, why should you be able to do so just because you place the catalogue on the Internet?

However, even if consumer behaviour is an important issue whether an e-business effort will survive or not, it will not *per se* determine a success. A comparison between Webvan and Disco shows the context dependency. Disco is operating in a market where home delivery of groceries is well established since many years and they also adapted to customers scepticism about paying with credit cards via Internet. At the same time one can raise the question if Webvan had the appropriate knowledge about consumer behaviour in their target market?

Clas Ohlson is a good example of a development strategy that is consistent with the existing business idea. They had a long tradition of selling their product portfolio via traditional mail order. Both the assortment as well as the mail order system with infrastructures for information and goods was well suited in order to provide an established mass of customers with a value. The extension into the e-business arena was not a huge step for Clas Ohlson, since the back bone logistics and the customer handling system was already in place. There was no conflict with the traditional values and beliefs in the firm, since the basic logic of operations was the same. One could in fact argue that the opening of physical stores was a harder step to take, since that strategic choice implied a new direction and focus of the firm's core competencies.

Compared to mail order companies solely present on the Internet, as Net-on-Net, Clas Ohlson has, at the moment, an advantage of a financial strength based on the turnover in their traditional stores, which makes them less vulnerable for losses in their e-business branch. The same situation can be said to be present for Disco who can relay on the turnover from their traditional store, and allow them to find out how an e-business effort can be integrated into the overall strategy.

In the case of Lovesearch it can be claimed that the company has added a value compared to more traditional match making services. The customer doesn't have to wait several days for answers regarding potential partners and the chat and message function makes it possible to immediately get in touch with the other person. However, one might raise the issue whether the survival until now depends on the value adding services those are provided by Lovesearch, or if it depends upon the marketing efforts with the celebrities and the TV-channel involved? Or is it a combination of both these circumstances?

6. CONCLUSIONS

Even though one can argue that our empirical observations are not characterised by the depth needed in order to make clear normative statements about strategy formation, we do believe that we can use the analysis above to indicate topics of importance when considering e-business efforts. Naturally, this is based on our approach that even though some scholars believe that we experience new logic in the economy we still believe in some basic strategic virtues. The basic premise for survival is that a firm can provide value to someone outside the firm, a statement that is supported by the limited empirical observations in this paper.

A problem is though how to combine intentions with the influence of contingencies. If a strategic decision situation is context dependent and contingent, is it ever possible to give recommendation for managers...? Of course not in terms of detailed action plans, but we will here point out some issues that have to be dealt with:

6.1 A clear conception of the target market

First of all, all customers are not all alike and do not possess the same needs, wants and demands. Hence, there is a need for a clear conception of the target market of the firm, and an understanding of what kind of problems that can be solved for these customers.

6.2 A consistency between the defined market and the product system to be sold

If there is a defined target market and the needs, wants and demands of this market are defined as well; there is a possibility to define a product system to be sold to this market. The most important thing to remember here is that customers basically do not care about products and services as such, but the problem solution these products offer.

In most cases, the Internet as such does not provide a problem solution but function merely as a media for transactions. There are of course other cases, where the basic problem solution can be defined in terms of convenience, accessibility, time and other dimensions and the Internet is the best mean in order to achieve this. It is however important to understand the fundamental behaviour of the target market in relation to the specific product class, when determining the problem solution to be sold.

6.3 An understanding of the relation between market, product and the delivery/communication system

With a defined target market, a definition of problems to be solved and a defined problem solution, the way to make this happen needs to be defined. Even though it is impossible to define an absolute best practice, there has to be a consistency between market, product and the set of competencies, resources, supporting infrastructures and technologies used. Even though a firm might have a "perfect solution" to be sold on "the best web site", this way to sell the product has to make sense for the customer, otherwise there will be no sale. Some products are very hard to sell via mail order. These products will be hard to sell on the net as well, if it is perceived as mail order upgraded by an electronic brochure.

6.4 Act on the values and beliefs of the organisation

This final recommendation might be the most important, but at the same time the most difficult to relate to. When facing a situation of an intended strategic change, one has to understand the importance of the tradition and history of the firm. There are a lot of cognitive understandings of the firm's identity and it's raison d'être guiding future conceptions of the firm's activities. Any e-business effort intended needs to be consistent with this understanding of the firm, besides the need for consistency with competencies, resources and structures. The reason for this can be found in the fact that any firm has its tradition and a cognitive perception of this tradition among the staff. If there for example is a dominant idea that the firm is not a mail order firm, an e-commerce development will not make sense to the staff if it is perceived as electronic mail order. The most likely consequence will be that even if this electronic ordering system is introduced, the organization will act on the values and beliefs underlying the tradition of not being a mail order firm. In that case, actions in the firm might not be consistent with the way the firm approach the market.

REFERENCES

Boberg, P, & Boborg, N. (2001) Just add .se: Old companies in a new situation - A qualitative study of hybrid channel structures. Master's Thesis. Dept of Business Administration Umeå University.

Brache & Webb (2000) The eight deadly assumptions of e-business. Journal of Business Strategy 21(3), 13-17.

Campbell, A & Yeung, S. (1991) Brief Case: Mission, Vision and Strategic Intent Long Range Planning, Aug 1991

Chandler, A D. Jr. (1962) Strategy and structure: chapters in the history of the American industrial enterprise. Cambridge, MA: MIT Press.

Coupey, E. (2001) Marketing and the Internet – Conceptual Foundations. Upper Saddle River, NJ. Prentice Hall.

Davidsson, P. (1989); Continued Entrepreneurship and Small Firm Growth. Stockholm: Ekonomiska Forskningsinstitutet.

Davidsson, P. (1996); Kultur och företagande. in Johannisson, B., Lindmark, L. editors.Företag, Företagare, Företagsamhet. Studentlitteratur, Lund. p. 151-73.

Edling, L (2001) Hon gör affärer på Internet. www.aftonbladet.se/vss/ekonomie24/story/0,2789,24459,00.html (020225)

Evans, P & Wurster, T.S. (2000) Blown to bits – How the new economics of information transforms strategy. Harvard business school press. Boston.

Glick, B. (2000); boo.com's fall makes realism the fashion. http://www.vnunet.com/Analysis/1102339

Hackbart, G & Kettinger W. J. (2000) Building an E-business strategy. Information Systems Management 17(3), 78-93.

Hamel, G, Doz, Y.L., Prahalad, C.K. (1989) Collaborate with your Competitors and Win. Harvard Business Review. Jan-Feb. 1989:133-139.

Heft, D. (2001) Don't Cry for Argentina's Version of Webvan. www.thestandard.com /article/0,1902,24050,00.html

Mintzberg, H, Ahlstrand, B, Lampel, J. (1998) Strategy Safari. Hemel Hempstead. Prentice Hall.

Normann, R. (1975) Skapande Företagsledning. Arlöv. Bonniers.

Orlikowski, W J. & Robey, D. (1991) Information technology and structuring of organizations. Information Systems Research. 2(2), 143-169.

Platoni, K. (2001) The Last Mile. In: East Bay Express online. http://www.eastbayexpress. com/issues/2001-05-25/feature.html/1/index.html

Schubert, P, & Dettling, W. (2002) Extended Web Assessment Method (EWAM) – Evaluation of E-commerce Application from the Customer's Viewpoint. In: Proceedings of the 35th Hawaii International Conference on Systems Sciences.

Searle, J R. (1995) The construction of social reality. London. Penguin Books.

The Irish times (2000); Boo.com - like selling fresh air, claims liquidator. http://www.ireland .com/newspaper/breaking/2000/0602/breaking42.htm

Thong, J.Y. and Yap, C.S. (1995); An information technology adoption model for small businesses. in Kautz, K., Pries-Heje, J., Larsen, T.J., Sörgaard, P. editors.Conference Notebook: First IFIP 8.6 Working Conference on Diffusion and Adoption of Information Technology. Norsk Regnesentral, Oslo. p. 349-64.

MANAGING A PORTFOLIO OF SUPPLIER RELATIONS IN INTERNET-DRIVEN ELECTRONIC MARKET PLACES.

A theoretical discussion

MARTIN GRIEGER, HERBERT KOTZAB and TAGE SKJØTT-LARSEN
Department of Operations Management, Copenhagen Business School, Denmark

Abstract: Corporative buying has changed from simple purchasing to e-sourcing, which means transforming the interaction between companies from transactional to relational relations. The following paper presents the conceptual framework of a supplier-buyer portfolio, when sourcing is done over the Internet. The perspective chosen is Supply Chain Management. Differing between three types of internet-driven electronic market places (private, consortia and independent e-market), different cooperative business relations have to be set up by supply management.

Key words: Cooperative business relationships, Internet-based electronic marketplaces, portfolio model

1. PROBLEM

1.1 General introduction

Supply Chain Management (SCM) can be defined as the management of an entire set of business processes that produces and delivers products/services to the final customer (e.g. Cooper et al. 1997). These business processes refer particularly to the management of the product and return flows, procurement, demand management and/or order fulfillment. The center of SCM's attention is the design of relationships amongst the supply chain members (Schary and Skjoett-Larsen 2001).

Thereby, the Internet offers the supply chain new methods for streamlining the coordination within the supply chain. Leading firms have long recognized that one critical key success factor for SCM is e-dimension (e.g. Christopher 1998 or Lee 2000). A number of e-business models can therefore be used to erase cross-organizational boundaries between firms and their customers and/or suppliers.

One of these business models is the Internet-based electronic marketplace (IEMP), which we define for our purpose as a place on the Internet, where corporate (= business) buyers and suppliers (B2B) meet, trade, and collaborate. Most observers have assumed that IEMPs would come to dominate the B2B landscape. In combination with SCM, several authors mean that these two areas will contribute to the future success of companies and/or a network of companies (see e.g. Anderson and Lee 2000; Chaffey 2002; Nøkkentved 2000).

1.2 Research purpose, research question and methodology

At a first glance the two areas of SCM and IEMP might be contradictory, where SCM aims for collaboration, and IEMPs focuses on economic market transactions. But, concentrating at the procurement dimension of SCM, more and more companies buy their input factors over the Internet using IEMPs.

Consequently, we assume a further increasing of e-sourcing via IEMP within a supply chain and we expect procurement management to segment the vast number of existing IEMPs (see Grieger 2001) in a similar way as they differentiated their vendor base. While classical models focused on the volume of products purchased (ABC-model), more recent approaches refer to the evaluation of vendor relations (see e.g. Kraljic 1983, Cox 1996, Olsen and Ellram 1997, Bensaou 1999 or Helper 1993). In this manner, the successful management of strategic supplier relations was the research focus of their work.

Our research venture tries to answer the following question: How are IEMP's changing existing procurement management practices, which focused on the management of supplier relations.

Therefore, we will develop an IEMP-driven buyer-supplier relationship-portfolio, which can be applied to evaluate the attractiveness of any given IEMP for procurement applications. The purpose of the paper is to present our conceptual approach, which is part of an ongoing research project conducted at the Department of Operations Management at the Copenhagen Business School. The results of our research are based on an extensive analysis of literature within the areas of supply chain management, buyer-supplier relationships and IEMPs.

2. GENERAL PRESENTATION OF THE RESEARCH CONSTRUCTS

2.1 Strategic character of procurement relations

The procurement area is getting more and more strategic (see Schary and Skjoett-Larsen, 2001, 179). This is due to the transformation from transaction based purchasing to relationship oriented supply management. Helper (1993) characterized these strategies as "exit" (= arm's length relation) and "voice" (= obligational relation). However, assuming that a company has a huge vendor base (e.g. Wal-Mart has over 7,000 suppliers, see Kotzab 1997), a company will not manage all supplier relations the same.

Kraljic (1983) developed a product portfolio model based on the importance of purchasing and the complexity of the supply market. In his model the purchases are divided in four groups: Non-critical, leverage, bottleneck, and strategic products. While Kraljic focused on the power balance between the buyer and the supplier and proposed strategies based on the current power balance, Olsen & Ellram (1997) recommended that the purchases were categorized based on the relative supplier attractiveness and the strength of the relationship between the buyer and the supplier.

Cox (1996) is segmenting supplier relationships by examining the degree of competence and the degree of asset specificity. His supplier relations ranged from adversarial leverage to strategic alliance. Low asset specificity skills should be outsourced through arm's length relations using competitive market signals. Skills of high asset specificity (core skills) should always be controlled through internal contracts. Skills of medium asset specificity should be based on various forms of collaboration spanning from preferred supplier to strategic supplier alliance.

Bensaou (1999) has proposed a portfolio model of supplier relationships based on specific investments by both buyers and suppliers. Bensaou classified buyer-supplier relationships into four categories depending on the degree of specific investments from either party: market exchange, buyer captive, supplier captive and strategic partnership.

The idea behind any of these models was/is to manage the sourcing relationships in an economic way and as a consequence more and more companies have changed their sourcing strategies from multiple sourcing to single sourcing. Today, e-sourcing by using the various forms of IEMPs appears as an attractive alternative.

2.2 Forms of Internet-driven Electronic Market Places

We differ in our paper between three types of IEMPs, the independent, the private and the consortia IEMP.

Hundreds of entrepreneurs started *independent IEMPs* (also called dotcom-marketplaces) for a staggering variety of industries; from dairy farmers to casket makers. Few of these early pioneers have survived, and those that were able to sign up buyers and suppliers had trouble getting their members to do much buying online. Independent IEMPs provide at low costs an easy way to access a fragmented base of suppliers that are either difficult to reach, or are too numerous for companies to get their arms around. Independent IEMPs will find that their most favorable niches focus on low-risk trading activities, such as purchasing maintenance, repair and operations (MRO) goods and indirect materials. For example, Works.com focuses on trading MRO products. Similarly, ChemConnect trades commodity chemicals, thereby helping one of its largest customers, Dow Chemical, find new trading partners and make spot trades (Kalakota and Robinson 2000, Raisch 2001).

The early independent IEMPs faced numerous obstacles like they never got full support from key industry players (Wise and Morrison 2000). The independent IEMPs players ultimately failed to provide industries what they really needed in a B2B exchange – a way to automate current trading practices.

While these upstart marketplaces failed to gain support, leading players in key industries, such as General Motors and Boeing, believe in the benefits of the IEMPs. These giants have started, in their respective industries, to launch *consortium IEMPs* that address all the steps in the procurement process (Kalakota and Robinson 2000, Raisch 2001, Goldman Sachs 2000). Several consortium-led exchanges have gained attention. Transora, an exchange launched by 54 packaged-goods makers, plans to streamline every step in the supply chain, from purchasing raw materials to logistics, financing and insurance. Consortia IEMPs generally serve a medium-size or large and sometimes captive customer base, and thus might seek to become one-stop-shopping sources. Toward this end, many will develop MRO capabilities similar to independent IEMPs and form alliances with MRO-focused independent IEMPs – as well as with other specialized service providers – that leverage the latter's established capabilities and relationships.

Most industry consortiums also will want to develop considerable direct materials procurement and exchange functionality (e.g., comparative catalogues for specific products across consortium members' entire supply base).

Nevertheless, some companies will insist on procuring direct materials through their own *private IEMPs*. Such was the case with Toyota and Volkswagen, which both chose to work directly with their own suppliers rather than to join Covisint. If more than a few companies in an industry take this position, the direct materials procurement functionality of industry consortiums will be limited. However, a certain amount of ground could be regained through "expertise positioning": becoming the hub for industry news, expert forums and industry-specific standards. About 200 consortium IEMPs are expected to endure in the long term – primarily those that provide shared-service platforms to industries (Goldman Sachs 2000). For most, the principal challenge will be to spearhead cooperation among traditional competitors and respond quickly to market changes.

With private IEMPs, companies build their own trading interface to both suppliers and customers via the Internet. The private IEMPs application acts as a platform for both buy side and sell side participants. With this "do it yourself" approach, companies can build their own network, with their enterprise at the center. Private IEMPs allow companies to trade in public marketplaces, but separate their organization from the inevitable changes in the public B2B industry. In addition, private IEMPs allow companies to maintain and improve relationships with their select partners and suppliers, providing faster ramp-up to manufacturing and more efficient and predictable inventory levels. Private IEMPs often also specialize in design and planning support and cover often tools needed to plan and manage complex projects or processes. Applications may range from a simple activity, such as designing a marketing brochure, to optimizing a transportation network between a consumer product manufacturer and its retailers (Kalakota and Robinson 2000, Raisch 2001).

Private IEMPs will focus primarily on direct materials procurement and deep collaboration with trading partners, which are the capabilities that deliver the highest tangible value to most companies. They will have the most sophisticated IEMPs capabilities, the most sophisticated software applications and the deepest integration with their trading partners' ERP systems. Because of their direct materials focus, they are less likely to stress MRO capabilities, nor will they emphasize industry news, industry data or expert forums (unless they are the dominant industry player—like Microsoft—that defines standards in a given marketplace).

3. MEASURING THE EXTENT OF COOPERATIVE BUYER-SUPPLIER RELATIONSHIPS

3.1 Defining a cooperative business relationship in general

Research has posited various definitions and determinants of *cooperative business relationships* and also developed certain theories to explain the reasons why firms enter such relationships. Researchers use a lot of other terms for “cooperative business relationships” such as "(strategic) partnerships", "strategic alliances” or “collaborative relationship” as opposed to the traditional "arm's length", “transactional” or “non-cooperative” type of associations (Ellram 1990, Ellram and Cooper 1990, Werani 2001).

Some people might argue that slightly differences or a hierarchical order exist between the various terms. So one can say that a strategic partnership might be the most cooperative business relationship. However, literature presents a specific set of determinants of when a business relationship can be seen as cooperative or partner-like. E.g. for Campbell (1985) a cooperative business relationship only exists, if both buyer and seller choose a cooperative interaction strategy.

General characteristics that distinguish between cooperative and non-cooperative business relationships are long-term orientation (Heide and John 1990, Ganesan 1994 or Ellram 1990), relationship-specific investments (e.g. Tröndle 1987, Hallén, Johanson and Seined-Mohamed, 1991 or Håkansson and Snehota, 1995), frequency of interaction: Cooperative business relationships imply an intensive mutual coordination of partners, high degree of information sharing, seldom change of contact persons and mutual exchange of personnel between the partners (e.g. IMP Group 1982), asset specificity (Williamson 1985, Bensaou 1999, Cox 1996) and the adoption of norms (e.g. MacNeil 1980, Kaufman and Stern, 1988; Heide and John, 1992).

3.2 Searching for a cooperative business relationship in an IEMP-setting

Whether any IEMP need collaborative business relations or not might be due to following reasons (Anderson 2000, Nøkkentved, 2000, Kalakota and Robinson 2000, Raisch 2001):

- Data privacy: Many companies are not comfortable with the security and privacy levels of independent or consortium IEMPs. They also do not want to make their order patterns and prices visible to a third party. Private exchanges allow greater control over information.
- Functionality: By their nature, independent and consortium IEMPs must strive for functionality that serves a large variety of customers. For this reason, they are unlikely to implement the specialized functionality needed to support specialized inter-company trades or uniquely structured, collaborative relationships.
- Proprietary advantages: When an industry has only a few dominant players, those entities are more likely to build private exchanges to retain their competitive advantage. In other words, those leaders also are more likely to feel that aggregating purchasing volumes or sharing information disproportionately benefits their competitors.
- Avoidance of business risks: The liquidity and long-term success of many independent or consortium IEMPs is uncertain. Private exchanges give companies more control over their own risk.

Developing a set of general determinants to describe cooperative relationships for IEMP-sourcing strategies

The following table gives first an overview of specific determinants that describe a cooperative business relationship as found in the economic, marketing, organization and law literature.

These set of determinants, can also be used for building a buyer-supplier relationship portfolio in an IEMP-procurement setting, complete Campbell (1985) characteristics of a cooperative business relationship. Following Table 2 summarizes our determinants' operationalization.

Determinants	Literature Source	Definitions
Planning	MacNeil (1978); Noordewier, et al. (1990)	Planning focuses on the process by which the parties will continue the relationship;
Change of Contact persons	IMP Group (1982)	Relationships with relatively stable patterns of social interaction with the consequence of a lower degree of fluctuation of interaction partners should be present
Building trust	Kasper-Fuehrer and Ashkanasy (2001)	Three issues are necessary to built trust in interorganizational relationships: Communication of trustworthiness by reliable Information and Communication Technology, establishment of common business understanding, and strong business ethics
Frequency of interaction	Campbell (1985)	Cooperative business relationships imply an intensive mutual coordination of partners
Relationship-specific investments	Hallén, Johanson and Seined-Mohamed (1991); Håkansson and Snehota (1995); Tröndle (1987)	Necessity of an efficient coordination of all relationship activities. In this context, mutual adaptations, which have to be considered as relationship-specific investments are of utmost importance.
Sharing of Benefits and burdens	La Londe and Cooper (1989); Ellram and Cooper (1990); Gardner and Cooper (1988)	Acceptance of short-term burdens in expectation of longer benefits and burdens; "futuristic orientation";
Asset Specificity	Williamson (1985); Bensaou (1999); Cox (1996)	The degree to which an asset is redeployable or not
Interdependence	Cummings (1984)	The understanding that the loss of autonomy will be compensated through expected gains;
(Operational-) Information sharing	IMP (1982), Nøkkentved (2000), MacNeil (1978); Noordewier et al. (1990); Gardner et al. (1994)	Mutual sharing of relevant information, such as orders, inventory status, production schedules, promotions and sales forecasts
Knowledge Sharing	Howells and James (2000); Lee (2000)	Recognition that relationship's knowledge base is a valuable asset and that enlarging that knowledge base and improving its use can contribute to the competitiveness of the whole supply chain
Computer Linkages	La Londe and Cooper (1989); Lee (2000)	Software compatible with supplier's/buyer's system; Shared (logistics) information system
Corporate communication	La Londe and Cooper (1989);	Frequent Face-to-face planning/communication; High corporate level of communication on important issues; Many corporate levels of communication;
Extendedness	MacNeil (1978), (1980); Noordewier et al. (1990); Gardner et al. (1994);	Part of ongoing relationship with no sharp beginning and no clear endpoint, a long-term open-ended relationship.

Table 1: Defining the determinants of a cooperative business relationship

Determinants	**Definitions**
Planning	*Planning* integrates the operations of the two firms, smoothing the disturbances from expected and unexpected environmental factors. Specifically, planning focuses on the process by which the parties will continue the relationship. Therefore, one can assume that planning would lead to greater partnership satisfaction and future expectation of partnership satisfaction.
Change of contact persons	Especially the IMP Group (1982) has called attention to the importance of social interaction processes for the development of long-term business relationships. Since, as already noticed, particularly cooperative business relationships are expected to be based on long-term orientation, in such relationships relatively stable patterns of social interaction with the consequence of a lower degree of fluctuation of interaction partners should be present.
Frequency of interaction	Cooperative business relationships imply an intensive mutual coordination of partners
Relationship-specific investments	The interdependence of partners in cooperative business relationships (Tröndle 1987) points to the necessity of an efficient coordination of all relationship activities. In this context, mutual adaptations, which have to be considered as relationship-specific investments (Hallén, Johanson, Seined-Mohamed, 1991; Håkansson, Snehota, 1995), are of utmost importance
Sharing of benefits and burdens	*Sharing of benefits and burdens* refers to the willingness of both parties to accept short-term hardships with the expectation that the other party will do the same. La Londe and Cooper (1989) uses the term win-win/risk sharing. Specifically, it means acceptance of short-term burdens in expectation of sharing future benefits and burdens. For example, firms can reduce barriers to market entry by sharing burdens and risks with a partner; in return both firms will share in future benefits derived from entering the market. Thus, one can assume that this dimension will increase partnership satisfaction.
Asset specificity	*Asset specificity* is the degree to which an asset can be put to alternative uses. Assets used in the relationship that cannot easily be redeployed for uses outside the partnership, are deemed assets specific to the partnership. If the partnership already has a high degree of assets used specifically for the partnership, then one expects a high level of satisfaction with the partnership, since these assets cannot be easily put to other uses.
Interdependence	As firms join forces to achieve mutually beneficial goals, they acknowledge that each is dependent on the other. *Interdependence* results from a relationship in which both firms perceive mutual benefits from interacting and in which any loss of autonomy will be equitably compensated through the expected gains. Thus, the willingness to give up autonomy or control for the expectation of future gains is expected to contribute to partnership satisfaction (Cummings, 1984).

(Operational) information exchange	*(Operational) information exchange* refers to systems designed to provide timely, accurate, and efficient information exchange. Systems capable of accomplishing above, include electronic data interchange (EDI) systems. One would expect firms to invest the capital and time in operational information systems if they are satisfied with the partnership.
Knowledge sharing	*Knowledge sharing* refers to the recognition that the partners'/supply chain's knowledge base is a valuable asset and that enlarging that knowledge base and improving its use can contribute to the competitiveness of the whole supply chain. Whilst much of the management literature on organizational knowledge has focused on managing and measuring knowledge use within the firm, a number of studies have sought to explore how companies can access know-how and experience from outside the organization and effectively import and absorb that knowledge (Howells, James, 2000; Powell, 1998; Ruggles, 1998)
Computer linkages	*Computer linkages* requires the compatibility of the company's IT systems (ERP systems). Ideally, forms the overall network a hub-and-spoke system with the participants' internal information systems – that is, an ERP or other enterprise system – being the spokes (Lee, 2000).
Corporate communication	*Corporate communication* refers to frequent face-to-face planning and communication and a high corporate level of communication on important issues. Also many corporate levels of communication within the companies indicates a high degree of cooperation (La Londe, Cooper, 1989).
Building trust	Three issues are necessary to *built trust* in interorganizational relationships: Communication of trustworthiness by reliable Information and Communication Technology, establishment of common business understanding, and strong business ethics (Kasper-Fuehrer and Ashkanasy, 2001)
Extendedness	*Extendedness* in a partnering relationship refers to an ongoing relationship with no sharp beginning and no clear endpoint, a long term open-ended relationship. This dimension is conducive to partnership satisfaction

Table 2: Operationalizing the determinants of IEMP-driven cooperative business relationships

4. DEVELOPING AN IEMP-DRIVEN BUYER-SUPPLIER RELATIONSHIP PORTFOLIO

Based on our argumentation in the sections before, we present in Figure 1 our suggestion for a buyer-supplier relationship portfolio for IEMP-sourcing, where the x-axis evaluates the business relationship based on our determinants (see Table 3) and the y-axis refers to the number of IEMP participants (few, many; see Table 4). The model can be seen as an extension of the general proposal of Olsen and Ellram's "classical" purchasing relationship portfolio.

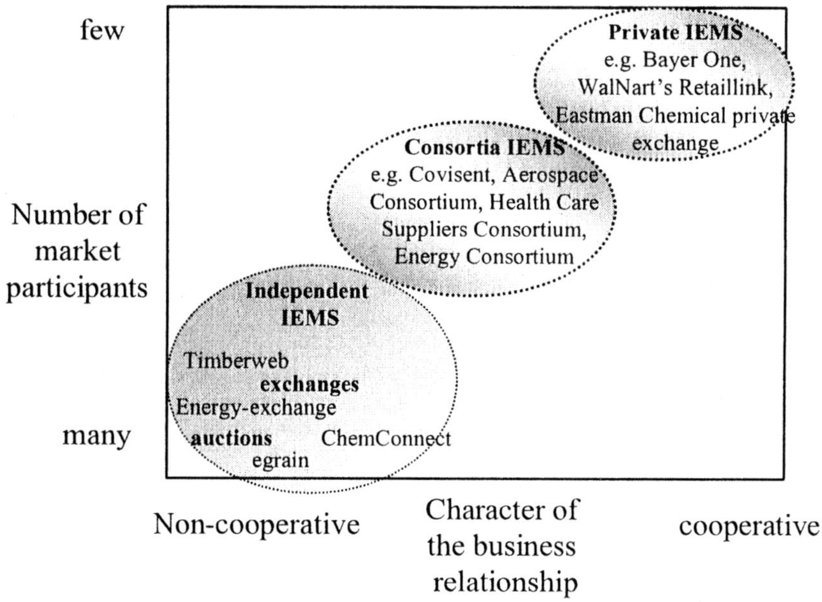

Figure 1. IEMPs portfolio model

While independent IEMPs provide a low cost and easy way to access a fragmented base of suppliers that are either difficult to reach, or are too numerous for companies to get an overview of (*many-to-many* structure), are the numbers of participants of consortia IEMPs smaller. The reason for this is that in consortia IEMPs, only a small group of large companies (*few-to-few* or *few-to-many* structure) combine their buying power, in which this few firms represent the highest concentration of market power (Kalakota and Robinson 2000). The consortiums provide an environment that compels buyers to purchase product by aggregating the industry's key suppliers and providing significant levels of product depth, breadth, selection, and service (Kalakota and Robinson 2000). Private IEMPs, on the other hand, allow companies to maintain and improve relationships with their own selected partners and suppliers (*one-to-few* structure) (see Table 4)

Determinants	**Market implications**		
	Private IEMP	Consortia IEMP	Independent IEMP
Planning	Important	Limited/important	Less important
Change of contact persons	Low	Limited	High
Frequency of interaction	High	Medium	Low
Trust building	Important	Important	Less important
Relationship-specific investments	High	High/Medium	Low
Sharing of benefits and burdens	Yes	Limited	No
Asset specificity	High	Medium	Low
Interdependence	High	Medium	Low
Operational information exchange	High	High/Medium	Limited
Knowledge sharing	High	Medium	No
Computer linkages	Hub-structure, Internet with firewalls	Internet with firewalls	"Open" system, limited ERP connectivity
Corporate communication	High	Medium	Low
Extendedness	Long-term	Long-term/short-term	Short-term

Table 3: Applying the determinants of cooperative business relationships to different forms of IEMPs

Number of market participants	**Market implications**		
	Private IEMP	Consortia IEMP	Independent IEMP
Description	few	medium	many

Table 4: Determining the number of IEMP-participants

5. DISCUSSION AND OUTLOOK

Future SCM has to consider IEMPs as significant contributors to the overall supply chain success. The goal of our paper was to show, how IEMP might change the management of supplier relations. We assumed that supply chain managers would develop differentiated IEMP-driven supply chain strategies (procurement), which cooperative business relationship management is dependent on the type of IEMP.

For that reason, we developed an IEMP-driven buyer-supplier-relationships portfolio, which we discussed on a conceptual level. Our model was built upon general determinants of a cooperative business relationship, which we adapted for IEMP-issues. Based on three different types of IEMP's we could see that in the case of sourcing over a private IEMP, collaborative characteristics such as the frequency of interaction, trust building, high relationship specific investments and a sharing of benefits and burdens have to be recognized for a successful sourcing strategy.

In a next step, we have to validate our suggestion, which we plan to realize by a case study approach concentrating on

- an empirical identification of the determinants of cooperative buyer-supplier relationships in an e-sourcing setting,
- an empirical analysis of their suitability and dependence towards our three IEMPs types (= independent, consortium and private IEMP) and
- the discovery of certain success criteria and limitations of e-based sourcing strategies, based on the different IEMPs types and their collaboration need.

REFERENCES

Anderson, D. L. (2000): *New Supply Chain Business Models – The Opportunities and Challenges*. www.ascet.com

Anderson, D. L. & Lee, H. L. (2000): *The Internet-Enabled Supply Chain: From the "First Click" to the "Last Mile"*. www.ascet.com

Bensaou, M. (1999): Portfolios of buyer-supplier relationships, *Sloan Management Review 40*, 4, pp. 35 – 44

Campbell, N. C. G. (1985): An Interaction Approach to Organizational Buying Behavior. *Journal of Business Research 13*, pp. 35-48.

Chaffey, D. (2002): *E-Business and E-Commerce Management*. Prentice Hall.

Christopher, M. (1998): *Logistics and Supply Chain Management. Strategies for Reducing Cost and Improving Service*. Financial Times, Prentice Hall. Second Edition. London, New York, San Francisco etc.

Cooper, M., Lambert, D. and Pagh, J. (1997): Supply Chain Management: More than a new Name for Logistics, *International Journal of Logistics Management 8*, 1, pp. 1 – 14.

Cox, A. (1996): Relational competence and strategic procurement management. *European Journal of Purchasing and Supply Management 2*, 1, pp. 57-70

Cummings, T. (1990): Transorganizational Development. *Research in Organizational Behaviour 6*, pp. 367-422.

Ellram, L. M. (1990): A Managerial Guideline for the Development and Implementation of Purchasing Partnerships. *International Journal of Purchasing and Materials Management 27*, 3, pp. 2-8.

Ellram, L. M. & Cooper, M. C. (1990): Supply Chain Management, Partnerships, and the Shipper-Third Party Relationship. *International Journal of Logistics Management 1*, 2, pp. 1-10.

Ganesan, S. (1994): Determinants of Long-Term Orientation in Buyer-Seller Relationships. *Journal of Marketing 58* (April), pp. 1-19.

Gardner, J. T. & Cooper, M. C. (1988): Elements of Partnership. In: Joseph E. McKeon (ed.), *Partnerships: A Natural Evolution in Logistics Relationships*. Cleveland: Logistics Resource Forum.

Gardner, J. T., Cooper, M. C. & Noordewier, T. (1994): Understanding Shipper-Carrier and Shipper-Warehouser Relationships: Partnerships Revisited. *Journal of Business Logistics 16*, 2, pp. 121-143.

Goldman Sachs (2000): *Internet: B2B e-Commerce. The consortium report*. Global Equity Research https://www.gs.com.

Grieger, M. (2001): *Electronic Marketplaces – An Overview and A Call For Supply Chain Management Research*. Proceedings of the Nordic Logistics Conference (Nofoma) in Island.

Hallén, L., Johanson, J. & Seined-Mohamed, N. (1991): Interfirm Adaptations in Business Relationships, *Journal of Marketing 55* (April), pp. 29.37.

Heide, J.B. & John, G. (1990): Alliances in Industrial Purchasing: The Determinants of Joint Action in Buyer-Supplier Relationship. *Journal of Marketing Research 27*, pp. 24-36.

Heide J.B. & John G. (1992): Do Norms Matter in Marketing Relationships? *Journal of Marketing*, 56, April, pp. 32-44

Helper, S. (1993): An exit-voice analysis of supplier relations. The case of the US automobile industry. In Grabher, G. (ed.), The Embedded Firm. On the Socioeconomics of Industrial Networks, Routledge, London, pp. 141-160.

Howells, J. & James, A. D. (2000): *Corporate Decision-Making on the Sourcing of Technological Knowledge*. Paper presented to 'Knowledge Management: Controversies and their Causes' Conference, University of Warwick, Coventry, UK, 10-11 Feb. 2000.

Håkansson, H. & Snehota, I. (1995): *Developing Relationships in Business Networks*, London, New York: Rout ledge

IMP Group (1982): An Interaction Approach. In: Håkansson, H. (ed.), *International Marketing and Purchasing of Industrial Goods: An Interaction Approach*. Chichester: Wiley, pp. 10-27.

Kasper-Fuehrer, E.C. & Ashkanasy, N.M. (2001), Communicating trustworthiness and building trust in interorganizational virtual organizations. *Journal of Management*, 27, pp. 235-254.

Kaufman P.J. & Stern L.W. (1992): Relational Exchange, Contracting Norms, and Conflict in Industrial Exchange, *Advances in Distribution Channel Research*, 1, pp. 135-159.

Kalakota, R. & Robinson, M. (2000*): e-Business 2.0 – Roadmap for Success*. Addison Wesley, Bosten, San Francisco etc.

Kotzab, H. (1997): *Neue Konzepte der Distributionslogistik von Handelsunternehmen*, Wiesbaden

Kraljic, P. (1983): Purchasing must become Supply Management. *Harvard Business Review*, 61, pp. 109-117.

LaLonde, B. J. & Cooper, M. (1989): *Partnerships in Providing Customer Service: A Third Party Perspective.* Oak Brook, Ill: Council of Logistics Management.

Lee, H. (2000): Creating Value through Supply Chain Integration. *Supply Chain Management Review*, Sept./Oct.

MacNeil, I., R. (1978): Contracts: Adjustments of Long-term Relations Under Classical, Neoclassical and Relational Contract Law. *Northwestern University Law Review 72*, pp. 854-905.

MacNeil, I.R. (1980): *The New Social Contract: An Inquiry into Modern Contractual Relations*, Yale University Press, New Haven.

Noordewier, T., John, G. & Nevin, J. (1990): Performance of Purchasing Arrangements in Industrial Buyer-Vendor Relationships. *Journal of Marketing 54*, October, pp. 80-93.

Olsen, R. F. & Ellram, L., M. (1997): A Portfolio approach to Supplier relationships. *Industrial Marketing Management 26*, pp. 101-113.

Nøkkentved, C. (2000): Collaborative Processes in e-Supply Networks – Towards Collaborative Community B2B Marketplaces. Research Report. PricewaterhouseCoopers.

Olsen, R. F. and L. M. Ellram (1997) A Portfolio Approach to Supplier Relationships, Industrial Marketing Management, 26, 2, pp. 101-113.

Powell, W.W. (1998): Learning from collaboration. *California Management Review 40*, 228-40.

Raisch, W. D. (2001): The eMarketplace – Strategies for Success in B2B eCommerce. McGraw-Hill, New York.

Ruggles, R. (1998): The state of the notion: knowledge management in practice. *California Management Review*, 40, 3.

Schary, P.B. and Skjoett-Larsen, T. (2001): *Managing the Global Supply Chain.* CBS Press, Copenhagen.

Tröndle, D. (1987): *Kooperationsmanagement – Steuerung interaktioneller Prozesse bei Unternehmenskooperationen*, Bergisch Gladbach, Köln: Eul.

Werani, T. (2001): *On the Value of Cooperative Buyer-Seller Relationships in Industrial Markets.* ISBM Report 2-2001. Institute for the Study of Business Markets. The Pennsylvania State University.

Williamson, O. E. (1985): *The Economic Institutions of Capitalism.* New York: Free Press.

Wise, R. & Morrison, D. (2000): Beyond the Exchange - The Future of B2B. *Harvard Business Review*, Nov.-Dec., pp. 86-96.

ADOPTION OF E-COMMERCE IN SMES: LESSONS FROM STAGE MODELS

ADA SCUPOLA
Department of Social Sciences, Roskilde University, Denmark

Abstract: The paper presents the results of an exploratory case study of early adopters of electronic commerce. The data have been analyzed by applying PriceWaterhouseCoopers stage model of adoption of e-commerce. This model has been used because it takes into consideration many factors such as adoption benefits and barriers, uses, evolution of e-commerce capabilities, and the measures that should be taken to increase adoption and diffusion of e-commerce in SMEs. The paper concludes that this model, while having many strengths, presents also some limitations, the most important being not taking into consideration the changes in the company capabilities and business processes that have to take place in order to go from one level to the next of e-commerce capabilities.

1. INTRODUCTION

It is believed that e-commerce could contribute to increase the market power and competitiveness of small and medium size enterprises (OECD, 1999). We adopt Zwass (1997) definition of e-commerce (here also called Internet commerce) as “the sharing of business information, maintaining business relationships, and conducting business transactions by means of telecommunications networks” and the European Parliament definition of SMEs according to which they are businesses with up to 500 employees (OECD, 1999). Furthermore, we focus on the business-to-business e-commerce conducted over Internet.

E-commerce is not, however, risk free for small companies as they often lack the resources, knowledge and understanding to take full advantage of these technologies. Therefore the need to better understand the process of e-commerce adoption and diffusion among SMEs. The question that this article addresses is: What are the stages through which e-commerce adoption unfolds and what are the characteristics of these stages?

Zaltman et al. (1973) found that within organizations the innovation process occurs in 2 stages. The first is a firm level decision to adopt the innovation called primary adoption. The second is the actual implementation including individual adoption by users, also called secondary adoption. However, even when the primary adoption decision has occurred, this is not a guarantee that the innovation will actually be implemented or used by the targeted users, as often there might be an assimilation gap (Gallivan, 2001). In explaining the adoption and diffusion of innovations, different types of models can be used such as "process models" and variance models. The stage models (which can be considered a sub group of process models) are based on the premise that the elements in the system move through a pattern of distinct stages over a period of time and that these stages can be described. According to Nolan (1973) two key characteristics of stage theory formulation are 1) the identification of elements and 2) the conception of their growth through time. The concept of an element is that it is generic to a particular field and that it can be specified by a set of attributes. The concept of growth over a period of time implies that the elements change as attributes expand or contract in number and nature. Well-known stage models in the diffusion of innovation theory are the ones developed by Nolan (1973), Prescott and Conger (1995) and Rogers (1995). However while these models focus on the adoption, implementation and diffusion of innovations in general and information technology in particular, very few stage models address the adoption, implementation and diffusion of Internet technology and e-commerce in particular. The characteristics of e-commerce and its evolution being different from the ones of other IT systems as Internet-commerce is based on complex, networked technologies that provide a seamless unified user interface to information systems within and outside the organization (Damsgaard and Scheepers, 1999).

The article is structured as follows. The following section is a review of the stage models of e-commerce adoption. The third section describes the research design and the data collection, while section four describes the case companies. Finally section 5 presents a summary of the results, while section 6 gives a short discussion and suggestions for further research.

2. REVIEW OF STAGE MODELS OF E-COMMERCE ADOPTION

The research on stage models adoption of e-commerce is mainly summarized in five studies (Table 1). Two studies, Quelch and Klein (1996) and Bickerton, Bickerton and Simpson-Holley (1999) provide general models of site development. Poon and Swatman (1999), Grant (1999) and PriceWaterhouseCoopers (1999) present stage models specific to SMEs.

Quelch and Klein's (1996) model consists of two evolutionary paths for web site development and therefore e-commerce adoption. These paths are different depending upon whether an organization is an already existing company or a start-up company with the purpose of doing business only on the Internet. The already existing company would be interested mainly in addressing the needs of existing customers and promoting and selling existing products. This company would follow the 'information-to-transaction model', consisting of the following sequential steps:

1. Promote brand image/ Provide product information.
2. Collect information about customers/ Perform market research.
3. Provide customer support and service.
4. Develop internal support and service.
5. Provide online transactions.

Examples of companies using this model are Federal Express and 3M. For a start-up company with the purpose of selling products through Internet, a 'transaction-to-information' model would typically be more suitable in order to build brand image, provide product support and win repeat purchases. Examples of companies following this model are Software.Net and CDNow. This model of site development consists of the following stages:

1. Provide online transactions.
2. Provide customer support and service.
3. Promote brand image/ Provide product information.
4. Collect information about customers/ Perform market research.

Model	Number of Stages	Focus of the model	Type of company
Quelch and Klein (1996)	Already existent company: 5 stages Internet-based only company: 4 stages	Web Site Development	Distinguishes between the already existent company and Internet-based only company
Bickerton et al. (1999)	3	Internet Technology Development	Any type of company
Poon and Swatman (1999)	3	Level of internal – external integration	SMEs
Grant (1999)	5	Company capabilities, mainly internal to the corporation	SMEs
PriceWaterhouse Coopers (1999)	5	E-commerce capabilities, takes into consideration external and internal factors	SMEs

Table 1. Overview of Stage Models of E-commerce Adoption in SMEs

Bickerton et al. (1999) has also developed a model of Internet technology development, based on 3 stages summarized below:

1. Internet presentation. In this stage the company chooses to publish information on the Web that can only be viewed trough the web browser. This stage is used to provide an image, to impart knowledge and values about the company, as well as to give access to information and to illustrate products or services.
2. Internet interaction. This stage allows for two-way communication between an organization and its customers. The system asks questions and the user supplies answers. At this stage, Internet technology becomes more then a purely electronic publishing tool.
3. Internet representation. In this stage the organization uses Internet technology to reorganize some of its business processes online. The technology executes a business process otherwise done by a person. This could be any activity as for example producing a new sales channel.

Poon and Swatman (1999) develop a stage model of e-commerce adoption mainly focusing on the level of integration between the internal company applications and Internet. This model suggests that integration will gradually increase as SMEs understand the potential benefits of e-commerce and that there will be no integration until a small enterprise sees these benefits. This is mainly due to the fact that the organizational processes have to be re-organized as a consequence of full integration. The model starts with minimum Internet-to-internal application integration, to limited Internet-to-internal integration to full Internet-to-internal application integration. The sequential steps are summarized below:

1. Purely inter-organizational exploitation
2. Selective local integration
3. Full local integration

Grant's (1999) model of e-commerce adoption among SMEs focuses on the competencies required for the transformation of a traditional business to an electronic business. It consists of five stages:

1. Immaturity: the company is not ready yet to start e-business;
2. On the Internet: the company reaches a stage of basic awareness;
3. E-commerce provisional strategy decided: a specific awareness to the business is reached and a plan is made to adopt e-commerce;
4. Ready to implement: the obstacles for the implementation are overcome, and finally
5. Implementation.

PriceWaterhouseCoopers (1999) also develops a five-stage model of SMEs e-commerce adoption based on the Internet capabilities a company has. They describe the steps as follows:

1. The cycle begins with the perception by SMEs of the opportunities and benefits offered by e commerce, such as greater access to international markets.
2. Based on their perceptions of opportunities and benefits, SMEs develop e-commerce capabilities.
3. As SMEs attempt to use the developed e-commerce capabilities, they experience a number of inhibitors to realizing their potential. The perception of these inhibitors may lead SMEs to develop less e-commerce capability than they might have done based solely on an assessment of opportunities and benefits. Inhibitors could include poor telecommunication infrastructure or gaps in the e-commerce capabilities of business partners.
4. The experiences or perceptions SMEs have with respect to opportunities and inhibitors influence what measures they believe should be taken by governments or other stakeholders to facilitate e-commerce adoption.
5. Previous stages in the cycle lead to the enabled benefits that SMEs actually experience. These experiences, in turn, influence their perception of the potential opportunities and benefits of e-commerce and contribute to another cycle of e-commerce development. (PriceWaterhouseCoopers, 1999, p. 8)

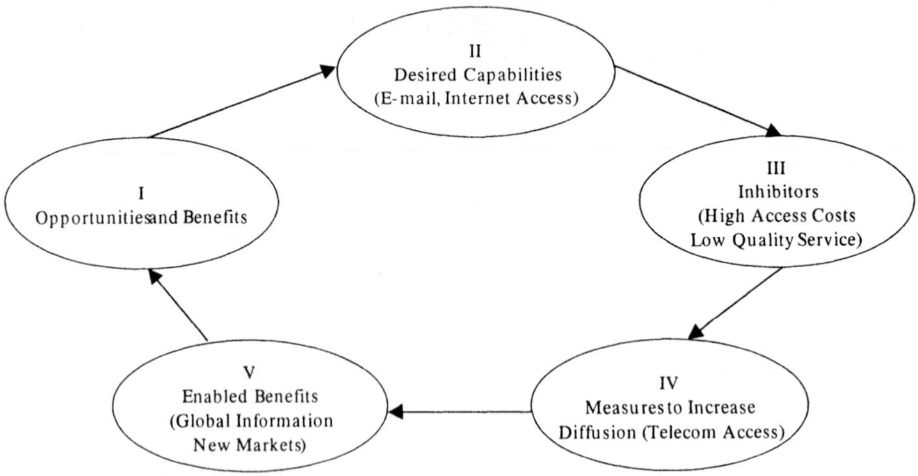

Figure 1. A Stage Model of SME's Adoption of B-to-B E-commerce

PriceWaterhouseCoopers, 1999

PriceWaterhouseCoopers distinguishes four levels of capabilities. Level 1 represents SMEs with very basic or no online capabilities, level 2 represents SMEs with a Web site, but no advanced capabilities, level 3 includes SMEs that are able to take orders and provide customer service on their web site, while level 4 represents SMEs that can make complete transactions and receive payment on their web site.

We can see that while Quelch and Klein (1996) and Bickerton et al. (1999) models focus on the web site characteristics and Poon and Swatman's model focuses mainly on the level of internal-external processes integration, Grant (1996) and PriceWaterhouseCoopers (1999) models are more comprehensive since they also take into consideration other factors such as capabilities. Furthermore, while Grant (1999) mainly focuses on the capabilities internal to the organization, PriceWaterhouseCoopers also take into consideration factors external to the organization such as government intervention, which is the reason why I choose this model to structure the analysis.

3. RESEARCH DESIGN AND DATA COLLECTION

I used exploratory case studies (Yin, 1994) of five SMEs in Southern Italy to understand the specific characteristics of the different stages through which the adoption and diffusion of e-commerce takes place. The companies, belonging to different sectors, have been chosen on the basis of representativeness and accessibility following the criteria of having had an Internet-connection for a period of at least 3 years and having a maximum of 500 employees. The data were collected with semi-structured interviews. In all the cases the person interviewed has been the owner also functioning as the CEO. The person to be interviewed had been suggested by the companies themselves after a first telephone contact.

The interviews have been conducted personally in spring 2001 and have lasted between 1.5 and 3 hours each. In addition the company's home page (when existing) has been visited. Each interview was transcribed and the data analyzed by keeping in mind the elements of the stage model.

4. COMPANIES DESCRIPTION

In this section, I describe the case companies, summarized in table 2, according to PriceWaterhouseCoopers model. In the discussion I put together stage I and II, and don't take into consideration stage V, since this is partially the same as stage I.

Company Number	**Type of Business**	**No. Of Employees**	**Capabilities Level**
F1	IT Consultants	80	Level 2: Simple Home page and permanent Internet connection
F2	Distributor	15	Level 3: Home Page and Online Selling Catalog
F3	Intermediary in the textile business	2 (Family Driven)	Level 1: Internet Connection, No Web Site
F4	Production and commercialization of textiles	300	Level 2: Home page internal-external integration
F5	Distributor	19 (family driven)	Level 2: Home Page and Permanent Internet Connection

Table 2. Companies Overview

4.1 Description of F1

F1 is a software house, offering consulting services to government, service sector and SMEs, with 80 employees. Recently they have started implementing business-to-business e-commerce for client companies.

4.1.1 Stage I and II

The CEO/owner recalls how when the Internet first came he was struggling to understand how they could use it and for what purpose. It was clear to him that there was much potential in this technology, but he did not know how to leverage it. He started therefore slowly building some capabilities in-house to leverage Internet technologies for consulting purposes. He decided for example to be an Internet provider, to hire consultants with web related experiences, to have an Internet connection, to have a web site, etc. Presently, F1 is at capabilities' level 2.

4.1.2 Stage III

It has not been easy for F1 to sell Internet related consulting services in the past and presently. This is mainly due to the fact that companies in other sectors according to F1 are still at the level of using computer systems for basic purposes such as accounting, word processing, etc. Some companies have a local area network, but very few understand the power of Internet technology. Therefore lack of knowledge and awareness have been the major barriers for F1 to sell its consulting services to local SMEs. They also admit that another major barrier is their (the consultants) inability to explain the potential of the technology to their customers in a simple way. Therefore for many years, even though they had developed basic web applications such as Home Pages and online catalogs, it was hard for them to sell these services, thus relatively been prevented from further developing human and Internet related capabilities.

4.1.3 Stage IV

As a result of their experience, they strongly believe that government intervention in terms of informational campaigns to increase awareness, tax incentives, etc. could be a viable way to increase the diffusion of e-commerce in SMEs.

4.2 Description of F2

F2 is a distributor, employees 15 people, and has a turnover of 5 millions EURO per year. This company imports products from the Middle East and resells them to 800 client companies all over Italy and abroad. They have 5 business agents that cover different parts of Italy. This company in Spring 2001 had had an online catalog for four months and already circa 5% of the business was done through Internet, but with already existing customers. It is possible for the client to log in the company with a password, look at the daily inventories, choose the type of product, the quantity wanted and then submit the order through the web site. They had not seen an increase in the number of clients yet as a consequence of the Home Page.

4.2.1 Stage I and II

F2, even though skeptical, adopted e-commerce in 1997 due to the fact that the owner had a friend that convinced him that e-commerce would be very useful for him and to make that investment. Soon F2 realized the benefits of e-commerce and decided to have an online catalog. However, they could just have a static home page providing basic information about the company and the company's products. It was, in fact, too complicated for them to update the catalog on a daily basis as required by their business due to lack of available technologies on the local market such as scanner and digital cameras. Only recently, after they have bought these complementary technologies, it has been possible for them to sell through a WWW catalog, because they can update it on a daily basis by themselves. The company capability level is 3.

4.2.2 Stage III

The main barriers preventing F2 at first from further using e-commerce were lack of complementary technology advances and affordable prices. As the prices of the digital cameras have become more affordable, they have invested also in further capabilities, both technical and human. Examples of human capabilities include training of one person to use the scanner, digital camera and uploading of the pictures into the system, as well as training about how to handle the online catalog. They acknowledge that there are still many of their clients, especially the smaller ones that do not have a computer or at least do not use Internet. We could therefore say that the lack of a critical mass among F2's clients is also another barrier. Among the benefits they have experienced cost savings and timesavings.

4.2.3 Stage IV

F2 also believes that government intervention in terms of awareness creating campaigns, training seminars, and government incentives such as tax-breaks for e-commerce based systems could contribute to an increase in the diffusion of e-commerce among SMEs. They also believe that the accessibility on the local market to complementary technologies such as the scanner and digital camera, the spreading of the English language and the introduction of the EURO could also further the diffusion of e-commerce

4.3 Description of F3

The third company (F3) are middlemen in the textile business, doing business mainly with abroad. They import the raw material and export the finished product, produced by local SMEs. They do not have a web site. They are not satisfied with the static web site that is a shopping window. They also showed concern about building a web site giving online access to their product collection because they are afraid that the competitors can copy what they are doing. Therefore they use Internet daily for business-to-business operations such as receiving and fulfilling orders, sending digital images of their products, communicating with their clients, and Internet banking. They said that Internet has contributed to increase the number of buyers per each client company they have, with an increase in the final total product sale.

4.3.1 Stage I and II

F3 started using e-commerce due to the perceived opportunities and benefits that it could offer them, especially in dealing with international markets. Their technical capabilities in Internet-commerce are however limited to an Internet connection. They are presently using e-commerce for market research, establishing contacts with new potential customers, order taking, order confirmation, sending images of their collection products as attachments after having scanned the products through the scanner, etc. Their capability level is one.

4.3.2 Stage III

While experimenting with e-commerce, F3 has realized its barriers and benefits. Among the major barriers they mentioned the lack of critical mass among the suppliers and the buyers, especially those located abroad. They say that many of their clients, especially in the past, did not want to use e-commerce because they felt that the security level for conducting web transaction was not sufficient enough. They have been thinking for some time to upgrade their technical system to either build a home page to provide information about the company or even to have an online catalog of their products, however they are afraid of loosing competitive advantage if they put many company information on the web. They are also afraid of setting an online catalog, because they feel that it is not secure enough. Among the benefits they have experienced cost savings and bigger access to international markets.

4.3.3 Stage IV

They believe that the main factors that could increase the diffusion of e-commerce are an increase in the security of the WWW system, the spreading of the English language and the introduction of the EURO. They have contacted many companies located abroad, but they cannot really establish any business because they cannot communicate. They were not aware themselves of any government intervention in terms of tax breaks, pilot programs, etc., but they said that they would be willing to experiment with more WWW capabilities if they did not have to make the whole investment by themselves.

4.4 Description of F4

F4 is a producer and seller of textiles. The company counts circa 300 employees with a turnover of 15 millions EURO per year. The internal and the external processes are interconnected. They have a home page, but don't have an online catalog because they are worried about the security. The company had started using Internet when none of their clients was using it. They have their own EDB department and do not believe in outsourcing, if Internet has to be used to achieve competitive advantage.

4.4.1 Stage I and II

F4 has adopted e-commerce in 1996 as soon as the WWW was introduced. At first they did not know exactly what to use it for, but the owner/CEO had a vision and a belief that it could be used to obtain a competitive advantage. Therefore they started developing some capabilities in e-commerce, both technical and human. They have installed a system that is integrated with Internet, and they have a firewall for protection. In that occasion they also have decided to hire two full time engineers that constitute the EDB department. These engineers are in charge of not only maintaining the computer and network systems, but to find always new ways to use both computer systems and e-commerce to decrease costs, increase market share, find new suppliers and customers, etc. F2's production department was completely automated in 1996, and they have automatic sewing and cutting machines, controlled by a computer located at distance. If an error occurs on a machine, most of the times it can be fixed online through the Internet 24 hours per day. F4 is at capability level 2.

4.4.2 Stage III

Even though F4 had an Internet connection and had integrated the internal and the external processes, for some years the company could really use e-commerce for just e-mail, market research, etc. as most of their suppliers and clients were not e-commerce adopters. However firmly believing in the technology they were not at all discouraged. Today they use Internet for many purposes, among which order taking, sending invoices, participation to e-auctions, establishing contacts with suppliers of untraditional products or to find lower-cost suppliers. However they do not have an online catalog yet, as they are afraid of loosing control on who is accessing it as they feel the password solution is not secure enough. They use CD-ROM to send the product collection, instead, because in this way they keep control on how many open the CD-ROM.

4.4.3 Stage IV

They did not really have any idea about what kind of measures could be taken to improve the diffusion of e-commerce. Having been themselves pioneers, they believe that government intervention in terms of tax incentives, funding, etc. is not really that important. If companies are interested in adopting e-commerce because they can see its advantages, then they believe that they are willing to make the necessary investments. However, they do agree that intervention to spread the use of English is very important. Another factor they considered important is the implementation of EURO.

4.5 Description of F5

F5 is a distributor of car parts. They import from all over Italy and distribute and sell to local SMEs, mechanics and private individuals. They have a static home page, but they are planning to make an advanced one with an online catalog of their products in order to sell on Internet. They have been having a permanent Internet connection for the last three years.

They are mainly using Internet for e-mail, but recently also for sending and receiving orders with suppliers and a subsidiary company located in a nearby city. Their use is limited to 3-5 messages per day. Their capability level is 2.

4.5.1 Stage I and II

F5 got the first Internet connection few years ago, it was a very simple connection and therefore they did not invest much technical or human capabilities in it. Their adoption was mainly due to technology push, that is they were hearing on the television, radio, about this technology and they decided to adopt it. However for circa one year and a half they were not really using e-commerce because they did not know what to do with it.

4.5.2 Stage III

Slowly, by trial and error this company has updated its e-commerce capabilities. At first they have been mainly using e-mail, then to receive orders from customers and sending orders to suppliers. Recently they have been using it more actively to search for new suppliers, especially on the international market and to send huge files over Internet with their subsidiary. This was a big saving of personnel resources for them, as they don't need a person to re-key the data with consequent mistakes. They are also considering of putting an online catalog to sell some products on the WWW. However, they are worried about security. The biggest barriers that have prevented them from expanding their e-commerce capabilities have been the difficulties in talking and negotiating with the consultants. They feel very unsecure because different consultants give different solutions, suggestions and prices and cannot really explain them what they can do with the system in simple, understandable terms.

4.5.3 Stage IV

They believe that to increase the diffusion of e-commerce it is important that the consultants are better trained to talk with people that are not expert of informatics and to explain in simple terms the potentiality of the system not only from a technical point of view, but also how it can support their business.

5. SUMMARY OF RESULTS

In this paragraph I discuss the factors characterizing each stage of PriceWaterhouseCoopers model found in the case studies. These results are summarized in Table 3.

5.1.1 Stage I and II

SMEs might adopt e-commerce due to the potential opportunities or benefits that they perceive this technology can offer as for example to increase competitive advantage (F1, F4, and F3). However, in my study I found that e-commerce adoption can also take place just-by-chance, because the owner of a company has for example a good friend that convince him to adopt e-commerce (F2). Other companies might adopt due to technology push (F5).

5.1.2 Stage III

After the decision for primary adoption has been made, the company starts experimenting with e-commerce (secondary adoption), thus realizing benefits, uses and inhibitors.

Uses. Usually SMEs start using e-commerce first mainly as a medium to exchange information (Poon and Swatman, 1999). As the level of awareness, experience and trust in e-commerce increases, SMEs start developing more capabilities and using it for more complicated business-to-business transactions, such as order taking and order confirmation from and to customers, price and inventory inquiries, document exchange and information sharing with buyers, suppliers and partners (e.g. transmission of invoices and images of product samples (F5)). Finally SMEs might be able to establish an online sale presence with an online catalog (F2) and to participate to e-auctions as buyers or sellers (F4) and to do Internet banking (F3) as also Poon (2000) has found. Eventually SMEs would reach external and internal integration (F4, partially F3). Most of the companies in this study are moving from capability level 2 to level 3 and to implementing internal and external integration. The complexity of a company's e-commerce capabilities is therefore a function of the level of awareness, trust and experience the SME has with this technology.

Barriers. As pointed out in other studies, also this study has showed that lack of competence, knowledge and awareness of the technology and its potentials is an important barrier to the adoption and diffusion of e-commerce among SMEs (Poon and Swatman, 1997). Internal resistance to change (F4) or implementation gap is also another important barrier. Poor communication between the IS consultants or IT specialists and the SMEs is

Stages of the PriceWaterhouseCoopers model of SMEs E-commerce Adoption	**Factors characterizing the stages found in the empirical investigation**
Stage I	Adoption Reasons: Perception of Opportunities and Benefits; Just-By-Chance (JBC); Vision of Getting a Competitive Advantage; Technology Push
Stage II	E-commerce Capabilities: Level 1-F3; Level 2: F1, F4, F5; Level 3:F2.
Stage III	Uses: Communication; Order Taking and Order Confirmation From and To Customers; Send Purchase Orders to Suppliers; Price and Inventory Inquiries; Document Exchange and Information Sharing with Buyers, Suppliers and Partners (E.g. Transmission of Invoices and Images of Product Samples); Market Research; Online Sale Presence; Participation to E-Auctions as Buyers or Sellers; Finding and Establishing Contacts with Suppliers or Partners; Internet Banking; Internal and External Integration
Stage III	Adoption Barriers: Lack of Competence, Knowledge and Awareness of the Technology and its Potentials; Internal Resistance to Change or Implementation Gap; Lack of Critical Mass of Suppliers, Customers and Partners Using Internet; Poor Communication Between SMEs and IS Specialists; An Online Sale Presence Might Decrease SMEs Competitive Advantage; Lack of Trust in E-commerce
Stage III	E-commerce Benefits: Contribution to internationalization; Increased Efficiency and Easiness to Do Business; Time Savings; Improved Communication Around the Clock; Administrative Cost Savings (Fax, telephone, postal service, paper); Increased Company Visibility; Increased Market Potential
Stage IV	Measures: Diffusion of Complementary Factors Adding Value to E-commerce (e.g. technologies such as digital image technologies, EURO and spreading of English) Government Intervention and Public Administration as User.

Table 3. Factors Characterizing the Stages of the Adoption of B-to-B E-commerce Emerged in the Case Studies

another important inhibitor as the consultants are not able to explain in simple terms what Internet can be used for (F1, F3, F5). SMEs fear that putting the product portfolio on Internet might decrease their competitiveness by giving away to competitors useful information (F3, F4). Lack of critical mass of suppliers, buyers and partners using e-commerce is also an important inhibitor. The critical mass has been lacking over the last years, but recently it is getting better.

Benefits. Benefits are the advantages that SMEs experience or expect to gain from the adoption of e-commerce. Improved communication around the clock, administrative cost savings, and increased efficiency and easiness to do business are the most important short-term benefits. Increased company visibility, market potential, and a contribution to internationalization are among the most important long-term indirect benefits (Poon and Swatman, 1999).

5.1.3 Stage IV

As SMEs experience with e-commerce, they also get an understanding of what kind of intervention should be taken to increase its diffusion and the business value that the adoption of e-commerce can bring to a small enterprise. This study's empirical investigation has found that the government and public administration are very important actors in promoting the diffusion of e-commerce. This can be achieved among others by promoting e-commerce use, raising awareness of e-commerce through informational campaigns, increase the quantity and quality of government services on the Internet especially by the local public administration.

Barua, Lee and Whinston (1996) develop a business value complementarity theory where the main idea is the construction of a multilevel model where the highest level variable is the dependent variable, the same that has to be optimized. The variables at the other levels are the independent variables. According to Barua et al. (1996) the exploration of complementarity among the independent variables could contribute to an increase in the value of the dependent variable. Milgrom and Roberts (1990) define two activities to be complementary if the profit or value created by doing both at the same time is greater then the sum of the individual profits from doing just one or the other.

If we use the business value modeling logic of Barua et al. (1996), then we can represent the variables that have to be optimized and the independent variables as in fig. 2. This figure means that in order to optimize the business value that e-commerce brings to a corporation it is important to explore the synergies among the complementary factors representing the independent variables of the model.

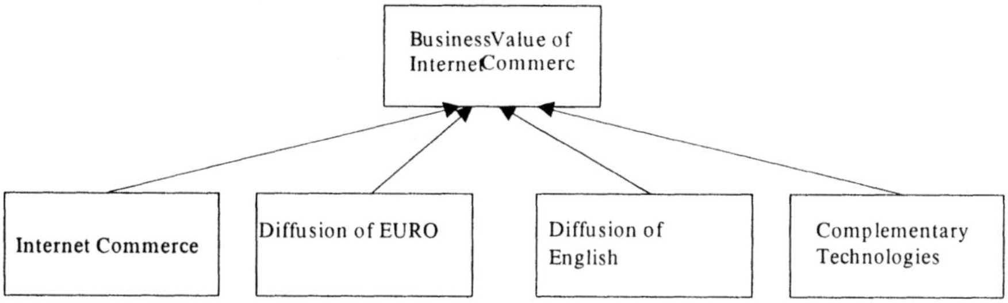

Figure 2. Business value compementarity model of e-commerce to SMEs

This empirical investigation has showed that complementary factors that could contribute to an increase in the business value of e-commerce to a small enterprise, especially regarding competitive advantage and internationalization, are the diffusion of complementary technologies such as digital imaging (F2), the implementation of the EURO (F2, F3, F4) and the diffusion of English as the common business language (F1, F2, F3, F4, F5).

6. CONCLUSIONS

It can be concluded that PriceWaterhouseCoopers model fits the data only partially. For example the first stage of the model takes into consideration only the opportunities and benefits that motivate SMEs for primary adoption of e-commerce, but it does not take into consideration other factors such as technology push and those situations that can fit under the category just by chance. Furthermore, regarding capabilities the model takes into consideration only the level of sophistication of the home page. With level one representing a company with no web capabilities and level four a sophisticated web site, where it is possible to order through an online catalog and to pay online for the products bought on Internet.

The model does not take into consideration, however, the company's capabilities that have to be either developed in house or acquired on the market to go from one stage to the next of web site development. These are also the problems that usually characterize the assimilation gap. The model also does not take into consideration the changes in the business processes that are required as a consequence of increasing the sophistication level of the home page, if e-commerce has to be conducted successfully.

These limitations can be however issues for further research. For example the model could be expanded with the capabilities, both technical and human that a company needs as a consequence of the evolution of the home page, as well as the required changes in the business processes. To do this, many more in depth case studies are necessary, as the empirical data on the basis of which these conclusions have been drawn are presently very limited.

REFERENCES

Barua A., Lee, S. C.H., Whinston A.B. (1996), 'The Calculus of Reengineering', *Information Systems Research*, Vol. 7, No. 4, pp. 409-428.

Bickerton, P., Bickerton, M, Simpson-Holley, K. (1999), *Cyberstrategy: Business Strategy for Extranets, Intranets and the Internet*, The Chartered Institute of Marketing, Oxford, United Kingdom.

Damsgaard J., Scheepers, R.' Power, Influence and Intranet Implementation, A Safari of South African Organizations', *Information Technology and People*, Vol. 12, No. 4, 1999

Gallivan, M.J (2001), 'Organizational adoption and assimilation of complex technological innovations: Development and application of a new framework', *Database for Advances in Information Systems*, Vol. 32, No. 3, pp. 51-85.

Grant, S. (1999) E-commerce for small businesses, in 'Proceedings of the 2nd International conference IeC '99', Manchester, November 1-3, 1999, pp. 65-72.

Milgrom, P., Roberts, J. (1992), *Economics, Organization and Management*, New York, Prentice Hall.

Nolan, R.L. (1973) 'Managing the Computer Resource: A Stage Hypothesis', *Communications of the ACM*, 16, 399-405.

OECD (1999), 'Business-to-Business E-commerce: Status, Economic Impact and Policy Implications', OECD Working Paper, NO. 77.

Poon, S., (2000), Business Environment and E-commerce Benefit-A Small Business Perspective, *European Journal of Information Systems*, Vol. 9, pp. 72-81.

Poon, S., Swatman, P. (1997) Small Business Use of the Internet: Findings from the Australian Case Studies. *International Marketing Review*, Vol. 14, No. 5.

Poon, S., Swatman, P. (1999) An Exploratory Study of Small Business E-commerce Issues, *Information and Management*, 35 (1999) pp. 9-18.

Prescott, M.B., and Conger, S.A. (1995). "Information Technology Innovations: A Classification by IT Locus of Impact and Research Approach," *The DATABASE for Advances in Information Systems*, Vol. 26, Nos. 2/3, pp. 20-41.

PriceWaterhouseCoopers (1999), SME E-commerce Study, Asia Pacific Economic Cooperation (APEC), Final Report, September 24.

Quelch, J. A., Klein, L. R. (1996), 'The Internet and International Marketing', Sloan Management Review, Spring, pp.60-75.

Rogers, E.M., (1995), The Diffusion of Innovations, 4th edition. Free Press, New York.

Zaltman, G., Duncan, R., and Holbeck, J.(1973). *Innovations and Organizations*, New York: Wiley & Sons.

Zwass,V. (1997), Foundations of Information Systems, New York, McGraw-Hill.

Yin, R.K.; Case Study Research Design and Methods, Second Edition, Vol. 5, Sage Publications, 1994.

E-GOVERNMENT BUSINESS STRATEGIES AND SERVICES TO CITIZENS

An analysis of the Australian e-tax system

JEFF CHAMBERLAIN and TANYA CASTLEMAN
Deakin University, School of Information Systems, Australia

Abstract: Governments are pursuing initiatives to deliver their services on-line in order to provide better service to citizens as well as to reduce their own business costs. Designing good applications is not just a matter of developing good technical solutions. The context in which the application will be used is also important. One application with the potential to benefit both government and citizens is on-line lodgement of personal income tax returns. Properly implemented, this could mean considerable savings of time and administrative costs for the government and provide citizens with an inexpensive, convenient and speedy way to complete their annual tax obligations. This paper analyses the development and implementation of the Australian on-line tax lodgement system known as e-tax. Analysis of data from the Australian Taxation Office (ATO) identifies patterns of e-tax use, characteristics of users and the users' evaluation of the e-tax system. The analysis indicates that e-tax is successfully used by a growing number of tax payers but that the up-take rates of e-tax are lower than might be expected. The spread of e-tax will depend on more than just the viability of the technical product. The ATO will need to deal with a variety of complex contextual factors in its plans to promote e-tax. This analysis highlights some broader issues related to electronic service delivery (ESD) and eGovernment.

1. INTRODUCTION

In recent years governments around the world have embraced the opportunities offered by conducting business over the Internet. Informed by a policy framework that emphasises efficiency and effectiveness in the way governments conduct their business, millions of dollars have been allocated to developing new on-line business models and practices that promise reduced operating costs, enhanced citizen services, improved applications of scarce resources and the rapid processing of business transactions. This has stimulated the implementation of thousands of government web sites and Internet based business and communications systems across the globe. Several years of such innovations provide valuable insight, particularly in relation to the achievement of their intended effects and ultimate successes.

The Australian federal government promotes the use of the Internet as an efficient and effective medium through which to conduct business and communication. Through its 'Government On-line' policy it prescribes requirements for government departments to deliver various services electronically (Government Online 2000). Consistent with this policy direction, the Australian Taxation Office (ATO) has innovated in this area by developing a number of strategies to deliver services and administer business electronically.

This paper examines one of the ATO's recent electronic initiatives, an on-line lodgement system for individual taxpayers known as 'e-tax'. The uptake of e-tax has fallen far short of government projections, raising questions about its ability to meet its objectives and how well it fits with the needs of the taxpaying public. Our purpose in this paper is to analyse comprehensive ATO data on e-tax use in order to understand its potential and limitations as an ESD initiative. We identify the situational factors that have influenced the success of this initiative and consider the implications for eGovernment and electronic service delivery (ESD) initiatives more broadly.

2. FACTORS IN GOVERNMENT ESD

Governments of the world have implemented many forms of ESD including on-line systems for voting; administering compensation claims and premium payments; completing surveys; accessing public records and obtaining permits and licences. Delivery of such convenience to citizens on-line has arguably enhanced governments' relationships with their constituents. Additionally, many cost savings have been achieved such as reduced publishing expenses; reduced telephone, mail, and front desk customer enquiries; streamlined procurement processes; a reduced need for public servants to key paper forms; enhanced data analysis and even increased advertising opportunities (Carberry 2000; Nabers 2000; Public Management 2000; Thibodeau 2000; The Economist 2000).

There are two main goals underlying initiatives for government on-line service delivery. These are increased government openness including better provision of citizen services and business process improvement (Chamberlain and Castleman, 2001). The prevailing motivation for eGovernment initiatives appears to be their potential to improve business processes. eGovernment initiatives are seen to maximise business efficiency and effectiveness. Such improvements relate primarily to the delivery of services to the public and information dissemination, typical transactions performed by governments everyday (Public Management 2000).

Business efficiency and effectiveness can be measured principally against the reduced costs of administering citizen transactions. Reduced transaction costs are presented as major arguments by governments in justifying business cases for implementation of on-line innovations. In this way governments also exercise their accountabilities to the public by demonstrating the effective allocation of public funds (Girishankar 1997; Colecchia 1999). In addition to transaction costs, effective allocation should include other considerations such as potential rates of on-line product diffusion, marketing methods and change management if such calculations are to reflect realistic outcomes. Governments and their administrations will ultimately be judged by the public; it is crucial therefore that eGovernment innovations everywhere, be implemented only where positive and realistic outcomes are, on the balance of probabilities, expected (Caddy 1999). Citizens expect, on the one hand, governments to operate efficiently and on the other hand, they expect governments to provide universally accessible services in ways that meet citizen's needs. Governments therefore need to find a suitable balance between implementing business efficiency gains and improved service delivery.

The Australian federal government is a good example of a government that follows these principles for ESD. In 2000 it announced an Internet strategy called 'Government On-line' which recognises that its own transition to the on-line environment is critical to instilling public confidence in that environment. The strategy includes provision for security, authenticity, privacy, accessibility, navigability, and standards (Government Online 2000).

- The four stated objectives of the Australian Government's on-line strategy are: An environment where virtually all government services are available around the clock to anyone;
- A complete range of high quality, low cost on-line services;
- Tailored services that are easy to use and allow people to interact with government in a way which is natural to them; and
- Bringing government closer to people to encourage people to interact with government.

It is within this policy framework that e-tax has been developed. Before turning to an examination of the implementation of this product, it will be useful to have a brief look at e-tax and the context in which it has been introduced.

3. E-TAX AND THE AUSTRALIAN CONTEXT

Australians are required to report annually to the ATO on their personal income for the purpose of tax assessment. There have been two main ways of submitting these reports.

- They may lodge paper returns which must be submitted between July and October. A kit of over 100 pages including forms and directions is available at newsagencies and ATO branch offices. The completed return is forwarded by post to an ATO branch office for processing which can take up to two months because ATO officers are required to check and key the information manually. The user is unlikely to receive a prompt refund. There is also a facility for electronic lodgement of paper returns through a post office.
- They may engage an accountant or tax-agent who will lodge using the secure ATO value added network (VAN). The ATO establishes a lodgement program with the tax professionals each year which extends beyond the July to October deadline required for other methods. To avoid late lodgement penalties, some individuals choose this lodgement method where they have been unable to complete their returns within the required time (ATO 2002).

Since 1999, taxpayers have had the option of e-tax. This secure, on-line tax return and lodgement program is downloaded by individual taxpayers from the ATO's Web site. It helps users determine whether they should lodge a tax return and, if so, asks a series of questions requiring user input to complete the actual return. A series of 'interview screens' guide users and intelligent rules built into the system ensure that only questions pertinent to each user are asked. The program includes worksheets for computations and various information and help screens. If they are entitled to a tax refund, users can elect to receive them via Electronic Funds Transfer (EFT). Users can print copies of completed returns for their records (McCarthy 1997; ATO 1997a; ATO 1997b; ATO 1998; ATO 1999a; Gliddon 2000). E-tax lodgement is available only from July to the end of October.

The e-tax program collates all of the typically required tax return data including information on the taxpayer's income, deductions, losses, tax offsets and rebates, the healthcare levy and any other adjustments. It also provides an estimate of the taxpayer's assessment (i.e., the dollar amount owing or refundable). Validation and consistency tests check the user's answers and figures and notifies her of incomplete items. 'Public Key' encryption technology is used to ensure the security, privacy, authenticity and integrity of the lodgement. Partly completed returns can be saved and several members of a household can use the software on the same computer after downloading their individual secure electronic keys and digital certificates.

In the original proof of concept documentation, business arguments presented in favour of the trial of the e-tax product included advantages for the service provider (ATO) as well as the tax payer. These included:

- the improvements brought to client assistance
- the ease of tax return preparation
- the speed of tax return preparation
- the reduction in compliance costs (for example, lodgement over the Internet), and
- a higher attainment of data quality by virtue of client keyed data and some software error checking (ATO 1997a)

These business arguments exemplify the efficiency and effectiveness objectives and rationales of governments when implementing such innovations. Efficiencies in this context related to such gains as expected reductions in processing and compliance costs and increased effectiveness in terms of client service and data quality. All arguments reflected the ATO's wider strategic plans in place at that time.

In the five years since e-tax was launched, a body of data on e-tax usage has been collected by the ATO. Our analysis uses this data to investigate the experience of the e-tax implementation to date and considers how successful the e-tax program has been in meeting its goals. We examine patterns of e-tax use to identify the factors which have influenced its adoption. More broadly, we look at how e-tax fits within the existing Australian taxation system and what Australia's e-tax initiatives suggests about government ESD initiatives and eGovernment.

4. METHOD

This analysis is based on tax lodgement data supplied by the ATO. This is a comprehensive set of de-identified national data for all personal income tax lodgements for the years 1998-2000 and is thus both complete and accurate. Although we had access to 2001 data, this was incomplete because returns submitted through tax agents were still permitted at the time the data was supplied. Most of our analysis in this paper is therefore based on data for 2000.

A total of 415,436 e-tax records were analysed, each of which included indications of lodgement type, income, deductions and rebates and the amount of tax refund or liability resulting from the tax assessment. The records also included demographic variables including occupation, sex, Australian residency, age and residence (by postcode regions). Data was formatted in Excel spreadsheet databases and pivot tables with assistance from the ATO.

Data on users' experiences of e-tax was also made available. An optional electronic survey of 26 questions, delivered through the e-tax software, was introduced in the 2001. It is automatically sent to the ATO upon lodgement of the individual's income tax return. The survey explores the reasons for using e-tax and the user's satisfaction with the e-tax product. By mid October 2001, 20250 individuals had completed the survey in relation to the 2001 lodgement year (this constitutes an 18% response rate). Summarised results of the survey were obtained from the ATO which we were able to analyse further for this study .

5. FINDINGS

In the 2000 tax year, 113,164 tax payers lodged their personal income tax returns using e-tax. This number was an increase from 26,015 in 1999 and grew to 273,952 in 2001. While this represents a rapid growth rate, e-tax lodgements in 2001 were only about three-quarters of the ATO forecasts and e-tax lodgements are still only 1% of the over 10 million lodgements as shown in Figure 1 .

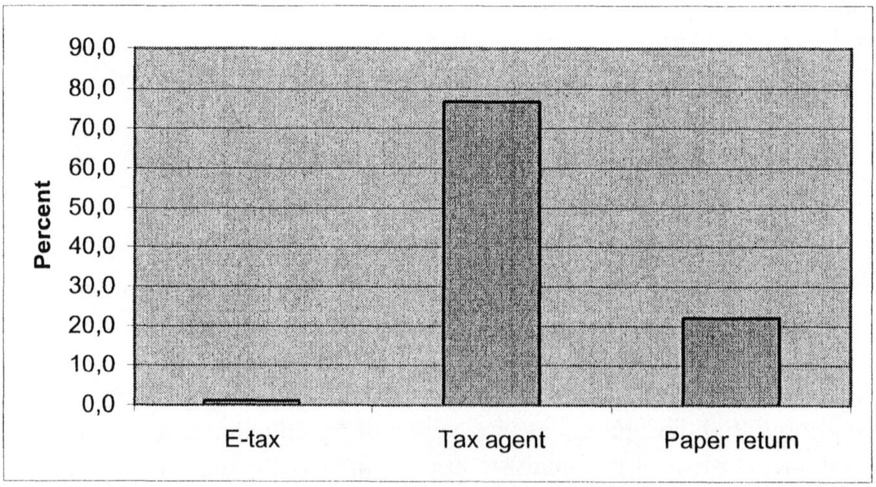

Figure 1. Methods of personal tax lodgement 2000

Source: ATO Mainframe data extract, November 2001

The vast majority (77%) of Australian taxpayers lodge their returns using the services of tax agents, with only 22% using paper returns. Lodgement types also reflect underlying differences in the two groups of taxpayers. As shown in Table 1, those using paper returns have, on average, lower incomes and fewer deductions than those using tax agents and claim a higher level of rebate (characteristic of lower income earners). The e-tax users have a profile much closer to that of tax payers who engage the services of tax agents than to those lodging paper returns.

	e-tax	**Tax agents**	**Paper return**
Income or loss	$35,241	$34,563	$24,360
Deductions	$1,351	$1,787	$856
Tax offsets and rebates	$730	$808	$818

Table 1. Mean Income, Deductions and Rebates per lodgement method in 2000

Source: ATO Environmental Monitoring System, Australian Taxation Office, November 2001.

How can we understand why the rate of uptake of e-tax lags behind ATO projections, despite its apparently high level of functionality? There are a number of reasons that might make e-tax less attractive than other lodgement methods and we investigate these possibilities by comparing data on the characteristics of e-tax users with other tax-payers.

5.1 Does the e-tax lodgement method work well enough?

The e-tax survey feedback is largely positive and when asked if they would use e-tax again in the 2002 year, 94% of respondents stated that they would. The remaining 6% were undecided. Most of these respondents were first time users; 67% of respondents had not used e-tax in the previous year. In response to the question, 'How satisfied or dissatisfied were you with e-tax?', 47% of respondents indicated that they were 'very satisfied' whilst a further 46% stated they were 'satisfied' (an over 90% satisfaction rate among the survey respondents). The e-tax product appears to be popular with the vast majority of its users who reported no significant technical problems either with downloading or lodgement.

5.2 Is e-tax too time-consuming and inefficient?

There is no indication that this is the case. In completing a personal income tax return using the e-tax software the user is 'interviewed' and is required to respond to a series of relatively straight forward questions with 'yes' and 'no' answers, not unlike responding to an expert system. The e-tax system analyses responses as it receives them and proceeds by asking the user only those questions pertinent to that user's tax affairs. This aids in the speed and accuracy of the completion of the return; in contrast, those using the paper kit must work through over one hundred pages of literature. Survey feedback revealed that 91% of respondents were either 'very satisfied' or 'satisfied' with the e-tax interview method. Eighty nine per cent of respondents considered this to be a 'very important' or 'important' feature of e-tax. Anecdotal evidence suggests that e-tax preparation can be completed in as little as half the time required for paper returns.

5.3 Is e-tax too complicated for the average taxpayer?

It is possible that e-tax is complicated and requires skill and education levels beyond those of most of the population. Survey questions related to the package's ease of use drew positive responses. Eighty per cent of respondents were either 'very satisfied' or 'satisfied' with the ability to locate e-tax on the ATO website and 90% believed that this was either a 'very important' or 'important' feature. Eighty seven per cent of respondents were either 'very satisfied' or 'satisfied' with the task of downloading the e-tax software from the Internet, whilst 81% indicated that they were 'very satisfied' or 'satisfied' with downloading the e-tax security software. Navigation scored an 85% approval rating and 91% were satisfied with the question-answer format of the product.

We also examined the occupations of e-tax lodgers on the premise that occupations are related to education and reflect, at least in broad terms, a taxpayer's ability to use complicated IT tools. Occupations were categorised as 'professional' or 'non-professional' from a list of 300 occupational descriptions. Examples of occupations considered to hold a professional status include judges, managers, scientists, teachers, lawyers and business professionals. Examples of occupations allocated a non-professional status include hairdressers, cabinet makers, sales representatives, taxi drivers, and construction workers.

The growing proportion of non-professionals among e-tax users indicates that the product is suitable for ordinary taxpayers. Analysis over the three lodgement years reveals a gradual decline in the proportion of e-tax users who were professionals from 43% in 1999 to 31% in 2001. Non-professionals increased from 57% to 65% of e-tax users over the same period. The remaining respondents did not state their occupations.

5.4 Is e-tax only attractive to people who want a quick refund?

It is not uncommon for taxpayers to receive a refund at the end of each financial year. An advantage of e-tax is the speed with which a tax return can be lodged and a refund provided. We might expect that this method of lodgement will be particularly attractive to taxpayers expecting to receive a refund and of much less interest to those who expect to pay additional tax. The speed of refund is likely to be a factor in e-tax use since an analysis of refunds revealed that most e-tax lodgers receive a tax refund. Figure 2 shows the patterns of refunds and debits for all e-tax users over the three years 1999-2001. Since the great majority (86%) of e-tax users gained a tax refund, the speedy lodgement and return process facilitated by e-tax is a significant incentive.

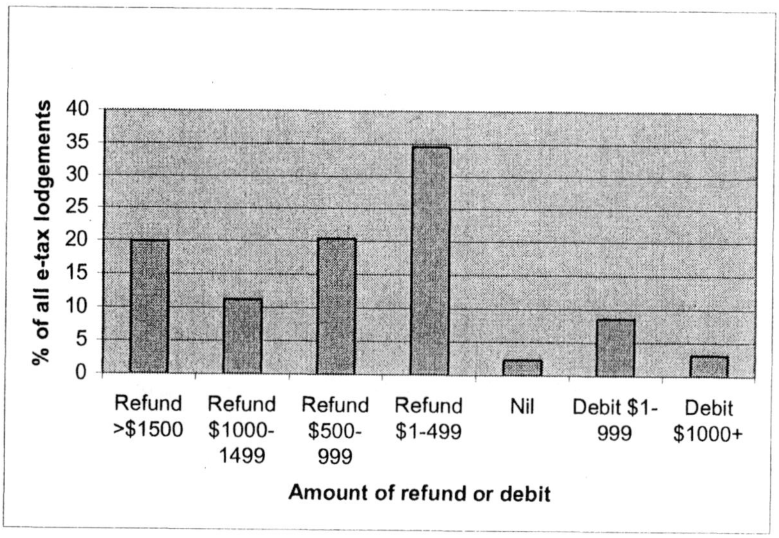

Figure 2. e-tax assessment outcomes 1999 - 2001

Source: ATO Mainframe data extract, November 2001

The survey data, however, indicate that convenience was even more important than getting a 'fast refund'. Respondents were asked to indicate the importance of various factors considered to be motivators for e-tax adoption. The distribution of survey responses shown in Figure 3 shows the percentage of respondents who considered these 'very important' and 'important' as motivators to their use of the e-tax innovation.

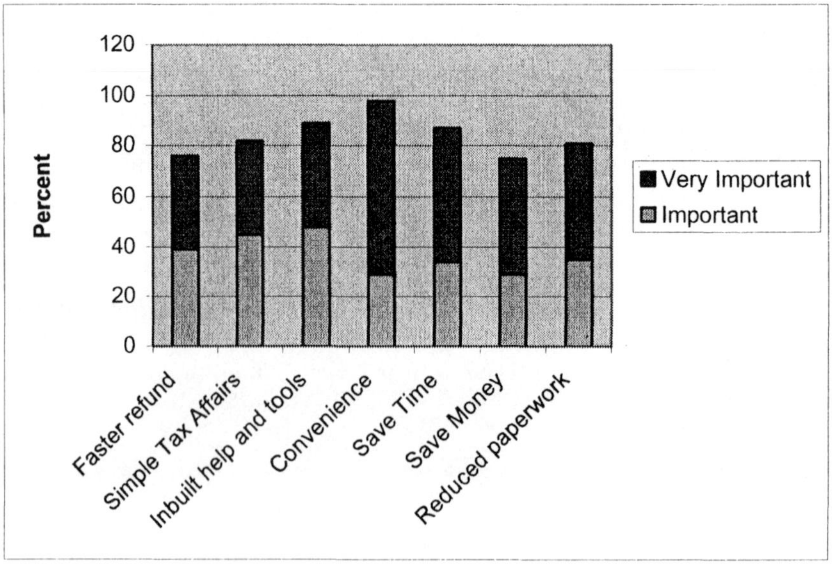

Figure 3. Reasons for using e-tax

Source: E-Tax 2001 User On-line questionnaire summary as at 15th October, 2001, Australian Taxation Office.

It is interesting to note that overall, saving money and accessing faster refunds are rated least important (though still representing a sizeable majority of users). 'Convenience' was the most common reason (98% of respondents cited this) followed by access to instant on-line help and tools offered in the e-tax product (89%) and the time-saving benefits of e-tax (87%).

5.5 Is e-tax inadequate for more complex tax issues?

It may be that e-tax is either not able to deal with higher levels of complexity in tax matters or that it is perceived as being inadequate for these purposes. It is true that e-tax does not cater for those required to complete the more complex types of income tax returns (e.g., more non-salary income relating to companies, funds, partnerships and trusts) but this would not account for the large difference between the level of e-tax use and those choosing to use tax agents. There is no direct measure of income tax complexity available for this analysis but we can reason that people with higher incomes and those who claim more deductions will have more complex tax affairs.

The data presented in Table 1 showed that e-tax users had relatively high median incomes compared with those using the paper return and those using tax accountants. This may indicate that e-tax is likely to be suitable for those with more complex tax affairs. However, e-tax users claimed a lower level of deductions than those using tax agents which would suggest that their tax arrangements are indeed less complex. The decision to use a tax agent, of course, may reflect not an inherent taxation complexity but the tax agents' ability to identify more or larger deductions than the taxpayer is able to do.

Survey figures give further insight on this point. Eighty-two per cent of respondents said that they used e-tax because their tax affairs were simple and straightforward. We conclude that while the e-tax application is not able to deal with very high levels of complexity, it can cope with a fair range of tax issues and that the users seem satisfied.

5.6 Does e-tax prevent taxpayers from maximising their tax deductions?

There is some support for this view. As indicated above, by far the most common form of lodgement is via tax accountants who provide advice in addition to filling out and lodging the returns. (Most lodge the returns they prepare for clients electronically via a VAN). Engaging an accountant provides the taxpayer with an added assurance that all tax deductions available to individuals have been considered and included in income tax returns where possible. The figures presented in Table 1 above reveal that lodgements through tax agents contain the highest average level of claims for deductions of the major lodgement methods. These figures in Table 1 above suggest that using tax accountants does help tax payers increase their deductions, thus reducing their tax liability.

If it is the case that tax agent lodgements are more effective in increasing tax deductions, this will diminish the attractiveness of e-tax. Even though e-tax may provide users with prompts to alert them to the deductions that they might claim, it may not be able to match (or may not be perceived to match) the ability of tax accountants to identify allowable deductions.

5.7 Has e-tax been poorly publicised or promoted?

It is possible that the reason many taxpayers do not use e-tax is that they are not aware of it or find it difficult to locate the web site to access it. An ATO marketing strategy document prepared in April 2001 reveals that the 'growth in use of e-tax has occurred with only moderate promotion mainly through 'business as usual' ATO channels. Examples of such channels include counter and telephone enquiries and advertising within the paper-based tax kit literature and other brochures. The e-tax on-line survey reveals that 37% of users either heard or learned about e-tax via advertising in the tax kit. Figure 4 reveals the sources from which users heard about or learned of e-tax for the 2001 lodgement year.

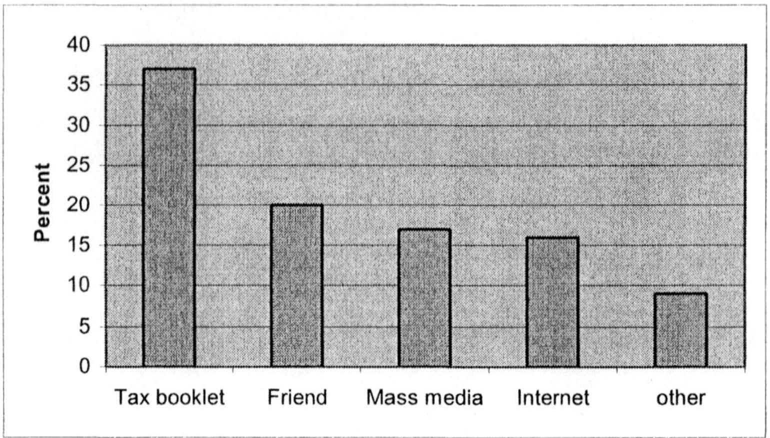

Figure 4. How users learned about e-tax - 2001

Source: ATO, e-tax User Survey, 2001

The fact that so few e-tax users learned about it through the mass media indicates that the publicity strategy for e-tax is inadequate and that it is not sufficiently promoted through public channels. The majority of users found out about it through what appear to be mainly adventitious processes. Without a public information campaign, it is unlikely that the diffusion rate of e-tax will rise swiftly. This finding also suggests, however, that a well-designed public information campaign could lift the use of e-tax considerably.

6. DISCUSSION

Our examination of e-tax concludes that it is a well developed, high quality product that works well and meets the Government's objective of providing high quality on-line services. It is freely available over the Internet and can be downloaded securely via the ATO's web site. It is arguable, however, whether the e-tax product can be considered a *low cost*, on-line service. Heavy costs must be borne by the ATO to sustain the product's life and whilst e-tax is offered free to taxpayers, a series of typically hidden client costs are also beginning to emerge, such as the need for a private ISP account, ISP download charges and download time as well as hard disk space requirements (ATO 1999c; Gliddon 2000; Madden 2000; Petrillo 2000; Preston 2000; Thomas 2000; Walker 2000; Fitzsimmons 2001; Neff 2001; NOIE 2001a; NOIE 2001b).

Costs incurred by the ATO include those associated with the development and currency of the product; technological and infrastructure requirements; project management and administration; and marketing and communications (ATO 1999b; Thibodeau 2000; ATO 2000a; ATO 2000b). Although we were not able to determine actual project costs, a project of this magnitude could cost several million dollars. This, coupled with a relatively small user base gives rise to a relatively high transaction cost. For example, a conservative estimate of say, A$3 million for total e-tax expenses in the 2001 year against the 2001 user uptake of 273,852 individuals, equates to a very high cost of $10.95 per transaction. This poses a problem in that e-tax as an electronic initiative should offer cost savings but may, at least in the short term, add to costs. It is unlikely that such a movement in estimated transaction costs would be endorsed in any business case for innovation as such costs, in an eGovernment project, would represent an ineffective allocation of public funds. However, it may be defensible as part of Government's other goals, *viz*, provision of services to citizens and leaders in the movement to an on-line environment.

The implementation of e-tax illustrates the kinds of quandaries that can confront governments, even when they pursue reasonably straightforward initiatives and where the technical systems work well. We have identified several issues that governments must deal with.

6.1.1 Managing complex sets of requirements among different groups of clients

The patterns of e-tax adoption clearly show that this mode of lodgement is appropriate only for taxpayers with access to the internet and with the IT skills to allow them to use it with confidence. Those lodging paper returns will often be people who have little prospect of being able to manage e-tax, either because of their income and education levels or because of their unfamiliarity with the Internet. Over the long term, the lack of IT skills and internet connection should decline as a barrier to the use of e-tax but this will not be a quick process. There will, arguably, always be a need to provide the option of paper-based returns, at least at the taxpayer end. Taxpayers who are unable to use e-tax will include many elderly and disabled people as well as those without computer access. Since potential e-tax users will need to be recruited from current paper users, this goal will be increasingly difficult to achieve. E-tax users currently are more similar (in income and demographic terms) to taxpayers who lodge via tax agents, yet e-tax cannot provide the same level of tax advice and assistance as the professional accountant. What advantage lies in encouraging tax payers to use e-tax rather than tax accountants? Because accountants lodge returns electronically, there is no reason for the ATO to encourage their clients to move to e-tax to enhance government business efficiency. However, having implemented the e-tax system, it must be continued if the government is not to disadvantage tax payers who prefer to lodge their own returns electronically. Ironically, the ATO may face the choice of either disadvantaging e-tax users (if the system is discontinued) or sustaining an uneconomic channel.

6.1.2 Managing ESD in light of different stakeholder interests

Aggressive moves to recruit taxpayers to e-tax from among those who currently use tax agents would clearly be inappropriate. Not only are there no business advantages for the ATO, but it would be highly inflammatory to take on such an influential professional group and threaten their livelihood. While a number of taxpayers may switch to e-tax from tax accountants, it is unlikely that this will be publicized or promoted by members of the industry themselves. As with so many other eCommerce issues, governments must tread a thin line in balancing their own interests with the business interests of the private sector. There is potential for government on-line initiatives to have consequences for the commercial market that were not anticipated.

6.1.3 Effective and feasible strategies for promoting electronic and on-line channels for business between government and citizens

One of the clear findings from our analysis was that the promotion of e-tax was ineffective and could be enhanced to recruit more users. Lack of publicity about the product and the incentives for using it probably contributed to its disappointing usage rates. One can imagine an advertising campaign or even an incentive scheme to increase e-tax use. If this campaign were to encourage a shift from paper returns, all the ramifications are likely to be positive, even if there are limits to the number of people who are capable of shifting. However, any significant inroads into the clientele of tax accountants is, as pointed out earlier, likely to create difficulties for the ATO. If a good business case were to be made for such a campaign, the costs of that campaign would need to be outweighed by the efficiency gains of a significant increase in e-tax uptake.

6.1.4 Adjustments in administrative processes and/or legal requirements to facilitate the move to ESD

E-tax predominantly services those individuals seeking speedy return processing and tax refunds. Only a small minority of e-tax users are required to pay more tax following lodgement of their returns. This brings into question the real need for individuals to lodge income tax returns in the first instance, at least by those individuals expecting to receive refunds. The ATO has already received tax revenue from this group. Should legislation be revised to alter the existing lodgement paradigm, for example, eliminating the need for individuals to lodge income tax returns at all? In scoping business change for efficiency and effectiveness, eGovernments should eliminate all unnecessary processes, in particular administrative transactions. Should an eGovernment business process improvement exercise, in the first instance, comprehensively question the existence of, and need for, an existing process by weighing it against transaction costs and other variables, and then eliminating it before even proceeding with the development of re-engineered on-line solutions?

6.1.5 The policy and political issues in balancing the dual goals of improved services to customers and increased business efficiency

Do the actual and perceived efficiencies of the e-tax product outweigh and justify the expensive maintenance and preservation of it? Should a high quality, on-line product be maintained to serve a fortunate minority at an unrealistic cost per transaction to sustain a philosophical construct founded upon the notion of democratic process fuelled by the hope of increased on-line interaction between government and citizens? Should a merging of technologies be considered, for example, synthesising the tax agent VAN and e-tax technologies and methods into a single lodgement channel with a view to consolidating development and maintenance expenses? Does eGovernment threaten or enhance democratic process, particularly increased government openness, by reducing administrative channels through consolidation, thereby forcing user fit but offering consistency in approach to a wider population?

7. CONCLUSION

Our purpose in this paper was to analyse comprehensive ATO data on e-tax use in order to understand its potential and limitations as an ESD initiative. Our findings show that despite disappointing uptake levels, e-tax performs well and is popular with its users. But there are questions about its appropriateness and attractiveness to a wider group of taxpayers. Various factors in the Australian taxation context have influenced the success of this initiative, including the heavy use of tax agents and the lack of access to computer and internet facilities by a significant proportion of the tax-paying population. This case shows clearly the conflicts that may arise between government goals of improving their own business efficiency and their obligations to a variety of stakeholder groups in the population. In the case of e-tax, efficiency goals suggest that either some degree of coercion is required to achieve an economic use of e-tax functionality or that e-tax itself should be abandoned as an uneconomic product. Either of these raises policy and political problems.

Governments will continue to search for business process efficiencies and effectiveness and will embrace the Internet wherever feasible to do so. The key is to do this without compromising its obligations to its citizens, whilst maintaining accountability for implementing efficient, effective, risk managed innovations that deliver publicly accessible, affordable, simple and necessary services.

REFERENCES

ATO, 1997a, 'EPack pilot planned for October', *The ATO Updater Online*, Jul/Aug 1997.

ATO, 1997b, 'e-tax trial scheduled for October', *The ATO Updater Online*, July 1997.

ATO, 1998, 'Epack gets go ahead for Taxtime 98', *The ATO Updater Online*, Feb 1998.

ATO, 1999a, 'e-tax ready for 1999 tax season', *The ATO Updater Online*, Apr 1999.

ATO, 1999b, A new tax office for a new tax system, *Australian Taxation Office*, May 1999,

ATO, 1999c, Tax and the Internet, *Australian Taxation Office*, 1999,

ATO, 2000a, Online eBusiness Strategy, Version 2.2, *Australian Taxation Office*, Sept 2000,

ATO, 2000b, 'ATO prepares for E-commerce prime time', *The ATO Updater Online*,Feb 2000.

ATO, 2002, Tax Return Deadline Approaches, *Media Release - Nat 2000/95*, http://www.ato.gov.au/content.asp?doc=/content/Corporate/mr200095.htm, Last Accessed, 11/02/2002,

Caddy, J., 1999, 'Engaging the citizen leads to better results', *Public Management Forum*, vol. 5, no. 3.

Carberry, J., Steins, C., 2000. 'G2B Web Sites', *Tech Trends*, Nov/Dec 2000, p.20-24.

Chamberlain, J., Castleman, T., 2001. National Governments doing business on-line: An Australian look at current practice and future hazards. *Sixth CollECTeR Conference on Electronic Commerce*, Dec. 3-4,2001 Coffs Harbour, Australia.

Colecchia, A., 1999, Defining and measuring electronic commerce. Towards the development of an OECD methodology. *Conference on the measurement of electronic commerce*, Singapore, Organisation for Economic Co-operation and Development.

Fitzsimmons, C., 2001, 'E-tax takes a commercial turn', *'The Australian'*.

Girishankar, S., 1997, 'Feds get down to business with latest E-commerce push', *Internet Week*,No. 688. p.18-19.

Gliddon, J., 2000, 'E-tax spells tax easy', *Bulletin with Newsweek*, Vol. 118, No. 6230. p.83.

Government Online, 2000, Government Online - The Commonwealth Government's Strategy, *Department of Communications Information Technology and the Arts*, April 2000,

Madden, B., 2000, 'TaxPack goes online', *Personal Investor*, Vol. 18, No. 6. p.11.

McCarthy, J., 1997, 'Electronic Tax Pack to be piloted during 1997', *The ATO Updater Online*, Feb/Mar 1997.

Nabers, M. S., 2000, 'E-government portals open doors for business', *Austin Business Journal*, p.38.

Neff, D., 2001, 'Connecting citizens to government online', *San Diego Business Journal*, Vol. 22, No. 23. p.14.

NOIE, 2001a, Access and Equity, *National Office for the Information Economy*, http://www.noie.gov.au/projects/access/index.htm, Last Accessed, 07/06/2001,

NOIE, 2001b, Equitable Online Access, *National Office for the Information Economy*, http://www.noie.gov.au/projects/access/online_access/index.htm, Last Accessed, 07/06/2001,

Petrillo, J. J., 2000, 'Government's use of web has winners and losers', *Government Computer News*, Vol. 19, No. 5. p. 24.

Preston, M., 2000, 'E-Government US-Style', *New Statesman*, Vol. 129, No. 4517.

Public Management, 2000, 'A guide to e-government and e-commerce', *Public Management*, vol. 82, no.7. p.1.

The Economist, 2000, 'Quick Fixes', *The Economist*, vol. 355, no. 8176. p13.

Thibodeau, P., 2000, 'E-Government spending to soar through 2005', *Computerworld*, vol. 34, no.17. pp. 12-13.

Thomas, T., 2000, 'High hopes for online tax returns', *Business Review Weekly*, Vol. 22, No. 25. p.82.

Walker, R. W., 2000, 'Many govt. sites don't heed users' needs, study finds', *Government Computer News*, vol. 19, no. 16. p. 57.

THE IMPLICATIONS OF E-COMMERCE FOR SOFTWARE PROJECT RISK: A PRELIMINARY INVESTIGATION.

KENNETH J. STEVENS[1] and GREG T. TIMBRELL[2]
[1]*School of Information Systems, Technology and Management, University of New South Wales, Australia*
[2] *Information Systems Management Research Group, Queensland University of Technology, Australia*

Abstract: When a business introduces the use of e-commerce applications the software related business risks the business faces change. A corresponding change may also occur in the risks faced by the developers of the e-commerce applications. Unrecognised changes in the risks involved in software projects have considerable implications for a business. This paper reports the outcomes of the preliminary phase of a study into the implications of e-commerce for software project risk in financial institutions. Firstly, the analysis draws on the e-commerce and systems development literatures to determine the differences between e-commerce development projects and traditional development projects. Four key areas of difference were found between traditional projects and e-commerce including changes in the development process outcomes, changes in the development processes and methods, changes in stakeholder groups and changes in determining application requirements. Secondly, the differences are analysed against a set of software project risk factors from a recent reputable study. Each of the risk factors was affected in some way. Some of these impacts appear to be temporary, while others appear highly dependent upon the individual circumstances of the organization undertaking the project. Some risks did, however, appear to be permanently increased or decreased, thus signalling a fundamental difference in the overall risk profile of e-commerce projects when compared to traditional projects. Whether the impacts are temporary, contextual or permanent, they all have implications for way in which risk in e-commerce software projects is assessed and managed.

1. INTRODUCTION

The introduction of internally developed e-commerce applications had challenged traditional notions of software development within information technology divisions (Earl & Khan, 2001). E-commerce software application stakeholder groups have broadened considerably; requirements definitions cannot be solicited as easily; timeframes have shortened; and methodologies for e-commerce application development have yet to reach the maturity of traditional software development projects. A consequence of these developments is a change in the software project risk profiles of e-commerce application development.

This paper describes the initial phase of a study of e-commerce software project risk, being undertaken in the finance industry in Australia through the Security Industry Research Centre of Asia Pacific (SIRCA). The unit of analysis of the study is the software project and the main research question is "what are the risks facing e-commerce software projects, and how are they best managed?" The planned research involves case studies of e-commerce application development projects in a number of leading financial institutions. Financial institutions are of particular interest because of their reliance on credible and reliable performance of secure transactions, which makes them particularly sensitive to risks regarding the systems that process the transactions. Many of these systems support e-commerce or are linked to e-commerce applications. These systems also underpin the e-commerce systems of many other businesses. The outcomes of this study will be not only relevant to the finance industry, but also to their customers and partners in providing online commercial activities.

Before the empirical phase of the study can commence, an understanding of how software project risk differs between traditional software projects and e-commerce software projects needs to be developed, so that the research can be properly focused. This paper presents an initial analysis, based on the literature, of the possible impact of the differences between e-commerce projects and traditional process on software project risk. Firstly, the paper provides a background to software project risk. Following this is analysis of the recent literature that distils the differences between traditional software projects and e-commerce software projects. The impact of these differences on software project risk factors is then analysed and discussed. Finally, the paper provides conclusions, outlines the limitations of the analysis undertaken and discusses the implications of the findings on the anticipated study.

This paper provides an insight into differences in software project risks between traditional and e-commerce software projects and should be of interest to those engaged in the research or practice of software project risk management.

2. BACKGROUND

E-commerce is variously defined in literature. For the purposes of this study the definition adopted is a 'broad usage that includes all business that takes place between a business and its customers or a business and other business that is electronically mediated via the Internet'. E-commerce applications (or information systems) are those software applications that facilitate these exchanges [10].

E-commerce has become one of the major factors that will determine the future survival or success of organizations and is seen by many to signify a fundamental shift in the way in which organizations operate, interact and compete (Holsapple & Singh, 2000). Incorporated within this shift are changes in the risks that businesses engaged in e-commerce face. Freeman (2000) notes "Internet risk becomes an increasingly significant component of business's operational risk" and O'Neil (2000) notes "typical business risks, such as loss of revenue, business interruption, fraud and loss of reputation, are magnified for businesses engaged in e-commerce". Other e-commerce related risks identified in the literature include liability for content, reputation and security (Jorgensen, 1988), extortion, business interruption, third party liability (Ceniceros, 2000), technical threats to content, legal and commercial risks, denial of service attacks (Wright, 2001) and customer-expectations risk, reputation risk, security risk (McNamee & Chan, 2001). These risks are the business risks that arise though the use of e-commerce applications and are considered to be software risks.

As the risks faced by business' change when e-commerce applications are brought into operation, corresponding changes may also occur in the risks faced by the developers of e-commerce applications. Unrecognised changes in each of these risks could have far-reaching implications for business and project alike. It appears that researchers and professional groups are beginning to recognise nature of software risk attributable to e-commerce, however little work has been undertaken into the software project risk faced by e-commerce projects. Yan and Paradi (1999) found that the characteristics of e-commerce success in these institutions include a need

[10] This definition does not include software / hardware that form part of the communications infrastructure and is in line with the distinction that is made between a traditional application and the operating system.

for a high tolerance to risk and a capacity to deal with the risks, suggesting understanding e-commerce related risks is fundamental to the success e-commerce systems and a worthwhile research pursuit.

2.1 Software Project Risk

One consistent factor influencing project success is the various risks associated with developing projects (Jiang & Klein, 2001). Experience has shown that risk management must be of critical concern to the project managers, as unmanaged or unmitigated risks are one of the primary causes of project failure (Royer, 2000). The high failure rate of software projects is often attributed to managers not taking prudent measures to assess and manage the risk involved in projects (Keil, Cule, Lyytinen & Schmidt, 1998), however, risk assessment and management in regard to software projects, is something that is done minimally, if at all (Smith, McKeen & Staples, 2001).

Schmidt, Lyytinen, Keil & Cule, (2001) define software project risk as the product of uncertainty associated with project risk factors and the magnitude of potential loss due to project failure, where a risk factor is defined as a condition that can present a serious threat to the successful completion of a software development project. Software project risk management is the assessment and management of those risk factors that are present or arise during the software development project. The scope of software project risk is limited to the software development project only, and only those factors that can impact on the outcomes of the development process are considered. This constraint distinguishes software project risk from the broader concept of software risk[11]. Organizational impacts and the business risks that may arise from the subsequent use of a software application are considered "down stream" of the software project risk.

Software development risk, as defined by Barki, Rivard & Talbot, (1993) and in the software engineering literature (such as Gluch, 1994), is incorporated within this definition of software project risk, as it is seen as slightly narrower construct.

Appropriate risk assessment and management methods in regard to these risks have been found to improve the overall handling of the software

[11] Software risk is variously defined in the information systems and software engineering literature. Definitions range from a very board notion that incorporates all risks that can be related to the use of software within the organization (including development projects), such as Sherer, 1995, and Longstaff, Chittister, Pethia & Haimes, 2000, and to some extent Higuera & Haimes, 1996. It is also defined very narrowly and similar in meaning to the use of software project risk in this paper, as in Ropponen & Lyytinen, 1997. In this paper the software risk is used its broad sense.

development related risks (Ropponen & Lyytinen, 1997) and hence improve the likelihood of project success, or at least assist to guard against it's failure.

2.2 Software Project Risk Factors

Software project risk factors are the 'sources' of risk to a software project. They are those factors that can have a detrimental impact upon one or more of the success criteria of a project, such that they cause the project to run over time, cost more than anticipated or result in the application not having the functionality or usefulness required. The factors that apply to a specific project are seen to constitute that project's risk profile.

Numerous lists and taxonomies of risk factors exist (Barki et al., 1993, Boehm, 1991, Sherer, 1995, Moynihan, 1997, Ropponen & Lyytinen, 2001). A recent empirical study (Keil et al., 1998, Schmidt et al., 2001) undertook a Delphi study of project managers in Finland, Hong Kong and the U.S.A. to determine a ranked list of current risk factors. The "top 11" of these factors, as presented in Keil et al., (1998) are given in the table below:

Rank	Risk Factor
1	Lack of top management commitment to the project
2	Failure to gain user commitment to the project
3	Misunderstanding of requirements by the developers
4	Lack of adequate user involvement in the project
5	Failure to manage end user expectations in regard to the projects outcomes
6	Changing scope and / or the objectives of the project
7	Lack of required knowledge / skills in the project personnel
8	Lack of frozen requirements, such that the requirements continue to change throughout the development project
9	Introduction of new technology
10	Insufficient / inappropriate staffing
11	Conflict between user departments

Table 1. Top 11 Software Project Risk Factors (Keil et al., 1998)

The Keil et al., (1998) study did not appear to have captured these risk factors in regard to any particular type or class of application, so these factors considered generic' and applicable to systems development in general. It is assumed that these factors represent traditional software developments, given their similarity to other findings (Barki et al., 1993). Any substantial differences between e-commerce development projects and traditional development projects may change the relative importance or applicability of these risk factors. The following section seeks to determine the differences between e-commerce development projects and traditional development projects and then analyse the impact of those differences on software project risks.

3. ANALYSIS AND RESULTS

The analysis involves two steps. Firstly, the differences between e-commerce development projects and traditional development projects are considered and; secondly, these differences are analysed against a set of software project risk factors.

3.1 E-Commerce Project Differences

Like any systems development, the development of e-commerce applications is a complex task (Standing, 2002), however, there is evidence to suggest that the e-commerce development process is different from what has come before. Earl & Khan (2001), in a study of an e-commerce specific IT department, found a variety of new practices and procedures particular to e-commerce were evolving.

To understand better the general nature of these evolving differences, a review of the e-commerce and systems development literature was undertaken. The analysis considered each phase of the development process, the approaches to development, development tools used, and project management practices.

Areas of Change	**Noted Key Differences**
Development outcomes	Applications built with an expectation of a short life
Development processes, methods and techniques	Less structured methods More iterative / evolutionary techniques Modularised development Development timeframe is significantly shorter
Stakeholders	Much broader stakeholder groups Multiple internal user groups Multiple external user groups Greater diversity in computer skills, domain knowledge, culture and language.
Scope and Requirements	Considerably more volatile Multiple reference groups

Table 2. Key Differences Between Traditional and E-Commerce Development Projects

The differences found have been grouped into four categories. These categories 'emerged' from the analysis and are not meant to be mutually exclusive. A summary of the key differences is set out in Table 2 and discussed at length below.

3.1.1 Changes in development outcomes

The significant costs of traditional systems development efforts typically necessitate the long-term use of an application to achieve an acceptable return on investment. Many of the current development practices are geared towards generating systems that are sufficiently robust and flexible to allow long effective lives.

E-commerce development, however, appears to be different. Earl & Khan, (2001) found a shift in development ethos from "built to last" to "launch and learn", resulting smaller systems that are considered disposable. Standing (2002) maintains that the entire notion of project completion is now inappropriate because of the need to constantly modified and update systems. The new goal in the development process appears to be 'time to market', as reflected in shorter development timeframes and the new outcomes of the development process are small, highly modularised, components that are added, used, then redeveloped or scraped as required.

3.1.2 Changes in development processes, methods and techniques

Standing (2002) states "the popular assumption is that processes, methods and techniques used for applications developments have changed radically as the focus of applications has moved from the traditional information systems domain to the Web". These changes include:

Firstly, a change in the development ethos to "more like craft than engineering" approach which involves "much learning by doing and a sense of being free from rules" (Earl & Khan, 2001).

Secondly, few traditional methodologies are considered appropriate for the development of e-commerce applications (Standing, 2002). Earl & Khan (2001) also found a move from the traditional waterfall method to a "new-venture" style of development because the waterfall method was considered too linear, too long, lacking in appeal to creative designers and could not cope with continuous change. The issue of the linearity within the development cycle is also address by Gordijn, Akkermans & van Vliet, (2000) who found "design decisions about e-business models and the associated information systems architecture cannot be sequentially made in a decoupled way, because business and technology considerations are strongly linked". Gordijn et al., (2000) also note the inadequacy of current methodologies because of their focus on discovering requirements rather than creating requirements. A number of studies offer alternative development methodologies for e-commerce and web development. Li, Chen & Chen, (2000) and Howcroft & Carroll, (2000) propose novel ways to undertake e-commerce developments, which are quite dissimilar to traditional application development methods.

Thirdly, the composition of the development teams appears to have changed. Earl & Khan (2001) note the need for multi-disciplinary teams that include users, technical types and creative types. Standing (2002) likens the e-commerce development team to that of a film production team.

Finally, the timeframe in which e-commerce applications are developed appears to be somewhat shorter than that allowed for more traditional projects. Earl & Khan (2001) report that some respondents in their study indicated that projects would only be undertaken in they could be completed in less than three months. Hammar-Cloyd, (2001) notes that many e-commerce developers are "under pressure to develop new applications faster" and Li et al., (2000) found faster revision cycles have lead to a blurring of development and maintenance phases.

3.1.3 Changes in stakeholder groups

A number of key differences the nature of stakeholders in e-commerce development and traditional development exist.

Firstly, the number of stakeholder groups involved in a development project has increased dramatically. Standing, (2002) notes that many web-based system are multi-functional, requiring user representatives from throughout the organization. Users external to the business, in the form of customers, suppliers and so on, are also now included in the stakeholder group. . This broadening of the stakeholder group has implications for the development of e-commerce systems including the funding, the potential for conflict between the user groups in regard to the systems requirements, the need to integrate the e-commerce system with multiple internal systems, the acceptance of the developed system and the management of its ongoing evolution and maintenance.

Secondly, the expanded user base is considerably more diverse. As the internal user groups are identifiable, assumptions to be made about their computer competency, business knowledge, language and culture. It is difficult to see how these assumptions could be made about the external users, as considerable diversity would exist in each of the above areas, thus posing considerable implications for the requirements of an e-commerce system.

3.1.4 Changes in requirements

A number of clear differences exist in the determination of the requirements for an e-commerce application and a more traditional application.

Firstly, the elicitation of requirements is seen as problematic as the requirements may simply not exist. Eliciting requirements is dependent upon users understanding the needs of the underlying business activities. In the case of e-commerce, where the system is good proportion of the underlying activities, the requirements many have to be created from scratch rather than discovered (Gordijn et al., 2000).

Secondly, the requirements will need to be elicited from the broader user base. Such diverse reference groups are bound to increase requirements conflict between stakeholder groups. The lack of underlying business models would tend to exacerbate these conflicts (Gordijn et al., 2000). The articulation of the requirements in regard to the new external user group is also problematic in terms of who actually articulates them.

Thirdly, the potential diversity of the external user base creates a considerably expanded set of requirements to accommodate different skill and knowledge levels, different languages, different data formats and conventions (Hasselbring, 2002), integration with both internal and external legacy systems and so on. These differences have implications not only for the main functionality, presentation and data of the system but also for ancillary functions such as online help.

Finally, it is apparent that the requirements for e-commerce systems are far less stable than other systems. The relative newness of the systems, the incremental nature of the development approach, the rapid evolution of the underlying technology and the competitive pressure from business units all seem to create a situation in which the requirements are in almost constant flux (Earl & Khan, 2001).

3.2 Impact of project differences on software project risk

In the above analysis, several key differences were noted between the e-commerce and traditional development projects. To gain an understanding of how these differences translate to a change in the risk profile of an e-commerce software project, an analysis of a common set of software project risk factors against these changes was required. The set of risk factors used in the analysis are from Keil et al., (1998)[12]

The analysis involved considering each risk factor in light of the differences between e-commerce and traditional software projects. The impact of each difference was considered in light of three perspectives: the direction of change in the factor; the permanence of the impact on the factor; and effect of context on of impact, as discussed below.

3.2.1 The direction of change in the factor

Each factor was considered in the light of each difference as to the extent to which the difference would cause change in the operation of that factor:

- Decrease - in that the operation of the factor would be diminished, hence contributing to a reduction in the project risk.
- Little or no change – in that the operation of the risk factor would remain more or less unchanged.
- Increase – in that the operation of the factor would be exacerbated, hence contributing to an increase in the project risk.

A simple three-point scale (increase, decrease or little or no change) has been used to categorize the direction of the change to keep the analysis simple.

3.2.2 The permanence of the impact on the factor

Each factor was also considered in regard to the permanence of the impact. The distinction between temporary and permanent effects appeared important as in terms of how the changes in the risk might be managed and how it might change over time.

3.2.3 The extent of context of impact on the factor

The impact of each factor was also considered in regard to the extent to which variation in the risk factor would be more attributable to the individual circumstances of an organization rather than in response to the fact that development was an e-commerce development. This perspective

[12] Keil et al., (1998) undertake a Delphi study of software development project managers from the USA, Hong Kong and Finland, providing strong validity. The study is also relatively recent, but no so recent as to already include the effects (if any) of e-commerce development.

was important as it accommodates situations where credible arguments could be mounted for change in the risk factor either way.

3.3 Results of analysis of the impact of development differences on risk

The analysis of four areas of difference (as set out in table two) against the eleven risk factors (as set out in table one) across the three perspectives discussion above resulted in a large and interesting data set. A summary of the analysis is set out in the following table.

In the table, the column "Risk Factor" lists each of the risk factors from Keil et al., (1988). The factors are ranked in order of importance, as per the study. The column "Expected change in factor" provides an estimation of the change in each risk factor in terms in light of the aggregated effect of all of the differences between e-commerce projects and traditional projects. Where this change is considered temporary or highly contextual, then this is also noted.

	Risk factor	**Expected change in factor**
1	Lack of top management commitment to the project	Little or no change as highly contextual
2	Failure to gain user commitment to the project	Decrease
3	Misunderstanding of requirements by the developers	Increase (and temporary)
4	Lack of adequate user involvement in the project	Decrease
5	Failure to manage end user expectations in regard to the projects outcomes	Decrease (highly contextual)
6	Changing scope and / or the objectives of the project	Increase (partially temporary)
7	Lack of required knowledge / skills in the project personnel	Increase (temporary)
8	Lack of frozen requirements, such that the requirements continue to change throughout the development project	Increase
9	Introduction of new technology	Increase (temporary)
10	Insufficient / inappropriate staffing	Increase (temporary)
11	Conflict between user departments	Increase

Table 3. Summary of Impacts on Risk Factors

3.4 Discussion of impact on individual risk factors

The key points that arose of the analysis of each factor are discussed below.

3.4.1 Lack of top management commitment to the project

Top management support has been the "bug bear" of information systems projects for many years. The operation of this factor in regard to e-commerce is difficult to understand. On one hand, if management sees e-commerce are important to the business's future than support may be forthcoming, on the other hand, the historical precedence that makes this item the single most important risk factor in the Keil et al., (1998) study, would suggest that management will pay scant attention to e-commerce. We suggest that in this regard the impact of the factor is highly contextual, in that it will operate in different ways in different organizations influenced by factors other than the fact they the development is e-commerce.

3.4.2 Failure to gain user commitment to the project

We suggest this factor should decrease, as e-commerce developments appear to be more inclusive of users. Identifying the appropriate users from which to gain commitment could be difficult and may dampen any effect.

3.4.3 Misunderstanding the requirements by the developers

An increase in this factor is expected because of the volatility of the requirements, the increased number of stakeholders, increased conflict between stakeholder groups, and difficulties in determine "what the customer wants". It is expected that as the organization learns how to develop e-commerce systems that the propensity to misunderstand the requirements may diminish.

3.4.4 Lack of adequate user involvement in the project

Like Factor 2, this factor should probably decrease, as the literature is clearly pointing towards more inclusive development teams. The sheer number of differing user groups could dilute any decrease.

3.4.5 Failure to manage end user expectations in regard to the project outcomes

Like Factor 3, this factor is expected to increase because of the volatility of the requirements, the increased number of stakeholders, increased conflict between stakeholder groups, and difficulties in determine "what the customer wants". This factor is exacerbated by apparent difficulties in understanding the requirements of external users, as they are outside the business and it becomes difficult or inappropriate to determine their needs. A diverse user group will yield diverse expectations.

3.4.6 Changing scope / objectives

In a similar manner to Factor 2, the overall objectives of the systems may be difficult to "pin down", until the capability of the technology is well understood. In a more permanent change, the ongoing volatility of the requirement can make scope and objective decisions more difficult. The noted change in development ethos towards more short term, disposable systems, may partially ameliorate this impact.

3.4.7 Lack of required knowledge / skills in the project personnel

A temporary increase is expected to occur until necessary skills are obtained. The different composition of project teams could exacerbate the increase for some time.

3.4.8 Lack of frozen requirements

A permanent increase is expected to occur in this factor as our analysis indicates that the new hallmark of e-commerce development is the fluidity of the requirements. The shorter time frame for development would seem to act to restrict the impact on this factor, as any problems that arise from incorrect functionality could be quickly overcome within the next iteration of the development cycle.

3.4.9 Introduction of new technology

A temporary increase is more likely to occur until the technology is understood and absorbed into the IT infrastructure and architecture. The ongoing development and release of new technologies (web-based programming languages / tools, communication technologies and the like) is likely to prolong the impact on this factor.

3.4.10 Insufficient / inappropriate staffing

A temporary increase is expected to occur until necessary skills are obtained. The different requirements for project team composition of project team could exacerbate the increase for some time.

3.4.11 Conflict between user departments

We believe this factor should increase in line with the increased number of stakeholders / user groups.

3.5 Discussion of results

The analysis suggests that a number of definite and significant differences between e-commerce development projects and traditional development project either exist or are beginning to emerge. Numerous differences where found. Some we expect to be "temporary" or "contextual". Temporary effects were those noted differences that related the novelty of the application, rather than the fact that it is an e-commerce application being developed. Contextual effects were those noted differences that related more the circumstances of the business undertaking the development. Other, more permanent differences were also noted, where it is the nature of the e-commerce applications themselves that cause the difference. Each of these difference effects requires a different response to managing the development risks associated with that effect.

A key goal of the analysis articulated in this paper was to determine the specific hypotheses to explore using case study methods. Case study is appropriate because of its ability to explicate the rich context needed to explore the risk determinants across a diverse stakeholder group in a contemporary setting and compare these with recent developments in software development project risk generally. Case studies also seek to 'understand' (in a phenomenological or hermeneutic sense) the meaning held by a subject or group rather than 'explanation' (as produced by a scientific 'explanation') (Gable, 1994). It is proposed that data will be collected using techniques as semi-structured interviews, participant observation, and sifting project team meeting records and other relevant project artifacts to explore the hypotheses derived from the expected differences listed and summarised in table 3.

4. CONCLUSIONS

The investigation presented in this paper sought to gain an initial understanding of the differences between e-commerce software projects and traditional software projects and to analyse these differences in regard to their impact on software project risk. An analysis of the literature revealed a number of changes in the outcomes of the project, the project methods and process, the stakeholders involved and the requirements of e-commerce applications.

When these differences are analysed against a set of software project risk factors from a recent reputable study (Keil et al., 1998), each risk factor was affected in some way. Some of these impacts appeared to be temporary, while others appeared highly dependent upon the individual circumstances of the organization undertaking the project. Some risks did, however, appear to be permanently increased or decreased, thus signalling a fundamental difference in the overall risk profile of e-commerce projects when compared to traditional projects. Whether the impacts are temporary, contextual or permanent, they all have implications for way in which risk in e-commerce software projects is assessed and managed.

4.1 Limitations

The paper suffers from a number of limitations. Firstly, the paper only seeks to examine the impact of the development differences in respect of known risk factors and, as such, ignores the possibility of identifying factors unique to e-commerce. Secondly, the assumption that the risk factors used relate to "traditional" software development projects rather than e-commerce projects may incorrect. If the participants in the Keil et al., (1998) study (from which the risk factors are drawn) did consider e-commerce projects in their responses then the analysis in this paper may indeed be double counting the impact of e-commerce development on risk factors. Thirdly, e-commerce projects and traditional projects have been used in a generic sense, without regard to the actual considerable variation in applications within these two categories. It has been assumed that risk factors would apply equally to all to e-commerce applications and this may not be the case. Subsequent phases of this research will need to address each of these limitations, however, given the preliminary nature of the initial phase of the research reported in this paper, the limitations do not detract significantly from the overall conclusions.

4.2 Implications to project managers and researchers

The analysis in this preliminary study proposes two ideas. Firstly, there is a marked difference between e-commerce software projects and traditional software projects and secondly, these differences have material implications for the risk factors of software project risk.

The key implication of these differences for project managers is the need to reassess their understanding of the risks they face when undertaking e-commerce projects and reassess the techniques that they use to manage and mitigate those risks. Project managers also need to ensure that their risk assessment mechanisms allow them to look beyond the usual risks.

The key implication for these findings for researcher it the need to undertake further work to better determine the nature of the differences in e-commerce and traditional projects, the subsequent impact on software project risks factors, and the way in which the risks may be best managed. In regard the proposed research study outlined at the beginning of this paper, the outcomes of initial analysis presented above provides more than adequate grounds to proceed to the next phase of the proposed research.

REFERENCES

Barki, H., S. Rivard, J Talbot (1993), 'Toward an Assessment of Software Development Risk', *Journal of Management Information Systems* **10**(2), 203-225.

Boehm, B.W. (1991), 'Software Risk Management: Principles and Practices', *IEEE Software* **8**(1), 32-41.

Ceniceros, R. (2000), 'Managing e-commerce risks', *Business Insurance* **34**(4), 29.

Gable G. (1994), 'Integrating case study and survey research methods: an example in information systems', *European Journal of Information Systems*, **3**(2), 112-126.

Hammar-Cloyd, M. H. (2001), 'Designing User-Centered Web Application in Web Time', *IEEE Software* **18**(1), 62-69.

Earl, M. and B. Khan (2001), 'E-Commerce is Changing the Face of IT', *MIT Sloan Management Review* **43**(1), 64-72.

Freeman, E. Q. (2000), 'E-Merging Risks: Operational Issues and Solutions in a Cyberage', *Risk Management* **47**(7), 12-16.

Gable, G. (1994), 'Integrating case study and survey research methods: an example in information systems', *European Journal of Information Systems* **3**(2), 112-126.

Gordijn, J., H. Akkermans, H. van Vliet (2000), 'Value Based Requirements Creation for Electronic Commerce Applications', *in* 'Proceedings of the 33rd Hawaii International Conference on Systems Sciences', Hawaii, Jan 4-7, pp. 1915 –1924.

Gluch, D. P. (1994), 'A Construct for Describing Software Development Risks', Technical Report CMU/SEI-94-TR-14, Software Engineering Institute, Carnegie Mellon University.

Hasselbring, W. (2002), 'Web Data Integration for E-Commerce Applications', *IEEE Multimedia* **9**(1), 16-25.

Higuera, R. P. and Y. Y. Haimes (1996), 'Software Risk Management', Technical Report CMU/SEI-96-TR-012, Software Engineering Institute, Carnegie Mellon University.

Holsapple, C. W. and M. Singh (2000), 'Electronic Commerce: From a Definitional Taxonomy Toward a Knowledge-Management View', *Journal of Organizational Computing and Electronic Commerce* **10**(3), 149-170.

Howcroft, D. and A. Carroll (2000), 'A proposed methodology for web development' *in* 'Proceedings of the 8th European Conference on Information Systems', Vienna, July 3-5

Jiang, J. J. and G. Klein (2001), 'Software Project Risks and Development Focus', *Project Management Journal* **32**(1), 4-9.

Jorgensen, L. (1998), 'Connection to Risk? Managing the exposures of cyberspace', *Risk Management* **45**(2), 14.

Keil, M., P. E. Cule, Kalle Lyytinen and Roy Schmidt (1998), 'A Framework for Identifying Software Project Risks', *Communications of the ACM* **41**(11), 76-83.

Longstaff, T. A., C. Chittister, R. Pethia and Y.Y Haimes (2000), 'Are we forgetting the risks of information technology?' *Computer* **33**(12), 43-51.

McNamee, D. and S. Chan (2001), 'Understanding E-commerce Risk', *Internal Auditor* **58**(5), 60-61.

Moynihan, T. (1997), 'How Experienced Project Managers Assess Risk', *IEEE Software* **14**(3), 35- 41.

O'Neill, D. T. (2000), 'Evaluating banks' e-commerce risks', *American Agent and Broker* **72**(11), 36-46.

Ropponen, J. and K. Lyytinen (1997), 'Can software risk management improve systems development: an exploratory study', *European Journal of Information Systems* **6**(1), 41-50.

Ropponen, J. and K. Lyytinen (2001), 'Components of Software Development Risk: How to Address Them? A Project Manager Survey', *IEEE Transactions on Software Engineering* **26**(2), 98-112

Royer, P. S. (2000), 'Risk Management: The Undiscovered Dimension of Project Management', *Project Management Journal* **31**(1), 6-13.

Schmidt, R., K. Lyytinen, M. Keil, and P. E. Cule (2001), 'Identifying software project risks: An international Delphi study', *Journal of Management Information Systems* **17**(4), 5-36.

Sherer, S. (1995), 'The Three dimensions of Software Risk: Technical, Organizational and Environmental', *in* 'The Proceedings of the 28th Annual Hawaii International Conference on Systems Science', Hawaii, January 3-6, pp. 369-378.

Smith, H. A., J. D. McKeen and Sandy D. Staples (2001), 'Risk Management in Information Systems: Problems and Potentials', *Communications of the Association for Information Systems* **7**(1).

Standing, Craig (2002), 'Methodologies for developing Web applications', *Information and Software Technology* **44**(3), 151-159.

Wright, A. (2001), 'Controlling Risks of E-Commerce Content', *Computers and Security* **20**(2), 147-154.

Yan, G., and J.C. Paradi (1999), 'Success Criteria for Financial Institutions in Electronic Commerce', *in* 'The Proceedings of the 32nd Annual Hawaii International Conference on Systems Science', Hawaii, January 5-8, pp. 341-348.

FRAMEWORK FOR PARTICIPANTS' RECOGNITION OF KEY SUCCESS FACTORS IN ELECTRONIC MARKETPLACES

ROSEMARY STOCKDALE and CRAIG STANDING
Edith Cowan University, Perth, Australia

Abstract: The development of electronic marketplaces has been prolific in the last five years and the pressure for companies to participate, before they have determined how to recognise the benefits and pitfalls, has been intense. This has left prospective participants facing a wide variety of choices in the selection of potential trading sites, in a marketplace that is both dynamic and immature. Although there are different drivers pushing companies towards participation, an appreciation of how electronic marketplaces are developing their trading models can support the selection process and enhance the trading experience of theparticipants.

Electronic marketplaces were selectively chosen and analysed against key success factors, previously identified in the literature, to examine how market makers are recognising the issues they need to address in developing their marketplaces. The analysis also highlights concerns that remain in regard to some of the key success factors, particularly in the areas of security, technological infrastructure and neutrality. The findings are used to provide a framework that facilitates recognition by prospective participants of the key success factors of an electronic marketplace and the issues surrounding them and thereby contributes to the selection of a trading site to meet a company's requirements.

1. INTRODUCTION

Electronic commerce has led to great changes in the way business to business trading has been conducted over the last few years, and enabled businesses to connect with each other in a way that requires new thinking in every area of commerce. The turnover from business to business e-commerce is anticipated to exceed $800 billion by the end of 2002 (Bowles, 2002) and is forecast to rise further in the next five years. However, the problem of introducing a new mindset to cope with fundamentally new principles in the digital economy (Lee, 2001) is aggravated by the pressure for rapid involvement before companies have assimilated the demands and pressures of the new business environment.

This is evident in the development of electronic marketplaces and the impact these are having on complex procurement and supply chains. E-marketplaces have been developed in virtually every industry and service sector, offering participants the facility to buy and sell a vast variety of goods and services to a wider array of potential customers than ever before. The speed of development has led to a complex, dynamic and immature environment that is bewildering for many companies and there is a reluctance to participate on the part of both buyers and sellers (Aberdeen Group, 2001; Deeter-Schmelz, Bizzari, Graham, & Howdyshell, 2001; Wise & Morrison, 2000). Nevertheless, indications from industry groups are that an increasing share of procurement transactions are moving to the online environment and non-participation will therefore be damaging to individual companies as majority participation gathers pace (Aberdeen Group, 2001; Downes & Mui, 1998; Forrester Research, 2000; Gartner Consulting, 2000; Sculley & Woods, 2001).

The profusion of e-marketplaces, the speed of transition to the electronic environment, the variety of business models and the varying requirements of different industries and service sectors cloud an already confused marketplace picture. Despite the confusion, there is immense pressure on companies, not least from their shareholders and directors (Banham, 2000), to move quickly to the electronic marketplace. Often they do so without a full understanding of what benefits they can accrue from participation and how they should recognise the factors that contribute to the development and success of e-marketplaces.

Using previously identified key e-marketplace success factors (Standing, 2001), this paper analyses how selected marketplaces are recognising these factors to highlight issues that remain to be addressed in electronic marketplace development. This enables a framework to be offered to facilitate the identification of key success factors by prospective participants to support their choice of an electronic marketplace that meets their company requirements.

2. ELECTRONIC MARKETPLACES

Definitions of electronic marketplaces are very diverse ranging from Malone's 'information-technology based governance mechanisms' (Malone, Yates, & Benjamin, 1987) to Bakos's more buyer-seller orientated 'interorganisational information system that allows the participating buyers and sellers in some market to exchange information about prices and product offerings' (Bakos, 1997). More recently, the US Federal Trade Commission has defined them more broadly as ' a distinct system of suppliers, distributors, commerce service providers, infrastructure providers and customers that use the Internet for communciations and transactions' (Federal Trade Commission, 2000).

The proliferation of these marketplaces in the last five years has resulted in a wide diversity of ownership and business models and many different classifications have been offered to provide some level of clarity to a dynamic environment (Kaplan & Sawhney, 2000; Lee, 2001; Piccinelli, Di Vitantonio, & Mokrushin, 2001; Raisch, 2001; Sculley & Woods, 2001). It is not possible to assess the number of electronic marketplaces on the Internet, although estimates of globally operating ones range from 800 to 1000 (Hurwitz, 2000; Tedeschi, 2001). This number cannot be maintained and there are forecasts of considerable consolidation taking place in the next two to three years (Forrester Research, 2000), which raises the question of which market makers are likely to continue to exist and what will contribute to their ability to survive.

2.1 Ownership of e-marketplaces

Many companies formed e-marketplaces to gain early mover advantage and to establish a critical mass of buyers and sellers to maintain a competitive edge in an increasingly fluid market environment (Bakos, 1991). Many of the early market makers were either intermediary companies, financed by venture capital, such as Freemarkets (http://www.freemarkets.com), or individual, technology companies such as IBM (http://www.ibm.com). More recently there has been an increase in industry consortia marketplaces, resulting from unprecedented cooperation between rival companies; for example the creation of Covisint (http://www.covisint.com) by a consortia of automobile companies including General Motors, Ford and DaimlerChrysler. Other sites have developed from associations between intermediaries, technology companies and industry participants such as Egreencoffee (http://www.egreencoffee.com).

The trend towards more industry coalition e-marketplaces is affecting the survival of some of the earlier dot.com businesses (Spiegel, 2001) and leading the latter to re-invent their presence in the market either as service companies or consortia partners. Pressure is also caused by the unsustainable proliferation of e-marketplaces; for example over 17 major e-marketplaces were identified in the mining industry in January 2001 (Ludeman, 2001) and 28 in the forest and building products industry (Industry Canada, 2000). While monopolies of marketplaces in individual industries would not be tolerated by governments, an optimal number of sites is likely to emerge from the current situation. Forrester Research estimates that less than 200 e-marketplaces will survive within two years (Forrester Research, 2000). This underlines the need for prospective participants to have some awareness of the issues that may affect the likelihood of survival when selecting a potential marketplace.

2.1 Trading models

At the most simplistic level, e-marketplaces can be defined as either horizontal or vertical, although this is no longer such a clear cut separation. Some larger vertical marketplaces such as Quadrem (www.quadrem.com) have moved beyond mining and metals to a more 'complete solution' to the procurement needs of their customers. Also, a number of horizontal marketplaces enable the purchase of industry specific goods through such offerings as Freemarket's Quicksource facility. An understanding of the transaction mechanisms and the levels of services offered by electronic marketplaces therefore offers an insight into potential trading models.

2.1.1 Transaction Mechanisms

While some marketplaces offer a variety of transaction mechanisms, others offer only one or two. As electronic marketplaces evolve, changes in the way firms are sourcing goods take place as they adapt to market developments. There is a wide variety of transaction mechanisms, some of which are very complex while others offer very simple identification services. They fall within five groups as follows:

- Catalogues - Catalogues are either individual vendor or multi-vendor. In addition to the traditional catalogue tasks of product representation, classification and search, online catalogues offer information, the ordering of goods and services, payment facilities, customer support, feedback and participation in corporate activities (Stanoevska-Slabeva & Schmid, 2000).
- Auctions - Auctions are the most visible face of B2B e-marketplaces and there are more than 30 different auctions formats currently in use (Davis, 2001). The most common formats are the seller-driven auction, based on

the traditional auction house method, and the buyer-driven reverse auctions.

- Exchanges - The exchange mechanism closely resembles the offline trading exchanges for commodities and near commodities and hosts competitive, anonymous bidding between buyers and sellers.
- Storefronts - The storefront mechanism offers participants the opportunity to maintain an open Webpage within the marketplace site.
- Negotiation - In the negotiation model, the marketplace acts as an intermediary for transactions and supports the posting of bids or quotes and allows for responding businesses to make their offers. The e-marketplace may accept the full role of intermediary and thereby maintains anonymity between the participants.

2.1.2 Additional facilities

Market makers use facilities additional to the buying and selling mechanisms to attract participants to their marketplaces and value-add facilities have been identified as a key success factor in marketplaces (Standing, 2001). Choudhury et al., (1998) identified different levels of service that are offered by e-marketplaces, developing from trading hubs that support the identification of potential trading partners to more complex models offering selection and, increasingly, execution services. These transaction orientated execution services may range from payment services through to logistics, customs forms, insurance, tracking of goods, escrow and currency exchanges. A further range of facilities identified in e-marketplaces includes information services: for example industry events, research papers, tutorials and news. Some e-marketplaces offer a community site model which offer a full range of facilities relevant to a specific industry, the benefits of which are well documented (Downes & Mui, 1998; Hagel & Armstrong, 1997; Raisch, 2001).

2.1.3 Benefits of e-marketplaces

The reported benefits to companies that are trading through e-marketplaces are compelling and suggest that cost savings being experienced by companies are considerable. Lucking-Reiley and Spulber (2000) report that online transactions could 'reduce costs by a factor of five or ten or more.' The following list of cost saving efficiencies was assembled from a search of current periodicals and journals:

- lower procurement costs
- lower search costs

- reduced administration costs
- reduced development time
- integrated global suppliers
- cuts in inventory holdings
- up-to-the-minute order tracking
- a strengthening of relationships with commercial partners
- exposure to a global market

The scope of the individual marketplace will determine how many of these benefits can be experienced by the participants of a particular marketplace. The element of choice in selecting an e-marketplace is often constrained by traditional partners or the positioning of major industry players. However, in open e-marketplaces where entry barriers are low, there are opportunities for smaller companies to bid for business with larger companies who were previously inaccessible.

3. KEY FACTORS OF SUCCESSFUL E-MARKETPLACES

The business press offers several factors which are believed to be key to the success of an e-marketplace (Standing, 2001) and these are summarized in Table 1.

4. METHODOLOGY

A detailed analysis of twelve electronic marketplace websites, representative of a wide variety of industries and marketplace models, was made to determine the extent to which key success factors, identified from the literature, are being addressed.

4.1 Selection of the websites

A list of e-marketplaces, trading on the Internet, was compiled from a search of the business press, academic journals and the use of the altavista (www.altavista.com) and yahoo (www.yahoo.com) search engines. Some industries are better served by electronic marketplaces than others and therefore a diverse range of industries was selected to give a broader view of how prevalent the recognition of key success factors is. The twelve sites were selected to represent a range of criteria as shown in Table 2.

Key Success Factor	Notes
Critical Mass	Sufficient number of participants to ensure effective running of an e-marketplace. Low entry costs, designed to attract new participants also encourage memberships of multiple e-marketplaces which has implications for income streams as it disperses the transactional value of suppliers' activities.
Income streams	Identified income streams include: transaction related fees membership/licensing fees sales of industry information value-add service fees advertising and marketing sales of accumulated marketing data.
Security	A secure environment in which to exchange commercially sensitive and financial information.
Level of independence	The ability to offer a neutral environment in which participants can trade without fear of compromise. The Federal Trade Commission reports that over-inclusive ownership by industry consortia could raise concerns of exclusion practices (FTC, 2000)
Technology infrastructure	Issues of: technological complexity resulting in additional costs to participants (e.g. hardware, software, training etc.) software standards
Relationship management: **Trust** **Privacy**	Trust can be signalled using criteria based on those outlined by Smith et al (1999) in relation to business-to-consumer e-marketplaces: Online community facilities allows interaction and the sharing of positive references (Kollock, 1999) Links from other trusted sites Unbiased product information from third parties Existing reputation (brand name) Commercial firms also offer authentication, validation and transaction services Privacy raises issues of maintaining industry relationships and safeguarding sensitive information.
Fulfilling participants' needs (value-add)	Market makers need to achieve a form of competitive advantage to attract participants and maintain profits (Bakos, 1991). In identifying and incorporating a relevant range of facilities to meet, or exceed, participants' needs, e-marketplaces can increase viability. The advantages of community sites are well-documented (Hagel & Armstrong, 1997) and the use of community site facilities has the capacity to create trust and enables the e-marketplace to act as a one-stop portal for industry participants.

Table 1. Key success factors

E-market-place	Industry	Ownership Model	Entry Barriers	Geograph-ical Range	Languages	Partici-pants
Quadrem	mining, minerals and metals industry	Industry consortia	Open	global	English, French, Spanish, Portuguese	Industry-wide suppliers/ buyers
Covisint	automobile industry	Industry consortia	Open	global	English, Japanese	manu-facturers and their suppliers
Con-verge	hi-tech goods	Industry consortia	Open	global	English	whole-sale distri-bution
Appliance-zone	consumer appliances	Inter-mediaries	Open	Europe	English, French, German	whole-salers/ high st. retailers
Paper Exchange	pulp and paper industry	Inter-mediaries	Open	global	English, French, German, Italian, Spanish, Finnish, Swedish	industry wide suppliers and buyers
Egreen coffee	coffee trade	Inter-mediaries	Open	global	English, Spanish, Portuguese	com-modity traders
E-greenbiz	green industry products	Inter-mediaries	Open	USA	English	small/ medium wholesalers
Cargo finder	transportation (shipping)	Inter-mediaries	Open	Dutch based (global)	English	service sector
58K	printing	Inter-mediaries	Industry regi-stered printers	USA Europe	English, French	medium to large scale service sector
Telemerc	telecomms	"vendor neutral"	Open	global	English	reselling products and services
Retailers Market Xchange	convenience stores and small business retailers	Inter-mediaries	Open	USA	English	small busineses
Ecfood	food and beverages	Inter-mediaries	Certified suppliers , invited buyers	global	English	'large industry players'

Table 2. Selected electronic marketplaces

A preliminary examination of the websites was made to check the criteria in Table 2 and to further define the profile of each e-marketplace by clarifying their methods of transacting business.

4.2 Methods of transacting business

	Auctions	Storefronts	Negotiations	Catalogues	Exchange
www.quadrem.com	X		X	X	
www.covisint.com	X		X	X	
www.converge.com	X		X	X	X
www.appliancezone.com			X	X	
www.paperExchange.com	X	X	X	X	X
www.Egreencoffee.com			X		X
www.E-greenbiz.com	X			X	
www.cargofinder.com			X		
www.58k.com	X		X		
www.telemerc.com	X	X	X		X
www.RetailersMarketXchange.com	X			X	
www.ecfood.com	X	X	X	X	

Table 3. Methods of transacting business offered by the electronic marketplaces

All but one e-marketplace offered two or more methods of transacting business. The most common facility offered for transacting business was negotiation, closely followed by auctions (no distinction has been made with reverse auctions) and catalogues. The exchange facility, which is used for commodities and commodity-like products, was offered by only a third of the e-marketplaces and storefronts by a quarter.

All the sites had some level of value-add facilities. For transaction based facilities, four e-marketplaces offered identification and selection services with execution of transactions being completed externally, usually via email and five sites offered full execution services with financial and logistical support. Three marketplaces were unclear, but it is thought that they offered, or were developing, execution services. Other value-add facilities are discussed in the findings.

4.3 Analysis of the websites

Although the analysis of websites is a recent area of study, many disciplines have moved towards an examination of them particularly in regard to judging the purpose of specific websites and assessing the effectiveness of their design (Gibson and Ward, 2000). This study however, is concerned with identifying the presence of specific factors on the websites and a content analysis approach was selected as the best method for identifying the presence of specific data. An awareness of both manifest and latent content analysis strategies (Berg, 2001, p243) enables a more interpretive approach to be taken, to account not only for the physical presence of elements, but also for an awareness of the underlying meanings that may exist.

Key success factors	Words and word groups sought
Critical mass	Names of major industry suppliers as participants, percentage growth rate, percentage of participant market, average transaction size, 'we have critical mass', number of participants, number of product lines
Income streams	Fees, transaction fees, licensing fees, commission, advertisements, percentage cut
Security	'highest levels of security', security statement, security guaranteed, security company participation (e.g. logo), secure environment/site
Level of independence	Statement of ownership, no affiliations, not affiliated to.., independent, neutral
Technology infrastructure	Technology standards, industry standards, technology partnerships, infrastructure
Relationship management: **Trust** **Privacy**	Community facilities, links to other trusted sites, third party endorsement, validation, feedback, maintenance of partner relationships Privacy statement
Fulfilling participants' needs (value-add)	Any words or word groups that relate to facilities offered in addition to buying and selling transactions e.g. news, chat rooms, what's new etc.

Table 4 Concept coding scheme

A coding scheme was developed using concepts as the unit of analysis; the key success factors were listed with groups of words that related to each factor (see Table 4) and the marketplace sites examined for the presence of these words or groups of words. The use of word groupings allows for verification of the analysis while not confining it to rigid constraints that ignore the apparent differences in the diversity of the various marketplaces. A coding form was used for each website to record the details found and to allow for comparisons to be made.

5. FINDINGS

The twelve e-marketplaces discussed displayed a wide diversity of approaches in developing their sites and the range of facilities offered was very broad. The findings are given under the individual key success factor headings to clarify the issues:

5.1 Critical mass

Market makers recognised the need to achieve critical mass if their sites were to function effectively and were aware that a degree of transparency was required to persuade prospective participants that their marketplace was attracting other suppliers and buyers. A majority of the e-marketplaces showed figures indicating the number of registered buyers/sellers, the growth rate of transaction turnover or the number of product lines available. For example, 58K.com in which 3,680 printers participate, has a 'growth rate of 3% daily' and E-greenbiz.com has over 4,000 companies with 46,000 product lines. Only three e-marketplaces did not give figures or directly address the subject of critical mass, although each of them gave details of the size of the market they were addressing.

5.2 Income streams

Prospective participants need to consider the issues of costs when entering a marketplace and whether they wish to be tied in by licensing fees or prefer the pay-per-transaction methods of some marketplaces. Examples of five of the identified income streams were found, although four sites did not explain how income was raised and it was not possible to ascertain what income model they used. Table 5 shows where multiple income streams were found. It is likely that other forms of income generation are being developed and used, but these cannot be identified without fuller access to the e-marketplaces (for example, income from hosting storefronts for suppliers).

Details of income generation through the sales of accumulated market data was not available, although it is evident from the privacy statements given on a number of sites that market data is accumulated in this way.

	Transaction fees	Licensing Fee	Advertising	Value-add service fees	Sales of Industry Information
www.quadrem.com					
www.covisint.com	X	X			
www.converge.com	X			X	X
www.appliancezone.com					
www.paperExchange.com	X			X	
www.Egreencoffee.com	X				X
www.E-greenbiz.com					
www.cargofinder.com	Currently free		X		
www.58K.com	X				
www.telemerc.com	Currently free		X		
www.RetailersMarketXchange.com	X			X	
www.ecfood.com					

Table 5. Income streams identified in the e-marketplaces

5.3 Security

The structure of the marketplace had an influence on how the security of the sites was addressed by the companies. E-marketplaces that offered only identification and selection processes (and therefore did not carry information on financial transactions) addressed the question of privacy rather than security. However, the larger industry consortia sites had strong statements assuring participants that security was 'paramount' and two offered security help for 'company IT desks'. Several sites relied on strategic partnerships with expert security companies to indicate their commitment to security issues. Two e-marketplaces carry the Verisign logo (http://www.verisign.com) although it is interesting to note that the status of one is 'revoked' and the other is 'expired', which raises concerns about the commitment these marketplaces really have towards security or the stability of the marketplace itself.

5.4 Level of independence

Only three sites did not carry statements asserting their independence as an e-marketplace. The remaining nine companies all carry statements ranging from 'E-greenbiz.com does not own any products nor is affiliated to any industry participant' to Appliancezone's statement that they are an independent, neutral company funded by venture capital. Industry consortia sites were particularly clear in stating that, although ownership is shared amongst industry players the e-marketplace companies were completely independent.

5.5 Technology infrastructure

Four marketplaces mentioned technological infrastructure or addressed the question of standardization, three of which gave statements regarding the latter. One smaller company showed an awareness of the technical complexities that might concern its less technologically advanced customers, while two of the largest state that their sites are standardized on XML. One consortia company is developing its own technology standards.

5.6 Relationship management

Two facets of relationship management were considered: trust and privacy.

i. *Trust.* Evidence of the awareness of the need to engender trust in prospective participants was based on criteria previously identified by Smith et al., (Smith, Bailey, & Brynjolfsson, 1999) and Kollock, 1999 as indicated in Table 1. Three sites were found to have incorporated an online community aspect to their marketplaces. Two marketplaces incorporated links to websites of organisational bodies that were established within the relevant industries, although it was not possible to trace links back from other sites to the e-marketplaces. Two marketplaces requested feedback from visitors, encouraging unbiased product information. Five marketplaces had no identified criteria for signaling or engaging trust, although two sites recorded other aspects that could signal a measure of trust (validation of suppliers through an existing industry register and participation in community-based initiatives). No direct use of existing reputation was discernible although all the e-marketplaces gave lists of their strategic partnerships to give credence to their sites.

ii. *Privacy* statements were given on all the sites relating to protection of data. Four e-marketplaces included a facility to enable buyers and suppliers to maintain relationships (both new and established) by communicating and transacting in private within the market site. While several of the e-marketplaces gave assurances that information accumulated on participants would not be disclosed to a third party, there were few assurances that amalgamated data would not be collated. Indeed, at least two of the major industry consortia sites have statements that visitors will be blocked from their sites if they disenable the cookies that allow data collection.

5.7 Fulfils participants' needs (value-add)

The ability to address individual customer requirements and thereby build loyalty-enhancing relationships is seen as a major contribution to e-marketplace success (Lee, 2001). The range of facilities identified in the marketplaces under review indicated that market makers were moving towards enhancing the basic buying and selling functions with facilities likely to enhance the benefits realisable by participants. Of the wide range of facilities identified some occurred in a number of sites (e.g. industry news) and others (e.g. completion of customs paperwork) in only one site. E-marketplaces that incorporated an online community site had the largest range of added facilities such as tutorials, book sales, chat rooms and industry information. The larger companies offered more value-add in respect to transaction-related facilities: for example, data warehousing, logistics and financial services, transaction tracking and virtual project workspace. The more specialised sites had industry-related value-adds. For example a commodities site offered futures quotes both in real-time (paid for) or delayed time (free) while the food industry orientated its value-add towards requirements in the food industry relating to health and safety, ingredient listings and standardized ingredients.

6. DISCUSSION

The findings from the website analysis provide a view of how market makers are addressing the key success factors in their marketplaces. The findings are visible through the website and are therefore available to prospective participants enabling them to make more informed decisions about which marketplace may suit their individual needs. The findings are discussed with regard to their relevance to prospective participants, and then summarized into a framework to facilitate businesses' determination of whether the market makers' approach to key success factors is appropriate for their own requirements.

6.1 Recognition of key success factors

The key success factors are all addressed in a variety of ways across the range of e-marketplaces, with greater levels of awareness being shown to some factors. For example, a high level of awareness of the importance of critical mass is shown by all the e-marketplaces. They demonstrate the need to show that they have sufficient participants for an effective trading site by such methods as citing the number of participants or product lines. They are encouraging new participants through a range of initiatives, including an initial 'try before you buy' phase, free transactions, site tours and lengthy FAQ sections. The factor of security was also strongly addressed by all the sites with the use of strategic partnerships with security companies as the favoured method of showing commitment to the issue. Whether this approach to security is sufficient to secure confidence in participants is uncertain.

Another area that was keenly addressed by all the e-marketplaces was the issue of ownership. All declared their independence notwithstanding their ownership, although in the case of the industry consortia it remains an open issue subject to close scrutiny by government bodies (FTC, 2000). One dominant ownership model may emerge as the most enduring, but in the current dynamic environment the issue of neutrality remains ambivalent.

In contrast to these well-addressed factors, the factor of technology is approached in a piecemeal way with a third of the marketplaces mentioning standardisation, but only one displaying real concern that participants' questions on the subject should be addressed. The lack of a common technological standard has switching cost implications if participants need to invest in diverse technologies to access different trading sites, so reducing flexibility in the electronic environment. The impact of fragmentation will be stronger if the larger consortia marketplaces move towards establishing their own standards and thereby locking in smaller participants. However, commitment to one marketplace may become more common if the anticipated consolidation of e-marketplaces is as concentrated as forecast.

Income generation was another factor that is addressed in a more fragmented way. Although the most common model remains the charging of transaction fees it is not possible to ascertain which income streams are viable sources of revenue. For example, it is not clear if the sale of futures quotes generates profit or is a value-add facility. Advertising revenue, a potentially valuable income, must be weighed against any negative images of neutrality or quality. One marketplace charged a one-off licensing fee that could have switching cost implications for small suppliers, reducing their ability to participate in several e-marketplaces.

Differences also remain between the marketplaces on how they approach the issue of signaling trust. The smaller companies utilise user friendliness and community orientation, while the larger companies use guided tours and presentations to display openness. None of the e-marketplaces used feedback from customers to promote trust with new participants. Overall, there is potential for developing more effective strategies for engaging the trust of marketplace participants and broadening the opportunities to promote loyalty amongst them. The issue of privacy between buyers and sellers, however was well recognised and the e-marketplaces all displayed privacy statements.

The remaining success factor is the e-marketplaces' ability to fulfil participants' needs and they are all very aware of the need to provide more services than purely transactional ones. Some companies were developing the online community model where the value-add covers a much wider range of facilities than more functional sites, which offered minimal value-add. This is perhaps a reflection of differing customers' needs within complex, fast moving industries and the greater functionality required by others. Additional value-add facilities are being introduced as e-marketplaces gain experience and participants and there are many examples of innovative approaches to value-add, supporting the more transactional mechanisms of the marketplaces.

6.2 The Participants

In the confused and dynamic environment of electronic marketplaces there are a wide variety of sites for prospective participants to consider. Their initial selection may be dictated by several factors including the level of service required, following established trading partners onto their selected site, the geographic reach of the marketplace or the brand name of the market makers.

These factors may influence decisions and replace an in-depth appraisal of the marketplace particularly in a climate where the pressures to participate in the electronic environment are immense. Identification of the key success factors from a preliminary inspection of a website can support the decision to participate in a particular marketplace, especially where the competition amongst them is strong and the environment is uncertain.

Table 6 summarizes the findings above to provide a framework that enables prospective participants to ascertain what key success factors can be determined from a website. This can be used to support the choice of an electronic marketplace that has awareness of the factors contributing towards its own success and that also matches a participant's specific requirements. Where access to the e-marketplace is restricted, preventing an assessment of the key success factors, this in itself raises the question of openness to prospective participants.

Key success factors	Issues
Critical mass	- Is the e-marketplace aware of the need for critical mass? - What visible evidence is there? - How large a segment of the market do they have?
Income streams	- What revenue streams are evident? - Do the payment methods indicate switching costs? - Who pays any transaction fees (buyer/seller)? - Are there any up-front licensing fees? - Is there advertising on the site? - What types of companies are advertising? - Are there service fees for value-add facilities?
Security	- What statements about security are evident? - What strategic security partners do they cite? - If a security service provider is used is the service valid?
Independence	- Who owns the marketplace? - If this is not clear, what implications could there be?
Technical information	- Is technical support offered? - Does the site have common technological standards? - Is any commitment to integration required? - What switching costs may be incurred through meeting technological standards?
Relationship management	- Trust - How does the e-marketplace signal its commitment to establishing and maintaining trust? - Privacy - What evidence of commitment to privacy is available?
Fulfils participants needs (Value-add)	- What value-add facilities are useful/attractive? - What do they cost? - Are they current and reliable? - What value do they add to participation in the e-marketplace?

Table 6. Framework to enable identification of key success factors in an e-marketplace

7. LIMITATIONS

The analysis of a diverse range of electronic marketplace websites has, necessarily, certain limitations. This research has studied the websites in the role of an external visitor, accessing the information that is available to prospective participants, before they register as a buyer or seller. This enables an examination of the level of recognition for the key success factors by marketplaces and highlights issues that arise from success factors that are not being adequately addressed. Further research is needed to test the issues and questions raised above against different e-marketplaces within the same industry and to ascertain the full decision making process of businesses seeking to participate in electronic marketplaces.

8. CONCLUSIONS

Using the seven key success factors, previously identified, in this study it has been possible to see that e-marketplaces are recognising many of the issues they need to address if they are to develop their potential. While some of the key success factors are being well addressed by the e-marketplaces, there remain areas of concern in the future development of marketplaces, particularly in the areas of security, technology infrastructure and ownership.

Although there are different drivers pushing companies towards participation, an appreciation of how electronic marketplaces are developing their trading models can support the selection process and enhance the trading experience of the participants. The proposed framework facilitates recognition by prospective participants of the key success factors and the issues surrounding them and can contribute to the selection of an e-marketplace that meets their company requirements.

Once the key success factors have been addressed more fully and participants have gained experience in the electronic marketplace environment, it is perhaps the value-add facilities offered that will encourage participants to favor one e-marketplace over another. The level of innovation already evident in marketplaces and the diversity of offerings show that this key success factor is the one that enables the greatest degree of differentiation to be achieved by market makers. If this is the case, the value-add facilities will play a greater role in contributing to marketplace survival when the consolidation of the marketplaces occurs.

REFERENCES

Aberdeen Group. (2001). e-Procurement: Finally ready for prime time Vol 14/2. Boston: Aberdeen Group, Inc.

Bakos, Y J (1991), A strategic analysis of electronic marketplaces. MIS Quarterly Vol 15(3): pp. 295-310

Bakos, J. Y. (1997). Reducing buyer search costs: implications for electronic marketplaces. Management Science, vol 43(12) pp 1676-1692

Banham, R. (2000). The B-to-B virtual bazaar. Journal of Accountancy Vol 190(1): pp 26-30

Bowles, J. (2002). B2B picks up steam. Net-Markets-Alert Mailing List, 6 March 2002.

Choudhury, V., Hartzel, K.S.,& Konsynski, B. R. (1998) Uses and Consequences of Electronic Markets: An Empirical Investigation in the Aircraft Parts Industry. *MIS Quarterly*, vol 22(4), pp 471-507

Davis, B. (2001). Under the hammer. Professional Engineering, vol 14(3), pp. 45-46.

Deeter-Schmelz, D. R., Bizzari, A., Graham, R., & Howdyshell, C. (2001). Business-to-business online purchasing: Suppliers' impact on buyers' adoption and usage intent. Journal of Supply Chain Management, vol37(1), pp 4-10.

Downes, L., & Mui, C. (1998). Unleashing the killer app: digital strategies for market dominance. Boston: Harvard Business School Press.

Federal Trade Commission. (2000). Entering the 21st Century: Competition policy in the world of B2B electronic marketplaces.: The Federal Trade Commission B2B Public Workshop.

Forrester Research. (2000). The e-marketplace shakeout [Webpage]. Forrester Research. Retrieved 19 April 2001, from the World Wide Web: http://www.forrester.com/ER/Baseline

Gartner Consulting. (2000). Importance of the security and management of E-marketplaces (White paper). San Jose: Gartner Group.

Hagel, J., & Armstrong, A. G. (1997). Net gain: expanding markets through virtual communities. Boston: Harvard Business School Press

Hurwitz. (2000). E-marketplaces: Issues, risks, and requirements for success (A Hurwitz Group White Paper). Framingham, MA: Hurwitz Group Inc.

Kaplan, S., & Sawhney, M. (2000). E-Hubs: The new B2B Marketplaces. Harvard Business Review, May-June.

Kollock, P. (1999). The production of trust in online markets. Advances in Group Processes, vol 16, pp 99-123.

Lee, C.-S. (2001). An analytical framework for evaluating e-commerce business models and strategies. Internet Research: Electronic Networking Applications and Policy, vol 11(4), pp 349-359.

Lucking-Reiley, D., & Spulber, D. F. (2000). Business-to-Business electronic commerce. Journal of Economic Perspectives, Vol 15(1), pp 55-68.

Malone, T. W., Yates, J., & Benjamin, R. I. (1987). Electronic Markets and Electronic Hierarchies. Communications of the ACM, Vol 30(6), pp 484-497.

Piccinelli, G., Di Vitantonio, G., & Mokrushin, L. (2001). Dynamic service aggregation in electronic marketplaces. Computer Networks, 37, pp. 95-109.

Raisch, W. D. (2001). The eMarketplace. Strategies for success in B2B ecommerce. New York: McGraw hill.

Sculley, A. B., & Woods, W. A. (2001). B2B exchanges. The killer application in the business-to-business Internet revolution. New York: HarperCollins.

Smith, M D, Bailey, J and Brynjolfsson E (1999) Understanding digital markets: Review and Assessment. in Brynjolfsson and Kahin (Eds), Understanding the Digital Economy, Boston: MIT Press. (viewed 12 March 2001) Available online at: ecommerce.mit.edu/papers/ude

Spiegel, R. (2001). Gotcha! Traditional industries stole the e-marketplace initiative from dot-coms. Now what? ecommerce business Wednesday 28 February 2001 Available online at: www.ecommercebusinessdaily.com/archive/ECBFA121800-93154asp (viewed 1 March 2001)

Standing, C (2001), The characteristics of successful e-marketplaces. Proceedings of the Pacific Asia Conference on Information Systems

Stanoevska-Slabeva, K., & Schmid, B. (2000). Internet electronic product catalogs: an approach beyond simple keywords and multimedia. Computer Networks, vol 32, pp. 701-715.

Tedeschi, B. (2001). Some business to business marketplaces showing staying power. New York Times, pp. www.nytimes.com (accessed 2 November 2001).

Wise, R., & Morrison, D. (2000). Beyond the exchange: The future of B2B. Harvard Business Review, November-December, pp 88-96.

INTEGRATING E-COMMERCE INTO THE RETAIL SUPPLY CHAIN

A Roadmap for Implementation

BOB ROBERTS[1] and GLYN THOMAS[2]

[1]*School of Computing & Information Systems, Kingston University, United Kingdom*
[2]*HP Consulting, United Kingdom*

Abstract: E-commerce systems in the supply chain extend beyond inter-organisational transfer to an integrated and optimised information flow across a value chain. Adoption of such systems, however, has proved extremely difficult since they span organisational boundaries and involve interaction with external entities such as trading partners and third parties that may have different and conflicting interests. In addition, adoption of such systems typically involve significant changes to organisations' culture, structure, business relationships and working practices. This retail sector case study is based on an eclectic mix of methodologies and considers an approach to implementing an Internet based solution to support the supply chain of a department store whose supplier mix precludes a dictatorial approach by the retailer. A challenge in doing this has been in choosing the appropriate method at each step. The introduction of electronic commerce, for example, can cause a change in the internal and external relationships. This is highlighted by looking at the value system of the cross enterprise links which are being changed and the effect on the internal value chain. To enable the implementation a number of different approaches were crucial to understanding the stakeholder requirements, to optimise the information flows and to realise the potential for redesigning business processes. Whatever the technical option chosen for implementation of electronic commerce there is a need to understand the business processes and identify the information flows to optimise the value added in the supply chain. The paper concludes with a roadmap of the methods for analysing the needs for successful e-commerce implementations from a technology, business process and organisational perspective.

1. INTRODUCTION

E-commerce systems in the supply chain extend beyond inter-organisational transfer to an integrated and optimised information flow across a value chain with application to application dialogue between organisations and associated changes in operations and functions. Adoption of such systems, however, has proved extremely difficult since they span organisational boundaries and involve interaction with external entities such as trading partners and third parties that may have different and conflicting interests. In addition, adoption of such systems typically involve significant changes to organisations' culture, structure, business relationships and working practices. This evolution to even tighter integration through Internet enabled collaborative interrelationships and interdependencies in the supply chain therefore requires analysis from political, cultural. operational and technological dimensions.

This introduction is followed by section 2 which reviews the literature concerning the development of electronic commerce in the supply chain and identifies a common theme of the holistic implication of e-commerce implementations through from earlier EDI implementations through to e-markets. Section 3 summarises the research methods adopted in the case study to analyse and to provide an understanding of these wider issues. Section 4 deals with the case study which provided a rich environment in which the methods were applied to understand the implications of implementing internet based EDI to support supply chain management in the retail environment. The concluding section argues that the approach applied in the case study may have generic applicability in understanding not only of the capability of the underlying technology, but the impact of its deployment on supply chain processes, the optimisation of data flows to enable good information management and the opportunities for redesigning the extended value chain.

2. A REVIEW OF ELECTRONIC COMMERCE IN THE SUPPLY CHAIN

Today's typical supply chain is often complex, as it comprises multiple networks of customers, trading partners and distributors, each with their own set of requirements. It is also characterised by fragmentation made up of a geographical spread with a mixture of proprietary systems and manual processes. In such a configuration a supply chain is only as good as its weakest link. Inter-organisational business process automation and technical integration represent significant challenges that are obviously greater than those faced internally within organisations. However, the links are not only made up of the enabling technology. With increasing depth of collaboration, interpersonal and inter-organisational relationships, trust and communication also become critical factors in ensuring the exchanging and sharing of information.

Traditional electronic data interchange (EDI) and the benefits to be gained from its implementation have been understood for many years. EDI can be implemented purely as a data transfer mechanism with manual intervention at either end but this has limited benefit. To optimise benefits EDI needed to be integrated into internal and external organisation systems (Chan & Swatman 1998). The true goal of EDI therefore goes beyond inter-organisational transfer to an integrated and optimised information flow across a value chain with application to application dialogue between organisations and associated changes in operations and functions (Sokol 1995, Swatman & Fowler 1994).

With EDI there has been a large growth in efficient stock control initiatives such as JIT (Just in Time). Initially established in manufacturing, industries such as retail are now particularly active with initiatives such as QR (Quick Response), VMI (Vendor Managed Inventory) and ECR (Efficient Consumer Response), fuelled by the large number of products and suppliers that need to be controlled. In some areas such EDI based programs have become a requirement rather than a differentiator (Donington & Hall 1994) and allied to this is the development of electronic catalogues and EDI for advanced information such as planning, price and product information. Such initiatives reflect the need to link supply chain constituents into a tightly knit network of communications and functionality for competitive advantage.

Poirier and Bauer (2000) refer to supply chain management as an approach that continuously improves an organisation's integrated processes for product and service design, sales forecasting, purchasing, inventory management, manufacturing or production, order management, logistics, distribution and customer satisfaction. Such an approach requires a company to take an external view of its business environment and then collaboratively identify the vital supply chain processes that will differentiate the network for mutual benefit. Poirier & Bauer (2000) also argue that businesses will be increasingly compelled to learn how to use e-commerce technologies in collaboration with other business or risk failure in this new digital business environment. Alt et al (1999) suggest a complimentary relationship between electronic commerce and supply chain management with the former concentrating on shaping information and contracting activities (for example through electronic catalogues) while the latter is mainly concerned with planning processes and the flow of goods. This convergence of supply chain management and e-commerce provides the opportunity to provide integrated network collaboration. However, there is a need to examine this phenomenon from the perspective of the power dynamics within and between organisations which to some extent set the agenda for what strategies are possible for firms.

The ubiquitous presence of the Internet and associated low cost network access has facilitated the more widespread use of inter-organisational communications and information sharing. The Internet has brought new possibilities for Business to Business (B2B) trading, especially with small and medium sized enterprises (SMEs) who previously considered the financial and resource cost of EDI prohibitive (Roberts & Thomas 2000). Some companies, such as Sainsburys supermarket in the UK are now using the Internet to establish EDI links with small suppliers previously not on-line to them (Goodwin 1998). The use of such community extranets for collaboration and for managing the supply chain can extend the organisation by enabling communication up and down the supply chain and transform relationships with suppliers and clients (Chan & Davis 2000, Senn 2000).The Value Added Networks (VANs), which traditionally acted as third parties and provided EDI services over proprietary networks, have reworked their strategies to include the Internet. WWW based services, for example, have been launched that enable large companies to receive documents such as HTML based purchase orders from small firms that traditionally have not used EDI software and VAN services (Threlkel & Kavan 1999, Roberts & Thomas 2000). New intermediaries have also appeared providing services to facilitate the marketplace via such value added services as specialised directories, brokering, referral, and supplier certification (Butler Group 2001, Tang et al 2001). These various developments now point to full scale business to business electronic commerce becoming a reality on the Internet or on community extranets.

Collaboration in the supply chain is driven by far more than simply the desire to control costs as it provides the basis for addressing the traditional gap between customers needs and supplier performance. Harris and Parfitt (1996) stress that in order to have an electronic commerce strategy there need to be an understanding of the components of electronic commerce, their inter-relationship and impact on traditional business processes. The term electronic commerce is used here to refer to not just a single technology but a combination of technologies, applications, processes, business strategies and practices necessary to do business electronically (Taylor & Berg 1995). Implementation can promote co-operation between partners and those organisations that develop mutually beneficial relationships can compete more effectively (Roberts & Mackay 1998). Electronic Commerce therefore needs to be viewed in the context of its wider impact in enabling business process redesign, the opportunities it offers for exploiting information, the challenge of integration with internal systems and its implementation through supporting technologies and applications.

There is also an increasing interest in trading through Internet based electronic marketplaces and exchanges. Initiatives such as Global NetXchange (www.gnx.com) and Transora (www.transora.com) reflect the developments in B2B Exchanges with a retail focus. Friedman (2000) suggests that the term "SupplyWebExchange" best describes how established supply chain management techniques and industry trading practices will eventually integrate with the evolution of the B2B digital environment. The common theme is one of providing collaborative solutions over the Internet including procurement and supply chain management. The promise for all participants is for a more reliable, efficient and responsive supply chain with specific benefits in areas such as reduced operational costs, shorter lead times, lower inventory and improved customer service. UK supermarket Tesco, for example, claims to have nearly reclaimed its $2 million investment after only a few months (Mathieson 2000). However, recent reports on emerging B2B exchanges indicate the reluctance of suppliers, and SMEs in particular, to participate based on a scepticism of win-win promises as they fear that exchanges will cut into profit margins or turn their products into commodities (Baldi 2001, Butler Group 2000, Poirier & Bauer 2000). Glick (2002), for example, reports that BuyIT, which is an independent and U.K. government backed forum created to share the experiences of different organisations with e-commerce processes, hosted workshops to examine the concerns of suppliers about e-marketplaces. The feedback reflected supplier concern and wariness that such initiatives were driving down costs at the expense of suppliers.

Building a successful B2B model is not an easy task and requires a clear understanding of a number of issues including the structure of the supplier base, where the inefficiencies are in the value chain and how IT ready potential partners are (Mercer 2000). Shared benefits are crucial to the concept of a value network where a collaborative approach enabled through a digital network binds closely integrated business communities (Bovet & Martha 2000, Bresslet & Grantham 2000). Whatever the technical option chosen for implementation of electronic commerce there is a need to understand the business processes and identify the information flows to optimise the value added in the supply chain.

3. RESEARCH APPROACH

The case study used an eclectic mix of methodologies to define the business practices and areas of change required by the retailer. A challenge in doing this was choosing the method at each step. Soft Systems (Checkland & Scholes 1990) led to the conceptual model and real world comparison but thereafter a selection of elements of tools and methodologies were used including process models and the value chain (Porter 1985). One problem was to find methodologies leading on from the Soft Systems Methodology for analysis and presentation of the various information sources in a fashion which is integrated but not overly complex. The tools used satisfied this requirement but are not necessarily the only approach.

Soft Systems Analysis (SSA) was used on the project because at the start of the work the situation was unclear. It was known that the company was trying to improve their supply chain but there appeared to be a number of inter-related issues and the positioning of electronic trading in this was not clear. Furthermore, there were no clear measurable objectives. Problem areas had been identified but there were no defined business targets. The viability of this approach is also confirmed by Chan and Swatman (1994) who claimed that, while they had not identified an appropriate modelling technique for the process of EDI integration, Soft Systems Methodology might prove to be the appropriate approach because it allows for multiple viewpoints, comparison with the real world and subsequent refinement of the model.

At the start of the study it was thought that the issues would relate primarily to the retailer and their internal supply chain control but this approach also highlighted the additional interrelated area of the rate of take up by the suppliers and how this was affected by the responsiveness of the service provider and level of involvement of the partners. Soft Systems helped to coalesce the issues into two main themes. The use of process model diagrams for the conceptual models provided a further framework for considering the real world activities and for defining and presenting the tasks, issues and recommendations.

The information gathered was used to carry out a cultural analysis of stakeholders and roles involved in the situation and also to consider the situation as a whole by means of a rich picture, identifying such issues as inter-departmental processes, interaction with partners, system integration, timescales and constraints. The holistic approach of Soft Systems Analysis highlighted areas of concern with the progress of implementation and with how the company intended to integrate the use of I-EDI into its existing organisation, processes and IT systems. From the rich picture (figure 1) two main problem themes were therefore extracted; issues in getting I-edi started with suppliers and requirement for a strategy for using I-edi within the supply chain.

An analysis of intervention (i.e. client, problem owner, problem solver) was produced which identified gaps in the ownership of these problems. A parallel activity of Political Analysis (via Stakeholder analysis) showed that there were a number of stakeholders (primarily the Buyers) who were not involved in the systems development, i.e. this was being approached as an IT problem when much writing recommends that implementing EDI is foremost a business problem. This analysis involves considering those parties affected by the implementation and those in a position to have an affect on the implementation from the standpoint of the current situation and the ideal or target situation.

From the rich picture, tasks and issues were derived which were used as a basis for comparing the real situation with a conceptual model. Conceptual models are about activities and the aim of the organisation was to change how they operated in the ordering and receiving parts of the cycle (albeit through having more consistent and higher quality information). For these reasons it was decided to use a process based approach to this part of the analysis to produce static models (figure 2). This was a useful way of documenting the two problem areas and identifying areas for possible improvement.

The next stage of the study took the process models produced for the supply chain and used these as the basis for a more structured set of interviews with staff and for activities to follow the supply chain processes in action and to identify the paper chain. The objective of this approach was to capture the information needs for each step of the supply chain and to identify how this was provided within the company. This was captured in tabular form and then represented in deployed flow chart form. The advantage of the flow charts is that they graphically show the movement of information between departments and roles in the organisation (with an implied time line). By including the existing information systems and by introducing colour and shape it can quickly be seen what information is on paper and also where new information is created (or value added). This enabled potential intra-departmental changes to be identified and also pointed to the inter-departmental information links such as the goods received note (GRN). The understanding of the usage this produced also allowed the requirements placed on the technology to be revisited with regard to interfaces into other systems (such as accounts) and processes along with usability aspects of the selected system.

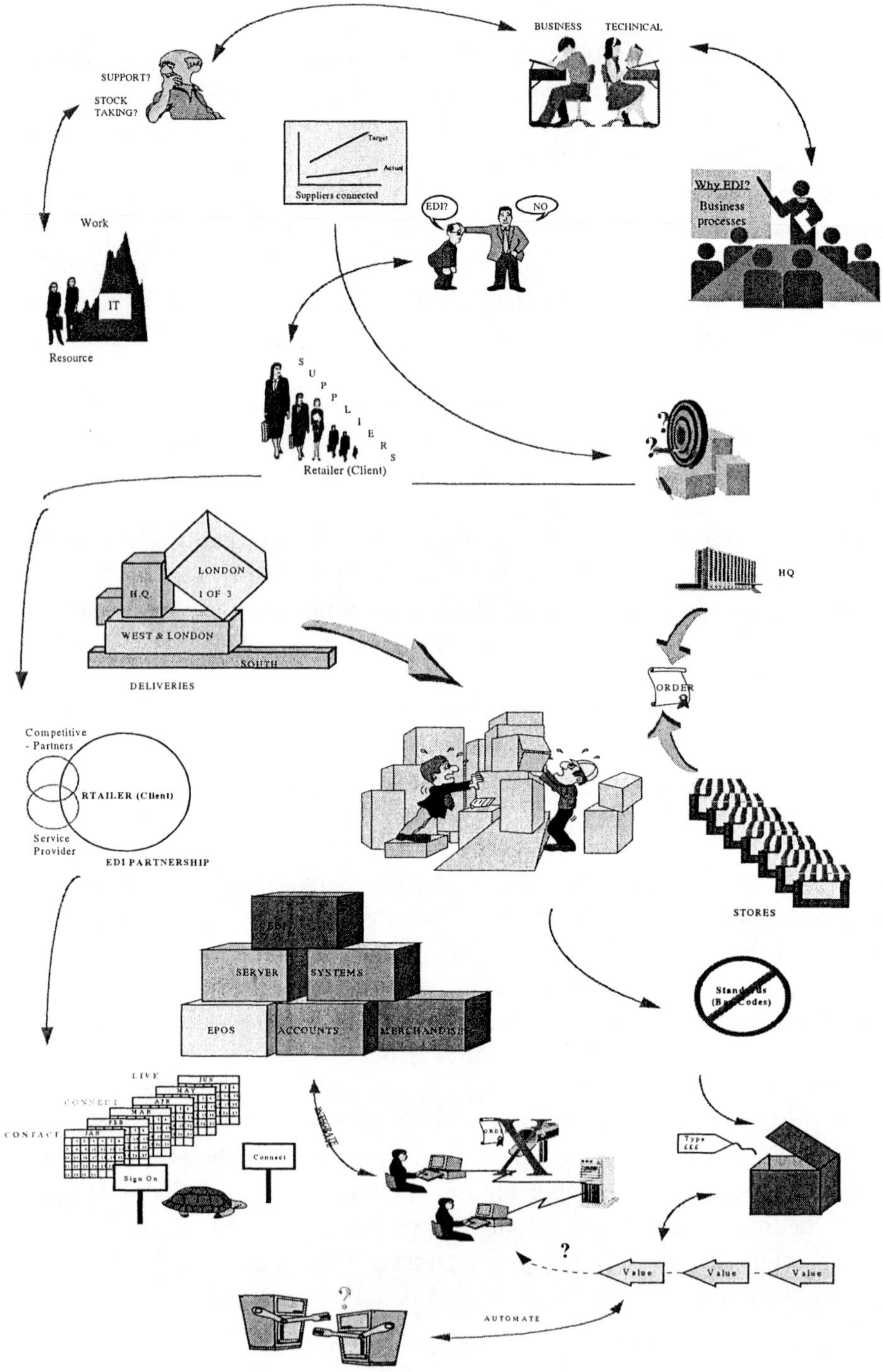

Figure 1. Rich Picture

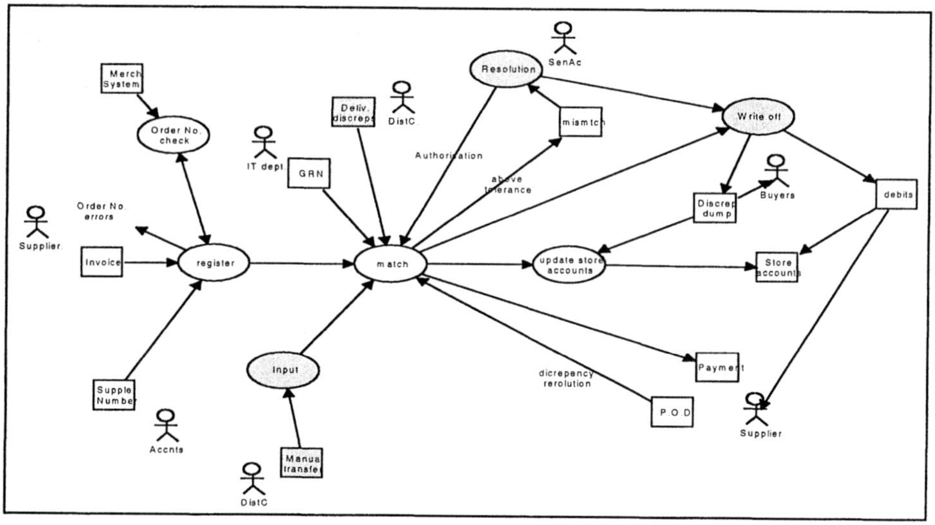

Figure 2. Sample Process

4. CASE STUDY

4.1 Background

The case study is based on a department store chain who are competing against some of the largest organisations in the UK retail industry. A critical success factor to remaining competitive is to increase the effectiveness of their supply chain especially with regard to removal of errors and reduction of inventory holdings. An established way of achieving this is the use of EDI. However the traditional approach to EDI was not a financially acceptable option for the company and many of its suppliers. They have therefore adopted an innovative approach to using features of traditional EDI combined with internet technology to overcome this barrier.

The e-commerce infrastructure was established on the basis of collaboration i.e. through the shared development / common adoption of technical standards and process norms, and the joint funding through partnership with competitors of infrastructural elements and intermediary services. A key element in provision of these intermediary services was a partnership with a third party technology provider to ensure access to the appropriate infrastructure and 'know how' and also to have a positive influence on future service development.

The company has a varied product line, including items as diverse as toys, furniture, perfume, glassware and clothes, which are structured into major departments. The departments are managed independently within each store but the product range for a department will be set by a buyer operating across all stores. In providing this product range they trade with 2500 suppliers. These range from large internationals to small specialist suppliers. Overall they operate with over one third of a million stock-keeping units (SKUs). The range and product volumes can also vary with seasonal trends and events. Added to this the orders can be placed either by a number of corporate central buyers or, within certain bounds, by staff within individual stores. Suppliers may deliver goods to a main distribution centre or direct to a store, however the stores are generally supplied via the distribution centre which also carries out checks, inspection and ticketing on supplier deliveries.

4.2 The supply route

Stock generally flows through the distribution centre. When a delivery is received in the distribution centre it needs to be checked against orders. Due to the mix of delivery types and the lack of external coding all deliveries have to be debatched. Vetting will take place against a copy of the order which is system printed or hand-written depending on the products and the source of the order. Order system inconsistencies then require manual totalling of the value of the delivery for system input. Lack of consistent supplier bar-coding and ticketing necessitate the further step of each package being opened so that individual items can be ticketed and finally batched for shipment to store. (See figure 3).

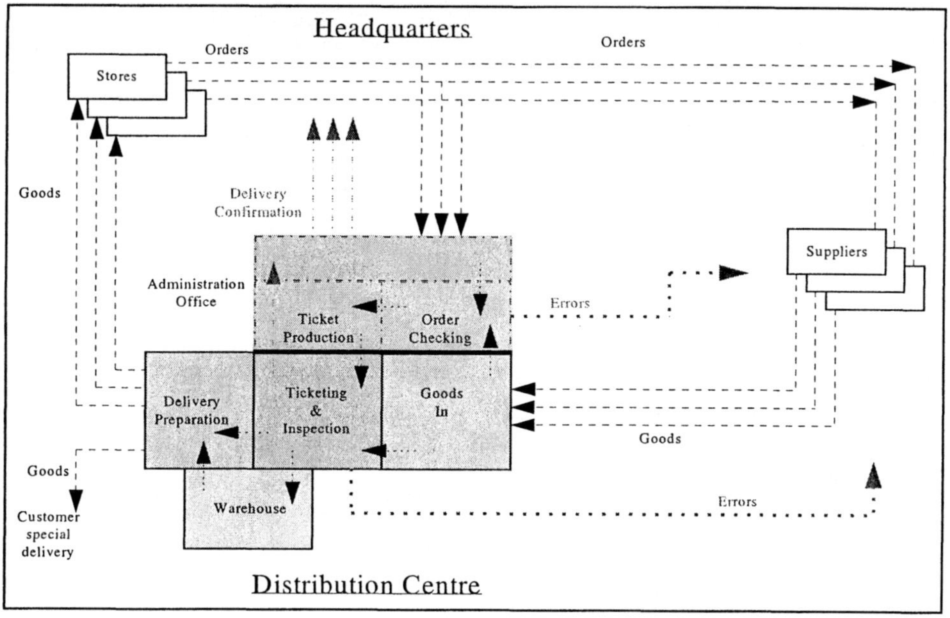

Figure 3. Supply process

4.3 Effect on the Value Chain

The introduction of e-commerce will cause a change in the internal and external relationships of a company. This can be highlighted by looking at the value system of the cross enterprise links which are being changed and the effect on the internal value chain.

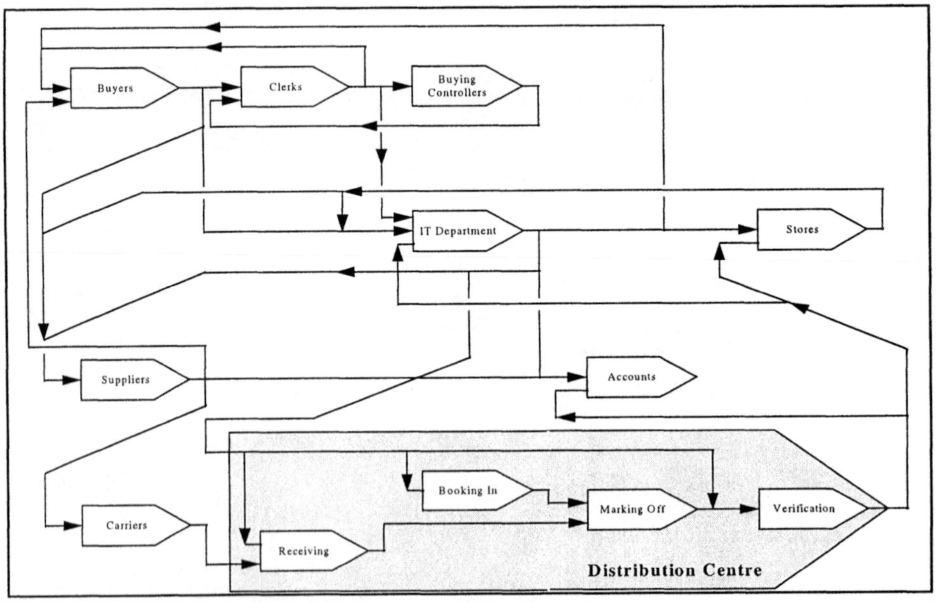

Figure 4. Current Value System (Supply)

For the retailer the upstream supply chain currently involves suppliers and carriers (see figure 4). In this diagram the linkages between the departments, organisations and roles involved in Ordering, Receiving and Paying are shown.

As can be seen from (figure 5) the introduction of e-commerce will alter these relationships. The distribution centre will still receive goods and information from the carriers but information from the suppliers will also now be supplied (via the IT department) to the distribution centre in the form of an electronic advance shipping note (ASN). There will also be a change in flow through the distribution centre. The direct link between the distribution centre and accounts will be diminished to discrepancy reporting only. New product information will be sent by suppliers only to the IT department who will format it for buyers' approval. The stores and buyers can place all orders through the corporate system and these will be sent electronically to the suppliers. The direct link for orders from buyers and stores to suppliers can be removed. Similarly paper invoices sent directly from suppliers to accounts can be replaced by electronic invoices delivered to accounts via the IT systems.

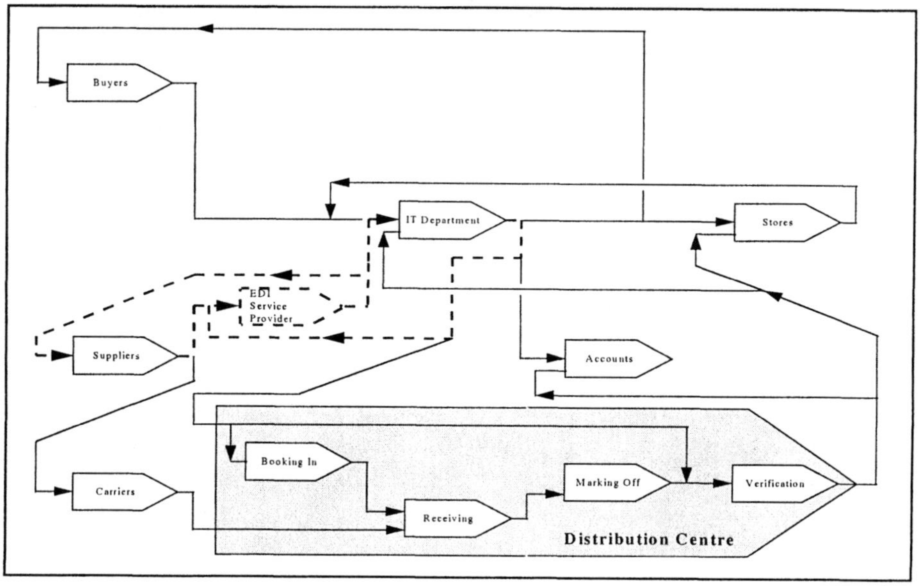

Figure 5. Value System (Supply) with I-edi

The addition to the system (shown in dotted lines) is the third party service provider who will become an intermediary for all routine traffic to and from the suppliers, including replacing the previous fax based order link from the IT department. This highlights the importance of the relationship with the service provider. The role of the IT department is also emphasised. With proper use of I-edi there should be increased flow of information to and from the suppliers and the IT department will be the single point of contact for information in and out of the retailer. Although single points of contact have potential risks such as performance it is considered be most effective to run EDI in such a fashion. The implication is that the IT department also becomes the one support organisation to handle all I-edi issues between the retailer and its trading partner base and therefore needs an established relationship with the service provider's helpline.

4.4 Implications of case study

The case study highlights the importance of information in facilitating the flow of goods in an effective, consistent and reliable manner. The advantage that the openness of the Internet can bring needs to be supplemented by reaping the benefits of integrating e-commerce into current business processes. To be successful businesses need to become more effective in managing the extended enterprise and co-ordinating the internal and external partners in the supply. The redesign of value added activities in the case study, for example, reflects the key role of the service provider in the realisation of reduced order cycle times, more accurate information and other benefits identified in the section on business drivers. Similarly, the meeting of demand and supply through catalogues offers real gains in efficiency and accuracy and the case study analysis highlighted the importance of the IT department as the focal point for all catalogue changes.

4.4.1 Relationship with Suppliers and Service Provider

A number of recommendations were identified which will change the working relationship with suppliers. An increasingly important consideration is the organisational and management implications of operating a virtual organisation with another company in a key position. With I-edi, as can be seen from the value chain, the service provider will become an integral part of the company's operation. Once the retailer have several hundred suppliers linked electronically they will themselves also be linked intimately with the service provider. Items such as their availability requirements, legal considerations (e.g. audit), and their strategy in terms of price commitments and long term partnering with the service provider therefore become prime considerations for the retailer. Furthermore the relationship with the specialist service provider will require development through the identification and fostering of common interests as well as formal agreements.

4.4.2 Internal relationships

The potential changes due to implementation of an electronic trading system raise a number of structural issues, for example within the Buying and IT departments:

Direct ordering by stores from suppliers representatives can be removed, thereby changing internal and external relationships.

Buyers can be more empowered on a day to day basis by the removal of manual authorisation processes so alternate periodic check and authorisation levels need to be introduced.

Buyers have been the contact point for suppliers. However I-edi usage implies that the IT department should be the interface for catalogue information.

In controlling catalogue updates the IT department will be monitoring responsiveness of approvals by Buyers. It could be seen as unsatisfactory to have an operational unit place demands on a business function. Buyers need to be actively involved in the I-edi programme and recognise it as a tool to use, with the information systems providing support to the Buyers for business decisions. This was also found to be the case in BT's implementation of e-commerce in supply management (Roberts & Mackay 1998).

The company has a small IT department. With the introduction of I-edi they become more critical to the business in three areas:

They provide a greater level of functionality to the business therefore it is essential that they have a sufficient support capability.

They will be a contact point for suppliers with I-edi related problems so again this capability needs to be sized and assessed.

They will be the focal point for changes and for ensuring that information is up to date and especially for managing the peaks, such as the fashion season changes, in a cost effective manner.

5. CONCLUSIONS

The paper uses a case study to give a retail sector perspective on the use of different methods and approaches to understand the impact of implementing electronic commerce within a particular environment. Traditionally e-commerce has been fostered by a strong technology push but it is clear from this case study that the inherent potential of Internet based EDI can only be realised through a holistic understanding of implementation issues.

The digitisation of ordering and product information has implications for transaction costs and information availability. However, there is also a risk of increasing costs and mismanagement unless the full process and organisational implications are identified. Mutual understanding between communicating partners is a lot more complex than just the exchange of data and a soft systems approach can be a powerful tool to highlight key issues and stakeholder concerns. The methods discussed in this paper vary in their scope but include both an analysis of the internal business processes of the retail organisation as well as highlighting the inter-organisational issues with suppliers and the service provider.

Findings from the case study indicate the importance of cultural factors in establishing a suitable environment in which collaboration and information exchange may take place and flourish. This requires a social environment based on consultation both internally and externally with suppliers and partners. Creating such a background appears to be a case of cultural evolution but the role of management vision and commitment through clear leadership in setting the general climate is critically important.

Politics, power and influence are important to consider in the context of e-commerce as availability of low cost technology does not guarantee either volume of users nor a willingness to use the medium to support new ways of working. Lack of commonality and congruence of objectives may create major barriers. It was clear that some companies preferred to continue using existing manual processes that they knew would work with a minimum of problems, rather than radically overhaul existing business practices and systems to implement electronic links. Another key source of frustration was that their trading partners were often not on the same level in terms of IT skills, budget, staff availability etc. In addition to important political and vested interests within the organisations there were also differences in perception between the constituents of the extended enterprise. Building relationships is a difficult process but having an intermediary in the position of the e-commerce platform provider may also be perceived as intervening in established relationships. Evidence from the case study also highlighted many instances of the disparity between the language used to articulate the desire to collaborate and the commercial reality of how power is exercised in implementing the practice. These issues limit the extent to which collaboration is feasible and impact on how benefits in such scenarios are distributed.

The research also highlighted the organisational inhibitors such as how the different cultures of organisations can result in tensions and lack of trust and how lack of consultation may lead to considerable resistance to change both within and between organisations in the inter-organisational environment. Finally, the research also highlights the difficulties that organisations may have in adapting their working practices to reflect and support the collaborative nature of relationships supported by e-commerce.

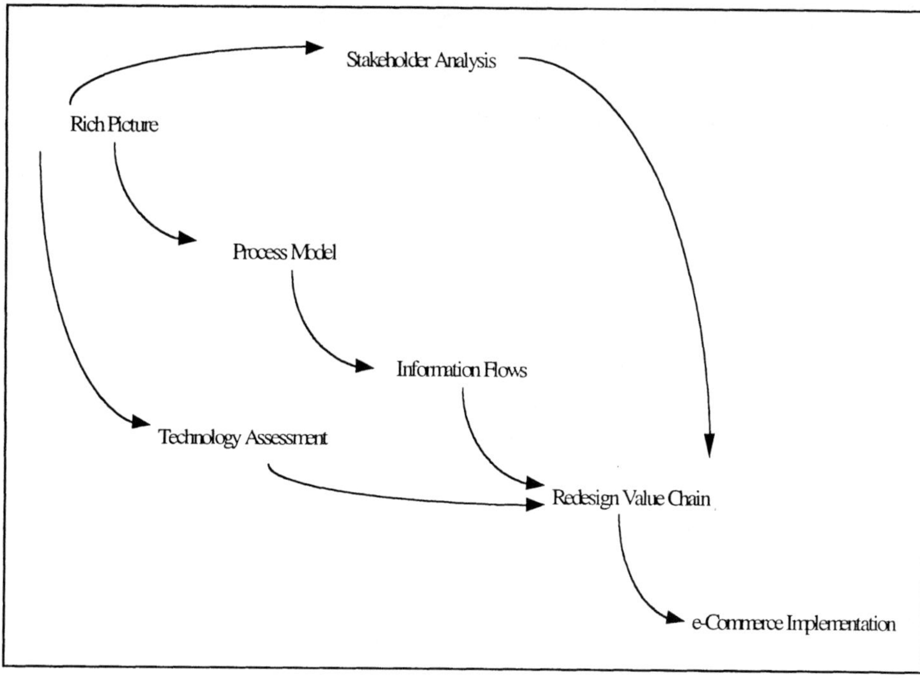

Figure 6. Roadmap

A suggested roadmap is outlined in figure 6 but this is not intended to be prescriptive and is intentionally eclectic in the variation of approaches. The authors believe that the methods used in the case study have generic validity independent of the specific technology employed. Whether the implementation is traditional EDI, internet based EDI or other variations via B2B exchanges, capturing the spectrum of inter related issues concerned with an e-commerce implementation requires a rigorous and inclusive analysis. It is vital to ensure an understanding not only of the capability of the underlying technology but the impact of its deployment on supply chain processes, the optimisation of data flows to enable good information management and the opportunities for redesigning the extended value chain. In parallel with this activity is the requirement to accommodate stakeholder concerns and to understand how e-commerce can influence the organisation's culture and business practices.

REFERENCES

Alt, R., Osterle,H., Reichnayer, C. & Zurmuhlen, R., (1999), Business Networking in the Swatch Group, International Journal of Electronic Commerce & Business Media, 9 (3), pp 169-174

Baldi, S. & Borgman, H.P. (2001), Consortium-based B2B e-Marketplaces - A Case Study in the Automotive Industry, *Proceedings of Fourteenth Bled Electronic Commerce Conference*, Bled, Slovenia, June 26-26, Volume 1, pp. 591-615

Bovet, D. & Martha, J., (2000), *Value Nets: Breaking The Supply Chain To Unlock Hidden Profits*, Wiley

Bressler, S. E. & Grantham, C.E., (2000) *Communities Of Commerce*, McGraw Hill,

Burgess, L. and Cooper, J. (1998), Quality of service in the electronic supply chain: the role of the internet in marketing strategy. *Proceedings of Eleventh International Bled Electronic Commerce Conference.*

Butler Group (2001), E-Supply Chain: Modelling The Supply Chain in the New Market Economies, Concept Report Volume 1, Butler Direct Limited

Chan, S. & Davis, R.V. (2000), Partnering On Extranets for Strategic Advantage, Journal of Information Systems Management, Winter 2000, pp. 58-64

Chan, C. and Swatman, P.M.C, (1998), EDI implementation: A broader perspective. *Proceedings of Eleventh International Bled Electronic Commerce Conference.*

Checkland P. & Scholes J. (1990), *Soft Systems Methodology In Action*, Wiley, Chichester

Donington, J.H. & Hall, D. (1994), The EDI Report, Published by Unicom Consultancy

Friedman, T.H., (2000), SupplyWebExchange: The Changing Landscape Of The Retail Supply Chain, *Retail Automation, 20(5)*, September-October

Glick, B. (2002), Forum Promotes On Line Trade, *Computing*, 9th May 2002 p.8

Goodwin.,W. (1998), Paperless billing for Sainsbury's. *Computer Weekly*, 26th November

Harris, B. & Parfett, M.(eds), (1996), *The Electronic Commerce Handbook, NCC*

Kalakota, R. & Whinston, A.B., (1997), *Electronic Commerce: A Manager's Guide*, Addison Wesley Publishing

Mathieson, S., (2000), Tesco's Retail Exchange Pays Rapidly For Itself, Computing, 16th November 2000, p.10

Mercer Management Consulting Report, (2000), *Beyond The Exchange: Promising Business Models For The Next Round Of B2B Commerce*, http://www.nmm.com/documents/B2B_comm_v5.pdf

O'Conner, J. and Galvin, E. (1998), *Creating Value Through eCommerce*. London: FT Pitman Publishing

Poirier,C.C. & Bauer, M.J. (2000), *E-Supply Chain*, Berrett-Koehler Publishers

Porter, M. E.., (1985), Competitive Advantage, New York, The Free Press,

Roberts, R. and Mackay, M., (1998), IT supporting supplier relationships: The role of electronic commerce. *European Journal of Purchasing & Supply Management 4 (1998), Elsevier Science Ltd.*

Roberts, R. & Thomas, G. A., (2000), Collaberative Approach to Implementing an Extranet in the Retail environment: A Case Study. *Proceedings of Eleventh International Bled Electronic Commerce Conference.*

Senn, J.A. (1996), Capitalising On Electronic Commerce - The Role of the Internet in Electronic Markets, *Information Systems Management*, 13(3), pp. 15-24

Sokol, P.K., (1995), *From EDI to Electronic Commerce: A Business Initiative*. New York: McGraw Hill Inc

Swatman, P.M.C. and Fowler, D.C., (1994), A model of EDI integration and strategic business reengineering. *The Journal of Strategic Information Systems (incorporating International Information Systems)* - Butterworth-Heinemann Ltd

Tang, J.E., Shee, D. Y. & Tang, T., (2001), A conceptual model for interactive buyer-supplier relationship in electronic commerce, *International Journal of Information Management*, 21, pp. 49-68

Taylor, D & Berg, T., (1995), The Business Value Of Electronic Commerce, *Strategic Analysis Report R-617-121*, Gartner Group, September

Threlkel M.S. & Kavan, C.B., (1999), From traditional EDI to internet -based EDI: managerial considerations, Journal of Information Technology, 14, pp. 347-360

Tung, L., Whye, B.Y.H. & Chin,E., (2001), The Role of Trust in Business-to-Business Electronic Commerce, *Proceedings of Fourteenth Bled Electronic Commerce Conference*, Bled, Slovenia, June 25-26, Volume 1, pp. 19-40.

INTEGRATION OF AN INTERNET-DRIVEN SUPPLY CHAIN FOR A MEDIUM-SIZE E-COMMERCE COMPANY

RICKI MAURICI[1] and JACOB L. CYBULSKI[2]
[1]*Glue Ltd., Marlow, Bucks, United Kingdom*
[2]*School of Management Information Systems, Deakin University, Australia*

Abstract: This research aimed at discovering the benefits and challenges of integration across a company's e-supply chain. The research involved a single case study of an Australian e-commerce company. In our work, we first formed a framework of benefits and challenges for e-supply chain integration, which was based on the beliefs held by management consultants. After conducting interviews with various organisational stakeholders of an e-commerce company, we found that although some of the elicited opinions matched those expressed by consultants, others provided their refinement in respect to a medium size, rapidly evolving, start-up company. We also discovered challenges, seemingly ignored by the consultants, which concerned changing market conditions and limited economies of scale perceived as seriously impeding SCM integration. Also, the ability to develop and maintain scalable and effective information systems was found to impact the capacity to integrate services across the e-supply chain. The case study's single most important contribution was to bring to our attention the importance of organisational and environmental maturity in the strategic planning of the supply chain management process.

1. INTRODUCTION

The traditional view of a supply chain is that of a network of entities through which material flows from suppliers to consumers. Generally, raw materials providers (suppliers) sell to component manufacturers, who sell to final assembly manufacturers, who distribute their products through wholesalers, distributors, dealers, and retailers to the final customers (Kaarma et al., 1999). A primary objective of traditional supply chain management is the minimization of the "total cost of transportation, warehousing, inventory, order processing and information systems" (Warkentin et al., 2000). Traditional supply chains are "push" models, empowered by manufacturers, suppliers and distributors (Kaarma et al., 1999). Usually, companies would utilise various third party providers or transportation services to warehouse and distribute products down the supply chain to wholesalers and other partners.

Traditional supply chains have been designed in a time of modest competition and slow response time and so are mostly outdated for the e-business environment. Hence SCM strategies need to be flexible in order to handle changing supplier priorities and commitments and increased competition (Billington, 2000). Prior to the influx of improved supply chain techniques (e.g. ECR and CPFR) and e-commerce technologies, the very structure of a traditional supply chain attracted a number of inefficiencies. For instance, the communication of demand had to go through many partners before finally reaching the manufacturer. The resulting distortion at each partner led to degradation in the quality of the information needed to manage the supply chain (Lee *et al.,* 1997; Taylor, 2000). As a result, for most products, transportation carriers find it difficult maintaining profitable equipment and driver utilization, the supply chain contains more than twice the inventory required for adequate customer service and products are handled several times too many (Kalakota *et al.,* 1999, pp. 199).

Currently, the trend in supply chain management is directed toward companies integrating their information systems to their suppliers and to their suppliers' suppliers, as well as their downstream partners (Lee *et al.,* 1997). It seems that supply chains are evolving from current enterprise-centric "push" models to more collaborative, partnership-oriented models. In fact, in some cases, e-commerce has allowed companies to interact directly with their customers. This is particularly true in an *Internet driven* supply chain, where companies are less focused on the actual product and more on the individual consumer (Chandrashekar *et al.,* 1999; Kaarma *et al.,* 1999). Thus, unlike a traditional supply chains, the emerging e-supply chains are non-linear and they cover planning, directing, and controlling product flow, services, and information from a firm's suppliers' *suppliers* to its customers' *customers* (Warkentin *et al.,* 2000).

As a result of SCM integration strategies, new supply chain models have emerged, e.g. *integrated made-to-stock, continuous replenishment* and *built-to-order* (Kalakota *et al.,* 1999, pp. 217), which eliminate some of the problems in the traditional and the older e-supply supply chains, thus resulting in reduced overheads, improved quality and control of information and product flows, better resource allocations, reduced inventory costs, and more efficient fulfilment. At the same time, however, the emerging e-supply models also bring new challenges for organisations engaging in e-commerce and e-business, e.g. the need for inter-organisation consistency in IT infrastructure, the possibility of cultural or management incompatibilities between collaborating organisations, elevated costs and complexities of implementing an integrated supply chain models, etc. The need for the subtle balance between the benefits and challenges of SCM integration attracted our attention, and hence lead to this research.

2. RESEARCH METHOD

The question guiding our study was: "What are the Benefits and Challenges of Integration Across the E-supply Chain of a Medium-Size E-commerce Company?" We specifically focussed on the medium-size e-commerce companies, as those organisations are the most representative in the maturing e-commerce market. Our research was conducted during the years 2000 and 2001, however, the bulk of the material was collected before the dot-com crash, and so the study captures the opinions characteristic for organisations operating in a relatively stable market.

As we aimed at obtaining in-depth insights into factors affecting supply chain integration, we thus decided to conduct a single case study. Such case studies normally allow an organization to be investigated in great detail in a short time, thus, enabling to reveal its deep structure (Cavaye, 1996), which could then provide a business context to a range of relevant issues to be instilled within the case (Zikmund, 1997). Due to the limited time and resources, we decided not to use multiple case studies, as they require lengthy or superficial investigations.

Our study included the support and participation of an Australian on-line retailing organisation, which for the purpose of this paper we shall call *Enterest Pty Ltd.* Enterest was founded in 1999 and offered an extensive range of products, to include books, music and videos, games and toys, health and sporting goods, electrical goods, clothing and accessories. Being in the retail business, their supply chain included the management of sourcing, warehousing and delivering products to the customer and between partners in the chain. Enterest also considered SCM integration as a top priority in their approach to optimising their business processes. Enterest's management had extensive logistics, IT infrastructure and supply chain knowledge and experience.

In addition to Enterest, a brief preliminary investigation was carried out with a consulting firm, specialising in systems integration and management. They were interviewed in order to obtain some initial insights into the benefits and challenges of SCM integration in Internet start-ups in Australia and the US. As SCM integration is still an emerging and innovative area, the insight provided by this firm assisted the research by further validating the literature survey in the area.

Face-to-face, semi-structured interviews were then used as the primary source of the case study data (Yin, 1994; Walsham 1995). We interviewed a number of different Enterest staff, which included the Business Manager, CIO, Director of Merchandise and Marketing, Business Analyst, Logistics Director, and the Fulfilment Manager who worked for a major Enterest supplier organisation. Each interview lasted between ¾ hour and 1 hour and covered the general areas of interviewee responsibilities and interests (see Table 1). In addition to interviews, company documents and reports were obtained and analysed as necessary.

The collected data was then analysed qualitatively (Miles & Huberman, 1994, pp. 10-11). All interviews were fully transcribed (Neuman, 2000, pp. 277), validated by the participants and then reduced and transformed (Zikmund, 1997), resulting in the categorisation of collected data and in annotation of transcripts with marginal remarks. Additional tables and narratives were finally used to support the data display for analysis and drawing conclusions (Darke *et al.*, 1998).

Participant **Issues discussed**	**Business Manager**	**CIO**	**Director of Merchandise & Marketing**	**Business Analyst**	**Logistics Director**	**Fulfilment Manager**
Responsibilities	☒	☒	☒	☒	☒	☒
Market Environment	☒	☐	☐	☐	☐	☐
Company Background	☒	☐	☐	☐	☐	☐
Benefits of Integration	☒	☒	☒	☒	☒	☐
IT Capabilities	☐	☒	☐	☒	☐	☒
Partner IT capabilities	☒	☒	☒	☒	☒	☒
E-supply chain Structure	☐	☐	☒	☐	☒	☐
Challenges to Integration	☒	☒	☒	☒	☒	☒

Supplier Relationships	☐	☐	☒	☐	☒	☒
E-supply chain goals	☒	☒	☒	☒	☒	☒
E-supply chain features	☐	☐	☐	☐	☒	☒
E-supply chain mgmt.	☐	☐	☒	☐	☒	☒
Multi-channel Strategy	☒	☐	☒	☐	☐	☐
Order Fulfillment	☒	☐	☐	☐	☒	☒
Duration	**60 mins**	**45 mins**	**50 mins**	**45 mins**	**2 X 45 mins**	**65 mins**

Table 1. Issues Discussed with the Enterest Stakeholders

3. BENEFITS OF SCM INTEGRATION

In this case study each participant was asked why they believed Enterest would benefit by implementing integrated e-supply chain strategies in their business. Although the responses given were quite diverse, three major classes of benefits clearly emerged, i.e. reduction of costs and increase in efficiency, adoption of more effective management and planning practices, and finally, marked improvement in customer service.

3.1 Reduced Costs and Increased Efficiency

In e-business, companies can reduce costs and accelerate order cycles by linking their business processes to those of their partners. In terms of inventory, companies should aim to reduce the lag between placing orders and receiving the inventory level update in order to improve their ability to provide real time inventory (Abbas & Brown, 2000).

Enterest believed there is ample opportunity to reduce costs throughout their e-supply chain, particularly in their major suppliers' warehouse, where many of Enterest-ordered products were picked and packed ready for shipping. Also, by improving efficiencies in their partner's warehouse, Enterest had been able to cut costs substantially. This was necessary for Enterest to remain competitive and for its overall longevity.

> "If we can buy products for less, if we can ship them for less, if it costs us less to manage them, then our supply chain is working" (Business Manager).

As indicated by Director of Merchandise & Marketing, the benefits of an efficient e-supply chain also extended to the customer whilst still allowing Enterest to maintain control over their margins.

At the distribution centre, there were a number of areas Enterest achieved efficiencies, with many other opportunities left for improvement. One of the ways was to change the type of packaging of their products.

> "In terms of supply chain efficiency that's one area where we've taken significant cost out of our supply chain. One, in the cost of the packaging, and two in the labour attached to doing that" (Logistics Director).

In addition, Enterest fulfilment could also be greatly improved by automation, as the labour-intensive and inefficient process deployed in the warehouse inhibited the Enterest's e-supply chain scalability. Although a cross-docking system was in use at Enterest, only two of its suppliers were able to effectively support it.

3.2 More Effective Management and Planning

An e-supply chain environment encourages the evolution from limited information sharing to rich information sharing (Warkentin *et al.,* 2000). Providing suppliers with performance feedback are one way to improving supply chain partnerships, by offering suppliers a clear indication of their position relative to competition (Abbas & Brown, 2000). Other advantages of real time collaboration and true partnerships include lower levels of inventory, improved cash flows and a substantial reduction of the *Bullwhip* effect (Anderson, 2000). Collaborative planning, forecasting and replenishment (CPFR) aims to improve the relationship a retailer and a manufacturer sharing forecasts via two-way interactive communication (Walton, 2000). However, intensive collaboration and communication in e-supply chain also needs high flexibility so as to avoid unnecessary dependencies between trading partners, and so they could also effectively deal with changes in market demands, suppliers changing priorities and commitments, customers acting upon their shifting preferences, and competitors turbulence (Billington, 2000; Chandrashekar *et al.*, 1999).

Integration across Enterest's e-supply was recognised to be advantageous by supporting management in their planning and decision-making. It was seen to improve visibility and accessibility of shared data and knowledge, and it aimed to reduce overall inventory levels:

> "We're a multi-channel business now, but in terms of online e-tailing, there's definitely a need to do that (integrate) to ensure that our inventory levels are as low or accurate as possible. So they're accurate in terms of the projected forecast. In terms of our other channels of distribution they need to be as

integrated with our suppliers as possible simply to achieve critical mass and efficiencies in the system" (Logistics Director).

However, Enterest's lack of further e-supply chain integration had limited the level of information flows with their customers, suppliers and other business partners. The company, however, aimed to improve the visibility among partners and use the customer data to monitor their level of satisfaction. Enterest's SCM planning was also improved by increasing consistency in product availability to facilitate their cross-docking system:

"We are providing consistency throughout our supply chain, and part of that involves our cross-docking between Enterest and [partners]. In the past the timing of it was very unreliable" (Logistics Director).

Enterest also aimed to include suppliers in their SCM planning processes, to improve the overall management of their e-supply chain:

"The future sees equal and opposite provision of information so that suppliers are able to do capacity planning, rate of sale, and sourcing of information from our site so that they can be involved in the planning process. Doing so they can see ahead of time that for example if we have a runaway success the suppliers are able to tap into our system for that product and gage a rate of return so that they can plan what our forward estimates are going to be" (Director of Merchandise & Marketing).

Enterest expended considerable effort to improve their business by focusing on developing warehousing and logistics systems. Enterest believed that their existing cross-docking system was one of the most important steps in that direction.

3.3 Improved Customer Service

Customer satisfaction creates more demand, and in turn can increase overall sales and revenue. But it requires extending the range of the available products and an increase in the production rate of in-demand goods (Fisher, 1997). In an e-supply chain, recruiting specialised companies for product variations can extend the product range (Chandrashekar *et al.,* 1999). However, with an extended product range, customer demand becomes almost impossible to predict. Thus, by utilising the *built-to-order* e-supply chain, such uncertainty can be alleviated by offering customers variety and filling orders quickly without the need to stock excess inventory (Fisher, 1997). Also, with the flux of advanced SCM solutions, companies can plan collaboratively with their partners and reduce order cycles, thus, early detection of exceptions in a supply chain network allows correct reaction in *real* time (Anderson, 2000). Including the Internet in the end-to-end supply chain, also allows customers to directly access product information, place orders, track shipments and pay freight bills, thus, making it easier for customers to do business with companies (Kaarma *et al.,* 1999).

In the long-term, it was clear that Enterest aimed to become the 'one stop shop' for customers, thus increasing the range of products and services available to them. Their strategy was to integrate products from suppliers rather than going into direct competition with them. With this model, Enterest believed that suppliers and manufacturers would have the opportunity to leverage off their e-commerce expertise and position in the market space by providing a virtual store that acts as a 'shop' for their products:

> "Enterest focuses on the supply chain as a means to an end. The means to an end is satisfying the customer requirement, so it's the customer in the first place that tells us what they want. What Enterest needs to do is meet those customers needs, and managing it on the supply chain is part of managing the customer need" (Director of Merchandise & Marketing).

However, in the short term it was important for Enterest to be up to date with innovative technologies in order to facilitate a one-on-one relationship with customers, and to assess their current customer service performance, and compare and contrast it to their competition.

> "The real success for a lot of retailing will be to manage a one-on-one relationship with customers. Having the technology capable of managing what might be half a million customers, knowing that a particular customer is interacting with us at any particular time, and they have these peculiar needs. Using the technology to manage that is where true CRM customer relationship management will start to add value both to the customer and to Enterest" (Director of Merchandise & Marketing).

Finally, by providing visibility and information feedback to the customer service centre, Enterest have gained better understanding of the reasons why their warehouse was contacted. Enterest used this information to anticipate warehouse requests and, as a result, improved their overall customer service levels.

3.4 Summary of Enterest E-Supply Chain Integration Benefits

Our study confirmed the three major areas of benefit recognised by other researchers in e-supply chain integration, i.e. reduction of cost and increase of efficiency, better management and planning processes, and improvement in customer services (in both B2C and B2B models). Table 2 lists these benefits (in rows) and attributes them (by cross) to statements made by different study participants (in columns).

	Participants / Benefits	Business Manager	CIO	Director of Merchandise & Marketing	Business Analyst	Logistics Director
Cost & Efficiency	Company Profits	☐	☐	☒	☐	☐
	Reduced E-Supply Chain Costs	☒	☐	☐	☒	☐
	Reduced Investment & Real Estate	☐	☐	☒	☐	☐
	Improved E-supply Chain Efficiency	☒	☐	☒	☒	☒
	Increased Order Fulfilment Speed	☒	☐	☐	☐	☐
Management & Planning	Better Management & Planning	☐	☒	☐	☐	☒
	Reduced Inventory Levels	☐	☐	☐	☐	☒
	Improved Understanding of Business	☐	☒	☐	☐	☐
	Visibility Across the E-supply Chain	☐	☒	☐	☐	☐
Customer Service	Better Choice and Variety of Products	☐	☐	☐	☒	☐
	Improved Customer Service	☒	☐	☒	☒	☒

Table 2. Benefits of Integration across Enterest's E-supply Chain

Other, less reported, benefits of SCM integration at Enterest varied depending on the participant (refer to Table 2). The CIO believed integration would improve visibility allowing Enterest a better understanding of their business. The Director of Merchandise & Marketing claimed that a well-integrated e-supply would increase profits and allow Enterest the ability to reduce their overall investment in SCM. The Business Manager believed that integration would speed up the order fulfilment process, from the store web site through to its warehouse. The Logistics Director thought that further integration would improve their warehousing processes, including collaboration with suppliers by lowering overall inventory levels.

4. CHALLENGES OF SCM INTEGRATION

Management consultants in e-supply chain integration, such as those involved in our study, identify three main classes of challenges facing mature e-businesses, i.e. challenges due to incompatible culture of collaborating organisations, due to inadequacy of human and financial resources allocated for the e-supply ventures, or due to difficulties in maintaining continuous improvement in integration and collaboration. Less experienced, start-up or rapidly changing organisations face many more challenges, some of which we identified in Enterest and which we classified into three major categories, i.e. business, infrastructure and external challenges.

4.1 Business Challenges

For the effective SCM in e-business, participating organizations need to adopt an appropriate business model and culture, which could facilitate inter-organisational integration, sharing of skills and knowledge, and enable change in response to market forces (Parr *et al.,* 1999). This could be achieved by good management practices, such as selective staffing, process measurement, motivation and self-management (Zhang & Zhang, 1995). Organisational and personal role boundaries need to be clearly defined, and leadership and accountability set as priority in organisational context (Abbas & Brown 2000). At the same time, collaboration between partners and within their organisations is paramount for companies aiming to fulfil their strategic SCM goals in their e-supply partnerships (Chandrashekar *et al.,* 1999; Lambert *et al.,* 1999).

These were in fact the main challenges for Enterest. Since its inception, Enterest suffered from a lack of process integration with their partners, particularly their suppliers. Enterest believed that further integration with all partners would benefit customers by improving visibility of information in order to meet customer expectations:

> "The challenge at the front end, before the order, is to have relationships with suppliers over time using as much electronic technology as possible to be able to source product availability in real time, to meet the customers requirements" (Director of Merchandise & Marketing).

In addition to suppliers, Enterest have experienced some difficulties integrating with their warehousing partners. These problems involved integrating Enterest's web site ordering system with the order fulfilment system using EDI, which was shown to be sub-optimal for the internet-driven e-commerce supply chain.

Parts of the inter-organisational network in the Enterest's e-supply chain was created due to the company's deficiency in some of its core competencies, e.g. the lack of knowledge in end-to-end planning in warehousing and logistics. This resulted in a decision to outsource order fulfilment to a third party provider. The other reason was a faster time-to-market for their rapid product rollout strategy. The CIO explains Enterest's decision to outsource:

> "Well we didn't have the core competency in picking and packing. And we didn't have the warehouse facilities. We identified we needed to be able to handle a lot more in terms of throughput, and a lot faster than we were simply

capable of building the infrastructure to supply. So we had to find it somewhere" (Chief Information Officer).

It was also clear that Enterest SCM skills were lacking on the supplier's end as well. As a result, Enterest were faced with the challenge of understanding and proposing the best way to integrate with all their suppliers. This was achieved by standardising their software and allowing the suppliers to easily connect into their IT systems. Such an approach was to improve not only their data communication facilities but also improve their business processes and facilitate collaboration between partners:

"We're like a central pond with lots of little fish (small suppliers) that we have to deal with. So we should deal with them all in the same way, and standardise our communication. This may include the way they bill us, the way we give them money and the way they send products. If all that fits in nicely then it's a lot more efficient for us" (Business Manager).

Standardising the collaboration between Enterest and all their suppliers was extremely challenging. Although Enterest's partnership increased their time-to-market, it also increased overall complexities by requiring increased management of their overall e-supply chain. These complexities added further pressures to Enterest as they continued to introduce new products and departments in their business whilst trying to improve relationships with their existing suppliers.

Managing Enterest and championing the company's e-supply chain strategies was another of its serious business challenges. Although Enterest had an entire team of people accountable for facilitating integration and performance measurement, some of its members, however, felt that due to market pressures challenging Enterest daily, forward planning for further integration with their suppliers was not as critical as day-to-day operations.

"We are, I mean we are looking at monitoring our suppliers and determining how we can achieve better service from them and how we can integrate further into their business...But I mean what you're talking about now is forward planning. It's not until our business becomes a mature business that we will be able to look at those opportunities. At the moment we don't have the luxury of time to look at those opportunities but in retrospect we probably should" (Logistics Director).

To counter-balance this not so uncommon opinion, CIO firmly asserted on another occasion that future planning was fundamental to the company business. One of those fundamental issues was to establish trust between Enterest and its suppliers. As part of trust building, Enterest devised some benchmarks and established service levels that were agreed upon by all parties. Having done that, Enterest actually struggled to measure and meet those service levels to the suppliers' satisfaction. On the other hand, many

Enterest's suppliers and partners were also unable to deliver their services as promised. Hence, this lack of trust and communication posed a significant barrier to Enterest's ability to further integrate across their e-supply chain.

Constant struggle with the limited capital and large warehousing and delivery costs are common in today's e-business, which includes Enterest. By descending down the Internet boom, the company had to re-evaluate their approach to e-commerce by sharply focusing on cost cutting, which meant holding more of their major selling lines and decreasing their entire product range, thus undercutting any other concerns, which also included the sophistication in the e-supply chain:

> "We've got limited capital, so we've got to budget everything up. We've got to spend X amount on IT and X amount on logistics and distribution, and X amount of money to buy certain things, so we have to prioritise what we buy. So at the moment its more important for us to get a stable website, and a great product offering, and we want to make it easy for customers to buy online, rather than the worrying about the biggest supply chain issues which at the moment won't have much impact because the scale is not there" (Business Manager).

Yet the Logistics Director felt that Enterest were not sufficiently focussed on SCM integration as opposed to other parts of the business like merchandise and marketing. Not surprisingly, Enterest staff in general believed that one of their biggest problems lies in disparate systems and disparate interfaces, and the enormous complexities involved with integration of inter-company systems.

4.2 Infrastructure Challenges

One of the major symptoms of a lack of SCM integration is the 'bullwhip' effect (Lee *et al.,* 1997), which we consider a major fault in the inter-organisational infrastructure, rather than a common business challenge. There are two major causes of the bullwhip effect, i.e. long resupply lead times and multiple demand-forecast updates, with common symptoms of excessive inventory, poor product forecasts or poor customer service due to unavailable products. In e-commerce, this effect is amplified even further as demand variability is much higher (Fisher, 1997). Lee *et al.* (1997) suggest information sharing, channel alignment and operational efficiency as possible remedies for bullwhip effect, and the new SCM initiatives such as ECR, VMI and the direct built-to-order e-supply chain (all previously mentioned) have been introduced specifically to reduce the effect.

Enterest staff understood that integration reduces the negative effects associated with sub-par management of their e-supply chain. They realized its importance because there are fundamental differences between their business and the traditional retailer.

> "The thing we have different from traditional retailers is that when a traditional retailer is out of stock, the customer doesn't see the product and therefore doesn't know whether they want to buy it. With online retail, when we have that product on our site, whether or not we've got the product in stock the consumer can expect to buy that product. So we require the ability to manage 'out of stock' product, and in a more time effective manner than a traditional retailer, who doesn't actually know they're losing a sale" (Director of Merchandise & Marketing).

In order to increase the accuracy of Enterest stock estimates and to improve product visibility in the supply chain, the company Business Analyst was particularly concerned with the technological solutions to support obtaining and manipulating real-time data correctly, e.g. with EDI or XML. Another Enterest's plan to address these challenges was to implement a new ERP system into their business that would improve integration among business units and between partners. Unfortunately, many of the Enterest's suppliers lacked the technological infrastructure to support high-tech real time visibility and delivery. As a result Enterest were forced to negotiate with their suppliers to upgrade their own IT infrastructure.

4.3 External Challenges

In the course of our study, we were amazed to discover the whole group of challenges, neglected by the consultants in e-supply chain integration, especially those we talked to. The class of challenges that we identified were deeply rooted in various strategic factors, which we determined as external to the organisations in the supply chain, e.g. market forces, economies of scale and maturity, the issues of market growth as compared with the scalability of the available technology. It wasn't surprising, however, that it was the Enterest's higher management, who were particularly concerned with these strategic issues.

The constantly changing nature of the marketplace creates a challenge for Enterest in deciding what hardware and software investments to make. In terms of SCM applications the CIO believed this area was still in its "juvenile" phase:

> "We use some 3rd party services for particular marketing related services. We can utilise those sorts of services provided by an external ASP. Actually most of those facilities are available at the marketing level but not at the supply chain level or the logistics level. The logistics levels are still maturing in the market" (CIO).

In particular, Enterest needed to constantly seek the best solution for their web site infrastructure.

Enterest had also been challenged with the limited economies of scale, and as a result, needed to remain highly flexible to changing customer requirements. This included their decision to acquire the services of four independent transport providers, to facilitate deliveries to different customers in different locations. Enterest viewed electronic marketplace as very unstable and, as the Director of Merchandise & Marketing explained, until Enterest's scale approached its critical mass, they would be limited in terms of their margin capability and their ability to effectively integrate with suppliers:

> "Because we're in start up mode and are just growing with the economies we are precluded from taking for example, Asian sourced product, where margin capability is a lot easier because you have to buy and contain a lot. We don't want to be in that business yet because that means we are making a long-term prediction that what our buyers choose is what our customers want" (Director of Merchandise & Marketing).

Consequently, in the short term Enterest were limited to using a form of wholesale aggregation on site in Australia, to acquire their products. This presented Enterest with a real challenge until they were able to improve their economies of scale to acquaint some of the traditional bricks and mortar, large size retailers. For example, many suppliers including traditional businesses have been reluctant dealing with Enterest directly because they only accounted for a small proportion of their business. Enterest, however, strongly believed that their situation could improve over time, which would be dependent on Enterest's ability to drive further sales and revenue to their business, as well as, having the e-supply chain infrastructure that would enable them to become *"one of the largest movers of these external products"* (Business Analyst).

In order to maintain scalable systems that were flexible to variability in demand, Enterest had to scale up in their own information technology, which included hardware and software systems. They had to provide additional facilities for order handling, in order to deal with sudden drops and rises of order volumes. Depending on the relative urgencies, in some cases Enterest's approach had been to immerse more people in the problem area. However, the CIO believed that issues of scalability and growth are industry-wide and cannot be dealt with properly without strong prior understanding of the e-commerce industry as a whole, which requires more research in the area.

5. DISCUSSION AND CONCLUSIONS

Having completed our study of a single e-commerce company, we gained a number of insights into the benefits and challenges of e-supply chain integration in a medium-size e-retail company.

Surprisingly, previously identified benefits of SCM integration were more perceived than actual. Some of these benefits included faster order fulfilment, inventory reductions and improved supplier partnerships. Though Enterest's actual benefits were also substantial, e.g. improved customer service and a reduction in costs through improved e-supply chain efficiencies. At the time of the study, Enterest were still to gain the main benefits of SCM integration, e.g. the long-term competitive advantage through increased revenue growth. Interestingly, the challenge of dot-com crash proved very sobering for Enterest, and so and after a series of downfalls and recoveries, the company reduced its alliances, staff, services and products.

Table 3 lists challenges observed to face Enterest (in rows) and attributed (with crosses) to the study participants (in columns). We classified these challenges into three generic categories related to business, infrastructure and external factors (the latter seemingly elusive to management consultants, see the shaded area in Table 3). Some of these challenges prevented Enterest from further SCM integration; others impacted the actual process of integration. To our surprise, many challenges showed clear inter-dependencies between internal and external factors, e.g.

1. As Enterest were in a constant state of flux growing rapidly from a small to a medium size e-commerce company (internal), they lacked organisational and financial capacity to stabilise changing market conditions and to react flexibly to external pressures (external);
2. Being an immature start-up business (internal), Enterest faced difficulties in utilising economies of scale, gaining organisations' trust to form alliances, and developing the necessary communication channels to integrate with its business partners (external);
3. As Enterest operated in quite immature technological environment (external), Enterest and its partners' information systems lacked the necessary scalability and complexity (internal) to effectively respond to continuous market growth and variability.

By looking at these dependencies, it was evident to us that many of the Enterest's supply chain integration barriers could be significantly reduced by forward planning for change in organisational and environmental maturity.

	Participants / Challenges	Business Manager	CIO	Director of Merchandise & Marketing	Business Analyst	Logistics Director	Fulfilment Manager
Business Challenges	Lack of process integration across partners	☐	☒	☒	☒	☐	☐
	Lack of knowledge & skills in logistics and SCM	☒	☒	☐	☐	☒	☐
	Achieving effective vision and leadership	☐	☒	☒	☐	☒	☐
	Establishing trust and open communication	☐	☐	☒	☐	☒	☒
	Cost & complexity of integrated e-supply chain	☒	☒	☒	☐	☒	☐
Infrastruct. Challenges	Inconsistent or out-of-date data - the bullwhip effect	☐	☐	☒	☒	☐	☐
	Lack of infrastructure or resources for collaboration	☐	☐	☒	☒	☐	☒
External Challenges	Changing market conditions	☒	☒	☐	☐	☐	☐
	Limited Scale & Maturity in B2C E-commerce	☐	☐	☒	☒	☐	☒
	Capability in maintaining scalable & effective IS	☐	☒	☐	☒	☐	☐

Table 3. Challenges of Integration across Enterest's E-supply Chain

Managing change has been previously noted as essential in effective supply chain strategy (Easton, *et al.*,1998). It has also been acknowledged as important to manage the continuing evolution of supply chain capabilities (Kalakota & Robinson, 2001, pp 292-295) and the gradual improvement in the supply chain processes (Fawcett & Magnan, 2001, pp 44, 49). The impact of organisational and environmental maturity on the supply chain management process, as brought to our attention through this case study however, is still to be widely recognised as significant in the supply chain strategic planning and yet to be considered as an integral part of the accepted supply chain integration models (Bowersox et al., 2002, pp 174-179; Supply-Chain Council, 2002).

In our future work, we hope to further explore the issue of organisational and environmental maturity in supply chain strategic planning and to follow up the case study reported in this paper with a multiple case study, which would allow us cross-organisational analysis of various internal and external factors affecting organisations' ability to deal effectively with change.

ACKNOWLEDGEMENTS

As much of the work reported in this paper was conducted when both authors were at the University of Melbourne, Department of Information Systems, we'd like to thank its staff and students for their encouragement to complete this research.

REFERENCES

Abbas, D., & Brown, N (2000): *Aspects of E-Commerce Supply-Chain Integration.* Cambridge Technology Partners: Richmond.

Anderson, D.L., & Lee, H.L. (2000): "The Internet-Enabled Supply Chain: From the "First Click" to the "Last Mile"", in *http://anderson-d.ASCET.com*: ASCET.com: Supply Chain Integration.

Anderson, G. (2000): "From Supply Chain to Collaborative Commerce Networks: The Next Step in Supply Chain Management", in *http://anderson-g.ASCET.com*: ASCET.com: Supply Chain Integration.

Billington, C. (2000): "Supply Chain Strategy: Real Options for Doing Business At Internet Speed", in *http://anderson-g.ASCET.com*: ASCET.com: Supply Chain Integration.

Bowersox, D.J., Closs, D.J. & Cooper, M.B. (2002): Supply Chain Logistics Management, Boston: McGraw-Hill.

Cavaye, A.L.M. (1996): "Case Study research: a multi-faceted research approach for IS". *Information Systems Journal.* 6: p. 227-242.

Chandrashekar, A., & Schary, P.B. (1999): "Toward the virtual supply chain: The convergence of IT and organisation". *International Journal of Logistics Management.* 10(2): p. 27-39.

Corbett, C.J., Blackburn, J.D., & Wassenhove, L.N.V. (1999): "Partnerships to improve supply chains". *Sloan Management Review.* 40(4): p. 71-82.

Darke, P., Shanks, G., & Broadbent, M (1998): "Successfully Completing Case Study Research: Combining Rigour, Relevance and Pragmatism". *Information Systems Journal.* 8: p. 273-289.

Easton, R., Brown, R. & Armitage, D. (1998): "The dynamics of change in the supply chain: Translating supply chain strategies into action", in Gattorna, J., *Strategic Supply Chain Alignment: Best Practice in Supply Chain Management*, Hampshire, England: Gower Pub. Ltd, p 446-468.

Fawcett, S.E. & Magnan, G.M. (2001): *Achieving World-Class Supply Chain Alignment: Benefits, Barriers and Bridges*, Center for Advanced Purchasing Studies, http://www.capsresearch.org.

Fisher, M.L. (1997): "What is the right supply chain for your product?" *Harvard Business Review.* 75(2): p. 105-116.

Fisher, M.L., Hammond, J.H., & Obermeyer, W.R. (1994): "Making supply meet demand in an uncertain world". *Harvard Business Review.* 72(3): p. 83-93.

Kaarma, E., & McCarter, J., & Hsieh, R (1999): "Electronic Commerce: Supply Chain Management and Policy Issues, Global Trade, Transportation, and Logistics Program", in *depts.washington.edu/gttl/htdocs/conf99/ecpaper.html.*

Kalakota, R., & Whinston, A (1997): *Electronic Commerce - A Manager's Guide*: Addison-Wesley, United States.

Kalakota, R., & Robinson, M. (1999): *e-Business - Roadmap for Success*. Massachusetts, US: Addison-Wesley Longman.

(2001): *e-Business 2.0 - Roadmap for Success*. Massachusetts, US: Addison-Wesley Longman.

Lambert, D.M., Emmelhainz, M.A., & Gardner, J.T. (1999): "Building Successful Logistics Partnerships". *Journal of Business Logistics*. 20(1): p. 165-177.

Lee, H.L., Padmanabhan, V., & Whang, S (1997): "The bullwhip effect in supply chains". *Sloan Management Review*. 38(3): p. 93-102.

Miles, M.B., & Huberman, A.M. (1994): *Qualitative Data Analysis*: SAGE Publications.

Neuman, W.L. (2000): *Social Research Methods - Qualitative and Quantitative Approaches*. Fourth ed. Boston: Allyn and Bacon.

Newton, C.J. (2000): "Demystifying E-Fulfillment: AMR Research Report on Supply Chain Management for April 2000", in *www.amrresearch.com/SCS/reports /0004scsbody1.asp*: AMR Research.

Parr, A.N., Shanks, G., Darke, P. (1999): *Identification of Necessary Factors for Successful Implementation of ERP Systems, New Information Technologies in Organizational Processes: Field Studies and Theoretical Reflections on the Future of Work*. Boston/Dordrecht/London: Kluwer Academic Publishers.

Peet, J. (2000): "E-Commerce - Shopping around the web". *The Economist* (February 26): p.1-38.

Supply-Chain Council (2002): "Supply-Chain Operations Reference-Model: Overview of SCOR Version 5.0", www.supply-chain.org.

Taylor, D.H. (2000): "Demand amplification: has it got us beat?" *International Journal of Physical Distribution & Logistics Management*. 30(6): p. 515-533.

Walsham, G. (1995): "Interpretive case studies in IS research: nature and method". *European Journal of Information Systems*. 4(2): p. 74-81.

Walton, B. (2000): "From Supply Chain to Collaborative Network: Case Studies in the Food Industry", in *http://walton.ASCET.com*: ASCET.com: Supply Chain Integration.

Warkentin, M., & Bapna, R., & Sugumaran, V (2000): "The Role of Mass Customisation in Enhancing Supply Chain Relationships in B2C E-Commerce Markets". *Journal of Electronic Commerce Research*. 1(2): p. 1-17.

Yin, R.K. (1994): *Case Study Research: Design and Methods*. 2nd Ed: Sage Publications.

Zhang, H.C., Zhang, D. (1995): "Concurrent Engineering: an overview from manufacturing engineering perspectives". *Concurrent Engineering: Research and Applications*. 3(3).

Zikmund, W.G. (1997): *Business Research Methods*. Fifth Ed: The Dryden Press.

CONSUMER CHOICE, INFORMATION PRODUCT QUALITY, AND MARKET IMPLICATIONS

GENNADI KAZAKEVITCH AND LUBA TORLINA
Deparment of Economics, Monash University and School of Information Systems, Deakin University Melbourne, Australia

Abstract: The paper concerns with the peculiarities of consumer choice in information product markets. This is a multidisciplinary study based on both information system research and microeconomic theory. An extension is introduced to the conventional general theory of consumer choice for explicitly taking into account the impact of information product quality on consumer behaviour. Multiple quality characteristics, considered against the price of product, are an essential reason for consumer choice of high tech product in general and information product in particular. We assume that consumers are able to aggregate their preferences of multiple product characteristics into a product preference order. On the supply side, the product quality characteristics incur costs. In the case of information product, those costs are the costs of the first copy, and marginal costs are near zero. All of the above constitute the distinctive characteristics of the competitive mechanism in the digital economy and in information product markets. A model, based on the game theory is used to consider two special cases. The first one deals with monopolistic competition for a share of the market with a limited number of customers. Conditions are derived for IT firm survival. The second one considers conditions at which a monopoly is able to successfully introduce a new version if its information product.

1. INTRODUCTION

The phenomenon of electronic commerce is relatively new. This year Internet reaches 33, the age blessed with maturity and wisdom. The use of Internet for commerce and business is much younger. For about a decade we watch the explosion of electronic commerce applications, and fast growth of e-business as an important subset of Information Economy. As for any business, key issue for electronic business is achieving success and being competitive. Despite the short history of this phenomenon, we witness examples of spectacular rises and collapses of companies starting a journey into the untravelled lands of virtual space.

There are many problems leading to failures. One of them is inability to recognise how new technology can change the delivery method and physical form of information, and pose a serious threat to otherwise highest quality product (E.g. Encyclopedia Britannica. See E-Commerce survey (2000), Torlina et al (1999)). A typical reason for Dot.com crashes in 2001 was minimal knowledge of the specifics regarding information markets. Subsequently, their business models and market strategies failed to accommodate particular features of information products and services, especially those offered via digital channel such as the Internet. The success stories are convoluted. For example, there is an ongoing debate about product quality, business methods, marketing and competitive strategies of Microsoft. Is Microsoft a successful innovator taking advantage of Information Economy, or a ruthless monopolist using the worst practices to retain their leading position? These questions were discussed, for example in BBC news (2001), Economides, N. (2001), Torlina & Kazakevitch (2001b).

Contradicting messages from practice about e-business successes and fiascos are under scrutiny and investigation by researchers from different perspectives and disciplines.

The goal of this paper is to establish a link, from the theoretical perspective, between the quality of information products, consumer choice and market success of information product provider. We are suggesting an integrated approach to understanding the consumer and producer behaviour in information product markets.

The theoretical framework and models developed within suggested approach are applicable to a wide range of information products in digital form, especially multi-functional, such as software and complex IS products, e.g. information systems, e-commerce applications, communications software, and on-line services. We investigate market structure of such products, market behaviour of both consumers and producers, conditions for survival, and competitive success for companies with significant information component in their products or services.

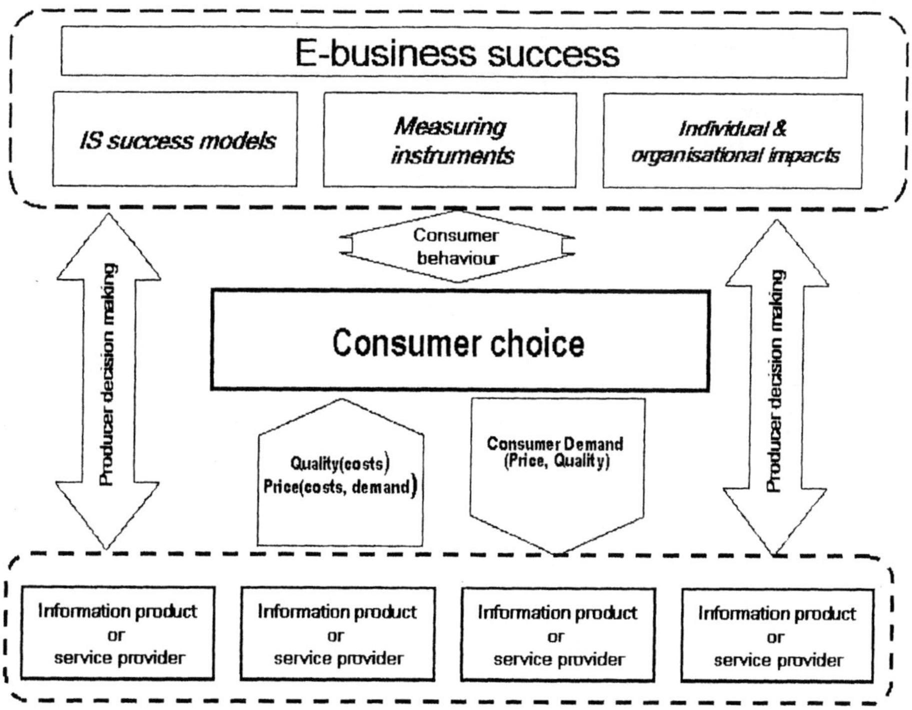

Figure 1. A conceptual model of e-business success

This is a multidisciplinary study based on both information system research and microeconomic theory. Figure 1 shows the conceptual framework of this study. First of all, we consider findings from an extensive information systems research in the area of information systems quality modeling, measuring, determination, and investigation of factors leading to information systems success. Secondly, we incorporate these findings into a model of consumer choice based on quality perception. Our approach radically differs from the traditional one, where consumer demand depends only on prices, and product quality is not explicitly included in the theory (See for example Varian & Varian, 1984). In e-business, the information component of product or service always needs to be taken into account. As was shown in Torlina & Kazakevitch (2000), product valuation, in such a case, is more complicated and essentially depends on specific characteristics of information products. The third component of our research framework includes a supply-side model. Consumer valuation and demand play key roles in price determination in information markets, and therefore, in the formation of a market equilibrium. The model captures the interrelation of producer costs/quality/price decisions and customer quality/demand feedback.

We use this approach to integrate and extend our earlier models and to analyse elements of consumer behaviour in information product markets where suppliers exercise considerable market power. One of them, initially discussed in Torlina & Kazakevitch (2001a), incorporates quality variables into the traditional theory of monopolistic competition, to allow application of this theory to information product market strategies, where several companies compete for their market shares within a limited customer base. In another one (initially introduced in Kazakevitch & Torlina, 2001b), the traditional economic analysis of monopoly market is modified to include specific characteristics of information products. This model allows for some conclusions about economic limitations to the quality of information products supplied by monopolies or companies, like Microsoft, occupying a considerable market share. In particular, we consider possible profit-optimising strategies towards issuing updates to existing products, inevitably leading to quality compromise.

We believe that this paper contributes to the better understanding of consumer decision making patterns, and therefore, may help in better planning product development and marketing strategies by information product suppliers.

2. MULTIPLE QUALITY CHARACTERISTICS OF INFORMATION PRODUCTS, AGGREGATION AND CONSUMER CHOICE

For a number of years, different aspects of information product quality have been of wide interest to the academia and industry alike. In the field of information systems research the most developed and widely used models, which integrate different aspects of IS product quality, and capture users' individual perceptions are: the model of IS success (DeLone & McLean, 1992), Technology Acceptance Model (Davis, 1989), End-user computing satisfaction measuring instrument (Doll & Torkzadeh, 1988), User Information Satisfaction (Ives & Olson, 1984). On the basis of these models, and identified dimensions of success, hundreds of measures, scales, measuring tools have been developed, and numerous model modifications have been suggested.

The main problems with these models are that there is no consensus among researchers on how to define information system success, which measures should be used, and what are the significant factors. The findings of individual cases are not robust, and vary considerably depending on application type, stakeholders and users involved, organisational settings, and external conditions (Seddon 1996, Seddon et al, 1998). At the same time, the approach can be very useful for early application evaluations, or pre-purchase decisions. (Doll et al, 1998)

A number of authors distinguish the success factors, significant for the adoption of information products from the success factors of continued usage. The findings in E. Karahanna, Straub & Chervany (1999) have important implications for theory and practice. Their study provides some evidence that adoption is solely influenced by normative considerations, while continued usage is determined by attitudinal factors. These findings can help software producers and potential buyers to select most suitable product development and implementation strategies.

Information product variety and quality available under different market conditions have been discussed in economic literature. Varian (1998) describes different forms of versioning information products available due to flexibility of digital media. Varian (1993) shows that under specific market conditions software providers are more interested in designing easy to learn interface, rather then invest in a better software functionality. Waterman (1991) analyses welfare tradeoffs between product quality and variety under the conditions of different pricing arrangements (direct payments from consumer versus advertiser's supported products), and fixed or varying investments in the first copy of information product. Meanwhile, the literature pays more attention to the supply side, cost structure, and pricing mechanisms, then to the demand side and consumer choice factors.

To summarise the above, the quality of an information product is a complex matter and may include product content and functionality, user interface, ease of learning, warranty, service and support provided, and many other things. "Quality" may be the *perceived quality,* which may include both real improvement as well as a successful marketing component. The latter may also appear to be a marketing hype.

For the purpose of this study, we assume that multiple sources of value embedded in the information product, including both tangible and intangible components should be reflected in the product quality and price determination. Each information product, like any high tech one, may be distinguished by a considerable number of quality features. In this section, we will introduce some extensions to the standard consumer choice theory, to demonstrate, from the theory viewpoint, a rationale for consumer preferences of one product to another based on multiple quality characteristics.

According to the standard theory of consumer choice, a consumer is faced with possible consumption bundles of n goods. Bundles differ by a quantity of each of the goods consumed. A rational consumer will always choose a most preferred bundle from the set of feasible alternatives, where feasibility is restricted by the consumer's budget and the prices for goods included in the bundle (See, for example, Varian, 1984). Meanwhile, the standard theory does not explicitly take product quality into consideration.

There is no reason why this theory can't be applied to a subset of the consumption bundle, provided that a fixed budget is allocated for such a subset. Initially, we consider a very special case:

- Just one type of information product;
- Multiple quality characteristics ($\mathbf{q} = (q_1, ..., q_n)$);
- Dollar market values – "prices" $\mathbf{p} = \mathbf{p}(\mathbf{q}) = (p_1(q_1), ..., p_n(q_n))$ attached to each of the quality characteristics (the nature of these dollar values will be discussed in the next section);
- The price for the product is a function of "prices" for quality characteristics $p = p(\mathbf{p})$; and
- Fixed budget constraint (y) (the maximum amount of money available for the purchase of this good).

The consumer chooses the variant of the product that maximizes *utility* (U) or *satisfaction* at given budget constraint y. Utility depends on quality characteristics ($U = U(\mathbf{q})$) as like, according to the standard theory, it depends on the quantity of goods in the bundle. $U(\mathbf{q})$ is a monotonic transformation. That is, if one set of qualities is preferable to another one ($\mathbf{q}_1 \prec \mathbf{q}_2$) then $U(\mathbf{q}_1) < U(\mathbf{q}_2)$. Consumer choice is based on utility maximization at given budget constraint:

$$\begin{aligned} &\max U(\mathbf{q}) \\ &\textstyle\sum_j p_j(q_j) \le y \end{aligned} \qquad (1)$$

The two-dimensional case of the problem (1) allows for a geometrical illustration, analogous to the standard theory (Figure 2).

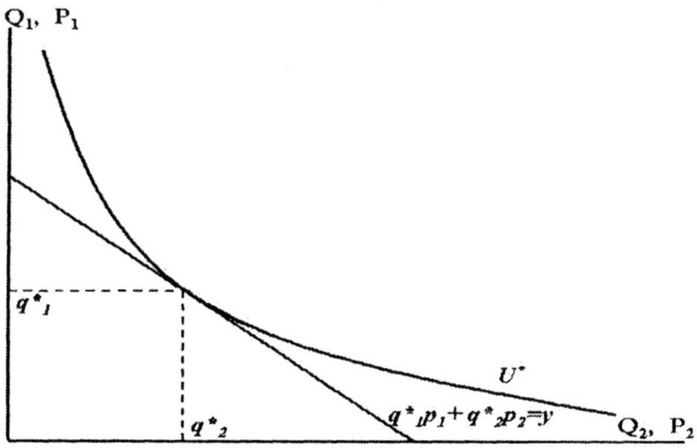

Figure 2. The combination of quality characteristics that maximizes consumer's utility.

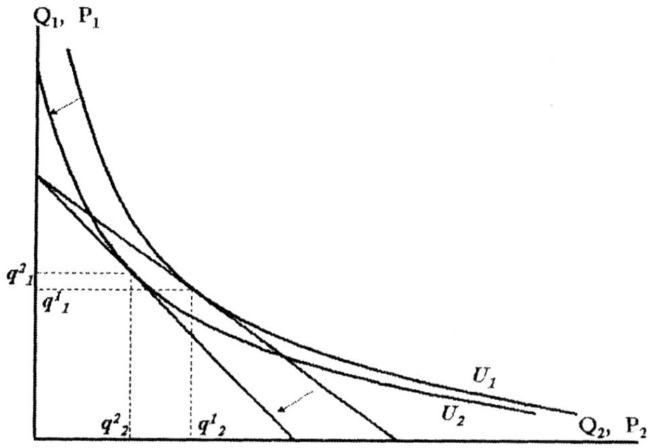

Figure 3. Consumer's reaction on increase in the "price" for one of the quality characteristics.

The curve U^* in Figure 2 as well as curves from U_1 and U_2 in Figures 3 and 4 are ***quality indifference curves.*** Each of them represents different combinations of qualities q_1 and q_2 delivering the same level of satisfaction consumer gets form the consumption of one unit of information good. The consumer prefers the product variant and corresponding level of satisfaction (utility U^*), where the combination of quality characteristics q_1 and q_2 fully utilizes the budget y at given prices p_1 and p_2.

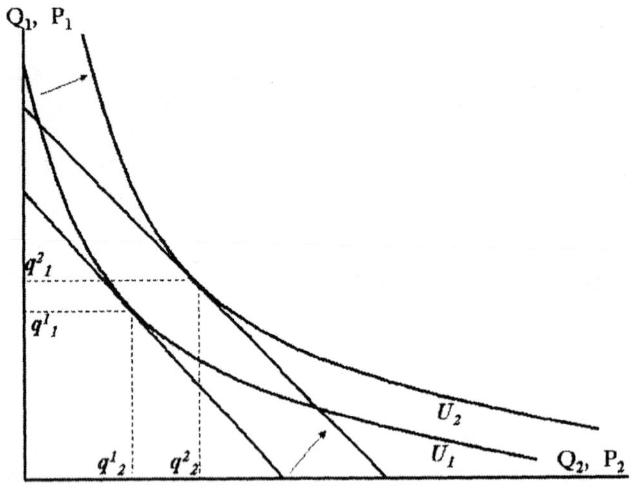

Figure 4. Consumer's reaction on increase in "real" budget.

The conclusion from the standard theory, with regard to consumer's reaction on change in prices or budget, can be also re-interpreted for this model.

If one of the quality characteristics (q_2) becomes more expensive (Figure 3), then the whole product becomes more expensive. This diminishes the real value of the budget allocated for the purchase and shift from higher (U_1) to lower (U_2) level of satisfaction. Also, if increase in the "price" for this quality feature is transparent to the consumer, then the consumer preference may be shifted to other quality parameters. The opposite conclusions apply if one of the quality characteristics becomes cheaper.

Figure 4 illustrates one of two situations: either the allocated budget increases; or decrease in the "price" for a particular quality feature is not transparent to consumer and just as decrease in price for the product. This corresponds to increase in utility from (U_1) to (U_2) and increase in both level of both quality features demanded.

The consumer, therefore, accepts multiple quality characteristics of information product as the "bundle of qualities maximizing his/her satisfaction. The utility function can be considered as a theoretical function aggregating the quality characteristics into a scalar variable from the consumer perspective. At the same time, price for the product can be considered as a sum of market values of all quality characteristics $\sum_j p_j(q_j)$.

Transition from the utility of single consumer to the group/community utility can be done similarly to the theory of trade. It is based on the perception of the similarity of tastes within a particular group or community of customers, which allows for considering group, common or average preferences.

3. INFORMATION PRODUCT QALITY AND PRODUCTION COSTS

In this section we consider the nature of dollar values – "prices" attached to each of the quality characteristics of information products, from the supply side, and their link with the cost of production.
From the supply side perspective, core information products possess some distinctive characteristics and properties, which take their extreme form when information products are digitized. See Varian and Shapiro (1998) for discussion of information products costs structure. Torlina et al (1999) discuss different categories of information products and implications of their conversion to digital form on value attributes. Whinston et al (1996), Wigand et al (1998), Willcocks et al (1997) discuss essential properties of information and digital goods.
Those properties include:

(i) Multiple and heterogeneous sources of value embedded in the product itself;
(ii) Specific cost structure - high fixed costs, near-zero variable costs and zero marginal cost. Initial fixed costs, including usually high marketing and promotion expenditure, in most cases are sunk costs, that is, they cannot be recovered if a product fails;
(iii) Extreme economies of scale - in the general case of an information good there are no natural or economically justified limits to production of additional copies;
(iv) No direct interconnection between costs spent on first copy production and product price: and
(v) Consumers valuation and demand are key price determinants.

In the case of information product, fixed costs are the costs of the development of the first copy of product. We assume that, in the short run, the quality q_i depends upon the costs C_i of the production of the original copy:

$$q_i = q_j(C_j)\text{, where } \frac{dq_j(C_j)}{dC_j} > 0;\ C_j \in \mathbf{C}_j \subset \mathbf{R}^+.$$

Here and below, differentiability of functions within continuous intervals of independent variables is assumed by default.

For the purposes of this model we also assume, that there is no problem of aggregation of functions $q_i = q_j(C_j)$ into a scalar function $Q = Q(C) = Q(\sum_j C_i)$.

4. MONOPOLISTIC COMPETITION AND INFORMATION PRODUCT QUALITY

The model is based on the common understanding of market behaviour. The company's objective is profit maximisation. The willingness of the company to supply is elastic and increases with increase in price. The consumer's objective is utility maximisation. The consumer demand is elastic and decreases with the increase in price. The model incorporates the generic assumptions characterising the monopolistic competition.

We consider a market for an information technology product that satisfies the conventional properties of monopolistic competition (See for, example, H.L. Varian, 1984; G. A. Jehle, 1991). The market consists of n mono-product firms. The products $i \in [1,n]$ are viewed by the buyers as close though not perfect substitutes for one another. Therefore, each of the sellers can be considered as the monopolist of its particular product variant with a limited degree of monopoly power. Such a monopolist is enjoying a monopoly power and making economic profit during only a short period of time from the introduction of a unique product or technology until such a technology becomes available to rivals, or until a new "more innovative" product is introduced by a rival.

The following specific features of the monopolistic competition in the IT sector discussed in previous sections are incorporated in the model. Traditionally it is assumed that the cost functions are identical across firms. We assume that the firms are characterised by different cost functions. In general case marginal cost is non-zero. For information market zero marginal cost assumption is essential. In general, technology is perfectly available to existing and new market participants. We assume that cutting-edge technology does not spill over immediately. For the time being, each firm possesses some unique product-attributable elements of otherwise common technology. These unique elements make the product variants different. The differences are viewed by the buyers as differences in quality characteristics. We consider the simplest case when all the quality characteristics of each product can be aggregated into a *scalar quality characteristic.* Increase in quality generates increase in consumer demand. Increase in quality can be achieved by a firm only through increase in the cost of the first copy. Each firm is characterised by its cost elasticity of quality.

The model describes the competitive behaviour of the IT firm in the information product market.

Aiming initially at covering first copy costs and then at earning profit, IT firm struggles for consumer demand and invests in the competitive quality of its product.

Increase in quality can be attained only at additional costs. The firms are characterised by generally different cost functions. Therefore, the incremental cost of increase in quality differs from one firm to another. Each of the firms sets the price to cover the costs and to earn profit, depending on anticipated demand. Different incremental costs allow them different degrees of freedom in setting a minimum price, which covers the firm's costs and returns a normal profit. On the demand side, increase in quality causes increase in demand. Increase in price causes decrease in quantity demanded. The total change in demand for a product of a particular firm can be negative or positive and varies from one firm to another. The firms' cost-quality decisions affect their relative competitive positions.

To ensure economic profit, relative increase in demand, associated with increase in quality per unit of relative increase in cost should not be offset by relative decrease in demand per unit of relative increase in price. Otherwise, the firm is not competitive.

As it was mentioned earlier, we assume the case where all the quality characteristics of each of the products i can be aggregated into the scalar quality characteristic q_i. We assume quality functions for each of the firms as defined in the previous section. This means increase in the value of the quality variable as the result of increase in costs within a particular range of costs $\boldsymbol{C}_{\mathrm{i}}$ for a particular firm *i.* However, it does not say anything about comparison between the values of quality variables of two firms. They depend upon the differences between the cost functions of different firms. In other words, a greater costs of firm i compared to firm j generally can lead to a lower value of the quality variable of firm i, as it is viewed by buyers. In the long run, the quality can be also improved using technological innovations, which are not directly associated with the cost C_i.

The key assumption about the IT product is that the costs C_i associated with the first copy of the product is the actual total cost of production of the first and any further number of copies: $C_i = C_i(y_i) = const$ or, in other words, marginal cost is equal to zero.

The demand y_i for product *i* is measured in the quantity of copies. We assume that the same buyer does not simultaneously purchase two analogous products from two different competitive sellers. Therefore, it is possible to measure total demand for all the variants of the product (**y**) by adding together the number of copies sold by each of the firms:

$$y = \sum_{i=1}^{n} y_i \, . \quad (2)$$

We assume that demand conventionally negatively depends upon the price p_i as well as upon the demand for the competitive products $y_{-i} = \sum_{j \in [1,n];\, j \neq i} y_j$. Based on (2) it can be measured as $y_{-i} = y - y_i$. It also positively depends upon the quality variable q_i. Therefore, the demand for product *i*, as viewed by a seller *i*, can be represented as a function: $y_i = y_i(p_i, y_{-i}, q_i(C_i))$ or its inverse

$$p_i = p_i(y_i, y_{-i}, q_i(C_i)) \, . \quad (3)$$

Even though non-conventional demand functions are assumed, we model such a market as a non-coalition game with profit as pay functions. In other words, each of the firms maximises its profit:

$$\Pi_i = y_i p_i(y_i, y_{-i}, q_i(C_i)) - C_i \rightarrow \max \, . \quad (4)$$

We are also adopting the standard behavioural hypothesis. Firm *i* makes its product/expenditure/price decision assuming the other firms' behaviour will be constant.

The first order equilibrium conditions for (4) appear to be more sophisticated than for the standard model:

$$y_{i,}\left(\frac{\partial p_i(y_{i,} y_{-i}, q_i(C_i))}{\partial y_{i,}} + \frac{\partial p_i(y_{i,} y_{-i}, q_i(C_i))}{\partial y_{-i,}} \frac{\partial y_{-i}}{\partial y_{i,}}\right) + p_i(y_{i,} y, q_i(C_i)) = 0 \, ; \quad (5)$$

$$y_{i,}\left(\frac{\partial p_i(y_{i,}y_{-i},q_i(C_i))}{\partial y_{-i,}}\right)=0\,;\ (6)$$

and

$$\frac{\partial p_i(y_{i,}y,q_i(C_i))}{\partial C_i}y_i-1=0\ (7)$$

Combining (5) and (6) gives:

$$y_{i,}\frac{\partial p_i(y_{i,}y_{-i},q_i(C_i))}{\partial y_{i,}}+p_i(y_{i,}y,q_i(C_i))=0\ (8)$$

The interpretation of the equilibrium conditions is rather difficult in the general case (7) - (8). However, a meaningful interpretation can be obtained at the assumption of the separability of the demand functions in the Cobb-Douglas form:

$$y_{i,}=aC_i^{\alpha_i}p_i^{\beta_i}(y-y_i)^{\gamma_i}\,,\ (9)$$

where $\alpha_i>0$ is *the cost elasticity of demand.* It is positive because it contributes to the quality of the product, and the quality is positively related to demand. $\beta_i<0$ is the conventional negative price elasticity of demand. $\gamma_i<0$ is the elasticity of demand for product *i* with respect to the demand for the competitive variants of the product. It is negative because, in the short run, within a given capacity of the market, the demand for product *i* decreases, with increase in demand for competitive products.

The inverse form of (8) is:

$$p_i=p_i(y_i,y_{-i},q_i(C_i))=\frac{1}{a}C_i^{-\frac{\alpha_i}{\beta_i}}y_{i,}^{-\frac{1}{\beta_i}}(y-y_i)^{-\frac{\gamma_i}{\beta_i}}\,.\ (10)$$

Substituting (9) into (7) and (8) after some transformations gives the following equilibrium conditions:

$$p_i y_i = -\frac{\beta_i}{\alpha_i} C_i \quad (11)$$

and

$$\frac{1}{\beta_i}\frac{1}{y_i} + \frac{\gamma_i}{\beta_i}\frac{1}{y - y_i} + 1 = 0 \quad (12)$$

Equation (12) means that the distribution of demand among the competitive firms does not depend upon the absolute level of prices. It is determined, however by relative values of the parameters of elasticity. Meanwhile, (11) is the key condition for the understanding of the IT firm's *i* situation in the market. It means that the firm earns a positive profit only if

$-\frac{\beta_i}{\alpha_i} > 1$ or $-\beta_i > \alpha_i$.

Combining the last inequality with the interpretation of the elasticity parameters in (9) gives the following theoretical outcomes with regard to the ability of the firm producing an information product in making a positive economic profit. At zero marginal costs, firm *i* absorbs the equilibrium distribution of demand (y_i) following from (12)). At this value of demand, the equilibrium price (p_i) and cost level (C_i) are established. To ensure economic profit, relative increase in demand, associated with increase in quality per unit of relative increase in cost, should not be offset by relative decrease in demand per unit of relative increase in price. The case, when the inequality $-\beta_i > \alpha_i$ is not held, means that the firm's technology is not capable of delivering a competitive level of quality per unit of its costs.

5. MONOPOLY AND QUALITY OF A NEW VERSION OF INFORMATION PRODUCT

In this section, we consider a special case where the information product is supplied by a monopoly. The monopoly has captured a particular market share and the overall number of users is limited. For simplicity, we restrict our consideration to a one-product company. The only way for such a company to keep its market share, and to continue extracting revenue, is to eventually offer a new version of the information product.

Like in the previous section, we assume that quality variable q depends upon the cost of the production C of the original copy of a new version:

Therefore, the demand for the IT product, as viewed by a monopoly, can be represented as a function:

$$p = p(y, q(C)), \quad (13)$$

with $\frac{\partial p(y,q)}{\partial q} > 0;\ q \in \mathbf{Q} \subset \mathbf{R}^+$ and $\frac{\partial p(y,q)}{\partial y} < 0;\ y \in \mathbf{Y} \subset \mathbf{R}^+$

However the willingness of the market to accept a higher price diminishes with each next increment in quality: $\frac{\partial^2 p(y,q)}{\partial q^2} < 0;\ q \in \mathbf{Q} \subset \mathbf{R}^+$. Even though, a non-conventional demand and cost functions are assumed, we can consider the conventional monopoly's profit maximization problem as:

$$\Pi = yp(y, q(C)) - C \rightarrow \max, \quad (14)$$

The first order equilibrium conditions for (14) appear to be different to the standard model:

$$y\frac{\partial p(y,q(C))}{\partial y} + p(y,q(C)) = 0; \quad (15)$$

$$y\frac{\partial p(y,q(C))}{\partial q}\frac{dq(C)}{dC} - 1 = 0 \quad (16)$$

Condition (15) is equivalent to the condition $\frac{dy}{y} = -\frac{dp}{p}$. It means that, at zero marginal costs there is no optimal scale of production, which would maximise profit. Meanwhile, due to the decreasing demand, increase in the volume of sales requires and allows for a proportional decrease in price.

Condition (16) or $y\frac{\partial p}{\partial q} = \frac{dC}{dq}$ means that there is an optimal combination of the cost of the first copy, price and the volume of sales, which says by itself about a limited incentive for expenditure for quality.

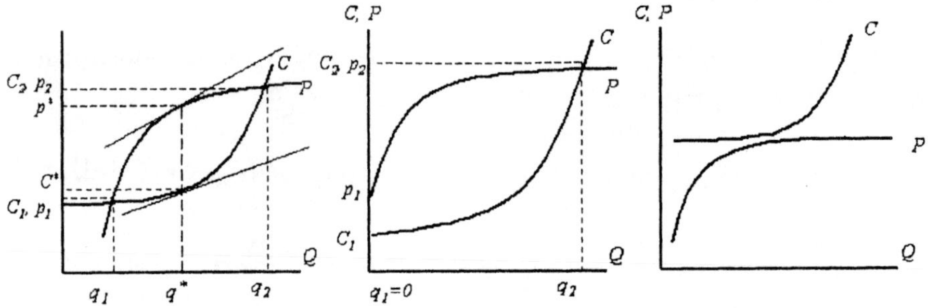

A B C

Figure 5. Quality-price-cost relationship at a constant volume of sale.

The case of fixed output ($y=y^*$), however, appears to be especially interesting. This case corresponds, for example, to the situation where a monopoly attempts to convince all the customers to buy a new version of its product. At a fixed output (Figure 5), the price as a function of quality is represented by a convex upward curve. In contrary, the cost as a function of quality is represented as a convex downward curve. Therefore, in the general case, (Figure 5A) the quality is feasible within the interval $q_1<q<q_2$. Outside of this interval, the price, at which all the customers accept the new version, appears to be below the cost of the first copy. Therefore, a better quality, beyond q_2 is infeasible. Figure 5B corresponds to an extreme case, where the customers accept any quality improvement at a price corresponding to such an improvement. However, as in the case A, the quality is limited by q_2. Figure 5C demonstrates the opposite extreme where neither quality improvement is affordable by the company due to prices acceptable by the customers lower than costs. Thus, a new version is not feasible.

6. CONCLUSION

The paper provides some insight into the competitive mechanisms of e-business success. We link e-business success to specific characteristics of information products and e-business services.

The traditional theoretical approach to market structures and competition has been modified to include factor quality of information products and services as an endogenous variable.

In the traditional monopolistic competition a partial monopoly power is achieved by releasing an innovative product. The monopoly power ends with rivals gaining access to the new technology and taking over some of the leader's market share. Meanwhile, the rivals' cost functions are not distinguished. In contrary, the essential feature of the information product or service markets, considered in this paper, is different firms' cost functions. This allows concluding that an essential condition of a firm's survival and competitiveness depends on its ability to contribute to the quality of its information product or service with less than proportional increase in cost components that may affect the product's minimum price.

As long as the monopoly is concerned, we show the economic constraints that such a company faces on the quality of the information product or service. The existence of such constrains causes limitations of the quality of products supplied by monopolists. In particular, this partially explains the phenomenon of Microsoft building financial success on products, continuously generating customer complaints.

This theoretical analysis of competition in information product and service markets, provided in the paper, may be applied to developing practical e-business strategies.

REFERENCES

Bakos, Y., (1998), The Emerging Role of Electronic Marketplaces on the Internet, *Communications of the ACM*, August 1998

BBC news (2001) Microsoft vs the US Justice Department (Full trial coverage) http://news.bbc.co.uk/hi/english/in_depth/business/2000/microsoft/default.stm ,

Davis, F. (1989), "Perceived usefulness, perceived Ease of Use and User Acceptance of Information Technology", *MIS Quarterly* 13 (September)

DeLone. McLean, (1992) "Information Systems Success: the quest for the dependant variable", *Information Systems Research*, March(3,1)

Doll, Torkzadeh, (1988) "The measurement of end user computer satisfaction", *MIS Quarterly* 12 (June)

Doll, et al., (1998), "Using Davis's Perceived Usefulness and Ease-of-use Instruments for decision making: a confirmatory and Multigroup Invariance analysis". *Decision Science*, vol 29, no 4

E-Commerce survey (2000), *The Economist*, February,

Economides, N., (1999), Competition and Vertical Integration in the Computing Industry, *Competition, Innovation, and the Role of Antitrust in the Digital Marketplace*, Eisenach J.A. and Lenard, T. M.,(eds.) Kluwer Academic Publishers,

Economides, N., (2001), 'Analysis and News of US v. MS'; http://raven.stern.nyu.edu /networks/ms/top.html

G. A Jehle (1991), *Advanced Microeconomic Theory*, Prentice-Hall.

Garrity, A., Sanders, G., (1998), *Information systems Success Measurement*, Idea group publishing

Ives, B. and M.H. Olson (1984), User Involvement and MIS Success: A Review of Research. *Management Science*, 30 (5), 586-603.

Karahanna, E., et al (1999) "Information technology adoption across time: a cross-sectional comparison of Pre-adoption and post-adoption beliefs", *MIS Quarterly*, June

Lancaster (1975), Socially Optimal product differentiation, *American Economic Review* 65, Sept.,

Seddon, P. (1996) "IS success: one underlying construct or many inter-related factors?", *Proceedings of ACIS96 conference.*

Seddon, P.,Staples, D., Patnayakuni, R., Bowtwll, M.(1998), 'The IS effectiveness matrix: the importance of Stakeholder and system in mesuring IS success', *Proceedings of ICIS98 conference*, Helsinki, Finland, pp.165-176

Shapiro, C, Varian, H. (1998) *Information Rules: A Strategic Guide to the Network Economy.* Harvard Business School Press

Torlina L., Kazakevitch G.,(2001a) Market Structures and Competition in Digital Economy, ECIS2001 conference proceedings, June 2001

Torlina L., Kazakevitch G.,(2001b) A monopoly Strategy towards a New Version of Information Product or why Microsoft products do not become much better ACIS2001 conference proceedings, December, 2001.

Torlina L., Seddon P., Corbitt B, (1999) Attributable characteristics of goods and services in Electronic Commerce, *Global Networked Organisations,* 12 Bled Electronic Commerce Conference, Vol 1.

Varian, H., (1998), Markets for Information Goods;
http://www.sims.berkeley.edu/~hal/people/hal/

Varian, H., (2001), 'High-Technology Industries and Market Structure'; http://www.sims. berkeley .edu/~hal/people/hal/

Varian H.L., Varian H. R., (1984) *Microeconomic Analysis*, W.W. Norton & Company

Varian, H., (1993) 'Economic 'Incentives in Software Design', http://www.sims.berkeley.edu/~hal/people/hal/

Waterman (1991), Diversity and Quality of Information Products in a Monopolistically Competitive Industry, *Information Economics & Policy*, Vol.4 (4)

Weber, B., (1998), 'Elements of Market Structure for On-line Commerce', ch. in. *Information Technology and Industrial Competitiveness: How IT shapes Competition,* Kemerer, Ch. F. (Ed), Kluwer Academic Publishers, Pp. 15-32

Wigand,R., Picot, A., Reichwald, R., (1997), *Information, Organisation, and Management*, Wiley & Sons

Willcocks, L., Feeney, D., Islei, G., (1997), *Managing IT as a Strategic Resource*, McGraw-Hill

Wilkin, C., R. Carr, and B. Hewett (2001): Evaluating IS Quality: Exploration of the Role of Expectations on Stakeholders' Evaluation. In W Van Grembergen (ed.), *Information Technology Evaluation Methods and Management* (pp. 111-129), Idea Group Publishing, Hershey, Pennsylvania, USA.

ON-LINE RETAILING: AN INVESTIGATION INTO THE SUCCESS FACTORS

WILLIAM GOLDEN, MARTIN HUGHES and PATRICIA GALLAGHER
Department of Accountancy and Finance, National University of Ireland

Abstract: This research is a descriptive study to identify some of the factors that contribute to the successful use of e-business. The research was focused on the retail Industry in Ireland, and more specifically on existing on-line retailers of Irish made gifts. The study was conducted using a postal survey. The research found that specific organisational factors – early adoption of web technology, internal IS/IT expertise, having an e-business strategy, and a person who champions the e-business project – does result in more successful e-business presences. Further, the research found no evidence to support the belief that certain product types are more likely to be successful on the web.

1. INTRODUCTION

Electronic commerce is said to overcome barriers to trading internationally hence making companies truly global without the need for a physical presence in another country. With over 90 million people worldwide claiming Irish descent, they represent a potential lucrative export market that can be reached cost effectively by leveraging the capabilities of electronic commerce.

The Crafts Council of Ireland (www.ccoi.ie) estimates that 66% of the crafts industry is located in rural areas. Therefore the Internet presents a great opportunity for these companies to overcome location disadvantages. While the retail market in Ireland is said to be worth in excess of IR£20 billion a year, the Crafts Council estimates that the gross turnover of the crafts industry is £92 million per annum.

This paper presents a descriptive study conducted with the aim of determining some of the factors that contribute to the success of retailers using electronic commerce to perform effectively in export markets. The focus of this research is on Irish export retailers in the crafts sector.

2. LITERATURE REVIEW

Electronic commerce has the potential to revolutionise the retail industry. Like other revolutions, some firms will be more adept at riding the new wave than others. The key factors that will enable organisations to be more successful in their adoption of web based e-commerce are twofold – organisational factors and industry specific factors.

2.1 Organisational factors influencing web site success

"The first man gets the oyster; the second man gets the shell." (Andrew Carnegie).

Some commentators believe that many of the successful companies on the web owe their success merely to the fact that they were first to exploit the capabilities of the Internet as a channel for business (Enders & Jelassi, (2000), Mellahi & Johnson, (2000)). While De Figueiredo (2000) points out that first movers will have some advantage and early movers have the highest website stickiness.

However, Golder & Tellis's (1993) study of first mover firms found that first movers did not enjoy exceptional and sustained benefits. Kerin et al. (1992) also support the view that being first to market does not automatically ensure dominant market share or long-term rewards.

Bhatnagar, Misra, & Rao (2000) state that the companies who are successful on the Internet have previous technological experience. Companies that have staff with IT skills and an IT department in their business will be more successful when operating online (Bhatnagar, Misra, & Rao, 2000). Mellahi & Johnson (2000) conclude after conducting a case study on Amazon.com, that the critical resources in the electronic commerce industry that result in competitive advantage are largely intangible assets and capabilities, such as innovation, technical expertise and knowledge. Thus, the technological experience and knowledge that companies have are critical factors in determining success in electronic commerce (Savin & Silberg, 2000).

Venkatraman (2000) comments that a business strategy that fails to recognise the Internet is destined to fail. A recent KPMG survey shows that mangers are aware of the need to execute a web strategy to complement existing business models (Venkatraman, 2000). They point out that it is critical for traditional retailers to begin to clearly define their web strategy.

Griffith & Krampf (1998) indicate areas which managers can build an e-business strategy on: online sales which are consistent with the definition of retailing; communication which involves advertising, promotion and building corporate brand image; and customer service where the Internet provides a rare opportunity for retailers to provide exceptional customer service by being both accessible and responsive.

Venkatraman (2000) points out that every company will need to develop a strategy for the dot-com world and ultimately, business strategy will be dot-com strategy. Vision, governance, resources, and alignment are the stepping-stones to a successful web strategy (Griffith & Palmer, (1999), Venkatraman, (2000), Hackbarth & Kettinger, (2000)).

Many organisations lack a central decision maker for e-business and need someone to oversee all aspects of e-commerce including e-commerce strategy development and implementation (Schuette, 2000). Barry (2000) and Bergstein (2000) found that companies who have a web champion to run, maintain, and update their web site have a higher number of hits and repeat visits than web sites that do not have an appointed web champion. An individual with responsibility for the web project is an important factor in successful e-businesses (Chen & Leteney, (2000), De Figueiredo, (2000)).

The maintenance of a fully interactive web site involves thorough background planning. Competitors who spend time and effort designing well thought out web presences will most likely gain from the mistakes made by businesses that proceed without planning (Van Doren et al., 2000). Indeed, the difference between success and failure on the web often hinges on how carefully people sift through details and fine-tune trivial plans (Brown et al, 1999). A case study conducted by Chan and Swatman (2000) revealed Internet based e-commerce requires the same amount of planning and foresight as any previous form of e-commerce, even though it may appear simpler. In another study Spiller & Lohse (1997) investigated the effects of effective customer interfaces on traffic and sales in online stores. They posit that the promise of electronic commerce, and online shopping in particular, will depend to a large extent upon the interface and how people interact with the computer.

2.2 Retail specific factors influencing web site success

Kiang et al. (2000) contend that product characteristics play a major role in the successful marketing of a product on the Internet. Phau & Poon (2000) state that one weakness of the Internet is that it can realistically reproduce only two of our five senses – sight and sound. Therefore this limitation will restrict the types of products that are saleable on the Internet. Peterson et al. (1997) classified products and services for sale on the Internet versus a retail store along three dimensions: cost and frequency of purchase; value proposition; degree of differentiation. In general, when purchase fulfilment requires physical delivery, the more frequent the purchase and the smaller the cost, it is less likely that there is a good 'fit' between a product and Internet based marketing. Along the second dimension, Internet related marketing is particularly well suited to certain types of intangible or service related goods (i.e. those based on digital assets). The third dimension reflects the degree to which a product or service is differentiable. When products are capable of significant differentiation, the Internet can serve as an effective segmentation mechanism for guiding buyers to their ideal product (Peterson et al., 1997).

Enders & Jelassi (2000) further this point to say that any products that can be delivered in a digital format are likely to experience a radical shift towards online retailing because the customer has no substantial reason to visit a physical store. The Economist Shopping Survey (26th February, 2000) shows the simplest distinction is between 'high touch' and 'low touch' goods. High touch items are goods that consumers would prefer to see and touch before they purchase whereas low touch items are more standard items such as books, CDs, and computers.

Merchandise represents the full range of products the retailer offers to potential customers. The merchandise a retailer holds defines the store for the customer (Reardon & Hasty, (1997), Berman & Evans, (1994), Lindquist, (1975), Chen & Leteney, (2000)). Christensen & Tedlow (2000) point out that in categories ranging from books to chemicals, web stores can offer a selection that no bricks and mortar store can match. Customers prefer a store with a large selection (Spiller & Lohse, (1997), Ng, Pan, & Wilson, (1998), Enders & Jelassi, (2000), Walsh & Godfrey, (2000)). Spiller & Lohse (1997) found that many retailers do not take advantage of adding rich product descriptions with many just transferring paper catalogues directly onto the web.

David Pottruck, president of Charles Schwab & Co., first used the phrase 'Clicks & Mortar' as he described the company's efforts to coordinate all its services. Pottruck predicted that future business success would not hinge on a battle between bricks and mortar companies against online efforts, but in successfully integrating the two – "the marriage of the best of the physical world and the best of technology". Chen & Leteney (2000) point out that Internet retailers are being forced to recognise the importance of having a physical presence. De Figueiredo (2000) further stresses this by arguing that if traditional companies do not establish effective electronic commerce ventures to compete with their own core businesses, others will. Selling through existing physical stores and through Internet channels allows retailers to leverage the strengths of each channel with stores and websites working well together thus increasing sales at both (Chen & Leteney, (2000), Quinn, (1999), Gulati & Garino, (2000), Enders & Jelassi, (2000), The Economist, (26th February 2000)). Gulati & Garino (2000) point out the benefits that integration offers such as cross promotion, shared information, purchasing leverage, and distribution economies. Despite all these advantages, Enders & Jelassi (2000) point out that as retailers move online, they also face challenges such as organisational restructuring and the adaptation of the existing distribution infrastructure to the new requirements of the online market. Conversely, many Internet retailers who have so far focused solely on the Internet aim to expand their access to new customers by moving into the physical front end of the value chain by adding physical retail stores (Enders & Jelassi, 2000).

3. RESEARCH METHODOLOGY

This research is a descriptive study to identify some of the factors that contribute to Irish retailers using e-business successfully. In order to assess to what extent the on-line presences were successful three measures along the customer-purchasing model were chosen – Browsing, request for information and purchase. These measures were assessed as follows: (1) the number of hits per week to the website, (2) sales leads generated as a result of the website and (3) turnover generated directly from the website.

These success measures were used to test two proposed hypotheses:

H1: Organisational factors influence the success of the web site.

- H1a: Early adopters are more successful
- H1b: Organisations with higher levels of IS/IT expertise are more successful
- H1c: Organisations with an e-business strategy are more successful
- H1d: Organisations who have a web champion are more successful
- H1e: Organisations who engage in planning are more successful
- H1f: Organisations who spend more on the development of their web site are more successful

H2: Retail specific factors influence the success of the web site.

- H2a: The characteristics of the products being sold influence the degree of success achieved

H2b: Organisations with larger online product catalogues are more successful

H2c: Organisations with an integrated "clicks and bricks" strategy are more successful.

The primary research was conducted by a postal survey. The sampling frame used was that of companies registered to any of fifteen Irish web directories under the categories 'gifts' or 'arts & crafts'. Gifts are defined as items given as presents or articles suitable for presents. Arts and crafts are defined as products created using a particular skill and sold as gifts or products for personal use. The main areas of manufacturing in the Irish craft industry are pottery, glass, textiles (particularly knitwear), furniture, and quality giftware. Irish craft businesses are typically small in scale and are geographically widespread, but taken nationally the industry is a significant employer. Each website was visited to ensure that the company sells online.

The questionnaire was mailed to 280 companies along with a personally addressed covering letter to the relevant person in the company. Of the 280 questionnaires mailed, 122 were returned for a response rate of 43.5%. Of these 122, 44 were returned after a second mailing of the questionnaire was sent to companies who had not responded after two weeks.

Non-response bias was assessed by treating responses received after the deadline given (two weeks after the first mailing of the questionnaire) as being representative of non-respondents. Chi-Square significance tests were used to test for significant differences between the first respondents and the late respondents in the study. The early and late respondents did not differ significantly (at $p < .05$) on the measures of success (hits, revenues, and sales leads) and the other variables tested including e-business strategy, web champion, IS/IT expertise and product characteristics.

The results of the questionnaires were analysed using SPSS version 10.1. The responses were first analysed using statistical measures such as means, standard deviations and frequencies. For more advanced statistics, the Chi-square test for independent samples was used. The chosen level of confidence for the research was $\alpha = .05$.

4. PROFILE OF ORGANISATIONS

The majority of companies have been in business for more than 8 years (58.5%), with only 4% of companies being in business for less than 1 year. The organisations surveyed are early adopters of e-business within their industry – only 17% believe that their competitors adopted e-business before them. In addition, the majority developed a website on their own initiative and not as the result of any outside pressure. Not only have these firms adopted e-business, but the majority (81%) are also generating revenue directly through their web site.

The main reasons for getting involved in e-business were to acquire new customers (93%), to gain international exposure (90%), to advertise (79%), to overcome the company's location disadvantage (60%), to provide online customer support (59%), to gain cost savings (41%) and to gather customer information (31%). As such, the main motivator for e-business adoption was as a sales mechanism rather than as a means to cut costs, or improve business processes.

The expectations of companies with respect to sales and competitiveness have been realised for the majority of the companies. 79% believe it has created new business, 68% believe it gives them a competitive edge, 62% have increased their sales in export markets. With respect to cost savings and business process improvements only 39% believe that e-business speeds up the delivery of their product and 35% believe that it has resulted in substantial cost saving.

The use of e-business is changing the industry structure within which these firms operate. Firstly, it is increasing competition within the industry (only 17% believe it is not), and secondly it is giving rise to dis-intermediation – 40% have cut out intermediaries in the sales process and e-business has allowed 84% of companies to sell directly to their final customers.

4.1 Metrics of success

75% of firms are receiving between 1 and 500 hits to their website per week, (with 26% receiving less than 50 hits per week, 26% receiving between 101-500 hits per week and the remaining 23% receiving between 50-100) (Figure 1). Of the 25% who received more than 500 hits per week, 8% receive more than 5,000 hits per week.

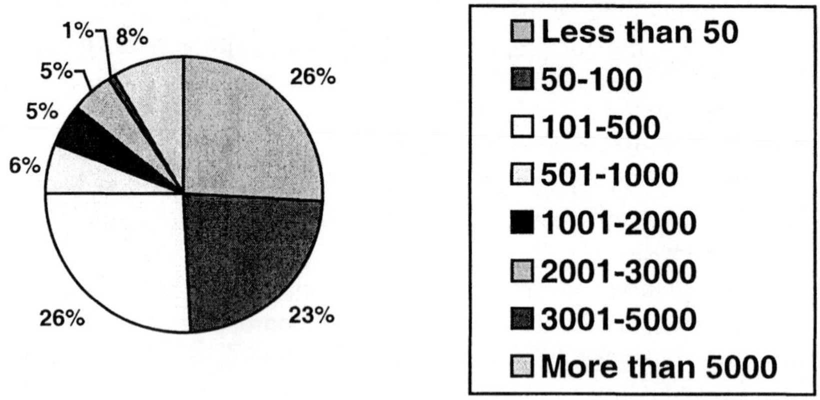

Figure 1. Number of Hits per Week

Nearly half of the respondents (49%) believe that 1-20% of sales leads are generated as a result of the website, while a further 12% consider that 21-40% of sales leads are generated as a result of the website (Table 1). Another 21% of companies believe that anywhere between 41% and 100% of sales leads are generated as a result of their Internet presence. However, 17% of respondents thought that none of their sales leads were generated through the website.

% of Sales Leads Generated from Website	% of Companies
0%	17%
1-20%	49%
21-40%	12%
41-60%	6%
61-80%	3%
81-100%	6%
Don't Know	7%

Table 1. % of Sales Leads Generated from Website

The third measure of success is turnover generated by the website. A small percentage of firms (8%) are generating between 81-100% of their revenue from the website (Figure 2). A further 9% are generating between 21% and 80% of revenues from their website. However, most companies (64%) are only generating between 1 and 20% of revenues from the website. Despite these promising figures, a further 20% of companies are generating no revenue at all from their website.

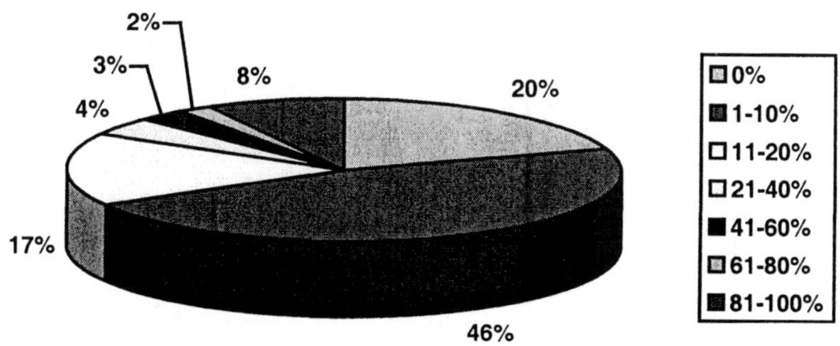

Figure 2. % of Annual Turnover Generated by Web site

5. FINDINGS

The study found that significant relationships do exist between some of the organisational factors hypothesised and the web site success measures. The extent and the nature of these relationships are presented in Tables 2 and 4.

Organisational Drivers of web site success	Number of Hits per week		Number of Sales leads generated		Amount of revenue generated	
	Chi Square	Cramer's V	Chi Square	Cramer's V	Chi Square	Cramer's V
1st Mover Advantage						
Length of time on WWW	.005	.005	.005	.005		
Exploit before competitors	.011	.011	.006	.006		
IS/IT Experience						
Level of IS/IT	.003	.003	.007	.007		

expertise						
E-business Strategy						
Formal e-business strategy	.000	.000	.025	.025		
Integrated e-business strategy	.000	.000	.025	.026		
Champion						
Leader of e-business project	.000	.000				
Planning of Website						
Security of customer information	.012	.012				
Security of payment						
Ease of Navigation			.006	.006		
Ease of use of checkout	.032	.032				
Minimising customer effort in the purchase process			.025	.025		
Full Product Catalogue					.005	.005
Uses customer profiles to anticipate future needs			.022	.022		
Development Costs						
Money spent developing Web						

Table 2. Organisational drivers of web site success

5.1 Organisational drivers of web site success

Two metrics were used to assess the extent to which firms were early-adopters of web technology – years using the web, and extent to which they believe they were early adopters of the technology. Companies who adopted e-commerce early gain significantly more hits, and sales leads. However, these hits and sales leads do not turn into significantly more online revenue.

The majority of the firms (55%) believe that they exploited the capabilities of the Internet before their competitors. The early exploiters of the web gain significantly more hits and sales leads, however these are not converted into hard cash in terms of online sales. Early adopters are reaping rewards in terms of visitors to their site and subsequent sales enquiries but these are not being converted online.

The research examined whether there was a difference in how successful a company was depending on the level of IS/IT expertise in the company. 12% of the companies surveyed have an excellent level of IS/IT expertise in their organisation, 38% have above average levels of IS/IT expertise. 32% cited an average level of expertise with the remaining 13% and 5% falling into the below average and poor categories respectively. Those with better IS/IT expertise were significantly more successful in terms of hits and sales leads generated, but not in online sales.

The extent to which an e-business strategy had a positive outcome on success was assessed using two measures – the extent to which a formal e-business strategy existed and how well this e-strategy was integrated into the business strategy. 54% of firms have an e-business strategy in place while the remaining 46% do not have an e-business strategy. The results show a significant relationship exists between the existence of an e-business strategy and both the number of hits and the amount of sales leads generated. However, no statistical significance to on-line turnover was found.

56% have integrated e-business and business strategies, while 17% do not have. Having integrated strategies results in significantly more hits and generates more sales leads, but not online revenue. Thus there is partial support for the idea that an e-business strategy leads to a more successful e-business.

78% of companies have a person who leads the e-business project in their company. Having such a champion significantly improves the number of hits that a site generates, but does not bring significant benefits in the other two success measures – sales leads generated and online revenue.

The research investigated the extent to which firms engaged in planning prior to launching their web site. The majority of firms actively pre-planned their web presence. However, such planning only has a limited impact on the success of the website. Attending to the needs of customers in terms of securing their information and making it easy for them to use the shopping cart facilities improves the number of hits, but not the amount of revenue generated.

When planning the design of the website, the following were considered important	Strongly Disagree	Dis-agree	Neutral	Agree	Strongly Agree
Security of customer information	3%	6%	24%	27%	41%
Security of payment	4%	3%	17%	24%	53%
Ease of navigation	1%	2%	6%	30%	62%
Site search facilities	2%	9%	28%	28%	34%
Ease of use of checkout facilities	3%	3%	23%	38%	33%
Minimising effort in the purchase process	1%	3%	17%	27%	51%
Full online product catalogue	1%	7%	17%	40%	35%
Interactive features	39%	27%	24%	4%	4%
Detailed company information	6%	3%	27%	44%	20%
Projection of a favourable corporate image	3%	2%	12%	36%	47%

Table 3. Planning Issues undertaken during Web design

Making the site easy to navigate and minimising the effort to complete a purchase increases the number of sales leads, but again not revenues generated. The only planning element that does significantly improve the revenue generating capabilities of the site is deciding to put the full product catalogue of the company on-line from the beginning.

Some firms also continue the planning process once the web-site is live. 43% use the customer profiles generated from the website to anticipate future needs and requirements of customers. Those who engage in this activity are significantly more likely to generate increased sales leads from their e-business activity. As such, proactive management of customer information obtained via the web site can yield successful results in terms of providing a more customised and focused product offering.

59% of companies spent between £1 - £5,000 developing their website, a further 22% spent between £5,001 - £10,000, while another 14% spent between £10,001 - £50,000 and 5% spent more than £50,000 developing their website. The amount of money that a company spends on its web site is not significantly related to any of the measures of success.

5.2 Retail specific drivers of web site success

Part of this research sought to assess the extent to which certain traits unique to retail impacted on the success of a web site. In particular the significance of the products' characteristics, the number of products for sale and the extent of integration between bricks and clicks was assessed.

Retail specific factors of web site success	Number of Hits per week		Number of Sales leads generated		Amount of revenue generated	
	Chi Square	Cramer's V	Chi Square	Cramer's V	Chi Square	Cramer's V
Product Characteristics						
Easy to ship						
Largely information-based						
Small value item						
Little need for touch/feel						
Customised to individual needs						
Clicks & Bricks						
Webstore that complements other channels			.003	.003		
Retail outlets as the key to acquiring customers			.044	.044	.014	.014
Products						
Amount of products for sale on the website						

Table 4. Retail specific factors of web site success

The results show no statistical significance between any of the characteristics of the products being sold on-line and the measures of success. 65% of companies have a product that is easy to ship. However, this fact does not result in higher revenues, a higher number of hits or a higher number of sales leads. Also, even though the literature presents one of the main advantages of online selling as the ability to customise products, there is no significance between customisable products and any of the three success measures, despite the fact that 42.4% of companies sell products that are customisable to individual customer needs. The other characteristics - small value item, little need for touch/feel and largely information based - also had no significant impact on the success measures for on-line retailing.

Product Characteristics	Strongly Disagree	Disagree	Neutral	Agree	Strongly Agree
Easy to ship	5%	5.9%	23.5%	34.5%	31.1%
Largely Information based	34.5%	25.2%	27.7%	10.1%	2.5%
Small Value Item	16.8%	21%	28.6%	21%	12.6%
Little need for touch/feel to evaluate product	12.6%	21.8%	30.3%	21.8%	13.4%
Customised to individual needs	11.8%	17.6%	20.2%	21.8%	20.6%

Table 5. Characteristics of products being sold online

21% of the companies surveyed had more than 100 products available on their website, with a further 21% offering between 50 and 100 products. The breadth of the product offering on a web site did not influence its success – no significant relationship was found in respect of any of the measures of success.

The majority of the companies use multiple sales channels to sell their products with only 11.5% selling exclusively on the Internet. Other outlets used include retail outlets (70%), mail order (50%) and 3rd party sellers (27%). The companies are export focused - 37% have exports that account for in excess of 40% of their annual turnover. The web site is seen as a complementary sales channel for the majority of companies (62%). Those who use the web as a complementary sales channel gain significantly more sales leads from their e-business presence. At a more specific level, 43% of companies believe that retail outlets are the key to acquiring new customers (26% believe the are not). Companies who believe that they are presently dependent on retail outlets for new sales generate significantly more sales leads and on-line revenue from their web site.

6. CONCLUSIONS AND FURTHER RESEARCH

The presence of specific organisational factors – early adoption of web technology, internal IS/IT expertise, having an e-business strategy, and a person who champions the e-business project – results in more successful e-business presences. In particular the extent to which these organisational factors are present greatly improves the degree to which customers seek information from, and enquire about products on a retailer's web site. However, these same organisational factors do not significantly impact the amount of sales completed online. This however may be due to the fact that customers are using retail websites to gather information, but still prefer to complete the transaction in a physical store. Support for this interpretation is provided in that 75% of firms see their web site as a source of sales leads.

It is a commonly held belief that certain product types are more likely to be successful on the web – this study found no evidence to support this view point. In addition, the number of products on offer through the web site is not a good predictor of the likely success of the web site. The extent to which a retail company integrates its web presence with its physical presence is likely to produce significant success for the web site in terms of sales leads generated and online revenues.

This study was descriptive in nature and also limited in scope. Further research is required to further investigate the conclusions drawn in this research. In particular, there is a need to replicate the study using a wider, or alternative, population sample as this study was confined to Irish retail organisations that sell giftware on-line.

The web site success measures presented in this paper could be broadened and developed in future research. For example, other measures of success that could be incorporated into future studies include customer loyalty, customer satisfaction and cost reductions achieved.

REFERENCES

Anonymous (2000). Shopping around the Web - A Survey of E-commerce. The Economist.

Barry, J. (2000). Avoid the pitfalls of going from bricks to clicks. Internetweek. 796: 19-20.

Bergstein, M. (2000). Digital Strategies - Look before you leap, Diamond technology partners.

Berman, B. and J. R. Evans (1994). Retail Management: A Strategic Approach, Prentice Hall.

Bhatnagar, A., S. Misra, et al. (2000). "Why some consumers are online shoppers while others are not." Communications of the ACM 43(11): 98-106.

Chan, C. and P. M. C. Swatman (2000). "From EDI to Internet commerce: the BHP Steel experience." Internet Research-Electronic Networking Applications and Policy 10(1): 72-82.

Chen, S. and F. Leteney (2000). "Get Real! Managing the Next stage of Internet Retail." European Management Journal 18(5): 519-528.

Christensen, C. M. and R. S. Tedlow (2000). "Patterns of Disruption in Retailing." Harvard Business Review 78(1): 42-48.

De Figueiredo, J. M. (2000). "Finding Sustainable Profitability in E-commerce." Sloan Management review Summer 2000: 41-52.

Enders, A. and T. Jelassi (2000). "The Converging Business models of Internet and Bricks and Clicks Retailers." European Management Journal 18(5): 542-55-.

Golder, P. N. and G. J. Tellis (1993). "Pioneer Advantage - Marketing Logic or Marketing Legend." Journal of Marketing Research 30(2): 158-170.

Griffith, D. A. and R. F. Krampf (1998). "An examination of web-based strategies of the Top 100 US retailers." Journal of Marketing Thoery & Practice Summer 1998: 12-20.

Griffith, D. A. and J. L. Palmer (1999). "Leveraging the Web for Corporate Success." Business Horizons Jan/Feb 1999: 3-10.

Gulati, R. and J. Garino (2000). "Get the right mix of bricks and clicks." Harvard Business Review 78(3): 107-114.

Hackbarth, G. and W. J. Kettinger (2000). "Building an E-Business Strategy." Information Systems Management(Summer 2000): 78-93.

Kerin, R. A., P. R. Varadarajan, et al. (1992). "1st-Mover Advantage - a Synthesis, Conceptual-Framework, and Research Propositions." Journal of Marketing 56(4): 33-52.

Kiang, M. Y., T. S. Raghu, et al. (2000). "Marketing on the Internet - who can benefit from an online marketing approach?" Decision Support Systems 27: 383-393.

Lindquist, J. D. (1975). "Meaning of Image." Journal of Retailing 50(4): 29-38.

Mellahi, K. and M. Johnson (2000). "Does it pay to be a first mover in e-commerce? The case of Amazon.com." Management Decision 38(7): 445-452.

Ng, H.-I., Y. J. Pan, et al. (1998). "Business Use of the World Wide Web: A report on further investigations." International Journal of Information Management 18(5): 291-314.

Peterson, R., S. Balasubramanian, et al. (1997). "Exploring the implications of the Internet for Consumer Marketing." Journal of Academy of Marketing Science 25(4): 329-346.

Phau, I. and S.-M. Poon (2000). "Factors influencing the type of product/services purchased over the Internet." Internet Research 10(2): 102-113.

Quinn, C. (1999). "How Leading edge E-commerce companies are marketing, selling and fulfilling over the Internet." Journal of Interactive Marketing 13(4): 39-50.

Reardon, J. and R. Hasty (1997). Retail Management, McGraw-Hill.

Savin, J. and D. Silberg (2000). "There's more to e-business than point and click." The Journal of Business Strategy 21(5): 11-13.

Schuette, D. (2000). "Turning E-Business barriers into strengths." Information Systems Management Fall 2000: 20-25.

Spiller, P. and G. L. Lohse (1997). "A Classification of Internet Retail Stores." International Journal of Electronic Commerce 2(2): 29-56.

Venkatraman, N. (2000). "Five steps to a Dot-Com strategy: how to find your footing on the Web." Sloan Management Review 41(3): 15-29.

Walsh, J. and S. Godfrey (2000). "The Internet: A new era in customer service." European Management Journal 18(1): 85-92.

GOVERNANCE FOR E-BUSINESS KNOWLEDGE MANAGEMENT SYSTEMS

RODGER JAMIESON
SEAR – Security E-Business Assurance Research Group, School of Information Systems Technology and Management, University of New South Wales, Australia

Abstract: When introducing E-Business Knowledge Management (EBKM) systems into organisations, management should carefully assess the risks and threats to these systems to ensure that they are well-secured and controllable and do not leave the organisation exposed to unwanted litigation or adverse publicity. This paper addresses this concern by raising IT governance risk issues and suggesting security and control features that may be put in place to protect both the EBKM systems and the organisation. The paper also addresses research in progress in this area, namely, to gather details of risks and controls via a survey and to undertake a case study of an organisation with a mature EBKM strategy which has considered the risks, security and controls for KM.

1. INTRODUCTION

E-business systems are increasingly being deployed throughout organisations. Knowledge is an extremely valuable resource which allows organizations to share knowledge amongst its employees and customers and often forms part of e-business systems. Knowledge management (KM) is a "...multi-disciplined approach to achieving organisational objectives by making the best use of knowledge." (Standards Australia HB275-2001). KM is also defined as "...a broad collection of organisational practices and approaches to generating, capturing, disseminating know-how and other content relevant to the organisation's business". (Stephen Denning, World Bank 2001).

Organizations operate in a fragile world and are subject to natural disasters, terrorism, cyber terrorism, e-crime, and a range of other threats to its information and knowledge resources and systems (CSI, 2001). Unfortunately there are risks and consequences associated with knowledge management systems, which if not adequately controlled and audited, and may breach privacy concerns and legislation. In order to protect knowledge assets from these threats, organizations should put in place appropriate security and control measures to counter these threats. The management process involved in considering threats and appropriate security measures is called risk management. This paper addresses these issues and provides a framework and guidelines for management to provide assurance over their EBKM systems.

The paper will first consider the senior management viewpoint from a risk management perspective. The risks security and control mechanisms involved in EBKM will be outlined using the knowledge management framework provided by Standards Australia. The paper will also consider privacy issues related to the capture and use of knowledge in an organization's knowledge management systems. Finally the paper will address the research in progress to gather details of risks and controls via a survey and to undertake a case study of an organisation with a mature KM strategy which has considered the risks security and controls for EBKM.

2. RESEARCH OBJECTIVES

The objectives of this research are to:

- understand risk management as it applies to knowledge management;
- identify risks associated with knowledge management;
- identify security and controls that may assist in preventing, detecting or correcting the risks associated with knowledge management; and
- understand the implications of privacy legislation to knowledge management systems and repositories.

In order to achieve these objectives the research will undertake a survey of knowledge management within organisations from a risk management perspective. In addition, detailed case studies will be undertaken with organisations having a mature KM environment in order to understand their methods of controlling risks within the KM environment.

3. THEORETICAL BACKGROUND – RISK MANAGEMENT

Strategically, it is important to ensure that knowledge management is an issue that is being considered by the corporate and IT governance committees. Knowledge management governance should ensure that the objectives of knowledge management are part of the strategic planning process and both the corporate and IT strategic planning levels. When considering the key issues of EBKM security, controls, and audit assurance of KM infrastructure and systems, it is important that a risk management strategy be considered and that the internal and external IT auditors and security personnel be consulted in this process. These personnel will be able to provide advice on identifying risks and abuses within EBKM systems, and helped to place appropriate security and controls to help mitigate these risks and threats. Guidance in this area may also be found from the IT Governance Institute in their document on Information Security Governance (IT Governance Institute, 2001).

Before discussing risk management in detail we will consider the different framework and models of knowledge management and then investigate whether risk management is considered as part of these frameworks. Holsapple and Singh (2000) consider that there is a need for KM frameworks that will provide researchers with a holistic view, common ground, consistent terminology and units of analysis across a variety of research settings. Earl (2001) argues that practitioners need frameworks so that they can understand both KM initiatives and investments that are possible and identify those that make sense and are feasible. A review of the literature revealed a number of KM models or frameworks for systems development. These include knowledge management models in the KM review by McAdam and McCreedy (1999) distinguishing between knowledge categories models, intellectual capital models and socially constructed models of KM. Another taxonomy of KM strategies is provided by Earl (2001) who identifies three schools – technocratic, economic and behavioural, which are very similar is essence to the categorisation of McAdam and McCreedy. Alvi and Leidner (2001) classify six knowledge perspectives and ten knowledge types or categories and then proceed to discuss the knowledge processes of knowledge creation, storage and retrieval, transfer, application and the enabling role of IT is KM activities. Their contribution is to focus on knowledge processes and enablers and considers the concept of a knowledge life cycle. Handzic and Hasan (2002) provide a further review of knowledge frameworks by adapting the work of Handzic (2001) which extends the intial work by Handzic and Jamieson

(2001). They propose an integrated KM framework (refer figure covering organisational environment, technological infrastructure, knowledge processes, organisational knowledge and knowledge measurement.

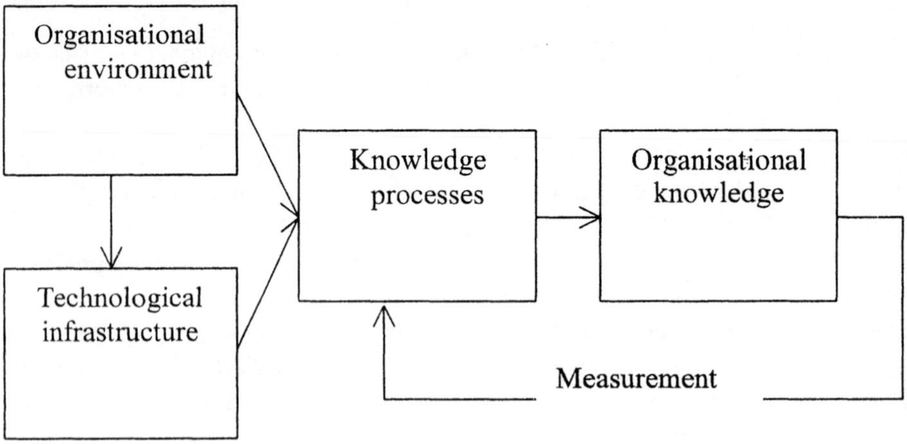

Figure 1. An Integrated KM Framework (Handzic, 2002)

Various authors Nonaka (1991), Ruggles (1997), Angus et al. (1998), Jackson (1999), Wensley (2000), Tyndale (2001), Robinson et al. (2001), have also suggested frameworks or models for knowledge development. These are compared in Table 1. The problem with all of these frameworks is that they do not explicitly discuss risk management as an important component of the KM development process.

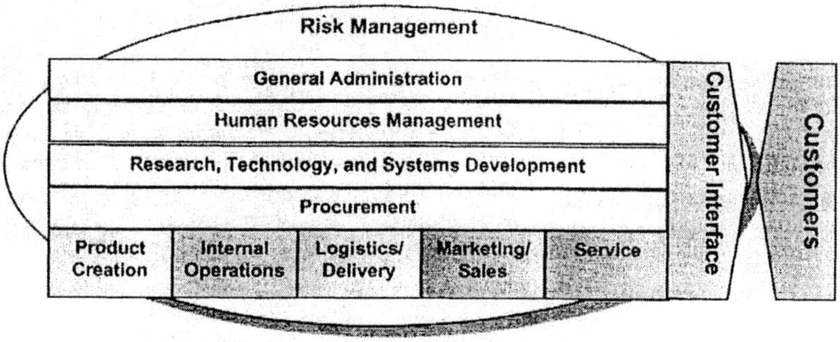

Figure 2. Risk Inherent in the Banking Industry using Porter's (1995) Value Chain

Source Ribiere, V. & C Chou (2001)

Phase	One	Two	Three	Four	Five
Nonaka's KM Model (1991)	**Socialisation**	**Externalisation**	**Combination**	**Internalisation**	
Ruggles (1997)	**Generation** Acquisition Synthesis Creation Fusion Adaption	**Codification** Auditing Categorisation	**Transfer** Face-to-Face Collaboration Dissemination		
Angus et al. (1998)	**Gathering** Pull Searching Data Entry	**Organising** Cataloguing Filtering Linking Indexing	**Refining** Contextualising Mining Projecting Compacting Collaborating	**Disseminating** Flow Push Sharing Notify	
Jackson (1999)	**Gathering** Pull Searching Data Entry / OCR	**Storage** Filtering Linking Indexing	**Communicat'n** Sharing Collaboration Group discussion	**Synthesis** Analysis Creation Contextua-lisation	**Dissemination** Push Publishing Notification
Wensley (2000)	**Generation** Communication Culture Barriers	**Codification** Conceptual analysis Rules	**Refinement** Rule deduction Filtering Classification	**Transmission** Assimilation Face-to-Face	
Tyndale 2001	**Creation** Capture	**Organisation** Interpretation	**Distribution** Publishing	**Application** Process	

KDLCM	Generation Gathering Absorption Assimilation	Filtering Codification Categorisation Amalgation	Face-to-Face Dissemination Transmission	Change Revise Amendment Review	
McGrath & Walsh (2001)	**Acquisition**	**Codification / Storage**	**Dissemination / Fabrication**	**Application / Use**	'based on Martensson (2000)
Robinson et al. (2001) IMPaKT	**Define Business Goals** Identify business & improvement measures	**Assess Implic'ns for Orgn K-Base** Indentify existing K Determin K gap Develop KM initiatives	**Assess Impact** Assess results product Asses performance		
Aust Std HB275-2001	**Knowledge Alignment** Context Analysis Planning	**Knowledge Processes** Sharing Acquisition Creating	**Knowledge Foundations** Culture Technology Sustaining Systems		

Table 1. Comparison of KM Frameworks
(Adapted from Tyndale (2001) p 668)

Ribiere and Chou (2001) do discuss risk management as background to their discussion of KM in the banking environment (refer Figure 2) but do so by suggesting that KM could help the risk management process via the use of knowledge maps rather than the KM using risk management as a technique. However, they do mention that trust and confidence are essential elements in banking and that by implementing KM, banks may be able to strengthen the trust and confidence factor that results from solid customer relationships, and use KM as a strategy for customer retention and acquisition. The problem is that trust may be broken quite easily in KM systems that are not well protected and this may lead to lack of confidence and customer loss – hence the importance of risk management for KM. While identifying where KM can assist risk management Ribiere and Chou (2001) miss the opportunity to see the benefits that risk management might offer to KM.

Standards Australia provides a Framework for KM and refers to risk management in relation to Establishing Priorities and Sustaining Systems for Knowledge Management (Standards Australia International, HB275-2001, 2001: refer section 3.2.1b p13-15; section 5.3.1 p47; and Appendix C p53-54). Standards Australia sees risk areas involving:

- Project
- Strategy (Alignment)

- Process
- Foundations

However, risk management is broader than this and should also refer to identifying risks, security and controls for EBKM infrastructure and systems. The use of the Risk Management Standard AS/NZS4360 (Standards Australia, 1999) should also be considered by the IT governance committee. This risk management process is shown in Figure 3. The IT governance committee needs to appoint persons to carry out this risk management process. We suggest the Chief knowledge Officer of the organization together with the IT internal auditor/security officer are appropriate persons to carry out this task. IT audit standards (ISACF, COBiT 3rd Edition, 2000) and the IT governance framework developed by the IT Governance Institute (ISACF, K-Net, 2001) should also provide guidance in this area.

The KM risk management team should firstly identifying the KM assets (including personnel, systems, infrastructure and networks, locations) and then identifying risks associated with these assets. The next phase involves identifying existing controls and security measures over these assets and then analysing the risks by determining the likelihood, consequence and level of the risks. The risks are then evaluated and prioritised, and an action plan drawn up to implement the recommendations for additional KM security and control measures to counter or mitigate the identified KM risks. For some KM risks, management may accept the risk, thereby self-insuring against that risk. During this process it is important to communicate with management and staff involved in KM about the findings from the risk management process, and solicit from them suggestions for improving KM security and controls. This process is not just carried out once and then forgotten, but should be monitored and reviewed on a continuing basis by the KM governance committee.

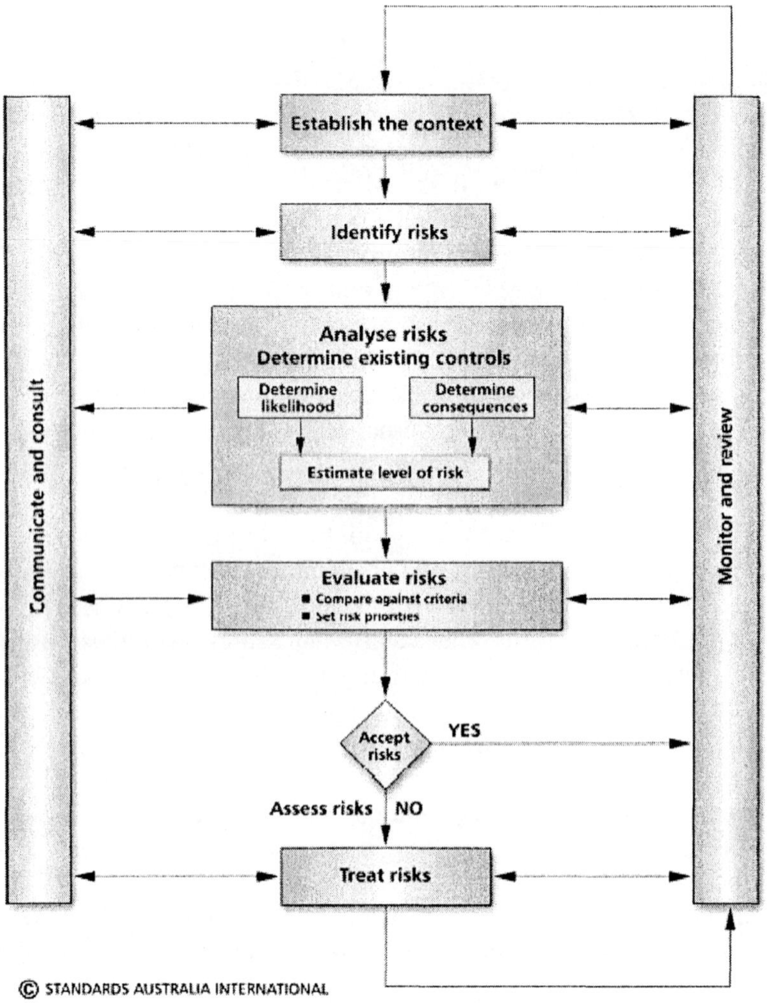

Figure 3. The Risk Management Process

Source: Standards Australia International, 2001, p14

Details of EBKM security and control mechanisms will be covered later in the paper.

The IT governance committee will also need to consider which KM technologies will be employed throughout the organization. EBKM Technologies include:

- retrieval engines,
- content management,
- document and records management,

- learning systems,
- automatic classification systems – neural networks, linguistic or semantic processing systems,
- intelligent technologies – AI, regression & correction, expert systems, case-based reasoning, data and text mining, rule-based systems, and
- archiving.
- Each of these technologies has their own risks and associated security and controls mechanisms. However, these technologies need to be considered in light of a knowledge management framework and are just one part of the knowledge foundations required to support the knowledge processes within an organization. To illustrate, standards Australia has formulated a knowledge management framework to guide practitioners setting up knowledge management within their organizations. Such a framework is depicted in Figure 4.

3.1 Risks within EBKM

The joint Computer Security Institute and the FBI Computer Crime and Security Survey (CSI, 2001) provide details of the types of risks, security breaches and attacks that organizations are facing in today's turbulent environment. Table 2 provides a selection of risks in the EBKM environment that need to be taken into account by management, security and auditor personnel - refer Jamieson and Handzic, (2002).

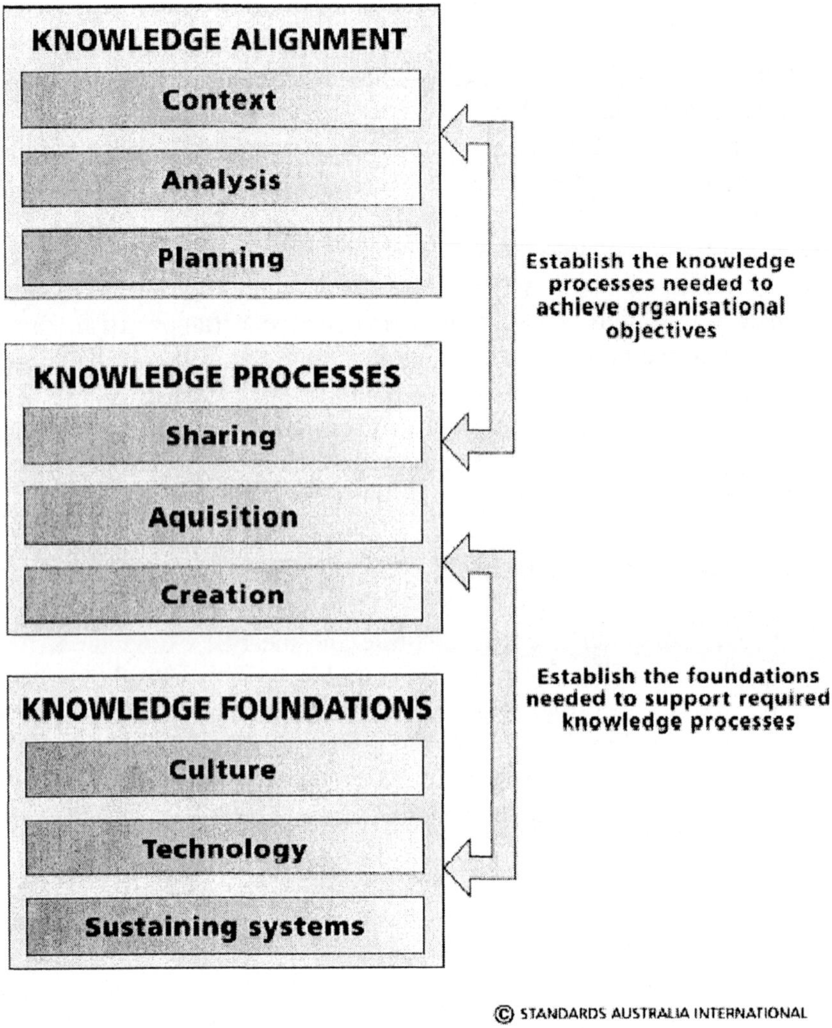

Figure 4. Knowledge Mangement Framework (Standards Australia International, 2001, p5)

Risks, Security/Controls, and Privacy

Selection of Risks within EBKM	
Strategic/Planning	mismatch of EBKM strategy to corporate and IT strategies unidentified or excessive costs especially maintenance and support overlooked essential EBKM functionality
Accidental or intentional	damage loss modification destruction use to/of specialized EBKM or traditional IT hardware used to run EBKM systems, EBKM software, knowledge repositories, as well as feeder software and associated data bases. Loss or incapacitation of key EBKM experts, knowledge engineers, programmers, or knowledge maintenance personnel, is also of concern.
Fraud and computer abuse	substitution/deletion of knowledge repositories obscure placement of forward chaining demons within the knowledge base if expert systems or knowledge based systems are part of the EBKM systems unauthorised access to EBKM systems or EBKM management/audit trails modification, deletion or insertion of EBKM information when passing through a network, communications or other layers of operating or support software such as data warehousing. This includes other application software when linked or integrated with EBKM systems.
Other Exposures	inability of imbedded EBKM software to recover/restart EBKM hardware, infrastructure or software failure - especially real-time monitoring or imbedded systems lack of knowledge use histories (audit trails) in hardcopy and/or magnetic/optical form inadequate trace facilities in EBKM/KB software for debugging and EBKM/KB testing EBKM systems knowledge not based on best expert's knowledge, reasoning, and explanations Inadequate control of and access to EBKM repositories poor quantity or quality of EBKM personnel poor management, supervision and control of the EBKM application and repositories if held elsewhere to IT department, eg. under R & D inadequate training and supervision of EBKM personnel inadequate EBKM hardware/software maintenance legal liability for reliance on EBKM opinion when that opinion caused loss of life, damage or monetary loss inadequate EBKM documentation of tools, environment and applications

Table 2. Selection of Risks in the EBKM Environment

As well as these risks EBKM management should be cognisant of the security and control considerations applicable to the EBKM environment.

3.2 Security and Controls for EBKM

Holsapple and Joshi (2000) provide an investigation of factors that influence the management of knowledge in organizations. One of the managerial influences on EBKM is *control* which involves two critical issues of protection and quality of the knowledge resources. They believe that the protection of knowledge resources from "... loss, obsolescence, unauthorized exposure, unauthorized modification, and erroneous assimilation is crucial for the effective management of knowledge"(Holsapple and Joshi, 2000, p240). They argue that management needs to consider knowledge validity (accuracy, consistency and certainty) and knowledge utility (clarity, meaning, relevance and importance) when establishing sufficient controls to govern knowledge quality. The security and controls discussed in this paper are concerned with knowledge validity. Considerations associated with operational EBKM systems are presented below and are summarized in Table 3 – refer Jamieson and Handzic, (2002).

Selection of Security and Controls in the EBKM Environment	
EBKM Hardware :	Sensitive knowledge access: key locked equipment restricted/controlled boot up procedures biometric access controls encryption provisions Up-to-date documentation Regular audits of EBKM equipment Logging and follow-up of all reported faults EBKM back-up: strategy equipment EBKM maintenance: diagnostic aids documentation EBKM environmental considerations: uninterrupted power supplies or voltage regulators air conditioners physical protection barriers to restrict physical access Security infrastructure

EBKM Software	Automated procedures for EBKM access control Valid software license agreements Up-to-date documentation EBKM software integrity checks Appropriate EBKM maintenance strategy EBKM software upgrade controls Logging and follow-up of all reported software faults EBKM repository encryption EBKM explanation facilities if using expert systems or KBS: HOW facilities WHY facilities Help facilities EBKM repository integrity checking Restricted screen/report output and knowledge document delivery Separate development and run time versions Graphical layouts of EBKM repository Cross reference listings Knowledge dictionary or thesaurus maintenance access and controls Knowledge use trace facilities Knowledge use or consultation case history maintenance if KBS Audit trail logging of all activity Certified by major consulting/accounting firm
EBKM Development	EBKM development methodology followed Separate EBKM development from production EBKM Appropriate design documentation Validation and testing of EBKM systems Quality assurance/control review Auditor involvement in EBKM development reviews Separate development and production EBKM source libraries Separate development and run time versions of EBKM software
EBKM Applications	Systems access security (password as minimum) & strong authentication Smart Cards Secure Client (IPSec) Digital Certificates Correct option setting for run time versions Edit facilities for data input Knowledge repositories/KB encryption Reasonableness checks Output review by competent EBKM personnel Hardcopy or magnetic/optical collection of case histories Management/audit review of audit trails Good application documentation Unauthorised copying protection Back-up and recovery

EBKM Network Controls	Internet, Extranet or Intranet access controls Virtual Private networks (VPN's) – site to site VPN Gateway Transmission encryption of Knowledge in transit Public Key Infrastructure (PKI) Dedicated connections Firewalls
EBKM Human Resources	Management commitment to EBKM strategy Assign responsibility for: EBKM development EBKM production operations EBKM disaster planning Adequate training of EBKM personnel Supervision and management of EBKM personnel EBKM Information Centre Segregation of duties Mandatory vacations Personnel security checks Maintenance supplier vetting

Table 3. Selection of Security and Controls in the EBKM Environment

An example of security and control concerns is provided in the following section in relation to knowledge repositories.

3.3 Security and Control Concerns with Knowledge Repositories

There are a number problems associated with knowledge repositories. One of problems involves where the knowledge repositories are located and who is responsible for them and their security. If the knowledge repositories are controlled in the same way as corporate databases, then they may fall under the security that is given to all other major IT systems. However, if the knowledge repositories are located within an end user environment on a knowledge server then these systems may not be well controlled. As a result, knowledge management systems may have no systems access security, inadequate monitoring, and lack of adequate backup and recovery procedures and facilities. If this is the case then management may need to review the security over these knowledge management systems and apply the same procedures as they would over their corporate IT systems. With knowledge repositories we need to ask questions as to who is responsible for placing documents within the repository, how is access to these documents controlled, and who is responsible for the disposal of the documents for disposal.

Some organisations have setup knowledge centres within the various divisions of their organisation. These knowledge centres are responsible for the addition, maintenance and review of documents placed within the knowledge repositories. These knowledge centres should also be responsible for the security and accuracy of information and knowledge that is placed within the repositories. Personnel in these knowledge centres should also be responsible for the setting up and maintenance of the knowledge dictionary or thesaurus for the organisation. The knowledge dictionary is very important to the organisation as it holds the key to accessing the many documents held within knowledge repositories. Knowledge held in documents within the knowledge repository is indexed and accessed by the terms within the knowledge dictionary. Therefore, protection over the knowledge dictionary is equally as vital as security over knowledge repositories. A person having access to the knowledge dictionary in a covert or incompetent manner may in fact intentionally or accidentally destroy or corrupt key terms within the knowledge dictionary. They may in fact destroy the whole knowledge dictionary or substitute another in its place. Rebuilding of the knowledge dictionary may in fact take person days of effort and in fact may be impossible to reconstruct, thereby causing the organisation significant losses due to the inability to access documents within the knowledge repositories.

Another concern is with the knowledge held within the knowledge repositories. Firstly, how are documents held within the knowledge repositories, are they encrypted or held in a clear text form? Secondly, are all documents held in a form that cannot be altered, or are these documents in an open form so that many people within the organisation may have assess to substitute, modify or delete them. If the documents are held in an Acrobat PDF form, then document security features may be enabled that provides protection on features such as content accessibility, print, change, extract or copy, altering author comments and fields, and document assembly. Adobe Acrobat also provides password protection and encryption over the document and over the documents security features.

Three important concerns relating to security include confidentiality, integrity, and availability (IT Governance Institute, 2001). Confidentiality involves ensuring that the knowledge held remains confidential and is only used for the purposes to which that knowledge was collected. Confidentiality also implies that there may be degrees of confidentiality associated with a document. For example there may be three levels of confidentiality namely, open access, commercially in confidence, for management eyes only. These levels of confidentiality need to be carefully thought through by an organisation so that they come up with their own method of grading information and then allowing that information to be used, so that only authorised personnel within the organisation that have appropriate clearance will have access to the knowledge held at that level. Confidentiality relates closely to privacy concerns discussed in a later section.

Integrity is an issue fact may be overlooked by those responsible for the knowledge management system. Integrity of relates to be knowledge being held in the knowledge repositories current and correct overtime. Integrity implies that the knowledge in the knowledge repository will remain current and correct or accurate, overtime. This embodies the ideas of accuracy of the knowledge and also the currency of knowledge. In the knowledge management system a lack of accuracy or currency of knowledge held may involve the organisation in serious loss, damage to reputation, or severe financial exposure as a result of decisions made on the basis of that knowledge. Thus, it is important to audit the knowledge held within the knowledge repositories to ensure that that knowledge is current and correct overtime. Integrity also relates to the security of the knowledge held. If an unauthorised person has access to knowledge held within a document then they may substitute, modify or delete knowledge and therefore compromised the accuracy and integrity of the knowledge incorporated within the document.

Monitoring of knowledge use is also an important concern. It is important for an organisation to be able to track who has access the knowledge documents in the repository, when that document was accessed, what was done to the document during the access, and if tracked, what use was made of the knowledge. Many knowledge management systems may not have the auditing and monitoring facilities to allow this to be tracked and captured. Others may have the facility within the knowledge management system but this facility may not have been enabled. In other cases the logs from the monitoring system may not be kept for an appropriate length of time.

Availability of the knowledge repository is also an issue that needs to be addressed. It is of no use to have a knowledge repository that is unavailable to knowledge workers around the globe. This may arise through some unfortunate incident which may have destroyed the knowledge repository or prevented access to this repository. Examples may include an act of cyber terrorism or actual terrorism, accidental mishaps leading to the deletion of key knowledge repositories, or an attack that may render communication lines to the repository inoperative.

Availability requires that an organisation's knowledge infrastructure including communication lines, knowledge servers and knowledge systems are all operational and are securely protected from penetration. Should such a disaster occur, it is important that a fallback facility is pre-arranged so that the organisation may keep operating as usual after a disaster occurs, by switching to those fallback facilities. It is a must that key knowledge systems and associated knowledge repositories are backed up and held securely off-site. Many organisations are using electronic vaulting as one of their backup and recovery strategies.

3.4 Privacy

Zannes (2000) discusses the conflicts between security and knowledge sharing. In the act of knowledge sharing we may unwittingly compromise the privacy of the knowledge in the repositories. So, privacy is an important issue to address when discussing knowledge repositories. In many countries there are privacy legislation for both public and private sectors. Privacy legislation usually requires that an organisation informs all persons, from whom the organisation is soliciting knowledge or information which is going to end in a knowledge repository, of certain key privacy tenets affecting how the information or knowledge solicited from them will be used and retained in the knowledge repository. Contributors need to be informed of what information or knowledge is being captured in the first place and then informed as the use for which that information or knowledge will be used in the future. It is then the organisation's responsibility to monitor who has access to that knowledge, who maintains the knowledge, and how that knowledge is used a within the organisation. If there is open access to knowledge documents within the knowledge repository, this may seriously compromised centres criteria of privacy legislation within the organisation. For example, even when an organisation is capturing knowledge from persons using the World Wide Web then they may need to have a privacy statement on the Web for their knowledge management system that informs the users /contributors of the privacy conditions that will apply to knowledge being given. Breaches of privacy in EBKM systems may cause lack of trust by customers/contributors and even leave the organization open to legal liability.

Many countries either have privacy legislation or are currently implementing legislation. In Australia, new national privacy laws came into effect on December 21, 2001 under the Privacy Amendment (Private Sector) Act 2000. The privacy legislation is based on 10 key National Privacy Principles (NPPs) (Privacy Commissioner, 2001):

1. *Collection* - only collect information relevant to your organisation by fair means and not in an unreasonable intrusive way. For EBKM, this means having a clear, coherent and specific privacy policy stating who your

organisation is, what knowledge your are collecting, who will see the knowledge, why you need the knowledge and what will happen if you don't have the knowledge.

2. *Use and disclosure* - you cannot disclose personal information unless it is for a specific need and customers/contributors would reasonably expect you to do so. Knowledge users/contributors are trusting your organisation when they give you personal information, and its in your organisation's best interest not to abuse that trust in any way. Make sure that you run any questionable ideas past your organisation's privacy officer, legal representative or privacy consultant.
3. *Data quality* – make sure the personal information you collect, use or disclose is accurate, complete and up-to-date. For EBKM systems, this involves ensuring that the personal information or knowledge captured in knowledge repositories remains current and correct. This may involve offering a Web self-service portal to the knowledge repository so that customers/contributors can notify you of any changes or make changes themselves to their personal information or knowledge stored in the knowledge repository.
4. *Data security* - an organisation needs to take reasonable steps to protect personal information from misuse and loss from unauthorised access, modification or disclosure. There is need to destroy or eliminate identifying details from information you no longer need for a specific purpose. For EBKM, this means implementing appropriate security measures that both protect the personal data and knowledge stored in knowledge repositories (e.g. by encryption) and prevent unauthorised access to the repositories and/or use of that knowledge (e.g. by authentication, systems access control, and activity logging).
5. *Openness* - an organisation must document it's personal information management policy and make this policy available to anyone who asks for it. For EBKM, this entails publishing the EBKM personal information management policy on a web page prior to customers/users entering the EBKM site, and includes links to your privacy policy on your web site. Also consider auditing and certification of your privacy policies through such organisation's as the Australian Privacy Compliance Centre (www.privacycompliance.org), and eTick administrator of the Australian Privacy Seal Audit and Certification (APSAC) program.
6. *Access and correction* - organisations are to let customers see information held on them and must be able to correct any incorrect information held. For EBKM, this involves either an online self-service portal or a K-Centre providing procedures for customers/contributors to update incorrect or changed information/knowledge via email, fax or call Centre.

7. *Identifiers* -organisations cannot use the same identification number or code that another organisation has assigned to a particular customer. This is in order to prevent aggregation of customer or client data from multiple sources. For EBKM, this means that the organisation should develop its own process for identifying customers/contributors and ensure that they do not communicate customer/contributors identifiers when sharing this information with other organisations including multiple divisions of a company.
8. *Anonymity* - where practicable individuals must have the option of not identifying themselves when entering into transactions with an organisation. For EBKM, this entails that we do not demand personal information just to allow customers/contributors to enter our knowledge repositories site. The EBKM systems meet built with the basic level functionality that is available to anybody, and the second tier offering extra value add-ons if a customer/contributor offers you more information about themselves.
9. *Transborder data flows* - organisations should not transfer information out of Australia unless the recipient is in a jurisdiction where privacy is up to the NPP standards and the recipient is likely to uphold customer/contributor's privacy. Organisations should get approval for these transfers wherever possible. For EBKM, this means great care should be taken with whom knowledge and personal information is to be communicated. Compromising customers/contributors privacy may seriously damage organisation's reputation and may even lead to legal liability.
10. *Sensitive information* - do not collect sensitive information about people unless they have provided authorisation, or would authorise it but cannot, or the organisation needs the information to benefit public health or safety. Although the law does not define 'sensitive', this principle is intended to protect medical records and other health-care related information. So for EBKM systems holding personal information and knowledge about customers'/contributors' medical or health records, the organisation should seek legal advice before implementing knowledge systems dealing with this type of information and knowledge.

Many knowledge management systems interact or form a key component of customer relation management (CRM) systems. The privacy principles and implications outlined above should be seriously taken into account by KM when developing and implementing these systems.

4. RESEARCH IN PROGRESS

The research methodology consists of the following phases: literature review; survey of risk management risk, security and controls, and privacy within organisations, followed by detailed case studies with global organisations having mature EBKM in order to study their approach to risk management of EBKM. The research framework set out above help to frame the research by setting out the risks, security and controls which should be relevant in a EBKM environment, the survey discussed below will assist in the verification of these risks, security and controls providing a breadth of coverage. This will be followed by a series of case studies to gain depth of knowledge and verification in this area.

To date a survey is under preparation which will identify risk management practices for EBKM within organisations. The survey will help to identify a ranked importance set of EBKM risks, security and controls measures. This should provide guidance to organisations when undertaking knowledge management governance, as well as providing a framework for management implementing EBKM security and controls within their organisations. Privacy is an increasing concern for organisations and the survey should help to provide guidance to organisations as to the impacts of privacy on EBKM. The survey will be run online using Australian Chief Knowledge Officers or their designates as the participants in the study.

Currently the first case study is underway with Schlumberger, a global organisation, which is a gas and oil exploration company operating within 150 countries, provide global knowledge management for their organization. This organisation needs a global infrastructure to enable knowledge management by both intranets within the company and extranets to link their customers and divisions to worldwide knowledge repositories. A global secure infrastructure is needed to guarantee bandwidth and some of the security technologies employed include VPN (virtual private network), PKI (public key infrastructure), and encryption. The results of this and other case studies will provide best practice guidelines for EBKM management in the areas of risk management, security and privacy.

5. CONCLUSION

This paper has presented the challenge of appropriate security and control of the knowledge management systems. The literature review has revealed a major problem that risk management is not explicitly factored into the current EBKM development frameworks and models presented in the literature. The only framework that mentions risk management is from

Standards Australia (2001), but even this framework does not provide any guidance as to how this should be implemented. The development of a more detailed risk and security framework in this author's research should act as a catalyst in the EBKM area to ensure appropriate governance of EBKM systems under development and in operation. Research in this area as to the validation and importance of appropriate risks, security and controls for EBKM and their incorporation into a research framework, should then provide guidance to EBKM management in the security and control of the EBKM environment. Results from case study analysis should also provide best practice guidelines for EBKM management. Neglect of these concerns may lead an organisation being exposed to destruction of key EBKM resources, unwanted litigation and adverse publicity. By considering EBKM governance and the use of appropriate risk management methodologies and techniques, the CKO and his team responsible for knowledge management should be able to put in place appropriate security and control measures over the knowledge management environment, systems and repositories to counter these risks.

REFERENCES

Alavi M. and Leidner D.E. (2001), Knowledge Management and Knowledge Management Systems: Conceptual Foundations and Research Issues, *MIS Quarterly*, 25/1, March, 107-136.

Angus, J., Patel, J. & J. Harty (1998), *Managing Knowledge*, Addison Wesley Longman Publishing Co.

Capshaw, S. (2000); "The knowledge audit", *Knowledge Management*, May,, 25-26.

CSI (2001), "2001CSI/FBI Computer Crime and Security Survey", *Computer Security Issues and Trends*, Computer Security Institute, 5, 1, Spring, 1-18.

Debenham, J.K. & J. Clark (1995), "The Knowledge Audit", *Robotics and Computer-Integrated Manufacturing*, Elsevier Science, 11, 3, 201-211.

Denning, S., World Bank *in* Doyle, S. (2001), "A Little Knowledge Can be a Dangerous Thing: Issues in Knowledge Management", *Proceedings from Oceania CACS 2001*, Information Systems Audit and Control Association, Canberra, ACT, 23-26 September.

Doyle, S. (2001), "A Little Knowledge Can be a Dangerous Thing: Issues in Knowledge Management", *Proceedings from Oceania CACS 2001*, Information Systems Audit and Control Association, Canberra, ACT, 23-26 September.

Dolye, S. (1997), "Securing Electronic Documents", KPMG Global Knowledge Management Respository.

Earle, M. (2001), Knowledge Management Strategies: Toward a Taxonomy, Journal of Management Information Systems, Vol 18, No 1, 215-233.

Handzic, M. & H. Hasan (2002), Integrated Km Frameworks, in Handzic, M. & H. Hasan *Studies in Knowledge Management*, forthcoming.

Handzic, M. and R. Jamieson (2001), "A Knowledge Management Research Framework for Electronic Commerce", *Proceedings of the IFIP TC8 Working Conference on Electronic Commerce*, Salzburg, Austria, 22-23 June, 2001.

Handzic M. (2001) Knowledge Management: A Research Framework, in *Proceedings of the 2nd European Conference on Knowledge Management*, Bled, Slovenia, 8-9 November.

Holsapple C. W. & M. Singh (2000), "Electronic Commerce: From a Definitional Taxonomy Towards a Knowledge Management View", Journal of Organisational Computing and Electronic Commerce, Vol 10, No 3, 149-170.

Holsapple, C. W. & K. D. Joshi (2000), "An Investigation of Factors that Influence the Management of Knowledge in Organizations", *Journal of Strategic Information Systems*, 9, 2-3, 235-261.

Horricks, B. & J. Moss (1993), *Practical Data Administration*, Hertfordshire, UK: Prentice-Hall.

ISACF (2000), *COBIT: Control Objectives for Information and Related Technology*, 3rd Edition, Rolling Meadows, IL: IT Governance Institute and Information Systems Audit and Control Foundation.

ISACF (2001), *K-Net, Global Knowledge Network for IT Governance, Control and Assurance*, Rolling Meadows, IL: IT Governance Institute and Information Systems Audit and Control Foundation, URL = www.isaca.org/knet.

IT Governance Institute (2001), *Information Security Governance: Guidance for Boards of Directors and Executive Management*, Rolling Meadows, IL: Information Audit and Control Foundation.

Jackson, C. (1999), Process to Product – Creating Tools for Knowledge Management, Conference in Lisbon Portugal.

Jamieson, R. (1991), *Auditing Expert Systems*. Research Monograph No 3, Carol Stream, Illinois: EDP *Auditors Foundation Inc.*

Jamieson R and Handzic, M. (2002): A Framework for the Security, Control and Assurance of Knowledge Management Systems forthcoming in Holsapple, C., *Handbook on Knowledge Management*, Springer-Verlag, Heidelberg (in press).

Joseph, E.C (1999), "Knowledge Management Audits", Proceedings of the International Conference on *Technology and Innovation Management, PICMET*, 1, p442.

Kalakota, R. and A. B. Whinston (1996), *Frontiers of Electronic Commerce*. Reading, MA: Addison-Wesley.

Malhotra, Y. (2002), Why Knowledge management Systems Fail?: Enablers and Constraints of Knowledge Management in Human Enterprises, forthcoming in Holsapple, C., *Handbook on Knowledge Management*, Springer-Verlag, Heidelberg (in press).

Martin, E., Ferguson, D., Lewis, S., Lynch, N. & S. Doyle (1996), *Data Administration Practice in Federal Government Organisations: A Pilot Study*, University of Canberra (unpublished).

McAdam, R. & S. McCreedy (1999), A Critical Review of Knowledge Management Models, *The Learning Organisation*, Vol6 No 3, 91-100.

Nonaka, I (1998), The Knowledge-Creating Company", in Harvard Business Review on Knowledge Management. Harvard Business School Press, Boston.

Nonaka, I. (1991), The Knowledge Creating Company", *Harvard Business Review*, Vol 69, No 6, 96-104.Privacy Commissioner (2000), *National Privacy Principles- Extracted from the Privacy Amendment (Private Sector) Act 2000*, URL = www.privacy.gov.au/publications /npps01.html.

Ramos, D. (2001), "The Auditor's Role in IT Governance", *Information Systems Control Journal*, 5, 23-24.

Ribiere, V. & C Chou (2001), Knowledge Management in the Banking Industry, in *Proceedings of the 2nd European Conference on Knowledge Management*, Bled, Slovenia, 8-9 November.

Robinson, H. S., Carrillo, P., Anum,ba, C. J. & A. M. Al-Ghassani (2001), A Conceptual Framework for Improving Management Performance through Knowledge Transformation, in *Proceedings of the 2nd European Conference on Knowledge Management*, Bled, Slovenia, 8-9 November.

Ruggles, R. (1997), Knowledge Management Tools, Oxford, Butterworth-Heinermann.

Standards Australia (2001), HB275-2001, *Knowledge Management: A Framework for Success in the Knowledge Era.*, Sydney, NSW: Standards Australia International Limited.

Standards Australia (1999), *AS/NZS 4360:1999 Risk Management.* Sydney, NSW: Standards Australia International Limited.

Standards Australia (1996), *AS4309 Records Management*, Sydney, NSW: Standards Australia International Limited.

Tyndale, P. (2001), The Organisational Knowledge Development Life Cycle: From Knowledge Creation to Knowledge Application, *Proceedings of the 2nd European Conference on Knowledge Management*, Bled, Slovenia, 8-9 November.

Wong K., Ng, B., Cerpa, N. & Jamieson R. (2000), "An Online Audit Review System for Electronic Commerce", *Proceedings of the 13th Bled Electronic Commerce Conference 2000*, Bled, Slovenia, June 20-23.

Wright M. (2001), Risk Based Auditing and Risk Management, ISACA Technical Seminar, Information Systems Audit and Control Association, 8 November, Sydney.

Zannes, E. (2000), Knowledge Management in Industry and Government: The Conflict between Security and Knowledge Sharing, *Proceedings IEEE 34th Annual International Carnahan Conference on Security Technology*, 2000.

THE VALUE OF E-PROCUREMENT MODELS IN B2B EXCHANGES – AN AUSTRALIAN EXPERIENCE

DOUGLAS THOMSON and MOHINI SINGH
School of Business Information Technology, RMIT University, Australia

Abstract: This paper presents a theoretical e-procurement model that was developed for a large multinational Australian corporate as a business plan as the company moves from traditional paper and EDI based processes to e-procurement. The model provides a framework for optimising e-procurement processes while enhancing interrelationships between buyers and sellers. The multi-disciplinary framework is based on value propositions specific to a single corporate, or to a buyer consortium using e-markets to facilitate B2B exchanges. The e-markets that facilitated the B2B exchanges or that were set up to facilitate the B2B exchanges comprised many founding shareholder enterprises, some of whom are both buyers and sellers in the B2B exchange arena. The impact of the model on e-procurement, the role of e-markets and resulting issues after implementation are discussed in this paper. The values of e-procurement models in B2B exchanges have also been highlighted. The model presented in this paper provides the framework for optimising these systems and processes and their relationships using e-enablement of the procurement process.

1. INTRODUCTION

Corporates around the world are implementing e-business, and are looking for guidance as to how this may be best achieved. Australian businesses have variously considered the adoption of the Internet as a pervasive tool for communication, research and as a medium of business. These changes have created competitive global pressures which are intense, but are aided by an improved ability to cope with complexity through use of the enabling Internet based technology. This growth in competition can be explained by the confluence of new technology with old needs

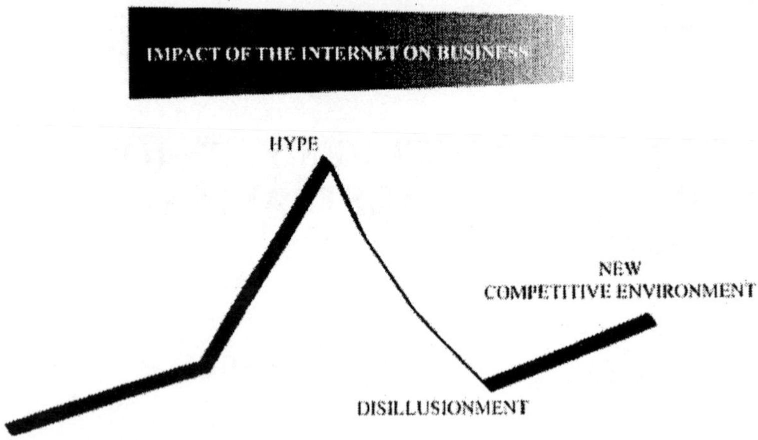

(Kinney, 2000).

B2B e-commerce in Australia is in a state of evolution as firms become accustomed to doing business electronically. With an increased emphasis on e-procurement as an accepted B2B e-commerce application, Australia has seen a proliferation of third party e-markets facilitating e-procurement. These e-markets are both consortia based as well as private. More recently however, consolidation of e-markets has taken place due to high operating costs and lengthy implementation time, the need for effective revenue models and the need to continuously adapt to new business models.

The Australian Bureau of Statistics Report on Business Use of Information Technology (2000) indicates that from June 1998 to June 2000 the proportion of Australian businesses accessing the Internet increased from 29 percent to 56 percent, while those with a web site increased from 6 percent to 16 percent. Australian companies using and developing Internet business tools generated revenues of 28 billion dollars in 2000 and 2001, which represents around 4.3 per cent of Australia's GDP. Use of e-commerce in Australia is becoming widespread. The Australian National Office for the Information Economy (NOIE) Report (2001) states that 55% of the firms surveyed indicated that they had complemented their traditional business activities with e-commerce, and 62 % realised some cost savings and greater efficiencies. Some B2B e-commerce in Australia developed from B2C e-commerce applications beginning with sell-side capabilities such as providing buyers with product and service information and allowing buyers to place orders online. Some B2C best practices such as searchable online catalogues and shopping cart functions are implemented as B2B sell-side transactional capabilities, with online access to fulfilment data, informing the customer of expected shipping date, delivery date and shipping status provided either by the seller or a third party logistics provider. With the developments in B2B e-commerce, Web-based e-procurement is the most important application by both large business organizations and governments in Australia. E-procurement benefits include achievement of volume purchases, wider choice of buyers and suppliers, lower costs, better product quality, improved delivery, and reduced paperwork and administrative costs.

2. LITERATURE REVIEW

E-procurement is the electronic integration and management of all procurement activities including purchase request, authorisation, ordering, delivery and payment between a purchaser and a supplier (Chaffey, 2002). Rayport and Jaworski (2002) refer to e-procurement as a B2B e-commerce application with Web-based functions that allow employees of a buying organization to purchase goods and services and allow suppliers to manage and communicate the fulfilment of the purchase orders submitted. This includes catalogue management, requisition, control and approval, receiving and exception processing, and financials and payment processing. Thomson and Singh (2001) advocate that e-procurement processes include sourcing of buyers and sellers, a digital catalogue of products, online bidding, ordering, payments, goods dispatch notices (fulfilment), logistics and supply chain management.

Businesses buy a diverse set of products and services, ranging from paper clips to computer systems, from steel to machinery. At the broadest level these purchases have been classified by Kaplan et. al. (2000) into manufacturing inputs and operating inputs. Manufacturing inputs are raw materials and components that go directly into the manufactured product or manufacturing process. Manufacturing inputs tend to be 'vertical' in nature, because the finished products they go into are industry specific. They are sourced from industry specific suppliers and distributors, and they require specialised logistics and fulfilment mechanisms. Operating inputs include indirect materials and services that do not go into finished products. These are sometimes called MRO (Maintenance, Repair and Operating) inputs which include industrial supplies, capital equipment, services and travel related goods. With the exception of capital equipment and some industrial supplies operating inputs are generally classified as 'horizontal'.

An 'e-marketplace' is a platform for collaboration between buyers and sellers (Matthewson, 2001). The benefits of e-Marketplaces suggested by many include significant cost reductions through process integration; faster channels of communication, reducing order-to-delivery lead times; cost-effective identification of new suppliers, products and services; greater price transparency for both buyers and sellers; increased reach and larger customer bases, plus lower acquisition costs for new customers; statistical reports on market activity, creating more accurate forecasts and better responsiveness to changing conditions; elimination of inefficient purchasing procedures; reduction of anti-competitive practices and industry cartels; improved staff productivity, by allowing them to concentrate on key relationships outside the marketplace environment (Matthewson, 2001).

An 'e-market' functions as a trusted intermediary whose well-integrated business procedures and technology save costs and streamline the purchasing and sales processes (Swedish Trade Council, 2001). In the year 2000, e-Markets proliferated at an astounding rate because of the increased potential for adoption of e-procurement in the global B2B e-space. For buyers, e-markets can lower purchasing costs while reaching new suppliers. For suppliers e-markets can lower sales costs and can help the supplier reach new customers (Chaffey, 2002). The large amount of bid, order and transaction management for B2B procurement requires assistance from e-markets (Thomson and Singh, 2001). The most important intermediary in B2B exchanges are e-markets. E-markets support e-procurement by enabling efficiency gains from better pricing of goods and services, cost savings in the administration of procurement processes, consolidation of buyers' sub entities into a single buying unit, and reduced costs through purchasing aggregation for some items. Other intangible benefits include improvements in operations support, employee productivity, visible purchasing habits of business partners and supplier performance. Reduction in procure to pay cycle time, streamlined procurement operations, avoidance of costs associated with outsourcing procurement, and cost savings in invoicing, financing, goods insurance, and delivery are achieved (McGagh, 2000). E-markets help suppliers by lowering administrative costs; use standard catalogues which can be quickly updated; effectively target and access a wider range of buyers; and lower inventory and warehousing costs (McGagh, 2000). Other opportunities include lower marketing, selling and service costs, an expanded product and service offerings, improved cash flow through improved inventory turns and accounts receivables, pull versus push orientation with buyer organisations, a more detailed insight into a buyer's purchasing needs, and immediate responsiveness to a buyer's needs and virtual product or service bundling (McGagh, 2000). By facilitating e-procurement, e-markets can collect revenue from transactions and associated services. Revenue model options include charging a percentage or flat rate on each transaction, annual subscriptions, levees, payment for services and so on.

For each e-market participant, benefits vary according to the participant's position. As buyers go to the e-marketplace for e- procurement, suppliers may not have any choice but to join in. Most suppliers are also potential buyers, therefore the net effect is an increasing participation in e-enabled procurement. Systematic sourcing and spot sourcing of goods and services dominate business purchases and are based on corporate strategic marketplace servicing decisions. Systematic buying through negotiated contracts with pre-qualified suppliers is often relationship oriented and contracts are longer term, usually of the order of one to three years. Spot sourcing is fulfilment of an immediate need, typically of a commoditised item for which it is less important to pre-qualify the suppliers and by relying on a known, standard product (Thomson and Singh, (2001), Chaffey, (2002), and Christiaanse, et al (2001)).

3. PROPOSED E-PROCUREMENT MODEL

The proposed e-procurement model covers business buy-do-sell processes i.e. the technology for procure to pay, the transaction marketplace, and the value/supply chain as shown in Figure 1:

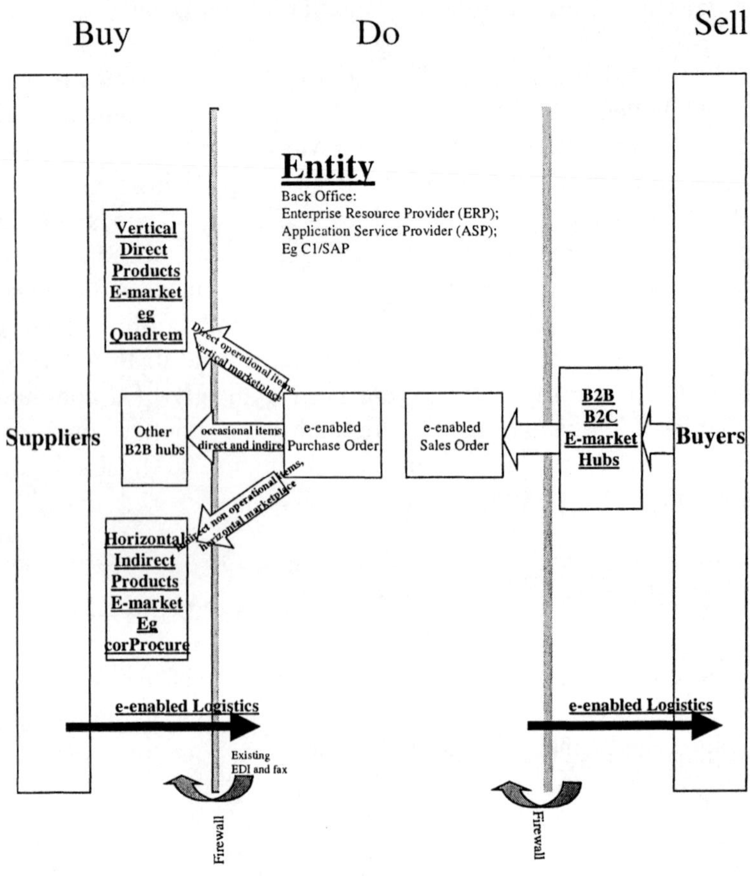

Figure 1. The E-procurement Business Environment End-to-End Process: Buyer to Supplier

The above diagram illustrates the plan for e-enabled procurement using the Internet. It was developed as an initial plan for an Australia based global corporate, BHP Pty Ltd. A more detailed process plan (below) shows the complex atypical e-procurement steps, which are in numbered sequence.

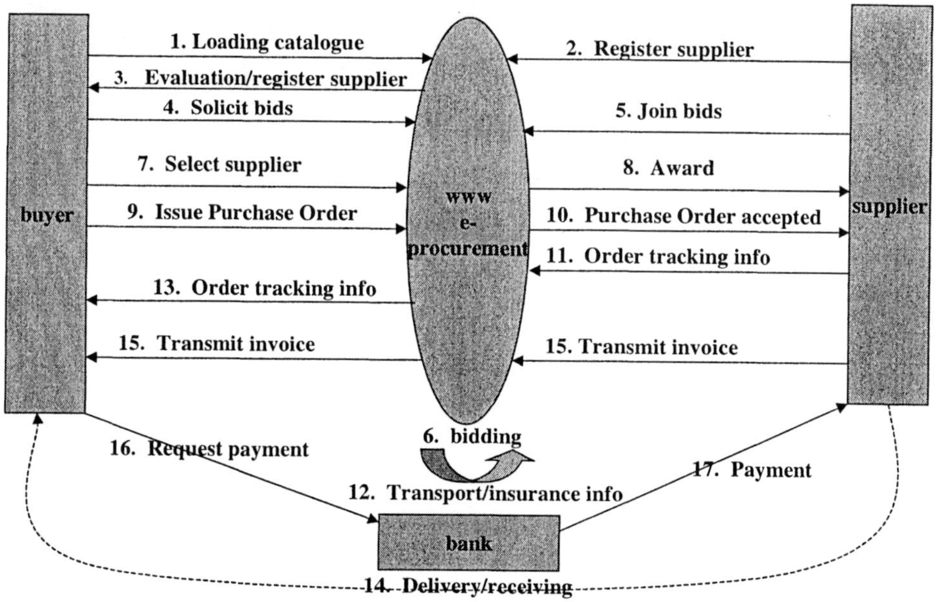

Figure 2. A typical E-procurement process

3.1 Theoretical Business Model for E-procurement

This theoretical business model (Figure 3) was developed as a business plan for e-procurement for BHP, a large Australian multi national organization. The model is based on the three major multi-disciplinary dimensions of e-enabled procurement: firstly, e-enabled marketplaces for buying and selling; secondly, e-enabled supply chain/value chain logistics for timely, cost effective delivery; and thirdly, e-enabled technology for procure to pay processes and the interrelationships between these processes.

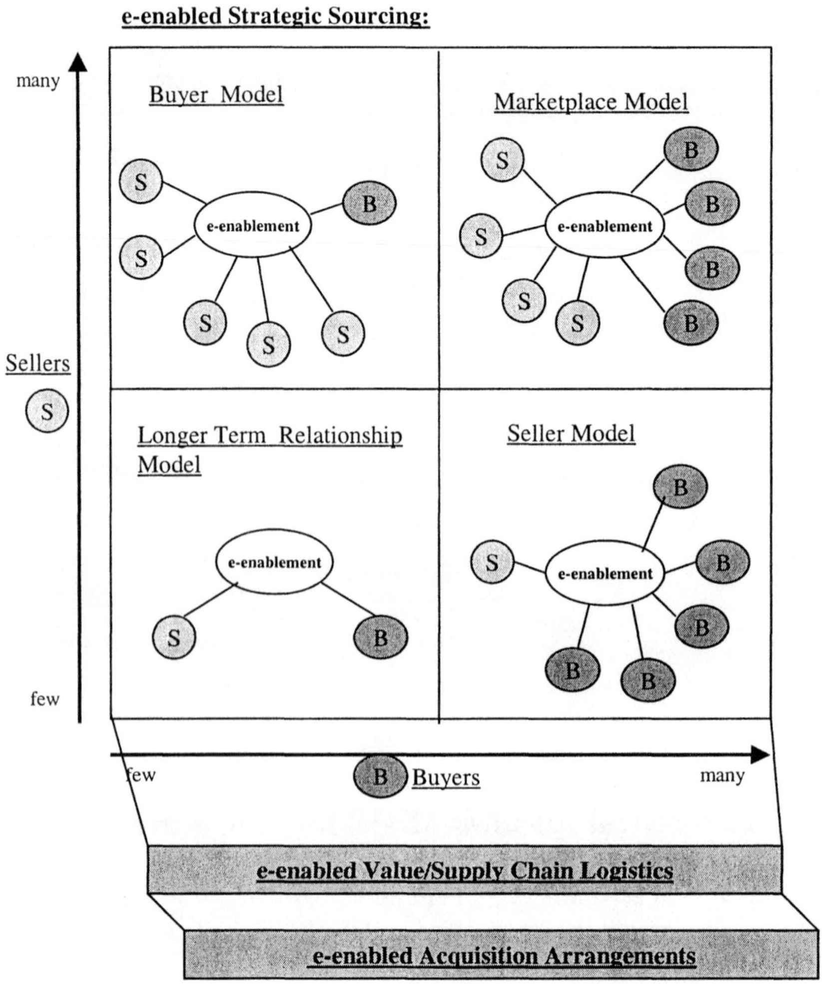

Figure 3. Theoretical Business Model for E-enabled Procurement

Product demand and supply arrangements are often based on high volume low value items and low volume high value items in the approximate proportions 80:20. For example, typical spend across two financial years by the Australian Department of Defence is shown in the following Table 1 (Thomson, 1997):

Australian Department of Defence's actual spread of spend and the number of associated transactions for two Financial Years:

Value Bracket of Procurements	FY 1 No of Transactions	FY 1 Value ($m)	FY 2 No of transactions	FY 2 Value ($m)
$150m and over	4	1404	2	1515
$100mto $150m				
$50m to $100m	3	178	4	306
$20m to $50m	7	195	6	187
$10m to $20m	18	241	12	177
$5m to $10m	28	191	28	197
$1m to $5m	193	395	253	549
$100k to $1m	2221	590	2205	583
$30k to $100k	4746	250	4410	231
$2k to $30k	43769	327	42035	309
Total	50989	3768	48955	4054

Table 1

Source: Thomson, JD (1997) *'Purchasing Statistics Bulletin 1989/90 to 1995/96'*, pp7, Department of Defence, Canberra, February.

This shows that there are typically relatively few high value items but many low value items. For e-procurement and e-markets, this leads to market and product structuring and differentiation. Typically, this may be demonstrated as follows:

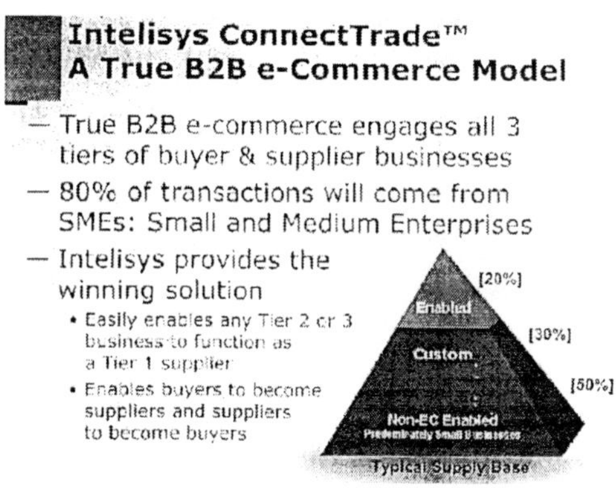

Figure 4. B2B E-commerce Model

The pyramid in Figure 4 shows how this can be translated to the B2B marketplace. Reflecting this and the demand/supply relationships, each quadrant in the e-marketplace model has its own particular application, the knowledge of which will enable product placement based on selected value drivers. For example, low value high volume products will more likely be in the 'marketplace quadrant', while high value low volume items are more likely to be in the 'longer term relationship' quadrant. The four quadrants of the model and their relationship with the e-supply/value chain and e-acquisition/technology arrangements are briefly explained in the following sections, followed by case studies to demonstrate the model.

3.2 Marketplace Quadrant (many buyers and sellers)

The Marketplace Quadrant is appropriate where additional value may be created through third party mediation of the matching process between buyers and sellers, or through aggregation of buying or selling volumes. This quadrant is particularly appropriate for low value high volume products, spot buying and sourcing in cross industries (horizontal) and within industry (vertical) markets for non-core (indirect) business products (Kaplan, 2000).

The value proposition for buyers and sellers is that aggregation reduces transaction, search and marketing costs and mediation improves supply/demand matching. In this quadrant revenue generation potential for e-markets is expected to be high. This quadrant is strategically complex because of existing alliances, contracts, and supply/value chains in the Australian B2B exchange arena.. The focus is on the price of undifferentiated product. This tends to ignore the repercussions of supply/value chain issues, 'value for money' tender selection and the need for smoothly functioning new technology and skills to connect buyers, suppliers and if involved, e-markets.

This quadrant in the model was important for BHP for the purpose of procuring families of largely undifferentiated products commodities such as stationery, or standard service requirements such as catering and cleaning. It also supports indirect spot purchases. Commodities are catalogued and presented in some detail by sellers, and industry specific catalogue items are easily provided in detail, such as assemblies, sub assemblies, components, etc.

3.3 Buyer Quadrant (few Buyers, many Sellers)

The buyer quadrant is appropriate in cases where there are a large number of potential sellers and this may result in multiple or fragmented formats, where the buyer is able to leverage buying power through the use of say, reverse auction tools. A reverse auction is where a supplier's winning bid is the lowest, rather than the highest, so suppliers compete against each other through an auction process to win the auction by making the lowest bid. Buyers can demand supply through these processes, so forcing the many suppliers to comply with the buyer's e-technology, requirements and processes.

The value proposition for the one or few buyers, in this case BHP, is that they can demand a common format for all electronic applications, specifications and contracts across all sellers; enforce compliance through workflow and supply chains; achieve process efficiency; automate and integrate back office systems to achieve seamless purchase and accounting efficiency. In this quadrant, power is with the buyer. The use of an e-market increases the potential buying power of the buyers. The sellers could end up incurring costs while upgrading systems and integrating with buyer backend systems. Implications for the e-marketplace are that there could be a large number of suppliers selling commodity items with high supply costs relative to the value of the items.

3.4 Longer Term Relationship Quadrant (one buyer, one seller)

The Longer Term Relationship Quadrant is appropriate for items requiring a high degree of planning between buyers and sellers either in the design stage or in fulfillment, typically strategic items. The importance of planning can be either due to technical complexity or demand characteristics driven by a time or phased requirement.

The value proposition for buyers and sellers is that concurrent design leads to reduced cycle time and improved manufacturability because the suppliers are part of the buyer's supply chain. Supply chain integration between buyers and sellers also improves customer service. Strategic relationships lead to few buyers and sellers, which can result in improved service, and reduced risks due to immature technical solutions. This was needed at BHP for the procurement of many contracted items such as critical expensive capital items. E-marketplace exchange enables the procurement of customised engineering and capital equipment from a small number of specialised suppliers, and sourcing of products where supply assurance may be more important than price. Because these are often high value low volume items, the role of e-markets in the transactions is likely to be less, as the transactions are often made on the basis of one-to-one. However, where there are a number of large buyers who can agree on timing and product, buyers may be able to exert buying power even though the relationship becomes one-to-one on contract signature.

3.5 Seller Quadrant (few sellers, many buyers)

The Seller Quadrant is appropriate for situations where the supplier hosts differentiated or value added products, often on its own Web site. The product for sale is not a commodity, and the seller is a monopoly or differentiated oligopoly of the product. Buyers are forced to buy from a limited number of suppliers. At BHP, this was included because BHP wished to test e-procurement processes on the sell side or customer side. BHP tried the sale of guaranteed quality diamonds from its Ekati mine, and some resources which were differentiated on the basis of their chemical composition.

The value proposition in this quadrant is that the seller aims for monopoly/oligopoly advantage through ownership of a differentiated product. The buyers have but one or a few suppliers, e-markets or e-catalogues to procure from, with facilities often provided by the supplier. Buyers/customers may be faced with the costs of integrating their technologies with the seller's web site or back office MRP/ERP/legacy systems, or accepting seller technological assistance in servicing the transactions. The supplier has marketplace power.

3.6 E-Enabled Supply Chain/Value Chain Logistics

Supply chain management is the coordination of material, information and financial flows between and among all the participating parties (Kalakota and Robinson 2000). It is an important entity of e-procurement for timely acquisition of goods and services. Logistics is common across all business buy, do (manage) and sell functions. With the advent of e-commerce, traditional logistics is being radically transformed to meet the demands of agile, high-velocity, granular approach (Bayles, 2001). There are two main components to e-enabled logistics. These are the supply chain itself, and the e-enablement of logistics. E-enablement of supply chains may lead to disintermediation, reintermediation, or infomediation of some businesses in the supply chain, based on the contribution of the participants in the chain. The three alternatives for such arrangements are that the buyer can reach back or the manufacturer can reach forward, or a new intermediary such as an e-market can add new value.

On both the sell side and the buy side, it is necessary to provide an underpinning delivery service. To deliver within a specified time frame and to have a returns policy, there is a need to process each web placed order for personalisation, to track the order status, and to keep the customer informed. Organisations with logistics services already in place will have an advantage, since logistics may well become a new '*core*' business within the e-enabled company. E-enabled supply chain logistics fulfilment options include insourcing, outsourcing and virtual warehousing through suppliers. Logistics e-fulfilment requires a high degree of flexibility in infrastructure, people, and IT skills to adjust to various product mixes and unpredictable demand patterns. Whether e-fulfilment logistics is in-house, outsourced or virtual, costs of technology upgrades, re-engineered business process and an infrastructure to support logistics has to be put in place to attain efficiencies. Disintermediation of intermediaries is an increased possibility when using e-supply arrangements, because the buyer can more easily go 'global' to the supplier manufacturers more easily.

3.7 E-Enabled Acquisition And Procure To Pay Processes.

The technological infrastructure of the procure-to-pay and back office processes of the supplier, buyer and e-marketplaces may be one of the major barriers to e-procurement, together with the availability and training of the staff to operate the new systems successfully. E-enabled logistics order fulfilment process starts once the on-line customer clicks the 'buy' option. It is then the responsibility of an order management logistics system to confirm inventory availability, manage each item, make delivery arrangements, and track the order through its lifecycle to completion on confirmation of its delivery by the carrier. This integration is not easy to achieve.

4. APPLICATION OF THE MODEL AND FINDINGS

During 2000/2001, the proposed model was implemented at BHP to e-enable the procurement processes. The outcome of the application of the model is discussed in the following sections.

4.1 Marketplace Quadrant - Product: Photocopy Paper.

Participants	'horizontal' e-marketplace CorProcure. Participant buyers were the 14 major Australia-based corporate founding shareholders of corProcure, suppliers were major Australia-based paper suppliers; reverse auction engine was provided by Price Waterhouse Coopers(PwC)

E-Exchange Conditions	Specific time, date, & payment in AU$, Delivery facilitated by corProcure, with PwC the contracted reverse auction engine agent; Request for Quotation and Specification issued prior to auction after considerable discussion and meetings by corProcure and PwC with buyers and suppliers; corProcure set a very low reserve price for the auction which was based on a knowledge of the current supplier's prices provided by current buyers.
Expected Outcome	Reduced up front costs for buyers and suppliers, online e-catalogues provided by suppliers which could be compared, e-search facilities, e-ordering, approval and payment, Reduced inventory for buyers and suppliers, possible disintermediation of some paper distributors
Actual Outcome	No bids were made by any supplier.
Issues	Selection of this apparently 'easy' commodity may not have been the best choice in retrospect; Existing relationships between buyers and suppliers and the supply chain proved difficult to break; The new unproven method of e-procurement was another issue.

Table 2.

4.1.1 Discussion.

The failure by the e-market corProcure to successfully orchestrate this reverse auction was due to a number of factors including supplier lack of knowledge of or confidence in the new e-procurement processes, supplier lack of trust in reverse auctions; supplier concern about e-payment processes not being in place and difficult/costly to get the required technology and trained people into place; supplier preferment of existing buyer/supplier contracts and the difficulties associated with existing contract end dates to be matched to new contract start dates; draconian terms and conditions of the contract by the e-market and its consultant on behalf of the buyers (or an anticipation that this was the collective buyer's requirement); supplier's very low margins on A4 paper meant possibly an unrealistic reserve price was set for the reverse auction. Because this commodity was often used by suppliers as a 'loss leader' for other of their stationery products, suppliers may have hesitated to bid in an auction which would have split the paper away from the other stationery items being sold at much higher margins as part of an overall deal with a buyer; there was a concern that the paper ordered in such large quantities in such a short time period could not be matched by the Australia based manufacturers.

corProcure was an open independent regional internet based procurement marketplace for buying and selling indirect goods and services. It was a horizontal exchange business which was established by Amcor, AMP, ANZ, Australia Post, BHP, Coca-Cola Amatil, Coles Myer, Fosters, Goodman Fielder, Orica, Pacific Dunlop, Qantas, Telstra and Wesfarmers to create a B2B web based buying and selling exchange for indirect goods. CorProcure's plan was to use technology to seamlessly connect buying and supplying trading partners in order to extract maximum value from the supply chain for all participants.

The existing A4 paper supply chain arrangements were not disintermediated into the potential e-supply chain, as anticipated by some of the buyers and suppliers (Figure 5).

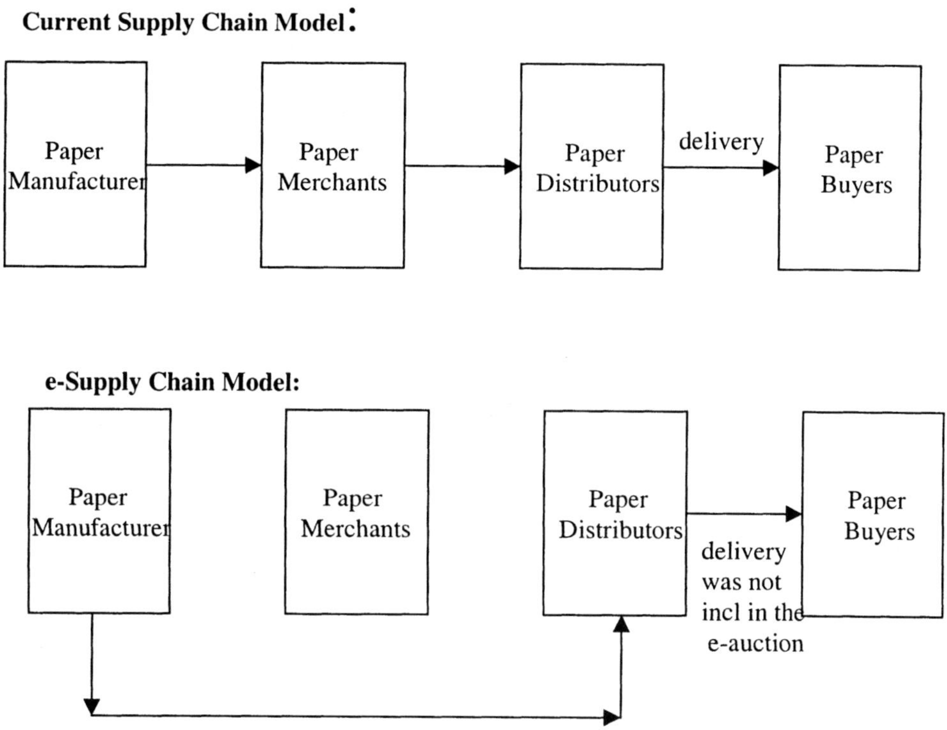

Figure 5. Current and Potential e-Supply Chains

The Australian consumer watchdog (ACCC) was kept informed about the proposed auction by the e-market corProcure, but did not become involved because the amount of paper being auctioned was a very small part of the total Australian marketplace in A4 paper. However, conditions set by the ACCC concerning marketplace collusion by buyers or sellers were met. The corProcure e-market trial was perhaps premature. In retrospect, selection of A4 paper may not have been a good choice because it tended to be one part of an overall value chain/supply chain process and supplier marketing strategy. The e-market found it difficult to develop a strategy around these issues, transaction technology was not in place connecting the e-market and all participating buyers and sellers. The e-market failed to provide a value proposition either for itself or for the suppliers involved. In so doing, it failed to provide a value proposition for the buyers or its founding shareholders. The e-market corProcure has subsequently been purchased by one of its founding shareholders, Australia Post, in December 2001.

4.2 Buyer Quadrant – Product: Hotel Rooms and Services.

Participants	One multinational corporate buyer; reverse auction agent FreeMarkets©; many (50-55) ***, ****, ***** star hotel room suppliers in Sydney and Melbourne.
E-Exchange Conditions	Facilitated by reverse auction agent FreeMarkets© operating from Pittsburg USA &Aust, Request For Quotation & Information available to suppliers online 1 week in advance; FreeMarkets© detailed market analysis took 4 weeks; FreeMarkets© interviews with both suppliers and buyer; FreeMarkets© thorough training of buyer and suppliers in the e-marketplace reverse auction process.
Expected Outcome	Cost and time savings; Better value for money while retaining the same quality of hotel accommodation for employees; improved budgetary control; improvements in information flow between buyer and seller; reduced maverick buying; improved payment processes; enhanced relationships between buyer and suppliers.
Actual Outcome	Very successful outcome facilitated by professional e-market reverse auction agent (FreeMarkets©);

Issues	Technology and training of suppliers and buyers; business model; Demonstration of benefits by reverse auction agent to buyers and suppliers; value proposition for all; trust established by all in the process and in the reverse auction agent.

Table 3.

4.2.1 Discussion

Benefits to BHP included e-procurement delivery process cost and time savings. These were each estimated at around one third to one fifth of the traditional procurement process. Overall contract savings achieved were around 12.5% of the value of the contract sum, in a market not expected to show any savings at all. Figure 6 indicates the outline reverse auction process:

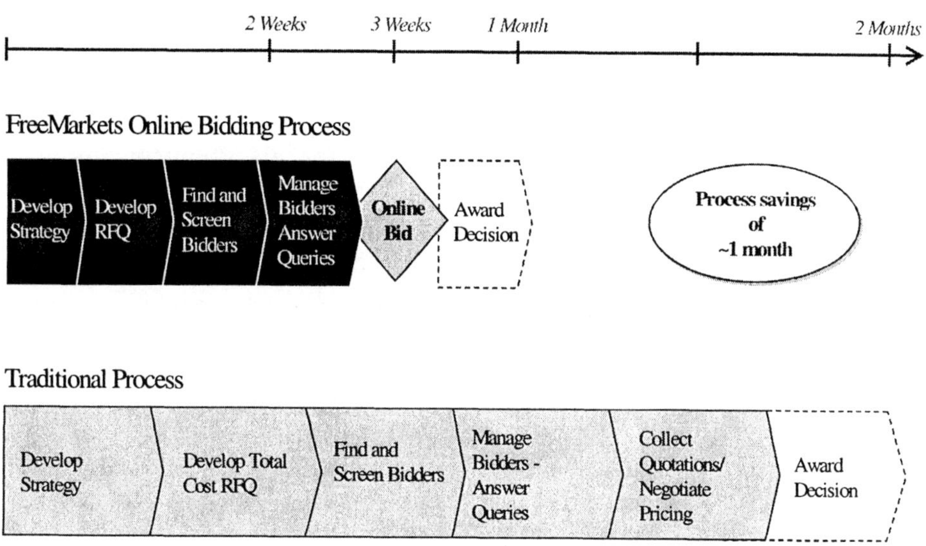

Figure 6. Freemarkets Online Bidding Process versus Traditional Process-Time Savings

Because the selected suppliers were to be listed and BHP employees allowed to use these suppliers only, maverick or off the list buying by BHP employees reduced to almost zero. Since the number of suppliers awarded contracts and able to be used by employees was significantly reduced from previous, payment processes for both suppliers and buyer were expected to be improved. Contract award was made on the basis of 'value for money', not simply 'lowest price'. This was achieved by FreeMarkets© finding out the most used services by the buyer's employees and setting a percentage of the room rate for the supply of these services. When the reverse auction had closed, the buyer assessed the bids made. After discussion with the lowest several bidders of each 'event', the buyer awarded contracts for a specified guaranteed number of 'room nights per annum' to the 'best value for money' bidders. Because there were two or three bidders awarded contracts for each level of hotel or 'event', competition between these suppliers for the guaranteed number of rooms per annum was expected to continue over the 12-month life of the contract. Previous well performing suppliers were awarded for their service because the buyer awarded contracts to a number of these suppliers despite the fact that they did not necessarily bid the lowest hotel room rate. Relationships between the buyer and suppliers were based on trust, established during the pre-auction period. No 'dummy' auction bids were permitted, and all suppliers could see on their screens what bids were being made at what time. No supplier knew which bidder made which bid, and the auction was continuously extended by a minute if a bid was made within the last minute. The whole auction took only a few hours. It was an open and transparent bid process, bound legally at the end of each 'event' auction by the reverse auction agent contacting the lowest bidders directly to confirm their bid and record the transaction as legally binding. There was equality and equity of bidding arrangements for all suppliers, and no difficulty in obtaining supplier interest. This was a great success. The value proposition for both buyer and sellers could be clearly demonstrated by the e-market reverse auction agent, and the latter achieved a value proposition for itself.

4.3 Seller Quadrant - Product: Diamonds.

Participants	Seller BHP 'Aurias' diamonds strongly marketed to marketplace buyers/customers to e-procure differentiated diamonds over the web from its web site
E-Exchange Conditions	Specific BHP 'Aurias' web site set up, with diamond inventory and price available to buyers; each diamond differentiated by a guarantee and quality certificate

Possible Outcomes	Anticipated possible disintermediation of some distributors, wholesalers or retailers; consumers drawn to site and transaction as a result of heavy marketing and promotions, and cost reduction for buyers by buying direct 'from mine to you'. Seller BHP 'Aurias' wanted to gain marketing, branding and sales e-experience through a 'proof of concept' approach.
Actual Outcomes	Partial success
Issues	Security; Product emotional and relationship value to customer; special product characteristics such as 'touchy feely' issues; trust in process and transaction; technology.

Table 4.

4.3.1 Discussion

In this seller quadrant, the role of BHP and its 'Aurias' diamonds brand was reversed in that BHP was the seller and its customers the buyers. The product selected was a special differentiated product where the seller anticipated a monopoly ie differentiated diamonds through guarantees, quality, and web site sales. While some web site sales were made, buyer /consumer resistance occurred since the product was expensive, buyers wanted to see and assess the goods before buying and committing to transacting large sums of money electronically. There was found to be a strong buyer preference to see and touch the product, rather than buy over the web. From BHP's perspective, there was consideration that some differentiation of the supply chain might occur. Figure 7 indicates the usual diamonds supply/value chain compared to an optimized e-diamonds supply/value chain. The anticipated outcome of this quadrant in the model was to reach the buyers directly, so disinter mediating the middle enterprises and reducing the overall supply costs.

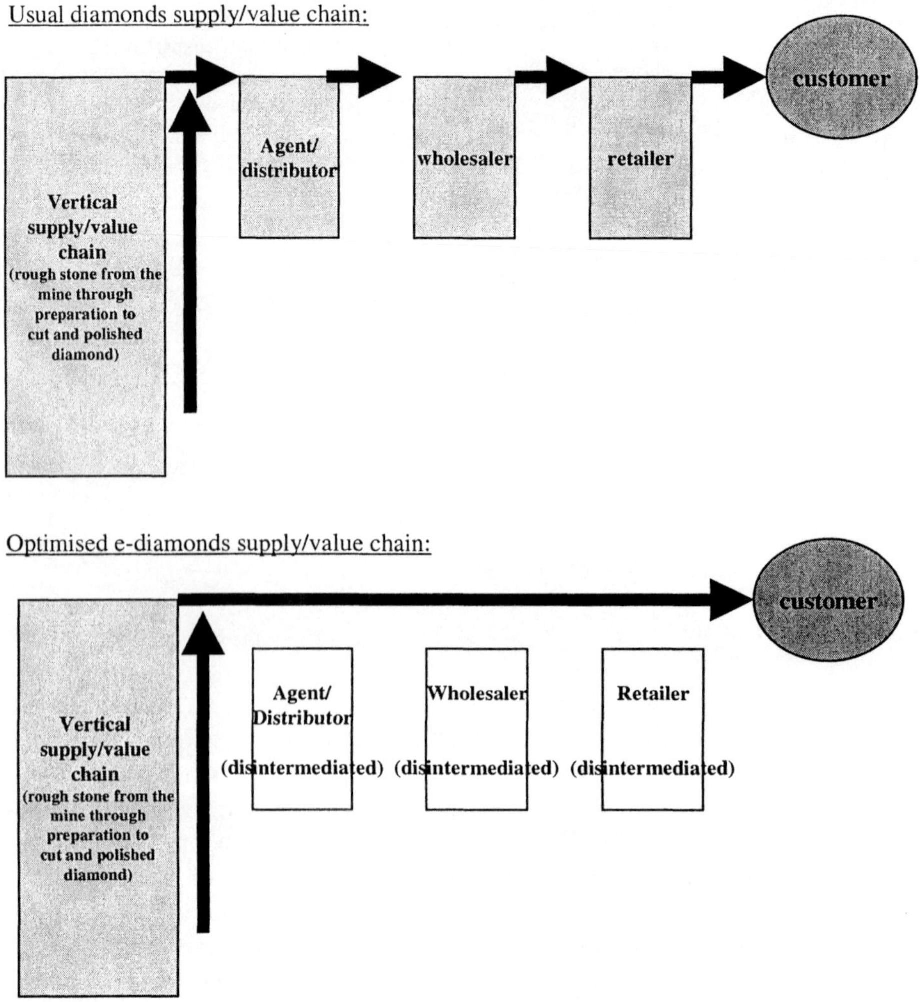

Figure 7. Usual versus Optimized e-Diamonds Supply/Value Chain

While this application was tested with a specific product, the product itself may not have been such a good choice because of its value and special characteristics. However, while this was not immediately successful the seller BHP and its 'Aurias' brand and e-market achieved much e-experience in this '*proof of concept'* trial. The business model is being adjusted to go global.

4.4 Longer Term Relationship Quadrant - Product: Capital Equipment

Participants	Multinational buyers and sellers of major capital equipment items ie 'vertical' products. Use of e-market Quadrem
E-Exchange Conditions	contracts for few items of high value, using Quadrem
Anticipated outcomes	Anticipated possible disintermediation of some distributors, wholesalers or retailers; consumers drawn to site and transaction as a result of heavy marketing and promotions, and cost reduction for buyers by buying direct 'from mine to you'. Seller BHP 'Aurias' wanted to gain marketing, branding and sales e-experience through a 'proof of concept' approach.
Actual Outcomes	Partial success, but improving with time
Issues	Major industry items of high value are usually of a strategic nature with fewer suppliers. This may not be as conducive to an e-market place based bidding process. However, because of the 'whole of life' relationship issues of the product, the value of e-markets and e-procurement lies in the passage of post contract information and in the pre contract award process.

Table 5.

4.4.1 Discussion

This quadrant of the model covers major items of capital equipment and strategic industry related products where supply assurance is more important for the buyer than price. The risks for BHP is that a monopoly situation may be set up with specific suppliers so increasing BHP's vulnerability, unless another source of supply is also able to be contracted. However, this is sometimes not possible. BHP is choosing this route with the assistance of the 'vertical' e-market Quadrem. Quadrem aims to reshape procurement for the global mining and metals industry by establishing a B2B internet based marketplace by end 2001. Shareholders are Alcan Aluminium Limited, Alcoa Inc., Anglo American plc, Barrick Gold Corp, BHP, Corporacion Nacional del Cobre de Chile (CODELCO), Companhia Vale do Rio Doce (CVRD), De Beers Consolidated Mines Ltd., Glencore Int AG; Imerys, Inco Limited, MIM Holdings; Newmont Mining Corporation, Noranda Inc., Normandy Mining, Pechiney, Penoles; Phelps Dodge Corporation, Rio

Tinto, the Votorantim Group, WMC Limited, and Morgan Stanley Dean Witter. With the demise of corProcure, Quadrem is expected to move into much of the horizontal space as well, so providing its shareholders, buyers and suppliers with a complete service.

5. CONCLUSION

The model was developed to provide a roadmap and guidance to the e-enabling of the procurement process at BHP, an Australian global mining, minerals and metals resources enterprise which has since merged with Billiton. Considerable time and effort was put into the development of the model. It is based on a thorough review of literature on B2B exchanges, is therefore generic and easily applied to different situations, enterprises and environments.

The model highlighted the benefits of e-procurement, the roles of exchange partners and intermediaries. However, each of the four quadrants of the model had differing success in delivering benefits to BHP. This is the subject of further research.

The model did provide a strong, flexible e-procurement framework which can be modified and implemented in the future even though the technology, marketplace environment, and supply/value chains may change.

REFERENCES

Australian Bureau of Statistics Report 8129.0, 'Business Use of Information Technology', December, 2000.

Bayles, D., 2001, E-Commerce Logistics and Fulfillment, Prentice Hall, New Jersey.

Chaffey, D., 2002, E-Business and E-Commerce Management, Prentice Hall, Great Britain.

Christiaanse, E., Sinneker, R. and Mossinkoff, M., 2001, The Impact of B2B Exchanges on Brick and Mortar Intermediaries: The Elemica Case', 9th European Conference on Information Systems, Bled, Slovenia, June 27 – 29, pp 422 – 432.

Kalakota R. and Robinson M, 2001 *'e-Business: Roadmap for Success'*, Addison –Wesley, Canada.

Kaplan, Steven, Sawhney and Mohanbir, 2000, 'E-Hubs: The New B2B Marketplaces', Harvard Business Review, May/June 2000, Volume 78, Issue 3, pp 97.

Kinney S (2000) 'An Overview of B2B and Purchasing Technology', Freemarkets, Pittsburg, PA.

McGagh J (2000), *'From Vision to Technology to Value'*, Rio Tinto,

Matthewson, J. A., 2001, 'e-Business a jargon-free practical guide', Butterworth Heineman, Boston;

NOIE Report (2001, 'B2B E-Commerce: Capturing Value Online', Commonwealth of Australia/

Rayport, J. and Jaworski, B., 2002, introduction to e-commerce', McGraw-Hill / Irwin MarketspaceU, New York.

Swedish Trade Council www.emarketservices.com/about_emarket_places/main.htm

Thomson,D., 1997, : *'Purchasing Statistics Bulletin 1989/90 to 1995/96'*, pp7, Department of Defence, Canberra, February

Thomson, D., 2000, A Macro Level Business Model for E-Enabled Procurement, MBA Thesis, Victoria University, Melbourne, Australia.

Thomson, D. and Singh, M., 2001, 'A Macro Level Business Model For E-Enabled Procurement', CollEcTeR Conference, Coffs Harbour, December 3-4.

E-COMMERCE AND HUMAN RESOURCE MANAGEMENT: THEORETICAL APPROACHES AND ISSUES FOR THE BANKING INDUSTRY

YVETTE BLOUNT[1],
TANYA CASTLEMAN[1] and PAULA M.C. SWATMAN[2]
[1] *Deakin University, Melbourne, Australia Affiliation*
[2] *Deakin University, Australia and University of Koblenz-Landau, Germany*

Abstract: Electronic commerce technologies are changing the way that work tasks are conducted and thus has significant implications for the way organisations manage their human resource functions. Although the impact of IT on work and employment has been the subject of research, little attention has been paid to electronic commerce and its effect on work organisation and HR management. This paper examines existing literature on how eCommerce technologies have shaped workplace management, with particular attention to the banking industry. It proposes a conceptual framework for identifying and understanding these changes in the context of the business pressures faced by banks in the highly competitive retail banking environment.

1. INTRODUCTION

The human resource management perspectives associated with the implementation of eCommerce technologies are not well understood in the Information Systems discipline. The purpose of this paper is to identify some of the issues involved in understanding the impact of eCommerce on the way employment is organised and managed. We have focussed on the banking industry as our example because of the importance of banking to eCommerce development and its role as a leading user of eCommerce and IT applications. Lessons from the banking sector will be relevant for many other industries that are developing in similar directions (such as the insurance or education sectors). The current shortage of literature on the implications of eCommerce for employment suggests that further research is needed in this area, as are theoretical models which incorporate the new approaches to organising production and the inter-organisational relationships which eCommerce creates.

The banking and finance industries are significant because they face cutting-edge technological and strategic issues at an earlier stage than other industries (Dewan and Seidmann, 2001). This makes banking a key industry in which to observe the impacts of the implementation of eCommerce on the design of work and the management of employment relationships. It will contain lessons for other industries which are yet to move down the eCommerce path. Technologies such as Automatic Teller Machines (ATMs), Electronic Funds Transfer, intranets, telephone and internet banking have made banking accessible in many more formats and have assisted the industry to reduce costs in a competitive and increasingly global environment.

There has been intense interest in the implementation of IT and eCommerce in this industry sector and its contribution to the ongoing tensions between the banks and their *customers* (BRW, 2001). eCommerce and the internet have enabled major changes in the way banks deal with their retail customers. In the past, customers conducted their banking business at a branch and received highly personalised customer service which involved customers and staff in face-to-face trust relations (Wells and Wolfers, 2000; Hughes et al., 1999). New fee structures, bank closures and staff cuts have left customers with little choice but to use technology such as ATMs (Connolly and Thomas, 2000). The implementation of eCommerce in banking has been greeted by customers with a mixture of enthusiasm for the convenience it affords and concern about lower levels of traditional service provision, an issue which has caused widely-publicised conflict between banks and their customers.

Other conflicts caused by eCommerce implementation in this sector, however, have not received the same degree of attention. Tensions between management and employees in the adoption of eCommerce are as significant as the tensions between customers and their financial institution. eCommerce is changing the way people perform their jobs and the way in which they are themselves managed. Banking employees have a new working environment, which includes greater job insecurity than previously, new skill requirements, work redesign and changes in career paths (Jesse, 1997; Scott & Walsham, 1998). Managers have to deal with these issues while putting in place strategies to attract, motivate and retain proficient employees, while at the same time having to develop new competencies themselves.

This paper begins by summarising some of the key eCommerce applications in the banking industry. We then discuss three conceptual approaches for understanding the impact of IT on employment and industry changes associated with the global economy and IT. We consider the impact of eCommerce on employment in the banking industry. We propose a composite framework for further investigating the impact of eCommerce on employment and conclude by outlining a program for further research.

2. ECOMMERCE IMPLEMENTATION IN THE BANKING INDUSTRY

Banks have not only been early adopters of eCommerce, but other businesses' move to eCommerce has been highly dependent on the electronic financial infrastructure that banks provide. Awad defines eCommerce in banking as consisting of: 'procedures that support commercial activities electronically or via networking to apply to bank-to-bank, bank-to-customer or bank-to-vendor' (Awad, 2000:144). The banking sector has implemented IT and eCommerce technologies over several decades. They developed Electronic Data Processing (EDP) centres to centralise operations and were using Electronic Funds Transfer (EFT) over secure networks to communicate between themselves as early as the 1970s (Game & Pringle, 1984; Kalakota and Whinston, 1997). Since then, technologies such as Automatic Teller Machines (ATMs), electronic funds transfer and point of service banking via retail terminals, phone banking, intranets and internet banking have assisted banks and financial organisations to streamline their business processes still further.

Banks and financial institutions around the world have implemented different business strategies and models. Although some of the smaller banks, credit unions and building societies have chosen to have no Web banking and to rely on branches and ATMs, the medium to large banking organisations are encouraging customers to switch to the Web for the cost advantages this channel offers (Jordan & Katz, 1999). In the USA, large organisations such as FleetBoston, Citigroup and Wells Fargo are offering a one-stop shop, which includes real time balances, corporate research and stock trading. Although there are Internet-only banks which have no bricks and mortar branches (Jordan and Katz, 1999) they do not appear to have been successful. The most viable option for most banks is to develop on-line applications while maintaining some level of in-person service.

A Jupiter Media Metrix study in the USA found that brick-and-mortar banks with a multi-channel customer approach are thriving in the Internet era, although online-only banks are struggling. From July 2000 to July 2001, unique visitors to online-only banking sites dropped from 1.2 to 1.1 million, an 8.1% drop. In the same timeframe unique visitors to multi-channel banks such as Chase, Wells Fargo and Citibank rose from 6.4 to 13.4 million, a 110.5% increase. The report's authors suggest that online-only banks can still carve out a niche by building some physical distribution points (including ATM's) and by targeting specific audiences. For example, Affinity Bank targets well-off retirees, the Naval Federal Credit Union has pioneered the concept of ATM's on naval ships and G&L Bank serves gays and lesbians by allowing them to pool assets to obtain loans, which other banks are reluctant to do (Koller, 2001).

Controlling costs in the banking sector is a key management objective and this industry has been keen to convert customers to online media and to utilise eCommerce, as it is significantly cheaper than face-to-face transactions and has additional benefits. According to the Australian Bureau of Statistics (Trewin, 1999-2000), the main benefits of internet use according to the banking industry were: better access to information and services, ability to facilitate business across different time zones, broader client exposure, improved customer satisfaction and reduced business costs. Chou (2000) argues that the Internet provides an excellent opportunity for business communications and transactions as it allows organisations to establish direct links with current and new customers while being able to deliver new products and services. For example, the Advance Bank in Germany decided to implement a virtual bank to stay competitive and gain access to a larger customer base without incurring the huge costs of putting in place a large branch network (Jelassi & Enders, 2000).

Awad (2000) observes that the combination of computers, the internet and information technology have become a feasible substitute for labour- and paper-intensive banking processes. In sum, the main drivers for eCommerce in the banking sector are: (1) increasing efficiency (2) improving the level of service offered (3) increasing flexibility (4) improving control over operations (5) reducing operating and labour costs (Aungles, 1992; Game and Pringle, 1984; Child, 1985) and (6) being able to respond more effectively to competition and to gain access to customers outside the organisation's geographical area in an increasingly global market (Jelassi & Enders, 2000). The industry holds a positive view of technological changes such as the ATM, phone banking and the utilisation of the internet (Awad, 2000), which do not require face-to-face interaction between customers and branch staff.

3. CONCEPTUALISING THE IMPACT OF ECOMMERCE ON EMPLOYMENT: IMPLICATIONS FOR HR STRATEGIES IN BANKING

When reviewing the literature, we found many theories and perspectives such as the technological determinist perspective (Sabel, 1982; Markus & Robey, 1988), the socio-technical approach (Mumford, 1999), the Marxist theories (Braverman, 1975) and feminist views (Wajcman, 1993; Game and Pringle, 1984) used to explain technological change (Knights & Murray, 1994). We were unable to find, however a comprehensive theoretical model that would assist us to understand the human resource issues when implementing eCommerce technologies and business processes.

We have identified three particularly useful theoretical perspectives dealing with workplace issues, which incorporate IT explicitly into their analyses. None of the three deals directly with eCommerce, but they all provide useful concepts for understanding its relevance to human resource issues – as well as for grasping the emerging principles of organisational management in a global, networked economy.

eCommerce has become an important part of the ability of financial institutions and banks to strategise and compete (Awad, 2000). The implementation of eCommerce necessitates a redesign of work tasks and consideration of how employees are managed to ensure that the investment in these technologies is realised. Each of the three perspectives discussed suggests areas for exploration and conceptual tools to analyse the relationships between eCommerce and HR management.

3.1 Child's labour process approach

Child (1985) developed his framework within a labour process model, which highlights the structure of employee-manager relations. He argued that management does not focus primarily on the labour process when investing in new technology, but that there are implications that could be seen as an unfolding of managerial strategy. 'New technology' includes information technology, microelectronics, software and communications facilities (Child, 1985: 112) and, of course, eCommerce (which he did not explicitly identify). Managers justify the changes to the labour process by reference to new technologies and response to competitive pressures (Child, 1985: 117). Child identified four interrelated management strategies which typically incorporate new technology.

These strategies consists of the **elimination of direct labour** through automation or flexible production systems, **contracting** in which the employee is re-cast as an independent contractor and paid for an agreed amount of labour time, **dissolution of traditional job demarcations** where workers perform a range of tasks that extend traditional job and skill boundaries and finally the deskilling and **degradation of jobs** in which the skill, knowledge and control is removed from the workers and vested in management (a strategy typical of Taylorism).

Several of the trends Child identified are evident in the banking industry. For example, during the last decade, banks in the US and Australia have been downsizing their organisations by closing branches and reducing their staff levels through redundancies, early retirement and natural attrition (Jesse, 1997). Many traditional banking jobs have declined or disappeared altogether, for example typists, secretaries, tellers and bookkeepers, and have been replaced by ATMs and other technologies. Employees at different levels of a bank will be affected in a different way by the eCommerce evolution. The elimination of direct labour strategy is concentrated in the middle and bottom layers of the employment hierarchy (Adler, 1991).

The employees in lower ranks, for example call centre employees and customer service representatives, have little input into the information technologies that are implemented. This layer tends to be where most of the automation and computerisation takes place (Adler, 1991). The implementation of an eCommerce strategy often means the integration of front and back office functions. Closing branches and increasing automation would suggest that many of these jobs would be replaced by computerisation of tasks requiring fewer employees to do the work. Jesse (1997) found that in the United States, fewer staff were required in both the new delivery channels, such as the internet, and those channels that were being radically altered such as retail branches. eCommerce technologies are a driver of labour reduction, often resulting in staff redundancies (Jesse, 1997).

Nor are professionals and middle managers immune to the effects of IT and eCommerce implementation. The more automated the organisation becomes, the fewer employees are needed at management level. The position of branch manager, for example, has come to involve less discretion in making decisions. For example, something as basic as approving a loan is automated by using computerised credit checking (Scott & Walsham, 1998). With greater automation and centralisation, there are also fewer branch offices, with a consequent diminution in career path offerings.

Changes in terms of employment and outsourcing have had a significant impact on the workforce in the banking industry. In Australia, employment in banking grew until 1990, after which it first declined and then levelled off. The occupational profile from 1986 to 1994 changed significantly – the proportion of clerical workers fell, while professional and technical workers, or those in the middle of the pyramid, increased. From the mid 1980s to the late 1990s part time employment in the banking and finance sector rose from 10.2% to 17.7%, mostly filled by women (Venn & Smith, 1999). There is a developing trend away from full-time clerical positions, which are easiest to automate.

In the US Jesse (1997) found that as labour management receives more attention, there is a greater likelihood of outsourcing functions such as credit scoring, some sections of human resources, payroll, purchasing and marketing. Jesse (1997) argues that managers in the Australian banking sector will increasingly utilise outsourcing (and part time workers) to improve their management of staffing requirements, as better use is made of technological innovations. If a job is downgraded from full-time to part-time, the benefits for the employee are also downgraded. If the job is outsourced, there is often no guarantee that the job will be the same or consist of the same benefits. The labour relations issues are passed on to another party.

Some apparently non-core areas of banking such as property management and securitisation are being outsourced, which means that the banks do not need to staff these areas themselves. This trend is shown clearly by the fact that the industries engaged in communications, computing, accounting, legal, property and telecommunications as part of an enlarged finance industry (FBCS industries) have been growing by over 50 percent compared to the industry average of 20 percent in the seven years to 2000. Employment in each of the broad categories of the FBCS industries has grown while overall employment in the banking sector itself has declined (Trewin, 1999-2000).

Child's framework highlights the different interests that managers and employees have in the employment setting. Different economic forces shape their actions and they experience the impact of technology in divergent (as well as convergent) ways. However, Child does not deal with some important issues that relate to eCommerce implementation such as the role of training or how managers deal with conflicting objectives that they need to attain such as reducing costs (including the rationalization of staff), while at the same time satisfying more demanding customers.

3.2 Zuboff's theory of Informatisation

A different perspective is provided by Zuboff (1988:57) who analysed the implications of information technology for job design. She argued that while computer-based automation is removing the human element from the business process (or deskilling workers), the "informating" (adding information and analysis to data) power of technology creates pressure for "profound re-skilling" by increasing the explicit information content of job tasks thereby reconfiguring the nature of work. Zuboff contends that even if the managerial purpose in implementing new technology was to control or deskill, managers themselves have their own pressures and issues to deal with while implementing new technology which may negate these intentions. In the "informated organisation", she asserts, the rigid separation of mental and manual labour is dysfunctional, distinctions between white and blue collar workers no longer exist and there is an intellectualisation of work tasks which results in the organisational skill base being more equal across the enterprise (Zuboff, 1988: 393).

Ideally, the organisation becomes a learning organisation, which translates to the expansion of knowledge by each member of the enterprise. Organisational structures become more flexible, individuals are in a position to align themselves to jobs they are best suited to and managers will have to become more open and participative. In Zuboff's 'informated' organisation, employees become more intellectualised as they deal with the new information technology. The intellective skill is applied by analysing the problem, determining the data required for analysis and the application of the analysis to improve performance. That is, employees in this type of organisation need to use higher order analysis and conceptualisation with a view to improve the way in which data are assimilated, interpreted and responded to. Managers in this scenario are responsible for task related learning and educating others (Zuboff, 1988: 397). Frenkel et al. (1995) support this view and contend that as workers' discretion increases to meet the variable requirements of customers, control by technology and bureaucratic control will be superseded by "info-normative" control (which can be described as control based on data objectification or performance indicators; and employee accommodation or commitment to performance standards). Information technology enables these trends but does not inevitably lead to the creation of a culture in which employees and citizens are empowered and fulfilled through the application of that technology.

Davidow and Malone (1992) suggest that Management Information Systems have replaced middle management's role of providing an information channel through which senior management can obtain business information and communicate orders to more junior employees. Computer networks are able to provide information about the status of operations more efficiently and effectively than the people they replace. This has to all intents and purposes reduced the layers of management required to run an organisation. Increasingly, employees will organise their own tasks and deal directly with customers, while computers will provide the information middle managers used to transmit. Management have a different role which consists of setting goals, measuring results, directing strategy, putting work processes in place and establishing the environment in which these processes will work effectively (Davidow & Malone, 1992:167). In a virtual organisation, managers will be in a position where they will not only have to manage traditional subordinates but also employees from other departments brought in for projects, part-time employees and other people that work for other related organisations such as suppliers (Davidow & Malone, 1992).

There is evidence of the processes that Zuboff (1988) theorised in other contexts. The skill demands of more sophisticated technical systems means that employees are generally moved from more repetitive, semi-skilled positions to ones involving more autonomy and/or skill (although if they are not able to make the transition to higher skill levels, they may lose their jobs altogether). This polarisation of outcomes (some jobs becoming more skilled while others are automated and disappear) makes training, deployment and career planning issues important ones for human resource management.

Employment changes in banking have followed the trends suggested by Zuboff in a variety of ways. In the Australian banking sector, for example, from 1979 to 1993 there was a reduction in the proportion of workers without post-school qualifications, and after 1990 workers with post-school qualifications outnumbered those without (Venn & Smith, 1999) which suggests that workers are becoming more skilled. As the banking sector moves further into the eCommerce era, workers will be expected to become still more flexible and multi-skilled. Jesse (1997) observes that the competencies or skill sets for banking roles are changing. There is greater importance given to sales in front line roles dealing directly with customers. There is also a general broadening of competencies for those in management. These skills include change management, change resilience, flexibility, technological awareness, a high level of interpersonal skills, team work skills and the commitment to continual learning (Jesse, 1997). These new skill requirements will become more pronounced as eCommerce becomes more established. Zuboff's concepts explain these trends (which Child's does not) and complements Child's framework by identifying 'informatising' aspects of job design, although the two approaches come from very different starting points.

For many employees, developing the relevant skills will pose some problems as they will require, in most cases, a significant amount of retraining. This may create tensions as management attempts to put in place the most appropriately skilled workers for the changing job positions.

Workers unable or unwilling to change will find that their positions and skills quickly become redundant.

The effects of eCommerce on employment in the banking sector raise many issues for human resource management. These include managing recruitment and retention of highly skilled employees in a competitive environment. Job decline, relocation, increased working hours and deskilling (Pinsonneault and Rivard, 1998; Adler, 1991) are serious issues but may be less challenging in the longer term than managing new skill development, including responding to customer demands, and being competitive in a global context. In this context, de-skilling strategies will not meet the challenges of managing the sector's workforce. In a case study of a French bank, management believed that low-level clerical jobs could be 'de-skilled' since with the implementation of new computer technology these workers would not require knowledge of banking procedures. This approach caused considerable difficulties with data integrity and incorrect transactions (Adler, 1991) and management had to rethink the training and cognitive skills required for people performing these functions. In the competition to recruit skilled employees for specialist positions, banks must manage their human resource functions to provide intrinsic as well as financial incentives. Designing jobs in line with the principles outlined by Zuboff will address this issue to some extent.

Zuboff's perspective offers a useful balance to Child's bleak account by identifying the positive potential of technologies for work design, increased employee autonomy and intrinsic job satisfaction. However, her account still focuses primarily on the organisation and even on the activities of individual employees. The implications of eCommerce extend beyond the boundaries of the individual worker and the bounded enterprise to incorporate networks and interorganisational working arrangements, in some cases virtual organisations. This requires a perspective that can accommodate the shifting of the boundaries of work performance.

3.3 Managing post-fordist organisations

A third perspective provides an analysis which includes changes in the ways that organisations operate in relation to trading partners and customers, arguing that there has been a major shift in systems of production to more flexible, dispersed and responsive processes. There are many interpretations of what forms of work organisation are emerging and how this is changing workplace relations (e.g., Frenkel et al 1995, Littler, 1991, Webster, 1995). We have used the work of authors who conceptualise this transition as change from a Fordist to a post-Fordist organisation of production (see

Webster, 1995; Piore & Sabel, 1984, Clegg 1990; Thompson and McHugh, 1995). Clegg (1990) argues that the modern organisation is essentially Taylorist / Fordist with the key characteristics of rigidity, technological determinism as well as differentiated and deskilled jobs. Individuals, by virtue of their office exercised authority and control to achieve productivity and efficiency. Although this control has been limited by the costs of surveillance and control, the hallmarks of the Fordist organisation are stability, control, hierarchy and formality (Thompson and McHugh, 1995: 167). By contrast, a post-fordist organisation is flexible, decentralised and participative with jobs de-differentiated and multi-skilled (Clegg, 1990). The post-Fordist mode of flexible specialisation is associated with flexibility of employees, flexibility of production and flexibility of consumption. Customers demand differentiation in the products and services they receive, i.e. flexibility of consumption, which requires organisations to produce more variety in their products to satisfy this change in consumption behaviour (Littler, 1991, Webster, 1995, Economist, 2001, Agarwal et al., 2001). Littler (1991) argues that 'flexible specialisation', from an industrial relations perspective may be associated with worker participation where management create a more consultative working environment. The 'build to replenish' production model, for example, changes the way production lines operate entirely: 'everything is brought to the worker, as if he were a surgeon' (Economist, 2001: 4).

While the term 'post-Fordism' has been useful for conceptualising new business and social relationships, not all authors have been persuaded that the post-Fordist work and the new, flexible workforce concept of post-Fordism really offers the blessings it may appear to offer in an eCommerce context (Maruyama, 1993). It may create a less secure and more fragmented job and career structure. The ability to work from home, indeed, the whole tele-working concept which was originally a somewhat unrealistic philosophy of happy mothers working at home beside their contented babies has, in fact, given way to driven executives working all hours and in all places, using their laptops and mobile phones to stay in contact, even on aeroplanes and in trains.

eCommerce, both as a set of technologies and a set of business practices, has been an integral part of the post-Fordist transition. The ability to provide 24x7 service support, help-desks, outsourcing, individualised customer profiles, and so on, are all dependent on technologies we associate with eCommerce. They also enable the removal of management layers, out of office work and the redesign of jobs. These technologies are essential for the transition from a Fordist to a post-Fordist structure by facilitating flexibility, responsiveness, customisation and new organisational structures. They also facilitate global networks and the internationalisation of business, tying together of markets, currencies and organisations (Clegg, 1990).

This perspective provides a powerful set of concepts for understanding the issues involved in the introduction of eCommerce technology and its effects both within an employment organisation and with customers and trading partners.

If the theorists of post-Fordism are correct, then the traditional personnel management approaches will not encourage the autonomy, responsiveness and independence required of employees. This is especially the case in industries such as banking where IT has automated the more routine jobs and employees are now more educated and skilled. They are likely to resist Fordist management regimes and the very nature of their work is not likely to lend itself to those strategies. However, HR management also needs to support organisational strategies that are competitive in the post-Fordist environment. This requires a transformation in the organisational ethos as well as an evolution of specific HR practices.

Figure 1 shows how different Human Resource strategies are related within a wider context. The banking industry relies on economies of scale to stay competitive while at the same time having to become more flexible in a more customer driven environment. Economies of scale are achieved by utilising technologies such as eCommerce to automate jobs (thereby eliminating them), to move customers to a self-service delivery channels or to deskill certain jobs – a deskilling/fordist strategy. On the other hand, eCommerce technologies have allowed organisations to develop specialised and customised products and services that require employees to become more skilled in an "informated" environment – an up-skilling/post-fordist strategy.

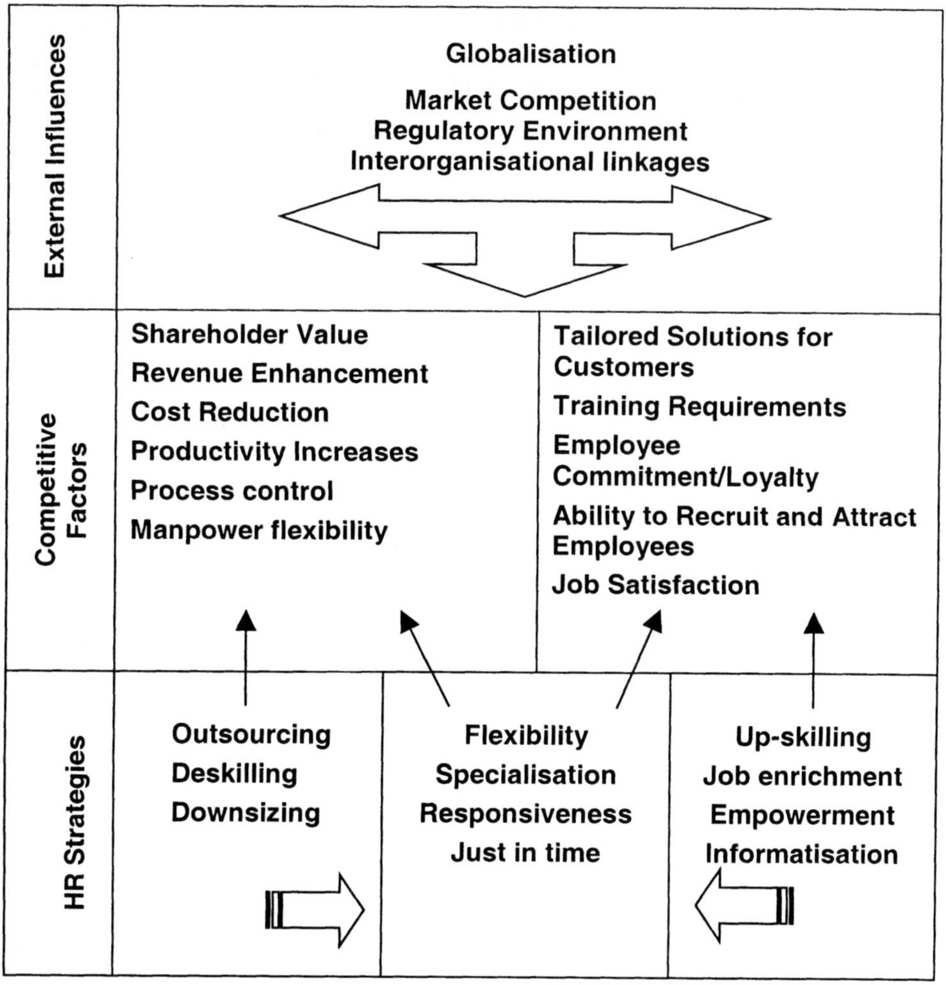

Figure 1. Human Resource Strategies in a Global Competitive Environment

Management, particularly in an industry such as banking, need to be aware of external influences such as globalisation, market competition and government policies when making decisions about the implementation of eCommerce technologies and the resultant effects this has on stakeholders. At the same time, the implementation of eCommerce technologies will have an impact on the way jobs are designed, how employees are recruited and retained, how training is conducted and how employees are supervised.

Each of the frameworks examined in this paper has limitations when used in isolation. However, drawing on the three frameworks offers us a more complete way to analyse the relationship between eCommerce and the HR issues in the banking industry. Taken together, the three frameworks suggest that banks and other enterprises face competing business goals and competing strategies for achieving them. In fact, even these perspectives may not be sufficient to explain all the factors in the industry environment. While globalisation shapes many business practices, it is not unfettered. Governments still exert their own influence on employment issues through their regulation of both labour practices and aspects of the finance market. In contrast to Australia and the US, German law prohibits the State-based banks (such as the various state-owned banks) from closing branches. Although these banks are introducing Internet-based payments (very popular in Germany) to try to reduce calls on branches, thus allowing them to reduce staff numbers, the branches themselves remain and provide a financial hub for village life across the country.

We will draw on this composite framework to investigate the HR implications of electronic commerce implementation in the banking and finance sector in the Australian context, especially as they relate to service provision to retail customers, who increasingly expect the kind of service provided in the post-Fordist context.

4. CONCLUSIONS AND A PROGRAM FOR FURTHER RESEARCH

This paper has discussed three theoretical perspectives for understanding the employment implications of eCommerce with a focus on these issues in the banking industry. Each perspective is useful for understanding the complex issues that eCommerce implementation raises for human resource management. Child's framework is helpful for understanding some implications of eCommerce for HR management strategies which entail reducing costs and increasing control, but it is limited by its focus on intra-organisational issues and traditional organisational structures. Zuboff's perspective points to the transformative potential of technology and the need for HR management to expand skills and empower employees to make better use of the technology. But her approach also concentrates on the localised context. By drawing on theories of post-fordism, the interorganisational and sector-wide issues can be addressed. This perspective highlights the increasingly global, fast-paced, flexible and customer-focused nature of competition.

A composite approach provides a good conceptual framework for understanding how the potential of eCommerce technologies for job loss and degradation can be addressed and managed to help banks remain competitive in a globalising marketplace for financial services, one in which consumers will seek a high quality of service. Banks need to find a way to manage these employee relations issues while grappling with the issue of how to gain competitive advantage and derive profit from new eCommerce business processes and technologies.

The employment impact of eCommerce in the banking industry provides a fertile area for investigation. A better understanding of the design, adoption, implementation and management of such technologies is needed.

Our research will address several specific questions suggested by the literature on organisational sociology and human resource-employee relations management.

- To what extent will eCommerce accentuate or undermine the use of a Fordist approach to business in the banking sector?
- What current HR strategies do banks use to give them competitive advantage in the consumer banking market?
- How do banks link eCommerce implementation and HR management to attract and retain retail customers?

Change management strategies are needed to deal with eCommerce implementation over the long term, not just for a given round of change. Future research should focus on the technological shapers of the labour process(es) and the dynamic relationships between eCommerce implementation, market pressures and human resource management strategies. The lessons learnt from the banking industry are relevant to a wide range of other organisational contexts.

REFERENCES

Adler, P. (1991). 'New Technologies, New Skills', *Technology and the Organisation of Work*. Geelong, Victoria, Deakin University Press.

Agrawal, M., Kumaresh, T.V. and Mercer, G.A. (2001) "The False Promise of Mass Customisation". McKinsey Quarterly. Vol 3. [Available Online] www.mckinseyquarterly.com/article_page.asp?tk=519677:1089:2&ar=1089&L2=2&L3=38 [Accessed: 23 February 2002].

Aungles, S. B. and S. R. Parker (1992). *Work, Organisations and Change Themes and perspectives in Australia*. Sydney, Allen & Unwin.

Australian Banking & Finance. (16 July 2001). Wingspan crashes to earth. Australian Banking & Finance: p20.

Awad, E. M. (2000). The Structure of E-Commerce in the Banking Industry: An Empirical Investigation. *Proceedings of the 2000 ACM SIGCPR conference on The 2000 ACM SIGCPR conference, 2000,* Illinois USA.

Battellino, R. (2000). 'Australian Financial Markets: Looking Back and Looking Ahead', *Reserve Bank of Australia Bulletin*: 16-25.

Blackburn, P., R. Coombs, et al. (1991). Information Technologies, The Service Sector and the Restructuring of Consumption. Technology and the Organisation of Work. Geelong, Victoria, Deakin University Press.

Braverman, H. (1974). Labor and monopoly capital; the degradation of work in the twentieth century. New York, Monthly Review Press.

BRW (2001). 'Good Bank, Bad Bank', *Business Review Weekly (BRW),* Vol. 23. Available: www.brw.com.au/stories/20010125/8618.htm (25 January 2001)

Causer, G. and C. Jones (1996). "Management and the Control of Technical Labour." *Work, Employment & Society,* Vol. 10, (No. 1): 107-123.

Child, J. (1985). 'Managerial Strategies, New Technology and the Labour Process', *Job Redesign Critical Perspectives on the Labour Process.* D. Knights, H. Willmott and D. Collinson. Aldershot, England, Gower Publishing Company Limited: 107-141.

Clegg, S. R. (1990). Modern Organizations: Organization Studies in the Postmodern World. London, SAGE Publications Ltd.

Connolly, C. and G. Thomas (2000). 'Is Your Local ATM Accessible?' *Australian Consumer Association Choice,* Available 203.166.10.91/articles/a101731p1.htm (October 2000)

Chou, D. C. (2000). 'A Guide to the Internet Revolution in Banking', *Information Systems Management,* Vol. 17, (Issue 2): 51-58.

Davidow, W., H. and M. S. Malone (1992). The Virtual Corporation. New York, United States of America, Harper Collins.

Dewan, R. and A. Seidmann (2001). "Current Issues in E-Banking." Communications of the ACM Vol. 44(No. 6): pp31-32.

Economist (2001). "Mass Customisation: a long march". The Economist. [Available Online] www.economist.com/displayStory.cfm?Story_ID=691227 [Accessed: 23 February 2002]

Finance Sector Union. (2001). FSU Campaign Against Bank Closures, LaborNet. 2001 (www.labor.net.au/news/95.html).

Frenkel, S., M. Korczynski, et al. (1995). "Re-constituting Work: Trends Towards Knowledge Work and Info-normative Control." Work, Employment & Society Vol. 9(No. 4): 773-796.

Game, A. and R. Pringle (1984). *Gender at Work.* London, Pluto Press.

Hughes, J., O'Brien, J. et al. (1999). 'Getting to know the 'customer in the machine'. *Proceedings* of the international ACM SIGGROUP conference on supporting group work, Phoenix, Arizona.

Jelassi, T. and A. Enders (2000). 'Branch-less and Internet Banking: The Advance Bank in Germany'. *Proceedings of the 13th International Bled Electronic Commerce Conference,* Bled, Slovenia: 200-212

Jesse, H. (1997). 'New Technology and Distribution Strategies - Future Impact on Workforce Planning'. *The Australian Banker,* Vol 111, No. 1: 28-33.

Jordan, J. and J. Katz (1999). 'Banking in the Age of Information Technology', *Regional Review,* Vol. 9 (Issue. 2): 24-30.

Kalakota, R. and A. B. Whinston (1997). *Electronic Commerce A Managers Guide*, Reading, Massachusetts, Addison-Wesley, Inc.

Knights, D. and F. Murray (1994). Managers Divided: Organisation Politics and Information Technology Management. Chichester, John Wiley & Sons Ltd.

Koller, M. (29 August 2001). Online Banks Still Struggling, Internet Week. (update.techweb.com/cgi-bin4/flo?y=eEVp0Bg8ak0H30RmX0Aj)

Littler, C. R. (1985). Taylorism, Fordism and Job Design. Job Redesign Critical Perspectives on the Labour Process. D. Knights, H. Willmott and D. Collinson. Aldershot, England, Gower Publishing Company Limited: pp10-29.

Littler, C. R. (1991). Technology and the Organisation of Work. Geelong, Victoria, Deakin University Press.

Markus,L.M. & Robey,D. (1988) Information Technology and Organizational Change: Causal Structure in Theory and Research. *Management Science* 34, 583-598.

Maruyama, K. (1993) "Is the Japanese Production System Post-Fordism?". Keizai Hyoron. February.

Mumford, E. (1999). Routinisation, Re-engineering, and Socio-technical Design Changing Ideas on the Organisation of Work. Rethinking Management Information Systems An Interdisciplinary Perspective. W. Currie and B. Galliers. New York, Oxford University Press Inc.: pp28-44.

Piore, M. J. and C. F. Sabel (1984). The Second Industrial Divide: Possibilities for Prosperity. New York, United States of America, Basic Books Inc.

Pinsonneault, A. and S. Rivard (1998). 'Information Technology and the nature of managerial work: from the productivity paradox to the Icarus paradox?' *MIS Quarterly,* Vol. 22 (No. 3): 287-312.

Reserve Bank of Australia, (1996). The Future of the Financial System. *Reserve Bank of Australia Bulletin*: 9-13.

Scott, S. V. and G. Walsham (1998). 'Shifting boundaries and new technologies: a case study in the UK banking sector'. *Proceedings of the International Conference on Information Systems*, Helsinki, Finland.

Venn, D. and G. Smith (1999). 'Technological Change and Employment in the Australian Finance Industry', *Australian Journal of Labour Economics,* Vol. 3 (No. 2): 113-129

Thompson, P. and McHugh, D. (1995) *Work Organisations: A Critical Introduction* 2nd ed., Houndmills, Macmillan Press

Trewin, D. (1999-2000). Finance Australia. Canberra, Australian Bureau of Statistics: 108 pages.

Trewin, D. (2000-01). Finance Australia. Canberra, Australian Bureau of Statistics: 94 pages.

Webster, F. (1995). Theories of The Information Society. London, Routledge.

Wells, N. and J. Wolfers (2000). 'Finance with a Personalized Touch: The banking industry has sure benefited from new technologies, but how can we ensure customer satisfaction?', *Communications of the ACM* (Vol. 43 No. 8): 31-34.

Wajcman, J. (1993). The masculine mystique. Pink Collar Blues: Work, Gender & Technology. B. Probert and B. W. Wilson. Melbourne, Melbourne University Press: pp20-40.

Zuboff, S. (1988). In the Age of the Smart Machine: The Future of Work and Power. Oxford, UK, Heinemann Professional Publishing Ltd.

Zwass, V. (1996). "Electronic Commerce: structures and issues." International journal of electronic commerce Vol. 1 (No. 1): pp. 3-23.

WHEN E-BUSINESS BECOMES K-BUSINESS.....WILL IT BE 'A NATURAL ACT'?

DEREK BINNEY[1] and MAGED ISHAK[2]
[1]*Chief Knowledge and Technology Officer (CKTO) for Computer Sciences Corporation (CSC) – Australia*
[2] *Faculty of Science, The University of Technology, Sydney, Australia*

Abstract: This paper proposes that the next wave of electronic business (e-business) will move from current transaction based e-business to the merging of e-business and knowledge management, and that organizations that have already internally adopted knowledge management (KM) will find the transition to this next wave of e-business a natural and sustainable act. The first part of the paper explores recent trends and forecasts pertaining to e-business and KM, concluding that organizations are moving towards a more networked economy where partnerships, collaboration and knowledge sharing will complement current transactional e-business, and that successful KM requires a balance between technology and organizational change interventions. The second part of the paper explores the issues associated with establishing a knowledge-sharing culture in preparation for the next proposed evolution of e-business by presenting interim results of a current study into the adoption of KM practices by staff in a global IT services company. Instantiating various adoption models, the study investigated time of adoption and potential factors that influenced the adoption of 2 KM applications by 283 survey respondents. The findings of this research are interpreted in light of the proposed next wave of e-business, providing additional considerations and actions that organizations may take to successfully participate in the evolution of e-business in a more knowledge sharing based networked economy.

1. INTRODUCTION

Although e-business has been with us for nearly a decade businesses use of e-business has been mostly informational or transactional and is still in the early stages of adoption and diffusion(Elliot 2002). E-business is seen by some as just another 'selling and distribution channel'(Needham 2002) though some are seeing the 'e-Opportunity[13]' as a chance to re-engineer business(Feeny 2001). Based on a review of the literature and our experience as practitioners in the field of e-business and KM we propose that the evolution of e-business, which we call the next e-wave, is moving beyond transactional e-business and building towards a world of partnerships, collaboration and knowledge sharing. We feel this evolution implies the merging of current e-business and a collective discipline currently known as Knowledge Management (KM) and will create a new knowledge-sharing era of e-business, one we could call k-business.

As this evolution takes place it will enable new highly interconnected organizational designs and models – it will also pose new questions and challenges. As organizations use e-business technologies to experiment with new forms of relationships to create and leverage new business opportunities, they will begin to redefine their traditional organizational boundaries. They will also pose new and interesting questions: what are the organizational boundaries?, how do I work with people who are both competitors and partners?, what knowledge do I value and must keep in house to protect vs. that which can be shared for mutual advantage or marketed and sold?. Organizations will also be asking their staff to behave differently – to collaborate and share knowledge with others – often former competitors – from outside of their own organization. Is this too big an ask? As organizations plan to exploit the evolution of e-business, will they be asking their staff to extend an existing KM system and its implied knowledge-sharing behaviors or will organizations be asking their staff to operate in the evolving e-business world and simultaneously develop a knowledge-sharing culture?.

Current KM literature proposes and recommends KM adoption theories based either on generic organizational change theories (Senge et al. 1999) or subjective views of the factors considered by consultants or interviewed managers as significant to an organizations success in KM and achieving a 'knowledge sharing culture' (Chiem 2001; Tissen, Andriessen, & Deprez 1998). There appears to be little empirical research into the factors that influence KM adoption and the timing of the KM adoption by *individuals* in a system. This paper explores the issues associated with establishing a knowledge-sharing culture by presenting the interim results of a recent study into the adoption of KM practices by staff in a global IT services company. Using Diffusion of Innovation and Collective Behavior theory as its theoretical foundation, the study looks at factors influencing the adoption

[13] E-Opportunity is a term coined by Feeny.

and timing of the adoption of the selected KM applications seen as relevant to the future knowledge-sharing based e-business.

The findings and their interpretation provide an empirical case study foundation for strategists and planners planning to establish KM systems and a knowledge-sharing culture internally in an organization as a pre-cursor to evolving their current e-business investments.

These propositions on the evolution of e-business, research results and interpretations are developed and discussed as follows. Section 2 provides a summary of e-business and KM today and proposes the knowledge-sharing evolution of e-business. Section 3 presents the study method and a general discussion and interpretation of the study results. Section 4 interprets the study results in light of the proposed evolution of e-business and contains a number of observations and recommendations for those planning to be part of the proposed evolution and then leads to some concluding remarks.

2. E-BUSINESS AND KNOWLEDGE MANAGEMENT – COMBINING FOR THE NEXT E-WAVE.

This section of the paper reviews e-business and KM today and develops the proposition that the evolution of e-business will be the convergence of these two disciplines. This convergence will allow new levels of organizational design based on dynamic organizational boundaries, communities, conversations and knowledge sharing. It concludes by suggesting that this evolution will require actions involving both technology and organizational change.

2.1 E-business Today

E-business today can be viewed in two dimensions; the business dimension and the consumer dimension. The business[14] dimension of e-business today is the world of business to business (B2B), business to consumer (B2C) and business to employees (B2E). Business' external use of the net and net technology has primarily been informational (or promotional), e.g. www.xxx.com sites, or transactional. Business' transactional use of the net ranges from net markets serving B2B needs through to consumer support for on-line purchasing or service support.

[14] Whilst the term business is used in the paper the propositions apply equally to government. Refer(Baum & Di Maio 2000) for a discussion on the 4 phases of e-Government being Presence, Interaction, Transaction and Transformation.

There is increasing discussion and some action about the opportunities to the redesign business and on the 'e-Opportunities' the net represents(Feeny2001; Powell 2000; Rozwell & Berg 1999; Schulman & Raskino 2001). Most of this discussion is focused on transactional and supply chain applications. Business' primary motivations for adopting of e-Business remain economy, service, new lines of distribution and speed. The current growth in investments and activity in the e-business space continues to be the implementation of existing technologies and transactional capabilities in an increasing range of industries, and new applications, across a broadening spread of organization types and sizes(Elliot2002). Ie More participants and an increasing range of available transaction types.

Consumers' use of the primary e-business delivery platform (the Net) is not limited to interacting with business. Consumers personal use of the Net includes communication and knowledge sharing between themselves using e-mail, bulletin boards, chat rooms and other collaborative tools that support the voluntary exchange of knowledge[15] provides an interesting insight into the possible evolution of e-business. The topics covered in these exchanges can range from topics of personal interest, personal interactions/contacts and views on products and services – their application and quality. The underlying conversational model allows many people to interact and share their information, opinion and, or knowledge. This knowledge sharing is uncensored, voluntary and without organizational boundaries. The consumer Net use is a world of conversation. Levine et al observe that now and increasingly in the future, 'Markets are conversations'. (Levine et al. 1999).

Businesses use of these collaborative technologies and applications internally to promote information and knowledge sharing also provides an indicator to the possible evolution of e-business. Business has begun to explore the external application of these collaborative technologies as we see the emergence of Extranets to facilitate virtual teaming between organizations[16].

Where will businesses' use of the internet head? Feeny (Feeny2001) proposes the e-Opportunity has three dimensions e-Operations, e-Marketing and e-Service and gives some insight into the next e-wave in his discussion of e-Service. Another likely directions are as a transactional platform for device-to-device communication. Yet another is as a key-enabler of new forms of organizational design – the blurring of organizational boundaries

[15] The individuals involved in this dimension may be in the general public or behind the organization's firewalls.

[16] These early interactions are often discrete and one-off based around a commercial opportunity, project or product development, and involving small and defined players from the parties involved.

and the emergence of community based organizational designs, conversations and knowledge sharing. (De Gues 1997; Levine, Locke, Searls, & Weinberger1999; Wenger 2001)

We propose that the pointers to the evolution of e-business lie in the convergence of current personal use of the Net (collaboration and knowledge sharing), the extension of businesses first steps towards B2B collaboration and virtual teaming and the forecast new organizational models based on collaboration and community based organizational design.

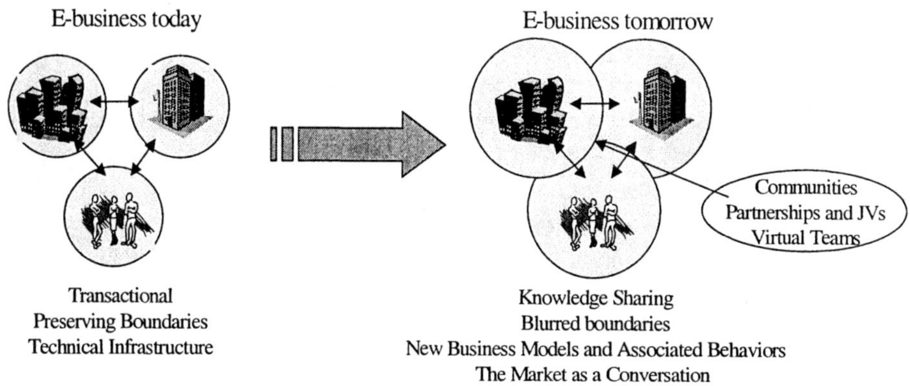

Figure 1. The proposed evolution of e-business

This proposition implies the marriage of e-business and a collective discipline currently known as Knowledge Management, the following section introduces some key KM concepts and applications relevant to this marriage and sets the scene for the research to be reported into the adoption of KM.

2.2 Knowledge Management Today

'Know how' is a term covering an organizations competencies and the skills of its people, its intellectual property and internal systems and its external relationships such as alliances, partners and customers(Sveiby 1997). KM can be seen as the coordinated effort to create and leverage an organizations 'know-how' value. Many writers see an organization's 'know-how' as its most valuable asset. (Davenport & Prusak 1998; Edvinsson & Malone 1997; Leonard 1999; Nonaka 1987).

KM covers a range of applications and technologies. Binney (Binney 2001b) provides a framework for this diversity, called the KM Spectrum, that established that the KM applications discussed in the literature can be categorized.

Knowledge sharing in the evolving e-business model will likely take two forms, the sharing of explicit or codified knowledge and the sharing of tacit, personal or social knowledge. In this light the KM Spectrum categories of interest in the context of this paper are 'Asset Management KM' and 'Innovation and Collaboration KM'. The *Asset Management KM* category is where individuals and organizations contribute and reuse their explicit knowledge. Where this explicit knowledge has value to parties outside an organization there is a commercial opportunity to exploit this value with consumers, client organizations, partners and, or alliances. The *Innovation and Creation KM* category is of interest as it offers the opportunity for organizations to partner in new ways in order to create new, often virtual, organization structures and, or to collaborate in the development of new products, services and innovations. The collaboration and community model aspects of *Innovation and Creation KM* offer a new model for B2B operational interactions using collaborative technologies. On the B2C side communities offer an interesting model for consumers to interact with an organization and its individuals directly across organizational boundaries.

Organizations are using net technologies internally to develop intranets that provide a knowledge environment supporting their KM applications. A successful knowledge environment is seen as one that leverages existing explicit and tacit knowledge through reuse and contact mechanisms, and fosters the creation of new knowledge through real-time collaboration within virtual teams and knowledge communities[17]. To be of sustainable value these KM environments require responsiveness from the participants and currency of content (aka knowledge assets). A sustainable KM environment requires an organizational culture supportive of this responsiveness and knowledge sharing. Where organizations do not have a strong 'knowledge-sharing' culture organizational change interventions are normally required. It is increasingly recognized that establishing a knowledge environment requires a balance between implementing enabling technologies and organizational change interventions aimed at establishing a knowledge-sharing culture(Binney 2001a); (Leonard1999; Senge, Kleiner, Roberts, Ross, Roth, & Smith1999).

2.3 E-business – Tomorrow

The business focus of KM initiatives to-date has been on the creation and leveraging of know-how value internal to that organization. As discussed

[17] Innovation and Creation KM in the KM Spectrum

earlier there is an emerging business model where the boundaries and distinctions between organizations are being blurred and dynamically defined. Internet technology is allowing the creation of areas where parties can interact and do business – beyond transactions – into the world of knowledge sharing, collaboration, conversations and communities(Drucker 1988; McDermott 2000; Wenger2001). Another aspect of this emerging organizational model is one where conversations take place and significant knowledge is shared between parties as part of the way work is done.

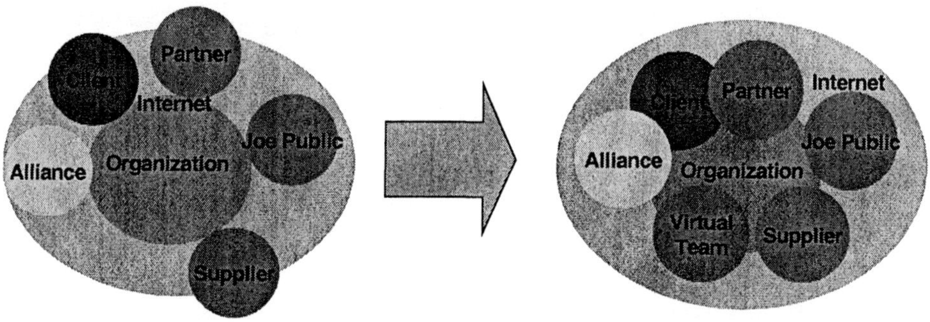

Figure 2. Envolving Business Models'

This new model offers business the opportunity to extend current B2B e-business to define and operate new partnerships and alliances aimed at the creation of new knowledge and products (innovation) when both parties contribute some of their know-how to create something new (Nonaka1987). The model also has the potential to extend B2C e-business beyond the e-Service opportunity proposed by Feeny (Feeny2001) in the direction foreseen by Levine et al(Levine, Locke, Searls, & Weinberger1999), where the 'Market (and all its interactions) is a conversation'.

How does an organization prepare for the evolution of e-business? We propose that organizations need to be prepared in two areas. The first is concerned with the effort required to establish the necessary technology environment, the second is concerned with the effort required to establish and sustain the necessary cultural environment.

Establishing the technical environment – Most current e-business systems have been designed for external use. In contrast most organizations are still designing their internal knowledge management and intranet systems with a view that they will only ever be used internally. Given that most organization's knowledge systems have been designed on this premise, they need to be re-architected to allow the 'opening up' of the organization. The literature is starting to recognize some of these issues at least as far as

IT support (Colville 2000) and security(Zannes 2000) are concerned. There has been little discussion on the areas IT will need to address which include shared domain issues such as security, content classification and segmentation, approaches to the integration with other parties' heterogeneous I/T environments and on self-service collaboration.

Establishing and sustaining cultural environment – An internal knowledge environment needs people to participate in terms of contributing assets, reusing assets, taking the time to interact with others by participating in communities and, or responding to requests for assistance. We propose that an external knowledge sharing environment will need the same conditions ie a knowledge sharing culture. As discussed earlier, the literature indicates that establishing a 'knowledge-sharing culture' requires varying degrees of organizational change interventions. As we shall see from the study results presented in the next section this takes time and the factors that influence individual adoption and participation in knowledge sharing vary between types of knowledge applications and vary over time.

3. RESEARCH METHODOLOGY

This section of the paper reviews a current study into the influences that affect the adoption and the timing of adoption of KM applications. The study was developed to investigate generic models applied to a wide range of social changes and their applicability when instantiated to KM as an innovation requiring changed behavior. The design of this study aimed to investigate and understand the adoption and the timing of adoption by individuals in an organization of selected KM applications.

3.1 Research Design

The core proposition to be tested in the research is 'that an individual's adoption of KM applications and the timing of that adoption is significantly affected by the identified potential influencing factors'. The 7 identified influencing factor categories are listed in Table1. Influencing Factor Categories and their Primary Source. Diffusion of Innovation and general Organization Design models of adoption provided the theoretical foundation for this research.

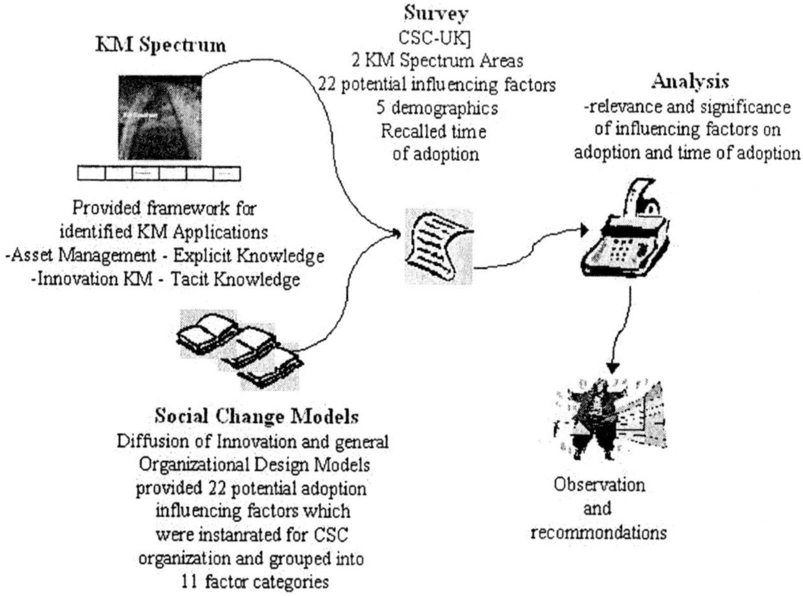

Figure 3. Overview of Research Model

The tool used to test the hypotheses derived from the core proposition was a survey of staff in CSC-UK. The survey instrument was designed using to collect the following the following groups of data.

The first group of data pertained to awareness, use and recalled time of adoption (first use) of the two KM applications. The recalled time of adoption questions asked *when the identified application was first used* in the nominated time increments over the past 5 years. The next group of data pertained to potential factors, which could affect the adoption of the identified KM applications. Diffusion of Innovation and general Organization Design theory was used to drive and instantiate the 22 potential adoption influencing factors to be tested in the survey. Diffusion of Innovation theory suggests that innovations are adopted over time by different adopter types with each adopter type having distinctive adoption influences or motivations. Diffusion of Innovation theory posits that the process of adoption is a social process where individuals adopt an innovation at different rates based on a mix of influencing factors including connectedness, relative advantage, risk minimization, complexity, observability and opinion leaders. (Rogers 1995). The generic Diffusion Theory potential influencing factors were instantiated for the target audience in CSC based on interviews and a review of CSC's internal documentation pertaining to their KM system. The Organizational Design factors such as trust and encouragement, which appeared in the general KM literature, were also used. (Davenport & Prusak1998) The final group of data were demographics.

To assist with the analysis, the questions relating to these groups of variables were aggregated and binary versions of the aggregated variables generated – these binary versions are indicated by '_B'. The following table maps these potential adoption-influencing factors to the generic factors identified in Diffusion of Innovation and Organizational Design Theory..

Influence Factor Category		
Source	Survey Category [and number of discrete tested factors.]	Terms used in this paper
Diffusion Theory		
Connectedness	Internal Connectedness [2]	IC_B
	External Connectedness [2]	EC_B
	Overall Connectedness [2]	OC_B
Relative Advantage	Relative Personal Advantage Factors [8]	PLF_B
Risk Minimization		
Complexity	Ease of Use [1]	Ease_B
Observability	Role Influenced Respondent [1]	Role_B
Opinion Leaders		
Organizational Design	System Level Factors [8]	SLF_B
Demographics	Respondents Role [1]	RRole
	Organization Unit [1]	Org
	Age [1]	Age
	Gender	Gender

Table1. Influencing Factor Categories and their Primary Source

The survey was designed to be completed in less than fifteen minutes. A pilot survey was conducted with 6 participants. The results from the pilot survey were discard. The survey contained questions requested by the survey sponsor in addition to those developed to test the research hypotheses – these sponsor-based questions were not included in the analysis.

The core proposition and the generated hypotheses were tested using different statistical methods. The tests were done in two stages, first at the binary aggregated influence factor level, as per the above table, and second, where the elements were found to be relevant in the first stage, at the survey variable level – Figure 4 provides an overview of the tests.

The first test used was a test for the relevance of the influence factor category. 95%confidence intervals (CI) was generated for each of the binary influence factor category variables and if the lower bound of the CI was greater than 50% influenced, then the factor was assessed as relevant, or of interest to the relevant population[18]. The second test used the same binary variables and tested for influence factor affect on the decision to adopt (Y/N) using a Chi-Squared Cross tabulation test for the binary adoption influence category variable vs binary adoption variable. The third test tested for affect on time of adoption for the cases where adoption had occurred using a Chi-Squared cross tabulation test for binary adoption influence category variable vs time period of adoption for cases where adoption had already occurred.

For each significant influence factor category in the above tests two further tests were performed to see which elements of the categories contributed to the significance. Descriptive techniques were used to determine if certain elements were more prominent in the responses. Where appropriate these descriptive tests were supported by further Chi-Squared Crosstab tests or by Analysis of Variances - ANOVA – tests on the discrete influence factors. The following diagram summarizes the test used in the research.

[18] A lower CI level of 50% was selected based on personal experience that management will more readily focus on something which influence the majority of staff.

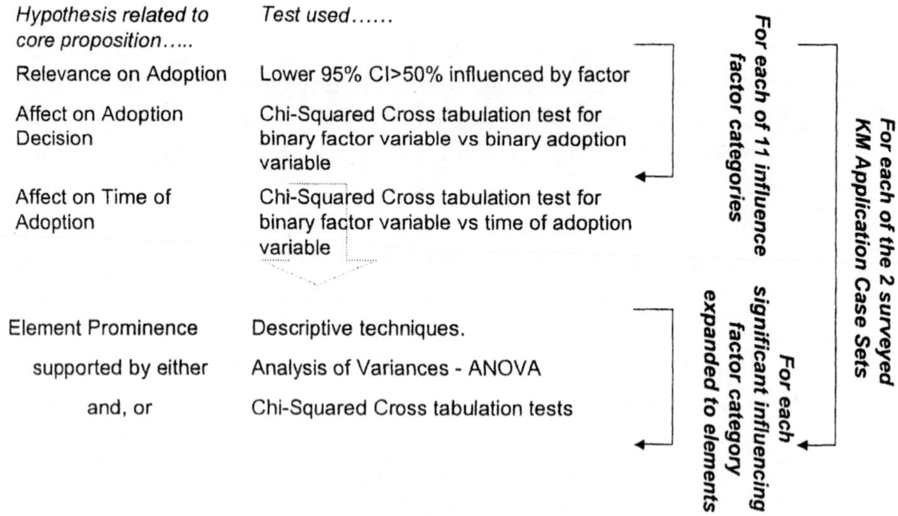

Figure 4. Overview of Tests Used in Research

In presenting the results, significance levels of 5% will be considered unless otherwise noted. The 95% confidence interval was generated using an Excel spreadsheet; all other analyses were conducted using SPSS Release 10.0.7 Standard Version.

3.2 Overview of CSC

Computer Sciences Corporation(CSC) is a US based multi-national company in the IT services sector. As indicated in its promotional literature(CSC Corporation 2001), CSC is a leading provider of information technology services to commercial and government markets worldwide. The services it offers include Consulting, Systems Integration and Outsourcing. CSC considers itself a knowledge-based company in that it's $US11.1billion annual revenues are generated by services based on the application of its employees' knowledge and experience, its accumulated IP and knowledge base, and a range of alliances with leading technology providers. Its 68,000 employees have access to a global web-based knowledge environment, called CSC Sources, which has evolved over the past decade. The KM applications used in the survey are part of this knowledge environment. CSC-UK is a fully owned subsidiary established in the UK in 1969. CSC UK has over 8,000 staff, is the fastest growing CSC division and accounts for approximately 33% of the CSC's revenues[19]. CSC-UK was selected for

[19] For additional information on Computer Sciences Corporation or CSC-UK go to csc.com.

this study due to its management's acknowledgment of the importance of KM to its business strategy, its history of promoting knowledge management applications and its relatively stable workforce over the period covered in the survey[20].

3.3 Results

The survey was conducted during September and October 2001. The survey was publicized on internal electronic bulletin boards asking people to visit the CSC-UK internet site and complete the survey. A total of 287 self-selected responses were received of which 4 responses were incomplete, deemed invalid and removed from the case set. The demographics; sex, age and length of service, of the 283 valid cases were compared to the corresponding CSC-UK population demographics, using the t-test for proportions differences, with the sample appearing representative of the overall CSC-UK population.

The self-selection technique of publicizing the survey being conducted and calling for voluntary responses means that there was no way of determining how many of the CSC-UK staff were aware of the survey and therefore determining the survey size and response rate. Whilst the demographics indicate that the sample is representative of the general population, the sample may be biased as the proportion of staff who didn't ever use the intranet and therefore by implication the KM applications (currently un-quantified) are not represented in the survey data. A sample size of 283 is statistically sufficient to produce reliable statistical inference for the factors examined in this study. It is understandable that further work of a qualitative nature would still be recommended in future work to strengthen the research model and emphasize, or otherwise, the findings of this research. In this sense, the survey tool conducted in this study and its results can be regarded as exploratory and as developing theory.

3.3.1 General Results of the Study

The following chart shows the cumulative adoption of the KM applications analyzed for this study.

[20] Whilst CSC-UK appears to have been achieving its growth rate without significantly increasing it's staff numbers.

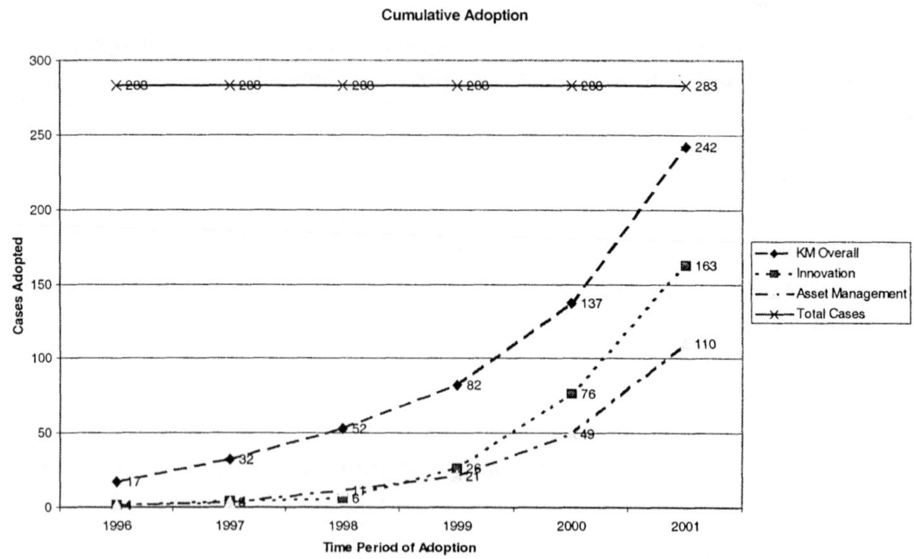

Figure 5. Cumulative Adoption

The proposition that individual adoption and therefore the diffusion of KM as an innovation are affected by certain influencing factors was supported in all case sets. The proposition that time of adoption is affected by certain influencing factors was supported for the KM Overall and Innovation case sets and rejected for the Asset Management case set.

At the time of the survey the following percentage of cases KM Overall (85%), Innovation (57%) and Asset Management (39%) had adopted the respective KM application. Assuming that the adoption process is not yet complete, as indicated by cumulative adoption slopes, then the survey is capturing a snapshot of the system in the process of diffusion rather than looking back at a system which has completed the diffusion process.

3.3.2 Detailed Results

The average time of adoption was for KM Overall (44.13 months), Innovation (51.68 months[21]), and Asset Management (50.78 months). The following table summarizes the test results. Relevant or significant results have been highlighted.

[21] Or 21.68 months when adjusted for general release of the communities application in mid-1999.

Adoption Type	Factor Category	95% Confidence Interval	Affect Binary Adoption χ^2 Test [p value] [Past% Future%]	Affect Processial Adoption Test χ^2 Test (p vaule)
KM Overall	slf_b	Relevant [100 100]		
	plf_b	Relevant [58 70]	Sig [.17][67 45]	
	role_b	Relevant [74 84]		
	ec_b			
	icl_b	Relevant [61 72]	Sig [.000][72 37]	Sig [.000]
	ocl_b	Relevant [75 84]	Sig [.006][82 63]	Sig [.000]
	ease_b	Relevant [81 90]		Sig [.010]
Demographics	rrole	N/a	Sig [.006]	
	org	N/a	Sig [.006]	
	age	N/a		Sig [.025]
	gender	N/a		
Innovation	slf_b	Relevant [100 100]		
	plf_b	Relevant [56 73]	Sig [.000][73 51]	
	role_b	Relevant [71 85]		
	ec_b			
	icl_b	Relevant [53 70]	Sig [.000][77 53]	Sig [.000]
	ocl_b	Relevant [68 83]	Sig [.013][85 73]	Sig [.011]
	ease_b	Relevant [81 94]	Sig [.000][77 55]	
Demographics	rrole	N/a		
	org	N/a		Sig [.000]
	age	N/a		
	gender	N/a		
Asset Management	slf_b	Relevant [100 100]		
	plf_b	Relevant [55 75]	Sig [.000][76 56]	
	role_b	Relevant [65 83]		
	ec_b			
	icl_b		Sig [.12][76 61]	Sig [.006]
	ocl_b	Relevant [65 82]	Sig [.21][86 75]	
	ease_b	Relevant [77 94]	Sig [.013][76 62]	
Demographics	rrole	N/a	Sig [.036]	
	org	N/a		
	age	N/a		
	gender	N/a		

Table 2. Summary Test Results - KM Overall, Innovation and Asset Management Case Sets.

The elements identified as a result of the exploratory Stage 2 tests (descriptive/ANOVA/Crosstab tests) are collectively presented in the following table for all three case sets. The identified elements are those that were seen to be significant amongst the elements aggregated for the above analysis of binary influence factors.

Factor Category	Identified Elements
slf	Encouraged to Research, Encouraged to Develop, Encouraged to connect, e-mail link
plf	Personal Effectiveness – Reuse, Personal Effectiveness – People, General recognition, Increase Skills
role	Peer same, supervising manager, Sources Staff UK, Sources Staff US[22].
course	Project Management, Catalyst (CSC's Methodology)

Table 3. Elements Identified in Stage 2 Tests

3.4 Generalized Results Discussion

This research provides evidence that establishing a knowledge-sharing culture, as defined by participation in the identified KM applications requires time to achieve a considerable level of participation. The average time of adoption and the current levels of adoption are: KM Overall - 44 months and 86% adoption; Communities[23] 21 months and 58% adoption and Asset Management 51 months and 39% adoption.

The results from the test of the potential adoption influencing factors investigated can be discussed in 3 groups. These groups are 1) those factors that were neither relevant nor significant, called *non-factors*. These non-factors are seen to have no significant impact on the decision or the timing of the decision to use a KM application, 2) those factors whose results were relevant but not significant – called *Environmental factors* as they can be considered as 'Pre and Necessary Condition' factors to adoption but did not affect the decision or the timing of the decision to use a KM application, and 3) those whose results were both relevant and significant in either, or both the decision to adopt and, or the timing of the decision to use a KM application – called *Adoption Factors*. The following table summarizes the results of this classification, which are then discussed with comments and interpretations in italics.

[22] In the Innovation sample Sources Staff US were not indicated, probably due to the maturity of the Knowledge environment when the communities application was implemented.

[23] . This figure has been adjusted for the re-launch of the Communities application in 1999.

Influence Factor Category	**KM Overall**	**Innovation**	**Asset Management**
System Level Factor (slf_b)	Environmental	Environmental	Environmental
Personal Level Factor (plf_b)	Adoption	Adoption	Adoption
Role Influenced Respondent (role_b)	Environmental	Environmental	Environmental
External Connectedness (ec_b)	Non-factor	Non-factor	Non-factor
Internal Connectedness (ic1_b)	Adoption	Adoption	Adoption
Overall Connectedness (oc1_b)	Adoption	Adoption	Adoption
Ease of Use (ease-b)	Adoption	Adoption	Adoption

Table 4. Potential Influencing Factor Category Classification

Environmental Factors

1. All influence factors derived from general Organizational Design theory were environmental. The factors of most significance in the System Level Response category were responses to; Encouraged to Research, Encouraged to Develop and Encouraged to Connect which indicate an environment existed in CSC where the importance to use the KM applications is generally acknowledge and encouraged. This environment, whilst possibly needing to be in place as a precursor to adoption, did not have an affect on the actual decision to adopt.

   KM deployment plans need to recognize and encourage knowledge-sharing behaviour as a pre-and necessary condition to adoption but these environmental factors do not directly affect the adoption decision.

2. When aggregated role was an environmental factor and did not have an affect on the decision or time of adoption. The influence of other people (roles) in the organization on personal adoption was greater than 74% across all cases but was not significant in its affect on time of adoption. On closer investigation ANOVA tests showed that the actual role indicated did vary over time. Initially the role influence came external to the UK, from US staff, moved to UK support staff and is currently coming from the roles of Peers and Supervising Manager24. The degree of influence also increased through this period with the roles of Peer and Supervising Manager indicated in approximately 40% responses. This progression appears to be consistent with diffusion theory where there is a need to observe and reduce risks associated with the adoption of an innovation. Executive management were not reported as having any significant affect on individuals' decisions to use a KM application.

[24] Overseas influence was not observed for the communities application that was introduced after the UK support organization was in place and after other KM applications had been in use for a number of years.

Focus on interventions that demonstrate use and benefit with an early focus on first line management to provide re-enforcement and encouragement and peers to provide observed use and benefit.

Adoption Factors.

1. Personal level factors that reflected personal effectiveness were more indicated than those that provided recognition or personal development. The Personal Level Factors of most significance were 'Personal effectiveness through reuse' and 'Personal effectiveness through connection to others in the organization'. The potential personal benefit through increase effectiveness had a significant affect on the decision to adopt but not the timing of the decision.

   Focus on interventions that stress and demonstrate improvements in personal effectiveness.

2. Attending internal training courses were indicated in over 70% of responses. The factor seemed the most significant of all factors on the decision and the timing of the decision to adopt was attendance at internal courses. The courses contributed most to this significance were those that taught methodology and project management disciplines.

   The deployment plan should incorporate references and reinforcements to KM applications and behaviours in internal training.

3. Ease of use was indicated as an influence in the decision to adopt but not the timing of the decision to adopt.

3.4.1 Non-factors

The only influence factor in the non-factor category was external connectedness. External connectedness had an inverse affect on adoption with the respondents who were more externally connected less likely to use internal systems. This could be due to the value derived from and, or effort taken to maintain external connections vs. the additional effort and value from internal systems. *This factor may become important where management is promoting both external knowledge-sharing and continued participation an organizations internal knowledge program.*

4. PREPARING FOR THE PROPOSED EVOLUTION OF E-BUSINESS - CONSIDERATIONS

This paper has proposed that organizations are moving towards a networked economy where partnerships, collaboration and knowledge sharing: that the evolution of e-business will involve the merging of current e-business and knowledge management. It further proposed that the KM Spectrum applications of most relevance would be those that focused on explicit and tacit knowledge sharing i.e. asset management and innovation KM. The current survey into the adoption of these KM applications has been presented and generalized observations on the adoption of KM drawn. These concluding thoughts look at the survey results in light of the proposed evolution of e-business and may assist strategists and planners charged with the responsibility of positioning their organizations to be part of the next e-wave. This positioning can start now by establishing an internal knowledge-sharing culture as a parallel or pre-cursor initiative, so that the move to a knowledge-sharing e-business of the future will be a natural and sustainable act.

For strategists considering the next e-Wave:

- Achieving a k-culture takes time, it doesn't happen overnight
- Adoption is not influenced by management or executive mandate

For those responsible for developing and implementing a knowledge management program

- Deployment and organizational change interventions need to address both environmental and adoption influence factors, they should combine Collective Behavior and Diffusion of Innovation models. Having established the environment, attention needs to be given to relative personal advantage factors such as increased personal effectiveness.
- The timing of the decision to adopt is influenced by others (roles) and the ability for adopters to observe usage, minimizing risk and have demonstrated its advantages – deployment plans should look for opportunities to promote peer observation and demonstrate personal advantage, rather than appealing to higher order organizational benefits.
- The relative importance of the influence factors varies over time - this needs to be considered in the deployment interventions and associated messages.
- Sustaining a shared knowledge environment between organizations as a new business model is potentially going to be more complex than sustaining an internal knowledge environment, especially when the shared environment involves the intersection of more than one organization – it may require sympathetic 'k-sharing cultures' in all

parties to add sufficient value to the individual participants and to be sustainable.

The proposed evolution of e-business may represent the progression of Peter Keen's 'reach and range' model of business interactions(Keen 1991) by taking the range dimension beyond 'multiple cross-linked transactions' as organization interact with other organizations, and potentially any 'net-enabled individual', in new, more meaningful, and conversational ways.

Finally returning to Levine and co,

> 'Corporate firewalls have kept smart employees in and smart markets out. It's going to cause real pain to tear those walls down. But the result will be a new kind of conversation. And it will be the most exciting conversation business has ever engaged in'. (pg xiii, (Levine, Locke, Searls, & Weinberger1999)).

Whether this conversation and collaboration is between organizations to create new knowledge and exploit new opportunities (evolving B2B) or provide new levels of customer intimacy and service (evolving B2C), we believe it will require a knowledge-sharing culture that is a 'natural act' in order to allow organizations to more easily reap the benefits of 'the most exciting conversation'. It is hoped that the discussion on the evolution of e-business to a future based on collaboration and knowledge sharing, combined with the interpretation of the research presented in the paper may increase your e-business strategic planning awareness and provide a more complete picture of the elements required to seek and achieve success in e-business as it evolves.

ACKNOWLEDGEMENTS

We would like to acknowledge the support of Dr James Guthrie, MGSM Sydney, for his thoughts, insights and valuable editorial work and Matthew Doucy, CSC-UK for sponsorship of the survey. The responsibility for the contents of this paper nonetheless remains entirely that of the authors. Please contact the authors via e-mail with any feedback or comments.

REFERENCES

Baum, C. & Di Maio, A. 2000, *Gartner's Four Phases of E-Government Model*, Gartner Group, Stamford, Ct., TU-12-6113.

Binney, D. 2001a, "The Knowledge Management Spectrum – the Human Factor.," in *Knowledge Management in the Socio Technical World - The Grafitti Continues*, 1 edn, E. Coakes, D. Willis, & S. Clarke, eds., Springer-Verlag, London, pp. 17-29.

Binney, D. 2001b, "The Knowledge Management Spectrum – Understanding the KM Landscape.", *Journal of Knowledge Management.*, vol. 5, no. 2, pp. 33-42.

Chiem, P. X. Trust Matters. Knowledge Management May, 2001, 50-55. 2001. San Francisco, Knowledge Management.

Colville, R. 2000, *E-Support Extends the IS Organization Beyond the Firewall*, Gartner Group, Stamford, Ct., SPA-09-7367.

CSC 2001, *CSC Knowledge Management Practice Guide* CSC.

CSC Corporation. CSC Fact Book. 1. 1-11-2001. El Segundo, CA, CSC.

Davenport, T. H. & Prusak, L. 1998, *Working Knowledge : How Organizations Manage What They Know* Harvard Business School Press, Boston, MA.

De Gues, A. 1997, *The Living Company* Harvard Business School Press, Boston, Mass.

Drucker, P. F. 1988, "The Coming of the New Oganization," in *Harvard Business Review on Knowledge Management*, Harvard Business School Press, Boston, MA, pp. 1-19.

Edvinsson, L. & Malone, M. S. 1997, *Intellectual capital :realizing your company's true value by finding its hidden brainpower*, 1st edn, HarperBusiness, New York.

Elliot, S. 2002, "Research Model and theoretical implications," in *Electronic Commerce: B2C strategies and models*, 1 edn, S. Elliot, ed., John Wiley and Sons, Chichester, UK.

Feeny, D. Making Business Sense of the E-Opportunity. Sloan Management Review 2001[Winter], 41-51. 2001. Cambridge, Ma, MIT.

Keen, P. G. W. 1991, *Shaping the Future - Busiiness Design through Information Technology* Harvard Business School Press, Boston, Ma.

Leonard, D. 1999, *Wellsprings of Knowledge - Building and Sustaining the Sources of Innovation* Harvard Business School Press, Boston, MA.

Levine, R., Locke, C., Searls, D., & Weinberger, D. 1999, *The Cluetrain Manifesto - The End of Business as Usual* Perseus Books, Cambridge, Ma.

McDermott, R. 2000, "Knowing in Community:*10 Critical Success Factors in Building Communities of Practice*", *IHRIM Journal* no. March, 2000.

Needham, K. More companies reject the Internet. Sydney Morning Herald . 2-19-2002.

Nonaka, I. 1987, "The Knowledge Creating Company," in *Harvard Business Review on Knowledge Management*, Harvard Business School Press.

Powell, J. 2000, *Changing Business Models and Roles: How e-Commerce is Changing Financial Services Institutions*, CSC, El Segundo, CA.

Rogers, E. M. 1995, *Diffusion of innovations*, 4th ed. edn, Free Press, New York.

Rozwell, C. & Berg, T. 1999, *How to Devise a Practical, Effective E-Business Strategy*, Gartner Group, Stamford, Ct., R-09-4033.

Schulman, J. & Raskino, M. 2001, *Gartner Predicts 2002: E-Business*, Gartner Group, Stamford, Ct., LE-15-1112.

Senge, P. M., Kleiner, A., Roberts, C., Ross, R., Roth, G., & Smith, B. 1999, *The Dance of Change - The Challenges of Sustaining Momentum in Learning Organizations - A Fifth Discipline Resource*, 1st edn, Doubleday/Currency, New York, NY.

Sveiby, K. E. 1997, *The new organizational wealth :managing & measuring knowledge-based assets*, 1st edn, Berrett-Koehler Publishers, San Francisco, CA.

Tissen, R., Andriessen, D., & Deprez, F. L. 1998, *Value-Based Knowledge Management: Creating the 21st Century Company: Knowledge Intensive, People Rich* Addison Wesley Longman, Nederland BV.

Valente, T. W. 1995, *Network Models of the Diffusion of Innovation* Hampton Press.

Wenger, E. Supporting communities of practice- a survey of community-oriented technologies. 2001, www.ewenger.com

Zannes, E. 2000, "Knowledge Management in Industry and Government: The conflict between Security and Knowledge Sharing.", *IEEE* pp. 160-169.

DESIGNING AN ONLINE SELF-ASSESSMENT TOOL UTILIZING CONFIDENCE MEASUREMENT

GRAHAM FARRELL[1] and YING K. LEUNG[2]
[1]*School of Information Technology, Swinburne University of Technology, Australia*
[2] *Department of Information & Communications Technology, Hong Kong Institute of Vocational Education*

Abstract: The convergence of multi-disciplined technologies to address and support the rapid evolution of e business is critical to the success of many ventures. There is an increasing demand for the availability of tools to assist in the evaluation and processing of information as it flows between the bodies involved. A tool that could predict and forecast expected occurrences with a stated level of confidence is considered to be extremely valuable and well worth pursuing. The area of Web based learning is rapidly becoming a fundamental component of corporate training areas and educational Institutions, with an increasing reliance on the delivery of their programs via the Internet or Intranet. The success of such programs is dependent on the marrying of Internet technology, Information systems, Human Computer Interaction and Educational Strategies while catering for the individual student.

This research investigates and evaluates the design of an innovative approach to a formative assessment that permits the participant to register their level of confidence. The system then provides enriched feedback and can predict the performance of the individual, reducing the number of failures. The system is based on the traditional Online Multiple Choice Questions format, but it facilitates a method of registering the level of confidence of the student's response to each of the options available, generating a score that reflects their level of understanding of the topic being considered. The iterative process of design and the results of a pilot program are discussed, and directions for further studies suggested.

1. INTRODUCTION

E-learning has in recent times become a major commercial enterprise. The supplying of quality education, at a global level, at a reasonable cost and with the additional convenience to the client, is seen to be a profitable opportunity. The cost efficiency of e-learning in the corporate sector is potentially so large that many substantial companies around the world are developing online materials for their in-house training or negotiating with established online education providers to do the same. In addition to this other organizations have established profitable business through the on-selling of material that they have developed.

Assessment plays a critical role in the educational process as both a means of grading and supplying valuable feedback to the students. The embracing of technology as an integral part of the delivery of education has increased the requirement for effective assessment systems to be available to the student, encouraging self-assessment at all stages of the learning experience. It is accepted wisdom that testing for the purpose of feedback should be an integral part of the sequence of learning activities rather than an interruption to that sequence. See Principles and Standards for School Mathematics (2000) for example.

In view of the commercial importance of e-learning, and the fundamental role played by assessment in the learning process, it is essential that we explore technologies and approaches that will improve assessment effectiveness in e-learning and its impact on the learning process. The e-learning removes the personal interactivity held within the classroom situation. The challenge for e-learning is to enhance the online learning experience with techniques that provide rich, personalized feedback to the individual student.

Traditionally both formative and summative methods of assessment have been reliant on the instructor to supply the feedback. With the ever-increasing demand to constrain delivery costs, resulting in increased student staff ratios, unintentional delays in supplying feedback to the student can occur to the disadvantage of both the student and the instructor. As a result often the most valuable feedback occurs at the final stages of the learning path generally too late to be of great value to the students' learning process and providing only limited feedback to the instructor. This situation tends to benefit primarily the group of students participating in the next scheduled delivery of the unit. To maximize the effect and value of feedback it must be instantaneous, an inherent characteristic of an online assessment tools due to the nature of the encompassing technology. The formative assessment feedback cycle should occur early, and then constantly throughout the duration of the learning experience.

Doebbert (1999) emphasizes the need for the student to develop skills in managing and controlling their learning, with the utilization of technology assisting in the process as they travel the educational path. Accordingly we are interested in looking at approaches to assessment, which help to place control of the learning in the hands of the student

This paper proposes and investigates the design of an innovative formative assessment tool, Multiple Choice Questions Confidence Monitor (MCQCM), using internet technology. The objective of the project is to develop a self-assessment system that provides enriched feedback to both the student and the instructor in order to benefit all those associated with the learning process. The self-assessment package is based on traditional Multiple Choice Questions. However it utilizes a method of students' registering their level of confidence for each of the options available. The package instantly generates a score that aims to reflect the students' level of understanding of the topic being considered. We discuss the initial design considerations and the corresponding pilot program that followed.

2. FORMATIVE ASSESSMENT

Black and William (1998) use the term "Assessment" as referring to the group of activities undertaken by both teachers and students in assessing themselves, providing both grades and feedback to modify teaching. They state that " such assessment becomes *formative assessment* when the evidence is actually used to adapt the teaching to meet the students needs". On the other hand it is generally accepted that *summative assessment* is a tool that has the primary objective of supplying a grade for the student.

Black and William (1998) refer to the learning environment as being a "Black Box", with input from pupils, teachers, parents and resources, with the consequential outputs being pupils with advanced educational standing. It is within this Black Box that they consider the role of Formative Assessment critical in the transformation of the students' educational standing, contributing to the raising of the national standards.

Marshall University (1999) provides a thorough comparative study of online course delivery software, identifying the active components of each package and the depth of their application. Not surprisingly, online assessment utilizing multiple choice questions format appears in all of the recommended packages such as Blackboard, WebCT, TopClass, Web Course in a Box, Toolbook, and others. They further state that only five of the identified ten packages that offer formative assessment also provide an effective feedback mechanism that directs the student to tutorial paths as a consequence of formative assessment.

Black and William (1998) sate that pupils too often " are content to get by". Perrenoud (1991) suggests that a solution would be for the instructors to "reconstruct the teaching contracts to counteract these acquired habits" with the inclusion of formative assessment as a key component of the learning process.

Resulting amended instructional paths instigated from formative assessment is critical for the students' success in navigating the learning path. We consider instruction and formative assessment not to be just strongly linked but inseparable components in the learning experience.

3. MULTIPLE CHOICE QUESTIONS AND THE ONLINE ENVIRONMENT

The general acceptance of the multiple choice question (MCQ) formats as both a formative and summative assessment tool has seen it extensively utilized in traditional education. This is mainly due to the ability of MCQs to assess a broad field of learning in a compact system that is quick to assess and offers student feedback without excessive cost. The ease of the adaption of the MCQ format to the Hypermedia environment produced fully integrated and automated systems, supplying instant feedback to the students' with suggested direction for further study.

MCQs offer an excellent method of assessing the students knowledge in areas deemed as either right or wrong. However, what about the "shades of gray" or fuzzier areas? Diamond and Forrestor (1973) define knowledge as asking the question "What do you know?" followed by the meta-question of equal importance "How sure are you of the answer to the question about what you know?".

Davidoff (1995) recognizes the need for a more thorough approach in assessing students in the medical arena. He suggests that a system designed to recognize "incomplete or partial knowledge", permitting the student to "hedge", would be greatly beneficial to the learning process. He further states that much of the medical knowledge is "incomplete, ambiguous and conflicting" and that the standard MCQ testing method does not facilitate or reflect the students' level of knowledge and their confidence in that level of knowledge. One of his main concerns is that MCQs recognize and reward those areas of knowledge that is either right or wrong, encouraging guessing and often leading to overconfidence, and he considers "miss-calibrated confidence" in medical education equally as concerning as lack of knowledge.

The scoring of MCQs has long been a point of discussion with serious consideration been given to various scoring models. Consequential scoring models designed for the purpose of eliminating guessing utilize complex scoring algorithms that aim to produce a reflection of the students understanding of the underlying concepts.

Brown and Shuford (1973) produced an MCQ calibrated scoring system "that encouraged honesty", designed to reflect the level of confidence in choosing the answer whilst severely penalizing the participant if they answered incorrectly. The primary objective of this scoring system is to identify students that are either overconfident or under confident.

Pollard and Clarke (1989) produced alternative MCQ scoring techniques designed to minimize random guessing due to the reward and penalty structure of the scoring system. Various institutions have used these methods however, to be effective, full understanding of the calculations involved in the grading schedule is required.

MCQs have traditionally required the student to identify the correct response from a list of possible answers. Traditionally the resulting score is based on the criteria of being correct or incorrect. Pollards (1985, 1986, 1993) extensive scoring mechanism aims to eliminate guessing by allocating a mark for each correct box ticked and each incorrect box ticked.

We see merit in this system but have concerns with the level of complexity in operation by the participant. The student must fully comprehend the consequences of his/her action. The system relies on the combination of boxes ticked with many variations that have to be considered.

Klinger (1997) utilized a system of scoring where the student nominated a position on lines joining the apexes in a triangular shape. Each of the apexes represented the three optional answers. He proportionally divided the lines joining the apexes into segments encouraging the student to nominate their level of confidence. The grade was then scored according to a graduated linear scale of logarithms, rewarding the student if they chose to declare that they were completely unsure of their answer.

This is also the case with other designed systems such as Paul's (1994) interactive response system that requires the student to choose an option demonstrating a level of confidence in their answer. With this system the student places the cursor within a grid area aimed to reflect the confidence of their choice. The system is presented to the student in the format shown in Fig 1. The student must negotiate the area with a mouse and click on the region that they feel portrays their confidence. Each of the three options are located at the vertices of the triangle and the closer the student positions the cursor to the vertex the more confident they are that it is the correct answer.

A corresponding score is then calculated. We have some initial concerns that this system could be difficult to use, as the regions appear to be cluttered at the vertices, and the scoring system for a centrally located choice of no commitment (.33 on the diagram) to any option scores a high 63.

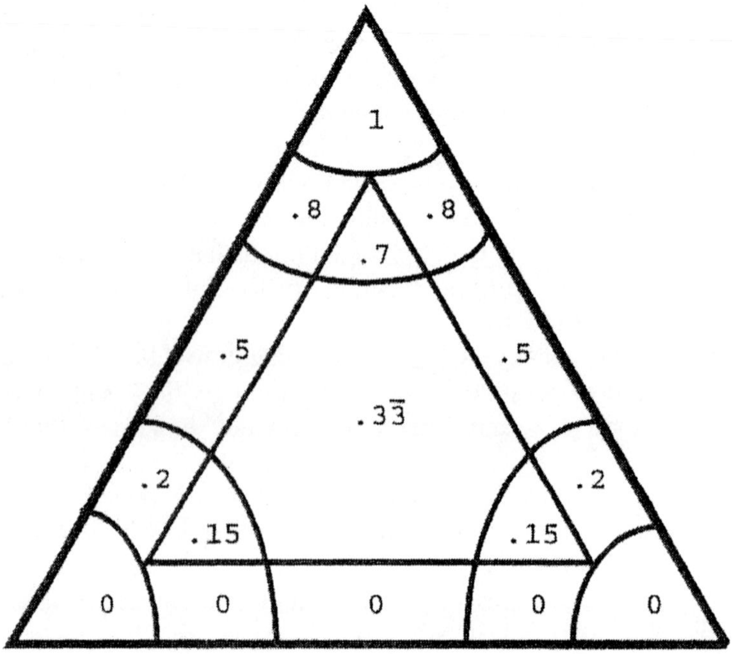

Figure 1. Confidence Measuring Template where the apex is the correct answer showing the consequential values awarded (Paul 1994)

We also consider the user interface to be difficult as it calls upon extreme cognitive load to be operable to a large group of participants.

Previous research has provided a good foundation for the development of formative assessment tools to the benefit of all concerned. The research of Pollard (1989) demonstrates the advantages of developing a scoring system that aims to reflect the students' understanding of the subject while Paul (1994), Brown and Shufford (1993) and Klinger (1997) all have demonstrated variations on systems designed to capture a numerical representation of the students level of knowledge.

The combination of this previous research with the rapid development of the Internet as a means of educational delivery and assessment encourages the designing, testing and evaluation of formative assessment tools that incorporate scoring systems aimed to reflect the level of confidence of the student, keeping them honest to themselves for their benefit.

4. THE MCQCM SELF-ASSESSMENT TOOL

The MCQCM is based on the traditional Multiple Choice Questions format, consisting of a stem with three or four options, as recommend by Kehoe (1995) and Frary (1995). The MCQCM is scalable to permit a variation on the available options as Frary (1995) states that the number of options can be restricted by the available sensible solutions.

In designing the MCQCM the following further criteria were considered, that is the self-assessment tool should:

- Be easy to use and not too demanding of the user.
- Utilize a scoring technique that is simple, placing the user in control of the consequences of their actions.
- Have good usability, engaging the user while exercising sound navigational properties for delivery across the Internet.
- Be able to capture and record the scores of the students as they participated in the exercise.

The final version of the MCQCM used for the trials was a result of considering all of the points culminating in the working prototype with the features described below.

The MCQCM:

- Permits more than one correct answer. This encourages the student to consider all options separately and not to identify what they consider to be the single correct answer and ignore the rest. The advantages of this system above the traditional MCQ format are as follows:
- Permits the instructor to word the options to closely examine the areas of study, eliminating the need to use easily recognizable distracters.
- Forces the student to consider all options carefully, increasing their exposure to associated areas within the topic.

The MCQCM was required to produce a score aimed to reflect the students' understanding of the concept being considered in each question. A simple scoring technique, easily understood by the student, gave the student control. Consequently, the students' were not surprised by the responses of the MCQCM and the cognitive load upon the user was minimized.

Each of the options within a question is scored separately on a continuum from –10 to 10, giving feedback for both correct and incorrect answers. If an option was True and the student moved the slide bar to the right towards the

True label then they would be rewarded with a positive grade depending on their recorded level of confidence. If the recorded level of confidence was 100% then the resulting score would be 10 marks, and so on for each decrement of 10 %.

The same scoring system applies for the situation where the option was False and the student moved the slide bar to the left towards the False label. The position of the slide bar would be recorded and the score would be a positive representation of the level of confidence, being 10 marks for 100% level of confidence. All positive scores were shown in Black.

If an option was True and the student moves the sliding bar to the left towards the False label then the student receives a negative score directly proportional to their recorded level of confidence. If the position is 100% the corresponding score is –10 and so on for decrements of 10%. The same scoring system applies to a situation where the option was False and the student moved the sliding bar towards the True label. All negative scores were shown in Red to ensure that the student realized that their response was incorrect. The final score for each option was given to the student after the completion of the test along with the correct answers.

This MCQCM is designed to reflect the students' level of understanding. The students' are placed in the position where they must clearly state their level of confidence, knowing that they would be proportionally penalized for an incorrect choice and proportionally rewarded for a correct choice. The MCQCM also permits the use of questions that have multiple correct answers, which requires them to identify all possible correct combinations and score accordingly. The design of the MCQCM is shown in Fig 2 .

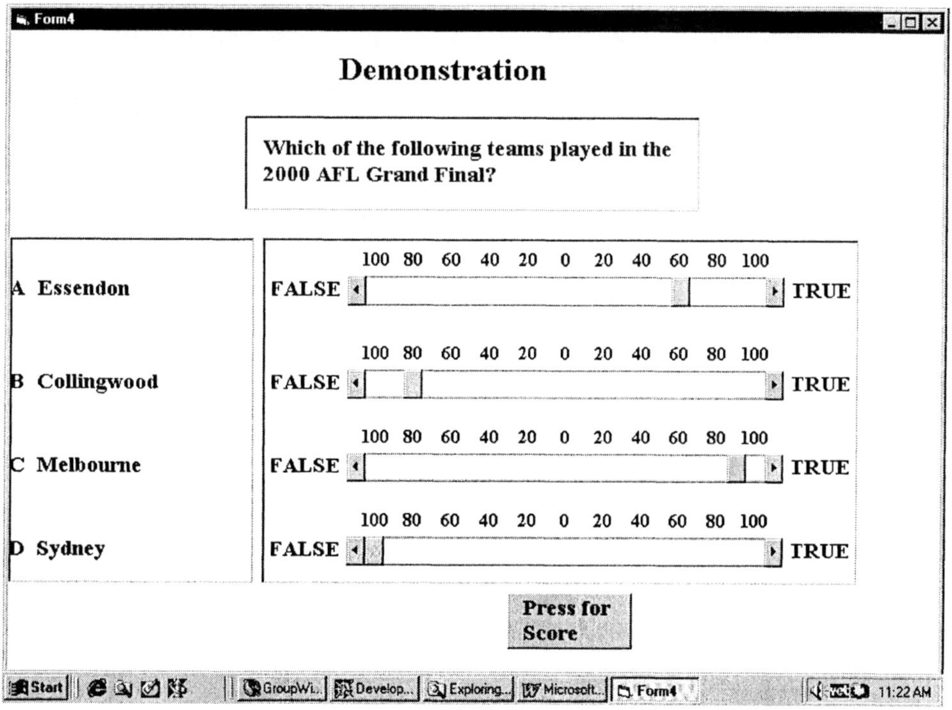

Figure 2. The MCQCM showing the demonstration screen used as part of the training

5. PILOT STUDY

During the development of the working prototype, discussions with experienced instructors about the functionality and design of the MCQCM identified the need to run an initial pilot program. Our objective was to elicit feedback from the operation of the prototype system.

We used Visual Basic to construct the interface with the ability to create individual data tables for each participant. The test responses from each of the participants were captured and displayed to them on completion of the exercise.

In keeping with recommendations for usability testing three males and three female students were invited to complete a test using the newly developed tool in the presence of the designers. The test consisted of five questions pertaining to an area of their study due to be formally assessed. Consequently the students perceived the test as advantageous to their study and were keen to participate.

To help the students become familiar to the self-assessment MCQCM they all participated in an introductory session that demonstrated the package in a non-threatening way. The students were initially required to respond to a general knowledge question set in their social environment. This question addressed a major, well-publicized, sporting event. After successful completion they started the formal test.

The subjects were all observed for the duration of the pilot program and the observations recorded. In addition they were also encouraged to verbalize their thought processes (Verbal Protocol) as they navigated the path of the test. On completion of the test they all participated in an interview session where they were asked a series of questions.

- Was the MCQCM easy to operate?
- Did you understand the scoring system that penalized for incorrect choices and rewarded for correct choices?
- Did you actively use the sliding bar to register your level of confidence freely?
- Did you understand the feedback display produced?
- Do you think that the feedback and resulting score would help you decide your study path?

6. OBSERVATIONS AND RESULTS

The initial introductory session required the subjects to use the tool in a non-threatening environment. This proved to be a successful exercise as they responded to the MCQCM in a relaxed manner. The students were then requested to complete the more formal part of the pilot program. It was observed that all students completed the test without any real operational concerns. However, despite the successful introductory session, there was still some initial apprehension in using the MCQCM.

It was apparent from their verbal protocol during testing they were not all together comfortable with the interface, due to the lack of familiarity. They also expressed concerns about being required to identify not only what they consider to be the correct options but also what they consider to be the incorrect ones. Some demonstrated hesitation registering their level of confidence in all of the options, but tended to only do so for the correct options.

The simple scoring system was well received. During the interview all of the subjects claimed to understand the method of calculating the score and consequently would react depending on their level of confidence to maximize their result. Further, all of the subjects stated during the interview that they understood the feedback, as it clearly reflected their responses. They also agreed that that the feedback would assist them in deciding their study path to improve their understanding of the topic.

It was observed, and confirmed during the interview, that the students tended to minimize the use of the slide bar for the first few questions. However, as the student became more relaxed with using the MCQCM, the use of varying levels selected on the slide bar increased.

All of the students requested for more opportunities to use the test as they considered it to be greatly beneficial in confirming their knowledge and highlighting their weaknesses in the topic covered.

7. DISCUSSION AND LIMITATIONS

The MCQCM was well received by all of the participants in the pilot program. The students appreciated the opportunity to use the self-assessment MCQCM and considered it beneficial in their preparation for the oncoming assessment task.

The students considered the MCQCM easy to operate and the method of scoring appeared to encourage risk taking, resulting in the students manipulating the MCQCM to their advantage. They increasingly used the sliding bar to register their confidence and confirmed that the feedback and consequential score was both comprehensible and helpful for further study direction.

A limitation was that the pilot program was not broad enough to give us any valid feedback about the biasness towards particular learning styles and gender. The students could neither demonstrate nor comment on these issues during their short exposure.

8. FURTHER WORK

The cognitive process of decision-making is to be explored to see if the choice of the option being either true or false is dominant in the participants mind, or if the expression of the level of confidence is the dictating factor. In simple terms, "is stating that you are 30% sure that the answer is false the same as saying that you are 70% sure that the answer is true?". These questions still need to be investigated and further trials completed in order to develop a tool to maximize the benefit to the students.

We intend on conducting a wider study to determine if the MCQCM is biased towards particular learning styles or groups of learners. Feedback would also be welcome on improvements or usability aspects of the interface aimed to improve the usability and thereby enhance the students' learning path.

An opportunity exists to apply the MCQCM to various other arenas that would benefit from the Web based technology, particularly e-comerce. Jamieson (1998) explored the application of an automated auditing tool (KASE) with great success that permitted the user to register their level of confidence of a particular situation being susceptible to fraud. An area of interest could be in registering consumer trust indexes.

REFERENCES

Black. P and William D (1998): Inside the Black Box: Raising Standards Through Classroom Assessment. *Phi Delta Kappan October 1998 Volume 80 Number 2 P 139-149* http://www.pdkintl.org/kappan/kbla9810.htm

Black. P and William D (March 1998): Assessment and Classroom. Learning *Assessment in Education, Vol 5 March* P. 7-74

Brown TA and Shuford EH (1973): Quantifying Uncertainty Into Numerical Probabilities for the Reporting of intelligence. *Defence Advanced Research Projects Agency Report R-1185-ARPA. Santa Monica, Calif., Rand Corp*

Davidoff F (Feb 1995): Confidence Testing- How to Answer a Meta-Question. *American College of Physicians Observer* www.acponline.org/journals/news/feb95/conftest.htm

Diamond GA, and Forrester JS (1983): An Epistemologic Model of Clinical Judgment. *Am J Med 75:* P129-137

Doebbert J (1999): Benchmarking the Learning Environment (Technology). *National Centre of Research in Vocational Education (Copa & Ammentorp press)* Chpt 5 vocserve.berkeley.edu/abstracts/MDS-1108/MDS-1108-CHAPTER-5.html

Frary R (1995): More multiple-choice item writing do's and don'ts. *Practical Assessment, assessment and evaluation ERIC Clearinghouse on Assessment and Evaluation.* Vol 4 (11) ericae.net/pare/getvn.asp?v=4&n=11

Jamieson, R. (1999): An Investigation of Auditor Decision-Making in an Information Systems Audit Domain, *Unpublished PhD Dissertation, University of New South Wales.*

Kehoe J (1995): Writing Multiple Choice Test Questions *Practical Assessment, assessment and evaluation ERIC Clearinghouse on Assessment and Evaluation.* Vol 4 (9) http://ericae.net/pare/getvn.asp?v=4&n=9

Klinger A (1997): Experimental Validation of Learning Accomplishment. *Frontiers in Education. Technical Report No. 970019*

Marshal University (1999): Comparison of Online Course Delivery Software Products. multimedia.marshall.edu/cit/webct/compare/comparison.html

Paul J (1994): Improving Education Through Computer Based Alternative Assessment Methods. *People and Computers Vol 9*

Perrenoud P (1991): Towards a Pragmatic Approach to Formative Evaluation. Assessment of Pupils' Achievement: Motivation and School Success *(Amsterdam: Swets and Zeitlinger)* P. 92

Pollard G (1985): Scoring in Multiple Choice Examinations. *Math. Scientists Vol 10 P 93-97*

Pollard G (1986): Scoring to Remove Guessing in Multiple Choice Exams. *Math Education Science Technology Vol 20 No2 P 33-36*

Pollard G and Clark D (1989): An Optimal Scoring System of Multiple Choice Competitions and an Analysis of Candidates Responses Under Two Different Methods of Scoring. *Mathematics Competitions* Vol 2 No 2 P33-36

Pollard G (1993): Further Scoring Systems to Remove Guessing in Multiple Choice Examinations. *Mathematics Competitions Vol 2 No 1 P 27-43*

Principle and Standards for School Mathematics (2000): *National Council of Teachers of Mathematics - Standards 2000 Project Chpt 2.*

STRATEGIZING FOR DISTRIBUTED KNOWLEDGE MANAGEMENT

MICHAEL HOLM LARSEN and MOGENS KÜHN PEDERSEN
Department of Informatics, Copenhagen Business School, Denmark

Abstract: Knowledge management is rarely found in a strategy context. Although some companies already have introduced the role of a chief knowledge officer, knowledge management is not treated as a strategic endeavour. Furthermore, contributions from an academic point of view are scarce in the field of the strategic issues of knowledge management. This paper contributes with some insight in pointing out the strategic question that knowledge management might provide answers for: The efficiency issue of strategic positioning. Furthermore, the paper emphasises the distinction between symmetric and asymmetric incentives in business relations, and on this basis identifies the notion of Distributed Knowledge Management as a means for creating efficiency strategies with symmetric incentives in business relations leveraging on information and communication technology exploitation. In this way a strategic agenda for knowledge management is identified.

1. INTRODUCTION

What kind of knowledge management activities is undertaken in companies? Are knowledge management projects merely considered as just another information technology or information system project? Has knowledge management actually reached the strategic agenda? Where does knowledge management fit in the strategic process? These are some of the questions that might be considered in relation to current practice of knowledge management in industry as well as in academia.

With the introduction of the notion of a "CKO", i.e. a chief knowledge officer (Davenport and Prusak 1998, Earl 1999), knowledge management is brought into the boardroom of companies - although the companies primarily are large firms.

According to Earl & Scott (1999) CKO's have two principal design competencies, i.e. that they are technologists meaning that they are able to understand which technologies can contribute to capturing, storing, exploring, and sharing knowledge, and they are environmentalists meaning that they have the ability to create social environments that stimulate and facilitate arranged and chance conversations or able to develop events and processes to encourage deliberate knowledge creation and exchange.

One reason why knowledge management from a strategic point of view is not diffused into most companies might be because there is little known about what strategic issues and questions knowledge management actually attack.

In practice knowledge management is rarely considered in a strategy context, and also little academic guidance is provided in literature. So far knowledge management is primarily treated as a tactical or an operational issue (Ruggles 1998, Davenport et al. 1998).

This paper provides some arguments on the kind of strategic questions where a knowledge management answer might prevail.

2. KNOWLEDGE MANAGEMENT - TACTICAL AND OPERATIONAL PROJECTS

What kind of knowledge management activities is undertaken in companies? Are knowledge management projects merely considered as just another information technology or information system project? Has knowledge management actually reached the strategic agenda? Where does knowledge management fit in the strategic process? These are some of the questions that might be considered in relation to current practice of knowledge management in industry as well as in academia.

With the introduction of the notion of a "CKO", i.e. a chief knowledge officer (Davenport and Prusak 1998, Earl 1999), knowledge management is brought into the boardroom of companies - although the companies primarily are large firms.

Ruggles (1998) has outlined a research agenda for knowledge management. He suggests a number of knowledge management activities, which are found in companies. The knowledge management activities are regarded from a process perspective of what can be managed about knowledge. These processes are: Generating new knowledge, accessing valuable knowledge from outside sources, using accessible knowledge in decision making, embedding knowledge in processes products, and/or services, representing knowledge in documents, databases, and software etc., facilitating knowledge growth through culture and incentive, transferring existing knowledge into others parts of the organisation, and measuring the value of knowledge assets and/or impact of knowledge management.

This research agenda is representative for most academic studies in knowledge management (e.g. Drucker 1988, Tampoe 1993, Wiig 1993, 1994, 1995, Davis & Botkin 1994, Miles et al. 1998, Demarest 1997, Ruggles 1998, Jordan & Jones 1997, Zack 1998, and Davis 1998). The list of knowledge processes shows that academia has focused on tactical and operational issues of knowledge management.

As this is the dominating research stream, the criteria for successful projects are not surprisingly also on a tactical or operational level. Davenport et al. (1998) suggest the eight most import criteria as being: Link to economic performance or industry value, technical and organisational infrastructure, standard, flexible knowledge structure, knowledge-friendly culture, clear purpose and language, change in motivational practices, multiple channels for knowledge transfer, and senior management support.

Although Davenport et al. (1998) point out the importance of linking a project to economic performance or industry value, this does not provide any substantial insight into how the knowledge management is related to the strategy, as focus primarily is on financial cost-benefit analyses.

We find the same conclusion regarding emphasis on tactical and operational issues of knowledge management when looking at the projects currently undertaken by companies. These projects are (Ruggles 1998): Creating an intranet, data warehouse/knowledge repository, implementing decision support tools, implementing GroupWare to support collaboration, create networks of knowledge workers, map sources of internal expertise, establish new knowledge roles, and launch new knowledge-based products or services

Earl (1999) argues that the firms need to have an information business mindset in their strategy making. Hence, Earl proposes firms to consider a convergence across industries towards the "information business". This raises three issues for business strategy making (Earl 1999, p. 163) which we here have related to knowledge management:

- "IT developments, threats and opportunities have to be included in strategy formation" In the knowledge management approach technologies and associated practices take precedence over a traditional value chain approach. IT is not only applied but built to fit information needs within the company and in between business partners.
- "The value creation potential of information has to be included in strategy formation." Knowledge management makes a difference to management decision when founded on business environmental attributes highly relevant to competitive advantage of products and processes.

- "The future has to be brought back into strategy-making in order to analyse, anticipate, and prepare for the information age." In the case of knowledge management, information anticipation being associated with adding specific information to environmental knowledge enhances the strategic-making capacity of management.

This motivates the research method of the paper. First, we will revisit the knowledge management literature from an ontological point of view because this might bring some insight to the general perspectives that need to be considered in a strategic context. Second, in order to identify strategic issues of knowledge management, we will provide the basic strategic questions to be answered in strategic positioning of the company. From this literature review a framework for "Strategizing for the Digital Business" is established combining strategic position directions and incentive strategies.

3. KNOWLEDGE MANAGEMENT ONTOLOGY AND REPOSITORIES

Knowledge management represents issues reflecting the need for solutions of routines insufficiently supported or supportable by the organisational structures of modern business. The scope of knowledge management encompasses individual competence and organisation memory, knowledge creation from tacit to explicit knowledge and the role of organisations in facilitating the creation of knowledge (Nonaka 1994). The ontology of knowledge management (KM) stated by Nonaka and Takeuchi (1995) is the individual, organisational and interorganisation domains.

The capability of information technology to serve human purposes using symbols is an integrated part of knowledgeable human behaviour. Information technology in this regard is a knowledge technology that processes meaningful symbolic behaviour to manage extended economic organisations (Konsynski 1993, Pedersen 1996).

In each of the three domains the knowledge aspect that IT supports is analysed. The reason why information technology is considered in this section is the appreciation that IT no longer solely should be treated as an enabler of business processes. In fact, IT in it self hold promises in a strategic scenario that the company might opt for.

The ontology of knowledge management is:

The individual domain: Learning from Japanese manufacturing quality models has inspired a new interest in knowledge creation and sharing (Nonaka 1994, Nonaka *et al.* 1994, Nonaka and Takeuchi 1995, Nonaka and Konno 1998, Lincoln *et al.* 1998). In these models knowledge is created within the corporation as a part and parcel of a co-operation process between workers and departments. Polanyi (1962,1966) provided the view of tacit and explicit individual knowledge. Nonanka and Konno's (1998) contextual knowledge creation in an organisational framework placed knowledge in a collective memory as social knowledge also known from Spender's view of social or organisational knowledge (Spender 1996). Whatever the industry, the social knowledge is achievable given the proper organisation is provided for, to process tacit knowledge (Takeuchi and Nonaka 1986).

In spite of reckoning tacit knowledge the promises of KM quickly move on to praise the value of explicit knowledge from individuals made available to the organisation after proper structuring and indexing of items. Creating the organisation's knowledge source is adamant to ensuring competitive viability of the company in adverse times when key personnel may leave for better performing competitors. That part of their knowledge that has been objectified into a knowledge repository remains with the company and thus confirms the idea of a pool of collective knowledge. This calls for establishing a knowledge repository.

The organisational domain: Knowledge management makes a public issue of what had previously been an asset of the individual member. The individual's knowledge consists in a mix of acquired formal qualifications and of job training as the merit of competence (Zuboff 1988). Today, knowledge is an asset when shared with other employees at the level of knowledge rather than at the level of functional tasks or as the product outcome of the division of labour. Thus it is the interchange of knowledge *qua knowledge* that represents the significant change in the management of knowledge from previous ways of managing knowledge. Ultimately, this implies to see the firm as a distributed knowledge system (Tsoukas 1996).

In recent years, competition has increasingly ruled out this knowledge management strategy and at the same time brought to the attention of management the opportunities for a focused use of information technologies for knowledge acquisition and dissemination within the organisation (Ciborra and Andreu 1996, Borghoff 1997, Davenport and Prusak 1998).

The following models moved on to offer a knowledge repository much inspired by enterprise resource planning models and the concept of centralised, corporate databases. In these models we find information quality issues along with best practice objectives that take knowledge across functional entities, between divisions or subsidiaries to make knowledge an organisational asset (Davenport and Klahr 1998). Disseminating knowledge was a matter of information retrieval and acquisition by each user as (s)he saw fit. Little or no decision support was offered from these repositories. What they offered were results of previous learning that only could be accessed if known to exist.

The inter organisation domain: A third kinds of models moved on to widen the scope of knowledge management by including business partners in a broader network of knowledge exchange. The supply chain attracted attention with its scope for increase of overall efficiency (Anderson et al 1997). In manufacturing and in particular in biotechnology and pharmaceutical industries the core capabilities of companies are based increasingly on knowledge-seeking and knowledge-creation. Learning about new innovation opportunities requires the companies to participate in technical communinities and building interorganizational linkages critical to the diffusion of knowledge, learning and technology development (Powell 1998).

The linear model of a knowledge flow of the demands of customers to dealers and distributors did not transform into value-added knowledge before considering the advantage from using the World Wide Web using rich information representations. In particular manufacturing and service suppliers in customer support knowledge took advantage of the Internet in moving knowledge beyond organisational boundaries (El Sawy and Bowles 1997, Hagel and Rayport 1997, Venkatraman and Henderson 1998).

Today, the distinction between knowledge management in manufacturing and in professional services may seem to be overridden by the experience of knowledge management projects crossing previously relevant lines of demarcation (Krogh and Roos 1996, Krogh et al. 1997and1998, Davenport et al. 1998, Ruggles 1998, Alavi and Leidner 1999). The classic questions of KM were how to motivate specialists to share their knowledge (Tampoe 1993), how to make employees capable to share knowledge (Ciborra and Andreu 1998), how to balance historical knowledge with current knowledge through "organisational learning" (Nonaka 1994) or through codification changes (Hansen et al. 1999). Another set of classic questions we are facing are the questions which and how to create incentive schemes for the exchange of knowledge (or just data) with various business partners. The collaboration tends to create clusters of companies working together more intensively than with others that are excluded from the intensive knowledge interchange (Powell 1998). The network perspective receives increasing interest in the management literature as "the future competition is not between companies, but between networks" (Kotler 1994).

The traditional dichotomy of acquiring information either in *reactive* mode (El Sawy and Pauchant 1988) with a specific decision to make or in *proactive* mode to scan and monitor the environment to detect problems requires a different decision management. Between the two we find a network of interdependent decision-makers all acting on information specificity that derives from knowledge specificity and time specificity taking advantage of computer networks (Choudhury and Sampler 1997).

Knowledge management therefore contemplates issues found in network theory exploring "co-specialised assets, joint control, and collective purpose" (Alstyne 1997:86).

The sequel to these business challenges has been the application of information technologies first represented in the acquisition of knowledge in a knowledge repository and later represented in network models like intranet and extranet (Davenport and Prusak 1998, Scott 1998). Knowledge management is bound to rely upon information technologies including networks, the technologies of processing, transmission and storage. On the one hand because these technologies continuously experience diminishing costs compared to wages and capital equipment and on the other hand because the organization of business is increasingly becoming one of interconnected networks of expertise and competence that require extensive collaboration across company boundaries. These forms of operations now challenge the concept of an enterprise repository that gives no access for the collaborating partners. How relevant and how representative of the knowledge creation will an enterprise repository become in a world of interorganizational knowledge linkages? Extranets are collaborative in principle and may therefore develop into the business partners co-specialized knowledge assets.

This article suggests that the rise of knowledge management should be tempered by the concomitant rise of decision support systems, though in a new framework, viz. the distributed knowledge management. The model of supply chain management relates a significant share of all trade to opportunities of knowledge management for efficiency purposes thus representing a significant part of all business models. The supply chain network has been shown to benefit from information technology in the order fulfilment process (Strader *et al.* 1998). Unlike previous, often hypothetical discussions of virtual organisations, a supply chain network decision support system provides an illustration of a robust knowledge based structure where the knowledge exchange enhance the performance efficiency of all participating in the network.

The model to be presented differs in a significant respect from other models catering only for knowledge relations discarding the specific nature of network business relations though stressing the decision support capability (Sridhar 1998). We argue that the exchange of asymmetric, specific knowledge in a network economy generates among all the participants a performance superior to that achieved without distributed knowledge networks.

Knowledge management is sparsely treated in the strategic literature – although the focus in resent years is intensified, cf. Zack (1999), Carneiro (2000), Helfat & Raubitschek (2000), Davenport & Völpel (2001), Bollinger

& Smith (2001), McEvily & Chakravarthy (2002), Mcnamara et al. (2002), Miller (forthcoming), and Tsang (forthcoming). Moreover, developing a knowledge management stand in the strategic positioning literature is not yet established.

Summing up this section, the review of the knowledge management ontology point to the importance that a company should be defined not only based on internal capabilities but in relation to the network in which it operates. From here the information system requirements can be derived.

4. KNOWLEDGE MANAGEMENT IN STRATEGIC POSITIONING

Strategy can be regarded from various points of view. An established point of view is the "Who, What, How" framework (Abell 1980). This framework proposes that the strategic position of a company is the sum of target customers (who), products and services (what), and the optimal way the company furnishes these efficiently (Markides 1997, 1998, 1999). This line of thought is by Applegate (2001) extended to encompass the evolution of an e-business strategy by considering the four issues of enhancement, extension, expansion and exit (p. 77). By enhancement is ment adding functionality or improving a product or service that is currently offered. Extension addresses the adoption of new business models or entering new businesses. Expansion means adding products and services within the existing business. Finally, exit point the options of eliminating a product or serviceline or leaving a business.

The competitive dynamics of markets impose upon management to follow-up on changing market structures and competitor behaviour, demanding on-going strategizing. Management has to consider regularly in which business they operate as well as the efficiency with which they operate, for example by reconsidering their core competencies in terms of opportunities for sharing, reusing or expanding competencies (Markides 1997).

In setting business right for strategizing the predominant guideline has been the value chain (Porter 1985) and the e-business imperative of the competitive forces of an industry (Porter 2001). The scope of this line of analysis is elaborated through complementors, which are participants in the value network from whom the customer buys complementary products or services, or to which suppliers sell complementary resources, cf. Ghemawat et al. (2001). Beyond the positioning framework Porter now stipulates the competitive advantages derived from clusters (Porter 1990, 1998a, 1998b): "Clusters are geographic concentrations of interconnected companies and institutions in a particular field" and "encompass an array of linked industries and other entities important to competition." While the geographic concentration is a codetermining factor of a cluster it is also "an alternative way of organising the value chain." Repeated exchanges, better co-ordination and trust "mitigate the problems inherent in arm's-length relationships without imposing the inflexibility of vertical integration or the management challenges of creating and maintaining formal linkages such as networks, alliances, and partnerships" (Porter 1998b: 78). The mutual benefits of clusters derive from this "organisational form that offers advantages in efficiency, effectiveness, and flexibility." Porter identifies the cluster effects upon competition as three: increase the productivity of companies based in the area; drive the direction and pace of innovation; stimulate the formation of new businesses that expand and strengthen the cluster itself. The cluster effects allow "each member to benefit as if it had greater scale or as if it had joined with others formally - without requiring it to sacrifice its flexibility."

The strategic option for knowledge management in clusters is to support business procurement, to exchange specialised information, and to offer complementarities like product complements and co-ordination of activities across companies' optimising on collective productivity (Porter 1998b).

The agenda of knowledge management previously limited to tactical and operational issues is now raising to strategic issues of the business. The Internet revolution has made network reconfiguration in Intranet and Extranet an issue in formulating digital based business strategies (Venkatraman and Henderson 1998). These strategies require a new knowledge management strategy: Which knowledge, to whom, and in which way?

In table 1 the strategic positioning framework of product-market and efficiency is associated with the nature of the incentive strategy. The asymmetric incentive strategy follows from unequal positions in the value chain reflecting strategies of competitive advantage (Porter 1980, 1985). The strength may be based in cost advantages, brands or other vehicles for differentiation in the market. The symmetric incentive strategy follows from the recognition of complementarities. The advance of the cost efficiency or strategic positioning of one partner benefits the other partners. In terms of knowledge management the advance of one partner depends upon the others and vice versa. There is a mutual incentive to enable the other partner to succeed because that facilitates and increases the probability of success for one self. Collaboration between companies at various levels of expertise reaches into strategic issues of product development and market strategies.

		Strategic Positioning	
		Product/Market	***Efficiency***
Incentive Strategy	***Asymmetric***	Value Chain	KM
	Symmetric	Cluster	DKM

Table 1. Strategizing for the Digital Business.

Moving beyond the boundaries of the firm into the extended enterprise (Konsynski 1993) elevates the virtual organising of business into a knowledge based strategy for a "dynamic portfolio of relationships to assemble and co-ordinate the required assets for delivering value to the customers" (Venkatraman and Henderson 1998:33). Their principles governing strategizing network reconfiguration cannot be found in a conception of knowledge management as purely an internal business affair. Business-to-business networks transcend the conventional image of value chains creating a complex exchange of specific information and in particular of specific knowledge (Choudhury and Sampler 1997).

In table 1 the concomitant of incentive strategies for knowledge management is also highlighted.

The *centralised* knowledge creation model promotes the idea of making knowledge available to the whole organisation as the purpose of knowledge management (Nonaka 1994, Nonaka *et al.* 1994, Nonaka and Takeuchi 1995, El Sawy and Bowles 1997, Favela 1997, Davenport and Klahr 1998). Here knowledge management (KM) faces the challenge how to ensure a dynamic updating of knowledge. The decision-making qualities of a relevant and timely information for decision support come to the fore in the concept of information specificity (Choudhury and Sampler 1997).

The alternative to a centralised knowledge management model, a *distributed* knowledge management model, generates knowledge amongst decision-makers in interdependent businesses on a continuous basis while redistributing the outcome for a time efficient knowledge use (Pedersen & Larsen 2001). The symmetries in knowledge and time specificity of the decision-makers ensure that knowledge creation in an actor network is an incentive compatible exchange of knowledge. Actor network theory captures the idea of a heterogenous, bottom-up and dynamic change of collaboration determined by the intermediary (here the specific information interchanged for knowledge creation) of the network (Callon 1991, Walsham 1997, Hull et al. 1999). Hence, DKM becomes a strategic issue as the company needs to decide "how" (cf. Abell 1980) to position itself in the value network in which it operates.

An example illustrating the strategic role of knowledge management is the findings by Granstrand et al. (1997). The study of 500 companies showed that the product portfolio compared to the portfolio of technologies could be described by the concept of distributed competences reflecting that their selection of a knowledge strategy exceeds the product strategy.

The centralised KM model consists in a conversion from individual, knowledge specificity into organisational, collective knowledge made available to all individuals where each individual user on an ad hoc basis converts the global knowledge into local decision support. In contrast, the distributed KM model requires another conversion. The focus is on the exchange of specific knowledge to network actors in a mutual value-adding network. Each actor appropriates information and submits enhanced information that in return becomes enhanced by other network actors at other destinations and thus return to the originator more valuable than when originated.

The actor network realises the exchange of a knowledge and time specific information thus taking responsibility for making knowledge creation available for decision by all actors in the network. The latter process also makes for the difference between a centralised KM system that is passive in regard to decision making and an active distributed decision support system that takes advantage of the knowledge specificity related to the different actors. And finally knowledge creation in terms of knowledge specificity encompasses both tacit and explicit knowledge since the same individuals or teams that create knowledge apply it (Polanyi 1962, 1966, Spender 1996). The emergent knowledge co-located with the actor results from acquired knowledge from the network merged with local, specific knowledge. Therefore emergent knowledge resides with the actor and does not have to cross the organisational boundaries of the collaborators. Only specific knowledge items are passed on in the actor network. This accounts for the symmetric incentive character of the network DKM model. Further, the collaboration between partners reflects their different roles and contributions reinforcing the economic complementarities of the cluster in which they participate. The strategic implications for product improvements and innovations follow.

5. CONCLUSION AND PERSPECTIVES

Knowledge management is seldom put into a strategy context. Although some companies already have introduced the role of a chief knowledge officer, knowledge management is rarely treated as a strategic endeavour. Also from an academic point of view few contributions are made in the field of the strategic issues of knowledge management.

This paper reviews the ontology of knowledge management as a basic understanding for creating business scenarios. The result of this review shows that a company should be defined not only based on internal capabilities but in relation to the network in which it operates or should operate to generate knowledge and new complementarities.

The primary contribution of this paper is a suggestion towards the kind of strategic questions that knowledge management might answer. The conclusion is that knowledge management contributes in the efficiency issues of strategic positioning.

Furthermore, the paper emphasises the distinction between symmetric and asymmetric incentives in business relation, and on this basis identifies the concept of Distributed Knowledge Management as a means for creating efficiency strategies with symmetric incentives in business relations.

Based on the issues raised in the paper, future research might then approach research questions as how to create knowledge-based strategic scenarios, raising further questions of how to incorporate symmetric incentive schemes in business relations. And raise the following issues on how to create knowledge-based business models, and how to test the viability and efficiently/effectiveness of the knowledge-based business model.

REFERENCES

Abell, D. (1980). Defining the business: The starting point of strategic planning. Englewood Cliffs, New Jersey: Prentice–Hall.

Adam, F., Fahy, M., and Murphy, C. (1998). A framework for the classification of DSS usage across organisations. Decision Support Systems, 22, 1-13.

Alavi, M. and Leidner, D. E. (1999). Knowledge Management Systems: Issues, Challenges, and Benefits. Communications of the Association for Information Systems. Vol. 1, Paper 5, January.

Alstyne, M. van (1997). The State of Network Organisation: A Survey in Three Frameworks. Journal of Organisational Computing and Electronic Commerce. 7,2&3) 83-151.

Anderson, E.; Day, G.; Rangan, V.K. (1997). Strategic Channel Design. Sloan Management Review, June. 59-69.

Applegate, L. (2001). E-Business Models – Making Sense of the Internet Business Landscape, pp. 49-101. In Dickson & DeSanctis (2001).

Badaracco, Jr. Joseph L. (1991). The Knowledge Link. Harvard Business School Press. Boston, Mass.

Bollinger, A.S & Smith, R.D. (2001). Managing organizational knowledge as a strategic asset. Journal of Knowledge Management. 5(1), pp. 8-18.

Borghoff, U.M. (1997). Information Technology for Knowledge Management. Journal of Universal Computer Science. 3(8), 835-842.

Callon, M. (1991). Techno-economic networks and irreversibility. In J. Law, ed. A Sociology of Monsters. Essays on Power, Technology and Domination. Sociological Review Monograph 38. London: Routledge.

Carneiro, A. (2000). How does knowledge management influence innovation and competitiveness? Journal of Knowledge Management. 4(2), pp. 87-98.

Chesbrough, H.W. and Teece, D. J. (1996). When is Virtual Virtuous? Organizing for Innovation. Harvard Business Review, 74, Jan-Feb. 65-73.

Choudhury, V. and Sampler, J. L. (1997). Information Specificity and Environmental Scanning: An Economic Perspective. MIS Quarterly, March 21(1) 25-53.

Ciborra, Claudio and Andreu, Rafael (1998). Organisational Learning and Core Capabilities Development: The Role of IT. in Information Technology and Organisational Transformation. Edited by R. Galliers and W.R.J. Baets. John Wiley and Sons Ltd.

Currie, W.L. & Galliers, B. (1999). Rethinking Management Information Systems. Oxford University Press.

Davenport, T. and Prusak, L. (1998). Working Knowledge - How Organisations Manage What They Know. Harvard Business School Press, Boston, MA.

Davenport, T.H. & Völpel, S.C. (2001). The rise of knowledge towards attention management. Journal of Knowledge Management. 5(3), pp. 212-222.

Davenport, T.H. and De Long, D.W. and Beers, M.C. (1998). Successful Knowledge Management Projects. Sloan Management Review. 39(2) Winter, 43-57.

Davenport, T.H. and Klahr, P. (1998). Managing Customer Support Knowledge, California Management Review 40(3) 195-208.

Davis, M.C. (1998). Knowledge Management. Information Strategy: The Executive's Journal. Fall, 11-22.

Davis, S. & Botkin, J. (1994). The Coming of Knowledge-Based Business. Harvard Business Review. September-October, 165-170.

Demarest, M. (1997). Understanding Knowledge Management. Long Range Planning. 30(3), 374-384.

Dickson, G.W. & DeSanctis, G. (2001). Information Technology and the Future Enterprise – New Models for Managers. Prentice Hall.

Drucker, P.F. (1988). The Coming of the New Organization. Harvard Business Review. January-February, 45-53.

Earl, M.J. (1999). Strategy-Making in the Information Age. In Currie & Galliers (1999), pp. 161-174.

Earl, M.J. and Scott, I.A. (1999). What Is a Chief Knowledge Officer? Sloan Management Review. Winter, Volume 40, No. 2.

El Sawy, O.A. and Bowles, G. (1997). Redesigning the Customer Support Process for the Electronic Economy: Insights from Storage Dimensions. MIS Quarterly December 457-483.

El Sawy, O.A. and Pauchant, T.C. (1988). Triggers, Templates and Twitches in the Tracking of Emerging Strategic Issues. Strategic Management Journal 9 (5) 455-473.

Evans, G.N. and Naim, M.M. and Towill, D.R. (1993). Assessing the Impact of Information Systems on Dynamic Supply Chain Performance. Logistics Information Management. 6(4), 15-25.

Favela, J. (1997). Capture and Dissemination of Specialized Knowledge in Network Organisations. Journal of Organisational Computing and Electronic Commerce 7 (2and3) 201-226.

Foss, N. J. (ed.) (1997). The Resource-based Perspective on the Firm. London: Routledge Kegan Paul.

Galbraith, J.R. and Lawler III, E.E. (1993). Organising for the Future. The New Logic for Managing Complex Organisations. San Francisco: Jossey-Bass Publishers.

Ghemawat, P. Collis, D.J. & Pisano, G.P. & Rivkin, J.W. (2001). Strategy and the Business Landscape: Core Concepts. Prentice Hall. Ghosh, A. K., 1998. E-Commerce Security. Weak Links, Best Defenses. Wiley Computer Publ. N.Y.

Granstrand, O., Patel, P.O. & K. Pavitt (1997) Multi-technology Corporations: Why they have "distributed" rather than "distinctive" core competencies. California Management Review, 39 (4), Summer, pp. 8-25.

Hagel, J. and Armstrong, A. (1997). Net Gain: Expanding Markets Through Virtual Communities. The McKinsey Quarterly, 1, 140-153.

Hagel, J. and Rayport, J. (1997). The Coming Battle for Customer Information. Harvard Business Review, January-February, 53-65.

Hammer, M. (1996). Beyond Reengineering. Harper Collins Publishers. N.Y.

Hammer, M. and Champy, J. (1993). Reengineering the Corporation – A Manifesto for Business Revolution. Harper Collins Publishers, New York.

Hansen, M. T., Nohria, N. and Tierney, T. (1999). What's your strategy for managing knowledge? Harvard Business Review 77 (2) 106-116.

Hax, A. and Wilde II, D.L. (1999). A Delta Model: Adaptive Management for a Changing World. Sloan Management Review 40 (2) 11-28.

Helfat, C. E. & Raubitschek, R.S. (2000). Product sequencing: co-evolution of knowledge, capabilities and products. Strategic Management Journal. 21(10-11), pp. 961-979.

Holland, C.P. (1995). Cooperative Supply Chain Management: the Impact of Interorganizational Information Systems. Journal of Strategic Information Systems. 4(2), 117-133.

Holtshouse, D. (1998). Knowledge Research Issues. California Management Review. 40(3), 277-280.

Huber, G. (1982). Organisational Information Systems: Determinants of Their Performance and Behavior. Management Science 28 (2) February. 138-155.

Hull, R.,V. Walsh, Green, K., and McMeekin, A. (1999). The Techno-Economic: Perspectives for Analysis and Intervention. Journal of Technology Transfer, 24. 185-195.

Johanson, J. and Mattsson, L.-G. (1987). Interorganizational relations in industrial systems: a network approach compared with the transaction-cost approach. International Studies of Management and Organisation. 17. 34-48.

Jordan, J. & Jones, P. (1997). Assessing your Company's Knowledge Management Style. Long Range Planning. 30(3), 392-398.

Keen, P. G.W. (1986). Competing in Time. Ballinger Publ.

Konsynski, B.R. (1993). Strategic Control in the Extended Enterprise. IBM Systems Journal, 32(1), 111-142.

Kotler, P. (1994). Marketing Management: Analysis, Planning, Implementation and Control. Prentice Hall.

Krogh, G. von and Nonaka, I. and Ichijo, K. (1997). Development Knowledge Activists. European Management Journal, 15(5), 475-483.

Krogh, G. von and Roos, J. (1996). Managing Knowledge - Perspectives on Cooperation and Competition. Sage, London.

Krogh, G. von, Roos, J. and Kleine, D. (1998). Knowing in firms - Understanding, Managing and Measuring Knowledge. Sage, London.

Larsen, M.H.; L.R. Franck, and Pedersen, M. Kühn. (1999). Frontline CALS – Extranet Enabled Support of Customer Relations Based on Product State Information. Proceedings of the 7th European Conference on Information Systems. Copenhagen, June, 302-319.

Leidner, D.E. (1999). Virtual partnerships in support of electronic commerce: the case of TCIS. Journal of Strategic Information Systems. 8(1) 105-117.

Lincoln, J. R. and Ahmadjian, C.L. and Mason, E. (1998). Organisational Learning and Purchase-Supply Relationships in Japan: Hitachi, Matsushita, and Toyota Compared. California Management Review. 40(3), 241-264.

Lomi, A. (1997). Markets with Hierarchies and the Network Structure of Organisational Communities. Journal of Management and Governance, 1, 49-66.

Markides, C.C. (1997). Strategic Innovation. Sloan Management Review 38(3) Spring, 9-23.

Markides, C.C. (1998). Strategic Innovation in Established Companies. Sloan Management Review 39(3) Spring 31-42.

Markides, C.C. (1999). A Dynamic View of Strategy. Sloan Management Review 40(3) Spring 55-63.

Mason-Jones, R. and Towill, D.R. (1997). Information Enrichment: Designing the Supply Chain for Competitive Advantage. Supply Chain Management. 2(4), 137-148.

Mason-Jones, R. and Towill, D.R. (1998). Time Compression in the Supply Chain: Information Management is the Vital Ingredient. Logistics Information Management. 11(2), 93-104.

McEvily, S.K. & Chakravarthy, B. (2002). The persistence of knowledge-based advantage: an empirical test for product performance and technological knowledge. Strategic Management Journal. 23(4), pp. 285-305.

Mcnamara, G.M. & Luce, R.A. & Tompson, G.H. (2002). Examining the effect of complexity in strategic group knowledge structures on firm performance. Strategic Management Journal. 23(2), pp. 153-170.

Meier, J. (1995). The Importance of Relationship Management in establishing Successful Interorganizational Systems. Journal of Strategic Information Systems. 4(2), 135-148.

Miles, G. & Miles, R.E. & Perrone, V. & Edvinsson, L. (1998). Some Conceptual and Research Barriers to the Utilization of Knowledge. California Management Review. 40(3), 281-288.

Milgrom, P. and J. Roberts (1992). Economics, Organisation and Management. Englewood Cliffs, N.J. Prentice-Hall International, Inc.

Miller, K.D. (forthcoming). Knowledge inventories and managerial myopia. Strategic Management Journal.

Nonaka, I. (1994). A Dynamic Theory of Organisational Knowledge Creation. Organisation Science, 5, 14-37.

Nonaka, I. and Konno, N. (1998). The Concept of "Ba": Building a Foundation for Knowledge Creation. California Management Review, 40(3), 40-54.

Nonaka, I. and Byosiere, P. & Borucki, C.C. & Konno, N. (1994). Organisational Knowledge Creation Theory: A First Comprehensive Test. International Business Review. Special Issue on Knowledge in Organisations, Knowledge Transfer, and Cooperative Strategies. 3/4, 337-351.

Nonaka, I. and Takeuchi, H. (1995). The Knowledge Creating Company – How Japanese Companies Create the Dynamics of Innovation. Oxford University Press.

Pedersen, M.K. & Larsen, M.H. (2001). Distributed Knowledge Management based on Product State Models - The Case of Decision Support in Health Care Administration. Decision Support Systems. Special issue on Knowledge Management. Volume 31, Number 1, pp. 139-158.

Pedersen, M.K. (1996). A Theory of Informations. The Business Cycle Model. Copenhagen. Samfundslitteratur.

Polanyi, M. (1962). Personal Knowledge: Towards a Post-critical Philosophy. University of Chicago Press, New York.

Polanyi, M. (1966). The Tacit Dimension. Anchor Day, New York.

Porter, M.E. (1985). Competitive Advantage. Free Press, N.Y.

Porter, M.E. (1990). The Competitive Advantage of Nations. Macmillan, N.Y.

Porter, M.E. (1998a). Clusters and the New Economics of Competition. Harvard Business Review. November-December 76(6) 77-90.

Porter, M.E. (1998b). The Adam Smith Adress: Location, Clusters, and the "New" Microeconomics of Competition. Business Economics. Washington, January 33(1) 7-13.

Porter, M.E. (2001). Strategy and the Internet, Harvard Business Review, March.

Powell, W.W. (1998). Learning from Collaboration: Knowledge and Networks in the Biotechnology and Pharmaceutical Industries. California Management Review, 40(3), 228-240.

Quintas, P. & Lefrere, P. & Jones, G. (1997). Knowledge Management: A Strategic Agenda. Long Range Planning. 30(3), 385-391.

Rayport, J.F. and Sviokla, J.J. (1995). Exploiting the Virtual Value Chain. Harvard Business Review, November-December, 75-85.

Riempp, G. and Nastansky, L. (1997). From Islands to Flexible Business Process Networks-Enabling the Interaction of Distributed Workflow Management Systems. Proceedings of the 5th European Conference on Information Systems.Vol. 1, 481-496.

Ruggles, R. (1998). The State of the Notion: Knowledge Management in Practice. California Management Review. 40(3), 80-89.

Sampler, J. L. (1998). Redefining Industry Structure for the Information Age. Strategic Management Journal 19. 343-355.

Scott, J. E. (1998). Organisational Knowledge and the Intranet. Decision Support Systems. 23, 3-17.

Shapiro, C. and Varian, H. R. (1999). Information Rules. A Strategic Guide to the Network Economy. Boston: Harvard Business School Press.

Spender, J.C. (1996). Organisational Knowledge, Learning and Memory: Three Concepts in Search of a Theory. Journal of Organisational Change Management, 9, 63-78.

Spinardi, G. and Graham, I. and Williams, R. (1997). EDI in the Scottish Health Service: Inter-Organisational Systems and Inter-Organisational Change. Journal of Strategic Information Systems. 6(3), 251-263.

Sridhar, S. (1998). Decision Support using the Intranet. Decision Support Systems, 23, 19-28.

Stalk, G. and Hout, T.M. (1990). Competing Against Time. N.Y. The Free Press.

Strader, T. J.; Fu-Ren Lin; Shaw, M.J. (1998). Information Infrastructure for electronic virtual organisation management. Decision Support Systems 23, 75-94.

Swatman, P.M.C., Swatman, P.A., and Fowler, D.C. (1994). A model of EDI integration and strategic business reengineering. Journal of Strategic Information Systems. 3(1) 41-60.

Takeuchi, H. and Nonaka, I. (1986). The New Product Development Game. Harvard Business Review, January-February, 137-146.

Tampoe, M., (1993). Motivating Knowledge Workers - The Challenge for the 1990s. Long Range Planning. 26(3), 49-55.

Teece, D. J. Ed. (1987). The Competitive Challenge. Cambridge. Mass.

Teece, D. J., (1987). Profiting from technological innovations: Implications for integration, collaboration, licensing and public policy. in Teece,1987).

Tsang, E.W.K. (forthcoming). Acquiring knowledge by foreign partners from international joint ventures in a transition economy: learning-by-doing and learning myopia. Strategic Management Journal.

Tsoukas, H. (1996). The firm as a distributed knowledge system: A constructionist approach. Strategic Management Journal, 17, Winter, 11-25.

Tunc, E.A. and Gupta, J.N.D. (1993). Is Time a Competitive Weapon Among Manufacturing Firms?. International Journal of Operations and Production Management. 13(3), 4-12.

Venkatraman, N. (1994). IT-Enabled Business Transformation: From Automation to Business Scope Redefinition. Sloan Management Review, 35, Winter 73-87.

Venkatraman, N. and Henderson, J.C. (1998). Real Strategies for Virtual Organizing. Sloan Management Review, 40 (1) Fall, 33-48.

Walsh, P. and Koumpis, A. (1998). Introducing the Concept of Information Supply Chains: the Buddy Project. Logistics Information Management. 11(2), 74-79.

Walsham, G. (1997). Actor-Network Theory and IS Research: Current Status and Future Prospects, in Information Systems and Qualitative Research. A.S. Lee, J. Liebenau, and J.I. DeGross (eds.), Chapman & Hall, London. 466-480.

Wang, E. T.G. and Barron, T. (1997). Computing services supply management: Incentives, information, and communication. Decision Support Systems 19, 123-148.

Webster, J. (1995). Networks of Collaboration or Conflict? Electronic Data Interchange and Power in the Supply Chain. Journal of Strategic Information Systems. 4(1), 31-42.

Wernerfelt, B. (1984). A Resource-based view of the firm. Strategic Management Journal 5, 171-180.

Wiig, K.M. (1993). Knowledge Management Foundations: Thinking About Thinking – How People And Organizations Create, Represent And Use Knowledge. Schema Press, Arlington.

Wiig, K.M. (1994). Knowledge Management – The Central Focus for Intelligent-acting Organizations. Schema Press, Arlington.

Wiig, K.M. (1995). Knowledge Management Methods – Practical Approaches to Managing Knowledge. Schema Press, Arlington.

Williams, T. (1997). Interorganisational Information Systems: Issues Affecting Interorganisational Cooperation. Journal of Strategic Information Systems. 6(3), 231-250.

Williamson, O. E. (1985). The Economic Institutions of Capitalism. New York: The Free Press.

Williamson, O. E. (1986). Economic Organization. Brighton: Wheatsheaf Books Ltd.

Williamson, O. E. (1994). Transaction cost economics and organization theory. In Smelser, N.J. and Swedberg,R. (eds) The Handbook of Economic Sociology. Princeton U P. 77-107.

Winter, S. (1987). Knowledge and Competence as Strategic Assets. In Teece, D. (edit.), (1987). The Competitive Challenge. New York, Harper and Row.

Zack. M.H. (1998). An Architecture for Managing Explicit Knowledge. Proceedings of the 6th European Conference on Information Systems, Aix-en-Provence, France, June 4-6, pp. 86-99.

Zack. M.H. (1999).Developing a Knowledge Strategy. California Management Review. 41(3), Spring, pp. 125-145.

Zuboff, S. (1988). In the Age of the Smart Machine.

SOFTWARE PACKAGES

What you always wanted to know when buying software but were afraid to ask

JAN DAMSGAARD[1] and JAN KARLSBJERG[2]

[1] *Dept. of Information Systems, Weatherhead School of Management, Case Western Reserve University, USA*

[2] *Dept. of Computer Science, Aalborg University, Denmark*

Abstract: This paper presents seven alerts that inform organizations and individuals buying software packages. The research is based on our own studies as well as a review of theoretical and empirical studies of modern information systems and the networks associated with these systems. The paper departs from a monolithic view of buying software as an atomic event that is based solely on the software's independent features and its immediate price. Instead we promote a pluralistic multi-organizational view of buying software as a continuous process of trying to match available packages with a base of already installed information systems while anticipating future needs. We have formulated seven alerts that both researchers and practitioners should consider when studying these building blocks of e-business.

1. INTRODUCTION

Software systems pervade our lives, both as professionals working in some organization, and as private persons. Such systems are not uniquely designed for each use situation, but instead they are built around some standard, that allows (and by exclusion disallows) communication with other software systems. Organizations and individuals alike therefore have to make decisions about which Internet browser and email program to purchase. And organizations are making substantial investments in terms of both money and time resources when it comes to the choice of organization-wide systems like financial software or enterprise resource planning (ERP) software, customer relationship management (CRM) software, network operating systems, etc. For these and many other software choices the notion of networking is important, as the acquired software will meet its full potential for the organization only when it is successfully integrated with other systems inside the organization, and in some cases even with systems of other organizations.

Very few organizations develop systems from scratch. Instead companies are buying standard software and adding it to a cumulative pool of standard systems that already exists in the organization. The result is that today an information system is not built as a "stand alone" micro cosmos; instead the system must obey many rules set by the installed base of existing IT systems in the organization with which it must interact in order to perform its intended function (Hanseth and Braa 1999). This paper argues for the urgent need to put the study of IT standards on the research agenda.

We wish to emphasize that the management of information technology standards is crucial in order to achieve the coherence of organizational information systems that is necessary to graduate from doing electronic commerce into doing electronic business. With some notable exceptions (e.g. Bensaou 1999; George 2000; Markus 2001), unfortunately IS scholars have so far had little advice to companies and CIOs on how to maneuver in the seemingly erratic world of standard based IS systems. This lack of advice is particularly alarming when it comes to developing e-business systems, as it is generally accepted that the e-business user interface is just the tip of the iceberg and that all successful e-business are built on top of a coherent and cohesive IT infrastructure made up of standard software systems. And there is ample evidence of e-businesses collapses due to lack of integration between different software systems.

2. SOFTWARE PACKAGES

In the early years of commercial use of computers (starting in the mid 1950s), all software systems were developed in-house out of simple necessity, since no software industry existed at the time (George 2000). As the software industry emerged, eventually most companies outsourced most of their software development to specialized software companies. Most software products were, however, still developed independently for each organization, i.e. there was little market standardization in the product, and little standardization in the production process. The next step was that each software producer developed its own set of standards in order to capture economies of scale in developing the software once for multiple customers

(Attewell 1992). This standardization also benefited the software buyers by lowering transaction costs as it was now possible to choose among a set of applications rather than merely choose among a set of software producing companies. Standardization also gives both producers and buyers of software a way of blackboxing knowledge by embedding it into the standardized components of the systems, thereby freeing resources for handling the exceptions (Scarbrough 1995).

For the purposes of this paper we define a standard software package as follows:

> A "standard software package" is a collection of software components that combined perform a set of generalized tasks that are applicable to a wide range of users (be they individuals or organizations). The software packaged is "standard" because the core components are identical across all of its implementations. Customization of the software may be performed to fit the software with use requirements unique to the individual implementations. This customization is implemented by adjusting program parameters, installing add-on modules, interfacing the software with other software systems, etc.

Three well-known categories of standard software packages are office application suites (including software like word processing, spreadsheets, and presentation software), database management software (DBMS), and enterprise resource planning (ERP) software. Some standard software packages require little customization on the part of the users before they are usable by an individual or an organization, while other standard software packages are mere tools on top of which the specific functionalities required by the user must be implemented in the customization process. In some cases, some customizations may be common among several customers, and the producer can then offer "standard customizations" on top of which only the site-specific customizations need be made. The German ERP producer SAP AG provides an example of this setup, since its system SAP R/3 exists in several standard customizations targeted at different industry sectors, e.g. chemical producing companies, retail store chains, and the pulp & paper industry.

Organizations are increasingly relying on standard software packages. George (2000) reports a threefold increase in the time corporate IS groups spend working on packaged applications from 1997 to 1998. The move from one-off implementations towards standard systems is accelerated by the increasing maturity of standard software packages due to economies of scale, and further by what looks like a flocking effect exhibited by the buyers of standard systems - creating winner-takes-all situations in many markets for standard software systems: large-scale consolidation on the producer side (Liebowitz and Margolis 1999; Shapiro and Varian 1999).

At first glance, these developments in the market for software systems may appear to be to great advantage for user organizations buying software since both the quality of products offered and the stability of the market increases. But as we shall illustrate in the seven alerts, standards have interesting properties that enable some or all participants in the market to use standards as a tool to attempt to manipulate the market.

It can be argued that in some large segments the market has narrowed down the range of options available to new buyers. For example bundling and co-branding agreements between hardware and software vendors often makes it impossible to buy a particular PC model without also paying for a license for Microsoft's Windows operating system. Another example concerns availability of particular versions of software products. Due to the high cost of supporting multiple versions of a software product, most software producers choose to let older versions expire, making it impossible for new users to buy a license to a particular version of the software which they may prefer over newer versions of the software.

We argue that strong effects of the market forces such as the two examples described above do not relieve the buying organization or individual from the responsibility of choosing the standards that suit their particular situations. Rather, these effects of the market forces make it all the more important for individual users and organizations alike to be aware of standardization issues and heed our standards alerts.

3. SEVEN ALERTS

3.1 Alert 1: When you buy a software package you join its network

The development from in-house development of software towards standard software packages puts the focus on standards and networks, since the users and producers of any given standard form a network (Shapiro and Varian 1999). Thus a decision to buy a particular product includes the implication of joining the network associated with the standard implemented by this product. The network is virtual in the sense that the members may not know each other, but they share a common interest in protecting their investments and therefore also in the evolution of the software. This is true whether or not the standard in question is a communication standard, because for all standards the adopters share common interests and communicate indirectly if not directly, for example through training and education of personnel, etc. (Shapiro and Varian, 1999).

The value of a network is determined by a combination of two factors: the number of members of the network and the interactions that take place in the network. First, Metcalfe's law (Shapiro and Varian, 1999) says that for a network with N participants, the potential value of the network is proportional to the number of possible interconnections in the network, which is N*(N-1) or approximately N squared. Thus the potential value of a network A with ten times as many members as a competing network B is not just ten times the value of network B, but a hundred times the value. Secondly, the network effects of a network are determined by the quantity and quality of actual interconnections and interaction in the network. If the network is sparsely connected because only few of the possible connections are realized, the network has little value; alternatively if the network enjoys rich communication and many interconnections, the members of the network reap large benefits of participating in the network.

Software companies own the network that is formed by their proprietary software and have the power to determine the evolution of the network. This power can be challenged, however, if a sufficiently large group of important customers agree to form a user group to influence the software producer's decisions regarding the software. Not all networks are subject to such power struggles based on the financial strength of the network's participants. By definition open standards are not owned by a single entity but rather by the community interested in the standard, i.e. the network of interested parties (Kindleberger 1983). Examples of open standards in information systems are most of the Internet standards such as the email protocols POP3 and SMTP (post office protocol 3, simple mail transfer protocol) which are implemented in every email client program used by Internet users worldwide regardless of which software producer developed the particular email client program.

The open source movement that lies behind applications such as sendmail and even operating systems such as Linux is a special case of open standards. In open source systems, the software producers not only comply with the specifications of an open standard, they also make the inner workings of their implementation freely available to other developers and encourage improvements to their software products. Thus a community of users and developers is designed specifically to prevent ownership and to promote shared software (Raymond 1997; O'Reilly 1998; Ljungberg 2000). The open source communities or networks surrounding various information systems appear unattractive to some user organizations because these networks lack central guidance which may lead to uncertainty in the future of the standard. Other organizations view these same properties of the open source networks as strengths since they protect the standard from the whims and opportunistic actions of individual stake holders, thus enhancing the continuity of the standard. We shall not conclude on this debate over open source here, but merely emphasize that organizations and individuals who choose to adopt a particular software package beware the intimate connection between any software package and its network.

3.2 Alert 2: Take a long-term perspective: Look ahead but reason back

Earlier when software was designed for a specific closed environment with well defined systems requirements, the focus was on immediate costs versus benefits when investment decisions were to be made. Often new software systems had both very short range and reach (Keen 1991; Weill and Broadbent 2000), i.e. they were standalone systems built to solve one particular task within a single organization, often even within a narrow setting in the organization. Thus, the buyer organization only had to consider short-range and short-reach implications of the software acquisition. As the standalone systems grew in numbers and size, a need emerged to move data between applications. The solution was standardized software platforms, e.g. operating systems, file systems, databases management systems.

Many standards choices made in the early stages of computer use in an organization or in an industry as a whole prove to have surprisingly durable consequences as both software standards and data have shown very long lifespans, as any organization with legacy systems can attest to. Now, in the age of open standards and interconnected systems it is vital for organizations to consider each standards choice as a long-range and long-reach decision with long-term implications, because the network is not limited to the users of that one application or standard. Rather the network includes a family of related and compatible software products, as well as a host of suppliers, institutions and other users surrounding this family of products. And it is important to choose the network that will provide the best long term benefits for the organization as the technologies of the network evolve. Further, the growing importance of system interconnections within the organization will mean that the standards choice has consequences for other parts of the organization whose software standards, implementations and interests may not originally have been considered in the decision process regarding the new software acquisition.

Two strategies for this choice are widely known as "best of suite" and "best of breed". In the "best of suite" strategy, the organization chooses the one best product or supplier that has the best all-round match with the organization's requirements. The reasoning behind this decision is to optimize the internal consistency between the various components of the overall system. The risk of this strategy is of course that of putting all of one's eggs in one basket, and that this trust may later prove to have been misplaced when the standard or vendor starts to move in a different direction compared with the organization's own requirements. In the "best of breed" strategy, the organization goes cherry-picking to find elements from several standards or suppliers that fit the organization's every requirement. The motivation behind this decision is to achieve optimal solutions. The risk - or rather the cost - of this strategy is that the system can be complicated to manage.

The evolution of many software applications is so that first an innovation is custom built by innovators and early adopters. Later several competing systems become available on the market (a breed of systems) and finally the systems become a commodity and bundled into a larger suite of standard software, like Microsoft Office Suite that contains a word processor, spreadsheet, presentation software, web site creation software, and database software. Awareness of this evolution trajectory for software applications helps the buying individual or organization focus on the potential long-term consequences of every software application acquisition.

We stress these long-term perspectives of software standards even as the pace of evolution in the computer industry reduces the effective lifespan of most products to very few years. When a personal computer is four years old, it is essentially unusable for any current software application. The machine will be at least an order of magnitude slower than contemporary computers, and very likely the replacement and upgrade parts for it have long since been unlisted by the supplier. Software products also typically have a high turnover with updates being released every year for most products. But the long lifespan of standards and data necessitates awareness that the standards choice involves participation in a network that may last one or two decades or longer.

An organization's initial choice of a standard software package for a particular task that has not previously been handled by a software package is a unique situation. There are fewer concerns about compatibility, both regarding existing technical systems, organizational processes, and knowledge management - old habits do not have to be unlearned. This situation is analogous to the choice of driving in the left side or the right side of the road. To the novice driver the decision is arbitrary; it does not matter in what side she drives. But to the experienced driver changing side represents a big challenge of "unlearning" as those of us who have tried it can attest to. The costs of changing to a different standard can be astounding to organizations with existing investments in technology and training.

3.3 Alert 3: When choosing a software package, there is safety in numbers

Earlier when ordering a software product an organization in effect committed itself to a particular (often local) producer and this producer's ability to produce added functionality as requirements grew. Now, as the commitments move from a local producer towards global producers and standards, user organizations must be wary of the development and evolutions of these standards and producers, a task that is likely much more demanding than keeping track of a single local producer.

As IT standards evolve and compete against each other, they may converge or diverge on some features, i.e. reaching or breaking compatibility with each other. As we shall describe in further detail in Alert 4, this development is caused by some party's perceived advantage in changing the degree of compatibility or interoperability between competing software standards. User organizations must be aware of the developments and seek to avoid the pitfalls of standards evolutions: blind alleys and one-way streets, which we describe next.

The blind alley scenario refers to the situation where an organization has chosen a standard that is now about to lose to competing standards. David (1986) uses the term "angry orphans" to describe the losing standards. He points out that such standards or technologies often show a sudden rapid development as they are losing the battle. For example the greatest speed of innovation in sail ships happened as the steam engine was taking over as the leading technology on the sea. Thus, though an organization should seek to avoid the blind alley scenario, the death throws of a losing standard may actually prove to be invigorating for the organization's IT systems. And if the losing standard manages to capture a niche market network, it may sustain itself for several years - or even perpetually, giving user organizations the choice of staying with the incumbent producer or the time to look for migration paths towards the wide boulevard, where there is safety in numbers. At other times the "angry orphans" may seek to counter the establishment of a new reign by holding on to resources that are critical for establishing a new. A good example is frequency allocation for cellular phones in the US where coalitions of companies providing first and second generation cellular phone services refuse to give up their control over a certain part of the radio spectrum, which in effect blocks a fast establishment of a third generation network.

A popular route taken by users who want to protect themselves against the blind alley scenario is the flocking strategy where users choose a standard based on the historic and current size and success of its associated network. As long as the network remains large, there will be a commercial incentive for both the original owner of the network as well as competing software producers to cater to the users of the standard. The risk for the users is that the network owner may end up being powerful enough to force users into a one-way street scenario.

The one-way street scenario describes the common situation where one is left with little choice when it comes to buying upgrades or expansions to existing systems. Often the purchase of a particular product in effect obliges the user to place future product purchases in the same product family, because the product or standard has low compatibility with other products or standards. This happens for example when the producer is ahead of the competition or if the producer has intentionally differentiated its implementation of the standard from the competition for competitive reasons rather than technological necessity. In this situation, the user organization may find itself so committed to the standard that the switching costs involved with moving to another software standard are prohibitive, and the organization is in effect locked-in to the standard software for better or for worse.

3.4 Alert 4: Focus on compatibility and avoid false gold

As we mentioned in Alert 2, the actual life expectancy of the data stored in software systems is often much longer than was expected at the time of the initial implementation. For user organizations this makes backward compatibility increasingly important, and the user organization must abstract from individual products and their features and instead focus on compatibility, product types and functionality.

In some cases several software products adhere to one common standard, enabling user organizations to choose among competing products based on other product features such as price, performance, usability, etc. Most often, however, compatibility is not a clear black and white issue because producers differentiate their products by adding proprietary features and unwarranted extensions to a standard (Besen and Farrell 1994; Shapiro and Varian 1998). Microsoft calls its execution of this competitive business technique "embrace, extend, and extinguish" (Kingmand 2001).

A user organization will often find these proprietary features attractive, but it is important to be aware that proprietary features are in reality false gold: Every time a proprietary feature is included in the organization's practice of use, the switching costs are raised, meaning that it will be harder to pull away from that producer if and when the organization should ever want to do so, for example when contracts are up for renewal or renegotiation. Instead, user organizations should keep their options open by staying close to compatible standards and look for gateway standards as a way to break an existing lock-in (David and Bunn, 1988). The break-down of standards happens in many cases where there is no central governance of the standard by a central player or authority, and even if such governance does exist standards often break down anyway as competitors test and extend the limits of the standard.

3.5 Alert 5: Choose a software package with an accessible base of knowledge

Earlier user organizations needed proprietary knowledge to operate the systems built especially for them. Today a standard system guarantees access to standardized knowledge both in its use and exploitation. Ideally, the network of organizations using a technology is matched by a network of individuals with knowledge and skills specific to this standard. If the two networks are not aligned, both user organizations and producer organizations will experience problems. One example of misaligned networks is that of ERP systems, where the number of organizations using ERP systems has not been matched by the number of people with knowledge about the setup and configuration of ERP systems, resulting in disproportionately high costs for the people component of ERP implementations.

Software producers employ various strategies for ensuring a network of knowledgeable users. One such strategy is to produce free or low cost versions of a product so people interested in the technology will be more likely to sample the products. One variation of this strategy is to make "academic versions" of the software available as free downloads or to bundle the products with textbooks used in educational institutions. Another variation is the bundling of products into product suites, resulting in a very wide distribution of even highly specialized software components (Shapiro and Varian 1999). By bundling feature-limited versions of the specialized software products, the vendor can even raise awareness about the products without serious loss of revenue from the sale of the full versions of the specialized software products. An example of feature limitation occurs in Microsoft's workstation (non-server) versions of Windows 2000 where the server modules (such as the web and file transfer protocol (FTP) modules) have been programmatically limited to ten simultaneous connections, effectively ensuring that organizations employing such services on some of their computers will invest in the much more expensive Windows 2000 server licenses for these computers.

A different strategy for building a network of knowledgeable users is formalization and institutionalization of the skills involved such as the establishing of authorized, branded training (courses and exams) for a technology, for example the multitude of titles in Microsoft's regime, such as

Microsoft Certified Systems Engineer. The process of institutionalizing skills is more complex for open standards such as open source products (sendmail, emacs, Linux, etc.) where there may be no single trusted certifying institution corresponding to the owner of the standard. Instead other forms of legitimization are used such as a person's ranking in recommender-systems such as discussion web sites for a particular product or community. Such online communities also make it very easy to see the contributions a particular member has made over the lifetime of the project, enabling potential customers or employers to get a quite detailed mental picture of the person's knowledge about a particular product, as well as her ability to explain technical issues to other users.

The co-development of the two networks (that of the technology and that of its users) has a high inertia to the point of being irreversible. The existing network of knowledgeable users of an incumbent standard forms an entry barrier that is hard to break through by a new, competing standard that has only a small network. If the new standard is owned and the owner is willing and able to invest in the standard, one way for the new standard to achieve a critical mass of users is for the standard owner to bear some or all of the switching costs for the users or user organizations willing to switch (Shapiro and Varian 1998; Shapiro and Varian 1999). Due to Metcalfe's law (see Alert 1) the owner of the network standard will be fighting an uphill battle until the networks are of comparable size. An alternative approach is to introduce gateway features into the new standard easing the transition from a competitor's product (David and Bunn 1988). When Microsoft Word was winning over the majority of the word processor market from WordPerfect they circumvented the knowledge barriers by providing WordPerfect users an easy passage. Microsoft Word featured two gateway technology features: An alternative user interface where Microsoft Word could be made to emulate the keyboard shortcuts of WordPerfect, and "Help for WordPerfect users" where the use of Microsoft Word was explained in terms that WordPerfect users could relate to. The latter feature still exists in the newest installment of Microsoft Word (Microsoft Office XP) that was released in 2001.

3.6 Alert 6: Choose a software package with the right type of standardization

Information technology standards are socio-technical constructs that comprise more than just technical specifications. Standardization can be achieved at many levels. Here we give an overview of the more common types of standardization, because it is important to choose the type that is right for the particular organization.

In standardization of output, the system's only compatibility restraint is that it must produce an output that can be used by the recipient users or systems. One example is that of web page production, where different users may use very different production techniques as long as their products fulfill agreed-upon requirements, such as a persistent look and feel when rendered on the five most popular web browser versions in use by the site's intended audience. This standardization strategy has the strength of allowing its users to optimize and personalize their data production methods without depending on consensus decisions. The strategy also has serious drawbacks if at any point in time the users need to share input or intermediate data. We would not recommend that this strategy be employed as the exclusive standardization strategy in an organization.

Standardization of user interface is a popular strategy employed to limit the training requirements as implementation decisions are guided by the similarities of the user interfaces. After some experimental implementations of information systems in a particular field, a dominant design emerges (Webster 1991; Teece 1997). Referring to web design Nielsen (2000) reasons that users spend most of their time on other sites, and therefore they prefer any new web site to be designed like the other sites they already know. As a consequence the dominant designs sometimes become static and end up as anachronisms when the surrounding systems change. For example the diskette icon featured in most MS Windows applications invokes the "save" function, even though few files are ever saved to diskettes these days, and some personal computers do not even contain diskette drives.

An organization might choose standardization of data files for one of two reasons, either seeking backward compatibility with existing data stored in legacy systems, or in an attempt to ensure access to the data using other information systems in the future. Employing this strategy, an organization can choose between a number of compatible software packages, thus bringing the simple advantage of choice in a market that may otherwise be dominated by a single producer. The disadvantage is that the user organization must abstain from using any proprietary features of the programs chosen (the false gold of Alert 4) in order to maintain data standardization. Examples of data standards with wide vendor support are the all-purpose information formatting language XML, the database language SQL, and Microsoft's rich text format (RTF).

More advanced modes of standardization of data interfaces include interconnectivity and interoperability (Bailey, McKnight et al. 1995). Interoperable information systems are able to communicate during the execution of a particular task. An everyday example is when the functionality of a electronic spread sheet program is employed by a word processing program to perform a calculation in a text document. More advanced implementations allow interoperability between systems running on different computers, even in different locations or different organizations. Recently implemented protocols such as Microsoft's .NET initiative and XML-RPC (extensible markup language - remote procedure call) allow relative simple runtime integration of information systems using standardized communication mechanisms over the common Internet. This will have far-reaching implications for the implementation of standard software packages and inter-organizational information systems in the coming years.

Organizations may choose standardization of skills by employing only people with a particular training or education, or if necessary to carry the cost of training new employees to some formalized level of training (see Alert 5). This strategy helps ensure uniform performance and results of the work carried out by the employees, and fewer control mechanisms have to be in place to assure the quality of the output produced. Organizations can choose two types of skills on which to standardize: specific or generic skills. Specific or proprietary skills encompass a user's qualifications with a particular product or product suite, where the skills are certified by the product producer or a trusted third party. Every major vendor in the technology market has such certification programs, and many are even updated on a continuous basis, forcing certificate holders to take new exams in order to preserve their certificate status. Generic skills are skills such as programming, business knowledge, etc. that can be acquired at universities or similar educational institutes.

3.7 Alert 7: Focus more on use and less on waiting

In 1965 Intel co-founder Gordon E. Moore famously predicted that the number of transistors that can be placed on a single integrated circuit would continue to double every 18 months for the next ten years (Moore 1965). The press dubbed this prediction Moore's Law, and though the initial predictions only dared include the time until 1975, the law has held true to this date as measured by the number of transistors incorporated in the top processor models from Intel over the years (Intel 2000). The popularized version of Moore's law states that for a constant price, computer performance doubles every 18 months. Software production actually has negative scaling: When a software product grows it inherently becomes more complicated and demands more development resources (Brooks 1995). But successful standard software packages mature with time, and innovation and market forces combine to establish a small set of dominant software packages from which new buyers can choose.

This may lead to a wait-and-see position for buyers until they can determine which packages will prevail (Au and Kauffman 2001). Our advice to buyers is not to fall into this trap for the following two reasons. First of all the winner will only emerge when companies actually buy software, so by being part of the selection process there is a greater chance that software that fits the needs of the company will succeed. Secondly change is inevitable and waiting only leads to greater discrepancy between a company's existing software base and the available software packages. In a worst case scenario from a buyer's point of view a late purchase of some package forces the replacement of the existing base of software.

Another trap buyers can fall into is waiting for the emergence of a software package that is a perfect fit with the buyer's requirements.

4. CONCLUSIONS

In this paper we have described and highlighted seven connotations that are related to buying a standard software package but less obvious than the two factors of price and immediate features. The seven alerts are depicted in table 1.

1. When you buy a software package you join its network
2. Take a long-term perspective: Look ahead but reason back
3. When choosing a software package, there is safety in numbers
4. Focus on compatibility and avoid false gold
5. Choose a software package with an accessible base of knowledge
6. Choose a software package with the right type of standardization
7. Focus more on use and less on waiting

Table 1. The seven alerts

We have advocated a broad, networked view of the purchasing process and argued that the purchase of a software package is not an atomic, stand-alone event similar to buying a piece of well established and packaged technology. Instead software packages are networked and built around standards that allow (and sometimes disallow (Wilson 2001)) more or less seamless connection to other software systems. We promote a pluralistic multi-organizational view of buying software as a continuous process of trying to match available software packages with a base of already installed software systems while anticipating future needs. We have formulated seven alerts that both researchers and practitioners should consider when studying these building blocks of e-business.

The first alert emphasizes that all software packages form networks of which their users become part. Secondly standards decisions should not only be based on immediate benefits but should take a long-term perspective, weighing in the past and the future. The third alert argues that the size and value of a network formed by a software package means that there is safety in numbers when buying software packages. The fourth alert states that even though additional features are attractive they may be deceiving and in effect lock-in the buyer to the software package, and therefore it is better to focus on compatibility. Alert number five stresses the importance of not only considering the artifact but also the entire support infrastructure and complementary assets surrounding the package. Software packages can be standardized along a number of dimensions, and alert six stresses the importance of choosing the right type of standardization. Finally alert seven urges the buyer to take an active part in the selection process and use of a software package.

We hope that these seven alerts will be used in practice by IT managers when evaluating different software alternatives. We have designed the alerts so that they each provide a particular yet practical concern when purchasing software.

One fruitful area of further research is the need to study in detail the evolution of information infrastructures built up by software packages, and how interoperability and standards decisions by software houses lead to success or failure for their software. Especially the time criticality and scalability of an e-business infrastructure is particularly interesting. We are in the midst of performing longitudinal field studies that follows the evolution of large-scale IT infrastructures that are comprised of a multitude of standard software packages.

ACKNOWLEDGEMENTS

This research was carried out as part of the PITNIT project. PITNIT is supported by the Danish Research Agency, grant number 9900102. URL: http://www.cs.auc.dk/research/IS/PITNIT/

REFERENCES

Attewell, P. (1992). "Technology diffusion and organizational learning: The case of business computing." Organization Science 3(1): 1-19.

Au, Y. A. and R. J. Kauffman (2001). Should We Wait? Network Externalities and Electronic Billing Adoption. Hawaii International Conference on System Sciences, Hawaii.

Bailey, J., L. McKnight, et al. (1995). "The economics of advanced services in an open communications infrastructure: transaction costs, production costs, and network externalities." Information Infrastructure and Policy 4: 255-277.

Bensaou, M. (1999). Electronically-Mediated Partnerships: The Use of CAD Technologies in Supplier Relations. Proceedings of ICIS 1999.

Besen, S. M. and J. Farrell (1994). "Choosing how to compete: strategies and tactics in standardization." Journal of economic perspectives 8(2 - spring 1994): 117-131.

Brooks, F. P. (1995). The Mythical Man-Month: Essays on Software Engineering, Anniversary Edition (2nd Edition), Addison Wesley Longman, Inc.

David, P. A. (1986). Narrow windows, blind giants and angry orphans: The dynamics of systems rivalries and dilemmas of technology policy. Technological Innovation Project - working paper no. 10.

David, P. A. and J. A. Bunn (1988). "The economics of gateway technologies and network evolution: Lessons from electricity supply history." Information Economics and Policy 3: 165-202.

George, J. F. (2000). The Origins of Software: Acquiring Systems at the End of the Century. Framing the Domains of IT Management: Projecting the Future Through the Past. R. Zmud. Cincinnati, Ohio, Pinnaflex Educational Resources, Inc.: 263-284.

Hanseth, O. and K. Braa (1999). Hunting for the treasure at the end of the rainbow: standardizing corporate IT infrastructure. IFIP TC8 WG 8.2 - New Information Technologies in Organizational Processes: Field Studies and Theoretical Reflections on the Future of Work, St. Louis, MO, Kluwer Academic Publishers.

Intel (2000). "Moore's Law", http://www.intel.com/research/silicon/mooreslaw.htm

Keen, P. G. W. (1991). Shaping the Future: Business Design Through Information Technology, Harvard Business School Press.

Kindleberger, C. P. (1983). "Standards as public, collective and private goods." KYKLOS - International review for social sciences 36 (1983): 377-396.

Kingmand, H. (2001). "The Microsoft Standard is Anything But" ZDNet News, http://www.zdnet.com/zdnn/stories/comment/0,5859,2784051,00.html

Liebowitz, S. J. and S. E. Margolis (1999). Winners, Losers & Microsoft, Competition and antitrust in High Technology. Oakland, California, The independent institute.

Ljungberg, J. (2000). "Open Source Movements as a Model for Organizing." European Journal of Information Systems 9(4): 208-216.

Markus, M. L. (2001). Process Integration In The Chemical Industry, (Working paper).

Moore, G. E. (1965). "Cramming more components into integrated circuits." Electronics 38(8).

Nielsen, J. (2000). "End of Web Design", http://www.useit.com/alertbox/20000723.html

O'Reilly, T. (1998). The open-source revolution. Release 1.0, Ester Dyson's Monthly Report: 3-26.

Raymond, E. S. (1997). "The Cathedral and the Bazaar", http://www.tuxedo.org/~esr/writings/cathedral-bazaar/cathedral-bazaar/

Scarbrough, H. (1995). "Blackboxes, Hostages and Prisoners." Organization Studies: 991-1019.

Shapiro, C. and H. R. Varian (1998). "The art of standards wars." California Management Review 41(2): 8-32.

Shapiro, C. and H. R. Varian (1999). Information Rules: a strategic guide to the network economy. Boston, Massachusetts, Harvard Business School Press.

Teece, D. J. (1997). Capturing Value from Technological Innovation: Integration, Strategic Partnering, and Licensing Decisions. Managing Strategic Innovation and Change. A Collection of Readings. New York, Oxford Press: 287-306.

Webster, J. (1991). Advanced manufacturing technologies: work organisation and social relations crystallised. A Sociology of monsters: essays on power, technology and domination. J. Law. London and New York, Routledge: 192-221.

Weill, P. and M. Broadbent (2000). Managing the IT Infrastructure: A Strategic Choice. Framing the Domains of IT Management: Projecting the Future Through the Past. R. Zmud. Cincinnati, Ohio, Pinnaflex Educational Resources, Inc.: 329-353.

Wilson, D. (2001). "Talkin' to Me? Not if AOL Has Its Way" Los Angeles Times, http://www.latimes.com/technology/la-000093189nov22.column?coll=la%2 Dheadlines%2Dtechnology

UNDERSTANDING E-BUSINESS COMPETENCIES IN SMES

a conceptual and operational approach

TOM R. EIKEBROKK and DAG H. OLSEN
Department of Information systems, Agder University College, Norway

Abstract: This paper reports on an ongoing project that aims to assist SMEs in the strategic use of e-business technology. We present the first stage of this project, where the goal is to identify critical types of competence that can enable or inhibit the successful use of e-business technologies. We start by describing the conceptual model of competencies and their relations to e-business success. Secondly, we describe the operationalization of this model into measures that are the basis for the subsequent survey used to identify critical types of competence related to e-business success for SMEs.

1. INTRODUCTION

One of the major characteristics of today's economy is the growth of e-business defined as business conducted over the Internet. All over the world both established companies and new ventures create new online businesses based on Internet technologies, which are therefore often referred to as e-business technologies, e-commerce solutions, etc. It is generally believed that e-business has the potential of increasing efficiency and effectiveness and hence generate substantial new value.

Research within the field of information systems (IS) economics show that the business value from IT investments in general is positive and highest in companies that not only invest in technology but also in organizational measures including training programs to leverage ITs potential (Brynjolfsson and Hitt, 1998). Most studies of the effects of IT-investments are done in the context of large firms, usually Fortune 500 companies, and there are very few studies of IT-value in smaller companies. In a recent study based on 441 small and medium-sized enterprises (SMEs) in Spain Dans (2001) found that IT-investments also gave a significant and positive business value in SMEs.

Moreover, in a recent study Amit and Zott (2001) argue that amongst IT-investments in general Internet technologies have the highest potential for value-creation through linking companies, its suppliers and customers in new and innovative ways. Amit and Zott further argue that this value potential of e-business is poorly understood both theoretically and in practice. In a European survey among Internet experts and online traders it was found that most companies did not consider e-business as a priority (Forrester Research, 1999). Among the major obstacles were lack of trained staff and co-ordination between internal departments. Knowledge and competence are increasingly emphasized by businesses in general as the most important competitive factor. In particular, small and medium sized enterprises suffer from resource poverty. In a similar European survey among SME managers it was found that the main obstacles to increased competence were high costs of courses, problems of internal organization of the attendance to the courses, bad quality of the training supply as well as difficulties in identifying training needs (E/1224, 1997). With the knowledge of key competencies, SMEs may spend their limited resources on factors that contribute the most to business value.

The purpose of this paper is to contribute to the theoretical and practical understanding of the nature and role of competence in utilizing e-business technology for the benefit of the business. In exploring this we are particularly concerned with the small- and medium sized companies. To do this, we begin with a review of the literature describing the company value of e-business, and the nature and importance of competencies needed to successfully utilize information technology including e-business solutions. Based on this review, we develop a conceptual model of e-business competencies and their relations to e-business value. In the empirical part of the paper we test the relevance of this model for SMEs through interviews with selected managers. These interviews also guide the operationalization of the model into a survey instrument. The final section of the paper presents a summary and conclusion of the theoretical and empirical work in the paper.

2. THEORY

There is an increased focus on individual achievement and productivity in the workplace (Stewart, 1997). In today's competitive environment, maximizing the potential of information technology in general and Internet technology in particular presumes that the technology is used well and not only adopted and used. Competence is a primary issue, as it enables employees to transform ideas into business value (Soh & Markus, 1995; Kanter, 1997), and as it leads to higher productivity (Higginbotham, 1997; Little, 1997).

Only a few studies have examined the relationship between information technology competence in general and business value. Also, the user competence construct is largely absent from prominent technology acceptance and fit models, poorly conceptualized, and inconsistently measured (Marcolin et al., 2000). Recent works show increased academic interest in this phenomenon.

Amit and Zott (2001) have explored the theoretical foundations for value creation in e-business in a recent study. Their review suggests that no single theory available in the entrepreneurship or strategic management literature today can fully explain the value creation potential of e-business. Rather, they argue that an integration of theoretical perspectives on value creation is necessary. Their proposed model is based on the concept of a business model, which describes how one or several companies (e.g. a company and its suppliers and customers) in co-operation can exploit business opportunities through the design, structure and governance of transaction content. With this as the level of analysis, they describe the potential of value creation in e-business in four interrelated dimensions, which are efficiency, complementarities, lock-in, and novelty. Efficiency relates to potential of reducing transaction costs as a result of utilizing e-commerce technologies. Complementarities describe the value potential of companies that cooperate in an e-business strategy and combine their products and services, technologies and activities. This combination can create value to customers as a result of reduced costs related to finding and ordering products and services, and to business partners as a result of utilizing interconnectivity of markets and possibilities of process integration. The third dimension, lock-in, describes the value potential of e-business as a result of switching costs where customers are motivated to repeat their transactions, and where business partners extend their relationships and also improve their current associations. As the last dimension in Amit and Zott's model, novelty describes how e-businesses can create value through innovations in the way business is conducted. Examples of such innovations are new ways of structuring transactions like web-based auctions and reverse markets. In the latter form potential buyers indicate needs and preferred prices to sellers. These examples show that e-business combines previously unconnected parties by utilizing new transaction technologies and by creating new markets.

2.1 IT Competence

According to Marcolin et al. (2000) and Basselier et al. (2001) the proliferation of approaches to the concept of competence has hindered the creation of a cumulative body of knowledge. Research has been conducted from a variety of approaches and areas of research, including psychology, human resource management, management, education and information systems. Partly, this confusion in the understanding of competence results from the interchangeable use of competence and performance, which confuses the understanding of process and outcome. Problems related to understanding and measuring competencies have caused many researchers to use performance as a proxy. In this study we will view an organization's access to competencies as a necessary but not sufficient factor to the successful implementation of strategies involving new technologies. We will primarily base our discussion and inclusion of potentially important areas of competence on studies within the IS field that include some form of outcome in either general or specific terms. Furthermore, since several studies point to the importance of the business manager in achieving successful implementation of strategies and technologies (e.g. Luftman et al. 1999; Papke-Shields and Malhotra 2001), we will also include studies which focuses on the business manager. In the interviews and in the survey we will also focus on business managers and hence assume that information from these will give a representative reflection of both relevant and critical types of competence in SMEs. Since the literature on e-business is more influenced by studies of bigger companies, we base our approach on the assumption that we can gain more understanding of e-business in SMEs by applying theories based on studies of businesses in general and adjusting them to the SME context.

2.1.1 Definitions and types of competence

In this emergent field of IS research there is yet little general agreement on how competencies should be defined and measured. There are different views concerning which elements competence consist of, and at what level of analysis these could be observed. In the IS field two streams of research considering the nature and importance of competence can be identified. Firstly, one stream concerns competencies needed at the company level of analysis and is influenced by similar studies reported in the management literature (e.g. Prahalad and Hamel, 1990). In particular, this stream is heavily influenced by the resource-based view of the firm (e.g. Barney, 1991) where competencies are regarded as resources defined as fundamental drivers of superior company performance. In addition, a distinction is made between resources and capabilities, where capabilities reflect the company's ability to combine resources in ways that stimulate performance. In general the goal of this research is to identify types of capabilities that are core in the sense that they can create a relative advantage to the company in it's effort of taking advantage of technology in relation to business needs. A persistent issue in this research stream has been to identify which types of competence in terms of resources and capabilities that are core and non-core to the business.

The other stream concerns the competencies at the individual level. This perspective holds that competence at the individual level is required for the creation of competence at the organizational level, or focuses simply on the competence requirements that individuals will be subject to (Lee and Trauth, 1995; Basselier et al., 2000). There is incomplete research at the individual level as is also reported in organizational research (Nordhaug, 1998).

Table 1 shows the level of analysis and definition of competence of the most significant recent contributions to the conceptualization of IS competence.

	Level of analysis	**Definition of competence**
Van der Heijden (2000)	Organizational level and IT management	IT core capabilities: organization-specific routines, processes, skills and resources
Feeny and Willcocks (1998)	Organizational level and IT management	IS core capabilities: organization-specific routines, processes, skills and resources
Sambamurthy and Zmud (1994)	Organizational level and IT management	Capabilities, skills and tacit know-how
Bharadwaj, Sambamurthy and Zmud (2000)	Organizational level	Critical IT capabilities
Basselier et al. (2001)	Individual level and business managers	IT related explicit and tacit knowledge
Lee and Trauth (1995)	Individual level and IS professionals	Critical knowledge and skills

Table 1. Approaches to the study of IS competence

IT-competence in business managers can be defined as "the set of IT-related knowledge and experience that a business manager develops over time which enables him/her to contribute effectively to the deployment of IT in the organization" (Basselier et al., 2001). Basselier et al. identifies five areas of knowledge that a manager should possess: technology, applications, system development, management of IT and access to IT knowledge. In addition to this knowledge, business managers' level of competence is increased by experience both at the project level and in the management of

IT. At the management of IT level, such activities are creation of IT vision, strategies and policies, budget, priorities of development, and communication mechanisms between IT and business people.

This area is perhaps most examined in the IT and related literature. In a literature review, Marcolin et al. (2000) observed three factors differentiating the measures of competence: Conceptualizations of competence, measurement methods and knowledge domains. The different conceptualizations identified by Marcolin et al. are associated with three outcomes from learning: cognitive outcomes, skill-based outcomes and affective outcomes (Kraiger, Ford and Salas, 1993). These outcomes represent different conceptualizations of competence, and can be used to understand differences in the effectiveness of the employment of technology (Marcolin et al., 2000).

What are less studied are the non-IT aspects of technology. It is generally accepted that such meta-skills as communication, social and leadership skills are necessary for successful IT professionals. To what extent such competence is needed in different organizational roles is a rich potential area of study. A growing body of research investigating the importance of alignment between business and technology has documented that having competencies in business strategy and IS strategies per se is not enough to successfully take advantage of new technologies (e.g. Luftman et al., 1999). Alignment which is defined as applying IT in an appropriate and timely way, in harmony with business strategies, goals and needs (King, 1995; Henderson and Venkatraman, 1993) can be viewed as one type of competence involving such meta-skills not related to technology it self. Thus, alignment as a competence involves combining and using the available competencies inside or outside of the organization in a way that realizes the strategic potential of new technologies in the company's business domain. Henderson & Venkatraman (1993) describes the process of alignment as a managerial role where the task primarily is to create a strategic fit between the external position of the organization in the competitive product-market arena and the internal design of an appropriate administrative structure that supports its execution. In achieving this alignment the organization must combine its available competencies on strategy and strategy formulation with competencies on technologies and internal operations. Alone, sophisticated technologies have no value without the competence that makes the organization capable of organizing its processes in a way that realizes the potential of the new technology and hence differentiate the organization from its competitors.

Knowing how to stimulate the active use and combination of relevant competencies is therefore important, but not straightforward. In an extensive longitudinal study of more than 500 companies in 15 industries, Luftman et al. (1999) identified factors that enables or hinders the successful alignment between business and IT strategies. Based on interviews with both business and IT managers, the results showed that one of the most important enablers of alignment was a business manager that recognized the potential value of IT, defined and communicated visions and strategies which included IT, as well as actively sponsored IT projects.

In a study of the manufacturing executive's role on business performance through strategic alignment, Papke-Shields and Malhotra (2001) found that both active involvement and influence from the business executive were important determinants of alignment which again had a significant influence on business performance.

2.1.2 Theoretical synthesis

There is general agreement in the literature that the successful use of IT assumes organizational and individual capabilities. There are different approaches to conceptualizing this phenomenon in the literature. Many terms are used in the IS field to describe organizations' capabilities. Some researchers describe this with terms like core capability (Feeny and Willcocks, 1998; Amit and Schoemaker, 1993; Penrose, 1959; Teece et al. 1997). Others use core competence (Sambamurthy and Zmud, 1994), explicit and tacit knowledge (Basselier et al., 2000) or distinguishes between cognitive, skill-based and affective dimensions of competence (Marcolin et al., 2000; Kraiger et al., 1993). We base our conceptualization on the integrative terms of Sambamurthy and Zmud (1994) that integrate organizational level concepts with individual level concepts. They view these dimensions as *organizational competencies* that exist of *organizational capabilities* (e.g. supportive organizational culture), *individual skills* (e.g. IT personnel skill base) and *tacit know-how* (e.g. individual experience in reorganization of work processes).

The literature on competence is so far more influenced by studies of IT-investments related to traditional business rather than e-business that highlights new and technology based interactions between companies. As a result, several models do not include competence on whether activities should be sourced within the company or within the e-business network. Such competence in sourcing and also in alignment can be viewed as secondary types of competence, where sourcing relates to obtaining and alignment relates to combining and use primary types of competence.

Most of the literature on competence is based on studies of relatively large companies. We need to adjust these models to fit smaller companies. It is very likely that smaller companies have fewer resources and as a result experience constraints to strategies and actions relevant to bigger companies.

The literature is not clear as to what these differences are. It is therefore necessary to test the conceptual model for its relevance to SMEs, which will be done in the next section.

3. THE CONCEPTUAL MODEL

The next step was to create a competence model that would work in our context. We performed a process of contrasting the dimensions of competence from the literature review in order to identify a common framework. The items of each dimension were clustered into appropriate dimensions for our study. We discussed the clusters and the items in terms of the significance for SMEs and e-business. Discussion with colleagues and open-ended interviews with SME leaders were used in this process. This process resulted in a model with six dimensions of competence as shown in figure 1. Our dimensions are elaborated below. Table 2 shows how our dimensions of competence relate to the dimensions in the literature review. Appendix 1 shows how our competence dimensions relate to the items of the most significant sources.

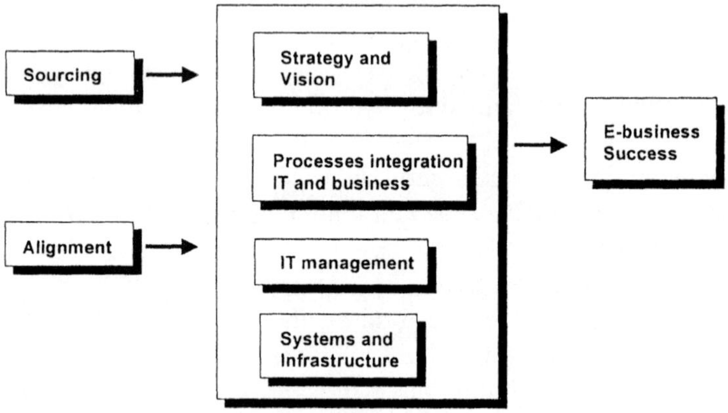

Figure 1. The conceptual model

	Strategy and vision	IT-Business process integration	IT management	Systems and Infrastructure	Sourcing and Alignment
Bharadwaj, Sambamurthy and Zmud, 2000					
IT business partnerships			x		X
External IT linkages				x	X
Business IT strategic thinking	X	X			x
IT business process integration		X			
IT management			X		
IT Infrastructure			x	X	
Basselier, Reich and Benbasat, 2001					
Explicit IT Knowledge					
Technology	x			X	X
Applications		x		X	X
Systems Development			X		X
Management of IT			X		x
Access to IT knowledge			X		x
Tacit IT Knowledge					
Experience			X	X	x
Cognition	X	X			
Feeny and Willcoks, 1998, van der Heijden, 2000					
Business IT Strategic Thinking(BIS)	X	x			x
IT management(ITM)			X		
Business Systems Thinking(BST)		X			
Relationship Building(RB)					X
Architecture Planning(AP)				X	
Making Technology Work(MTW)			X		
Informed Buying(IB)				X	
Contract Facilitation(CF)			X		
Contract Monitoring(CM)			X		
Vendor Development(VD)			X		
Sambamurthy and Zmud, 1994					
Business Development		X	X		X
External Networks					X
Line Technology Leadership		x			X
Process Adaptiveness		X		X	
IT Planning	X	x	X		X
IT Infrastructure			X		
Data Center Utility				X	
Lee and Trauth, 1995					
Technical Specialties				X	

Knowledge					
Technology Management Knowledge			X		
Business Functional Knowledge		X			X
Interpersonal and Management Skills			X		X

Table 2. The relation between the conceptual model and the major sources.

3.1 Strategy and Vision

This dimension describes the company's ability to envision the strategic potential of new e-business or e-commerce technology in its marketplace. The dimension both involves understanding the concept of e-business and how related new technology for e-commerce can represent threats and opportunities to the company. Included here is also the ability to understand and use strategic planning methods needed to develop an e-business strategy.

Strategy and vision as a variable will reflect the maturity of the enterprise in both understanding the e-business domain and what it means in terms of new possibilities and threats in the business domain. The variable will also reflect the organizational capability to develop plans, which describes how e-business will be put into action.

The importance of this variable was supported by our interviews with eight SME managers and two consultants specializing in IT and business issues in SMEs. The most important issues, according to these managers and consultants, were the visions and strategies related to the utilization of e-business and the implications of e-business on the work processes both within the SMEs and their business partners.

3.2 Sourcing and Alignment

Sourcing and alignment describes activities related to the company's ability to involve and take advantage of competencies inside or outside of the company in order to develop and implement strategies related to e-business. The importance of these variables is well documented in the literature. Sourcing refers to whether competencies will be build up internally or accessed from external sources, either through insourcing of competencies or outsourcing of activities where competencies are needed. When competencies are not sufficiently represented internally, the company must decide what strategy it will utilize to close this gap. Identified competencies could be build up internally through education programs or through recruitment of new personnel. Alternatively, the activity where competencies are needed could also be partly or totally outsourced to partners in the business network. The company could also implement some combination of these strategies. Sourcing of competence describes the process of gaining access to competencies inside or outside of the company.

Having access to sources of competence per se both inside or outside of the company is not enough for the successful use of competence. Work processes whether they are located inside or outside of the company, can be intertwined and dependent on each other. In the effort of designing new processes, or improving existing processes, the company must make competencies work together in order to realize the potential of information technology. The concept of alignment describes both the process of how different competencies represented in different sources are brought together and put into action, and the outcome of this process as a resulting level of alignment. Previous work on the alignment between business and IT shows that departments, business and IT experts must be brought together and involved in the effort of combining IT possibilities with business needs and opportunities. Relationships must be built between IT professionals and business unit managers. Research on both alignment and sourcing has documented that both the choices of alignment strategy and sourcing strategy are related to company performance.

In our model, sourcing and alignment represent meta or secondary competence that involve using and combining the primary types of e-business competence that the company possesses. The rationale behind this variable is that primary types of e-business competence are necessary but not sufficient for the successful use of these competencies. The company must also have secondary types of competence in terms of the ability to combine competencies in a relevant way in support of their visions and strategies.

3.3 IT-Business Process Integration

This variable describes the organization's capability of envisioning and implementing work processes made possible by new technologies. New business or IT work processes can be designed or old processes can be restructured in order to leverage the opportunities of new technology. Independent of which strategy is chosen, the company must have the necessary capability to identify and implement changes in business processes in order to increase process efficiency to the relevant level according to the technology chosen.

The notion that one must organize in order to leverage the potential of new technology has been wide spread in the IS literature. Empirical studies in the area of IS economics have also documented that productivity gains in

Fortune 500 companies from utilizing new technologies are higher in companies that organize themselves in ways that leverage the potential of the new technology (e.g. Brynjolfsson and Hitt, 1998). In a European study of 441 Spanish SMEs, Dans (2001) found a similar correlation between IT-investments and productivity for SMEs that can partly be attributed to organizational redesign. This means that companies must look for new and powerful ways of both organizing and managing their work processes. To do this, competencies are both needed in developing the new business model and in the subsequent implementation of this model in the organization. We describe these types of competence as IT-business process integration.

3.4 IT Management

IT management is activities related to the management of the IT function. This is activities such as IS planning and design, IS application delivery, IT project management, and planning for controls and standards (Bharadwaj et al., 2000; DeLone, 1988). Research on SMEs shows that these companies seldom have a defined IT budget or an explicit IT plan or strategy, and investments in technology are often driven by the owner, rather by any formal cost-benefit or strategic analysis (Ballantine et al., 1998; Dans, 2001). This was also supported in our interviews with eight managers from SMEs and two consultants working with IT- and business issues in SMEs, where IT management in general and the specific activities like formal and specific IT plans mentioned above, were perceived as less important in relation to e-business. As a result of this we do not define specific activities in IT management, but keep this at a more general level.

3.5 Systems and Infrastructure

This dimension refers to the foundation for enterprise applications and services, and is comprised of data, network, and processing architectures. Systems and infrastructure influence the reach and range of business opportunities available to firms in applying IT in their business strategies.

Successful use of e-business technologies involves both finding the right technology with a strategic potential to implement and having a technological and managerial infrastructure that can support it. This involves competence on available e-business solutions as well as on the importance of having or creating internal structures that can utilize the new solutions.

SMEs generally are dependent on a small number of customers to whom they sell a limited number of products. SMEs will thus often be heavily influenced by the e-business strategy of the dominant actor in the value chain, and be forced to conform to their solutions and technology (Ballantine et al., 1998), and thus the competence requirements defined by this. We have therefore reduced the level of detail in the specific competencies related to systems and infrastructure, and to a more general level. Our choice here was also supported by the interviews with SME managers and consultants who perceived competencies related to systems and infrastructure as of much less importance that competencies in vision and strategy along with competencies in integrating work process between business and IT. Furthermore, the interviews also revealed that several SMEs had experienced lack of control and autonomy regarding IT decisions that involved an important customer or business partner.

3.6 E-business Success

We define e-business success in line with Amit and Zott (2001) who describe the potential of value creation in e-business in four interrelated dimensions, which are efficiency, complementarities, lock-in, and novelty. Efficiency relates to possible reduction in transaction costs, whereas complementarities describe the value potential from combining products and services, technologies and activities with an e-business partner. The third dimension, lock-in, describes the potential value in creating switching costs from arrangements that motivate customers and business partners to repeat and improve transactions and relationships. The last dimension, novelty, describes value as a result of innovations in the way business is conducted (e.g. web based auctions, etc.).

4. DEVELOPMENT OF SURVEY INSTRUMENT

The conceptual model was developed in order to establish the dimensions of the survey instrument. This survey will later be used in identifying types of competence that are critical in realizing e-business value in SMEs in five European countries. Figure 2 depicts the phases in the development of the survey instrument. The initial conceptual model was developed on the basis of the literature review. The integration and relation of the major contributing articles to our initial conceptual model is organized in a matrix in appendix 1. The initial model was discussed with colleagues in a research seminar. This spurred some minor adjustments and a further literature review, which led to the final conceptual model. This served as input to the development of an operational model with the initial list of survey indicators.

We then conducted open-ended interviews with eight executives of Norwegian SMEs and two related consultants, as an additional reality check of this model, and as a guide to the further elaboration of our dimensions and specific indicators. Since small businesses most likely have different characteristics from large companies, the purpose of the interviews was also to include factors relevant to the context of small businesses. These interviews started open-ended to obtain possible fundamental changes or additions to our conceptual model. We then gradually narrowed the focus in the interviews to elicit more specific information. The outcome of this process led to an improved final conceptual model, which is assumed to be relevant for SMEs.

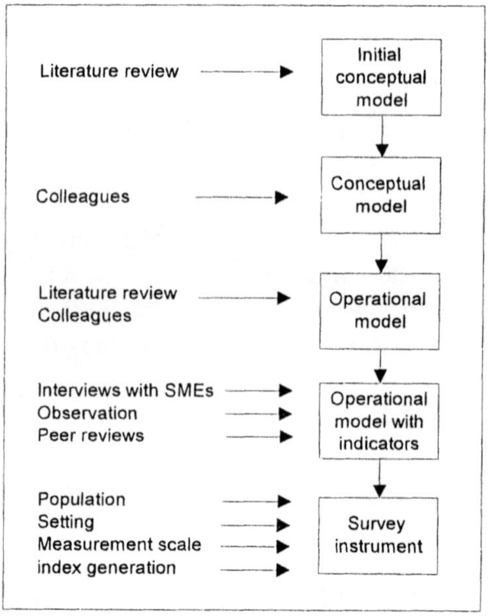

Figure 2. Phases in the development of a conceptual model and survey instrument

The list of indicators was turned into a preliminary list of survey questions. This list was subject to further refinement through pre-testing in a new sample of SMEs. The national partners of the ANTRA project subsequently translated the survey into Norwegian, Finnish, and Spanish, and surveys are currently being carried out in 3 industries in each partner country.

5. RESULTS AND DISCUSSION

Our review of the literature suggests that e-business competence can be conceptualized into the six dimensions of our conceptual model. The relationships between these dimensions and the major contributing articles are shown in the matrix in appendix 1. The review of the literature and the interviews with SMEs indicate that the general conceptual model is relevant also to SMEs. The survey instrument is presented in appendix 2.

The interviews also indicated that some types of competence are perceived by SMEs as more relevant than others in the context of e-business. SME managers and consultants considered competencies in strategy and vision, IT-business process integration, and sourcing as most important. Competencies in IT management, systems and infrastructure and alignment were considered relevant but less prioritized in relation to the other types of competence. Competence in sourcing was described as particularly important since this is strongly related to the importance of the local network to SMEs in general. Both managers and consultants described the local network of business partners as an important relationship since it is characterized by higher trust and less costs than partners outside of the local area. As a result of this, SMEs rest heavily on local partners and associates when issues of importance to their business are discussed.

The interviews also pointed to the influence of significantly bigger business partners. SMEs generally have small market shares. They are typically dependent on a small number of customers to whom they sell a limited number of products (Ballantine et al., 1998). SMEs will therefore most likely be influenced by the e-business strategy of the dominant actor in the value chain. In this case, SMEs will experience less autonomy in both choosing the appropriate technology and the related competencies. We have some support for this argument in our interviews with SMEs, and it should be investigated further. We have included control variables in the survey instrument to address this situation.

In this research we assume that developing and implementing an e-business strategy is an ongoing process in most SMEs. One interview, however, revealed that e-business was not perceived as a new issue. This SME had already and long ago implemented electronic communication and transactions with its major business partners. The technology used was not originally based on Internet but gradually this technology had been replaced by Internet solutions. This replacement was regarded as a pure technical issue and was now almost completed. As a result of this, the manager did not perceive e-business competence as relevant because the process of utilizing information technology to assist business transactions was close to its end. This interview show that some companies might perceive the issue of competence as irrelevant since the process of implementing e-business is ended. To control for this situation we have included items to measure this process in the survey instrument.

Our interviews and some studies in the reviewed literature suggest that SMEs experience a different reality than large companies. Some studies suggest that resources in general are much scarcer in SMEs, and managers or other personnel fill many roles at the same time. The use of formal planning methods and strategic plans per se is often limited. It is not clear in the literature how and when size of a company leads to specialization and formal structures. To more fully understand the differences between big and small companies we need more research into this issue. More research will increase our knowledge of what and when important conditions are in place and to what extent they can stimulate business development in general and e-business success in particular.

ACKNOWLEDGEMENTS

This paper benefited from work conducted under the ANTRA project that is partly financed by the EU Commision and the Leonardo da Vinci program.

REFERENCES

Amit, R. & P. Schoemaker (1993), 'Strategic assets and organizational rent', *Strategic Management Journal*, 14(1), 33-46.

Amit, R. & C. Zott (2001), 'Value creation in e-business', *Strategic Management Journal*, 22, 493-520.

Barney, J.B. (1991), 'Firm resources and sustained competitive advantage', *Journal of Management*, 17, 99-120.

Ballantine, J., M. Levy & P. Powell (1998), 'Evaluating information systems in small and medium enterprises', *European Journal of Information Systems*, 7, 241-251.

Basselier, G., B.H. Reich & I. Benbasat (2001), 'Information technology competence of business managers: a definition and research model', *Journal of Management Information Systems*, 17(4), 159-182.

Bharadwaj, A.S., V. Sambamurthy & R.W. Zmud (2000), 'IT capabilities: theoretical perspectives and empirical operalization', *in* 'Proceedings of the 21th International Conference on Information Systems', Brisbane, Australia, 378-385.

Brynjolfsson, E. & L.M. Hitt (1998), 'Beyond the productivity paradox: computers are the catalyst for bigger changes', *Communications of the ACM* 41(8), 49-55.

Dans, E. (2001), 'IT investment in small and medium enterprises: paradoxically productive?', *The Electronic Journal of Information Systems Evaluation*, 4(1), March.

DeLone, W.H. (1988), 'Determinants of success for computer usage in small business', *MIS Quarterly*, 12(1), 51-61.

Feeny, D.E. & L.P. Willcocks (1998), 'Core IS capabilities for exploiting information technology', *Sloan Management Review*, Spring, 9-21.

Forrester Research, (1999), *in* 'Connectis, Europe's E-business Magazine' 1(1),

E/1224, (1997), 'Training processes in SMEs: practices, problems and requirements'.

Henderson, J.C. & N. Venkatraman (1993), 'Strategic alignment: leveraging information technology for transforming organizations', *IBM Systems Journal*, 32(1), 4-16.

Higginbotham, J.S. (1997), 'The satisfaction equation', *R&D*, 39(10).

Kanter, R.M. (1997), '*The frontiers of management*', Boston, Mass., Harvard Business School Press.

King, J. (1995), 'Re-engineering focus slips', *Computerworld*, March 13.

Kraiger, K., K. Ford, & E. Salas (1993), 'Application of cognitive, skill based and affective theories of learning outcomes to new methods of training evaluation', *Journal of Applied Psychology* 78(2), 311-328.

Lee, D.M.S. & E.M. Trauth (1995), 'Critical skills and knowledge requirements of IS professionals: a joint academic/industry investigation'. *MIS Quarterly*, 19(3), 313-340.

Little, B. (1997), 'The have-nots of the new technology', *The Globe and Mail Monday*. Toronto, Canada.

Luftman, J.N., R. Papp & T. Brier (1999), 'Enablers and inhibitors of business IT alignment'. *Communications of the Association for Information Systems*, 1 (11).

Marcolin, B.L., D.R. Compeau, M.C. Munro & S.L. Huff (2000), 'Assessing user competence: conceptualization and measurement'. *Information Systems Research*, 11(1), 37-60

Nordhaug, O. (1998), 'Competence specificities in organizations', *International Studies of Management and Organization*, 28(1), 8-29.

Penrose, E.T. (1959), *The theory of the growth of the firm*, Oxford, Basil Blackwell.

Papke-Shields, K.E. & M.K. Malhotra (2001), 'Assessing the impact of the manufacturing executive's role on business performance through strategic alignment'. *Journal of Operations Management*, 19 (1).

Pralahad, C.K. & G. Hamel, (1990), 'The core competence of the corporation'. *Harvard Business Review*, May-June, 79-91.

Sambamurthy, V. & R.W. Zmud, (1994), 'IT management competency assessment: a tool for creating business value through IT', *Financial Executives Research Foundation*, Morristown, New Jersey.

SSB: 'Informasjonssamfunnet', Kvartalsrapport 1/2000. Norwegian Bureau of Statistics.

Soh C. & M.L. Markus (1995), How IT creates business value: a process theory synthesis, *in* 'Proceedings of the Sixteenth Conference on Information Systems', Amsterdam, The Netherlands, December, 29-41.

Stewart, T., 1997: '*Intellectual capital*', Doubleday Press, New York.

Teece, D.J., G. Pisano & A. Shuen, (1997), 'Dynamic capabilities and strategic management', *Strategic Management Journal*, 18(7), 509-533.

Van der Heijden, H. (2000), Measuring IT core capabilities for electronic commerce: results from a confirmatory analysis, *in* 'Proceedings of the 21th International Conference on Information Systems', Brisbane, Australia, 152-163.

Appendix 1. The relation between the conceptual model and the major sources.

	Strategy and vision	IT-Business process integration	IT management	Systems and Infrastructure	Sourcing and Alignment
Bharadwaj, Sambamurthy and Zmud, 2000					
IT business partnerships					
IBP1					X
IBP2					X
IBP3					X
IBP4			x		X
IBP5			x		X
IBP6					X
External IT linkages					
EIT1				x	X
EIT2				x	X
EIT3					X
EIT4					X
Business IT strategic thinking					
BIT1	X	X			x
BIT2	X	X			x
BIT3	X	X			x
BIT4	x	X	x		x
BIT5	x	X	x		
IT business process integration					
BPI1		X			
BPI2		X			
BPI3		X			
IT management					
ITM1			X		
ITM2			X		
ITM3			X		
ITM4			X		
ITM5			X		
ITM6			X		
ITM7			X		
IT Infrastructure					
INF1				X	

INF2				X	
INF3				X	
INF4			x	X	
INF5				X	
Basselier, Reich and Benbasat, 2001					
Explicit IT Knowledge					
Technology					
ET1				X	X
ET2				X	X
ET3	x			X	X
Applications					
EA1		x		X	X
EA2				X	X
Systems Development					
ES1			X		X
ES2			X		X
Management of IT					
EM1			X		x
EM2			X		x
Access to IT knowledge					
EK1			X		x
EK2			X		
Tacit IT Knowledge					
Experience					
TE1				X	
TE2			X		x
TE3			X		x
Cognition					
TC1		X			
TC2	X	X			
Feeny and Willcoks, 1998, van der Heijden, 2000					
Business IT Strategic Thinking BIS	X	x			x
IT management ITM			X		

Business Systems Thinking BST		X			
Relationship Building RB					X
Architecture Planning AP				X	
Making Technology Work MTW			X		
Informed Buying IB				X	
Contract Facilitation CF			X		
Contract Monitoring CM			X		
Vendor Development VD			X		
Sambamurthy and Zmud,1994					
Business Development					
BD1		X			
BD2		X			X
BD3					X
BD4		X			X
BD5					X
BD6					X
BD7			X		
BD8			X		
BD9			X		
External Networks					
EN1					X
EN2					X
EN3					X
Line Technology Leadership					
LT1		x			X
LT2					X
Process Adaptiveness					
PA1				X	
PA2		X			
PA3		X			
IT Planning					
IP1	X	x			x

IP2					X
IP3			X		x
IP4			X		
IT Infrastructure					
II1			X		
II2			X		
II3			X		
II4			X		
II5			X		
II6			X		
Data Center Utility					
DC1				X	
DC2				X	
Lee and Trauth, 1995					
Technical Specialties Knowledge					
TS1-18				X	
Technology Management Knowledge					
TM1			X		
TM2			X		
TM3			X		
Business Functional Knowledge					
BF1		X			X
BF2		X			X
BF3					X
BF4					X
Interpersonal and Management Skills					
IM1			X		
IM2			X		
IM3			X		
IM4			X		X
IM5			X		
IM6			X		
IM7			X		
IM8			X		
IM9			X		

IM10			X		
IM11			X		X

Appendix 2. The Survey Instrument

Country

O Finland O Norway
O Germany O Scotland
O Spain

INTRODUCTION TO RESPONDENT

This interview is part of a project that investigates the use of e-commerce or e-business in small and medium-sized companies in Europe. In this interview you will be presented with questions about e-business, which can be defined as utilizing technologies for conducting business over the Internet. This implies all types of business interactions over the Internet with suppliers, customers and other business partners.

We ask you to answer as correct as possible based on the knowledge you have of your company. This survey is anonymous and we guarantee that it will not be possible to trace any of the answers back to you and your company.

First some introductory questions:

BACKGROUND INFORMATION

1. Approximately, how many employees are there in your company? _____ **employees**
2. In what type of industry is your company?
   O **Tourism** O **Transport** O **Food & Beverages**
3. Does your company use web pages, e-mail or e-commerce systems for business purposes?
   O **Yes** O **No**
4. What types of e-business systems does your company use? (multiple responses possible)

O web pages whith information to individual customers about products or services
O web pages where individual customers can make orders
O web pages where companies can find information about products or services
O systems for electronic sales of products and services to other companies

O EDI solutions on the Internet
O systems that enables your suppliers to see information about your demand or production
O systems that integrates supply chains
O other

5. To what extent are IT activities in your company outsourced to external providers?

a very low extent 1 2 3 4 5 6 7 a very high extent

6. To what extent is your company informed about commercially available e-business systems?

a very low extent 1 2 3 4 5 6 7 a very high extent

7. To what extent is your company informed about providers of e-business related training?

a very low extent 1 2 3 4 5 6 7 a very high extent

8. To what extent has your company implemented its e-business intentions?

a very low extent 1 2 3 4 5 6 7 a very high extent

In the next section we would like you to assess your company's level of competence in various topics related to e-business. The questions are in the form of propositions. We ask you to give your evaluation of how accurately you feel that these propositions describe the situation in your company. If you find that any of the propositions are irrelevant, please indicate so by answering "not applicable". Please indicate how well you agree with the proposition by answering a number between 1: totally disagree and up to 7: totally agree.

STRATEGY AND VISION

TOTALLY DISAGREE *TOTALLY AGREE* *N/A*

1 2 3 4 5 6 7 ☐

The concept of e-business

9. Our company has a high level of knowledge of how e-business technologies can be of value to our business 1 2 3 4 5 6 7 □

10. Our company has a high level of knowledge of how our main competitor(s) use IT to support similar business areas 1 2 3 4 5 6 7 □

11. In general, e-business is well understood by my company 1 2 3 4 5 6 7 □

Strategic planning

12. Our company has a high level of knowledge of strategic planning 1 2 3 4 5 6 7 □

13. Our company has a well developed set of strategic planning techniques 1 2 3 4 5 6 7 □

14. In general, strategic planning is well understood by our company 1 2 3 4 5 6 7 □

SOURCING AND ALIGNMENT

Sourcing competencies

15. Our company has a high level of knowledge on outsourcing of activities to other companies 1 2 3 4 5 6 7 □

16. Our company has a high level of knowledge on how to use competencies in our business partners 1 2 3 4 5 6 7 □

Alignment competencies

17. In my company business and IT managers very much agree on how IT contributes to business value 1 2 3 4 5 6 7 □

18. In my company there is effective exchange of

ideas between business people and IT people 1 2 3 4 5 6 7 ☐

19. In general, my company is good at using the competencies it already has 1 2 3 4 5 6 7 ☐

20. In general, my company is good at using competencies represented in our business partners 1 2 3 4 5 6 7 ☐

IT-BUSINESS PROCESS INTEGRATION

Competence in Process Integration

21. My company is actively working with the impact of e-business on its business processes 1 2 3 4 5 6 7 ☐

22. In general, my company is good at reorganizing work to utilize new information technology 1 2 3 4 5 6 7 ☐

MANAGEMENT OF IT

23. My company's IT resources are effectively managed 1 2 3 4 5 6 7 ☐

24. My company is good at achieving the anticipated benefits from IT investments 1 2 3 4 5 6 7 ☐

SYSTEMS AND INFRASTRUCTURE

25. The systems infrastructure is very flexible in relation to my company's future needs 1 2 3 4 5 6 7 ☐

26. The IT systems make it possible for my company to effectively cooperate electronically with

business partners **1 2 3 4 5 6 7** ☐

In the last section we would like you to assess your company's experiences with the effects of its e-business efforts. We ask you to give your evaluation of what you feel has come out of your company's e-business efforts.

E-BUSINESS SUCCESS

Efficiency

Our e-business efforts have reduced costs by electronic order taking over the Internet **1 2 3 4 5 6 7** ☐

27. Our e-business efforts have made us able to deliver faster **1 2 3 4 5 6 7** ☐

28. Our e-business efforts have reduced costs in communication with suppliers and customers **1 2 3 4 5 6 7** ☐

Complementarities

29. As a result of our e-business efforts our products or services complement products or services from other suppliers **1 2 3 4 5 6 7** ☐

30. Our business efforts make it possible for other suppliers to complement our products or services **1 2 3 4 5 6 7** ☐

31. Our e-business efforts have made our supply chain strongly integrated to our partners' supply chains **1 2 3 4 5 6 7** ☐

Lock-in

Our e-business efforts make it more expensive for our customers or suppliers to replace us **1 2 3 4 5 6 7** ☐

32. Our e-business efforts have made our products and services more tailored to our customers' needs **1 2 3 4 5 6 7** ☐

Novelty

33. Our e-business efforts have made our company a pioneer in utilizing e-commerce solutions **1 2 3 4 5 6 7 ☐**

34. Our e-business efforts have made us cooperating with our customers or suppliers in new and innovative ways **1 2 3 4 5 6 7 ☐**

General

35. In general, my company has experienced very positive effects from its e-business efforts **1 2 3 4 5 6 7 ☐**

OTHER/CONTROL

Leader vs. Follower

There is a dominating customer or supplier who dictates our e-business efforts **1 2 3 4 5 6 7 ☐**

36. Our company is good at implementing changes in its organization **1 2 3 4 5 6 7 ☐**

37. Overall, my company has a high level of competence for utilizing e-business technology **1 2 3 4 5 6 7 ☐**

TRADITIONAL AUSTRALIAN MEDIA ORGANISATIONS ADOPTION OF THE WORLD WIDE WEB

DARREN BURDEN[1], PHILIP JOYCE[2] and JAMIE MUSTARD[3]
[1] *IT Department, Fairfax Pty Ltd, Australia*
[2] *School of Information Technology, Swinburne University of Technology, Australia*
[3] *School of Management Information Systems, Deakin University, Australia*

Abstract: The aim of this paper is it to identify whether Australian media companies moved online with a clear business model in mind or in an ad-hoc manner. In-depth interviews were conducted with four Internet media managers from two large Australian media organisations. All four had been involved in Web publishing from its early stages and had extensive knowledge of the development of Web publishing in the industry. The interviews focused on the period around the mid 1990's when the early development of the organisations' websites took place. We also review an analytical approach of examining narratives from research interviews developed by Davidson (Davidson 1997) and Mishler (Mishler1986a, 1986b).

1. INTRODUCTION

Information has been a commodity of large publishers and media organisations since the development of the first moving press in 1440. Such organizations are currently experiencing a revolution in the way information is handled, stored and disseminated. In the last 20 years there has been a new movement away from mechanical technologies to create goods to the buying and selling of information handled with electronic technologies. The rise of this information technology revolution – fuelled by the advances in communication and digital technologies – to disseminate and distribute data quickly and cheaply is changing the balance from large organisations to individuals.

Media organizations are of particular interest, as they are an industry that sells the basic material which information technology was spawned from, raw information or data. The information systems behind the media product are networks of digital data transmission. Telephones, Faxes, wire services, databases of old stories and computers to write the story on are the tools and services that media organisations use to create the final product: words, sound, vision. Media organisations have had a monopoly on information as the large capital needed to make your own paper, television or radio station (Smith 1980), but that is changing in the form of the WWW. The WWW has opened up an opportunity for potentially anyone to set up his or her own publishing company with very little capital. Web pages about your favorite hobby can be published and distributed across the globe in seconds, in what was once the domain of large publishers who had the capital to attempt such feats.

Currently, most Australian media organisations are providing some of their information product on the Web. There is an important distinction between an online retailer, who makes money from selling their goods online, and the media company that is giving away its goods, news and information, online. Even in the media industry there is a further distinction between publishers putting their narrowband content online and broadcasters putting their broadband content online. Broadcasters can't put all their TV shows on the Internet yet because of speed restrictions, but a newspaper company can, and do, put its journalists' stories online in text form.

From the outside it seems that many of the major publishers and broadcasters in Australia jumped on the WWW roller coaster, spending money on developing Web sites without any sound business justification. What is worse is that many of these businesses may have jumped onto the Web without any explicit information technology strategies, totally ignoring the possible impact of their new ventures on the organisation.

A report by Eric Meyer (Meyer 1995) for Newslink Associates in America was a strategic planning guide for online publishing by general circulation newspapers. Meyer addresses many of the issues and risks that newspapers needed to be aware of when moving into the new electronic media. This work is important because it could alleviate many of the fears and heal the burns that publishers perceived when they jumped onto the last 'new' electronic media, teletext and videotext, which were an expensive failure (Meyer 1995:1). It also attempts to show where online media will fit in with the newspaper businesses.

This paper explores whether Australian WWW media sites were built with a clear business model or in an ad-hoc manner. In order to investigate this idea there needs to be an understanding of why media organisations moved online. In particular, did established Australian media organisations move online with a clear business model or in an ad-hoc manner and were the strategic intentions of moving online in-line with the businesses objectives?

The paper is organised as follows. In section 2 we examine the Australian media industry. Section 3 describes the analytical approach of examining narratives that was used during this research. The research design and participants in the study are described in Section 4. Lastly, the main results of the study and conclusions are given in Sections 5, 6 and 7.

2. AUSTRALIAN MEDIA ORGANISATIONS

The importance of the Internet as a new way of distributing information for large media groups has not been ignored. All the large media organisations in Australia have some type of investment in online business (Burden 2000:6). Some organisations have separate sites for each masthead (i.e., corporate areas) while others have a single portal for various mastheads in the company. What is not clear from viewing online sites is their overall strategy for the online world and how they see it cohabitating with the paper (Petre and Harrington 1996:17).

The Australian online sites are all free media. They're free in the sense of free-to-air television, which doesn't cost to view but is paid through some other means, usually advertising. In a traditional newspaper circulation contributes to 20% of the overall income while advertising and classifieds bring in the remaining 80% (Meyer 1995:15). The *New York Times Online* originally had a general access fee but this was waived and consequently the number of visitors to the site doubled (Miller 1999). The traditional fee based transaction of newspapers is not used by any Australian media organisation. The only time some kind of fee may change hands is when a consumer wants to access a story stored in historical archives.

2.1 The Evolution of the Media and the Impact of the WWW

The distribution and control of information within media organizations have typically followed a mass medium system architecture, which is pyramid shape. Information comes into a point of news making or gathering and is distributed to a mass audience. The pyramid distribution of news not only applies to publishing, it is also relevant to television and radio news distribution as shown in figure 1.

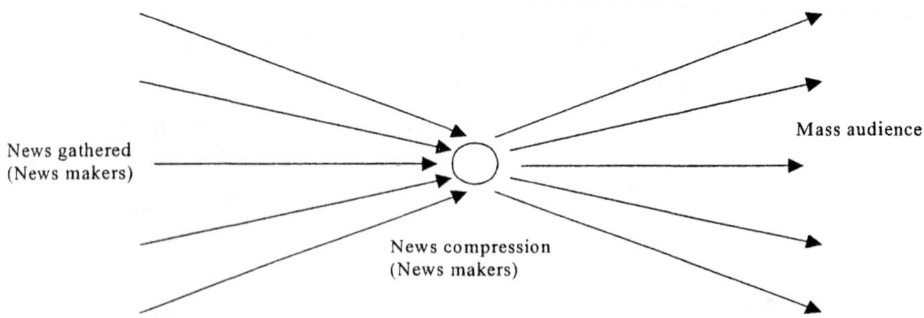

Figure 1. Mass media system architecture

The *news gathered* is the journalists, photographers, cameramen and wire feeds that are gathered by the news organisation at the *news compression* node. The news product distribution channel, whether it's television or newspaper, sends the same information to the *mass audience* or consumer (Newhagen and Levy 1998:11).

Internet based communication is distributed: changing the way information can be gathered and disseminated amongst consumers. The flow of information is no longer linear, but a complex network of sending and receiving nodes. Each node is a Web site, electronic bulletin board, email account or other Internet based tools, personal or organisationally controlled, that can have its own news or refer to news on other nodes within the network (Newhagen and Levy 1998:11). The Internet has provided a vehicle that separates the production and control from the newsmakers to the consumers, which is represented by the sender/receiver nodes capable of moving information over the architecture (Newhagen and Levy 1998:16). The interactivity of the architecture has allowed this change in news distribution.

2.2 Strategic Usage of the WWW by Australian Media Organisations

The Australian audience regularly using the Internet is greater than the audited circulation of *The Sydney Morning Herald* and *The Australian* (Petre and Harrington 1996:124). From June 1999 a Roy Morgan Research poll indicated that 47 % of Australians aged 14 or greater had accessed the Internet and 35% of those people accessed the Internet at least monthly (Research 2000). The Australian Bureau of Statistics indicate there has been steady growth in Internet usage in Australia, between 1998 and 1999 there was a 27% increase in home Internet access alone (ABS 1999). Moreover, the use of the Internet by professionals and managers is between 64% and 75% (Research 2000). This audience has become an opportunity for media companies and other companies to capture new and untapped markets.

The rush to capture new markets has however led to confusion and unreal expectations due to the lack of Web understanding (Schulman and Smith 1997:2). The strategic advantage that the WWW has opened up includes the opportunity for business to improve their "processes and customer interfaces to create a sustainable, competitive advantage" (Lawrence et al. 1998:8). According to Porter the Internet is going to affect every company in some way. Every company is full of information systems and those information systems reside in virtually every activity in the value chain, it's clear that the Internet is going to affect every company (Porter 1999). However, Porter points out that the effect is not going to be strategic or transformational on companies that have a physical product that have to be serviced. Although the WWW can be used to streamline parts of the value chain of these companies, the information-based companies (such as the media organizations) will be the most affected by the WWW technology.

The industries where the Internet is likely to be transformational are industries that are the most obvious cases, where what you are providing is the service or basic information itself - something like stockbrokerage or making a market like auctions or providing digital goods that are actually basic information goods (Porter 1999).

Clearly, any strategy developed by an organisation must encapsulate the current trends and technology used not only within the organisation but what is being used within the industry and in other industries. Some industries will be affected more than others, however, any well-developed strategy needs to be focused on providing services and goods that their consumers want and need.

3. EVALUATION OF THE AUSTRALIAN MEDIA ORGANISATIONS

The objective of this study is to gain an understanding into the adoption and implementation of Internet sites by Australian media organization that took place during the mid 1990's, as clearly started in the Introduction. Of particular interest was whether traditional media vendors followed any business models or assessed the strategic impact their move onto the WWW would have on their businesses. A major consideration of this work was the limited number of media organisations within Australia. Each of these media organisations have considerable synergies and a number of key employees have worked in many of these Australia media organisations. Moreover, there were a limited number of key employees from that period still in the industry. Information about this period would come from interviewing these people. In order to effectively capture this period of time it was decided to adopt a methodological approach to analyse the interview narratives that has previously been used by Davidson in information systems research (Davidson 1997). In the remainder of this section we review Davidson's approach drawing primarily on the work done by Davidson (Davidson 1997) and Mishler (Mishler 1986a 1986b).

3.1 Analysing narratives: a methodological approach

Davidson proposed a methodological approach for analysing interview narratives and applied it within the information systems field (Davidson 1997). This structural analysis tool is based on the theories of social scientist Mishler, and his theories of narrative analysis in *Research Interviewing: context and narrative* (Mishler 1986b) and *The analysis of interviews-narratives* (Mishler 1986a). It's a three-phased examination of structure, meaning and interaction context, which we cover in the next three subsections.

Category	Description
Narrator's perspective	Segments or use of language (e.g., "I" or "we" versus "they") in which the narrator reveals his or her perspective on events in the narrative.
Orientation/contextual descriptions	Segments in which the narrator provides contextual information which does not contribute to the movement of action through time. These are not always present.
Actors	Segments or use of language (e.g., "I" or "we" versus "they") which indicate who carried out actions or contributed to events depicted in the narrative.
Problematic situation	Segments in which the narrator describes his of her perceptions

	of the noncanonical or exceptional circumstances which motivates actions described in the narrative.
Goal/problem solution	Segments in which the narrator describes his or her perceptions of how the problematic situation could be or was resolved.
Actions and events	Narrative clauses segments: Actions are activities that occur during the time span of the narrative that have a strict temporal sequencing. Past actions or flashbacks serve as orientation clauses. Events are recognised changes in state, such as completion of an activity or arriving at a decision point.
Outcomes	Segments in which the narrator describes the perceived outcome of actions and events, such as resolution of the problematic situation by achieving the goal.

Table 1. Classification categories for narrative segments (Davidson 1997:130)

3.2 Structure Analysis

The first phase of structural analysis involves identifying the components of the interviewees' narrative accounts or descriptions. The narrative accounts are divided into segments of partial, complete or strings of sentences that contain distinctive information. The distinctive information is narrator's perspective, orientation/contextual information, actors, problematic situation, goal/problem solution, actions and events and outcomes. All these areas are outlined by Davidson (1997) and reproduced in *Table 1*.

3.3 Meaning: Global, Local, Themal

The second part of the analysis involves coherence relations. This attempts to reveal implicit meaning within the context of the narrative. The three general coherence relations that impart a form of unity into a narrative text are:

- Global coherence, which relates to the speaker's overall plan or intent for the narrative;
- Local coherence, which refers to the function of an utterance within the immediate text segment; and
- Themal coherence, which suggests the narrator's assumptions, beliefs, and goals that reoccur throughout the narrative. (Davidson 1997:126)

3.4 Interaction context

This last step attempts to assess the impact the researcher/interviewer had on the interviewee/participant during the interview. Davidson (Davidson 1997) drew on Mishler's (Mishler 1986b) suggestions that "narratives are a joint production of interviewer and interviewee which reflects ongoing shifts in the reciprocal dual roles of interviewer/interviewee and listener/narrator" (Davidson 1997:126). Mishler notes that the interviewer's role in the production of narratives has largely been ignored (Mishler 1986a, Mishler 1986b). At this point the interviewer describes their relationship with the interviewee and how this may have reflected in the answers that were finally given. The interaction context is described before the two main narratives are analysed. This is due to both research objectives were explored in the one interview.

4. RESEARCH DESIGN

In Australia most major media organisations are located in Melbourne and Sydney. Indeed, these organisations are amongst the largest stocks listed on the Australian Stock Exchange. With the growing use of information technology, especially in electronic commerce and the Internet, suitably skilled employees are now able to move between organisations and industries. Employees in Australian Media organisations are no exception. This research was mindful of employees moving not only within the Australian media organisations but also to unrelated industries. This made the selection of suitable interviewees that were prominent in the early development of the media organisations web presence difficult. Eventually, four key industry leaders from two of the largest media organisations were selected and requested to participant in the research. Of the four participants only one was still employed by the same media organisation. The other three were still in the Internet industry but they were not in the 'traditional' media industry anymore.

The data collection involved an interview with each of the four participants and was retrospective and semi-structured. Three of the interviews were face-to-face and one participant was interviewed over the phone. Full transcripts of the relevant data being analysed in this research can be found in Burden (2000). The questions revolved around questions on:

- Background information about each person;
- Was there a champion in upper-management?
- Did established Australian media organisations move online with a clear business model or in an ad-hoc manner?

- Were the strategic intentions of moving online in-line with the business objectives of the company?
- What was the revenue plan and what was the site providing to the core business?

The following section is a basic description of the companies and the participants within those companies. The ethical approval of this research requires the identity of the participants and their organisations not to be disclosed and are simply referenced as participant A, participant B, etc., and Media Organisation A, Media Organisation B. Each participant is referred to as "she" or "her" in the following descriptions.

4.1 Selected Organisations

Media Company A is a large Australian publisher that has had an online presence since early 1995. The company has metropolitan and country publications in Victoria and New South Wales. The company has also created a separate Internet company although this was not realised until the late 1990s. Participant B was involved with the first implementation of a Web site for Media Company A. Participant B's title was electronic publishing and information services (library) manager, this included CD-ROMS and other digital services; Internet responsibilities were a minor part in this role. Participant A took over from participant B in about 1996. The role was a combined IT manager and online publishing manager role for Masthead A1, which Participant A did until 1999. The major differences between these two people are Participant A had an editorial background and Participant B had a librarian background.

Media Company B is also a large Australian publisher that had an online presence since 1995. The company has metropolitan and country publications Australia wide. The organisation has had a separate multimedia company since it's Internet beginnings, but was originally focused with CD-ROMS. This was later changed to an Internet focus. Participant C was an editorial manager for Masthead B1, who was involved with the first Internet site for Media Company B, a few years later. Participant D came in as editor of Masthead B1's Web site in 1996, later moving into the separate Internet business of Media Company B in 1998. Participant D is still involved with Media Company B.

4.2 Interaction context

A section of the narrative analysis is the interaction context that defines the interaction between the interviewer and interviewee. This helps identify how the interviewer may have shaped the interview in the initial approach and the assumptions of shared knowledge.

4.2.1 Participant A Interview (Media Company A)

The context was a formal interview conducted with participant A in her work office. The interviewer had contacted the participant via email and then by phone. The interviewer had met the participant before this interview and knew some mutual friends in the media industry. The interviewer used these relationships to build a rapport with the interviewee, enhancing the likelyhood of participation. The interviewee and interviewer had some similarities in professional background and this also helped build a rapport.

4.2.2 Participant B Interview (Media Company A)

The interviewer initially contacted the participant via email and then by phone. The interview was conducted in a meeting room in Participant B's place of business. Prior to the interview the researcher and the participant had a coffee together to discuss what the research was about and professional work. At this point we discovered mutual colleagues. The interviewee used assumed knowledge during the interview, not describing some people and positions during the interview. While interviewing the researcher tried to keep the questions as open as possible but keeping them within the bounds of the topic of interest.

4.2.3 Participant C Interview (Media Company B)

The interviewer contacted the participant via email and then talked to her on the phone. The first time the researcher and participant spoke to each other the phone conversation went for about 20 minutes and covered topics that were peripheral to the research topics. The formal interview took place in the participant's office.

4.2.4 Participant D Interview (Media Company B)

The interviewer contacted the participant via email and then talked to the participant on the phone. From the first point of contact until the interview was conducted there was about a two-month lag as the participant and interviewee kept missing each other's suggested meeting times. After failing to be able to meet face-to-face a phone interview was decided to be the best way of conducting the interview. This interview didn't have the preliminary and post 'small talk' of the other interviews. The researcher felt a little less involved with this interview compared to the three prior interviews. This was the quickest interview of the four.

5. INDIVIDUAL NARRATIVE ACCOUNT: PARTICIPANT A

Analysing narratives is a voluminous task and text may contain many interwoven and partial stories. Therefore, we have selected only one of the participants and one of the research questions from this study to present the methodological approach, as outlined by Davidson, in depth. The full analysis of all participants and all research questions can be found in Burden (2000). In the following section we analyse the narratives of Participant A that were concerned with whether Media Company A moved online with a clear business model or in an ad-hoc manner.

5.1 Structure Analysis

The structural analysis focuses on the narrative clauses and creation of an abstract of the plot sequence through which the narrator organises her explanation for her and others' actions. The results of this analysis are shown in table 2 and all references refer to Burden (2000). This revealed:
- recognition that the Web was going to emerge as something important;
- preliminary research into the emerging industry; and
- the selection of a course of action.

In the first problem solving sequence there is a recognition that "something was going to happen to transfer a lot of information, distribution and publishing to electronic media". Other signs of the importance of the Web came from an advertising manager who "recognised very early that his customers were taking a big interest in moving some of their activities online," and this had all been recognised by the librarians first. Although there had been some Internet activity in Media Company A, participant A and 'others' were actively looking at what other people were doing by traveling overseas. There had also been some other multimedia projects that had been in the pipeline before the business interest in the Web heated up. The participant had also done some research in classified sites and especially real-estate sites; "we saw a couple of examples like that early property real estate site." The selection of a course of action was created from a classifieds bent, "we looked at that and thought, well, real estate is going to be the first one to go off because that looked as if it was a working model." The creation of any clear business model was complicated, as there were not many other models to go off either overseas, or in Australia. In fact participant A found that when she went overseas her understanding of what they were doing in her company was in "advance" of people overseas. The move online was hampered by a number of factors including not enough people or money and lack of editorial involvement, which is related to a lack of enthusiasm shown by people "you needed to work with."

Narrator's abstract	"I don't know whether they actually did, well ... I suppose there was a couple of stages" (p87:39-40)
Narrator's perspective	"So we were pro-active about it and some were not." (p87:12-13) "we also looked at next generation advertising systems which anticipated some Internet activity" (p87:68-69) "We found that when we went overseas that often our understanding of what we were doing and what we needed to do was in advance to some of the people who we spoke to over there." (p87:78-82)
Orientation/ contextual descriptions	"to a certain degree it was the champions of electronic media who persuaded the company to give them support ..." (p87:13-16) "the librarians were the first to see this happening if you like." (p87:18-20) "Media Company A in Sydney were very, very slow. Although that's not what they will tell you." (p87:34-36) "Basically it was planned outside the core organisation" (p87:48-49) "Newspapers overseas were very slow too, newspapers in the States were among the last people to wake up to the fact that the Internet was going to be important." (p87:70-73) "I've never thought that publishing newspapers online in newspaper form was a long term strategy anyway." (p87:93-95)
Actors	Person AR – Participant B, Library Manager of Masthead A1 (p87:16,47,49) Person AI – Library Manager of Masthead A2 (p87:17) Person AU – Advertising Manager, Masthead A1 (p87:29,67)
Problematic situation	"I think their reasons would have been that if something was going to happen to transfer a lot of information, distribution and publishing to electronic media then Media Company A had to at least make sure it was in there and it understood what was happening. Purely as a risk management exercise." (p87:6-12) "Under budgeted and user resourced for a lot of the time." (p87:25-26) "There was not much interest or enthusiasm shown by people who you needed to work with." (p87:26-28) "the advertising manager was one person who recognised very early that his customers were taking a big interest in moving some of their activities online ..." (p87:29-32) "Person AR used to publish Masthead A1 Web site without much involvement from anybody in editorial at all." (p87:49-51) "Nobody in Australia was doing anything." (p87:65) "There wasn't many models for newspapers to look at in terms of what the Internet was going to mean for them." (p87:76-78)

Goal/problem solution	Librarians began the sites as they saw the Importance of the Internet to the company, they got the initial support (p87:13-21) "we had a contractor in to build the Web site." (p87:56-57)
Actions and events	Mentions two failed ventures that his company was involved in (p87:40-47) Talks about the contractor building the news Web site but points out the core of the contractors work was the IT jobs (p87:56-59) Looked at real estate as the next big thing on the Web – as far as online classifieds go – but was wrong as employment was (p87:86-90) "A few of us from Melbourne did travel overseas, I and a colleague went over twice basically to an expo" (p87:56-68)
Outcomes	"we looked at that and thought, well, real estate is going to be the first one to go off because that looked as if it was a working model" (p87:86-89) "I suppose we looked at very basic early Internet classifieds and though that was pretty much what we had to do." (p87:90-92)

Table 2. Participant A – Did Australian media organisations move online with a clear business model or in ad-hoc manner?

5.2 Meaning: Local, Global and Themal Coherence in the Narrative of Participant A

In the analysis of meaning, the local, global and themal coherence of segments in the narrative of Participant A was considered. The researcher asked "how did Media Company A plan the move onto the World Wide Web?" (p87:37-38) she answered "I don't know whether they actually did. Well I suppose there was a couple of stages" (p87:39-40). This statement has local coherence as it introduces the events leading up to the company's move onto the Web. At the same time it is global as it serves as the abstract of the participants group of answers. Although coming in about a third of the way through the group of questions it sets the stage for participant grouped answers. At the third level, themal coherence, it describes the lack of an early global plan for the Media Company and its foray onto the WWW, save for small stages like the concentration on classifieds (p87:85-92), advertising (p87:29-32) or editorial development (p87:59-51).

The segment "there weren't many models for newspapers to look at in terms of what the Internet was going to mean for them" (p87:76-78) has global coherence. It is almost an excuse for the newspaper not to have a 'business model' as nobody else did. The infancy of the industry is almost a reason for lack of business plans as the participant says "newspapers overseas were very slow too" (p87:70-71) or 'our' meaning people within Media Company A had a greater understanding of what they were doing compared to colleagues overseas (p87:78-82). These bits of information deflect the enquiries about their business plans to a third party.

The statement "Media Company A in Sydney were very, very slow. Although that's not what they will tell you" (p87:34-36), has a themal coherence. This implies a separation in the company between the cities, and a lack of trust is also evident when the participant warns the researcher to be wary of lies when talking to people involved with Media Company A in Sydney. As far the segments relation to the business model question it shows that there was a separation of planning between the Sydney and Melbourne arms of Media Company A. At this point it must be noted that the researcher only talked to Melbourne based participants from Media Company A.

6. A COMPARISON OF NARRATIVES

A comparison of the different narratives between participants and companies is made regarding the manner in which the move online was made.

6.1 Media Company A

Participants A and B constructed the origins of the Web site and developed basis of a business plan. However, a number of differences did exist in solving the problem. In both cases the participants recognised that Web publishing was something that was going to be very important to the company. Participant A accredits this recognition to the librarian and the advertising manager at the time. Participant B is the librarian that Participant A indicates, she recognised the importance of the Web and consequently she personalises the beginnings as something she pushed, as someone who understood the medium and its purpose (p88:2-3,42-43).

At the next stage Participant A describes preliminary research that involved overseas trips, which in most cases showed her that in many cases Company A's understanding of the Web was in advance of other people in the industry. Participant B on the other hand is more concerned about the problems involved with creating a Web site, and the way she created solutions. Part of this solution was to show people the technology and how it could be used. She concentrates on the building of her knowledge, with information exchanges with experts from the United States. She also highlights the things that weren't available to her like sufficient human and dollar resources.

Participant A, who had come from editorial background had strong views on putting news online, "I've never thought that publishing newspapers online in newspaper form was a long term strategy" (p87:93-94), and was very focused on the classifieds side of the Internet business (p87:85-92). Participant B has a librarian background and was involved in very early use of the Internet in Media Company A was more focused on getting something online, and seemed more editorial focused. Interestingly Participant B worked very hard in the editorial area, by communicating with experts in the field (p87:49-53) after realising that they had a deficiency in the understanding of editorial matters (p87:39-40).

6.2 Media Company B

These narratives are similar in nature to company A. In both cases the narrative plot identifies a beginning that indicates people within Media Company B realised a Web presence was needed. Participant C personalised the sequence more than Participant D, because Participant C was directly involved with the first version of Web publishing within the company, Participant D got involved later. Participant C describes many of the problems with launching the site including no support and even an instance of voiced opposition (p90:13-16). Her largest focus was on the issue of copyright and how that made it more difficult to create a Web site as she had to rewrite copy from the newspaper or else the Union, which she doesn't support, would cause a strike within another organisation.

Participant D doesn't mention the copyright issue. She concentrates on the lack of monetary and technical support available (p92:17-22), as well as saying the Internet within the newspaper industry was "perceived more as a threat than an opportunity" (p92:25-26). Participant C also mentions budget problems with the implementation of the site (p92:93). When describing the Web site implementation, Participant D mentions that it was a "defensive strategy" (p92:4-7) which had a "hobbyist kind of approach" as it could disappear like "CB radio" (p92:41-43). Participant C segment of narrative about going head-to-head with Publisher C and Media Company A, who were already online, as well as the segment about stopping the white-anting of their classifieds market is a description of the defensive move online.

6.3 Comparison of Media Company A and B

Media Company B initial plan seemed to be in response to protecting their market or hedging their bets. In contrast Media Company A had a vague notion of the company having to be online, mostly driven by people like Participant A who could see the potential of the Web site to deliver information. All participants cited lack of resources, monetary, technical and even knowledge base, as problems with the initial implementation of the websites. Participant A and D, who were involved with the websites after Participants B and C respectively, were less personally involved with the implementation.

The planning of the websites wasn't a clear-cut document that was created and distributed amongst the Media Company, although participant D says there would have been 'something' like a plan circulated. Both companies created ad-hoc plans to begin with and there was no specific moment in any of the narratives that clearly identified the creation of a starting plan. In describing the situation in Media Company B, Participant D mentions "I couldn't grandeur this by saying we had a grand plan or vision from the start" (p92:33-37). Participant C explicitly states there was no clear planning until the Atlanta Olympics in 1996, "the whole 18 months, two years before then was very ad-hoc" (p88:65-66).

7. CONCLUSION

There was no official strategy, only a feeling that the companies needed to move online to protect their markets in classifieds and news disseminators. No participant was able to define a single clear plan in his or her approach to moving online as an Australian Media Organisation. Instead, they describe what types of influences made them shape a Web site. A typical sentiment inferred by Participant B defines the Web site as something that is born out of multiple fronts. There were ad-hoc business plans that sprang up from other business units within the companies. Working with people who understand where you are going to people who are threatened by the Internet, "none of these things are linear." In using the narrative approach outlined in Davidson 1997, we have been able to clearly identify the information contained in the narratives of the interviews.

REFERENCES

ABS (1999) Use of the Internet by households (Australian Bureau of Statistics, August, 8147.0)

Burden, D. (2000) Adoption of the World Wide Web by Traditional Australian Media Vendors (Thesis), Deakin University, School of Management Information Systems.

Davidson, E.J. (1997) Examining Project History Narratives: An analytic approach, in: A.S. Lee, J. Lawrence, E., Corbitt, B., Tidwell, A., Fisher, J.-a. & Lawrence, J.R. (1998) Internet commerce: Digital models for business (Brisbane, John Wiley & Sons Australia, Ltd).

Meyer, E. (1995) Tomorrow's news today (Pewaukee, News Link Associates).

Miller, S.C. (1999) Personal communications via email

Mishler, E.G. (1986a) The analysis of interviews-narratives, in: T.R. Sarbin (Ed) Narrative Psychology: The storied nature of human conduct (Londo, Praeger).

Mishler, E.G. (1986b) Research Interviewing: context and narrative (London, Harvard University Press).

Newhagen, J. and Levy, M. (1998) The future of journalism in a distributed communication architecture, (London, Lawerence Erlbaum Associates).

Petre, D. and Harrington, D. (1996) The clever country? Australia's digital future (Sydney, Pan MacMillian Australia).

Porter, M. (1999) The Net Won't Transform Everything, [Internet]. Inter@ctive Week. Available: http://www.zdnet.com/intweek/stories/news/0,4164,2381095,00.html [1 July 2000]

Research, Roy Morgan. (2000) Roy Morgan Research: Discover your edge, [Internet]. Roy Morgan Research. Available: http://www.roymorgan.com.au/ [July 1 2000]

Schulman, M.A. & Smith, R. (1997) The Internet strategic plan (Brisbane, Wiley Computer Publishing).

Smith, A. (1980) Goodbye Gutenberg: The Newspaper Revolution of the 1980s (Oxford, Oxford University Press).

THE NATURE OF WORK FOR EMPLOYEES IN A VIRTUAL ORGANISATION: THE VIRTUAL WORKER

VI-LAM TRUONG[1] and BRIAN J. CORBITT[2]
[1] *Price Waterhouse Coopers, Australia*
[2] *School of Information Systems, Faculty of Business and Law, Deakin University, Australia*

Abstract: This exploratory study aims to develop and offer some deeper understanding of the impact on work created by virtual organisations. This study seeks to understand: what are the advantages in the virtual arrangement that attracts the virtual workers? And what aspects of the virtual worker enable them to function in this working environment? Although the meanings of the virtual organization are varied, an adapted definition of the characteristics of the virtual organization is presented. The salient aspects of the virtual organization is the flexibility to meet the changing environment, its effectiveness in using electronic communication and the leveraging of strategic partnerships. Understanding virtual work is important as e-commerce and e-business strategies are adopted and implemented in organizations where flexible work practice is a key component of the business strategy.

1. INTRODUCTION

This study explores the nature of work for the virtual worker and offers some understanding of the impacts that working in the virtual environment can have on the virtual worker. This understanding may prove useful for researchers and practitioners. For practitioners, such knowledge and deep understanding will allow better consideration when developing virtual work arrangements, especially in e-commerce and e-business flexible working arrangements. Understanding the implications and nature of such work will allow academics to better cater for further research in this field. The aim of the study is to develop a deeper understanding of the impacts of virtual organisations on the virtual worker.

There is an increasing trend towards the adoption of the Internet and teamwork in modern organisations. New methods of conducting business have begun to revolutionalise work. VeriFone, a multinational organisation, operates with company management distributed globally (Stoddard & Donnellon, 1997). Microsoft uses virtual teams to support global corporate customers with interdependent customer needs crossing country boundaries (Jarvenpaa, Ives, & Pearlson, 1995). New organisational structures and working arrangements have increasingly been adopted. One of these new organisational structures is the Virtual Organisation. Castells (2001) argues that the new world of work is not only network but has encouraged the dissipation of work tasks.

2. VIRTUAL ORGANISATIONS

The meaning of what a 'virtual organisation' is varies. Definitions range from virtual communities that are free from geographical constraint (Van Alstyne & Brynjolfsson, 1996), to an organisation in which there exists no boundaries, with teams formed at need and which often consists of members from different countries (Jarvenpaa, Knoll & Leidner, 1998). Nohria & Berkley (1994) define the virtual organisation as one without clear organisational boundaries, with electronically based communication and storage. Venkatraman & Hendersen (1998) define virtualness as a strategic characteristic applicable to every organisation. Palmer & Speier (1997) describe a stable virtual organisation where there is a permanent core, which lays down the rules for collaboration with partner organisations. Another description of virtual organisations involves organisations that come together when a customer approaches them with an order or problem. Temporary collaboration relationships and shared leadership are formed (Davidow & Malone, 1992). Others define the virtual office to cover a variety of mobile and remote work environments (Davenport & Pearlson, 1998). Christie & Levary (1998) support that a virtual organisation involves continuously evolving networks of independent companies linked together to share skills, costs, and access to one another's markets and data.

These definitions provide an understanding into what virtual organisations' may be. For the purpose of this study, the researchers believe that certain characteristics are present in virtual organisations. Virtual organisations can exhibit certain attributes, which together make them more or less virtual. These attributes are represented in Table 1, adapted from Bultje & van Wijk (1998) and Jansen, Steenbakkers & Jagers (1999) and represent a workable definition of the virtual organisation for the purpose of this study.

Drawing on existing literature dealing with virtual teams and workers, it is evident that virtual workers share a common goal, without centralised buildings, physical plant, or other characteristics of a traditional organisation

Characteristics of Virtual Organisations	
core competency based	one identity
network of independent organisations	based on information technology
boundary crossing	no hierarchy
pooling of resources	changing participants
sharing of knowledge	participant equality
geographical dispersion	electronic communication

Table 1. Characteristics of the Virtual Organisation.

Adapted from Bultje & van Wijk (1998) and Jansen, Steenbakkers & Jagers (1999)

(Hartman & Guss, 1996; Staples, Hulland & Higgins, 1998); often operating across space, time and organisational boundary (Lipnacks & Stamps, 1999; Christie & Levary, 1998). The researchers propose then that the term Virtual Worker can be defined as: workers that perform their work at various locations, may be employed by a virtual organisation or work on assignments from various sources on a full-time basis.

3. RESEARCH RATIONALE

Virtual organisations have been made possible by the increasing sophistication of information and communications technology, providing new ways of conducting business (Dennis, Pootheri, & Natarajan, 1998; Fritz, Narasimhan & Rhee, 1998; Venkatraman & Hendersen, 1998). Organisations once confined by geography and differing time zones are now able to enable tasks from remote locations and at anytime (Davenport & Pearlson, 1998). New organisational structures and information technologies have impacted on the interactions of human and collaborative systems within and between organisations (DeSantis & Monge, 1998; Grabowski & Roberts, 1998). The Internet is the technology that has facilitated a solution where geographical distances and information exchange among people have been fundamentally altered (Van Alstyne & Brynjolfsson, 1996; Castells, 2001).

Virtual organisations no longer conform to Weber's model of bureaucracy or Taylor's scientific management (Fritz, Narasimhan & Rhee, 1998; Rittenbruch, Kahler & Cremers, 1998). These new organisations require new sets of management techniques and acceptance of different issues including work. This exploratory study aims to develop a deeper understanding of the impact on work created by virtual organisations. Traditionally, research within the field of information systems that deal with virtual organisations has focused on virtual teams, groupware, and communication (Vandenbosch & Ginzberg, 1997; Fritz, Narasimhan & Rhee, 1998; Jarvenpaa, Knoll & Leidner, 1998; Rittenbruch, Kahler & Cremers, 1998). There is a need for further research about virtual workers in the virtual environment, which traditionally, has been neglected in the research community (Hill, Miller, Weiner & Colihan, 1998). This study will enable a better understanding of the nature of work in order to aid further research in virtual organisations. In practice, human resource has long been regarded as a sustainable competitive advantage (Stroh & Caligiuri, 1998). Issues are raised when a radical structures or work arrangements are implemented. These issues include renumeration, supervision, quality control, promotional opportunities, or choice in the matter. The aim of this study is to develop a deeper understanding of the effects of virtual work on the virtual worker.

This research uses techniques couched in an interpretivist epistemology. To develop a deeper understanding of virtual work, within a distributed work environment, it is clear that interpretivist view of research will allow the researcher to understand the phenomenon of virtual work and capture the richness of data needed to engage a deeper understanding. In selecting the research method to subscribe to for this study, the researchers paid particular attention to the aims of the study, to ensure that the method used was appropriate for the type of research and outcomes required (Hamilton & Ives, 1982, Galliers, 1992; Shanks et al., 1993) to ensure rigor. As discussed above, the current research was based on the interpretivist tradition, although quantitative and qualitative methods contain many epistemological traditions (Yin, 1994; Lin 1998), qualitative methods were chosen for the current study. Quantitative research relies on the measurement of descriptive variables, to remove the effects of context, and to use inferential statistics in order to produce generalisable and reproducible results (Kaplan & Duchon, 1988). In the current study, the aim is not to test theory or measure any descriptive variable from the data and thus quantitative methods were not adopted. Rather resultant data was analysed and assimilated in order to draw logical implications. Qualitative research methods were chosen instead, in order develop the implications and suggestion from the data.

Qualitative research focuses on the meaning in the context or natural setting of the study, and is oriented towards exploration and discovery where the researcher attempts to make sense of the situation (Patton, 1990; Myers, 1997). Categories and meanings emerge from the data collected as the researcher develops an understanding of the situation (Kaplan & Duchon, 1988). The outcomes required by the researcher involve the discovery of important concepts, themes and implications, in the context of the virtual work environment. The study did not aim to, but did not consciously point the study away from, comparisons between virtual and conventional workplaces. The study aimed at developing a deeper understanding of the effects of virtual work in the context of virtual organisations.

Data collection was done through interviews using open-ended questions[25], which allowed the researcher to probe information and explanations from respondents to gain rich data. The researcher was able to stimulate the responses of the exemplars to be broader than that of a structured interview (Walsham, 1998), providing their view of the virtual environment. It also provides the ability to observe non-verbal cues and allows rapport and motivation for respondents to build (Williamson, 1999). Further, the researcher was able to control the focus of the interview and allowed the researcher the option to follow up on interesting leads in later interviews, perhaps in a further study to refine or test the findings of the current study. The interviews were held over a two-week period with the researcher meeting the participants for approximately 60 minutes. Other sources of information used by the researcher included press releases, the Internet, company documents and other sources of interest, regarding the virtual arrangement of the virtual worker.

There were three exemplars of virtual work drawn from a spectrum of distributed work arrangements. This concept is depicted in Figure 2. This forms a representative spread whereby themes and implications may emerge, despite the limited number of individual studies done.

Figure 1. Spectrum of Virtual Arrangements

Source: VL Truong (1999)

The use of three exemplars can be justified due to the rich data that was collected. In quantitative studies, the researcher knows beforehand the possible answers they would be able to receive, in qualitative research, the researcher cannot shield them from unknown information (Becker, 1996). The researcher of this study found that as the exemplars responded to the interview questions, more questions emerged which were probed and explored to extract further and richer information.

Although strictly speaking, there were only three case studies, after careful analysis of the data, the findings somewhat matched the findings in existing literature. According to Gummesson (1988), limited numbers of observations may not inhibit the findings to be generalisable, large amounts of generalisation may not lead to more meaningful generalisations. Generalisation from individual or many cases does not necessarily depend on statistical validity but the plausibility and cogency of logical reasoning used in describing and drawing conclusions from them (Walsham, 1993; McMaster & Vidgen, 1995).

According to Walsham (1995), the aim of data analysis in the current study can be described as interpretive generalisation, whereby the researcher aims to develop concepts, theories and implications that are valuable in the context of virtual work other than the particular situations of the exemplars. The current study will mainly draw on the information elicited from the interviewees. After the interviews were conducted, the transcription to hardcopy was made and verified by the exemplars. Data analysis of the three case studies was a reiterative process of reading, re-reading, sifting, and discussion of the field data to identify themes and issues, similar to methods applied in Walsham (1998). The sifting and discussion of the data involved similar techniques used in case study analysis, which consist of single or multiple case studies with multiple levels of analysis (Yin, 1984), most notably within case and across case analysis.

Open coding of the interview transcriptions were performed first in order to break apart and fracture the data analytically, leading to grounded conceptualisation (Strauss, 1987). Essentially this involved a line by line breakdown of the text, whereby emergent themes and concepts emerged. The next step involved the "within case analysis" of creating stories[26] from the data, or descriptions of the exemplar experience of virtual work; these stories are central to the generation of useful insight (Gersick, 1988; Pettigrew, 1988). The aim was to develop an intimate understanding of each exemplar experience in the process unique patterns emerge which allows generalisation across different exemplar experiences (Eisenhardt, 1989).

The next phase involved the use of "cross case analysis"[27] which further developed the generalisability of concepts emerged through analysis of common patterns across the exemplars (Eisenhardt, 1989). For example, a matrix including the exemplars and emergent concepts and implications was developed and analysed and was used to validate conclusions drawn. This analysis of the patterns emergent across cases forced the researcher to look beyond initial impressions evident in the data (Eisenhardt, 1989).

4. DISCUSSION

This study explores virtual work and its effects on the virtual worker. The literature on virtual organisations offers many insights to why organisations adopt virtual structures. However, little has been done in relation to what virtual organisations can offer the virtual worker. Two particular areas emerged from the analysis, the perceived benefits and problems that arise for the virtual worker, and the nature of the persona of the virtual worker.

4.1 Benefits and disadvantages for the virtual worker

This research would suggest the following about the benefits for the virtual worker.

4.1.1 Flexibility and Autonomy

Virtual organisations, due to its distributed nature can provide virtual workers with autonomy and flexibility (Davenport & Pearlson, 1998; Hill et al., 1998). According to Davenport & Pearlson (1998), mobile workers value flexibility and autonomy in virtual environments. Flexibility gives the virtual worker the ability to control when and how to work and autonomy provides the ability to control the output of work, providing virtual workers with a distinct advantage. Completing tasks independently without the assistance of others is extremely satisfying. One subject in Case Study 1 notes: "...ultimately a more satisfying way to work, because of the flexibility...the autonomy of work..."(Case Study 1 participant).

The data from this study suggests that flexibility and autonomy are important factors that attract workers to virtual situations.

4.1.2 Working Environment

In virtual organisations, each member is skilled in a particular area, creating an enjoyable working environment. As the virtual organisation is non-hierarchical and decentralised (Ahuja & Carley, 1998), each member is required to contribute significantly to each assignment (Christie & Levary, 1998). Van Alstyne & Brynjolfsson (1996) suggested that in the virtual community, all members are equal. This equality is also represented in some of the participants in that "...you don't get caught up in the politics and you have a specific time frame to finish off the work" (Case Study 2 participant). The subjects of the research suggest that, renumeration is performance based so non-productive, political games are useless in this environment. There will be limited politicking in the virtual organisation, as there are no benefits to the virtual worker who plays political games when performance is measured by productivity. This participants in this study suggests that in virtual organisations, due to its flat hierarchy and distributed structure, performance is more important than political manoeuvring. Each member is specialised in a particular area, they are respected in that area and this, according to the virtual workers studied, creates a good working environment.

4.1.3 Career Objectives

During the interviews, particular emphasis was given to the nature of assignments the virtual workers chose to conduct. All exemplars in the current study believe that the variety and scope afforded by virtual arrangements are advantageous for their career development. Their work and roles are not restricted as each assignment and assignment role is different, each has its own performance criteria and scope (Townsend et al., 1998). In one assignment they may be working for local government and in the next, providing their services to a major utilities company. One of the participants notes: "...if I were applying as a permanent position in to the utilities industry...I would not have gotten that...because I have different skill sets...in the interview I sold myself...now they offer me..." (Case Study 2 participant).

The virtual worker experiences a wide range of business environments and industries, giving the virtual worker the ability to build core skills and specialisations to improve their employability. Virtual workers are able to use these experiences to pursue particular interests or develop particular skills to market themselves in seeking further assignments. Career development opportunities in virtual environments are very attractive in allowing virtual workers to gain experience in a variety of industries.

Interviews generated in this research not only identified positive outcomes from working virtually, they also highlighted some of the disadvantages.

4.1.4 Getting Started and Keeping Afloat

The stories in the data suggest that a disadvantage one for workers in many virtual organisations is that they do not strictly employ the virtual worker, rather they are contracted for a given period. Once this ends, the relationship between virtual worker and the virtual organisation also ends (Grabowski & Roberts, 1998). One of the participants notes the nature of projects: "I work on multiple different tasks...multiple different projects. They tend to be short-term projects." (Case Study 1 participant). In these situations, management sees the virtual worker as third party employees (Dickerson, 1998), thus not many training or support facilities are offered. This may be because employee numbers are not fixed, increasing and decreasing when there are assignments. It is a personal issue for the virtual worker. In this situation, there may be a lack of organisational identity that binds the employee to an organisation (Wiesenfeld et al., 1998). One of the participants in Case Study 2 clarifies: "...one of the problems I face myself...if I don't work for two weeks...I don't get paid for two weeks...in (conventional) organisations...you still get paid for two weeks!" (Case Study 2 participant).

There are also costs associated with being a virtual worker, as one of the participants in Case Study 2 explains: "...you have to set up yourself to be in business for yourself like getting the work and buying the your own equipment to set up your SOHO... run your own business..." (Case Study 2 participant). Set-up costs to facilitate virtual work may be high. Marketing, training and accounting can be expensive. This discussion, albeit brief, supports Dickerson's (1997) findings that some disadvantages of virtual work involve the lack of training, support facilities and set-up costs, as virtual organisations need to be structured to achieve maximum flexibility for management (Dickerson, 1997).

4.1.5 Career Management

The flexibility afforded to the virtual worker may cause time management issues to arise. This research highlights the need for virtual workers to effectively manage their time, as often, they will not be able to walk away from the work. One of the participants clarifies: "...its difficult to set a particular time for your work...so work tends to impinge much more on your personal life...you can't really shut it away." (Case Study 1 participant). This may be explained that the decision to put in time to complete assignments are the worker's. The interviews suggest they put in the maximum amount of time in order to complete the work, often neglecting other areas of their lives. Career wise, the flat or non-existent hierarchy (Ahuja & Carley, 1998; Townsend et al., 1998), create difficulties in career advancement. One of the participants commented on the lack of career opportunities: "...less managerial career prospects...more team based...more responsibility..." (Case Study 3 participant).

New forms of organisations emerge as new technologies and methods of interactions are developed (Townsend et al., 1998), causing workers to alter their career advancement perspectives. This study suggests that disadvantages include the difficulty in career advancement as virtual organisations have flat hierarchies making upward movement difficult. It is suggested that the flexibility afforded by virtual organisations to the virtual worker dictates that they be adept at time management, lest they let work encroach on their personal lives.

4.1.6 An Isolated Environment

In virtual organisation literature, communication has been regarded as the medium that clarifies goals, relationships and responsibility between members (Grabowski & Roberts, 1998). Communication creates organisational identity (Wiesenfeld et al., 1998). In the virtual environment, communication is conducted through electronic means, which hinders the development of trust (Jarvenpaa et al., 1998). Electronic communication, if not managed properly is a disadvantage of the virtual organisation (Davenport & Pearlson, 1998; Fielding et al., 1998; Jarvenpaa & Leidner, 1998). One of the participants notes: "...you interact...across the limited communication channels...much more restricted on the ability to communicate, particularly in non-verbal fashion". (Case Study 1 participant).

New members coming into the organisation are required to develop trust and relationships. If face-to-face interactions are not possible, the virtual worker must overcome these difficulties of electronic communications but the lack of physical cues makes this difficult (DeSantis & Monge, 1998; Fielding et al., 1998). Reliance on electronic communications stems from the distributed nature of virtual work, as virtual workers work are isolated from each other. One of the participants explains:

"...because I'm here in Melbourne and it's difficult to interact with colleagues who basically are working out of Sydney." (Case Study 1 participant).

The virtual worker must deal with this issue to work effectively. Often, this isolation is not between the virtual worker and colleagues, but also between the virtual worker and the client. This creates issues such as the building of trust, organisation identification and virtual team dynamics (Jarvenpaa et al, 1998; Wiesenfeld et al., 1998). The analysis of data from this study suggests that isolation and the reliance on electronic communications is disadvantageous to the virtual worker.

4.1.7 Working Relationships

Working virtually will involve isolated periods of work. Relationships developed between the virtual worker and the client are often limited, as there are usually neither time nor benefits for the virtual worker to build strong relationships. One of the participants explains: "I just get the job done according to my brief and try to do it well to move on to the next job!" (Case Study 2 participant). If he/she does a good job, the client may offer him/her additional work or a permanent position. Professional relationships are built between the virtual worker and the client through the interactions required in performing their tasks. This relationship is often adversarial. One of the participants explains: "you're always on an adversarial position with the clients because they're always trying to get the best deal and your always trying to sell them the biggest deal." (Case Study 3 participant).

The advantages of flexibility and autonomy are offset by the need to deliver an acceptable product in the end. Davenport & Pearlson (1998) argue that a reason for organisations to adopt virtual structures is to increase productivity. The virtual workers of this study are often contracted for specific purposes within assignments. Being solely responsible, they are more accountable. New measures are needed for virtual arrangements (Ahuja & Carley, 1998). One of the participants explains: "I will be paid for the work I produce, and if I were paid on an hourly rate, much more consideration would be given to my productivity." (Case Study 1 participant).

The analysis of the data suggests these disadvantages of virtual work, which includes the adversarial relationships with clients and the need to be more accountable. No comparison is made between virtual and conventional work, although this participant does speculate on the nature of conventional and virtual environment accountability. One participant noted that "…working in an office environment is that people are much more putting in time...being in the office is much more important…if you're a virtual worker, that's not work…you're not actually producing an output…as a virtual worker, you're much more measured by the output…" (Case Study 1 participant).

This section has highlighted, albeit briefly, the benefits and disadvantages experienced by the virtual workers studied. Disadvantages included the start up and ongoing costs of becoming a virtual worker, the limited support and the limited training opportunities. Career wise, the virtual workers studied felt the lack of organisational hierarchy limited their upward movement within the organisation. Working relationships were not easily built, either between members or clients, as limited benefits are provided to the virtual worker that develops these relationships. Often, client relationships developed are adversarial. The nature of virtual work requires the virtual worker to be better accounted in the work they perform. The distributed work environment relies on electronic means of communication as members of the virtual organisation are often geographically dispersed. The virtual worker must overcome the isolation of virtual work. Second, the disadvantage of electronic communication is that it requires the virtual worker to communicate and create meanings over limited communication channels that lack the physical cues of face-to-face interactions. The advantages and disadvantages identified in this study are summarised in Table 12. Overcoming these difficulties in the virtual environment requires that virtual worker to have certain attributes. The following section discusses what some of these attributes that create a persona of the virtual worker.

Advantages:	**Disadvantages:**
Flexibility of Work Arrangement	Lack of Support
Performance Based Renumeration	No Training
Autonomy of Work and Responsibility	Time Management
Career Development	Career Advancement
Interest and Skill Sets	Isolation
Not Paramatised	Adversarial Client Relationships
Respect vs Power	Electronic Communication
Working Environment	Accountability of Work
	Virtual Worker Set-up Costs

Table 2. Advantages and Disadvantages of Virtual Work.

4.2 The persona of the virtual worker

The discussion from here focuses on the other theme that emerged in the research, the persona of the virtual worker. The researcher proposes that the following aspects represent a cautious look into the persona of the virtual worker. It can generally be seen that there are several dimensions in the persona of a virtual worker. The dimensions depicted in Table 3 were found throughout the analysis of the data. Each of these is evaluated in detail in the following discussion.

Working Methods	Work Autonomously Work Individually Contribute to Teams Self Directed Self Reliant
Communication Skills	Communication Electronically Communication Skills
Organisational Experience	Enjoy Being Part of Dynamic Organisations Enjoy Challenge Enjoy Change Enjoy Work Experienced in Change
Personal Traits	Flexible Good Manager of Self Skilled Task Oriented Dedicated Disciplined Motivated Work Ethic Personality Match

Table 3: The Persona of the Virtual Worker.

4.2.1 Working Methods

This dimension focuses how virtual workers are required to work. Virtual workers work in isolation, apart from team members and alone. The attributes in this dimension enable the virtual worker to work effectively. Being able to work autonomously enables the virtual worker to plan and produce work according to their knowledge and skills. So one important attribute is to be able to work autonomously (Davenport & Pearlson, 1998). One of the participants notes: "…autonomy. My style of work works best if I am left to get on with it." (Case Study 3 participant).

According to Christie and Levary (1998), the virtual worker must be self-directed and self-reliant, as there is a need for them to resolve any complications by themselves. As the virtual worker often works in isolation from others, there is a need for them to work individually. This does not mean that the virtual worker cannot work in a team environment. On the contrary, they must be able to contribute to teams when it is required

(Plishkin & Romm, 1997; Hill et al, 1998). One of the participants explains: "...we work as a team. So we have a project leader...I'm part of a team and...do the data gathering...(but) most of the work that I do is basically myself because I specialise in a certain area of the application and I do most of the work myself." (Case Study 2 participant). This aspect of the persona of the virtual worker allows them, when the need arises, to contribute and adapt to both environments. One of the participants explains this ability of virtual workers to adapt to isolated, team, conventional and virtual arrangements. "Working like a virtual worker gives you an added advantage, it enables you to adapt to any working environment, you only need your tools and off you go to get the job done". (Case Study 2 participant).

4.2.2 Communication Skills

This dimension involves the nature of communication conducted by the virtual worker. Communication within the virtual environment is different to that of other work arrangements. It involves electronic communication and face-to-face meetings, although virtual workers often lack informal conversation opportunities (Fielding et al., 1998). One of the participants explains: "...informal social interactions between co-workers can be very productive in terms of getting work done, disseminating information, understanding what everybody else is working on and helping to feed that back into your own work." (Case Study 1 participant).

Wiesenfeld (1998) has found that increased communication strengthens organisational identification. This reliance on limited communication channels causes that participants some concern for new workers starting in a virtual organisation. For example on noted that "...much more limited exchange of information...somebody new coming in to the organisation...would be much more difficult for me to work with and develop...rapport." (Case Study 1 participant).

The virtual worker must be able to communicate electronically and be computer literate (Christie & Levary, 1998), to build conversation, rapport and trust. One of the participants highlights the importance of communication in his role. "...means I find the client, I elicit the requirements, I build the model, I sell the model, I control the implementation. I make sure that there is no problem all the way through..." (Case Study 3 participant). The ability of the virtual worker to communication with clients is also required. Communications skills are required when meeting with clients, when collecting data and when presenting solutions to the client. Communication skills aid the virtual worker in conducting business. One of the participants notes: "...on the job you need to be able to express yourself and get to work with people on site as well…" (Case Study 2 participant).

4.2.3 Organisational Experience

This dimension deals with attributes that enable the virtual worker to cope with the nature of virtual organisations. Virtual organisations are flexible in structure, ever changing and dynamic (Davenport & Pearlson, 1998). The virtual worker must enjoy being part of a dynamic organisation, which requires them to continuously learn and develop new skills to cope with increasingly unstable trends in business. One of the participants clarifies stating that: "…so I undergo continuous learning because I think that's important...you need to be able to continuously improve yourself." (Case Study 3 participant).

Virtual organisations take advantage of their flexible nature to take the opportunities that arise in changing markets (Dickerson, 1998). Experienced in change, not only of the organisation itself but in organisational dynamics, the nature and scope of work and previous experience allows the virtual worker to better deal with change. One of the participant's situation involves: "…we are all experienced professionals…coming in to it as a new person in the industry or as a graduate…it would be very hard for them to adjust…you have to be a good time manager…" (Case Study 3 participant). The virtual workers in this study feel that the virtual worker must enjoy this change, enjoy the nature of such work and to enjoy the challenge of virtual work. One of the participants clarifies: "…one thing to be able to survive and the most important thing I think is to be able to get the work you enjoy doing, that's most important, at the same time getting paid for the work you do." (Case Study 2 participant). The results of the study suggest that the virtual worker must, most importantly, enjoy the work and challenge that come with the position.

4.2.4 Personal Traits

The following dimension deals with the personal traits provided in the interviews. The virtual worker should exhibit some of the following attributes to enable them to perform in this environment. The virtual worker is disciplined, dedicated, and motivated to perform the work assigned (Christie & Levary, 1998). Virtual work involves independent work. One of the participants summarises what attributes a virtual worker should exhibit. He noted: "…you have to be very dedicated…have to be fairly motivated…disciplined." (Case Study 3 participant).

Further, they should have the flexibility and work ethic to research and solve complications that arise in their assignments without referring to superiors (Davenport & Pearlson, 1998). One of the participants notes: "…need that kind of flexibility to be able to say…I've got to sit down, this is the work that I'm doing. If I can't figure out this problem or find a solution for it, then you actually have to sit down and do the research in your own time to solve the problem." (Case Study 2 participant). Virtual work requires that the virtual worker to be good managers of themselves and have the personality that enjoys the constant change, the challenge of assignments and the dynamics of a virtual organisation. Implying that the virtual worker is skilled in their chosen field, is task orientated in order to complete assignments and to excel in their work (Christie & Levary, 1998). One of the participants comments about achieving: "…if you succeed and, achieve and over achieve you stand out…" (Case Study 3 participant).

The persona of the virtual worker then appears to consist of four dimensions, each with its own set of attributes (Table 3). Further research is needed on the persona of the virtual worker to rigorously validate the findings of this study.

5. CONCLUSIONS

The main focus of this research has been to develop a deeper understanding of the effects virtual work on the virtual worker. In achieving this aim, the research unravelled the stories of three case studies involving virtual workers. Each story highlighted the background and future aspirations of the virtual workers. Attention was also paid to the profile of the virtual organisations, the role of information technology as the enabler of this new organisational form, the advantages and disadvantages of working virtually and the persona of the virtual workers interviewed as part of this study.

Autonomy and flexibility were suggested as the factors that were most important to the virtual worker. This related to autonomy to do their own work and flexibility to do their work when and where they chose. The main disadvantages discussed related to the isolation of the virtual environment, with the reliance on limited electronic communications, the lack of support and the lack of training contributing to the negative factors of virtual work. The discussion of the virtual worker persona was also reported in this paper. The persona of the virtual worker was reported to have four dimensions each with its own set of attributes salient to the ability of the virtual workers involved in this study to work virtually.

This study attempted to develop a deeper understanding of the effects of virtual work on the virtual worker. In developing this understanding the advantages and disadvantages of virtual work and the persona of the virtual worker was explored. Through the discussion of these suggestions, which can be described as tentative, it is anticipated that a deeper understanding of virtual work has in fact been developed and will frame continuing research, especially as they related to the work processes and work flows becoming evident in newly developing e-businesses.

This study has tapped into only two sections of the findings of a much larger study. Future research may involve further investigation of the remaining sections. These may be the role of information technology in the virtual organisation, as enabler of new organisational structures or driver of new opportunities for the virtual worker. This study draws evidence from both perspectives. Other areas requiring further investigation may involve the complete definition of the virtual organisation. This study presented the work arrangements of the virtual workers. These arrangements or contractual relationships may be further explored. Future studies may involve either the salient aspects of virtual work arrangements or a framework for developing virtual arrangements in organising virtual workers. Alternately, future research may attempt to expand on the topics of interest discussed by the current research. This may involve developing a total picture of the virtual worker to further refine and expand on the dimensions of the virtual persona. Another avenue of further research may involve the use of the advantages and disadvantages found, to more rigorously validate them through quantitative research. This allows for the development of more generalisable and rigorous set of attributes. This will further strengthen the notion that virtual organisations are a viable structure in today's information technology driven economy.

In practice, the implementation of the virtual structures imposes a wholly different set of expectations onto the worker. From a relatively stable working environment to one that focuses on change may and has often caused great stress. Organisations need to consider how their workers view the advantages and disadvantages of virtual structures. Organisations must ask themselves:

- Will the implementation of these structures provide real gains for the organisation and the virtual workers?
- What are the views of the current workforce?
- Are the advantages seen in this study seen by their employees?

These questions may guide organisations in implementing virtual structures, to ensure that the benefits of virtual work outweigh the disadvantages as evident in this study.

Understanding the persona of the virtual worker will also enable organisations considering virtual structures to assess the mental readiness of their employees. Questions organisations may ask of their employees may involve:

- Can adequate communication norms be developed to handle the reliance on electronic communications in virtual environments?
- Are the experiences of the employees able to cope with constant change?
- Do the employees exhibit the personal traits found in this study of virtual workers?

REFERENCES

Ahuja, M. K., & Carley, K. M., (1998) "Network and Structure in Virtual Organisations." *Journal of Computer Mediated Communication,* Volume 3, Issue 4, June.

Applegate, L. M., McFarlan, F. W., & McKenney, J. L., (1999) *"Corporate Information Systems Management, Text and Cases."* 5th edition, USA: Irwin McGraw-Hill.

Becker, S. H., (1996) "The Epistemology of Qualitative Research." in Jessor, R., Colby, A., & Schweder, R., (Eds) *"Essays on Ethnography and Human Development."* University of Chicago Press, Chicago.

Boudreau, M. C., Loch, K. D., Robey, D., & Straud, D., (1998) "Going Global: Using Information Technology to Advance the Competitiveness of the Virtual Transnational Organisation." *The Academy of Management Executive,* Volume 12, Issue 4, November.

Brousseau, E., (1990) "Information technologies and inter-firm relationships: The spread of inter-organisational telematics systems and its impact on economic structure." *Paper presented to the International Telecommunications Society*, Venice, June.

Bultje, R., & van Wijk, J., (1998) "Taxonomy of Virtual Organisations, based on definitions, characteristics and typology." in: *VoNet: The Newsletter* @ www.virtual-organization.net, Volume 2, Number 3.

Burrell, G., & Morgan, G., (1979) *"Sociological Paradigms and Organisational Analysis."* Heinemann, London.

Byrd, K., & Gulbro, R. D., (1998) "E-mail and the Organisation of Tomorrow." *Ivey Business Quarterly*, Volume 63, Issue 1, Autumn.

Castells, M (2001) *The Internet Galaxy,* Oxford, OUP.

Checkland, P., (1981) *"Systems Thinking, Systems Practice."* John Wiley and Sons, Chichester.

Christie P. M. J., & Levary R. R., (1998) "Virtual Corporations: Recipe for Success." *Industrial Management*, Volume. 40, Number 4.

Compeau, D., Higgins, C. A., & Huff, S., (1999) "Social cognitive theory and individual reactions to computing technology: A longitudinal study." *MIS Quarterly,* Minneapolis, Volume 23, Issue 2, June.

Davenport, T. H., & Pearlson, K., (1998) "Two cheers for the virtual office." *Sloan Management Review,* Cambridge, Volume 39, Issue 4, Summer.

Davidow, W., & Malone, M., (1992) *"The Virtual Corporation."* New York: Harper Collins.

Dennis, A., Pootheri, S., & Natarajan, V., (1998) "Lessons from the Early Adopters of Web Groupware." *Journal of Management Information Systems*, Volume 14, Number 4, Spring.

DeSantis, G., & Monge P., (1998) "Communication Processes for Virtual Organisations." *Journal of Computer Mediated Communication*, Volume 3, Issue 4, June.

Dickerson, C. M., (1998) "Virtual Organisations: From Dominance to Opportunism." *New Zealand Journal of Industrial Relations,* Volume 23, Issue 2, June.

Eisenhardt, K. M., (1989) "Building Theories from Case Study Research." *Academy of Management Review,* Volume 14, Issue 4.

Erben, K., & Gersten, K., (1997) "Cooperation Networks towards Virtual Enterprises." in *VONet: The Newsletter*, Volume 1, Number 5, December, @ www.virtual-organization.net.

Fielding, R. T., Whitehead, Jr. J. E., Anderson, K. M., & Bolcher, G. A., (1998), "Web-based development of complex information products." Association for Computing Machinery. *Communications of the ACM*, New York, Volume 41, Issue 8, August.

Fritz, M., Narasimhan, S., & Rhee, H., (1998) "Communication and Coordination in the Virtual Office." *Journal of Management Information Systems*, Volume 14, Number 4, Spring.

Gallegos, F., & Powell, S. R., (1997) "Telecommunications Networks in Virtual Corporations." *IS Audit & Control Journal*, Volume 3.

Galliers, R., (Ed.), (1992) "*Information systems research: Issues, methods, and practical guidelines.*" Blackwell Scientific Publications, Oxford.

Gersick, C. J. G., (1988) "Time and transition in work teams: Toward a new model of group development." *Academy of Management Journal*, Volume 31, Issue 2.

Glaser, B. G., (1992) "*Emergence vs Forcing: Basics of Grounded Theory Analysis.*" Sociology Press.

Glaser, B. G., & Strauss, A., (1967) *"The Discovery of Grounded Theory: Strategies for Qualitative Research."* Aldine Publishing Co, Chicago.

Glaser, B. G., (1978) *"Theoretical Sensitivity: Advances in the Methodology of Grounded Theory."* CA: The Sociology Press, Mill Valley.

Goldman, S. L., Nagel, R. N., (1993) "Management, technology and agility: the emergence of a new era in manufacturing." *International Journal of technology Management*, Volume 8, Numbers 1/2.

Goodman, P. S., & Darr, E. D., (1998) "Computer-aided systems and communities: Mechanisms for organisational learning in distributed environments." *MIS Quarterly*, Minneapolis, Volume 22, Issue 4, December.

Grabowski, M., & Roberts, K., (1998) "Risk Mitigation in Virtual Organisations." *Journal of Computer Mediated Communication*, Volume 3, Issue 4, June.

Gummesson, E., (1988) "Qualitative Methods in Management Research." *Studentlitteratur,* Stockholm.

Hamilton, S., & Ives, B., (1982) "MIS Research Strategies." *Information & Management*, Volume 5.

Hart, P., & Estrin, D., (1991) "Inter-organizational networks, computer integration, and shifts in interdependence: The case of the semiconductor industry." *ACM Transactions on Information Systems*, Volume 9, Issue 4.

Hartman, F., & Guss, C., (1996) "Virtual teams - constrained by technology or culture." *Proceedings of IEMC 96, "Managing virtual enterprises: A convergence of communications, computing and energy technologies."* Vancouver, BC, Canada: IEEE.

Hill, J. E., Miller, B. C., Weiner, S. P., & Colihan, J., (1998) "Influences of the virtual office on aspects of work and work/life balance." *Personnel Psychology*, Durham, Volume 51, Issue 3, Autumn.

Hirscheim, R., & Klein, H., (1992) "A Research Agenda for Future Information Systems Development Methodologies." In Cotterman, W. W., Senn, J. A., (Eds) "*Challenges and Strategies for Research in Systems Development.*" John Wiley and Sons, Chichester.

Jansen, Steenbakkers & Jagers, (1999) "Electronic Commerce and Virtual Organisations." *Proceedings of the 2nd International VoNet-Workshop*, Zurich, Special Issue eJOV, Volume 1, Number 1, September.

Jarvenpaa, S. L., & Leidner, D. E., (1998) "Communication and Trust in Global Virtual Teams." *Journal of Computer Mediated Communication*, Volume 3, Issue 4, June.

Jarvenpaa, S. L., Ives, B., & Pearlson, K., (1995) "Global customer service for the computer and communications industry." in Palvia, P. C., Palvia, S. C., & Roche, E. M., (Eds.), *"Global information technology and systems management."* Ivy League Publishing, Harrisburg.

Jarvenpaa, S., Knoll, K., & Leidner, D., (1998) "Is anybody out there? Antecedents of Trust in Global Virtual Teams." *Journal of Management Information Systems*, Volume 14, Number 4, Spring.

Kaplan, B. and Duchon, D., (1988) "Combining Qualitative and Quantitative Methods in Information Systems Research: A Case Study." *MIS Quarterly*, Volume 12, Issue 4.

Kekre, S., & Mudhopadhyay, T., (1992) "Impact of electronic data interchange technology on quality improvement and inventory reduction programs: A field study." *International Journal of Production Economics,* Volume 28.

Klein, H. K. & Myers, M. D., (1999) "A set of principles for conducting and evaluating interpretive field studies in information systems." *MIS Quarterly,* Minneapolis, Volume 23, Issue 1, March.

Kraut, R., Steinfield, C., Chan, A., Butler, B., & Hoag A., (1998) "Coordination and Virtualisation: The Role of Electronic Networks and Personal Relationships." *Journal of Computer Mediated Communication,* Volume 3, Issue 4, June.

Lacity, M. C., & Janson, M. A., (1994) "Understanding Qualitative Data: A Framework of Text Analysis Methods." *Journal of Management Information Systems*, Volume 11, Issue 2, Fall.

Lee, A. S., (1994) "Electronic Mail as a Medium for Rich Communication: An Empirical Investigation Using Hermeneutic Interpretation." *MIS Quarterly*, Volume 18, Issue 2, June.

Leedy, P. D., (1997) *"Practical Research: Planning and Design."* Sixth Edition, Prentice Hall, New Jersey.

Lin, C. A., (1998) "Bridging the Positivist and Interpretivist Approaches to Qualitative Methods." *Policy Studies Journal*, Volume 26, Number 1.

Lipnack, J., & Stamps, J., (1999) "Virtual teams." *Executive Excellence, Provo*, Volume 16, Issue 5, May.

Malone, T., & Rockart, J., (1993) "How will information technology reshape organisations? Computers as coordination technology." in Bradley, S., Hausman, J., & Nolan, R., (Eds.), *"Globalisation, technology and competition: The fusion of computers and telecommunications in the 1990s."* Harvard University School Press, Boston.

Malone, T., Yates, J., & Benjamin, R., (1987) "Electronic markets and electronic hierarchies: Effects of information technology on market structure and corporate strategies." *Communications of the ACM*, Volume 30, Issue 6.

Meyerson, D., Weick, K. E., & Kramer, R. M. (1996) "Swift trust and temporary groups." in Kramer, R. M., & Tyler, T. R., (Eds.) "*Trust in organisations: Frontiers of theory and research.*" Sage Publications, Thousand Oaks.

Myers, M. D., (1997) "Qualitative Research in Information Systems." *MIS Quarterly*, Volume 21, Issue 2, June. *MISQ Discovery*, archival version, June 1997, @ www.misq.org/misqd961/isworld/. *MISQ Discovery*, updated version, April 28, 1999, @ www.auckland.ac.nz/msis/isworld/.

Neuman, W. L., (1991) *"Social Research Methods: Qualitative and Quantitative Approaches."* Allyn and Bacon, Massachusetts.

Nohria, N., & Berkley, J.D., (1994) "The Virtual Organisations: bureaucracy, technology, and the Implosion of Control." in Helscher, C., & Donnellon, A., (Eds.) *"The Post-Bureaucratic Organisation: New Perspectives in Organisational Change."* Sage, Thousand Oaks.

Orlikowski, W. J. & Baroudi, J. J. (1991) "Studying Information Technology in Organisations: Research Approaches and Assumptions." *Information Systems Research,* Volume 2.

Palmer J. W. and Speier C. H., (1997) "A Typology of Virtual Organisations: An Empirical Study." in *Proceedings of the Association for Information Systems 1997 Americas Conference*, Indianapolis, August.

Patton, M. Q., (1990) *"Qualitative Evaluation and Research Methods."* (2nd Ed.) Sage Publications, Newbury Park.

Pettigrew, A., (1988) " Longitudinal field research on change: Theory and practice." *Paper presented at the National Science Foundation Conference on Longitudinal Research Methods in Organisations*, Austin.

Plishkin, N., & Romm, C.T., (1997) "The impact of e-mail on the evolution of a virtual community during a strike." *Information and Management*, Volume 32.

Powell S., & Gallegos F., (1998) "Securing Virtual Corporation." *Information Strategy,* Volume 14, Number 4.

Rittenbruch, M., Kahler, H., & Cremers, A. B., (1998) "Supporting Cooperation in a Virtual Organisation." in Hirschheim, R., Newman, M., & DeGross, J. I., (Eds.) *"Proceedings of the Nineteenth International Conference on Information Systems."* Helsinki, Finland.

Shanks, G., Rouse, A., & Arnott, D., (1993) "A Review of Approaches to Research and Scholarship in Information Systems." *Proc. 4th Australian Conference on Information Systems, Brisbane.*

Staples D. S., Hulland J. S., & Higgins C. A., (1998) "A Self-Efficacy Theory Explanation for the Management of Remote Workers in Virtual Organisations." *Journal of Computer Mediated Communication,* Volume 3, Issue 4, June.

Steinfield, C., Kraut, R., & Plummer, A., (1995) "The impact of interorganisational networks on buyer-seller relationships." *Journal of Computer Mediated Communication [Online],* Volume 1, Issue 3.

Stoddard, D. B., & Donnellon, A., (1997) *"Verifone."* Harvard Business School, 9-398-030, Harvard Business School Publishing, Boston.

Strauss A., (1987) *"Qualitative Analysis for Social Scientists."* Cambridge University Press, Cambridge.

Strauss, A., & Corbin, J., (1990) *"Basics of Qualitative Research: Grounded Theory Procedures and Techniques."* Sage Publications, Newbury Park.

Streeter, L. A., Kraut, R. E., Lucas, H. C., & Caby, L., (1996) "The impact of national data networks on firm performance and market structure." *Communications of the ACM.*

Stroh, K. L., & Caligiuri, P. M., (1998) "Increasing global competitiveness through effective people management. " *Journal of World Business*, Greenwich, Volume 33, Issue 1, Spring.

Townsend A. M., DeMarie S. M., & Hendrickson A. R., (1998) "Virtual teams: Technology and the workplace of the future." *The Academy of Management Executive, Ada,* Volume 12, Issue 3, August.

Urquhart, C., (1996) "Exploring Analyst-Client communication: using grounded theory techniques to investigate interaction in informal requirements gathering." *ACIS, Conference.* Proceedings

Van Alstyne, M., and Brynjolfsson, E., (1996) "Electronic Communities: Global Villages or Cyberbalkanisation?" *International Conference on Information Systems,* 1996 Proceedings.

Vandenbosch, B., and Ginzberg, M.J., (1997) "Lotus Notes and Collaboration." *Journal of Management Information Systems,* Volume 13, Number 3, Winter.

Venkatraman, N., & Hendersen C.J., (1998) "Real strategies for virtual organizing." *Sloan Management Review,* Cambridge, Volume 40, Issue 1, Fall.

MOBILE COMMERCE – THE CHALLENGES

NILMINI WICKRAMASINGHE
Cleveland State University, USA

Panel Members: **Stefano Perlusz**
Aalborg University, Denmark

Doug Vogel
City University of Hong Kong, Hong Kong

Heidi Winklhofer
Griffith University, Australia

PANEL REPORT

Only yesterday we were being bombarded with concerns about the new millennium, focusing on Y2K and possibilities of major technological disasters. Now the new millennium is here and one if not the defining feature of this new millennium is the Internet in particular Internet based e-commerce. One after another more and more e-"somethings" are constantly appearing. The newest sensation though, is not an e-"something" rather the mobile Internet, m-commerce or the mobile version of e-commerce. What then is m-commerce and what can mobile commerce do? Concisely, m-commerce has the potential to deliver anything the Internet can offer plus it gives the added advantage of mobility as well as being extremely user friendly.

M-commerce facilitates access to enterprise and commerce applications at anytime, anywhere and anyplace. Much of the literature focuses on business to business(B2B) and business to consumer (B2C) activities, which is essentially no different to e-commerce in general or is it? This is discussed by the panel by trying to compare and contrast what are the key differences between m-commerce and e-commerce, an m-vision versus an e-vision and m-business versus e-business.

Some of the key findings of the panel discussion include the following:

1. m-commerce identifies the PAN or personal area network
2. case study data highlights that the ubiquitous use of cellular technology makes privacy and data security issues a concern for users and provides, with age appearing to be a significant factor regarding relative tolerance
3. the characteristics that support the delivery of location sensitive and highly personalized user information make it also convenient to another sector not yet considered in e-commerce/e-business discussions; namely; business-to-employee (B2E) activities and communication. It is this B2E aspect that is a truly unique aspect of m-commerce.
4. while e-commerce has brought new ways of conducting business, m-commerce appears to be going a step further and bringing about new ways of how life will be lived
5. we should think of three key aspects when discussing m-commerce: mobility, locatability and greater personalization
6. m-commerce research should be cross-disciplinary including areas of economics, legal issues, marketing , sociology as well as technology

From the panel discussions and input from the audience it became evident that while m-commerce was not a paradigm shift per say, it was indeed an important area that will only continue to be a significant force for business in this 21st century.